ααααααααααααααααααααααααααααααααααααααααααααααααααααααααααααααααααααα
~~~~~~

Fishes:
An Introduction
to Ichthyology

Fishes: An Introduction to Ichthyology

PETER B. MOYLE
JOSEPH J. CECH, JR.

Department of Wildlife and Fisheries Biology
University of California, Davis

PRENTICE-HALL, INC.
Englewood Cliffs, New Jersey 07632

Library of Congress Cataloging in Publication Data

Moyle, Peter B.   (date)
    Fishes: an introduction to ichthyology.

    Bibliography: p.
    Includes index.
    1. Fishes.   2. Ichthyology.   I. Cech, Joseph J.
II. Title.
QL615.M64   597   81-12185
ISBN   0-13-319723-9   AACR2

Editorial/production supervision
   and interior design by *Ros Herion*
Cover design by *Suzanne Behnke*
Cover print by *Christopher M. Dewees,*
   Davis, California
Manufacturing buyer: *John Hall*

© 1982 by PRENTICE-HALL, INC., Englewood Cliffs, N.J. 07632

Printed in the United States of America

10   9   8   7   6   5   4   3   2

ISBN: 0-13-319723-9

PRENTICE-HALL INTERNATIONAL, INC., *London*
PRENTICE-HALL OF AUSTRALIA PTY. LIMITED, *Sydney*
PRENTICE-HALL OF CANADA, LTD., *Toronto*
PRENTICE-HALL OF INDIA PRIVATE LIMITED, *New Delhi*
PRENTICE-HALL OF JAPAN, INC., *Tokyo*
PRENTICE-HALL OF SOUTHEAST ASIA PTE. LTD., *Singapore*
WHITEHALL BOOKS LIMITED, *Wellington, New Zealand*

Contents

Preface

The emphasis of ichthyology has traditionally been on the systematics, anatomy, and distribution of fishes. Ecology, physiology, evolution, and behavior have generally been treated as minor, if interesting, sidelights. This view of ichthyology is a historic one; most of the prominent names associated with the field have made their major contributions with systematic, anatomical, and distributional studies. Today, however, most people who study fishes have interests and needs that extend beyond the traditional areas. They study fish for such reasons as to find ways of better managing fisheries or aquaculture operations, to determine the effects of human activities on aquatic environments, or to be able to use fish as handy animals with which to test ideas in such rapidly developing fields as ecology, physiology, behavior, and evolution. There is also a growing number of sophisticated amateur ichthyologists who study fishes to increase their understanding of the fishes they keep in aquaria or those they pursue with hook and line. Regardless of why fish are studied, those studying them still need the basic vocabulary and understanding of fish biology provided by the traditional areas of emphasis. The purpose of this book, therefore, is to provide that basic background, but to integrate it with recent developments in other areas, and to provide some feeling for the excitement being engendered by recent research on fishes.

In large part the book is designed to serve as a text in classes in fish biology. The large number of chapters and the numerous cross references within chapters are meant to provide instructors of such courses with flexibility in assigning readings in the text. We have assumed that the book will be used in conjunction with a laboratory manual of fish anatomy (of which there are many), keys to fishes (such as Eddy and Underhill 1978), and perhaps a collection of readings (such as Love and Cailliet 1979). The students we had in mind while writing were junior- and senior-level university students. However, we also hope that this book will prove to be a useful and palatable summary of recent developments in ichthyology for individuals who have been away from the college classroom for some time or for anyone else who needs an introduction to the most numerous, diverse, and fascinating of all vertebrate groups.

This book would not have been possible without the encouragement and help of many people. Gary Grossman, Donald Baltz, and Robert Daniels were especially helpful in providing references, discussion, and criticisms of many of the chapters. Timothy Ford, Lynn Decker, Bruce Vondracek, John Dentler, Wayne Wurtsbaugh, Jerry Smith, Daniel Varoujean, John Cornacchia, Michael Massingill, Stephen Mitchell, and other members of the University of California, Davis, Fish Research Collective, and numerous graduate and undergraduate students contributed valuable comments on various chapters and/or helped to keep our research programs going while we devoted time to writing. We benefited from discussions with Jeff Graham, Fred White, Hiram Li, Ken Gobalet, and Serge Doroshov. The reviews of selected chapters by Eugene Balon, Michael Bell, David Ehrenfeld, Dale Lott, John Radovich, Arnold Sillman, Randolph Smith, and Paul Webb are appreciated. Paul Feyen of Prentice-Hall, Inc., provided constant encouragement despite our numerous delays and procrastinations. Many of the figures were skillfully drawn by Alyne Lavoie-Ruppanner. Much of the manuscript was cheerfully typed by Donna Lombardo, who managed to correct many errors of spelling and grammar while doing so. Marjorie Kirkman assisted us in many ways but especially by keeping the departmental office running efficiently, making it much easier to accomplish our regular duties while the book was in progress. Finally, we are exceedingly grateful to our wives, Marilyn Moyle and Mary Cech, for permitting our marriages to survive and even grow stronger while the book was in progress, and to our children, Petrea and Noah Moyle and Scott and Gregor Cech, for keeping us from getting *too* serious about ichthyology.

PETER B. MOYLE
JOSEPH J. CECH, JR.

PART I

Introduction

ααααααααααααααααααααααααααααααααααααααααααααααααααααααααααααααααααααααα
~~~~~~

Introduction

Modern Fishes   The fishes are the most numerous and diverse of the major vertebrate groups. They dominate the waters of the world through a marvelous variety of morphological, physiological, and behavioral adaptations. The fishes include some of the most ancestral[1] and some of the most derived vertebrates. Their diversity is reflected in the large number of living species (about 20,000 to 22,000 by the estimates of Cohen [1970] or 18,818 according to Nelson [1976]) and by the wide variety of habitats they occupy. Various fish species can be found thriving in vernal pools, intermittent streams, tiny desert springs, the vast reaches of the open oceans, deep oceanic trenches, cold mountain streams, saline coastal embayments, and so on into a nearly endless list of aquatic environments.

Modern fishes consist of three major groups that have had separate evolutionary histories for at least 400 million years (Fig. 1.1). The most ancestral of these lines is the Agnatha (jawless fishes). Their heyday was 350 million to 500 million years ago, and they are represented in today's fish fauna by only about 50 rather specialized species of lampreys and hagfishes. However, the earliest agnathans were also the earliest vertebrates, and so they were ancestral to the two other major evolutionary lines, the cartilaginous fishes (Chondrichthyes) and the bony fishes (Osteichthyes).[2] Another major line, the Placodermi, flourished during the Devonian period but then died out, apparently leaving no

---

[1]The terms "ancestral" and "derived" are used throughout this book instead of the more traditional (and less objective) "primitive" and "advanced."

[2]Jarvik (1977) and others advocate that the term "Elasmobranchiomorphi" be substituted for "Chondrichthyes" and "Teleostomi" for "Osteichthyes," on the grounds that some "cartilaginous" fishes have bony skeletons and a number of "bony" fishes have cartilaginous skeletons.

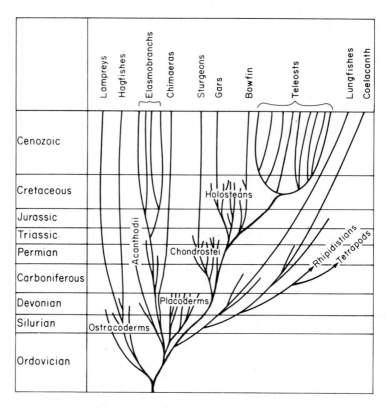

FIGURE 1.1 Presumed evolutionary relationships of major fish groups.

direct descendants. The cartilaginous fishes split into two distinct lines early in their history, the sharks and rays (Elasmobranchi) and the ratfishes and chimaeras (Holocephali). There are about 600 to 700 living species of sharks and rays and 20 to 30 species of chimaeras and ratfishes. The bony fishes also split into at least four lines early in their history, the lungfishes (Dipneusti), the crossopterygians (Crossopterygii), the bichirs (Brachiopterygii), and the rayfinned fishes (Actinopterygii). The lungfishes are represented today only by five species and crossopterygians by the single coelacanth species. The bichirs are a modern group of 11 species whose relationship to other bony fishes is uncertain. Living rayfinned fishes are generally broken up into three groups (infraclasses) representing the major stages of evolution to the advanced bony fishes: Chondrostei (sturgeons and paddlefishes, 25 to 30 species), Holostei (bowfin and gars, 10 species) and Teleostei (all others, 19,000 to 21,000 species).

It might be expected that most of this diversity of fishes would be contained in the oceans, because salt water covers over 70% of the surface of the earth, while fresh water covers only about 1%. By volume, 97% of all water is in the oceans, and 0.0093% is in freshwater lakes and streams (the remainder is in ice, atmospheric water, etc.) (Horn 1972). Surprisingly, only 58% of modern fish species are marine, while 41% are

4

freshwater inhabitants and 1% move on a regular basis between the two environments (Cohen 1970). The large number of species of freshwater fish is a reflection of the ease with which fish populations in landlocked waters become isolated from each other and thus have the opportunity to evolve into new species. The chances of populations becoming isolated are increased by the fact that most freshwater fishes are incapable of entering salt water, even for brief periods of time.

While the freshwater habitat consists largely of thousands of distinct "islands" of water in a sea of land, most of the saltwater habitat consists of open ocean, which is rather unproductive and lighted only in the surface layer. Only 13% of all fish species are associated with the open ocean: 1% in the surface layer (epipelagic fishes), 5% in the unlighted sections of the water column (deepwater pelagic fishes), and 7% on the bottom (deepwater benthic fishes). A majority (78%) of marine fish species (making up 44% of all fishes) live in the narrow band of water less than 200 m deep along the margins of land masses. An additional factor affecting the number of fish species found in an area is the annual temperature regime. In both fresh and salt water, a majority of the species are found in the warmer environments where annual temperature fluctuations are minimal.

Despite the diversity of fish habitats and the diversity of adaptations enabling fish to live in these habitats, most fish are readily recognizable as fish. The reason for this is that the physical and chemical characteristics of water impose a number of constraints on the functional design of fish. Most of the characteristics we recognize as fishlike are adaptations to allow the most efficient use of the aquatic medium by mobile vertebrate predators. The characteristics of water exerting the greatest influence on fish design are its density, low compressibility, properties as a solvent, and transparency.

Water is about 800 times denser than air. This greatly reduces the effects of gravity on fish and enables them to remain suspended in the water column with little effort compared to the effort required by most birds to stay airborne. In fact, most fish are neutrally buoyant, so virtually all muscular effort can be devoted to movement and little is wasted counteracting the pull of gravity. In addition, more thrust can be obtained by pushing against water than against air, as the futile flapping of a fish on land demonstrates. On the other hand, the high density of water means that it resists movement through it. Fish typically solve this problem by being streamlined to lower the resistance of the water to their swimming, by having a high proportion of their bodies devoted to the muscles needed for forward motion, and by having efficient means of shoving the body and tail fin against the water column to thrust the fish forward.

The resistance of water to motion is the result not only of its density but also of its virtual incompressibility. Movement through air is made considerably easier by the fact that air compresses slightly along bodies moving through it, flows by smoothly, and so does not have to be completely displaced. Water, in contrast, literally has to be pushed out of the way by organisms moving through it. This creates turbulence along the sides and in the wake of the organism and increases further the drag of the water. While the incompressibility of water creates problems for fish, they are also able to take advantage of it. Each fish has an extremely sensitive sensory system, the lateral line system, that can detect small amounts of turbulence and water displacement created either by its own motion or by the motion of other organisms or objects. Using this system, fish can detect nearby stationary objects, other fish, and food organisms. The lateral line system is particularly useful when visual cues are lacking. Fish (mainly teleosts) also use the incompressibility of water to help them in eating and breathing. Quick expansion of the mouth and gill chambers allows water to rush in, carrying food and oxygen into the chambers along with the water. This "pipette effect" is particularly well developed in fishes that feed on small, mobile organisms and results in jaw structures very different from those of terrestrial vertebrates.

While for the purposes of movement, feeding, and breathing of fish, water behaves as if incompressible, it can be compressed slightly. This is fortunate, because it enables sound to be carried. In fact, sound is carried farther and faster in water than it is in air (1433 m/sec versus 335 m/sec) thanks to the greater density of water. As a consequence, most fish have an excellent sense of hearing, even though they lack the external ears associated with hearing in terrestrial vertebrates. External ears are not needed because fish tissue is of roughly the same density as water and so is nearly transparent to sound waves. However, the sound waves can be intercepted internally by structures that are either much denser than water (otoliths) or much less dense than water (swim bladders). Since most fish can hear well, it is not surprising to find that many also make sounds for communication. A single toadfish, for example, when engaging in its courtship rites, can produce sound that may reach 100 db in loudness. The "silent world" of the oceans is largely a myth, at least as far as fish are concerned!

Perhaps the most important characteristic of water that enables it to support life, including fish, is its property as the nearly universal solvent. The waters of the world contain complex mixtures of dissolved gases, salts, and organic compounds, many of which are needed by fish to sustain life and are taken up either directly through the gills or indirectly through food organisms. The most important of the gases is oxygen, which is present in extremely small amounts compared to that found in air (1 to 8 ml of oxygen per liter of water; 210 ml of oxygen per liter of air). Although the gills of fish are incredibly efficient at extracting oxygen from water, the low availability of oxygen in water can limit the metabolic activities of fish. In fresh water, where oxygen supplies may become depleted, many fishes are able to breathe air at least for short periods of time. In order to extract what oxygen is available in the water, fish must expose a large, highly vascularized gill surface area to the water. As a consequence, other substances also may pass between the environment and the fish. Fish eliminate waste products (especially carbon dioxide, ammonia, and heat) through the gills, but they may also take up harmful substances, including pollutants such as heavy metals and pesticides. The large area of exposed gill also makes fish very sensitive to changes in the concentration of salts in the water, so relatively few fish are capable of moving between fresh and salt water.

A final important characteristic of water to fish is its low penetrability to light as compared to air. Even in the clearest water, light seldom penetrates deeper than 1000 m, and in most water the depth of penetration is considerably less. Since the lighted (photic) zone is the zone where primary production takes place and where grazing invertebrates are concentrated, it is not surprising that most fish are found there as well. Indeed, a majority of fish rely primarily on sight for prey capture and so have well-developed eyes, although most fish have extremely limited focusing abilities. It should be noted, however, that many fishes have developed sensory structures, such as barbels and electric organs, that allow them to find their way about at night, in muddy water, or in other situations of low light. Below the lighted zone of the oceans are complex communities of fish that produce their own light in photophores in order to signal each other and to attract prey.

As the following chapters will reveal, there are many exceptions to the preceding generalities about fish. Each fish species has its own unique combination of adaptive traits that enables it to survive in its own particular environment. The study of these traits and how they relate to each other and to the biological, chemical, and physical environment of fish is the essence of ichthyology.

Fish Classification   Although the describing of new taxa of fishes and the organizing of the taxa into systems that demonstrate the interrelationships among the taxa is no longer the primary occupation of most biologists who work with fish, it is nevertheless of fundamental importance. In order to understand the significance of the ecological, physiological, behavioral, and other types of adaptations of fish, their evolutionary relationships must be understood as well. Modern classification schemes are generally presumed to reflect the evolutionary relationships among fishes, since common structural features (upon which most schemes are based) presumably reflect common ancestry. Because our knowledge of most fishes is far from complete and because taxa higher than the species level tend to be somewhat arbitrary, refinements and changes to accepted classification systems are continually being proposed. Eventually these changes lead to new systems that may bear little resemblance to the old systems on which they are based. Indeed, the most prominent figures in much of the history of ichthyology were individuals who organized the recent

TABLE 1-1
A Comparison of the Classification Systems for Living Fishes of L.S. Berg with That of Nelson, Together with Names from Other Systems That May Be Encountered in the Literature[a]

Berg (1940)	Nelson (1976)	Other Systems
Superclass Agnatha	Superclass Agnatha	
Class Petromyzones	Class Cephalaspidomorphi	Classes Cyclostomata/
Order Petromyzoniformes	Order Petromyzoniformes	Ostracodermi
Class Myxini	Class Pteraspidomorphi	
Order Myxiniformes	Order Myxiniformes	
Superclass Gnathostomata	Superclass Gnathostomata	
Class Elasmobranchi	Class Chondrichthyes	Class Chondrichthyes[b]
Subclass Selachii	Subclass Elasmobranchi	Subclass Elasmobranchi
		Superorder Galeomorphii
Order Heterodontiformes	Order Heterodontiformes	Order Heterodontiformes
Order Lamniformes	Order Lamniformes	Order Lamniformes
		Order Orectolobiformes
		Order Carcharhiniformes
		Superorder Squalomorphii
Order Hexanchiformes	Order Hexanchiformes	Order Hexanchiformes
Order Squaliformes	Order Squaliformes	Order Squaliformes
		Order Pristioformes
		Superorder Squatinomorphii
		Order Squatiniformes
Order Rajiformes	Order Rajiformes	Superorder Batoidea
		Order Rajiformes
		Order Pristiformes
		Order Myliobatiformes
Order Torpediniformes		Order Torpediniformes
Class Holocephali		
Subclass Chimaerae	Subclass Holocephali	
Order Chimaeriformes	Order Chimaeriformes	
	Class Osteichthyes	Subclass Sarcopterygii
Class Dipnoi	Subclass Dipneusti	Order Dipnoi
Order Ceratodiformes	Order Ceratodiformes	
Order Lepidosireniformes	Order Lepidosireniformes	
Class Teleostomi		
Subclass Crossopterygii	Subclass Crossopterygii	Order Crossopterygii
Order Coelacanthiformes	Order Coelacanthiformes	
Subclass Actinopterygii	Subclass Brachiopterygii	Order Brachiopterygii
Order Polypteriformes	Order Polypteriformes	
	Subclass Actinopterygii	Subclass Actinopterygii
	Infraclass Chondrostei	
Order Acipenseriformes	Order Acipenseriformes	
	Infraclass Holostei	
Order Lepidosteiformes	Order Semionotiformes	
Order Amiiformes	Order Amiiformes	
	Infraclass Teleostei	
Order Clupeiformes		Order Isospondyli
	Superorder Osteoglossomorpha	
	Order Osteoglossiformes	
(Order Mormyriformes)[c]	Order Mormyriformes	
	Superorder Clupeomorpha	
	Order Clupeiformes	
	Superorder Elopomorpha	
	Order Elopiformes	

Berg (1940)	Nelson (1976)	Other Systems
(Order Anguilliformes)[c]	Order Anguilliformes	(Order Apodes)[c]
(Order Saccopharyngiformes)		
(Order Notacanthiformes)	Order Notacanthiformes	(Order Heteromi)
(Order Halosauriformes)		(Order Lyopomi)
	Superorder Protacanthopterygii	
	Order Salmoniformes	
(Order Galaxiiformes)		
(Order Giganturiformes)		
	Superorder Ostariophysi	
	Order Gonorhynchiformes	
Order Cypriniformes	Series Otophysi	Superorder Ostariophysi
	Order Cypriniformes	
	Order Siluriformes	Order Nematognathi
	Superorder Scopelomorpha	
Order Scopeliformes, in part	Order Myctophiformes	Order Iniomi, in part
	Superorder Paracanthopterygii	
Order Beryciformes, in part	Order Polymixiiformes	
Order Percopsiformes	Order Percopsiformes	
Order Gadiformes	Order Gadiformes	
Order Macruriformes		
Order Batrachoidiformes	Order Batrachoidiformes	Order Haplodoci
Order Lophiiformes	Order Lophiiformes	Order Pediculati
	Superorder Acanthopterygii	
Order Mugiliformes, in part	Order Atheriniformes	
Order Cyprinodontiformes		
Order Beloniformes		
Order Lampridiformes	Order Lampridiformes	
Order Ateleopiformes		
Order Beryciformes	Order Beryciformes	
Order Stephanoberyciformes		
Order Scopeliformes, in part		
Order Zeiformes	Order Zeiformes	
Order Syngnathiformes	(Order Syngnathiformes)	Order Solenichthys
Order Gasterosteiformes, in part	Order Gasterosteiformes	Order Thoracostei
Order Symbranchiformes	Order Synbranchiformes	Order Symbranchii
Order Perciformes, in part	Order Scorpaeniformes	
Order Dactylopteriformes	Order Dactylopteriformes	
Order Pegasiformes	(Order Pegasiformes)	
Order Perciformes, in part	Order Perciformes	
Order Thunniformes		
Order Mugiliformes, in part		
Order Chanduriformes		
Order Mastacembelliformes		
Order Icosteiformes		Order Opisthomi
Order Echeneiformes		Order Malacichthyes
Order Gobiesociformes	Order Gobiesociformes	Order Xenopteri
Order Pleuronectiformes	Order Pleuronectiformes	Order Heterosomata
Order Tetraodontiformes	Order Tetradontiformes	Order Plectognathi

[a]A classification down to the family level may be found in Chapters 13 through 23.

[b]The classification of Chondrichthyes under "Other Systems" is that of Compagno (1978).

[c]Orders in parentheses are not included in Berg's Clupeiformes or in the Isopondyli of C.T. Regan (as cited in Berg, 1940).

advances in the knowledge of fishes into "new" classification schemes. Most recent classification schemes are based in large part on that of Berg (1940). However, the provisional classification of the teleosts by Greenwood et al. (1966) has had a major impact on the thinking of systematic ichthyologists and has stimulated many further attempts at revising taxa within the teleosts. The 1972 symposium on *Interrelationships of Fishes,* edited by Greenwood, Miles, and Patterson (1973), indicates that considerable attention is also being paid by modern systematists to the other groups of fishes as well. Nelson (1976) has put much of this recent work together in a reasonable classification system that will be followed in this book. His system is compared to that of Berg in Table 1-1. The system used in this book deviates from that of Nelson mainly in the class Chondrichthyes, where the system of Compagno (1973) is followed down to the level of order, reflecting Compagno's convincing arguments that there are four distinct lines of elasmobranchs (sharks and rays) rather than just two. However, the families of Chondrichthyes used in Chapter 15 are largely the same as those of Nelson.

Supplemental Readings   Berg 1940; Boulenger 1910; Cohen 1970; Compagno 1973; Greenwood, Miles, and Patterson 1973; Greenwood, Rosen, Weitzman, and Myers 1966; Horn 1972; Hubbs 1964; Jordan 1922; Lagler, Bardach, Miller, and Passino 1977; Lurie 1960; Myers 1964; Nelson 1976; Norman and Greenwood 1975; Patterson 1977.

ααααααααααααααααααααααααααααααααααααααααααααααααααααααααααααααααααααααα
~~~~~~

Structure
and
Function

ααααααααααααααααααααααααααααααααααααααααααααααααααααααααααααααααααα
~~~~~~

Form and Movement

The great ecological diversity of fishes is reflected in the astonishing variety of body shapes and means of locomotion they possess. Indeed, much can be learned about the ecology of a fish simply by examining its anatomical features or by watching it move through the water. Equally important to students of ichthyology (if not to the fish) is that these features also form the basis of most schemes of classification and identification. The purpose of this chapter, therefore, is to provide an overview of (1) external anatomy, (2) internal support systems (the skeleton and muscles), and (3) means of locomotion.

External Anatomy Although life in water puts many severe constraints on the "design" of fishes, the presence of 20,000 or so species in a wide variety of habitats means that these constraints are pushed to their limits, resulting in many very unlikely forms. What could be more unfishlike, for example, than seahorses, deepsea gulper eels (Eurypharyngidae), or lumpfishes (Cyclopteridae)? Understanding the significance of the peculiar external anatomy of such forms practically requires study on a case-by-case basis. On the other hand, species that are more recognizably fishlike (Fig. 2.1) can usually be placed in some sort of functional category through the examination of body shape, scales, fins, mouth, gill openings, sense organs, and miscellaneous structures.

Body Shape Most fishes fall into one of six broad categories: rover-predator, lie-in-wait predator, surface-oriented fish, bottom fish, deep-bodied fish, and eel-like fish (Fig. 2.1).

Rover-predators have the body shape that comes to mind when

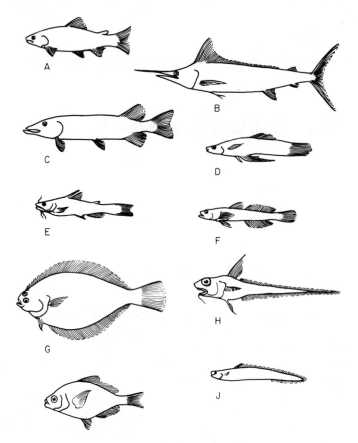

FIGURE 2.1 Typical fish body shapes: (A and B) rover-predator; (C) lie-in-wait predator; (D) surface-oriented fish; (E) bottom rover; (F) bottom clinger; (G) flatfish; (H) rattail; (I) deep-bodied fish; and (J) eel-like fish.

most people think of fishes: streamlined (fusiform), with a pointed head ending in a terminal mouth and a narrow caudal peduncle tipped with a forked tail. The fins are more or less evenly distributed about the body, providing stability and maneuverability. Such fishes typically are constantly on the move, searching out prey which they capture through pursuit. Examples include many species of minnows (Cyprinidae), bass, tuna, mackerel, and swordfish. The rover-predator body shape is also characteristic of stream fishes such as trout that spend much of their time foraging in current.

Lie-in-wait predators are mainly piscivores (fish eaters) that have a morphology well suited for the capture from ambush of fast-swimming prey. The body is streamlined, but it is also elongate, often torpedolike. The head is flattened and equipped with a large mouth filled with pointed teeth. In many species the mouth is largely contained in a long, pointed snout. The caudal fin tends to be large, and the dorsal and anal fins are placed far back on the body, often in line with each other. This arrangement of the fins gives the fish the large amount of thrust it needs to launch itself at high speeds at passing fish. The narrow frontal profile that these fish present, coupled with their cryptic coloration and secretive behavior, also makes them less visible to their prey. Members of this group include the freshwater pikes (Esocidae), barracuda, gars, needlefish (Belonidae), and snook (Centropomidae).

Surface-oriented fishes are typically small in size, with an upward-pointing mouth, a dorsoventrally flattened head with large eyes, and a posteriorly placed dorsal fin. The morphology is well suited for capturing plankton and small fishes that live near the water's surface, or insects that land on the surface. In fresh or brackish water that is stagnant, these surface-oriented fishes may survive by being able to take in, through the mouth, the thin layer of oxygen-rich water that exists at the air-water interface. Most surface-oriented fish are stocky-bodied fresh or brackish water forms, such as mosquitofish (*Gambusia*), many killifish (*Fundulus*), and the four-eyed fish (*Anableps anableps*), but a number of elongate marine forms, such as the halfbeaks and flying fishes (Exocoetidae), have similar adaptations.

Bottom fishes possess a wide variety of body shapes, all of them adapted for a life in nearly continuous contact with the bottom. In most such fishes the swimbladder is reduced or absent, and most are flattened in one direction or another. Bottom fishes can be divided into five overlapping types: bottom rovers, bottom clingers, bottom hiders, flatfishes, and rattails. Bottom rovers have a rover-predator-like body, except that the head tends to be flattened, the back humped, and the pectoral fins enlarged. Examples include forms as varied as North American catfishes (Ictaluridae) with large, terminal mouths, small armored catfishes (Loricariidae) with small, subterminal mouths, and suckers (Catostomidae), sturgeons, and carp, with fleshy, protrusible lips that are used to suck plant and animal matter off the bottom. Many teleost bottom rovers have small eyes and well-developed barbels (equipped with tastebuds) around the mouth, indicating their ability to find prey at night or in murky water. Many sharks, with their subterminal mouths, flattened heads, and large pectoral fins, can also be classified as bottom rovers.

Bottom clingers are mainly small fishes, with flattened heads, large pectoral fins, and structures (usually modified pelvic fins) that allow them to adhere to the bottom. Such structures are handy in swift streams or intertidal areas that have strong currents. The simplest arrangement is possessed by sculpins (Cottidae), which use their small, straight, and closely spaced pelvic fins as antiskid devices. However, other families of fishes, such as the hillstream fishes (Homalopteridae), gobies (Gobiidae), and clingfishes (Gobiesocidae), have evolved suction cups. Bottom hiders are similar in many respects to the bottom clingers, but they lack the clinging devices and tend to have more elongate bodies and smaller heads. These forms usually live under rocks, in crevices, or lie quietly on the bottom in still water. The darters (Percidae) of North American streams are in this category, as are many blennies (Blennidae). However, the latter family contains species that range in form from "good" bottom hiders to more eel-like forms.

Flatfishes have the most extreme morphologies of bottom fishes. Flounders (Pleuronectiformes) are essentially deep-bodied fishes that live with one side on the bottom. In these fishes the eye on the downward side migrates during development to the upward side, and the mouth often assumes a peculiar twist to enable bottom feeding. In contrast, skates and rays (Batoidea) are flattened dorsoventrally and mostly move about by flapping or undulating the extremely large pectoral fins. Not only is the mouth completely ventral on these fishes, but the main water intakes for respiration (the spiracles) are located on the top of the head.

The rattail shape is another type of body shape that has been independently evolved in both the Osteichthyes and the Chondrichthyes. Groups such as the grendadiers (Macrouridae), brotulas (Ophidiidae), and chimaeras (Holocephali) have bodies that end in long, pointed, rat-like tails and begin with large, pointy-snouted heads and large pectoral fins. These fishes are almost all inhabitants of the deep sea, and exactly why this peculiar morphology is so popular among benthic fishes is poorly understood. The fishes live by scavenging and preying on the benthic invertebrates.

Deep-bodied fishes are laterally flattened forms, with a body depth usually at least one third that of the standard length (distance from snout to base of caudal peduncle). The dorsal and anal fins are typically long, and the pectoral fins are located high on the body, with the pelvic fins immediately below. The mouth is usually small and protrusible, the eyes large, and the snout short. Deep-bodied fishes are well adapted for maneuvering in tight quarters, such as the catacombs of a coral reef, dense beds of aquatic plants, or tight schools of their own species. They are also well adapted for picking small invertebrates off the bottom or out of the water column. A majority of deep-bodied fishes possess stout spines in the fins, presumably because in the course of their evolution they have sacrificed speed for maneuverability and developed spines for protection from predators. Although most deep-bodied fishes are closely associated with the bottom, many open-water plankton feeders are also moderately deep-bodied. This is largely the result of a sharp ventral keel, which functions to camouflage these silvery fishes by eliminating ventral shadows, thus making them less visible to predators approaching from below.

Eel-like fishes have elongate bodies, blunt or wedge-shaped heads, and tapering or rounded tails. If paired fins are present, they are small, while the dorsal and anal fins are typically quite long. Scales are small and embedded, or absent. Eel-like fishes are particularly well adapted for entering small crevices and holes in reefs and rocky areas, for making their way through beds of aquatic plants, and for burrowing into soft bottoms. Examples of this group include the many eels (Anguilliformes), loaches (Cobitidae), and gunnels (Pholidae).

It is important to recognize at this point that these categories of body shapes are general groupings and, indeed, many fishes have shapes which have characteristics of more than one group or have shapes which are difficult to categorize.

Scales

The type, size, and number of scales can tell much about how a fish makes its living. The scales of bony fishes range from the heavy coating of bony ganoid scales possessed by gars (see Chapter 16), to a few large bony plates on the back, to a dense covering of lightweight cycloid or ctenoid scales, to no scales at all. Bony plates are large modified scales that seem to serve as armor on a number of bottom-oriented fishes, such as sturgeons (Acipenseridae), many South American catfishes, poachers (Agonidae), and pipefishes and seahorses (Syngnathidae). Such fishes are mostly rather slow in their movements. In contrast, typical scales usually cover the bodies of most free-swimming fishes, apparently providing some degree of protection from predators while not excessively weighing the fish down. Fishes that are fast swimmers or regularly move through the fast water of streams typically have many fine scales (e.g., trout), whereas those that live in quiet water and do not swim continuously at high speeds tend to have rather coarse scales (e.g., perch, sunfish). Scales of teleosts are of two basic types, cycloid and ctenoid. Cycloid scales are the round, flat, thin scales found on such fishes as trout, minnows, and herrings. Ctenoid scales are found on the "derived" teleosts (Acanthopterygii) and are similar to cycloid scales except they have tiny, comblike projections (ctenii) on the exposed (posterior) edge of the scales. The exact function of the ctenii is poorly understood, but they may improve the hydrodynamic efficiency of the swimming. Curiously, the tiny placoid scales of sharks may be an independently evolved solution to the same "problem," as they, like ctenii, make the exterior of the fish rough to the touch.

Although scales are usually considered an integral part of any fish, a surprising number of species lack them altogether or have just a few modified for other purposes. Such fishes are by and large bottom dwellers in moving water (e.g., sculpins), fishes that frequently hide in caves, crevices, and other tight places (many catfishes and eels), or fast-swimming pelagic fishes (swordfish, some mackerels). However, many fishes of these types that appear to be scaleless in fact have a complete coating of deeply embedded scales (most tunas, anguillid eels). It is also worth noting that many of the bottom-dwelling skates and rays do not have placoid scales, except as patches of bony armor or as spines (in sting rays).

Fins   As should be obvious from the section of
this chapter on body shapes, the various
combinations of location, size, and shape of the fins are closely associated with the different body shapes. Although the paired fins (pectorals,
pelvics) and unpaired fins (dorsal, anal, caudal, adipose) evolved together
as a system that simultaneously propels, stabilizes, maneuvers, and, often,
protects each fish, they will be discussed separately here, for convenience.

Pelvic fins are the most variable of the fins in position. In more
"ancestral" bony fishes, such as salmon, shad, and carp, and in sharks,
the fins are located ventrally, toward the rear of the fish (termed *abdominal* in position). Most of these fishes have rover-predator body
shapes, and the fins act as stabilizers. In more "derived" teleosts, many
of which are deep-bodied, the pelvics are more anterior, below the pectoral fins (*thoracic* position) and occasionally even in front of the pectorals (*jugular* position). In eels and eel-like fishes the pelvic fins are
frequently absent or greatly reduced in size, for ease of squeezing
through tight places. In bottom-dwelling fishes the pelvics are frequently
modified into organs for holding on to the substrate.

Pectoral fins are generally located high up on the sides of fishes
that depend on precise movements for picking prey from the bottom or
water column. In rover-predators they tend to be more toward the mid-
line of the fish, or below. In very fast-swimming fishes, such as tuna, and
in very deep-bodied fishes that pick prey from the substrate (bluegill,
many cichlids), the fins tend to be long and pointed. In slower-moving
rover-predators or other fishes that need more surface area for stability
while swimming, the fins tend to be more rounded. The pectoral fins
of bony fishes that rest on the bottom, such as suckers (Catostomidae)
and sculpins (Cottidae), are usually broad, rounded, ventral in position,
and spread out laterally. Some bottom fishes, such as the sea robins,
(Triglidae), have free rays in the pectoral fins that are used as "feelers"
to probe the bottom for buried invertebrates. Still other fishes use
enlarged pectoral fins for gliding (flying fishes, Exocoetidae), for true
flapping flight out of the water (freshwater hatchetfishes, Gasteropelecidae), or "flying" in the water, in the case of many rays (e.g., eagle
rays, Myliobatidae). In some fishes, such as the "flying" gurnards
(Dactylopteridae) and the tropical lion and turkey fishes (Scorpaenidae),
enlarged pectoral fins are apparently used mainly for display, either to
startle predators when suddenly opened (gurnards) or to signal predators (and conspecifics) to stay away from poisonous spines.

In contrast to the pectoral fins of bony fishes, the fins of sharks
are rather like rigid wings that can be moved but not collapsed. These
fins operate not only as stabilizers but also as "diving planes." Because
of the latter function, they are normally set at an elevated angle of attack to generate lift for the anterior part of the body; the heterocercal
tail provides lift for the posterior part of the body.

Dorsal and anal fins are generally long on rover-predators and deep-bodied fishes, for stability while swimming. In fast-swimming pelagic fishes, such as tuna and mackerel, the rearmost portions of both fins are frequently broken up into numerous finlets. When swimming at high speed, the forward portion of the dorsal fin in such fishes may fold into a dorsal slot, presumably to reduce the resistance the additional surface area would create; likewise, the pectoral fins of such fishes lie down into shallow pockets. However, even bony fishes that lack these specializations will collapse the dorsal and anal fins and fold back the pectoral and pelvic fins when putting on a burst of speed. Interestingly, this method of reducing drag is not available to sharks, although a number of the mackerel sharks are capable of swimming at quite high speeds.

Another group of fishes with long dorsal and anal fins are the eel-like fishes. Their fins frequently run most of the length of the body and may unite with the caudal fin; such a configuration is necessary for the anguilliform locomotion discussed later in this chapter. In eellike electrical fishes only one of the two long fins is developed. In such cases the fin is the principal means of propulsion, operated by sending waves of movement down the fin. The reason for this is that electric fishes must keep their bodies rigid while swimming, to maintain a uniform electrical field about them.

While long dorsal and anal fins are typical among "derived" bony fishes (Acanthopterygii), they are comparatively uncommon among other groups, such as the salmonids, minnows, catfishes, herrings, sharks, and skates. Aside from this phylogenetic correlation, short fins are most characteristic of bottom-dwelling or surface-oriented fishes.

The **caudal fin** has a shape that is strongly related to the normal swimming speed of a fish. The fastest-swimming fishes, such as tuna and marlin, have a stiff, quarter-moon shaped fin attached to a narrow caudal peduncle. Most rover-predator fishes, or other fishes requiring frequent sustained swimming to live, have forked tails, the deepest forks occurring on the most active fishes. Deep-bodied fishes and most surface and bottom fishes have tails that are square, rounded, or only slightly forked. The tails of most bony fishes are *homocercal*, with upper and lower lobes being about the same size, while in the Chondrichthyes, the tail is usually *heterocercal*, with the upper lobe being longer than the lower lobe. These two basic tail types do not so much reflect differences in ways of making a living as they do the evolutionary history of the fishes that have them (Chapter 12).

The **adipose fin** is a fleshy, dorsal appendage, without internal supporting rays, that is found in the trouts (Salmonidae), lanternfishes (Myctophidae), and various catfishes. Although located between the dorsal and caudal fins toward the caudal peduncle, the small size and lack of stiffening rays presumably dictate a minor propulsive role to this fin.

Spines. One of the most important attributes of the fins of fishes is the presence or absence of spines on the dorsal, anal, and pectoral fins. The importance of spines is indicated by the fact they have developed independently in a number of different groups of fishes. "True" spines are characteristic of most "derived" teleosts but especially the Acanthopterygii; such spines are solid bony structures without any segmentation and round in cross section. In contrast, the spines of fishes such as catfish, carp, goldfish, and North American spinedaces are just stiffened, thickened rays. Rays (lepidotrichia) are the main supporting structures of the fins and are segmented, dumbell-shaped in cross section, and often branched. This structure combines strength with flexibility. The spines that precede the dorsal fin possessed by some sharks are apparently modified placoid scales. Regardless of their structure and origin, spines are an effective and lightweight means of protection against predators. Dorsal, pectoral, and opercular spines are often located at the fish's center of mass, the usual target point of piscivorous (fish-eating) predatory fish (Webb 1978a). Besides being uncomfortable for a predator to bite down on, spines greatly increase the effective size of a small fish. This is because once the dorsal, anal, and pectoral spines are locked into place, the fish can only be grabbed by a predator that can get its mouth around the spines. By increasing its effective size through the use of spines, a small fish reduces the number of predators available to prey on it, because large predators are almost always fewer than small predators. As a consequence of this factor, well-developed spines are found mainly in small to medium-sized fishes that actively forage for their food. Bottom fishes that rely on cover or cryptic coloration to protect them usually are without spines or, if they are acanthopterygian fishes, have the spines reduced or softened.

Other Structures   The mouth tells much about the habits of a fish by its position, shape, and size. Not surprisingly, bottom-feeding fishes have downward-pointing (subterminal) mouths, while surface-oriented fishes have upward-pointing mouths. For most fishes, however, the mouth is at the end of the snout. The size of the mouth is usually directly related to the size of the preferred food organisms, as is its shape. Thus, fishes that feed on small invertebrates by suction have a small mouth surrounded by protractile "lips" that, when protruded, form an O-shaped opening (the shape with the maximum ratio of area to perimeter length). However, fishes that feed on large prey typically have an inflexible rim to the mouth, which is oval in cross section and frequently lined with sharp teeth. Beyond these general mouth types, the mouths of fishes can show extraordinary shapes that reflect specialized modes of feeding, as discussed in the chapters on the fishes of tropical reefs (Chapter 34) and tropical lakes (Chapter 30).

The **gill openings** of most bony fishes are covered by a thin and flexible bony operculum that is an important component of the "two-pump" respiratory system possessed by most fishes (Chapter 4). As a consequence, the gill openings and cover do not show a large amount of variability, except to be smaller on fishes with low activity levels than on fishes that are more active. In eels, the openings are typically reduced to a small hole, presumably because of the problems associated with raising and lowering the opercular bones under confined conditions. In the Chondrichthyes, the spiracles, used for the intake of water for respiration, are dorsally located in the bottom-dwelling skates and rays, laterally located in most sharks. In the most active species of sharks, however, the spiracular opening is greatly reduced in size because most of the respiratory water is forced through the mouth and across the gills while swimming.

Of the externally visible **sense organs** of fishes, the eyes perhaps tell the most about habits. The size of the eyes, relative to the size of the fish, vary both according to the methods used to capture food and according to the light levels under which the food is taken. Well-developed eyes are found in most fishes that are diurnal predators, although the largest eyes are present on fishes that feed mainly at dusk and dawn, such as the walleye (*Stizostedion vitreum*), or fishes that live near the limits of light penetration in the oceans (see Chapter 36). Many cave-dwelling fishes and deepsea fishes have either tiny eyes or none at all but typically do have extremely well-developed lateral line systems (Chapter 10).

Moderately small eyes are characteristic of fishes that do not rely on vision for feeding, but especially of fishes that prey on bottom-dwelling organisms. Such fishes often have well-developed barbels around the mouth for taste and touch (catfishes), or sensitive, fleshy lips (suckers, Catostomidae).

The **miscellaneous structures** found on fishes are as various as the fishes themselves. For example, males of species with internal fertilization have anal fins modified as intromittent organs, while the males of many species with external fertilization have their fins, sides, and head covered with nuptial tubercles (see Chapter 9). Most deepsea fishes and some nocturnal forms possess light organs (photophores). Many small bottom fishes have plantlike growths (cirri) on their heads and, occasionally, bodies that make them blend into the substrate better.

Skeletal System

For convenience, the skeletal system is considered here to have three main components, the vertebral column, the skull, and the appendicular skeleton (Fig. 2.2).

The **vertebral column** in fishes ranges in development from a cartilage-sheathed notochord (hagfishes), through a cartilaginous vertebral column (vertebrae without centra in lampreys but with centra in elasmobranchs), to one of partially ossified cartilage (ratfishes), to one of solid bone (teleosts). Although the centra (round centers of the vertebrae) are aligned in a series in fishes, the vertebrae lack elaborate interlocking processes, which are necessary in terrestrial vertebrates to counteract

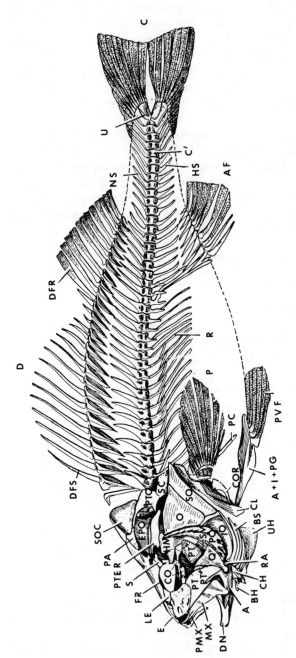

FIGURE 2.2 The teleost (*Perca*) skeleton: *A* angulo-articular; *A+PG* actinosts + interneural + pelvic girdle; *AF* anal fin; *BH* basihyal; *BS* branchiostegal rays; *C* caudal fin; *C'* caudal vertebral centrum; *CL* cleithrum; *CH* ceratohyal; *CO* circumorbitals; *COR* coracoid; *D* dorsal fin; *DN* dentary; *DFR* dorsal fin ray; *DFS* dorsal fin spine; *E* ethmoid; *EPO* epiotic; *FR* frontal; *HM* hyomandibular; *HS* hemal spine; *IO* interoperculum; *LE* lateral ethmoid; *MX* maxillary; *NS* neural spine; *O* operculum; *P* pectoral fin; *PA* parietal; *PC* postcleithrum; *PMX* premaxillary; *PO* preoperculum; *PT, PT', PT''* ecto-, ento-, *metapterygoid;* PTER *pterotic;* PTO posttemporal; *PVF* pelvic fin; *Q* quadrate; *R* rib; *RA* retroarticular; *S* sphenotic; *SC* supracleithrum; *SM* symplectic; *SO* suboperculum; *SOC* supraoccipital crest; *U* urostyle; *UH* urohyal. (Modified from Dean, 1895.)

gravitational forces. The gars (Lepisosteidae) are an exception to this rule and have interlocking vertebrae that resemble those of reptiles. This is presumably related to the heavy load of scaled armor they carry around. The vertebral column of fishes, of course, provides the structural base for swimming movements, and there is generally one vertebra per body segment. This system is admirably suited for withstanding the heavy compression load put on it by contractions of the large muscle masses during swimming.

Despite their apparent simplicity in structure compared to the vertebrae of terrestrial vertebrates, the vertebrae of fish are structurally specialized. The anteriormost vertebrae (the atlas and the axis) are structured for articulation with the skull. In minnows and catfishes (Cypriniformes) the upper portions of the first four to five vertebrae are actually separated from the vertebrae themselves and form a chain of tiny bones that connect the swimbladder to the inner ear, for acute hearing (Chapter 10). At the other end of the spinal column, the posteriormost vertebrae are modified into a series of flattened elements (penultimate vertebrae, hypurals, epurals, and urostyle), which articulate with the rays of the caudal fin. Between these two sets of highly modified vertebrae are the trunk vertebrae, most of which bear ventral (pleural) ribs. These ribs extend ventrally from centra and extend between adjacent muscle masses. In addition to the ventral ribs, most bony fishes also have dorsal ribs that extend between dorsal muscle masses but are usually just loosely associated with the vertebral column. When such ribs or intermuscular bones are well developed, as in minnows, suckers, and pikes, they can be a real nuisance and an occasional hazard to individuals who eat fish.

Both teleost and elasmobranch trunk vertebrae also feature dorsal (neural) processes which form an arch to accommodate the spinal cord. Through the length of these fish, the neural arches together compose the neural canal. In bony fishes the neural spine prominently extends from each neural arch to provide points of attachment for dorsal (epaxial) musculature. In like manner, fusion of the transverse processes produces a hemal canal ventral to the centra in the caudal vertebrae (posterior to the body cavity). The hemal canal carries the primary blood vessels supplying and draining all the caudal musculature (Chapter 5). A hemal spine extends ventrally from each hemal arch and provides a site of ventral (hypaxial) body musculature attachment. In laterally flattened teleosts both the neural and hemal spines are very long so as to give adequate support to the body musculature. They resemble a delicate "double comb."

The skull of fishes (Fig. 2.2) is an extremely complex structure, which represents a design compromise among frequently conflicting uses of the head region: it is the entry point for food and for water for respiration, the site of major sensory organs, a protective container for brain, gills, and other organs, the attachment site for many major muscle masses, and a streamlined entry point necessary for efficient swimming. In agnathans (lampreys and hagfishes) the skull is little more than a cartilaginous trough for the brain from which other cartilages are suspended to support the mouth parts and the gills. Superficially, the skull of the chondrichthyan fishes is also relatively simple; it consists of (1) a solid-appearing chondrocranium which is molded around the brain and sense organs of the head; (2) the jaws, which largely consist of the palatoquadrate cartilage (upper jaw) and Meckel's cartilage (lower jaw) supported by elements of the hyoid arch; and (3) the branchial cartilages, supporting the gills. Despite its simple appearance, the chondrichthyan skull is quite complex in many subtle ways (e.g., position and size of foraminal and fenestral openings, development of rostrum) and is important in the study of taxonomy and evolution.

The skull of bony fishes is an elaborate puzzle of articulating bones that differs from the elasmobranch skull in many fundamental ways, among them that: (1) the optic rather than the olfactory areas are well developed; (2) the relative positions of many of the elements are quite different; and (3) the important parasphenoid and opercular bones have no equivalents in the elasmobranchs. The skull of bony fishes is highly variable. Bones important in the skull of one group may be totally absent from another, and equivalent bones are often difficult to define among major taxonomic groups. However, for convenience, the skull can be divided into five elements: the neurocranium, the suspensorium, the jaws, the opercular bones, and the branchiohyoid apparatus.

The *neurocranium* is the braincase, the most solid portion of the skull, yet typically consists of 40 to 50 bones (counting the small bones around the eyes and optic region). In ancestral bony fishes, including the modern gars, the neurocranium is a solidly fused unit, with strong connections (often fused) to the other portions of the skull. In more "derived" bony fishes, while there remains a solid "core" of bone around the brain (the various frontal, parietal, occipital, optic, and sphenoid bones), the rest of the neurocranium and the skull are rather loosely articulated to provide the expansion capabilities needed for suction feeding and the "two-pump" respiratory system. Another development in advanced bony fishes is the presence of parietal and pterotic crests and the fossae ("trenches") between them on which trunk muscles insert. This reflects changes in methods of swimming.

Connecting the neurocranium and the jaws is a series of bones (hyomandibular, symplectic, quadrate, pterygoids, etc.) collectively called the *suspensorium*. This series of bones has undergone rather dramatic changes in shape, size, and position in the course of evolution from "ancestral" fishes to modern teleosts and to the tetrapods. The *jaws* have also undergone rather dramatic changes in bony fishes, related to the change from a firm biting mouth to a flexible sucking mouth. In the course of this change the principle bone of the upper jaw has changed from the maxilla to the premaxilla (see Chapter 12) and the principle bones bearing teeth have changed. In contrast, the principle bones of the lower jaw (dentaries) have remained fairly constant. The *opercular* bones have also remained fairly constant in bony fishes, although the teleosts have added an interopercular bone on each side to increase the efficiency of the operculum as a respiratory pump. In more "ancestral" bony fishes the interopercular bone is just another branchiostegal bone, part of the *branchiohyoid apparatus* that makes up the "floor" of the mouth and the support for the gills. The branchiostegal bones are a fanlike series of bones that make up the floor of the branchial chamber and provide much of its expansion capabilities, which are so important for suction feeding and respiration.

The **appendicular skeleton,** compared to the skull, is relatively simple, consisting of the internal supports for the various fins, most prominently the supports (girdles) for the pectoral and pelvic fins. In the Chondrichthyes the support for the pectoral fins consists of a series of caracoid and scapular cartilages that form a U-shaped bar attached to the fins on either end. The pelvic girdle is even simpler, consisting solely of a connecting bar, the ischiopubic cartilage. In bony fishes the girdles are more complex. In the pectoral fins the rays articulate with a series (usually five) of radial bones, which in turn articulate with the scapula and coracoid. These bones are attached to those of the cleithral series, but particularly the cleithrum itself, a large bone that is firmly united with the body musculature and is joined, via the supracleithrum, with the skull. The girdle of the pelvic fins of bony fishes is relatively simple, usually consisting of just one basipterygial bone on each side. These bones are usually united with each other or, in advanced teleosts, with the cleithrum of the pectoral girdle (when the fins are in the thoracic or jugular position). For the dorsal and anal fins, the internal supports consist of basal cartilages in the Chondrichthyes and a series of pterygiophores in the bony fishes (one series for each ray or spine in advanced forms). Because they interdigitate with the neural spines of the vertebrae, the dorsal pterygiophores are frequently called interspinous bones.

Muscular System   In almost all fishes, the large muscles of body and tail used for swimming comprise the majority of the body mass, although there are many other smaller muscles associated with the head and fins, often as parts of complex interacting systems. The body muscles are divided vertically along the body length into sections, the myomeres (myotomes), which are separated by sheets of connective tissue. The myomeres are basically shaped like a "W" on its side, so that they fit into one another like a series of cones. The myomeres on the right and left halves of the body are separated by a vertical septum. A horizontal septum separates the muscle masses on the upper and lower halves of the body. The upper muscles are called the *epaxial* muscles and the lower muscles the *hypaxial* muscles. In addition, there is usually a lateral band of muscles that run along or slightly below the midline of the fish.

On inspection, fish muscles can often be divided into red muscle and white muscle. Red muscle has many capillaries per cubic millimeter. The tissue appears red from the high concentrations of red oxygen-binding pigments in the blood (hemoglobin) as well as in the muscle tissue itself (myoglobin). The high capillary density and presence of the pigments insure the red muscle of an adequate oxygen supply for high levels of continuous swimming activity. Therefore, continuously active fish (e.g., bonito, marlin) have a large proportion of red muscle. In general, red muscle fibers metabolize fat aerobically, so that their power output is dependent on their oxygen supply. Fish of "intermediate" activity levels often have the lateral band of muscles, which is always red, well developed and/or have various red fibers scattered in the white muscle that makes up most of the body mass. For example, examinations of body muscle cross sections show that the greatest proportion of red muscle occurs in the lateral bands at the caudal peduncle in both bluefish (*Potatomus saltatrix*) and striped bass (*Morone saxatilis*). The red bands average 18.6% and 10.9%, respectively, of the total musculature in this region (Freadman 1979). Evolutionarily "derived" tunas (e.g., *Thunnus*) carry their red muscle bands deeper toward the body core than more "ancestral" tunas (e.g., *Sarda*), which leaves room for heat-exchanging vasculature in *Thunnus* (Sharp and Dizon 1978). Presumably this arrangement aids *Thunnus* in conservation of metabolic heat, permitting faster muscular contractions and higher swimming velocities (Chapter 3).

The white muscle fibers are thicker than the red, have a poorer blood supply, and have no high oxygen affinity pigment such as myoglobin. As one might expect from the characteristics of this comparatively poor oxygen delivery system, white muscle contraction is not as dependent on oxygen supply. White muscle usually converts glycogen to lactic acid via anaerobic pathways. Thus, white muscle is most useful for short bursts of swimming and dominates the muscle mass of moderately active to "sluggish" swimmers. For example, dogfish sharks have almost all white muscle and can use up 50% of available muscle glycogen in about two minutes (Bone 1966). After this burst of activity, the fish "repays it oxygen debt" by aerobic conversion of lactic acid.

Recently, "staging" in red and white muscular activity has been shown in several fishes (Roberts and Graham 1979). That is, white muscle fibers in chub mackerel, mosaic red and white mixed fibers in salmonids, and pink and white fibers in carp are recruited for swimming activity at sub-burst velocities. Roberts and Graham (1979) detected white muscle contractions from implanted electromyographic electrodes at swimming velocities as low as 2 body lengths per second in chub mackerel. Guppy and Hochachka (1978) have shown how shifts in muscle pH, oxygen tension, temperature, and biochemical substrates can reversibly alter aerobic and anaerobic enzyme activities in skipjack tuna white muscle. Thus, some species conform to the classical differentiation of red and white muscle function (e.g., bluefish, striped bass, and herring, [*Clupea harengus*]) while others (e.g., chub mackerel, rainbow trout, coalfish [*Pollachius virens*], and carp) show a broader range of "white" muscle activity (Freadman 1979).

Locomotion   Fishes move by a variety of means. The simplest means is the passive drift of many larval forms, but such drifters quickly metamorphose into forms more capable of active, directed movement. Although various fish species have evolved the ability to burrow, walk or crawl on the bottom, glide, and even fly, swimming is by far the most important means of locomotion.

To swim forward (or backward!), most fish utilize rhythmic undulations of part or all of their bodies or fins. In the former case, by sequential contraction of the myomeres, the body sides and fins exert force on the relatively incompressible surrounding water. The relatively stiff vertebral column provides compression resistance so that the body bends from side to side rather than shortening. Similarly, Wainwright et al. (1978) showed that the helical collagen network in the skin, the distal insertion of the myomeres, acts as an external tendon for more efficient transmission of muscular force to the tail in lemon sharks (*Negaprion brevirostris*). Changes in collagen fiber angle during swimming prevent loss of tension or skin wrinkling on the concave side of the shark.

Figure 2.3a shows how the lateral flexures at the appropriate angle of attack propel the fish forward. The flexures typically move backward along the body with increasing amplitude and at a speed somewhat greater than the forward progress of the fish. As this propulsive wave moves posteriorly, the water adjacent to the fish is accelerated backward until shed at the posterior margin of the caudal fin, producing thrust (Lighthill 1969) much as the propeller on a boat does. The more undulatory waves the fish can exert against the surrounding water, and the faster and more exaggerated the waves are, the more power can be generated. If other factors such as drag from body dimensions and shape are held constant, fish which generate more power can accelerate more quickly and swim at faster velocities.

Webb (1971) measured the mean wavelength of rainbow trout to be 0.76 times the fish length, a constant at all swimming velocities greater than 0.3 body lengths per second. To increase swimming velocity, trout increase both tail beat frequency (lateral movements per minute) and amplitude (lateral deflection per movement). The thrust (forward-directed force) generated by this propulsive wave is a function of forces produced by the body flexures and the rearward velocity of the propulsive wave,

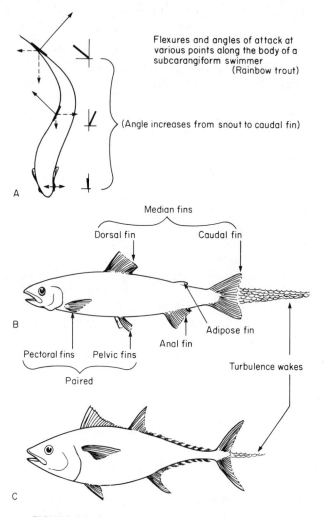

Flexures and angles of attack at various points along the body of a subcarangiform swimmer
(Rainbow trout)

(Angle increases from snout to caudal fin)

A

Median fins

Dorsal fin   Caudal fin

B

Adipose fin

Anal fin

Pectoral fins   Pelvic fins

Paired

Turbulence wakes

C

FIGURE 2.3 Generalized swimming features of fishes.

limited by decreased hydrodynamic efficiency at high tail beat frequencies and amplitudes. An inevitable consequence of this forward movement is a trail of vortices (turbulence) in the water behind the fish (Fig. 2.3b, c).

It should be obvious from the wide variety of body shapes of fishes that, despite the basic approach to swimming just discussed, there is considerable variation in just how fishes swim. It is possible to divide these swimming methods into four basic types: anguilliform, carangiform, ostraciform, and swimming with the fins alone (Fig. 2.4).

Anguilliform swimming, named after the common eel (*Anguilla*), is characteristic of flexible, elongate fishes. The whole body of such fishes is flexed into lateral waves for propulsion. Just as an oar surpasses a pole in rowboat propulsion, the flattened posterior surface of most eels improves their swimming efficiency. Typical eel median "fins" con-

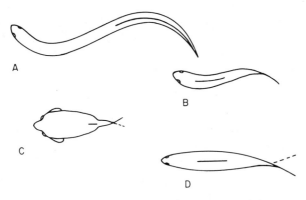

FIGURE 2.4 Swimming modes of fishes: (A) anguilliform; (B) subcarangiform; (C) ostraciform; and (D) carangiform.

sist of a continuous dorsal-caudal-anal soft-rayed fin extending around the posterior half of the fish. A similar fin configuration and swimming style is also found in such evolutionarily widespread groups as the marine gunnels (Pholidae), the anadromous lampreys (Petromyzonidae), and the lungfishes (Dipnoi). Anguilliform swimmers without a strict eellike shape include certain elasmobranchs (e.g., carpet or nurse sharks, Orectolobidae) as well as some teleosts, such as cod (*Gadus*), when swimming slowly (Wardle and Reid 1977). Species that undulate their bodies into less than one full wavelength, yet more than one-half wavelength (at speeds greater than one body length per second), are often placed in a separate movement category, of *subcarangiform swimming*.

Carangiform swimming is intermediate between the anguilliform and ostraciform extremes. Carangiform (jack-style) swimming involves throwing the body into a shallow wave (up to one half wavelength within the body length) with the amplitude increasing from very small at the head and anterior two-thirds of the body to large at the posterior edge of the caudal fin (Webb 1975a). The body shape of carangiform swimmers is typically fusiform, tapering to a narrow caudal peduncle and then broadening to a large, forked caudal fin. Species normally thought of as carangiform types (e.g., jacks, drums, snappers, tunas, mackerels) are swift swimmers.

The fastest-cruising fishes (tunas, billfishes, swordfish, lamnid sharks) combine the low-drag fusiform shape and carangiform swimming mode with a large, slim, lunate (moon-shaped) caudal fin for propulsion. With its "swept-back," tapered tips and "scooped-out" center, the lunate tail provides efficient power for fast underwater movement. Frictional drag is minimized by the "high aspect ratio" design of the tail. By having a small surface area per span length or distance between lobe tips (high aspect ratio), propulsive force is maximized while energy wasted on lateral displacement of water (and consequent creation of excessive vortex wakes) is minimized. The vertically large tail allows a greater mass of water to be accelerated to the rear, increasing forward thrust.

Ostraciform swimming, named after the boxfish family (Ostraciidae), contrasts greatly with the previous two styles of swimming. Instead of throwing their bodies into numerous waves, these fishes swim mainly by flexing the caudal peduncle. By contraction of the entire muscle mass on one side of their bodies and then the other, these swimmers oscillate the caudal fin to produce a sculling type of locomotion. Fishes with this type of locomotion, mainly the trunkfishes, cowfishes, and boxfishes (Tetraodontiformes), are generally encased in armor and rely on this armor (plus spines and toxins) to protect them from predators, rather than speed. The small, isocercal (not differentiated into lobes) caudal fin also is in keeping with their low swimming velocities.

Swimming with fins alone is characteristic of a surprising number of teleosts, including forms that will use their body musculature for swimming when high speed or sustained swimming is necessary. The ray-and-membrane fin design allows these fishes to undulate individual fins or fin pairs rather than their bodies to achieve precise movements. Examples of this type of swimming are found among, but not limited to, fishes inhabiting areas of dense vegetation or coral or rock reefs. The California sheephead (*Pimelometopon pulchrum*) and the birdfish (*Gomphosis tricolor*) of tropical coral reefs both utilize a rowing action of the pectoral fins for forward propulsion. In contrast, triggerfish (e.g., *Balistodies* and *Melichthys*) use alternate dorsal and anal undulations with some pectoral adjustments. The beautiful (and poisonous) lionfish (*Pterois volitans*) of shallow tropical waters moves by deliberate fanning of the caudal, anal, and second dorsal fins when the feathery pectorals and dorsal spines, capable of injecting the painful venom, are held erect.

Energetics of Swimming

The energy costs of swimming have long fascinated investigators. Many attempts have been made to measure the relationship between thrust and drag in swimming fishes. These have ranged from the pioneering efforts of Houssay (1912), who harnessed fish to a balance device which measured swimming power by measuring the weight lifted, to the more sophisticated efforts of Webb (1971), who attached wire grids or plastic plates of various resistances to the dorsal surface of fish swimming in a tunnel respirometer. Bainbridge (1958) showed that for goldfish, trout, and dace the swimming speed at any tail beat frequency increased for longer specimens. As a general rule, a doubling of body length corresponds to a 150% increase in velocity per body flexure. The relationship worked out for small fish is: $V = kL^\beta$, where V is the mean swimming velocity (in meters per second), L is fish length (in meters), k is a constant, and the exponent β has been determined experimentally, usually between 0.5 and 0.6 (Wu and Yates 1978). When sudden bursts of swimming are required, the value of the exponent β is typically about 0.8, a value determined for fish as varied as dace, goldfish, and barracuda. One factor which complicates this relationship is that smaller fish are typically capable of faster tail beat frequencies, which also can increase swimming velocities (Wardle 1975). However, when speed is normalized as body lengths per second, the relationship between speed and tail beat frequency becomes predictable for a range of fish lengths (Fig. 2.5a). When this information is coupled with that of Brett (1965) (Fig. 2.5b), Wohl-

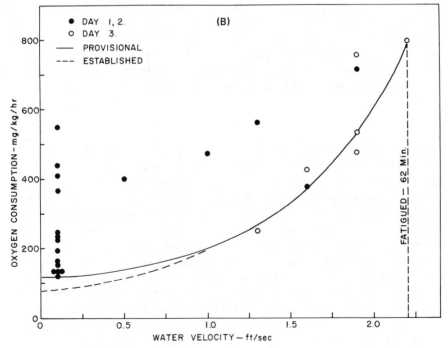

FIGURE 2.5 (A) Relationship between swimming velocity and frequency of caudal undulations (tail beats) for dace, *Leuciscus leuciscus*. (From Bainbridge, 1958.) (B) Relationship between swimming (water) velocity and oxidative metabolic (oxygen consumption) rate for juvenile sockeye salmon. (From Brett, 1964.)

schlag et al. (1968), and others who described the relationship between energetic costs and swimming velocities, estimates regarding a fish's metabolic demands can be made on free-swimming animals by counting tail beat frequencies (Feldmeth and Jenkins 1973).

Temperature is an important factor in the swimming dynamics and energetics of fishes. A 10°C rise in temperature (from 13°C to 23°C) is accompanied by a 22% decrease in water viscosity, which would presumably reduce hydrodynamic drag. Moreover, warm muscles tend to operate more efficiently by exerting more force per contraction. Stevens (1979) found that temperature acclimation produced effects on the swimming muscles of rainbow trout (*Salmo gairdneri*) and largemouth bass (*Micropterus salmoides*). At a constant swimming velocity, tail beat frequencies were lower (i.e., longer stride lengths) for both species acclimated to a higher temperature. Similarly, Webb (1978b) found that trout benefit from warmed environments by increased acceleration rates, which should enhance their attack success on prey. Chapter 3 discusses a vascular heat exchanger system found in several continuously cruising fishes which keeps red muscle mass up to 10°C warmer than the surrounding water.

Webb (1971) determined that the power required to propel a trout was exponentially proportional to the swimming speed (Fig. 2.6) and was approximately 2.8 times greater than that required to propel a *rigid* fish model of equal dimensions. In steady swimming, the average thrust will equal the average total drag on the fish. For the fish to keep moving, the inertial forces of motion must be larger than the viscous forces of the surrounding water. Thus, Reynold's number (Re):

$$Re = VL/v$$

is always greater than 1, where V is the mean swimming velocity, L is the length of the fish, and v is the coefficient of kinematic viscosity of the fluid. Values of Reynold's number typically range from 10^4 to 10^8 for fishes swimming normally (Wu and Yates 1978). Viscosity effects at such high Reynold's numbers are mostly confined to a thin boundary layer adjacent to the body surface, especially in the more streamlined fishes. In species (tunas, marlin, etc.) with small turbulence wakes (Fig. 2.4), the maximum thickness of the boundary layer (at the tail end) is generally not more than a few percent of the body thickness (Wu and Yates 1978). There is evidence that the mucus coating on a fish reduces the frictional drag (Rosen and Cornford 1971). It is also hypothesized that water expired from the opercular (gill cover) openings acts to smooth the flow of boundary water next to the body.

In studies of trout fast-start acceleration, Webb (1975) found that rainbow trout expend 18% of the total work of acceleration to overcome frictional drag. This study also demonstrated that both trout and green sunfish (*Lepomis cyanellus*) display uneven rates of acceleration during

32

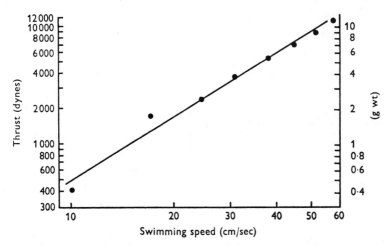

FIGURE 2.6 Thrust/swimming speed relationship for rainbow trout at cruising swimming speeds. (From Webb, 1971.)

a fast start initiated by a mild electric shock. These species initially tended to accelerate maximally. Even though velocity and distance covered increased with time, acceleration rate actually decreased in the milliseconds after a fast start. To capture prey or avoid predation from larger predators, this behavior would seem to have high survival value. Greater velocities would be attained and increased distances covered in a shorter time than with a constant acceleration rate at an increased energy cost of only 2% to 3% of the total expended.

Supplemental Readings   Alexander 1967; Bainbridge 1958; Moyle 1976a; Webb 1975a, 1978a, b; Wu and Yates 1978.

ααααααααααααααααααααααααααααααααααααααααααααααααααααααααααααααααααααααααα
~~~~~~

Buoyancy and Thermal Regulation

Morphologically, the gas-secreting structure of "closed-end" swimbladders found in "derived" teleosts and the heat exchange organs in some large, active, oceanic fishes are very similar. Both involve exchanges, of gas in one case and of heat in the other, across blood vessel walls in an ordered countercurrent (opposite direction) exchange network. Conceptually, this common factor brings these functionally somewhat disparate areas together in this chapter.

Buoyancy

Neutral buoyancy (weightlessness) allows fish to minimize the energy cost of staying at a particular depth to feed, hide, reproduce, or migrate. As an active fish can exert a *propulsive* force greater than 25% to 50% of its body weight for only brief periods, continuous effort to support its body by muscular effort alone would be energetically costly (Marshall 1966). It is not surprising, therefore, that various ways of achieving neutral buoyancy have evolved among fishes. Essentially four strategies[1] are recognizable: (1) incorporation of large quantities of low-density compounds in the body; (2) generation of lift by appropriately shaped and angled fins and body surfaces during forward movement; (3) reduction of heavy tissues such as bone and muscle; and (4) incorporation of a swimbladder as a low-density, gas-filled space.

The use of low-density compounds to reduce the overall density of the body is characteristic of most sharks and a few teleosts. In many sharks large quantities of lipids (specific gravity $\simeq 0.90$–0.92) and the

---

[1] The term "strategy" in this sense implies a direction dictated by the principles of natural selection. "Strategy" does *not* imply a conscious mode of action by the fish either at birth or during its life.

hydrocarbon squalene (sp. gr. $\simeq$ 0.86), found especially in the large livers, bring the total body mass toward neutral buoyancy in sea water (sp. gr. $\simeq$ 1.026). Furthermore, the characteristic heterocercal tail of sharks along with the "angles of attack" of the leading edges of the pectoral fins and the surface of the head provide additional lift while swimming. Hydrodynamic drag is minimized in the more pelagic sharks, which have relatively smaller fins and larger, fatty livers.

Among teleosts, only a few marine species such as the sablefish *Anoplopoma fimbria* (Anoplopomatidae), the pelagic medusa fishes (Stromateidae), and the shallow-water rockfish *Sebastes ruberrimus* (Scorpaenidae) use low-density (triglyceride) oils to lessen negative buoyancy (Lee et al. 1975). The oils are found mainly in the bones. At least one deepsea fish, *Acanthonus armatus* (Ophidiidae), has an enlarged cranial cavity (approximately 10% of the head volume) which is mostly filled with watery fluid (Horn et al. 1978). This fluid has a total osmotic concentration almost one half of those found in the plasma or perivisceral fluid and about one quarter that of the sea water environment. The cranial position of the "light-fluid" reservoir nicely balances most of the heavy body components (otoliths, gill rakers, pharyngeal teeth, and cranial spines) which are also located there.

Fishes of deep (more than 1000 meters) oceanic midwaters characteristically have reduced skeletal and muscular tissues. Food is scarce in these environments, and energetically expensive tissues to maintain such as swimbladders and expensive compounds to synthesize such as body lipids are usually reduced or absent. It is also likely that the cartilaginous skeleton (sp. gr. = 1.1) of elasmobranchs and some bony fishes is partly an adaptation to decrease body density. Bone has a specific gravity of 2.0.

The major problem with the preceding methods of regulating density is that they either greatly restrict the activity of the fish (reduced tissues) or make it difficult for the fish to regulate its density in response to changes in pressure with depth or to changes in the temperature and salinity of the water. The swimbladder is an "invention" of bony fishes that overcomes these problems and has no doubt been largely responsible for their success.

Swimbladders allow precise control of buoyancy because the volume of gas they contain can be regulated with comparative ease. Because of the increased density of sea water, fish and other objects are buoyed up more than in fresh water. Hence, with typical teleostean skeletal and body composition, swimbladders occupy about 5% of the marine teleost's body volume and about 7% of the freshwater forms.

Swimbladders are of two basic types, physostomous and physoclistous. Physostomous swimbladders have a connection (pneumatic duct) between the swimbladder and the gut. Physoclistous swimbladders lack this connection. Fishes with physostomous swimbladders include many of the more "ancestral", soft-rayed teleosts, including herrings, salmonids, osteoglossids, mormyrids, pikes, cyprinids, characins, catfishes, and eels (Marshall 1966). Physostomous fishes inflate their swimbladders by gulping air at the water's surface and forcing it through the pneumatic duct into the swimbladder by a buccal force mechanism (Fänge 1976). It is, therefore, not surprising that physostomes are largely shallow-water forms. Additional swimbladder inflation is needed for neutral buoyancy at deeper depths. As the maximum swimbladder inflation volume at the surface (1 atmosphere gas pressure) is halved with each 10 m descended, its buoyancy value is minimized with increasing depth. Thus, the amounts of gas needed at depth would be so great that it would be impossible for the fish to submerge!

Deflation of the physostomous swimbladder is accomplished by a reflex action, the *gass-puckreflex* (gas-spitting reflex), which is initiated when reduced external pressure makes the fish too light, releasing gas via the pneumatic duct into the esophagus. Pneumatic sphincter muscles (both smooth and striated muscle tissue), under nervous control, guard the entrance to the pneumatic duct. Fänge (1976) attributes the release of gas to a relaxation of the sphincter muscles, a contraction of smooth muscles in the swimbladder wall (under similar nervous control), the elasticity of the swimbladder wall, and contractions of body wall muscles. The importance of gas diffusion mechanisms (i.e., with the blood) for physostome swimbladder inflation or deflation is probably minimal. Although the number of species investigated is comparatively low, only a few species (e.g., eels [*Anguilla, Conger*]; whitefish [*Coregonus*]) show the richly vascularized wall structures specially adapted for gas exchange (Fänge 1976).

In contrast to physostomous fishes, fishes with "closed" (physoclistous) swimbladders have special structures associated with the circulatory system for inflating or deflating the swimbladder. Presumably because these structures "free" the fish from dependency on the surface, over two thirds of all teleosts (especially the more "derived," spiny-ray species) are physoclistous. A red organ or *rete mirabile* (meaning "wonderful net") is the source of inflation gas in these swimbladders. The rete consists of a tight bundle (rather than net) of afferent (running toward) and efferent (running from) capillaries surrounding each other (Fig. 3.1). This vascular arrangement provides for an efficient, counter-

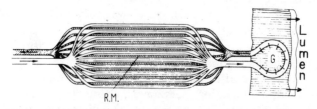

FIGURE 3.1 Schematic drawing of the capillary rete mirabile (R.M.) and "gas gland" (G) of the eel (*Anguilla*). The thickness of the swimbladder wall containing the "gas gland" is exaggerated. (From Kuhn et al., 1963.)

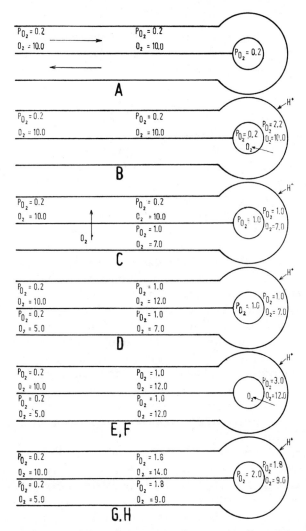

FIGURE 3.2 A numerical example of hairpin counter-current multiplication of O_2 by the rete of a fish swimbladder. The Root shift is exaggerated. For pedagogical purposes, the concentration mechanism is shown as occurring in steps with arbitrary intervals. Oxygen tensions (P_{O_2}) are in atmospheres, and oxygen concentrations (O_2) are in volumes % (= ml/dl). [From Steen, 1971, with permission, from *Comparative Physiology of Respiratory Mechanisms*. Copyright by Academic Press Inc. (London) Ltd.]

current exchange of blood gases, which allows gas pressure (and, therefore, volume) to increase or "multiply" within the swimbladder lumen. Figure 3.2 shows an example of how the hairpin countercurrent system secretes high concentrations of oxygen into the swimbladder of a physoclistous fish. Figure 3.2a shows blood saturated with oxygen arriving in the rete. Localized lactate secretions near the lumen end of the rete lower the blood pH, provoking a loss in hemoglobin oxygen affinity (Bohr effect) and capacity (Root effect, see Chapter 5). Oxygen is thus driven off the hemoglobin into the plasma, increasing the plasma oxygen partial pressure (P_{O_2}) (Fig. 3.2b). The P_{O_2} gradient (higher in plasma than in swimbladder lumen) forces oxygen to diffuse into the lumen until a P_{O_2} equilibrium is established between the two (Fig. 3.2c). As the blood P_{O_2} is somewhat elevated in the efferent vessel compared with the 0.2 atmospheres in the afferent vessel, oxygen moves from the efferent to the adjacent afferent vessels. This diffusive movement of oxygen proceeds efficiently along the length of the rete capillaries as a result of the countercurrent flow (see Chapter 4). The complementary movements of oxygen to the afferent vessels in the rete and to the lumen provide the "multiplication" of gas pressure needed to inflate the swimbladder, despite the crushing influence of hydrostatic pressures encountered in deep water. In this fashion the gas pressure in the swimbladder lumen is "multiplied" up to 300 atmospheres in some deepsea fishes. The longer the retial capillaries, the more complete is the gas exchange and the more efficient is the filling of the swimbladder at depth. Indeed, investigations on deepsea fishes show a good correlation between retial capillary length and habitat depth. Fish found between 1500 m and 3500 m may have retial capillaries 25 times longer than those of fishes found between 150 m and 500 m (Marshall 1971). Besides oxygen, a significant fraction (up to 40%) of the gas secreted into the swimbladder can be carbon dioxide from bicarbonate in the blood or gas gland metabolism (Fänge 1976). Even "inert" gases such as nitrogen can be concentrated in the swimbladder by the countercurrent multiplier. Addition of lactate as a solute lowers the solubility of blood for all dissolved gases ("salting-out" effect).

Deflation of the physoclistous swimbladder is accomplished by diffusion of gas back into the bloodstream via a richly vascularized area adjacent to the enclosed gases. As long as the partial pressure of the oxygen, nitrogen, or carbon dioxide is greater inside the swimbladder compared with the blood, diffusion back into the blood will occur in this area. This area may be an "oval" patch of densely packed capillaries on the dorsal wall of the swimbladder or may consist of the posterior lining of the swimbladder wall, the functional area of which is regulated by anterior/posterior movements of a mucosal "diaphragm."

Thermal Regulation   It is often assumed that all fish, as "cold-blooded" vertebrates, are always at the same temperature as their environment. The large surface area of the gills, which exchanges gases so efficiently (Chapter 4), also exchanges heat efficiently. As the blood circulates through the gills every 30 sec to 2 min (Davis 1970), heat produced from body metabolism can be quickly carried away from the fish by the water ventilating the gills.

However, the British physician John Davy noticed in 1835 that skipjack tuna caught for food were 10°C warmer than the water in which they were caught. Field studies also revealed that certain fishes "preferred" waters of particular temperatures over other, equally accessible areas. Thus, two possible methods of some internal temperature control became apparent: behavioral and physiological thermoregulation.

Behavioral thermoregulation concerns the movements of fishes from one water mass or area to another characterized by a warmer or cooler temperature. As temperature affects rates of metabolism and digestion so profoundly (Chapters 4 and 7), some fishes may "select" a particular temperature to conserve energy or to run their metabolic machinery (i.e., enzymes) at its most efficient temperature. For example, Brett (1971) found that sockeye salmon (*Oncorhynchus nerka*) select a warm temperature (15°C) at a depth of approximately 11 m to digest the food eaten at their dusk feeding during the short Canadian summer nights. In contrast, the fish go deeper (37 m) to 5°C water between the dawn and dusk feeding periods. Thus, during the longer daytime period, the fish conserve energy by lowering their body maintenance energy requirements in the colder water (Chapter 4).

Human-induced thermal changes in aquatic environments have further stimulated investigations of fish thermoregulatory behavior. For example, Neill and Magnuson (1974) consistently captured bluegill (*Lepomis machrochirus*), largemouth bass (*Micropterus salmoides*), longnose gar (*Lepisosteus osseus*), small rockbass (*Ambloplites rupestris*), pumpkinseed (*Lepomis gibbosus*), large yellow bass (*Morone mississippiensis*), and carp (*Cyprinus carpio*) in the heated outfall plume waters of an electrical power generating plant located on Lake Monona, Wisconsin. Evidence was collected that localized food sources (e.g., zooplankton for the bluegill, small fish for the longnose gar) influenced the preference of some of these species for the thermal plume area, which was 2°C to 4°C warmer (median temperatures) than adjacent areas during middle to late summer. However, concurrent laboratory studies using a shuttlebox apparatus showed that the consistent plume residents tested had higher preferred temperatures than the one species which consistently avoided the thermal plume, yellow perch (*Perca flavescens*).

Physiological thermoregulation in fishes, to a significant degree, is exhibited only by several continuous-swimming species. Each of the "warm-bodied" species leads a pelagic marine existence and has heat-exchanging retia mirabilia to conserve heat produced by the fish's metabolism (Carey et al. 1971). These fish also have the major arteries and veins for blood transport between the heart and gills and the heat exchanger located close to the skin (Fig. 3.3).

This enables them to transport the cool (i.e., near water temperature) blood to and from the heat exchanger without absorbing much of the heat produced by the swimming muscles. The structure of these retia is similar to that of the physoclistous swimbladder, gas-secreting retia described in the buoyancy section of this chapter. Essentially, by means of a honeycomb arrangement of afferent and efferent blood

FIGURE 3.3 Circulation in the muscles of a bigeye tuna: (A) segmental artery and vein; (B) vascular bands; (C) cutaneous artery; (D) cutaneous vein; (E) rete mirabile; (F) arterial branches from dorsal aorta. (From Carey and Teal, 1966.)

vessels, heat (instead of gas) is exchanged by convection across the walls of these many vessels running parallel to each other. No gases are exchanged in the heat-exchange retia because there is no localized acidification of the blood, such as by lactic acid in the swimbladder rete. Also, the larger vessel diameter (ten times as large: 0.1 mm rather than 0.01 mm) and thicker vessel walls (compared with the swimbladder rete capillaries) further slow the diffusion of oxygen molecules, which diffuse at a rate ten times slower than heat. Because of the countercurrent flow, the metabolic heat is efficiently conserved in the rete, which surrounds the red swimming muscles (Fig. 3.3). The efficiency of this heat exchanger is 95% as a thermal barrier between the gills and red muscle in skipjack tuna (*Katsuwonus pelamis*) (Neill et al. 1976).

Although the number and position of heat-exchanging retia varies among the various tunas and mackerels (Scombridae) and lamnid sharks (e.g., shortfin mako [*Isurus oxyrinchus*]) that possess retia, all of them are capable of fast, continuous swimming. As warm muscles can contract faster than cool ones, presumably the heat exchanger allows these predatory fishes to exert more swimming thrust and thus outswim the squid and smaller fishes that compose their diet. For example, the grouper (*Epinephelus*), which does not have the special circulatory adaptations for metabolic heat conservation, has an internal temperature of $0.3°C$ above that of the water it lives in, whereas the swimming muscles of albacore tuna (*Thunnus*) show a $12°C$ elevation (Carey et al. 1971). "Warm-bodied" fishes, however, do not have constant body temperatures (such as in mammals or birds) but have temperatures that fluctuate with that of the environment. The core temperature of the largest of these "warm-bodied" species, the bluefin tuna, seems least affected by environmental temperature, apparently because of the great thermal inertia that is inherent in large bodies. In some situations this may work to their disadvantage by causing overheating of the muscle mass when exercising. Thus larger tuna adopt a cyclical pattern of depth distribution to "cool off" below the thermocline if surface waters are too warm for continuous occupancy.

The ability of "warm-bodied" fishes to sense changes in their thermal environment may operate either by neural comparisons of temperature of the water (external surface of the fish) with that deep inside the body or by the blood temperature gradient across the heat exchanger (Neill et al. 1976).

Supplemental Readings   Carey and Lawson 1973; Carey et al. 1971; Carey and Teal 1966; Fänge 1976; Kuhn et al. 1963; Marshall 1966; Neill et al. 1976; Neill and Magnuson 1974; Neill et al. 1972; Steen 1971.

αααααααααααααααααααααααααααααααααααααααααααααααααααααααααααααααααααα
~~~~~~

Respiration

Respiration in an aquatic environment presents different problems when compared with respiration in air. Most terrestrial vertebrates have internal lungs that must be ventilated by bidirectional (tidal) movement of air to replenish the oxygen supply at the gas exchange surfaces. In contrast, most fish have external gills that are ventilated by a unidirectional flow of water, created either by branchial pumping or passively, by simply opening the mouth and operculi while swimming forward. Not having to accelerate and decelerate the water in a bidirectional pattern obviously saves the fish valuable energy. The fine sieve structure of the gills (Fig. 4.1) enables them to extract oxygen very efficiently from the water. This efficient oxygen uptake is vital to fish, since the dissolved oxygen content of water is very low. Water contains about $\frac{1}{30}$ as much oxygen per volume as the atmosphere above it. This low oxygen availability has undoubtedly contributed to the evolutionary development of the gills, which are characterized by large surface areas and extremely efficient gas exchange, and to the many, often bizarre, mechanisms some fishes use to extract oxygen directly from the air. The low availability of oxygen has also placed limits on rates of oxygen uptake and consequently on fish metabolism.

Gills	Gills are the main site of gas exchange in almost all fishes. The gills consist of bony or cartilaginous arches (Fig. 4.1) which anchor pairs of gill filaments. The numerous, minute secondary lamellae which protrude from both sides of each filament are the primary sites of gas exchange. The secondary lamellae are made up of thin epithelial cells on the outside and thin basement membranes and supportive pillar cells on the inside (Fig. 4.2), allowing blood cells to flow through the interior without significant changes in

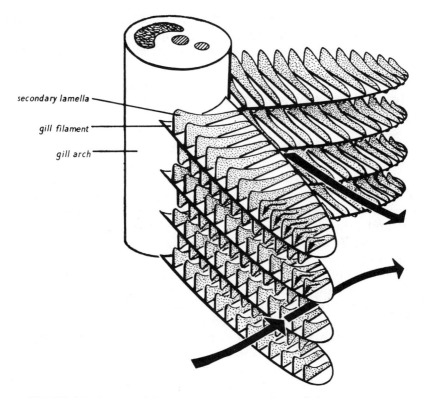

secondary lamella
gill filament
gill arch

FIGURE 4.1 Diagram of fish gill structure. Large arrows indicate direction of water flow; small arrows show direction of blood flow. (Modified from Hughes and Grimstone, 1965.)

shape (Hughes and Grimstone 1965). Oxygen is taken up by diffusion across the thin lamellar membranes. Because the blood and the water move in opposite directions, gas exchange efficiency is maximized by countercurrent exchange. Countercurrent flow insures a steady oxygen tension gradient along the entire diffusion surface. Thus the blood can be oxygen-saturated to a greater degree than with a parallel flow arrangement. Van Dam (1938) reported oxygen utilizations (extraction efficiencies) as high as 80% by a rainbow trout (*Salmo gairdneri*). When a parallel flow was experimentally induced by reversing the ventilatory

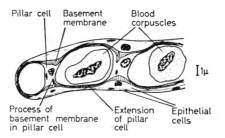

Pillar cell   Basement   Blood
              membrane   corpuscles

I 1μ

Process of   Extension   Epithelial
basement membrane   of pillar   cells
in pillar cell   cell

FIGURE 4.2 Section through secondary lamella. (Modified from Hughes, 1963.)

water in the tench (*Tinca tinca*), utilization dropped to less than 10% (Hughes 1963). The actual rate of oxygen uptake depends on the surface area of the lamellae, the thickness of the gill epithelia across which the oxygen moves, and the oxygen (tension) gradient across the membranes. Consequently, in order to increase rates of oxygen uptake from water highly active fishes typically have larger gill surface areas and extra thin gill epithelial layers (Table 4-1). In order to increase gill surface area, fishes have two main evolutionary "options": increasing the number of lamellae by spacing them more closely together and increasing the length of the lamellae. The latter "option" is seldom found because of the fragility of the delicate lamellae. Some tunas have evolved lamellae which are fused at the tips between adjacent filaments to add rigidity and hence protect the lamellae from damage from the high ventilatory flows (Muir and Kendall 1968). The close lamellar spacing and the thin epithelia usually associated with the lamellae of active fish both decrease the distance across which the oxygen in the water must diffuse to enter the blood and thereby increase the rate of diffusion. Gas diffusion rates also depend on the gas tension gradient across the respiratory surface. As oxygen diffuses from the water through the lamellar surfaces and into the relatively oxygen-depleted blood, diffusion slows or stops if fresh, oxygen-rich water is not continually provided. Renewing this water is called ventilation of the gills.

TABLE 4-1
Comparison of Gill Dimensions in Several Teleost Fishes

Species	Thickness of Lamellae (μ)	Lamellae (per mm)	Distance Between Lamellae (μ)	Distance Between Blood and Water (μ)	
Icefish (*C. aceratus*)	35	8	75	6	
Bullhead	25	14	45	10	Sluggish
Eel	26	17	30	6	species
N. tessellata	20	17.5	35	2	
Sea scorpion	15	14	55	3	
Trout (5 kg)	15	20	40	3	
Flounder	10	14	70	2	
Icefish (*C. esox*)	10	18	40	1	Active
Trout (400 g)	12	23	35	3	species
Roach	12	27	25	2	
Coalfish	7	21	40	<1	
Perch	10	31	25	<1	
Herring	7	32	20	<1	Very active
Mackerel	5	32	25	<1	species

Source: Modified from Steen and Berg (1966).

CH. 4   RESPIRATION

Gill ventilation. In most bony fishes ventilation is accomplished by synchronous expansion and contraction of the buccal and opercular cavities to provide a nearly continuous unidirectional flow of water over the gill surfaces. In the first phase of the pumping cycle, water enters the mouth by expansion of the buccal cavity. The water is then accelerated over the gills by a simultaneous contraction of the buccal cavity and expansion of the operculi. After the branchial cavity contracts, expelling the water out the opercular openings, the cycle begins again (Fig. 4.3). Interruptions of this cycle produce brief reversals of flow or "coughs" which fish use to clear foreign matter or excess mucus from the gills. The frequency of these coughs in brook trout (*Salvelinus fontinalis*), has been used as a sublethal indicator of excessive copper concentrations in fresh water (Drummond et al. 1973). The greater volume of water passed over the gills, the faster the "boundary" water is replaced at the lamellar surfaces, maximizing the oxygen tension gradient and, therefore, the diffusion rate. Sharks, skates, and rays use fleshy flaps of skin to create a ventilatory current through the branchial cavity.

Varying the ventilation volume is one adjustment that fish can make to influence the rate of gas exchange at the gills. Roberts (1975) has shown that at least one species from each of eight teleostean families ceases branchial movements and passively ("ram") ventilates at a high, "critical" swimming velocity. Presumably these critical velocities are evolutionarily determined to maximize energetic efficiency by using the swimming musculature both to propel the fish and to ventilate the gills adequately.

Another example of ventilation volume adjustments to influence gas exchange rates is exhibited by most fishes which encounter water

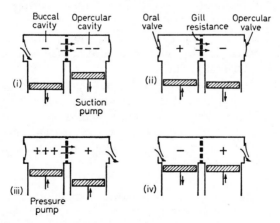

FIGURE 4.3 Diagrammatic representation of the two-stage (buccal and opercular) pump for ventilating the gills of bony and cartilagenous fishes. The first three phases actively pump water through the gill sieve. The last phase shown (iv) does not pump a significant flow but accounts for only a very brief part of the cycle. (From Hughes, 1963.)

TABLE 4-2
Means of Striped Mullet Ventilatory Responses to Hypoxia

Variable	Units	Ambient Conditions	Hypoxic Conditions
Inspired dissolved O_2 concentration	mg O_2/l	8.81	3.48
O_2 consumption rate	mg O_2/kg/hr	120.54	119.40
Ventilation volume	ml water/min	36	171
Ventilatory frequency	strokes/min	60	95
Ventilatory stroke volume	ml water/stroke	0.60	1.80
Percentage utilization of oxygen	%	66	39

Source: Modified from Cech and Wohlschlag (1973), with permission, from *Journal of Fish Biology.* Copyright by Academic Press Inc. (London) Ltd.

with low amounts of oxygen. In this case the oxygen tension of the inspired water is reduced and diffusion of oxygen across the gills slows as a result of the decreased oxygen gradient. The typical response to hypoxia is a higher ventilatory water flow. To increase the volume of water pumped over the gills, increases in either the number of buccal and opercular strokes per minute (ventilatory frequency) or the volume pumped with each stroke (ventilatory stroke volume) are required. Commonly a fish will increase both in response to hypoxic conditions (Table 4-2). Increases in ventilation volume maximize the oxygen tension difference by rapid displacement of water next to the lamellar surfaces. Even though the oxygen extraction efficiency per volume of water (or percent utilization) is often reduced at high ventilatory flows, a sufficient total amount of oxygen can normally be taken up to maintain respiratory homeostasis (Table 4-2).

Other sites of aquatic respiration. In some fishes a small amount of aquatic gas exchange takes place at areas besides the gills. For example, the upper lobe of the caudal fin of the longnose gar (*Lepisosteus osseus*) has an extra rich blood supply and is used to a minor extent to exchange gases. Diffusion through the skin is known to play an important role in the respiration of larval fish. Significant cutaneous respiration has also been implicated in some adult forms such as eels (*Anguilla* sp.) and the Antarctic icefish (*Chaenocephalus* sp.). However, because of a variety of limitations regarding surface area and blood supply, the contribution of cutaneous oxygen uptake is probably minor, especially in large fish (Holeton 1976).

Air-Breathing Fishes

Behavioral means have also evolved in fishes to cope with hypoxic water. Whereas some species swim to the surface and inspire the oxygen-rich water next to the atmosphere, others have evolved the ability actually to leave the water and breathe air. Other fishes which migrate short distances over land or are exposed to severe drought conditions have also evolved aerial respiratory adaptations. These adaptations range from modifications of the gills, to use of the skin, to special respiratory structures in the mouth and gut, to true lungs.

Modified gills. *Clarias batrachus*, the "walking catfish" of southeast Asia and more recently of southern Florida and other areas (Chapter 20), represents an example of a fish with modified gills. These catfish feature thickened, widely spaced lamellae on the dorsal side of the filaments and branched, bulbous dendritic structures dorsally emanating from the second and fourth gill arches. These dendritic structures resemble "respiratory trees" and reside in suprabranchial cavities (Jordan 1976). The thickened and bulbous shapes of these modified gills ensure adequate support in air. Ordinary gills, having numerous, closely spaced filaments and lamellae, tend to stick together and functionally lose much of their surface area when removed from water. Another requirement for respiratory surfaces is that they remain properly moist. *Clarias* apparently moves on land mainly when it is raining (Jordan 1976).

Skin. The extent to which fishes use cutaneous respiration is poorly known. It is best documented in eels (*Anguilla anguilla*), which can migrate short distances across land. By diffusion through a well-vascularized skin and to a lesser extent across the gills, they are able to use the atmosphere for respiration (Berg and Steen 1965). Desiccation of the body surface is avoided by limiting terrestrial sojourns to nocturnal movements through moist grass.

Mouth. Electric eels (*Electrophorus electricus*), in contrast to "true" eels, are among the obligate air-breathing fishes. This species has a well-vascularized area in the buccal cavity where most of its required oxygen is taken up. Whereas this region has a large surface area from surface convolutions and papillae, the gills have degenerated over evolutionary time. The electric eel surfaces at intervals of about 1 min to replenish the oxygen supply in its mouth and will drown if forcibly kept immersed (Johansen et al. 1968).

Two other genera which use modified areas of the mouth for aerial gas exchange are *Anabas*, the Asian climbing perch, and *Gillichthys*, the North American mudsucker. Both of these examples have evolved bimodal breathing capabilities to feed or escape predators by moving out of the water.

Gut. *Hoplosternum*, *Anicistrus*, and *Plecostomus* are three tropical catfishes which have parts of their gut specialized for oxygen uptake by actually swallowing air. In these and most other air-breathing fishes, elimination of respiratory carbon dioxide occurs primarily at a site different from that of oxygen uptake. Since the gut is not closely associated with the external environment, the highly water-soluble carbon dioxide is excreted primarily at the gills.

Lungs and swimbladders. Another example of a gas-specific exchange location comes from the famous lungfishes (Dipnoi). Like *Electrophorus*, the South American (*Lepidosiren*) and African (*Protop-*

terus) lungfishes are obligate air breathers. The latter forms have adapted to extensive drought conditions which may completely dry up their environments. By breathing air through a small vent to the atmosphere, these fishes survive extensive dry periods in the mud of dried-up lakes and rivers in an estivated state. When their habitats refill with water, they surface to inspire air into well-sacculated and heavily vascularized lungs. On the other hand, most of the carbon dioxide is eliminated directly into the water through vestigial gills. The Australian lungfish (*Neoceratodus*) is not subjected to such lengthy drought conditions in its natural environment and will perish if experimentally denied access to water for extensive periods. Other facultative air breathers which use a modified swimbladder for some gas exchange function include the bichir (*Polypterus*), the bowfin (*Amia*), and gars (*Lepisosteus*).

Fish Oxygen Requirements

Fish need energy to move, to find and digest food, to grow, and to reproduce, in addition to maintaining the body and internal environment. Energy stored in their food must be metabolically converted to power for these various bodily functions. Oxygen, along with an organic substrate, is needed for all oxidative metabolic processes. Oxidative (or aerobic) metabolic pathways are dominant in organisms which have a fairly reliable oxygen source because they are biochemically more efficient than anaerobic pathways. The amount of oxygen which a fish requires for these processes over a given length of time is called its oxygen consumption rate. Oxygen consumption rate can be affected by a variety of factors. Three of the most significant of these are body weight, level of activity, and environmental temperature.

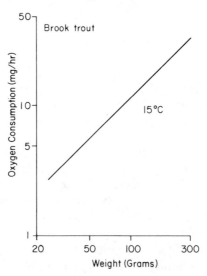

FIGURE 4.4 The influence of body weight on total oxygen consumption rate for brook trout (*Salvelinus fontinalis*) at 15°C. (Modified from Beamish, 1964.)

CH. 4   RESPIRATION

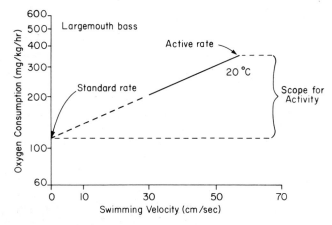

FIGURE 4.5 The effect of swimming velocity on the oxygen consumption rate of largemouth bass (*Micropterus salmoides*). Extrapolation back from the data to 0 cm/sec estimates the standard metabolic rate. Subtraction of the standard metabolic rate from the active rate gives the scope for activity. (Modified from Beamish, 1970.)

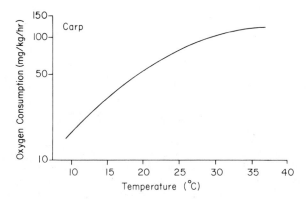

FIGURE 4.6 The influence of temperature on the oxygen consumption rate of carp (*Cyprinus carpio*). (Modified from Beamish, 1964.)

In general, larger fish use more total oxygen per hour than smaller fish do (Fig. 4.4), although per unit body weight, smaller fish use more oxygen than larger specimens. In similar manner, swimming fish use more oxygen than resting animals (Fig. 4.5). Moreover, fish in warmer water generally have higher oxygen consumption rates than those in cooler water (Fig. 4.6).

Experimental Techniques   The apparatus generally used to measure fish oxygen consumption (oxidative metabolic) rates is called a respirometer. A respirometer can be as simple as a stoppered bottle filled with water and containing a fish (Fig. 4.7a). This sort of container can be used *in situ* in field situations or as part of

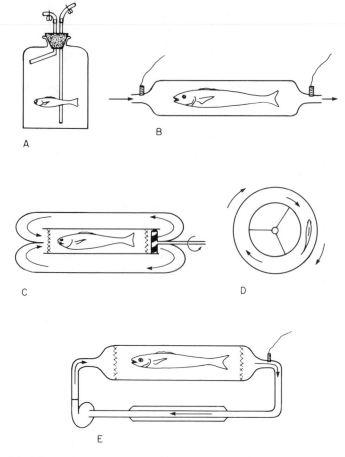

FIGURE 4.7 Fish respirometer diagrams: (A) static respirometer with inflow and outflow tubes for water samples; (B) flow-through respirometer with oxygen electrodes for measuring inflowing and outflowing oxygen concentrations; (C) Blazka-type swimming respirometer with a tube within a tube and a rotating impeller to circulate the water at various speeds; (D) annular-type swimming respirometer that rotates to move water; (E) Brett-type or tunnel respirometer with a pump to move water past fish.

an elaborate laboratory system with strict environmental control. Comparison of dissolved oxygen concentrations taken when the bottle is stoppered with those taken after the fish has consumed part of the oxygen will yield consumption rate data. Compared with this static system, flow-through respirometers (Fig. 4.7b) are useful for studies in which air-saturated water must be available to the fish over a long time period.

Conventional static and flow-through respirometers may be used to measure "routine" and, with special precautions, "standard" or "resting" metabolic rates of fishes. There are also several types of respirometers usable in measuring "active" rates of fish swimming at various velocities (Fig. 4.7c, d, e). In addition, this technique is commonly used to estimate standard metabolic rates by extrapolation back to a swimming speed of 0 lengths/sec (Fig. 4.5). Subtraction of the standard metabolic rate from the active metabolic rate yields the "scope for activity," which is a useful index in determining the relative amount of nonmaintenance energy reserves. Fishes with more reserves are better able to move, grow, reproduce, and resist diseases and parasitism.

Supplemental Readings Beamish 1964, Berg and Steen 1965; Cech and Wohlschlag 1973; Hughes 1963; Johansen et al. 1968.

αααααααααααααααααααααααααααααααααααααααααααααααααααααααααααααααααααα
~~~~~~

Blood and Its Circulation

Blood Fish blood, like that of other vertebrates and many invertebrates, is composed of blood corpuscles (cells) suspended in plasma that is circulated throughout the body tissues. The cells are of two basic types, erythrocytes (red blood cells, RBCs) and leukocytes (white blood cells, WBCs). In this section we will first describe the nature and function of erythrocytes and leukocytes, then briefly describe how these cells are enumerated, and finally discuss in detail the structure and function of hemoglobin, the oxygen-carrying pigment of the blood.

Both RBCs and WBCs are formed from hemocytoblast precursor cells which may originate from a variety of organs but usually mature after they enter the bloodstream. In hagfish the primary blood-forming site is the mesodermal envelope surrounding the gut (Jordan and Speidel 1930). Percy and Potter (1976) have shown that adult lampreys (*Lampetra*) synthesize blood cells from the fatty tissue dorsal to the nerve cord. Elasmobranch fishes produce erythrocytes from the organ of Leydig (situated in the esophagous), special tissue around the gonads, and especially the spleen. Splenic production of RBCs may consist either of immature erythrocytes or of cells which differentiate into erythrocytes after entering the blood (Fänge and Johansson–Sjöbeck 1975). Teleostean hemopoietic (blood-forming) sites are primarily the kidney and spleen (Satchell 1971). Fish bone has no marrow for hemopoiesis.

ERYTHROCYTES Red blood cells are usually the most abundant cells in fish blood (up to 3 million per mm^3). They contain hemoglobin and largely function in carrying oxygen from the gills to the tissues. Like the erythrocytes of other nonmammalian vertebrates, fish RBCs are

TABLE 5-1
Hematological Characteristics of Various Fishes

Species	Erythrocyte Number (cells $\times$ $10^6/mm^3$)	Hematocrit (%)	Hemo-globin Concen-tration (g %)	Mean Erythrocytic Volume (μ^3)	Blood Oxygen Capacity (volumes %)	Source
Spiny dogfish (*Squalus acanthias*)	0.09	18.2	—	650–1010	—	Thorson (1958) Wintrobe (1934)
Blue shark (*Prionace glauca*)	—	22.3	5.70	—	—	Johanson–Sjöbeck and Stevens (1976)
Oyster toadfish (*Opsanus tau*)	0.69	—	6.84	—	—	Eisler (1965)
Winter flounder (*Pseudopleuronectes americanus*)	2.21	23	5.36	107	8.30	Bridges et al. (1976)
Common carp (*Cyprinus carpio*)	1.43	27.1	6.40	186	12.50	Houston and DeWilde 1968
Striped mullet (*Mugil cephalus*)	3.08	26.9	7.14	88	8.36	Cameron (1970a)
Pinfish (*Lagodon rhomboides*)	2.66	32.9	7.59	124	7.78	Cameron (1970a)
Spotted sea trout (*Cynoscion nebulosus*)	3.25	32.2	6.99	99	8.56	Cameron (1970a)
Bluefish (*Pomatomus saltatrix*)	3.85	—	13.41	—	—	Eisler (1965)
Albacore (*Thunnus alalunga*)	—	—	17.20	—	—	Barrett and Williams (1965)

nucleated and show a wide range of sizes among different species. Elas-mobranchs typically have larger RBCs, although fewer in number, than teleosts (Table 5-1). Even within the teleosts, fishes having more erythrocytes per milliliter of blood generally have smaller RBCs. Within this group the more active species tend to have more erythrocytes than sedentary forms (Table 5-1). Perhaps the smaller cell size in these active forms presents a shorter mean diffusion path length for essential respiratory gases such as oxygen. Shorter path lengths and more erythrocytes would make the oxygen uptake at the gills and delivery to the oxygen-requiring swimming muscles more efficient.

Because the oxygen demands of fish vary with stage of life history and environmental conditions, the number of red blood cells per milliliter varies as a way of balancing the energy costs of producing RBCs with those of pumping blood to the tissues. Blood that is low in RBCs obviously has to be pumped through the body at a greater rate than

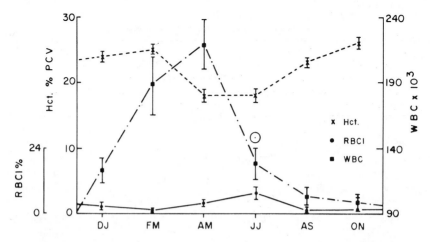

FIGURE 5.1 Bimonthly mean values (± SE) of microhematocrit, immature red blood cells, and leukocytes (WBCs) for winter flounder (*Pseudopleuronectes americanus*) from Casco Bay, Maine. The notation ⊙ signifies the highest mean RBCI, which occurred during the third week in June. (From Bridges et al., 1976.)

blood that is high in RBCs, if the oxygen demand is high. Since Cameron (1975) has demonstrated, for three species of freshwater fish, that the teleost heart requires up to 4.4% of the total energy of the fish, the number of RBCs can have a significant effect on its overall energy balance, including growth, etc. (Chapter 8). Indeed, rainbow trout (*Salmo gairdneri*) experimentally made anemic show significant increases in the volume of blood pumped by the heart (cardiac output) (Cameron and Davis 1970). However, when oxygen demands of tissues are relatively low, such as when water temperatures are low and the fish are not very active, large numbers of RBCs are not required and the number tends to drop (RBCs live up to 150 days, at least in tench [*Tinca tinca*], at 18°C, Hevesy et al. [1964]). Thus, in active fishes there are often seasonal changes in RBC production. For example, winter flounder (*Pseudopleuronectes americanus*) have a peak in RBC production in late spring and early summer in waters off Maine (Fig. 5.1). Cameron (1970) has shown that changes in RBC counts (and in total hemoglobin concentration, Hb) in pinfish (*Lagodon rhomboides*) are of some significance in meeting seasonal increases in respiratory demands. However, he points out that other adjustments, in erythrocyte size and in the rate of blood circulation, would also be required to meet the nearly tenfold change in respiratory metabolism associated with seasonal temperature extremes. In the striped mullet (*Mugil cephalus*) changes in RBC numbers and Hb are associated not only with seasonal temperature changes (Cameron 1970b) but also with spawning activity, with its high energy demands (Fig. 5.2). Increases in RBC number during the spawning season have also been recorded for fish as diverse as carp (*Cyprinus carpio*) (Fourie and Hattingh 1976) and the cichlid *Tilapia*

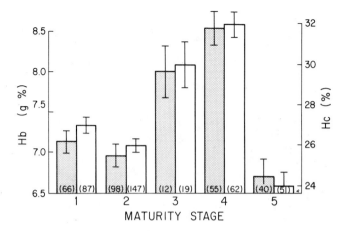

FIGURE 5.2 Mean hemoglobin and hematocrit levels at different reproductive maturity stages. Histogram bar heights indicate mean values; vertical lines indicate ±1 SE; numbers in parentheses indicate sample size; stippled bars indicate total hemoglobin concentration; open bars indicate percent of packed cell volume (hematocrit). Maturity stages: 1 = immature (gonads very small or absent); 2 = mature (gonads mature, but small); 3 = prespawning (gonads enlarged but not secreting reproductive products); 4 = ripe (reproductive products flow easily from fish); 5 = postspawning (gonads somewhat enlarged but empty). (From Cech and Wohlschlag, 1981.)

zilli (Ezzat et al. 1973), so the phenomenon may be widespread among teleosts. It is also worth noting that RBC counts may also be affected by other environmental factors, particularly pollutants. Destruction of erythrocytes through the inhibition of vital metabolic pathways in the cell appears to be one of the reasons chlorine in water is so harmful to fish (Grothe and Eaton 1975; Buckley 1976).

LEUKOCYTES White blood cells are less abundant (20,000 to 150,000 per mm^3) than RBCs in fish blood and function in a variety of ways in ridding the body of foreign material (including invading pathogens), along with providing a mechanism for blood clotting. Measurements of change in total WBC number or in the percentages of the various types can often lead to a better understanding of the physiological or pathological state of the animal. Circulating WBC number can also vary through the year in some fish species. Bridges et al. (1976) describe a pattern of total and differential (separate) WBC counts in winter flounder which generally shows an inverse relationship with fish condition or health. Sick individuals would presumably make more WBCs to synthesize antibodies, phagocytize bacteria, etc. A thorough review of fish leukocytes has been prepared by Ellis (1977). Sample photomicrographs of winter flounder blood cells are shown in Fig. 5.3. There are often several types of leukocytes found in fish blood, and different roles have been attached to their presence. The principal types of WBCs are lymphocytes, thrombocytes, monocytes, and granulocytes.

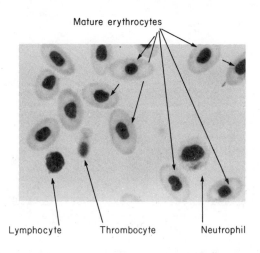

Mature erythrocytes

Lymphocyte   Thrombocyte   Neutrophil

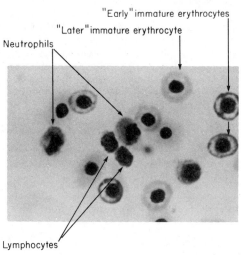

"Early" immature erythrocytes

"Later" immature erythrocyte

Neutrophils

Lymphocytes

FIGURE 5.3 Winter flounder blood cells.

Lymphocytes can vary in size (4.5 μm to 12 μm in diameter) among species. Their morphology, on the other hand, is more consistent. They are dominated by the nucleus, with only a narrow rim of basophilic cytoplasm in which there are a few mitochondria and ribosomes. The number of lymphocytes varies among species (and with counting technique!). Ellis (1977) found that 12×10^3 lymphocytes per mm^3 was the representative value for plaice. However, the number of lymphocytes can vary with season, following general WBC seasonal trends (Fig. 5.1). Teleostean lymphocytes appear to be produced by both thymus and kidney, although specific antigen responses may differ between cells produced by each organ (Ellis 1977).

The primary function of fish lymphocytes seems to be to act as the executive cell of specific immune mechanisms by means of antibody production. Klontz (1972) reported a large increase in cells resembling small lymphocytes in the kidney of rainbow trout, which was correlated with high antibody production, 2 to 3 days after antigen injection. Hildemann (1970) and Hogarth (1973) have described the accumulation of cells resembling small lymphocytes at the graft points of rejected tissue transplants in fish. There is also some evidence that fish lymphocytes may demonstrate phagocytic activity (engulfing foreign cells) or give rise to cells (e.g., macrophages) which have this ability (Klontz 1972; Weinreb and Weinreb 1969).

Thrombocytes of fishes may appear as spiked, spindle, oval, and lone nucleus forms in stained blood smears, prepared on microscope slides. The various thrombocyte shapes may well be different forms of the same cell, as changes in shape can be observed in live preparations. From his work on plaice, Ellis (1977) believes that thrombocytes originate in splenic tissue. Wardle (1971) has shown the function of thrombocytes in plaice to be the clotting of circulating fluids. Clots are produced by spreading of the thromocytic cytoplasm into long threads which cross-link the denuded nuclei, forming a fibrous network which traps circulating corpuscles.

Monocytes comprise a small proportion of the WBC population, unless foreign substances are present in the tissues or bloodstream. Thought to originate in the kidney, monocytes (termed "macrophages" by some workers) concentrate at and phagocytize foreign particles. Morphologically, therefore, the cell outline may be quite irregular from pseudopod formation.

Granulocytes are leukocytes with conspicuous cytoplasmic granules. There are three basic types: eosinophils, basophils, and neutrophils. The names of the three types reflect the comparative visibility of the granules when the cells are treated with acidic (e.g., eosin), basic, and neutral stains, respectively. Neutrophils are the most commonly encountered fish granulocyte, comprising up to 25% of the total leukocytes in brown trout (Blaxhall and Daisley 1973). In addition to the neutral-staining (e.g., gray) cytoplasm, fish neutrophils often have an eccentric nucleus which is divided into several lobes.

Granulocytes are formed in the kidney and the spleen to a lesser extent in teleosts (Ellis 1977). Fange (1968) determined the organ of Leydig to be the site of granulocyte formation in elasmobranchs. Granulocytic function is still open to question. Neutrophilis apparently migrate to sites of bacterial infection, where they may be phagocytic (Finn and Nielson 1971). Neutrophilia (i.e., increased numbers of circulating neutrophils) often corresponds to "stress" in rainbow trout (Weinreb 1958).

Basophils have been reported in goldfish, Australian lungfish (*Neoceratodus forsteri*), carp (except an Israeli strain), and Pacific salmon, but absent in the blood of anguillid eels, plaice, yellow perch (*Perca flavescens*), brown and rainbow trouts, and cyclostomes (Ellis

1977). Ellis (1977) also reported much confusion and contradiction in the fish hematological literature as to the presence or absence of eosinophils in fishes. Although still unclear, basophil and eosinophil functions seem related to antigen sensitivity, stress phenomena, and phagocytosis (eosinophils) (Ellis 1977).

CORPUSCLE-ENUMERATION METHODS Because of the presence of nuclei in both erythrocytes and leukocytes of fishes, electronic methods routinely used in clinical measurements of red and white cell number cannot be used for fish blood (Blaxhall 1972). The Neubauer-type hemocytometric method of blood dilution and counting in ruled areas in a microscope field is in common use. WBC abundance has been estimated by the height of the white cell layer (buffy coat) which settles between the red cell pack and the plasma when capillary tubes (e.g., for hematocrit determinations) are centrifuged. This buffy coat height or "leucocrit" has usefulness as a rough diagnostic tool in fish disease work. Microscopic examination is used to determine numbers of the various types of leukocytes.

HEMOGLOBIN Hemoglobin (Hb) is a respiratory pigment that vastly increases the binding power of the blood for oxygen. For example, in the Port Jackson shark (*Heterodontus portjacksoni*) at 20°C, 93% of the oxygen carried by the blood is reversibly bound to the hemoglobin while 7% is physically dissolved in the plasma at saturation (Grigg 1974). In colder environments the plasma percentage may increase (12% in the Antarctic nototheniid *Trematomus bernacchii* at -1.5°C). Indeed, the Antarctic crocodile icefishes (family Channichthyidae) carry no hemoglobin in their blood at all. The icefishes survive because (1) their metabolic oxygen requirements are low and the environmental dissolved oxygen is high in the consistently cold Antarctic waters; (2) their sluggish activity levels are adequate to catch sufficient quantities of the plentiful krill and small fish; and (3) special cardiovascular adaptations (e.g., comparatively large heart and blood volume with relatively low resistance capillaries) promote efficient movement of their blood (Holeton 1970).

Despite this evidence that some fish can get along without hemoglobin, its importance to most fishes is difficult to overstate. However, hemoglobin is not just a single type of molecule but really a class of structurally similar molecules that vary in their structure and in their affinity for oxygen under different conditions. This variability will become evident in the next sections on (1) hemoglobin structure; (2) the role of hemoglobin in blood oxygen affinity; and (3) factors affecting blood oxygen affinity.

Hemoglobin structure. Fish hemoglobin is of two basic types, monomeric and tetrameric. Monomeric hemoglobins consist of single-heme polypeptide molecules, each with a molecular weight of about 17,000. They are characteristic of lampreys and hagfishes (Agnatha).

Tetrameric hemoglobins are characteristic of all "higher" fishes. They are composed of four chains of amino acids (two α chains and two β chains), much like mammalian hemoglobins, and have molecular weights of approximately 65,000. There are many different kinds of tetrameric hemoglobins, and several kinds may be found in one fish! For example, four kinds of hemoglobin are found in rainbow trout blood (Binotti et al. 1971), two in American eel (*Anguilla rostrata*) blood (Poluhowich 1972), and three in goldfish (*Carassius auratus*) blood (Houston and Cyr 1974). The significance of synthesizing more than one hemoglobin type appears to be related to the different functional properties of each, so different combinations of hemoglobin types reflect adaptions to different environments or ways of life.

Multiple hemoglobins are especially adaptive in migratory species which experience considerable environmental variation. For example, the catadromous American eel has one hemoglobin which has a high oxygen affinity in saltwater and one with a high affinity in freshwater conditions. Poluhowich (1972) suggests that the polymorphic hemoglobins assist in the acclimation of these eels to environments of different salinity by maintenance of an approximately constant blood oxygen affinity.

The goldfish hemoglobins are functionally differentiable by their responses to temperature (Houston and Cyr 1974). Goldfish acclimated to 2°C had two different hemoglobins, while others held at 20°C and 35°C featured three. Because the observed concentration of the third hemoglobin did not exceed 12.5% of the total concentration in any individual, its physiological importance may be minor, and a warm-temperature function for this component has yet to be demonstrated. However, Houston and Rupert (1976) have shown that the third Hb can be made to appear and disappear with temperature changes from 3°C to 23°C and vice versa, respectively, within *3 hours*. Thus, this rapid synthesis of the third hemoglobin in goldfish probably stems from rearrangement of the α and β subunits in other hemoglobins rather than from synthesis of a new hemoglobin or production of a new type of erythrocyte.

Hemoglobin polymorphism for activity levels has also been hypothesized for species of suckers (Catostomidae). Powers (1972) has presented evidence that the desert sucker (*Catostomus clarki*) possesses a pH-insensitive hemoglobin which maintains a high O_2 affinity even when the O_2 affinities of other hemoglobins are drastically reduced from increases in circulating lactic acid from violent muscular activity. This species typically lives in fast water. In the same stream, however, lives the Sonora sucker (*Catostomus insignis*), which does not possess this hemoglobin. This species is therefore found mainly in the slower-water portion (e.g., quiet pools) of their streams.

Changes in hemoglobin types with age have also been demonstrated in fishes. Coho salmon, for example, show changes with the progression from alevin to fry to presmolt stages. Giles and Vanstone (1976) believe these changes are controlled genetically and may be related to known changes in the hemopoietic origin of the erythrocytes during development. Certainly the pattern of Hb's seems more fixed in developing cohos than in goldfish, as exposure of the salmon fry and pre-smolts to extremes of temperature, salinity, and dissolved oxygen produced no detectable variations (Giles and Vanstone 1976).

BLOOD OXYGEN AFFINITY   Figure 5.4a shows the blood oxygen dissociation curves of a Sacramento blackfish (*Orthodon microlepidotus*), and Fig. 5.4b shows those of a rainbow trout.   Hyperbolic curves like those from blackfish blood result from the paucity of interaction among the four subunit hemes (O_2-binding sites) characteristic of tetrameric molecules.   The subunit independence results in curves which are similar to those of the monomeric hemoglobin of agnathans. The steep, hyperbolic curve of the blackfish hemoglobin displays its ability to be 50% saturated with oxygen (half of the highest possible content, or half of capacity) at only 2 mm Hg P_{O_2} at 20°C.[1] This is termed the half-saturation value (or P_{50}) and reflects the affinity of the hemoglobin for oxygen. The low P_{50} of the Sacramento blackfish (2 mm Hg) indicates a high blood oxygen affinity. By comparison, the rainbow trout blood features a higher P_{50} (17 mm Hg) or *lower* blood oxygen affinity.

The importance of this difference is especially apparent in hypoxic environments (those low in dissolved oxygen). For example, if the P_{O_2} of the water is only 32 mm Hg (about 20% of air saturation), fish could only raise their arterial P_{O_2} to about 25 mm Hg in the gills, despite the efficiency of this countercurrent gas exchanger. At 25 mm Hg, the Sacramento blackfish can saturate its arterial blood to about 90% (Fig. 5.4a), whereas the rainbow trout will only be able to saturate its blood to about 65% (Fig. 5.4b). This ability to saturate the blood to the 90% level under these conditions is obviously an advantage to a fish living in poorly oxygenated water, such as sloughs, stagnant pools, or in hypolimnetic parts of lakes. The higher percent saturation achieved by the blackfish means that a greater content of oxygen is reversibly bound by the hemoglobin for transport to the tissues to meet the metabolic oxygen (content) requirements of the fish.

The evolutionary advantages inherent in the sigmoid curve characteristic of the trout include the unloading of oxygen at the tissues at a fairly high P_{O_2}. Typifying quite active fishes in well-oxygenated waters, the high P_{O_2} of the inspired water ensures full oxygenation of the blood while traversing the gills. Fishes with sigmoid curves with a fairly steep middle segment can unload and reload large quantities (contents) of oxygen over a quite narrow P_{O_2} range. This steep portion of the curve represents the physiologically most efficient P_{O_2} range for O_2 uptake and delivery for the species. As the steep portion of sigmoid curves is

---

[1]Note that 2 mm Hg P_{O_2} = partial pressure (P) of oxygen equal to 2 mm mercury (Hg) pressure.

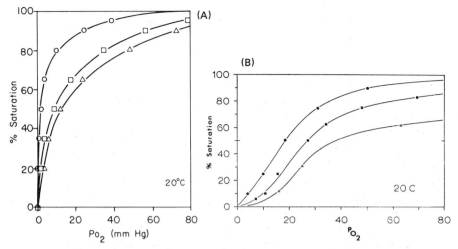

FIGURE 5.4 (A) Blood oxygen dissociation curves for Sacramento blackfish, equilibrated at 20° C and three P_{CO_2} levels: <1 mm Hg P_{CO_2} (circles), 5 mm Hg P_{CO_2} (squares), and 10 mm Hg P_{CO_2} (triangles). (From Cech, Mitchell, and Massingill, unpub. data.) (B) Blood oxygen dissociation curves for rainbow trout blood equilibrated at 20° C. Solid circles are data for 0 mm Hg P_{CO_2}, solid squares for 3 mm Hg P_{CO_2}, and open triangles for 7 to 8 mm Hg P_{CO_2}. (From Cameron, 1971a.)

usually shifted to the right (compared with hyperbolic curves), the active fishes with sigmoid curves operate most efficiently in well-oxygenated environments (streams, well-mixed oligotrophic lakes, shallow ocean areas).

Oxidized (rather than oxygenated) hemoglobin, which cannot function as a respiratory pigment, is termed methemoglobin (MetHb) and may occur in significant quantities in fish blood. Cameron (1971b) found 11% of the total hemoglobin in pink salmon (*Oncorhynchus gorbuscha*) was methemoglobin, as was up to 17% of the hemoglobin in hatchery rainbow trout. Although it is not clear why high percentages of MetHb occur in the few species examined, it is known that energy is required to reduce the MetHb back to the less stable, functional form (Cameron 1971b).

FACTORS AFFECTING BLOOD OXYGEN AFFINITY The dynamics of fish hemoglobin–oxygen binding and dissociation have evolved to optimize gas transport to oxidative tissue sites. Numerous factors can influence the blood oxygen affinity. Among the most important are pH, carbon dioxide concentrations, temperature, and organic phosphate concentrations.

Carbon dioxide concentration and pH effects are often interrelated and are physiologically the most important factors affecting blood oxygen affinity. Figure 5.5 shows the effect of pH and P_{CO_2} on winter flounder blood oxygen affinity. The decrease in affinity with decreasing pH or increasing P_{CO_2} (Bohr effect) normally works to "drive off" oxygen from the hemoglobin, thereby facilitating its diffusion to surrounding

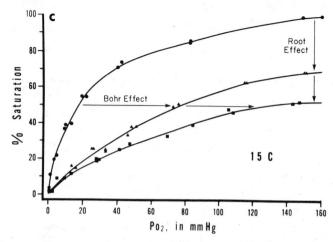

FIGURE 5.5 Blood oxygen dissociation curves of winter flounder (*Pseudopleuronectes americanus*) blood equilibrated to three levels of P_{CO_2} at 15°C. The notations ● = <1 mm Hg P_{CO_2} (mean pH = 8.02), ▲ = 8 mm Hg P_{CO_2} (mean pH = 7.48), and ■ = 24mm Hg P_{CO_2} (mean pH = 7.17). (Modified from Hayden et al., 1975.)

tissues. The Bohr shift is calculated by dividing the shift or change in log P_{50} by the change in pH associated with the shift. Table 5-2 shows that more active fish species tend to have larger Bohr shifts. This tendency would presumably be adaptive, as exercise provokes greater oxygen demands of the red swimming muscles. The larger Bohr effect would increase the O_2 diffusion rate across the capillary walls to meet this demand. Moreover, violent or high levels of sustained exercise activates the primarily anaerobic white muscles, incurring an "oxygen debt." Lactic acid, the glycolytic end product of this metabolism, decreases blood pH even further, thereby magnifying the Bohr shift.

The Root effect (Root 1931) is another pH/P_{CO_2}-induced shift, except that blood oxygen capacity rather than affinity is affected (Fig.

TABLE 5-2
Bohr Effects of Fishes Characterizing Various Activity Levels

Activity Level	Species	Temperature (°C)	Bohr Effect $\dfrac{\Delta \log P_{50}}{\Delta pH}$	Source
Lower	Brown bullhead (*Ictalurus nebulosus*)	9, 24	−0.31	Grigg (1969)
	Flounder (*Platichthys flesus*)	15	−0.55	Weber and DeWilde (1975)
Higher	Rainbow trout (*Salmo gairdneri*)	15	−0.57	Eddy (1971)
Highest	Atlantic mackerel (*Scomber scombrus*)	25	−1.2	Hall and McCutcheon (1938)

5.5). The Root shift is now thought of primarily as an extreme Bohr shift, and the molecular basis of this phenomenon may be associated with a special hemoglobin within a complement of multiple hemoglobins. Increases in P_{CO_2} or decreases in pH lower the O_2 capacity (O_2 content at 100% saturation). This effect is found only among fish hemoglobins and typifies species with swimbladders and retia mirabilia (red organs). Sharks have no swimbladders and no Root effect associated with their hemoglobins. As described in detail in Chapter 3, the unique features of these retial countercurrent exchangers and the Root effect makes swimbladder inflation possible at great depths. Baines (1975) found a large Root effect characterizing the hemoglobin of relatively deep-water rockfishes (*Sebastes*, Scorpaenidae) he studied off the California coast. More shallow water scorpaenids which have less extensive vertical migrational patterns had smaller Root effects. Finally, in the strictly shallow-water California scorpionfish (*Scorpaena guttata*), which has no swimbladder, no Root shift could be detected.

Winter flounder have no swimbladder yet display a significant Root effect (Fig. 5.5). Like many other teleosts that depend on vision to feed, winter flounder possess a choroid rete or countercurrent vascular organ behind the retina of the eye (Wittenberg and Haedrich 1974). The Root effect may play a significant role in delivering sufficient oxygen to the retina tissue, which has a high oxygen demand (Hayden et al. 1975).

Aspects of carbon dioxide transport in the blood are covered in more detail in Chapter 6, in the section concerning acid-base balance. Regardless, it is germane here to explain the CO_2 equilibrium curve

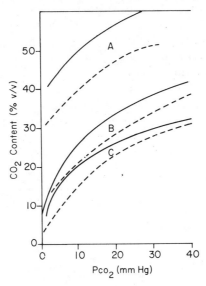

FIGURE 5.6 Representative carbon dioxide equilibrium curves: (A) *Cyprinus carpio*; (B) *Scomber scombrus*; and (C) *Salmo gairdneri*. Solid lines and dotted lines represent deoxygenated and oxygenated blood, respectively. (Modified from Grigg, 1974.)

which relates CO_2 loading (content) in the blood with the partial pressure of CO_2 (P_{CO_2}). There is typically significant CO_2 loading with little change in P_{CO_2} within the normal physiological range of P_{CO_2} (less than 10 mm Hg), with some flattening out at higher tensions (Fig. 5.6). CO_2-combining power is greater in fishes (e.g., carp) adapted to living in stagnant, high P_{CO_2} environments and is lower for fishes typifying low CO_2 habitats (e.g., trout and mackerel). Figure 5.6 also shows the increased CO_2 combining power of deoxygenated Hb (Haldane effect) due to the pH rise accompanying blood deoxygenation (Grigg 1974). The magnitude of the Haldane effect also varies among species.

Temperature effects on blood oxygen affinity and capacity of fish hemoglobins are most noticeable in stenothermal species. Figure 5.7 shows that increases in temperature depress both oxygen affinity and oxygen capacity of tench blood. The extra oxygen delivery to the respiratory tissues (e.g., from blood oxygen affinity loss) when oxygen demand is elevated by increased temperatures would seem to be an adaptive advantage. However, instead of exerting a selective effect like the Bohr shift (i.e., working primarily at the tissue sites where P_{CO_2} is high and/or pH is low), the temperature effect in these ectotherms works equally well at the gills! Thus, large temperature effects would not appear advantageous to species inhabiting environments that exhibit large temperature fluctuations or to species that move quickly from one temperature to a different one.

The effect of temperature on the oxygen affinity and capacity of hemoglobin can be quantified by the apparent heat of oxygenation (ΔH) from a form of the van't Hoff equation (Riggs 1970). The "living fossil" coelacanth (*Latimeria chalumnae*), living at the quite thermally stable depth of 200 m to 400 m in the ocean, has hemoglobin displaying a ΔH of -10.42 kcal/mole (Wood et al. 1972). The more eurythermal winter flounder of coastal marine environments has a hemoglobin ΔH of -7.7 (Hayden et al. 1975). Species confronting wide temperature variations such as the Sacramento blackfish in shallow California lakes and sloughs (Cech et al. 1979) and the globally migra-

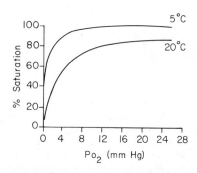

FIGURE 5.7 Oxygen dissociation of tench (*Tinca tinca*) blood at 5° and 20° C. (Modified from Eddy, 1973.)

tory bluefin tuna (*Thunnus thynnus*) (Rossi-Fanelli and Antonini 1960) display Hb Δ H values of –1.6 and –1.8, respectively.

Organic phosphate effects are also important in the reversible binding of fish hemoglobins with oxygen. Gillen and Riggs (1971) have shown that concentrations of naturally occurring organic phosphates can profoundly influence Hb-O_2 affinity. They found adenosine triphosphate (ATP) to be the primary phosphorylated compound in Rio Grande perch (*Cichlasoma cyanoguttatum*) and that ATP additions depress O_2 affinity, increase the Bohr effect, and modify heme–heme interactions. In carp RBCs, guanosine triphosphate (GTP) plays a greater role than ATP in blood oxygen affinity regulation (Weber and Lykkeboe 1978). Intraerythrocytic organic phosphate concentration decreases thus comprise another physiological mechanism for enhancing O_2 uptake efficiency in fishes exposed to warm (Grigg 1969) or hypoxic (Greaney and Powers 1978; Weber and Lykkeboe 1978) environments.

Circulation   The cardiovascular system of most fishes is a closed system typically consisting of a heart as the pump in line with branchial (gill) and systemic capillary beds connected by arteries and veins (Fig. 5.8). In contrast, hagfish circulatory systems have accessory inline hearts. Lungfish also differ with the presence of a pulmonary circulation and partial mixing of oxygenated and deoxygenated blood in the heart (Randall 1970). A variety of circulatory adaptations can be found in fishes having accessory respiratory surfaces, for example, in cavities, at the skin, in the gut (Satchell 1976). Given the diversity of circulatory adaptations in fishes, it is instructive to examine aspects of the cardiovascular anatomy to

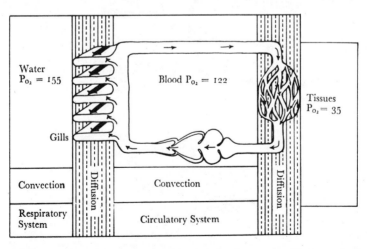

FIGURE 5.8 The sites of convective and diffusional transport of oxygen in the circulation of a fish. The partial pressures of oxygen quoted are those of aerated water, arterial and venous blood in *Salmo gairdneri*. (From Satchell, 1971.)

understand circulatory function better. Of paramount importance is the heart.

HEART STRUCTURE   Propulsion of blood through the circulatory system of the majority of teleostean and elasmobranch fishes is accomplished by a four-chambered heart, two chambers of which effect significant acceleration of the blood. All four chambers are in line and pump only venous blood. Except for a few air-breathing fishes, all flow of blood is to the gills. The heart and gills are closely associated, as fish hearts are located the farthest anterior of all the vertebrates. The heart is enclosed in a pericardium, which is more rigid in elasmobranchs than in teleosts (Satchell 1971).

The first chamber of the fish heart is the sinus venosus, which functions as a manifold. That is, venous blood from the hepatic circulation and the ducti cuvieri are collected in this relatively thin-walled chamber and directed to the atrium through the sino-atrial valve by a delicate lining of cardiac muscle (Fig. 5.9). While the sinus venosus provides the initial transition from smooth to pulsatile flow, the atrium provides the first significant circulatory acceleration of the blood. Compared with the sinus venosus, the atrium is a relatively large chamber which lies dorsal to the ventricle and funnels down to the atrio-ventricular ostium and two-flap valve.

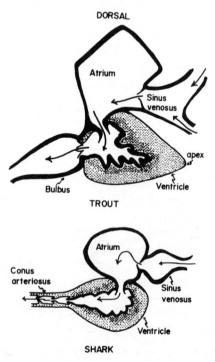

FIGURE 5.9 Diagrams of the heart in (A) a trout (teleost) and (B) a shark (elasmobranch). (From Randall, 1968.)

The ventricle is also a relatively large chamber featuring heavy walls of cardiac muscle (Fig. 5.9). It is pyramid-shaped in elasmobranchs and conical in teleosts, with the apex pointing posteriorly. The heavy muscle and efficient geometry of the ventricle provide the main propulsive force for circulatory flow. Ventricular walls are composed of two layers of muscle. The cortex is relatively dense cardiac muscle (myocardium) which receives oxygen and nutrients from the coronary artery. The cortex is well developed in active species such as skipjack tuna (*Euthynnus pelamis*) and rainbow trout, whereas sluggish species, such as toadfish (*Opsanus tau*), have a much reduced cortex (Cameron 1975). The inner layer consists of a spongy mesh supplied with oxygen and nutrients only by the venous blood it pumps.

In contrast to the atrium or ventricle, the fourth chamber (conus arteriosus in elasmobranchs, Agnatha, and holosteans; bulbus arteriosus in teleosts) does not increase the acceleration of the blood. It functions as an elastic chamber to dampen the extremes of pressure and intermittent flow from the ventricle into a less-pulsed, continuous flow to the ventral aorta and the gills. The bulbus wall consists only of elastic tissue and layers of smooth muscle and features no valves. Priede (1976) has summarized the functional morphology of the trout bulbus arteriosus. Conversely, the conus can have many valves (up to 72 in gars [*Lepisosteus*]!) as well as cardiac musculature in the walls. It is felt that the more rigid membrane (pericardium) that houses the heart in elasmobranchs produces a more active "rebound" between contractions of the heart, which assists in its filling from the veins. The conal valves insure that significant reverse flow of the blood back into the heart does not occur during this rebound. The conus is more poorly developed in cyclostomes, which have a single pair of valves.

Johansen and Hanson (1968) have summarized the differences in heart structure in lungfishes and amphibians associated with the evolutionary transition from aquatic to atmospheric breathing. The most dramatic difference is the partial division in the lungfish heart associated with the separate return of blood (pulmonary vein) on the left side of the heart from the lungs. This separate return emanates from a special pulmonary vascular circuit which is coupled in parallel with the normal systemic (body) and branchial (gill) circulation. The *partially divided* ventricle moves the arterial (from the lungs) and venous (from the body) blood through a bulbus cordis which largely maintains separation of the two flows by spiral ridges which twist throughout its length. The arterial blood is conveyed to the body, while the venous blood passes through the functional gills, some of it subsequently entering the lung. The extent of separation of flows in the heart correlates with the dependence on air breathing. The Australian lungfish (*Neoceratodus*), which cannot withstand lengthy air exposure, displays the least separation. *Protopterus* (African) and *Lepidosiren* (South American lungfish), which must withstand periodic droughts in their natural habitats, show more complete separation of flows. An excellent review of circulation in air-breathing fishes is provided by Satchell (1976).

MYOCARDIAL ELECTRICAL ACTIVITY   Typically for a vertebrate, most fish hearts are myogenic (i.e., no nervous signal from the brain is necessary for each heart beat) and show a complex electromyogenic wave form. Although the actual sites of the primary pacemaker nodes are still obscure, evidence gathered for some teleosts suggest islets of pacemaker cells in the sinus venosus and atrium (Satchell 1971). Kisch (1948) demonstrated that many areas of the myocardium can show pacemaker activity.

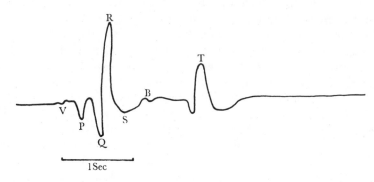

FIGURE 5.10   The electrocardiogram of the Port Jackson shark, *Heterodontus portusjacksoni*. (From Satchell, 1971.)

Fish electrocardiograms (ECG) showing the progression of electrical phenomena through a cardiac cycle are obtained by implantation of bipolar electrodes under the skin, commonly spanning the pericardial area. The electrodes are wired to an appropriate amplification and display system consisting of either an oscilloscope or physiological recorder. Figure 5.10 shows the ECG of an elasmobranch, the Port Jackson shark. The chronological sequence of chamber depolarizations (contractions) shows the synchronous movement of blood through the heart:

Wave	Chamber Myocardium Depolarized
V	Sinus venosus
P	Atrium
QRS	Ventricle
B	Conus arteriosus (elasmobranchs only)

The T wave is usually the only ECG wave visibly indicating chamber muscle repolarization (ventricle). Satchell (1971) presents a good discussion of cardiac electrical phenomena in fishes.

CARDIAC FLOW   The ventricular pumping rhythm induces the systolic (contraction)/diastolic (relaxation) rhythmic flow in the ventral aorta.

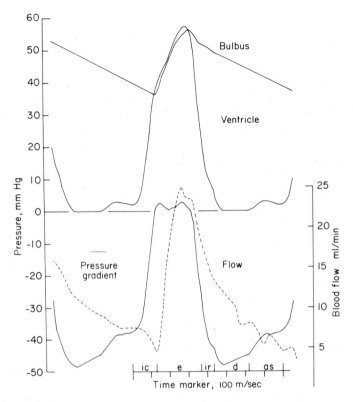

FIGURE 5.11 Rectilinear records of blood pressure during one heartbeat of a lingcod (2.0 kg, 15°C). (From Stevens et al., 1972.)

The bulbar pressure pulse dampening effect as measured in lingcod (*Ophiodon elongatus*) is seen in Fig. 5.11. The systolic/diastolic wave form of pressure is also detectable in the dorsal aorta, even though the branchial vascular network of the gills drops the blood pressure by $\frac{1}{4}$ to $\frac{1}{3}$. For example, in winter flounder, bulbus arteriosus mean pressure = 29 mm Hg and dorsal aorta mean pressure = 22 mm Hg. This difference (7 mm Hg) represents a 24% pressure drop through the gills (D'Amico Martel and Cech 1978).

Blood pressures in hagfish are very low despite the presence of the branchial and several accessory hearts. The various hearts work independently of each other to perfuse various parts of the body with blood (Randall 1970):

Hagfish Heart	Blood Source	Blood Destination
Branchial	Body, liver	Ventral aorta
Portal	Gut, anterior cardinal vein	Liver
Caudal	Subcutaneous sinuses	Anterior body

The hagfish caudal heart consists of a cartilaginous plate and attached skeletal musculature along with a pair of lateral sacs with valves to regulate the direction of blood flow. Movement of the muscles forces blood anteriorly.

Body undulations during swimming have also been implicated in blood flow in higher fishes. Satchell (1965) recorded increased blood flows in the caudal vein of a Port Jackson shark trunk preparation when electrical stimulation produced swimming-type movements. He also found valves in the caudal vein which allowed only anterior movement of the blood. Sutterlin (1969) described similar valves in the ventral segmental veins of brown trout (*Salmo trutta*). Isolated heart studies by Bennion (1968) reveal that increased filling volume (venous return) will produce an increased force of contraction (inotropism) by the heart. Mediated by stretch receptors in the myocardial wall, this response (Starling's law of the heart) acts to increase the volume of blood pumped per contraction (cardiac stroke volume or Q_{sv}). The cardiac stroke volume and frequency (heart rate or HR) determine the circulatory flow rate (cardiac output or $\dot{Q}$).

CARDIOVASCULAR CONTROL   Fish control their hearts and cardiovascular systems with several aneural and neural mechanisms. Venous return is one of the controls that can be produced by a variety of factors.

Aneural cardiovascular control is effected by changes in blood volume, by direct responses of heart muscle to temperature changes, and by secretions of various organs. Along with swimming movements in certain species, changes in blood volume will also affect venous return. Mobilization of blood into the general circulation has been associated with the spleen, liver, or a blood sinus in various species. Temperature acts as another aneural regulator of circulation by direct action on the pacemakers in the myocardium (Randall 1970). Table 5-3 shows the positive chronotropic effect (increased heart rate) of temperature on winter flounder as the water temperature increased from $10°C$ to $15°C$. These heart rate increases caused an elevated cardiac output at these temperatures, even though the amount of blood pumped per contraction did not change (Table 5-3). This increase in blood flow provides an increased delivery of oxygen throughout the body, which is operating at a higher metabolic rate (Table 5-3) at the warmer temperatures (Cech et al. 1976).

Secretions of hormones which effect either the heart or the relative constriction or dilation of the blood vessels represent an important category of aneural cardiovascular regulators in fishes. Catecholamines such as epinephrine affect both the heart and the resistance to flow in various vascular beds. Nakano and Tomlinson (1967) have shown that levels of circulating catecholamines (epinephrine and norepinephrine) rise with exercise in rainbow trout. Epinephrine stimulates heart rate increases at relatively low temperatures (e.g., $6°C$) and cardiac stroke

TABLE 5-3
**Values of Cardiovascular Variables of Winter Flounder
at Spring and Autumn Temperatures**

Variable[a]	Units	Mean $\pm$ SE (with Number of Fish) at:		Level of Significant Difference[b]
		$10°C$	$15°C$	
HR	Beats/min	$35 \pm 1(18)$	$62 \pm 2(18)$	<0.01
$\dot{V}_{O_2}$	ml/kg/min	$0.39 \pm 0.02(20)$	$0.66 \pm 0.03(20)$	<0.01
$\dot{Q}$	ml/min/kg	$23.1 \pm 1.6(16)$	$36.2 \pm 4.6(16)$	<0.01
Q_{sv}	ml/beat	$0.68 \pm 0.07(15)$	$0.60 \pm 0.07(15)$	NS
Body weight	g	$635 \pm 40(20)$	$681 \pm 42(20)$	NS

[a] Variable abbreviations: HR = heart rate; $\dot{V}_{O_2}$ = oxygen consumption rate; $\dot{Q}$ = cardiac output; and Q_{sv} = cardiac stroke volume.

[b] As determined by the t test (Snedecor and Cochran 1967).

Source: Modified from Cech et al. 1976.

volume increases in warmer water (e.g., 15°C) (Bennion 1968). Studies using blocking agents (e.g., inderal) have shown that the heart has receptor sites that are primarily epinephrine-sensitive. The interplay of temperature, myocardial stretching, and epinephrine as controlling mechanisms determine the frequency/stroke volume characteristics under the various conditions. Other studies have shown that primarily norepinephrine-sensitive receptors predominate in constricting systemic vascular beds, whereas epinephrine-sensitive receptors dilate gill vasculature in rainbow trout (Wood and Shelton 1975).

Neural cardiovascular control. The hearts of all fish except lungfish are innervated by a branch of the tenth cranial nerve (vagus) (Randall 1970). Stimulation of the lamprey vagus produces an increased heart rate (positive chronotropism), whereas elasmobranch or teleostean vagal stimulation slows the heart rate. As these stimuli mimic effects of acetylcholine (the substance that transmits impulses between neurons having chemical synapses), these fibers are termed *cholinergic*. Several factors may alter the level of vagal tone (level of fiber excitement), although stimuli threshold levels vary considerably between species. Light flashes, sudden movements of objects or shadows, touch, or mechanical vibrations usually promote a bradycardia (decreased heart rate) in teleosts and elasmobranchs by increasing the level of vagal tone. Atropine injections sufficient to block cholinergic innervation (the vagal nerve supply to the heart) attest to the neural origin of these responses. Stevens and Randall (1967) found no vagal tone in resting rainbow trout, but atropine injections into a largescale sucker (*Catostomus macrocheilus*) increased the resting heart rate from 38 beats per minute to 55 beats per minute. Swimming in this sucker also reduced the inhibitory vagal tone, thereby elevating heart rate. Rainbow trout also possess stimulatory fibers (rather than strictly inhibitory ones) from the vagus as an additional neural control mechanism (Gannon and Burnstock 1969).

Armed with such a variety of control mechanisms, fishes have much built-in flexibility for circulatory adjustments to environmental or other changes. For example, environmental hypoxia invokes a bradycardia, an increased cardiac stroke volume, elevated peripheral resistance of both branchial and systemic blood vessels, and enhanced gas exchange efficiency in many teleosts and elasmobranchs (Satchell 1971). Changes in gas exchange efficiency may be linked to changes in blood distribution in the gills (e.g., described as lamellar recruitment by Booth [1978]). The reflex bradycardia has been described for the California grunion (*Leuresthes tenuis*) and the California flying fish (*Cypselurus californicus*) during exposure to air (Garey 1962). Both of these species have "standard" gills and are exposed to the atmosphere for short time periods (e.g., only 42 sec for the flying fish and up to a few minutes for the spawning grunion; see Chapter 9). In contrast, the Indian climbing perch (*Anabas testudineus*), which has labyrinthine organs specialized for air breathing and spends much of its time out of the water, shows an initial tachycardia (increased heart rate) just after taking an air breath.

These circulatory patterns may be linked to maximization of oxygen uptake and delivery and, possibly, conservation of cardiac energy in the case of the bradycardic responses. Of course, to best understand the physiological response pattern of a fish to hypoxia (or any other change), the ventilatory, hematological, circulatory, and other affected systems must be considered as well. Apparently the receptors which detect low oxygen levels and provoke the bradycardia and increases in gill ventilation (see Chapter 4) are located on the dorsal part of the first gill arches in rainbow trout (Daxboeck and Holeton 1978; Smith and Jones 1978). Singh (1976) has pointed out the importance of carbon dioxide and pH (along with oxygen) receptors in the air-breathing *Anabas, Clarias,* and *Heteropneustes.*

The degree of cardiovascular control possible in fishes is demonstrated by the dogfish shark (*Squalus suckleyi*). Surgical closure of various gill slits prevented water ventilation of isolated gill arches. By selective vasodilation and constriction, blood was largely directed away from the nonventilated arches toward those receiving ventilatory irrigation (Cameron et al. 1971). As vascular resistance is a function of the fourth power of vessel diameter, minute constrictions or dilations of vessels will significantly affect peripheral resistance and flow. Thus, the dogfish successfully maintained an efficient ratio of water flow (ventilation) to blood flow (cardiac output). Ventilation/perfusion ratios of approximately 10:1 to 20:1 have presumably evolved in gill breathers as fish blood O_2 capacities approximate 10 to 20 times the oxygen capacity of water. The matched flows ensure efficient O_2 diffusion. Absolute matching (stroke to stroke) of the ventilatory water pump and the cardiac pump is relatively rare in fishes with few exceptions (e.g., rainbow trout in hypoxic water).

Supplemental Readings

Blaxhall 1972; Bridges et al. 1976; Cameron 1971a, b; Ellis 1977; Ferguson 1976; Holeton 1970; Houston and Rupert 1976; Randall 1970; Riggs 1970; Satchell 1971, 1976; Weber and Lykkeboe 1978; Wood and Shelton 1975.

αααααααααααααααααααααααααααααααααααααααααααααααααααααααααααααααααααααααα
~~~~~~

Hydromineral Balance

Living cells require an environment characterized by particular concentrations of certain substances (including ions) dissolved in water. Thus, in fishes, the internal environment must have the necessary combinations of dissolved salts, acidity, and dissolved organic compounds despite an external environment which may have a very different combination of these factors. Special problems such as movement between freshwater and saltwater environments or survival in habitats subject to freezing add to the complexity of maintenance of the appropriate internal environment in some fishes. The following sections concerning osmoregulation, ion regulation, freezing resistance, and acid–base balance address the "strategies," dynamics, and diversity of hydromineral balance in fishes.

Osmoregulation

The fishes can be divided into four groups or strategies of regulation of internal water and total solute concentrations. The first osmoregulatory strategy is used by the hagfishes (Agnatha, Myxiniformes) and is characterized by no regulation at all. The hagfishes are all strictly marine and are stenohaline (able to tolerate only a narrow range of salinities). Thus the hagfishes have a total salt concentration in their body fluids which is very similar to that of sea water, the only vertebrates with this characteristic (Schmidt-Nielsen 1975). They can be described as osmoconformers rather than osmoregulators. However, hagfish do not have to withstand large changes in internal osmolality (total dissolved solute particles), because they live only in marine environments of quite constant salinity. As Table 6-1 shows, however, hagfish do show some individual (Na^+) ion-regulatory ability (see the ion regulation section in this chapter).

TABLE 6-1
Plasma Solute Concentrations in MMols/Liter

Habitat	Species	[Na$^+$]	[Ca^{2+}]	[K$^+$]	Urea	Total Salts (mosm/1)
M	Hagfish (*Myxine glutinosa*)[a]	549	5	11	—	1152
F	Lamprey (*Lampetra fluviatilis*)[b]	120	2	3	—	270
M	Dogfish (*Squalus acanthias*)[c]	263	7	4	357	1007
M	Anglerfish (*Lophius americanus*)[d]	198	2	3	—	—
M	Moray eel (*Murena helena*)[b]	212	4	2	—	—
F	Bass (*Micropterus dolomieu*)[e]	140	3	3	—	—
F	Whitefish (*Coregonus clupoides*)[b]	141	3	4	1	—
	Sea water[f,g]	~450	~20	10	—	1000
	Fresh water[h,i]	<1	<1	<1	—	1-10

Sources: [a]Bellamy and Chester-Jones (1961); [b]Robertson (1954); [c]Murdaugh and Robin (1967); [d]Forster and Berglund (1956); [e]Shell (1959); [f]Schmidt-Nielsen (1975); [g]von Arx (1962); [h]Hutchinson (1957); [i]Royce (1972).

The second strategy is that which encompasses all marine elasmobranchs. Like most vertebrates, the elasmobranch fishes maintain an internal inorganic salt concentration equal to about $\frac{1}{3}$ that of sea water (Table 6-1). However, large quantities of organic salts (primarily urea, secondarily trimethylamine oxide or TMAO) in their blood bring the total osmotic concentration up to that of sea water (Table 6-1). The tissues and organ systems of these fishes are especially adapted for functioning with high urea concentrations. Whereas high concentrations of urea are toxic to teleosts, urea is *necessary* for the functioning of marine elasmobranch tissue! Despite a total salt concentration which approximates that of the sea, elasmobranchs possess considerable abilities to regulate the concentrations of individual ions. The coelacanth (*Latimeria chalumnae*) uses this osmoregulatory strategy as well.

The fishes using either one of these two strategies of osmoregulation have solved a major problem in the water balance. Water diffuses quite easily across thin membranes such as the skin, and especially those in the gills. Because the internal total salt concentration of these fishes mimics that of their environment, passive water influx (inflow) or efflux (outflow) is minimized.

The third osmoregulatory strategy is that of the marine teleosts. The salt concentration of their internal environment is approximately $\frac{1}{3}$ that of their environment (Table 6-1). Thus, they operate *hyposmotically* and tend to lose water continually by diffusion to the more saline environment. These teleosts continually replace lost water by drinking (ingesting) sea water. Naturally, this also results in a large intake of salts, which must be excreted at a concentration higher than that ingested. Special cells in the gill epithelium eliminate much of the excess salt via active transport. Teleost kidneys cannot produce a urine more salty than the blood (Schmidt-Nielsen 1975).

The fourth strategy has evolved in freshwater teleosts and elasmobranchs that operate *hyperosmotically*. As their internal environment (one-third the salt concentration of sea water) is more concentrated than their environment (Table 6-1), they are continually gaining water by diffusion. The excess water is continually excreted by well-developed kidneys as a large volume of dilute urine (up to one-third of the body weight per day). Control of diuretic (urine-producing) processes is influenced by blood pressure changes induced by pituitary hormones (e.g., arginine vasotocin) (Sawyer et al. 1976). Some salts are unavoidably lost through the urine and by diffusion through the gill tissues. Although some of these solutes are replaced with those taken in with food, most are taken up at the gills, using active transport mechanisms. Thus, an energy-requiring salt pump operates in special cells of the gills in these fishes as well, except that ions are pumped inward, rather than the reverse as exhibited by the marine teleosts. The remarkable Amazon stingray (*Potamotrygon*), a stenohaline freshwater species, displays an interior milieu strikingly similar to that of the freshwater teleosts with essentially *no* urea. The more euryhaline sharks, which can ascend rivers, have a urea concentration about one-third that found in the marine elasmobranchs.

Most fishes are stenohaline and have evolved the osmotic machinery needed to cope with the relatively constant salt concentration (whatever it may be) of their immediate surroundings. However, diadromous fishes (e.g., lampreys, salmon, eels), which move between freshwater and marine environments as part of their regular existence, must possess more versatility in dealing with environmental salinity. Keys (1933) moved an eel (*Anguilla anguilla*) from a freshwater environment to a marine one and measured an osmotic water loss from the body equal to 4% of the total body weight in 10 hours. The weight loss slackened as the eel began to drink sea water, and an equilibrium returned after 1 to 2 days. If Keys inflated a balloon in the esophagus of the eel, preventing the ingestion of sea water, the weight loss continued until the animal died of dehydration. Transfer of the eels from salt water into fresh water promoted a weight gain from passive water diffusion. The eels again reached an equilibrium in 1 to 2 days, when urine production increased to excrete the excess water.

Whether a fish is diadromous, freshwater, or marine, osmoregulation is usually one of the energy "costs" it has to "pay" just to stay alive. Indeed, growth rates of fishes may often be affected by how much energy they must put into osmoregulation. For example, Brocksen and Cole (1972) measured the food consumption and assimilation, growth, and oxygen consumption in several stenohaline fishes from the Salton Sea, California. Using test salinities of 29, 33, 37, 41, and 45 parts per thousand (ppt), they showed that juvenile bairdiella (*Bairdiella icistia*) grew more efficiently at 37 ppt when held at 25°C. In contrast, substantially more food was required at both higher and lower salinities.

On the other hand, sargo (*Anisotremus davidsoni*) showed optimal feeding efficiency at 33 ppt. Juvenile corvina (*Cynoscion xanthulus*) displayed optimal assimilation efficiency at 37 ppt. Wohlschlag and Wakeman (1978) demonstrated that another euryhaline sciaenid, the spotted sea trout (*Cynoscion nebulosus*), operates at maximum metabolic efficiency (maximum scope for activity) at approximately 20 ppt salinity (Fig. 6.1, p. 78), although it occurs under a wide range of salinities in estuaries.

Ionic Regulation

Even if a fish has blood that has nearly the same osmotic concentration as sea water, energy still must be expended in regulation of solutes because the concentrations of individual ions will differ between the internal and external environments. To maintain an optimal ionic composition, active, energy-consuming processes are needed. These processes, and the organs involved, vary considerably among fishes, although in terms of general "strategies" of ionic regulation fishes fall into five main groups: agnathans, elasmobranchs, saltwater teleosts, euryhaline teleosts, and freshwater teleosts.

Agnathans. The lampreys (Petromyzoniformes) and hagfishes (Myxiniformes) have had long, separate evolutionary histories (Chapter 12), and this is reflected in the distinctness of their methods of ion regulation. Lampreys have ion concentrations and regulatory mechanisms similar to those of teleosts and so will not be discussed any further here. Hagfishes, in contrast, are not only iso-osmotic with seawater but have a rather similar ionic composition as well, although some differences are detectable. For example, *Myxine glutinosa* demonstrates a sodium concentration [Na^+] somewhat greater than that of sea water (Table 6-1). The low Na^+ concentration in the secreted slime which coats its body probably helps maintain plasma [Na^+], as McFarland and Munz (1965) could find no evidence of Na^+ active transport across the gut, gills, or skin. The divalent ions Ca^{2+}, SO_4^{2-}, and Mg^{2+} are all present in lower concentrations in hagfish than in sea water. However, Mg^{2+}, K^+, SO_4^{2-}, and PO_4^{2-} are secreted into the glomerular filtrate by the mesonephric duct cells and appear in the urine at higher concentrations than in the plasma (Munz and McFarland 1964; McFarland and Munz 1965). Moreover, the slime has high concentrations of Ca^{2+}, Mg^{2+}, and K^+.

Elasmobranchs. While the retention of urea and other compounds has provided an efficient solution to the problem of water balance in sharks and their relatives, they still must eliminate the excess Na^+ and Cl^- they ingest. Excretion of these ions is in fact the principal function of the rectal gland, which is found only in elasmobranchs (Burger and Hess 1960) and the coelacanth. The rectal gland secretes a fluid which has Na^+ and Cl^- concentrations approximating those of sea water (twice those in the plasma) (Silva et al. 1977). In spiny dogfish (*Squalus acanthias*), rectal glandular secretions can be produced by hypertonic injections of NaCl into the blood stream (Burger 1962), and removal of the

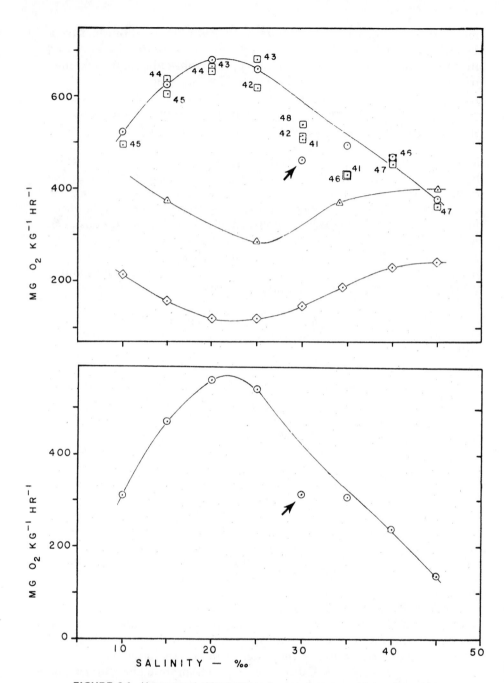

FIGURE 6.1 *Upper panel:* Metabolism of spotted sea trout (*Cynoscion nebulosus*) at standard (lower line, diamonds), routine (middle line, triangles), and maximum sustained activity levels (upper line, heavy points) over a range of salinities at 28°C. *Lower panel:* Scope for maximum sustained activity (maximum sustained rates – standard rates) over salinity range. Arrows indicate "depressed" values from fish in poor condition. (From Wohlschlag and Wakeman, 1978.)

rectal gland provokes steady increase in plasma [Na⁺] (Forrest et al. 1973). Silva et al. (1977) have shown that the Cl⁻ secretion rate into the lumen of the dogfish rectal glands is dependent on the Na⁺ concentration. These authors hypothesize that the movement of Na⁺ and Cl⁻ from the blood (or perfusate) across the glandular wall into the lumen results from both active transport "sodium pumps" catalyzed by the special enzyme Na⁺-K⁺-dependent adenosine triphosphatase (Na⁺-K⁺-ATPase) and from electrical forces inducing movement of these charged ions toward electrical homeostasis. The importance of the elasmobranch rectal gland (or Na⁺ and Cl⁻) excretion is also shown by its evolutionary *regression* in elasmobranchs adapted to fresh water (Oguri 1964).

Marine teleosts. Marine teleosts maintain a total ionic concentration in the plasma about $\frac{1}{3}$ that of sea water. Since most of the ions needed by the fish are present in excess in the environment, the principal method used by marine teleosts for maintenance of ionic balance is selective excretion, particularly of Na⁺ and Cl⁻ (Fig. 6.2). Since the gills have a relatively high permeability to monovalent ions, Na⁺ and Cl⁻ move passively from sea water into the plasma. In addition, when sea water is ingested to replace water which has diffused into the environment, monovalent ions, as well as water, are absorbed in the intestine. Teleostean kidneys are of little help in the excretion of these ions, as

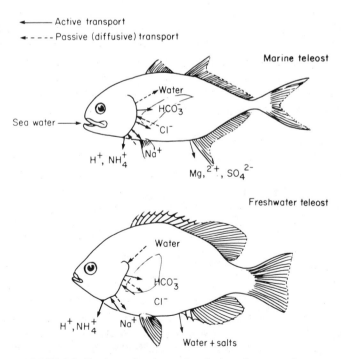

FIGURE 6.2 Passive and active routes of salt and water exchange.

they do not have the ability to form a urine more concentrated than the blood. Indeed, many marine teleosts (e.g., oyster toadfish [*Opsanus tau*], and plainfin midshipman [*Porichthys notatus*]) have an "evolutionary regressive" *aglomerular* kidney to minimize water losses! Instead, special large cells in the gills actively transport the excess monovalent anions against the concentration gradient back into the environment. Catlett and Millich (1976) describe these "chloride cells" as being larger than the flat cells of the gills specialized for respiratory gas exchange. The "chloride cells" feature an abundance of energy-providing mitochondria, display extraordinary development of cytoplasmic microtubules, and contain the Na^+-K^+-ATPase system also found in elasmobranch rectal gland secretory tissue. Utida and Hirano (1973) have shown that both Na^+-K^+-ATPase concentrations and numbers of chloride cells increase with increasing environmental salinity in gill preparations of Japanese eel (*Anguilla japonica*) (Fig. 6.3).

While the gills are the principal site of monovalent ion excretion, the kidneys do function in the elimination of excess divalent ions, such as Mg^{2+} and SO_4^{2-}. Such ions are present in only small amounts and so do not present the problems of the abundant monovalent ions. Much remains to be learned concerning more complex hormone interactions, such as cortisol (from interrenal tissue) effects on ion transport and permeability, with gill, kidney, and gut wall tissue.

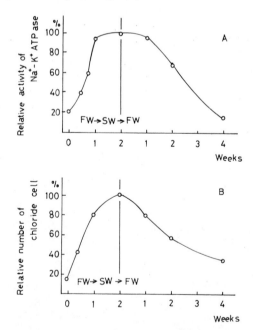

FIGURE 6.3 Changes in Na^+-K^+-ATPase activity and number of chloride cells following transfer from fresh water to sea water (FW–SW) and vice versa (SW–FW). (From Utida and Hirano, 1973; in W. Chavin, *Responses of Fish to Environmental Changes*.)

CH. 6   HYDROMINERAL BALANCE

Euryhaline teleosts. The study of euryhaline teleosts can provide considerable insight into the mechanisms and energy costs of ionic regulation because such fishes often endure dramatic changes in their external environments. Euryhaline forms can be divided into two categories: the estuarine and intertidal inhabitants, which experience continual shifts in external salinity dictated by tidal rhythms as well as wind, storm, or river flow variations, and diadromous species, which spend part of their life cycle in fresh water and part in salt water. As an example of the former group, Evans (1967a,b) studied the intertidal black prickleback (*Xiphister atropurpureus*), whose plasma [Na$^+$] and [Cl$^-$] levels are stable when individuals are immersed in dilutions of sea water down to 31% sea water. Na$^+$ and Cl$^-$ concentrations fall about 15% after transfer to environments with salinities between 10% and 31% of sea water. Salinities below 10% sea water are not in the tolerable range, apparently because of the prickleback's inability to retard Cl$^-$ losses from passive diffusion.

Towle et al. (1977) have documented changes in total Na$^+$-K$^+$-ATPase activity in the gills of the euryhaline mummichog (*Fundulus heteroclitus*) to environments of different salinities. As in the Japanese eels, Na$^+$-K$^+$-ATPase was high at 30 ppt salinity when compared with 16 ppt. However, they found intermediate enzyme activities associated with acclimation of this killifish to *freshwater* environments. Apparently the same enzyme may function to absorb Na$^+$ at low salinities and excrete Na$^+$ at high salinities.

In diadromous fishes changes in ion regulatory abilities are typically associated with ontogenic changes. Saltwater readiness in young trout and salmon ranges from a modest springtime rise in resistance shown by underyearling steelhead trout (*Salmo gairdneri*) and other trouts and chars to complete tolerance and survival in chum (*Oncorhynchus keta*) and pink (*O. gorbuscha*) salmon alevins! For most salmonids, tolerance of marine conditions develops in the spring, prior to the seaward migration of the silvery smolts (see Chapter 19). Hoar (1976) points out that although a "critical size" for saltwater tolerance has been implicated, the lengthening springtime photoperiods represent the most important factor in timing the changes. Pituitary hormones (e.g., prolactin), as elevators of the animal's awareness of photoperiodic and other stimuli, are presumably involved in this process. The prolactin-producing tissue in the anterior lobe of the pituitary (adenohypophysis) has been found to be more active while Pacific salmon are in fresh water.

Studies in species besides salmonids have also demonstrated the role of prolactin in preventing Na$^+$ diffusive loss in freshwater-adapted fish and in minimizing increases in passive Na$^+$ loss as euryhaline forms pass from sea water to fresh water. For example, hypophysectomy (removal of the anterior lobe of the pituitary where prolactin is synthesized) of freshwater-acclimated mummichogs promotes a marked drop in plasma electrolytes compared with sham-operated controls (Maetz et al.

1967). Ion-regulatory roles of fish prolactin have also been linked to stimulation of number and activity of skin mucus cells in the cichlid (*Cichlasoma biocellatum*) and to various physiological and morphological changes in kidney and urinary bladder of various species (see review by Ensor and Ball [1972]).

Excitement, handling stress, and activity provoke increased epinephrine (adrenaline) secretions which affect water permeability across gill epithelia in fish (Mazeaud et al. 1977). Thus, stress will invoke a loss of water in marine fishes and a water gain in freshwater fishes by increased water diffusion rates (Fig. 6.4). For example, Pic et al. (1974), using tritiated water, showed that water diffusion rates increased by 100% after epinephrine was injected into grey mullet (*Mugil capito*) adapted to either sea water or fresh water. Exercised *Tilapia nilotica* adapted to sea water displayed an increased plasma osmotic pressure (from water loss). The same fish experienced a decreased osmotic pressure (from water uptake) with exercise after adaptation to fresh water (Farmer and Beamish 1969). These osmotic problems can be especially severe in fish culture conditions where capture, handling, and transport stresses may be comparatively frequent. Transportation of excitable freshwater fish in salt solutions similar to their blood (isosomotic) has been used as a method to reduce handling mortality due to permeability changes (Hattingh et al. 1975).

It is apparent that gill ionic permeabilities in many species are also affected by the concentration of calcium (Ca) in the water, although the actual site and mode of Ca^{2+} action on the membrane has yet to be determined. The sodium efflux from the plains killifish (*Fundulus kansae*) in fresh water is reduced 50% when 1 mM calcium is added to the water (Potts and Fleming 1971). Calcium can also reduce Na^+ permeability across the branchial epithelia of fish in sea water, such as *Anguilla* (Cuth-

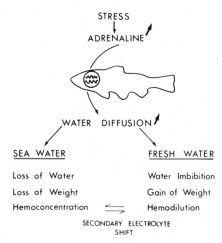

FIGURE 6.4 Interpretation of some stress effects on osmotic balance. (From Mazeaud et al., 1977.)

bert and Maetz, 1972). Carrier and Evans (1976) demonstrated that the euryhaline marine pinfish (*Lagodon rhomboides*) tolerates essentially fresh water (5 mM sodium) if 10 mM calcium is also present. Transfer of the pinfish to calcium-free fresh water stimulates substantial Na^+ efflux. Pinfish left in calcium-free fresh water for 2.5 hours died with less than 50% of the body Na^+ concentrations found in those acclimated to calcium-supplemented sea water. These results help explain why Breder (1934) observed several marine fish species living in a freshwater lake on Andros Island of the Bahamas. Analysis of this lake water showed it to have an unusually high (1.0 mM to 1.5 mM) calcium concentration.

Freshwater teleosts. The hyperosmotic state of the freshwater teleosts dictates that small ions such as Na^+ and Cl^- are continually being lost to the environment by diffusion across the thin epithelia of the gills (Fig. 6.2). Solutes are also continually lost in the large volumes of dilute urine which is produced to expel the excess water passively taken up by diffusion across the gills. Although some of the salts are regained via food sources, most of the Na^+ and Cl^- needed to regain internal ionic homeostasis is taken up by active transport mechanisms in the gills.

From the pioneering work of Krogh (1939) and of Maetz and Garcia Romeu (1964), a model describing ion-exchange mechanisms across the gills in freshwater teleosts has been formulated (Fig. 6.5). These ion-exchange mechanisms serve several functions besides maintenance of $[Na^+]$ and $[Cl^-]$ in the fish. The Na^+ exchange for NH_4^+ conveniently rids the fish of the principal waste product of protein digestive breakdown (see Chapter 7). Injections of NH_4^+ into the freshwater goldfish thereby stimulated Na^+ influx (Maetz and Garcia Romeu 1964). Both the Na^+ exchange for H^+ and the Cl^- exchange for HCO_3^- tend to main-

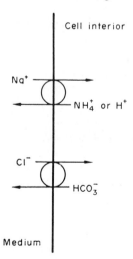

FIGURE 6.5 Model for the ionic exchange mechanisms at the apex (outer surface) of the transporting cells of the freshwater-acclimated teleost fish gill. (From Evans, 1975.)

tain internal acid-base homeostasis (see the acid–base balance section in this chapter). Thus, just two ionic exchange mechanisms provide for:

1. Maintenance of appropriate internal $[Na^+]$.
2. Maintenance of appropriate internal $[Cl^-]$.
3. Elimination of potentially toxic NH_3.
4. Elimination of metabolic CO_2 (as HCO_3^-).
5. Adjustment of internal H^+ and OH^-.
6. Maintenance of ionic electrical balance.

Evans (1977) reported results indicating the same exchange in four species of *marine* fish. Apparently *active* (besides passive) uptake of Na^+ and Cl^- via these active transport ion-exchange pumps may be *necessary* for adequate excretion of NH_4^+, H^+, and HCO_3^-. If this mechanism to take up Na^+ and Cl^- is functional in marine teleosts, one may ask why marine species are all not more euryhaline. After drinking rates, urine flows, and permeability differences have been considered, the relative inefficiency of NaCl *uptake* by the marine fishes compared with diffusional NaCl losses in fresh water probably represents the limiting factor (Evans 1975).

Freezing Resistance
As their body fluids are either hyperosmotic or isosmotic with their environments, hagfish, marine elasmobranchs, and freshwater teleosts are not subject to freezing as long as their environment remains unfrozen. However, because the marine environment has a higher salt concentration than their body fluids and consequently a lower freezing point, marine teleosts can freeze to death even though the water around them is still liquid. To prevent this, many cold-water, marine teleosts possess macromolecular "antifreeze" compounds (glycoproteins or proteins) in their blood serum. Apparently the hydroxyl groups on the glycoprotein molecules bond with oxygen molecules on the surface of the ice crystals forming in the blood, essentially coating them with antifreeze. Available evidence suggests that these "bound" ice crystals are thus prevented from increasing in size. Consequently demersal Antarctic fishes such as the naked dragon fish (*Gymnodraco acuticeps*), *Trematomus bernachii,* and *T. hansoni* can be found resting on anchor ice (DeVries and Wohlschlag 1969). An aglomerular kidney is considered part of the freezing-resistance system in Antarctic fishes, as the glycoproteins are conserved rather than filtered out of the blood. Moreover, energy is not needed for glycoprotein reabsorption, thereby lowering the energetic cost of low-temperature osmoregulation in these forms (Dobbs et al. 1974).

Duman and DeVries (1974a) showed that winter flounder (*Pseudopleuronectes americanus*) from Nova Scotian waters display seasonal changes in serum freezing point. Their serum freezing point is lowered from $-0.69°C$ during the summer (water temperature $17°C$) to $-1.47°C$

in the winter (water temperature -1.2° C). Macromolecular antifreeze production allowed this species to depress the freezing point of its serum adequately during the colder months. It was also shown that acclimation to cold temperatures alone promoted antifreeze production in several Nova Scotian fishes. However, a combination of both warm temperatures *and* long photoperiods was necessary as a "failsafe" system to lose the anitfreeze completely over a period of 3 to 5 weeks. From studies on the high cockscomb (*Anoplarchus purpurescens*) taken from cold Alaskan waters and from more mild California intertidal waters, genetically based population differences in antifreeze production are apparent. Upon acclimation to cold water, the Alaskan individuals were capable of producing the antifreeze compounds, whereas the Californian population could not (Duman and DeVries 1974b).

Acid-Base Balance   The control of internal acid-base conditions within a certain range is essential for life in fishes. It has been pointed out by Howell et al. (1970) that maintenance of a constant pH (hydrogen ion concentration) is critical in *homeothermic* animals. However, the ionization constant of water (K_w) changes greatly with temperature, and along with it the pH of neutrality of water. In fish and other ectotherms, the pH and pOH are regulated in parallel with the neutral point of water over a 30°C temperature range. Thus, these ectotherms are mainly regulating the OH^-/H^+ ratio (relative alkalinity) rather than pH.

At one time it was assumed that the internal relative alkalinity was controlled by gill ventilation (Albers 1970), much as in mammals in which hyperventilation "washes out" CO_2 from the lungs. This assumption was attractive because ventilation volume has been shown to be highly plastic in several fishes and because CO_2 is so soluble in water (see Chapter 2). Randall and Cameron (1973) have since demonstrated that changes in ventilation apparently play little or no role in acid–base regulation in rainbow trout. It is now known that fish maintain their extracellular relative alkalinity by adjustments of the bicarbonate equilibrium system, allowing ventilatory water flow to vary according to bodily oxygen demands. Dissolved carbon dioxide is hydrated and dehydrated in aqueous solutions according to:

$$CO_2 + H_2O \rightleftharpoons H_2CO_3$$

The carbonic acid formed ionizes according to:

$$H_2CO_3 \rightleftharpoons H^+ + HCO_3^-$$

As CO_2 is produced in the tissues as the product of oxidative metabolism, it diffuses across the capillary walls into the plasma. Part of the CO_2 dissolves in the plasma. A portion of this plasma CO_2 forces the above equilibria to the right, slowly forming HCO_3^- and lowering blood pH (increased [H^+]). Another part of the CO_2 diffuses across the membranes of the red blood cells (erythrocytes), and a fraction of this binds with the hemoglobin to form carbaminohemoglobin. As much of the hemoglobin may be in the reduced state (deoxygenated), the hemoglobin's CO_2 capacity is relatively high (see the discussion of the Haldane effect in Chapter 5). Further, much of the CO_2 in the erythrocytes is quickly hydrated to H_2CO_3 by the enzyme *carbonic anhydrase* and is then quickly ionized to HCO_3^- and H^+. These reactions proceed because the H^+ and HCO_3^- are taken up as quickly as they are formed. The hemoglobin binds and, therefore, buffers the H^+, and the HCO_3^- diffuses into the plasma (Davenport 1975). Because the HCO_3^- level in the plasma is much lower in the absence of the enzymatic catalysis, "excess" HCO_3^- produced in the erythrocytes diffuses into the plasma, establishing a HCO_3^- equilibrium across the erythrocytic membrane. However, as the H^+ produced in the erythrocyte is bound by the hemoglobin (neutralizing the hemoglobin's negative charge) and much of the HCO_3^- is diffusing into the plasma, the erythrocyte becomes more positively charged than the plasma. Because positively charged ions do not move easily across the erythrocytic membrane, Cl^- diffuses into the red cell to alleviate an electrical disequilibrium. Cameron (1978) demonstrated this "chloride shift" in erythrocytes of marine red snapper (*Lutjanus aya*) and the freshwater rainbow trout. The chloride shift brings more osmotically active particles (Cl^- ions) from the plasma into the erythrocytes. Thus, water enters these cells along with the Cl^-, ensuring an osmotic equilibrium. This induces some swelling of the erythrocytes and accounts for the volume of erythrocytes (hematocrit) in venous blood being 2% to 3% higher than arterial blood from the same fish (Stevens 1968).

As the venous blood enters the gills, 95% of the total CO_2 is in the form of plasma bicarbonate (Cameron 1978). The process described above works in reverse to release dissolved CO_2 gas to the environment (Fig. 6.6). The presence of carbonic anhydrase in gill epithelial cells rapidly promotes the HCO_3^-/Cl^- exchange described in the ion-regulation section. This gill membrane "chloride shift" accomplishes both the excretion of CO_2 as HCO_3^- and the uptake of Cl^- (Cameron 1976).

The osmotic problems fish face in maintaining their acid–base balance are among the main reasons they have a hard time surviving in highly acid waters, such as streams draining many mines or lakes contaminated by acid rains. Rainbow trout show significant increases in [H^+] and decreases in total CO_2 after two days exposure to water with a pH of 4. Compensatory rises in hemoglobin concentration apparently offset Root-shifted losses (Chapter 5) in blood oxygen capacity (Neville 1979). Another major problem in low-pH environments concerns excessive Na^+ losses from the body. From the Maetz and Garcia Romeu (1964) model of ion exchanges (Fig. 6.5) it is apparent that high external [H^+] could inhibit H^+ excretion necessary for Na^+ uptake. Leivestad and

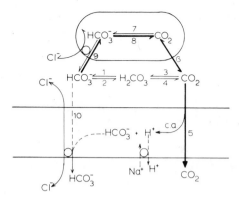

FIGURE 6.6 Principle pools and reaction pathways for CO_2 in the fish gill. Oval shape at top represents erythrocyte in plasma; middle region is gill epithelium, with the water medium toward the bottom. The notation c.a. denotes carbonic anhydrase. (From Cameron, 1976.)

Muniz (1976) attributed the death of brown trout (*Salmo trutta*) exposed to low pH conditions in the Tovdal River in southern Norway to extreme reductions in plasma NaCl.

Supplemental Readings

Cameron 1975; Carrier and Evans 1976; Davenport 1975; Duman and DeVries 1974a, b; Evans 1975; Hoar 1976; Maetz and Garcia Romeu 1964; Mazeaud et al. 1977; Randall and Cameron 1973.

CHAPTER **7**

ααααααααααααααααααααααααααααααααααααααααααααααααααααααααααααααα

Feeding, Nutrition, Digestion, and Excretion

Fish must have an energy source to run the body machinery (metabolism). They also require an adequate amount of essential amino and fatty acids plus vitamins and minerals to sustain life and promote growth. This chapter therefore examines feeding, food requirements, and the resulting dynamics in fishes.

Feeding   Fish can be classified broadly on the basis
                               of their feeding habits as detritivores,
herbivores, carnivores, and omnivores. Within these categories fish can
be characterized further as (1) euryphagous, having a mixed diet; (2) stenophagous, eating a limited assortment of food types; and (3) monophagous, consuming only one sort of food. A majority of fishes, however, are euryphagous carnivores. Often the feeding mode and food types are associated with the body form and digestive apparatus. For example, longer guts with greater surface areas typify species that feed on detritus and algae and take in a high percentage of indigestible material such as sand, mud, or cellulose. In contrast, carnivorous species tend to have shorter gut lengths. Among carnivorous fish, however, gut lengths are often greater in those fish that prey on small organisms (relative to their own size) than those that prey on large organisms. Thus, the herbivorous, euryphagous Sacramento blackfish (*Orthodon microlepidotus*) has a vastly longer gut than the carnivorous Sacramento squawfish (*Ptychocheilus grandis*), which feeds largely on other fish. The Sacramento hitch (*Lavinia exilicauda*) has an intermediate gut length (Fig. 7.1) corresponding to its diet of small zooplankters (Kline 1978). Digestive area can also be increased through the use of spiral valve intestines, found in the Chondrichthyes and in "ancestral" bony fishes, such as sturgeons and lung-

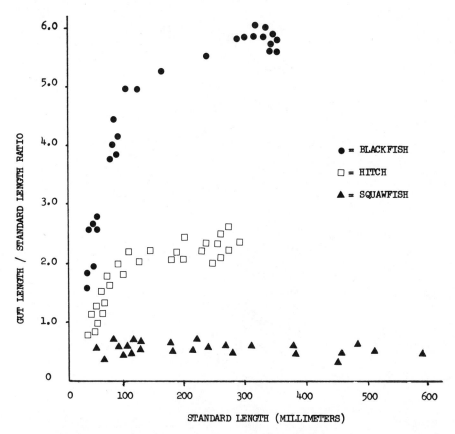

FIGURE 7.1 Relationship between the relative length of gut and fish standard length for blackfish, hitch, and squawfish. (From Kline, 1978.)

fishes. A spiral valve is a longitudinal fold which spirals down the length of the intestine, much like a spiral staircase down a lighthouse (Fig. 7.2).

Structures in the buccal-pharyngeal cavity often correlate with food type and feeding habits. For example, the pharyngeal pad (or palatal organ) situated dorsally at the entrance to the esophagus has been implicated in removing excess water from the ingested food of carp (*Cyprinus carpio*) (Jara 1957). In contrast, the pharyngeal valve hanging from the roof of the pharynx of scarid fishes probably assists in the placement of pieces of coral for grinding by the pharyngeal teeth and lubrication from epithelial mucus cells (Kapoor et al. 1975). Likewise, the bony or cartilaginous gill rakers which protrude from each gill arch can be specialized for modes of feeding (Fig. 7.3).

Many of these gill raker specializations can be found in the sunfish family (Centrarchidae). In piscivorous members of the family, such as the largemouth bass (*Micropterus salmoides*), the gill rakers are short, stout, widely spaced, and pointed. They function mainly in preventing the prey from escaping through (and damaging) the gills but may also

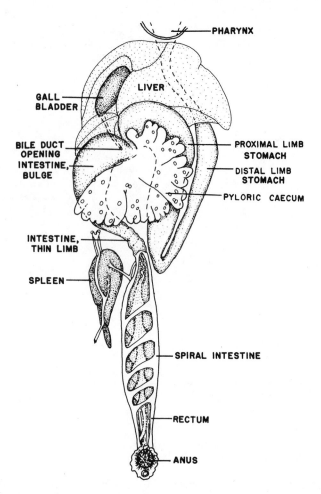

FIGURE 7.2 Viscera of the paddlefish showing spiral valve intestine. The proximal limb of the stomach normally lies in the mid-line of the coelom. The diffuse pancreas is omitted from this illustration. (From Wiesel, 1973.)

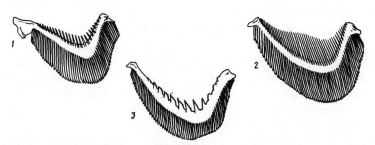

FIGURE 7.3 Gill-rakers of planktophagic and predatory fishes. (A) Neva whitefish, *Coregonus lavaretus*; (B) *Coregonus muksun* (Pall.); (C) pike-perch *Lucioperca lucioperca L.* The first two species feed on planktonic crustacea, and the pike-perch ingests larger prey. [From Nikolsky, 1963, with permission, from *The Ecology of Fishes.* Copyright by Academic Press Inc. (London) Ltd.]

partially descale fish as they pass by the rakers. The shortest and stubbiest gill rakers in the family are possessed by members, such as the redear sunfish (*Lepomis microlophus*), that are specialized for feeding on snails. Gill rakers of intermediate length, thickness, and spacing are found in euryphagous species, such as bluegill (*L. machrochirus*). The longest and finest gill rakers in the family are those of the crappies (*Pomoxis* spp.), reflecting the importance of zooplankton in their diets, which they "pick" individually from the water column. Among fishes in general, the finest, most closely spaced gill rakers are possessed by species which strain plankton out of the water, such as the Atlantic menhaden (*Brevoortia tyrannus*). Large schools of this abundant clupeid decrease the phytoplankton as well as the dissolved oxygen concentrations of the waters they swim through (Oviatt et al. 1972). Dense concentrations of the food organisms in the water stimulate faster swimming by the menhaden (to 2.5 body lengths per sec). Durbin and Durbin (1975) showed that the feeding response of menhaden is linked to the presence of comparatively large zooplankton or the larger phytoplankton rather than to much greater densities of the small phytoplankters, which are filtered less efficiently.

Mouth structure is also related to the feeding modes and habits of fishes. Mouth structure is highly variable, and this variability explains in part the evolutionary success of both teleosts and elasmobranchs (Chapter 12). The "ancestral" mouth consists of firm jaws lined with sharp teeth for grasping active prey. Such jaws are still possessed by many piscivorous fishes (such as barracuda and pike). More common among modern fishes are jaws modified for suction feeding. In suction-feeding fishes the jaw is shortened to limit the gape while the expansibility of the orobranchial (mouth and gill) cavity is maintained, resulting in increased water velocity through the smaller mouth when the cavity is expanded or contracted. In elasmobranchs, such as skates (Rajidae), rays (e.g., Myliobatidae), and nurse sharks (Orectolobidae), the strong oral suction created allows them to feed effectively on benthic invertebrates. In teleosts anterior extension of the hyomandibular bones and lateral expansion of the opercular apparatus allows the orobranchial cavity to enlarge quickly and create strong suction. Alexander (1970) trained fish to take rings of earthworm off the free end of a nylon tube connected to a pressure transducer and recorder. Negative pressures from –80 cm water (18°C) in the temperate black bullhead (*Ictalurus melas*) to –400 cm water (27°C) in the tropical butterfly fish (*Pterophyllum scalare*) were measured.

The feeding of many sharks represents an unusual type of predation, that of taking bites from prey larger than the predator. The sawtooth edges on the awl-shaped teeth of the lower jaw and the bladelike teeth of the upper jaw teeth, coupled with a head-shaking action, provide for efficient cutting through flesh of larger, slow-moving or disabled animals. The well-developed jaw musculature and the unique position of the hyomandibular cartilages provides support and positioning for the jaws when the mouth is open to effect a deep, gougelike bite (Moss 1977).   In contrast, filter-feeding elasmobranchs such as the basking shark (*Cetorhinus*), whale shark (*Rhinodon*), and manta rays (Mobulidae) have comparatively weak jaw musculature and reduced dentition.   Instead, numerous, elaborate gill rakers function to strain small organisms from immense ventilatory water flows.

Nutrition

Most of our knowledge concerning fish dietary requirements comes from experimental nutrition studies conducted on cultured species, primarily salmonids.   These studies have demonstrated the relative importance of dietary proteins, lipids, and carbohydrates for growth (anabolism) and for energy to run the bodily machinery (catabolism).   Proteins, which consist of chains of amino acids, seem to be essential mainly for growth, although they may also be used for catabolic functions.   The importance of proteins for growth has been shown in numerous nutritional studies that omit proteins containing amino acids the fish are not capable of synthesizing themselves.   For example, Halver (1957) fed experimental groups of chinook salmon (*Oncorhynchus tshawytscha*) diets devoid of single amino acids and compared their growth rates with control animals fed diets containing all the amino acids.   He found that their growth rates were greatly reduced because new structural proteins (for muscle, bone, etc.) could not be synthesized when one or more amino acids composing the specific protein chain were missing.   Missing amino acids can also provoke developmental vertebral abnormalities such as scoliosis and lordosis (Halver and Shanks 1960).   These nonsynthesizable amino acids therefore become "essential" in the diet of the fish.   Ten amino acids which have been shown to be essential for fish are arginine, histidine, isoleucine, leucine, lysine, methionine, phenylalanine, threonine, tryptophan, and valine.   The *quantities* of the various required amino acids needed, however, vary among species, and excessive amounts of any one acid may also be detrimental to growth and survival.

In wild fish, proteins are often an important source of energy for meeting metabolic demands.   For example, rainbow trout (*Salmo gairdneri*) in the wild feed largely on aquatic and terrestrial invertebrates, making protein a high percentage of their natural diet, far beyond what is needed for growth.   In cultured fishes, however, the protein fraction of the diet usually comes from fish meal and is a comparatively expensive part of the feed.   To minimize their monetary costs of operation, fish culturists include protein in quantities sufficient only for anabolic processes and substitute lipids or, especially, relatively inexpensive carbohydrates for a source of energy.   A significant energy cost is incurred in breaking down (hydrolyzing) the large, complex protein molecules. This cost is termed the *specific dynamic effect* (SDE) or *specific dynamic action* (SDA) and increases with the amount of protein in the diet.

Thus, Schalles and Wissing (1976) calculated that 12.6% to 16.1% of the ingested energy was used by bluegills to digest and assimilate diets containing 23.9% to 45.3% protein, respectively.

Carbohydrates and lipids constitute the other available energy sources in foods. In natural aquatic environments, lipids are found both in animal and plant sources, while carbohydrates are found almost exclusively in plants. The low digestibility of carbohydrates by carnivores such as trout and salmon contributes to the low energy value gained from their ingestion. A salmonid extracts only 1.6 kcal of energy from 1 g of carbohydrate fed, while gaining 3.9 kcal/g for ingested protein and 8.0 kcal/g for lipids. The salmonid culturist must thus balance the low feed costs of carbohydrate sources (e.g., grains and cereals) with their low nutritional value. Of the carbohydrates, monosaccharides are the most digestible, followed (in order) by disaccharides, simple polysaccharides, dextrins, cooked starches, and raw starches (Halver 1976). Some herbivorous and omnivorous fishes, such as anchovies (*Anchoa*), sea catfish (*Arius felis*), and channel catfish (*Ictalurus punctatus*) may utilize gut microbes to break down the plant structural carbohydrate, cellulose (Stickney and Shumway 1974). The bacteria having this cellulase activity are either maintained in the gut or regularly brought in with ingested detritus (Prejs and Blaszczyk 1977).

Lipids represent a rich source of energy for fishes in general. Besides their high specific energy value (8.0 kcal/g), they are also almost completely digestible (Halver 1976). The high lipid content of a diet consisting of small fish maximizes growth by sparing the ingested protein for tissue synthesis. For example, rapid growth rates are typically achieved by predaceous fishes such as the mackerels, billfishes, salmon, pikes, and sharks. Besides an energy source, lipids provide essential fatty acids. Fatty acids are used in the construction of fats or oils (triglycerides) to be stored by a fish for use as an energy source at a later time. A classic example is the Pacific salmon (*Oncorhynchus*), which accumulates lipids at sea and expends them while fasting during migrations upstream to spawn. Experiments with catfishes (*Ictalurus*) have shown that body lipids synthesized by fish for energy storage parallel those ingested in terms of saturation (completeness of hydrogen bonding of constituent fatty acid carbon chains) (Andrews and Stickney 1972).

The relative importance of lipids and proteins as energy sources is also shown by their mobilization by fishes during periods of starvation, which can be a regular occurrence in the life cycle of many fishes. For example, winter flounder (*Pseudopleuronectes americanus*) inhabiting coastal Maine waters fast while in deeper water during the period January to May (Bridges et al. 1976). Pacific salmon as well as Atlantic salmon and steelhead trout fast during their spawning migration. As no carbohydrates, protein, or fat are taken into the body during a fast, the fish must use compounds stored in body tissues. Savitz (1971) showed that bluegill utilize body protein and, especially, fat to meet body energy demands when fasting. The quantities of body fat and protein are significantly reduced in the starved fish, while inorganic content (ash) remains about constant. Protein depletion is presumably accomplished by the high concentration of proteolytic enzymes found in fish muscle (Siebert et al. 1964). Losses in body fat or protein as seen in bluegill are rarely reflected in significant body weight changes in the fish. Instead, the metabolized fat or protein is replaced by water to make up the body weight difference. For example, the whole body water content of sockeye salmon increased from about 60% to 77% during the spawning migration, while the sum percentage of lipid plus water was approximately constant at 80% (Idler and Bitners 1959). The familiar documentation of ascending salmon possessing an atrophied gut but still striking a fisherman's bait represents an interesting contradiction. Even if food were swallowed, the degeneration of the digestive tract and the significant decrease in gastric enzyme secretion indicate that very little of the food could be digested.

At the other end of the feeding spectrum, it is of interest to know what happens when fish have unlimited food available to them. In their investigation of unrestricted feeding in juvenile rainbow trout, Grayton and Beamish (1977) found that the trout held at 10°C would only consume just under 4% of their wet body weight per day of dry, prepared trout pellets. The trout would consume this quantity whether they were offered the pelletized food in unlimited quantities twice daily or up to six times a day. As one would expect, growth rate also did not vary with feeding frequencies from two to six feedings per day. In contrast, Balon (1977) describes deep-bodied, obese body shapes associated with an extreme abundance of food. Deep-bodied salmonids (including rainbow trout), pikes (e.g., *Esox lucius*), carps, and others have been described in cultured or natural environments where food is very abundant. As described in Chapter 8, fish tend to grow throughout their lives, but increase more in girth rather than length toward the ends of their lives.

Digestion   Digestion in fishes concerns the breakdown of foods by enzymatic and, in many cases, acidic secretions in the gut. The diversity of foods found in the guts of fishes attests to the variety of morphological and chemical adaptations which have evolved for digestion. The esophagus of fishes often contains many mucus cells and functions as a lubricated transit tube between the buccal pharyngeal cavity and the lower gut. The lower gut of many fishes (especially carnivorous ones) contains a true stomach, characterized by a smooth muscle "muscularis mucosa" layer of tissue. On the other hand, development of a gizzard (for masticatory as well as secretory digestive processes) as found in mullets and shad is a stomach specialization for microphagous food habits.

The gastric mucosa of the stomachs of carnivorous fishes produces a protease (protein breakdown) enzyme (e.g., pepsin) with an optimal activity at a pH of 2 to 4. Hydrochloric acid is also secreted by the gastric mucosa glands in these species, creating the low-pH environment. Gastric acid secretions are stimulated by stomach distension, which apparently activates cholinergic (mimicking acetycholine response) neural fibers. The "secretory" signals of these fibers to the acid glands can be blocked with injections of the neural-blocking agent atropine. The rates of both gastric acid secretion and of pepsin secretion are influenced by temperature. As temperatures increase (up to a point), the rates of secretion also increase. These increased secretions largely account for the threefold to fourfold increases in digestion rate that follow $10°C$ increases in temperature (Kapoor et al. 1975).

Proteins are also broken down in the alkaline medium of the intestine by the action of the enzyme trypsin. Trypsin is secreted by pancreatic tissue, which may be concentrated in a compact organ as in the mackerel (*Scomber*) or diffusely located in the mesenteric membranes surrounding the intestine and liver. Some fishes possess one or more pyloric caeca (see Fig. 9.1), which are blind pouches of secretory tissue located near the pyloric valve, at the stomach-intestine junction. Trypsin may be secreted from the caecal tissue or the pancreatic tissue, which commonly envelopes the caeca.

Fish also have enzymes which break down carbohydrates (carbohydrases) and fats (lipases). The pancreas appears to be the primary site of carbohydrase (e.g., amylase, which breaks down starch) production, although the intestinal mucosa and pyloric caeca represent additional production sites in various species. The pancreas is presumably also the primary site of lipase production. However, lipase activity has been found in extracts of the pyloric caeca and upper intestine as well as the pancreas in mackerel, menhaden, scup (*Stenotomus*), and sea robin (*Prionotus*) (Chesley 1934).

Both the presence and the quantity of digestive enzymes seem to correlate with the diet of fishes. Herbivorous and omnivorous fishes which have no stomachs also lack pepsin as a low-pH, proteolytic enzyme (Kapoor et al. 1975). However, omnivorous species have amylase activities in the gut many times that found in carnivorous species (Volya 1966).

Compounds broken down by actions of pharyngeal teeth, gizzards, and/or secretions of acid and enzymes are subsequently absorbed through the intestinal wall. Absorption (or assimilation) can be estimated by the difference between the quantity and quality (energy value in kilocalories or joules[1]) of the food ingested and of the feces excreted. These estimates are made even more precise when fecal nitrogen and calories from nonfood sources (e.g., sloughed gut wall) are taken into account.

---

[1]Note that 4183 joules = 1 kilocalorie (kcal).

TABLE 7-1
Vitamin Requirements for Growth[a]

Vitamin (mg/kg dry diet)	Rainbow Trout	Brook Trout	Brown Trout	Chinook Salmon	Coho Salmon	Carp	Eel	Goldfish	Yellowtail	Channel Catfish
Thiamine	10–12	10–12	10–12	10–15	10–15	R[b]	R	R	R	R
Riboflavin	20–30	20–30	20–30	20–25	20–25	7–10				R
Pyridoxine	10–15	10–15	10–15	15–20	15–20	5–10			R	R
Pantothenate	40–50	40–50	40–50	40–50	40–50	30–40		R	R	R
Niacin	120–150	120–150	120–150	150–200	150–200	30–50				R
Folacin	6–10	6–10	6–10	6–10	6–10	?				R
Cyanocobalamin	R	R	R	0.015–0.02	0.015–0.02	?				R
myo-Inositol	200–300	R	R	300–400	300–400	200–300				R
Choline	R	R	R	600–800	600–800	1500–2000				R
Biotin	1–1.2	1–1.2	1.5–2	1–1.5	1–1.5	1–1.2	R			R
Ascorbate	100–150	R	R	100–150	50–80	R		R	R	R
Vitamin A	2000–2500	R	R	R	R	1000–2000		R	R	R
Vitamin E[c]	R	R	R	40–50	R	80–100			R	R
Vitamin K	R	R	R	R	R					R

[a] Fish fed at reference temperature with diets at about protein requirement.
[b] R = required.
[c] Requirement directly affected by amount and type of unsaturated fat fed.
Source: From Halver (1972).

As in other animals, the metabolic conversion of biochemical compounds, either to provide energy or to synthesize other compounds (e.g., enzymes, structural proteins, stored triglycerides), requires particular cofactors to proceed. The cofactors which are largely unavailable in the body constitute the vitamins. The vitamin requirements of fishes probably vary somewhat with species, although only a few species (mostly of commercial value) have been investigated (Table 7-1). Dietary deficiencies of the vitamins that are essential for life and growth provoke a variety of physiological disturbances (Table 7-2). As with the research into essential amino acids, most of the vitamin deficiencies were determined by single vitamin deletions in an otherwise complete diet.

TABLE 7-2
Vitamin Deficiency Syndromes

Vitamin	Symptoms in salmon, trout, carp, catfish
Thiamine	Poor appetite, muscle atrophy, convulsions, instability and loss of equilibrium, edema, poor growth
Riboflavin	Corneal vascularization, cloudy lens, hemorrhagic eyes — photophobia, dim vision, incoordination, abnormal pigmentation of iris, striated constrictions of abdominal wall, dark coloration, poor appetite, anemia, poor growth
Pyridoxine	Nervous disorders, epileptiform fits, hyperirritability, ataxia, anemia, loss of appetite, edema of peritoneal cavity, colorless serous fluid, rapid postmortem rigor mortis, rapid and gasping breathing, flexing of opercles
Pantothenic acid	Clubbed gills, prostration, loss of appetite, necrosis and scarring, cellular atrophy, gill exudate, sluggishness, poor growth
Inositol	Poor growth, distended stomach, increased gastric emptying time, skin lesions
Biotin	Loss of appetite, lesions in colon, coloration, muscle atrophy, spastic convulsions, fragmentation of erythrocytes, skin lesions, poor growth
Folic acid	Poor growth, lethargy, fragility of caudal fin, dark coloration, macrocytic anemia
Choline	Poor growth, poor food conversion, hemorrhagic kidney and intestine
Nicotinic acid	Loss of appetite, lesions in colon, jerky or difficult motion, weakness, edema of stomach and colon, muscle spasms while resting, poor growth
Vitamin B_{12}	Poor appetite, low hemoglobin, fragmentation of erythrocytes, macrocytic anemia
Ascorbic acid	Scoliosis, lordosis, impaired collagen formation, altered cartilage, eye lesions, hemorrhagic skin, liver, kidney, intestine, and muscle
p-Aminobenzoic acid	No abnormal indication in growth, appetite, mortality

Source: From Halver (1972).

Excretion

Digestive breakdown of either lipids or carbohydrates yields water and carbon dioxide as end (waste) products. Water is either conserved, excreted, or diffused away depending on the salinity of its environment (Chapter 6).

Carbon dioxide enters into the bicarbonate equilibrium system, and most is excreted at the gills (Chapter 6). Protein digestion yields nitrogenous compounds in addition to carbon dioxide and water. In teleost fishes, these nitrogenous wastes take the form of ammonia, a potentially toxic substance. Thus, teleosts are primarily "ammoniotelic." Despite its toxicity, ammonia has many advantages over urea or uric acid as the chief excretory product of nitrogen metabolism as long as the animal resides in an environment with abundant water. First, the small molecular size and high lipid solubility permits nonionized ammonia (NH_3) to diffuse easily across the gills. Second, ionized ammonia (NH_4^+) is exchanged for Na^+ at the gills for maintenance of relative alkalinity and internal ion balance (Chapter 6). Third, conversion of ammonia to either urea or uric acid requires energy. Thus, in contrast to terrestrial forms, less energy is required to complete nitrogenous compound catabolism and, in teleost fishes, the end products resulting from this catabolism are largely released at the gills rather than the kidney. For example, carp and goldfish (*Carassius auratus*) excrete six to ten times as much nitrogen at the gills as at the kidney. Of the total nitrogenous excretion, 90% is in the form of ammonia and only 10% consists of urea (Smith 1929).

Elasmobranch fishes as well as the coelacanth (*Latimeria*) excrete urea as the primary nitrogenous end product (i.e., are ureotelic). As discussed in Chapter 6, much of the urea is retained in these marine fishes, giving their body fluids a near isosomotic relationship with their environment. The elasmobranch kidney filters urea from the blood plasma at the glomerulus. Much of the urea is subsequently recovered from the filtrate by active tubular resorption, preventing major "losses" of urea in the urine (Schmidt-Nielsen 1975).

Lungfishes, to varying degrees, possess the biochemical machinery to be either ammoniotelic or ureotelic. For example, the African lungfish (*Protopterus*) must sometimes endure extensive droughts. When the aquatic environment is drying up, *Protopterus* constructs a cocoon of mucus in the bottom mud and estivates there until the water returns. *Protopterus* is mostly ammoniotelic while aquatic but shifts to complete ureotelism while estivating and survives by metabolizing the proteins in its muscles. This shift is made possible by high concentrations of the necessary enzymes for urea production in its liver tissue (Janssens and Cohen 1966). Nontoxic urea may accumulate in the blood of estivating *Protopterus* to concentrations of 500 m mol/liter after a three-year estivation (Smith 1961). In contrast, the liver of Australian lungfish, *Neoceratodus*, possesses only 1% of the concentration of urea-synthesizing enzymes found in *Protopterus*. This finding is in accord with the obligatory aquatic habits of *Neoceratodus* (which also does not estivate).

Supplemental Readings

Andrews and Stickney 1972; Balon 1977; Budker 1971; Goldstein et al. 1967; Grayton and Beamish 1977; Halver 1972, 1976; Kapoor et al. 1975; Love 1970; Nikolsky 1963; Savitz 1971; Stickney and Shumway 1974.

ααααααααααααααααααααααααααααααααααααααααααααααααααααααααααααααααααα
~~~~~~

Growth

Most fish continue to grow throughout their lives. Consequently, growth has been one of the most intensively studied aspects of fish biology because it is a good indicator of the health of individuals and populations. Rapid growth indicates abundant food and other favorable conditions, whereas slow growth is likely to indicate just the opposite. Growth can be defined as the change in size (length, weight) over time or, energetically, as the change in calories stored as somatic and reproductive tissue. The energetic definition is particularly useful for understanding the factors that affect growth in fishes because ingested food energy (I), measured in calories, must emerge either as energy expended for metabolism (M) or growth (G), or as energy excreted (E) (Brett and Groves 1979). This can be simply expressed in the equation

$$I = M + G + E \qquad (1)$$

As explained in Chapter 4, metabolic energy expenditures can include calories expended for body maintenance and repair, for digesting food, and for movement. Excreted energy can take the form of feces, ammonia and urea, and the small quantities of mucus and sloughed epidermal cells of the skin. The remaining factor in the energy equation is growth.

Factors Affecting Growth   As growth is usually positive (e.g., increase in weight over time), a positive energy balance in metabolism is indicated. Metabolism is the sum of anabolism (the tissue synthesis or "building up" aspect of metabolism) plus catabolism (the energy-producing breaking of chemical bonds or "tearing down" aspect). Thus, the rate of anabolism exceeds that of catabolism in a growing fish. The principal factors controlling anabolic processes are growth hormones secreted by the pituitary and steroid hormones from the gonads (see next section). However, the rate of growth of fish is highly variable because it is greatly dependent on a variety of interacting environmental factors such as water temperature, levels of dissolved oxygen and ammonia, salinity, and photoperiod. Such factors interact with each other to influence growth rates, and with other factors such as the degree of competition, the amount and quality of food ingested, and the age and state of maturity of the fish.

Temperature is among the most important environmental variables. For example, growth in desert pupfish (*Cyprinodon macularius*) increases with temperature up to 30°C before falling off some at 35°C. Brett et al. (1969) measured the weight gain in fingerling sockeye salmon (*Oncorhynchus nerka*) at several ration (meal size) levels. As for pupfish, maximal growth rates are achieved at intermediate temperatures (15°C). It is also noteworthy in Brett's study that the maintenance ration (ration at zero growth) increased with temperature, reflecting the increased standard or maintenance metabolism (M in equation (1)) at warmer temperatures (Chapter 4). At any particular temperature, there often is an optimal ration for maximum growth. This is shown for the higher ration levels in juvenile reticulate sculpins (*Cottus perplexus*) at winter temperatures (Fig. 8.1). The more horizontal upper end of the growth curve indicates a significant decline in net growth efficiency (efficiency of ration utilization for growth at rations above the maintenance or "no growth" level); that is, the "extra" food consumed was not used efficiently for growth (Davis and Warren 1965). The fall data indicate a more equal net growth efficiency at various ration levels.

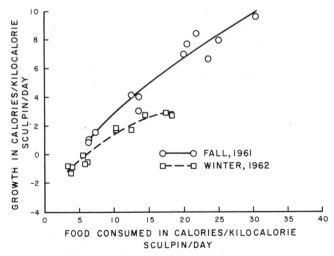

FIGURE 8.1 Relationships between rates of growth and food consumption for yearling reticulate sculpins at temperatures ranging from 8.3°C to 15.8°C during the fall of 1961 and from 3.9°C to 8.9°C during the winter of 1962. (From Davis and Warren, 1965.)

Dissolved oxygen levels, although temperature-dependent, are often by themselves an important factor affecting the growth rates of fishes. Stewart et al. (1967) measured a significant reduction in growth rate and food conversion efficiency in juvenile largemouth bass (*Micropterus salmoides*) when dissolved oxygen concentrations fell below approximately 5 mg/1 at 26°C. Presumably, the reduced ôxygen below this threshold precludes "extra," aerobic, energy-requiring activities such as growth and reproduction above maintenance energy costs. These fishes (called "oxygen regulators" and including largemouth bass, channel catfish [*Ictalurus punctatus*], striped mullet [*Mugil cephalus*], Sacramento blackfish [*Orthodon microlepidotus*], and others) maintain a homeostatic level of metabolism as oxygen levels are reduced. In some cases, attempts to swim to more favorable environments will be made by these species.

Ammonia is the primary excretory product of fishes, but if it is present in high concentrations, it will slow growth rates. For example, juvenile channel catfish display a linear drop in weight gain with increasing ammonia in their water (Fig. 8.2). The mechanism of growth inhibition by ammonia is still unknown. Obviously, this information has important applications in the culture of channel catfish. Culture systems designed to maximize growth rate must have either high flows of fresh water to carry excreted ammonia away or ammonia-removal systems such as green plants or "biological filters" utilizing appropriate bacteria. It is generally acknowledged that un-ionized ammonia (NH_3) in the water produces more toxic effects on fishes than an equal concentration of the ionized form (NH_4^+). As the relative proportion of the two forms depends on water pH, regular pH monitoring is an essential part of the operation of intensive freshwater fish culture systems. Although ammonia is a "natural" compound, its effects on fishes are typical of many pollutants, which also reduce growth rates when present at sublethal levels.

Salinity also affects growth rate. The euryhaline (broad salt tolerance) desert pupfish shows maximum growth rate at 35 parts per thousand (ppt) salinity compared with both higher and lower salinities (Kinne 1960). Growth is altered as other energy-demanding components (such as ion and osmoregulatory active transport systems) respond to environmental characteristics. These responses increase maintenance energy requirements (M), which will decrease growth rate (G) if I and E remain constant (Brett 1979). This topic is discussed more completely in Chapter 6.

Competition, either within or among species, for limited food supplies may slow growth. Swingle and Smith (1940) showed that bluegill (*Lepomis macrochirus*), a species in which the adults and young both eat virtually the same aquatic invertebrates and are not cannibalistic, become "stunted" when the population size reaches a particular level. Fertilization of the pond will increase the invertebrate food base and

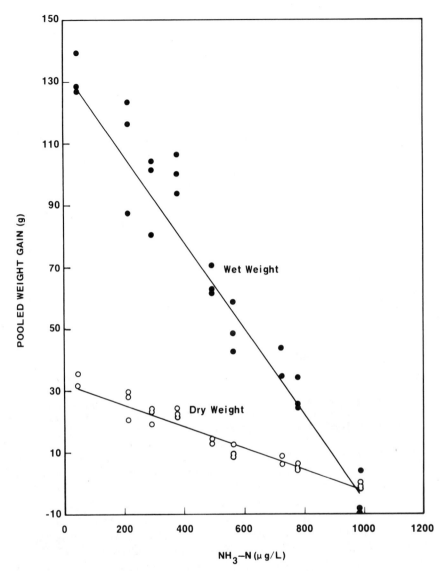

FIGURE 8.2 Effects of nonionized ammonia on growth, measured in terms of pooled weights of the fish in each aquarium. (From Colt and Tchobanoglous, 1978.)

consequently bluegill total biomass. However, the average size of the bluegills remains small as growth slows and some reproduction continues.

Food availability also interacts with other factors as well, particularly temperature, to affect the growth of fishes on a seasonal basis. For example, Gerking (1966) found marked seasonal differences in growth (length increases) in northern Indiana bluegill populations (Fig. 8.3). Bluegill growth was accelerated during the warmer months of plentiful food. Figure 8.3 also shows the reduced rate of growth (especially gains

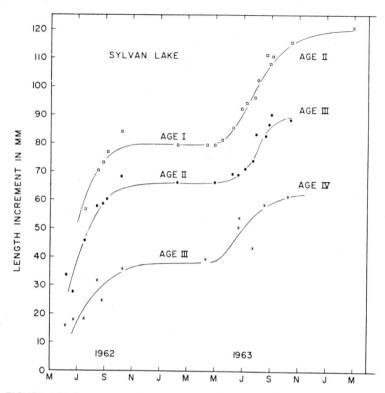

FIGURE 8.3 Seasonal gain in length of a population of bluegill (*Lepomis macrochirus*) by age groups. The growth increment varies with season and decreases with age and size. (From Gerking, 1966.)

in length) consistent with advancing age in bluegills, also typical of most other fishes. Striped mullet (*Mugil cephalus*) from south Texas coastal waters show cycles of seasonal growth similar to those of bluegills, except that growth virtually ceases during the warmest months of midsummer through midautumn. This leveling off of growth when food is abundant can probably be attributed to excessive water temperatures reducing assimilation efficiency (Cech and Wohlschlag 1975, 1981). Photoperiod (day length) may also affect seasonal growth phenomena. For example, Hogman (1968) found a close association between growth of lake whitefish (*Coregonus clupeaformis*) and seasonal photoperiod, but no relationship between the spring water temperatures and growth.

Age and maturity are usually the best predictors of relative growth rates in fishes, although the absolute growth rates are strongly influenced by environmental factors. Thus, fish typically grow very rapidly in length in the first few months or years of life, until maturation. Then increasing amounts of energy are diverted from growth of somatic tissues to growth of gonadal tissues. As a consequence, growth rates of mature fish are much slower than those of immature fish. Partly because of the amount of gonadal tissue, however, mature fish are typically heavier per unit of length than immature fish. This is reflected in their higher condition factor (K), an index of "plumpness":

$$K = \frac{W(100)}{L^3}$$

where W is the weight of the fish in grams and L is the length in centimeters. The condition factor is frequently used by fisheries biologists as an indicator of the health of a fish population. If the fish in a population have high K values, then there is probably plenty of food available to support both somatic and gonadal growth.

Growth Regulation

Photoperiodic and other factors affecting growth rates may well act through variations in hormone secretions. Fish growth hormone is synthesized in the alpha cells of the pars distalis (anterior lobe) of the pituitary gland (Donaldson et al. 1979). Removal of this tissue (hypophysectomy) results in a cessation of growth in species investigated (including poeciliids, salmonids, and sharks). On the other hand, mammalian growth hormone injections increase growth rates of juvenile coho salmon (*Oncorhynchus kisutch*), apparently because food conversion rates are improved. Possible mechanisms involved with this improved food conversion rate include stimulation of stored fat mobilization (for an energy source), positive effects on protein synthesis, or stimulation of insulin production or release (Markert et al. 1977). Thyroid and gonadal steroid hormones have also been used to increase growth in various species. For example, two synthetic androgens, dimethazine and norethandrolone, increased the growth rate of juvenile rainbow trout when either compound was added to a pelleted diet. These weight gain increases were due to both the increased protein synthesis rate and the improved food conversion efficiency (Matty and Cheema 1978). Hormonal enhancement of growth in fishes is reviewed thoroughly by Donaldson et al. (1979).

Growth Rate Measurements

Growth rate in fishes can be determined by measuring changes in size over time. In practice, it is usually measured by changes in body weight (mass) or length per unit of elapsed time. Growth rates of fishes are generally measured by one of five methods.

1. **Raise in a controlled environment.** A fish (or egg or larva) of known age is placed in a tank, small pond, or cage in a larger water body. Its length or body weight is measured at time intervals for growth rate calculations. This method is especially valuable for assessing growth of cultured fishes, as feeding rates, temperatures, etc. may be controllable.
2. **Mark and recapture.** A fish is marked (or tagged) and released when an initial measurement of size is made. The fish is recaptured at a future date and measured again. The growth rate is calculated from the

change in size over the time period the marked animal spent in its habitat. It should be established that the marking method does not significantly alter the behavior, feeding rate, etc. Marks may consist of clipped fin rays, liquid nitrogen "cold brands," pigmented epidermis from high-pressure spray painting, or flourescent rings on bones or scales (visible under ultraviolet light) from incorporation of tetracycline or 2, 4 bis (N, N' di-carboxymethyl-aminomethyl) fluorescein (DCAF) in the diet (Weber and Ridgway 1962; Hankin 1978). Tags may also vary considerably from externally attached discs, plates, and streamers to small, implantable metal rods detectable in a magnetic field. Although these fish provide more realistic data concerning growth rates in their natural setting, they are more difficult to recapture compared with those in which the first method is used.

3. **Length-frequency distribution.** Length-frequency distributions are produced by measuring the lengths of individuals sampled from a population and plotting the number of fish (frequency) of each length caught. This is especially useful as a technique with young fish, and the individual peaks often separate by age classes (Fig. 8.4). By comparing the mean lengths between age classes, one can determine approximate growth rates at various ages. For example, in Fig. 8.4 the difference between age class 0 (young of the year) fish and age class I (between second

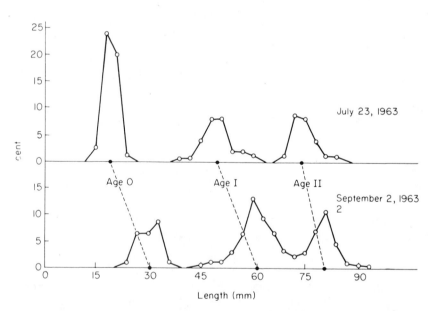

FIGURE 8.4 Percentage length frequencies of pond smelt, from Black Lake, Alaska, in middle and late summer. (Unpublished data from Fisheries Research Institute, University of Washington, Seattle, Washington, (From Royce, 1972.)

CH. 8 GROWTH

and first "birthdays") fish is 49 mm–20 mm = 29 mm. Thus, these grow at a mean rate of 29 mm (length) per year in their first year of life (when sampled in late July). In this example, the growth increment declines with increasing age from 29mm to 24 mm per year (between year classes I and II).

    4. **Back-calculation from rings on hard structures.** Juvenile fish have the same number of bones and scales as very old, much larger individuals of the same genetic stock when rearing takes place under similar conditions. And, for many species, the rate of growth in diameter of the bones, spines, and scales is proportional to the growth rate (length) of the fish. For many reasons scales are the hard structure most commonly examined. The relative transparency of scales, the ease of sampling them, and the minimal damage to the fish make them desirable to work with. Scales grow by fibroblast cells in the fibrillar plate region supplying collagen (a protein) and by calcification ($CaCO_3$) of the outer surface. Figure 8.5 shows the proliferation of cells at the scale margin which enlarge the diameter of the scale. These additions to the scale diameter are formed repeatedly at a relatively constant rate over time and are distinguishable as growth rings (circuli) when the scale is magnified (Fig. 8.6). Periods of slow growth are discernible in magnified scales as areas of closely spaced circuli. Closely spaced circuli may occur on an annual basis from:

    a. cold seasons decreasing metabolism and appetite, especially in temperate water,

    b. fasting periods associated with spawning and unavailability of food, or

    c. partial scale decalcification (resorption) in females with developing eggs and young.

These annual variations in the circuli pattern are termed annuli. Thus, age can be determined by counting the annuli, and fish lengths at each year can be back-calculated by measuring the linear distance (radius) from the "focus" of the scale to each annulus (Fig. 8.6). For example,

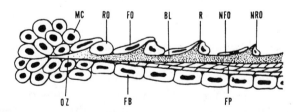

FIGURE 8.5 Schematic diagram showing the structure of anterior margin of a teleostean fish scale and the scale-forming cells. *BL* bony layer, *FB* fibroblast, *FO* flattened osteoblast, *FP* fibrillary plate, *MC* marginal cell, *NFO* necrotic flattened osteoblast, *NRO* necrotic round osteoblast, *OZ* osteoid zone, *R* ridge, *RO* round osteoblast. (From Kobayashi et al., 1972.)

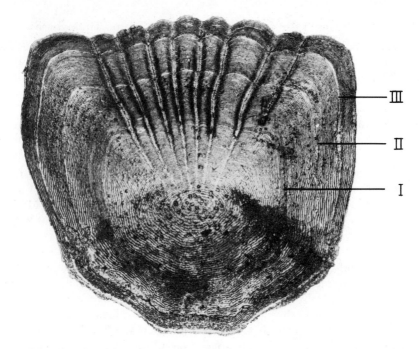

FIGURE 8.6 A scale of a kelp perch (*Brachyistius frenatus*) from Bodega Bay, California. Shown are three annuli (magnification = 14X). (Photo by Samuel Woo, Illustration Services, University of California, Davis.)

the length at n years can be calculated by using the following formula (Lee 1920):

$$L_n = a + \frac{(L - a)\,(V_n)}{V_r}$$

where L_n = fish length at n years
      a = a constant that often approximates fish length at time of scale formation
      L = fish length at time of capture
      V_n = scale radius distance from focus to nth annulus
      V_r = scale radius from focus to scale edge

From these back-calculations of length at different years, growth rates can be estimated. Table 8-1 shows back-calculated standard lengths for striped mullet from South Texas coastal waters.

    Daily increments of growth have been detected on fish otoliths ("ear stones") (Pannella 1971). The widths of these increments average 1 μm to 2 μm in larval anchovies (*Engraulis*) and 3 μm to 4 μm in larger hake (*Merluccius*) but are difficult to count where annular rings are formed. Thus, using daily growth increments for age estimates is particularly effective in young fishes (less than 1 yr) and in tropical species having poorly differentiated annuli (Brothers et al. 1976).

TABLE 8-1
Mean Back-Calculated Standard Lengths in Millimeters of Striped Mullet

Age Class	(n)*	Standard Lengths (mm)				
		I	II	III	IV	V
1+	(39)	132				
2+	(71)	127	194			
3+	(54)	122	188	234		
4+	(12)	125	178	227	266	
5+	(3)	127	183	213	249	286
Means		127	186	225	258	286
Growth increments		59	39	33	28	

*n = Sample size in each age class.

Source: From Cech and Wohlschlag (1975).

5. **Radiocarbon uptake method.** Ottoway and Simkiss (1977) describe a method where living fish scales, plucked from the epidermis, are incubated in a medium containing the simple amino acid glycine, which has been radiotagged with ^{14}C. The rate at which the ^{14}C glycine is incorporated into the collagenous structure of the scale after an incubation of less than 4 hours is measured by the level of beta radiation emitted by the scale. Faster growth rates of fish should accompany increased ^{14}C incorporation by the scale, as measured in a scintillation counter.

Supplemental Readings

Brett 1979; Brett and Groves 1979; Brett et al. 1969; Cech and Wohlschlag 1975; Colt and Tchobanoglous 1978; Davis and Warren 1965; Donaldson et al. 1979; Gerking 1966; Kinne 1960; Kobayashi et al. 1972; Markert et al. 1977; Matty and Cheema 1978; Ottoway and Simkiss 1977; Royce 1972; Stewart et al. 1967; Weatherley 1972; Webb and Brett 1972.

ααααααααααααααααααααααααααααααααααααααααααααααααααααααααααααααααααα
~~~~~~

Reproduction

The success of any fish species is ultimately determined by the ability of its members to reproduce successfully in a fluctuating environment and thereby to maintain viable populations. Since each fish species occurs under a unique set of ecological conditions, it has a unique reproductive strategy, with special anatomical, behavioral, physiological, and energetic adaptations.

Anatomical Adaptations   The reproductive strategies of fishes are often clearly reflected in the anatomical differences between the sexes. Internally, of course, the sexes of most fishes can be easily distinguished by examination of the gonads, at least during the spawning season. Both the testes of males and the ovaries of females are typically paired structures that are suspended by mesenteries across the roof of the body cavity, in close association with the kidneys. (Fig. 9.1). During the spawning season, the testes are smooth, white structures that rarely account for more than 12% of the weight of a fish, while the ovaries are large yellowish structures, granular in appearance, that may be 30% to 70% of a fish's weight. A few hermaphroditic species (mostly in the family Serranidae) have ovotestes, which are part ovary, part testes.

The testes are rather similar among the various groups of fishes, although the path of the sperm may show considerable variation. Thus, in lampreys and hagfishes (Agnatha) and in the Salmonidae the sperm are shed directly into the body cavity and exit through an abdominal pore or pores. In contrast, in the Chondrichthyes the sperm passes through a duct that is shared with the kidney and may be stored in a seminal vesicle for a short period of time before being expelled. A similar situation exists in most primitive bony fishes (Chondrostei, Holostei,

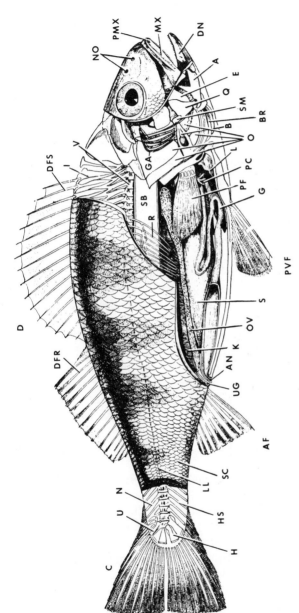

FIGURE 9.1 General anatomy of a teleost (*Perca*): *A* angulo-articular bone, *AF* anal fin, *AN* anus, *B* bulbus arteriosus, *BR* branchiostegal rays, *C* caudal fin, *D* dorsal fin, *DFR* dorsal fin ray, *DFS* dorsal fin spine, *DN* dentary bone, *E* ectopterygoid bone, *G* intestine, *GA* gill arches, *H* a hypural bone, *HS* hemal spine, *I* an interneural bone, *K* kidney, *L* liver, *LL* lateral line, *MX* maxillary bone, *N* neural spine, *NO* anterior and posterior nares, *O* opercular series and preoperculum bones, *OV* ovary, *PC* pyloric caecum, *PF* pectoral fin, *PMX* premaxillary bone, *PVF* pelvic fin, *Q* quardate bone, *R* ribs, *S* stomach, *SB* swimbladder, *SC* scales, *SM* symplectic bone, *U* urostyle bone, *UG* urogenital opening, *V* vertebral centrum. (Modified from Dean, 1895.)

Dipnoi), although a seminal vesicle is usually lacking. In teleosts there are usually special separate sperm ducts. The means of passing eggs from the ovary to the outside are similar to those for sperm, although special modifications of the oviducts (and/or ovaries) are common in fishes that retain the fertilized eggs and/or young, particularly if nutrients are supplied to the developing young by the mother (see the next section of this chapter).

While the internal differences between the sexes are generally obvious in mature fish, it is frequently difficult to distinguish the sexes externally. Indeed, many fishes which are mass spawners, but particularly pelagic forms, show virtually no sexual dimorphism or dichromatism (color differences), even when spawning. At the opposite end of the spectrum are fishes which are permanently and obviously dimorphic or dichromatic. Many of these species have internal fertilization, so the males have intromittent organs. In most such cases, such as sharks or poeciliid fishes (e.g., guppies), the intromittent organ is a modified fin. Because intromittent organs evolved independently in many groups, they show considerable anatomical variation, ranging from the barely noticeable thickening of the anal spine region of the surfperches (Embiotocidae), to the elongated movable anal rays of the Poeciliidae, to the complex claspers of the Chondrichthyes. Curiously, even in fishes without claspers it is common for the anal fin to be considerably larger in males than in females. This is particularly noticeable among suckers (Catostomidae).

While modified anal fins are common among fishes, perhaps the most widespread type of sexual dimorphism is size. In egg-laying fishes in which the males are territorial during the breeding season, the males are often larger than the females (as in salmon). However, in most fishes with sexual differences in size, it is the female that is larger or at least achieves a larger size. Thus the record-sized individuals of many species such as striped bass (*Morone saxatilis*) and sturgeon are females. Among live-bearing fishes, females as a rule are larger than males. What males may lack in size they often make up for in bright coloration. Sexual dichromatism is mostly a seasonal phenomenon among fishes, because bright colors that are likely to increase reproductive success by attracting mates are also likely to attract predators. Exceptions to this "rule" are found primarily among tropical fishes in which the breeding season lasts through much of the year, so the males are more or less continuously on display. Males of dichromatic fishes often have temporary structural modifications as well. Best known are the bizarre hooked mouths (kypes) and humps characteristic of many spawning salmonids. More widespread, however, are breeding tubercles and contact organs which Wiley and Collette (1970) noted were found in at least 25 families of fishes. Breeding tubercles are tiny, keratinized bumps that grow on the fins, head, and body scales during the breeding season. Contact organs are similar but have an internal core of bone as well. Both types of structures are found primarily in males on the parts of the body that are likely to come in contact with females or other males during the spawning season. These tubercles seem to function in assisting the males in maintaining contact with females during spawning, in stimulating the females during spawning, and in assisting the defense of territories and nests. For ichthyologists, the breeding tubercles and contact organs have proved to be very useful taxonomic tools, because the number and pattern differ among species.

Behavioral Adaptations   Fish have a fascinating array of reproductive behavior patterns. Not surprisingly, such behavior is highly adaptive and is strongly correlated with the overall ecology of each species and with its morphological adaptations. It is thus possible to construct an ecological classification of fishes based on their reproductive strategies, particularly as these strategies are manifested in behavior patterns and specialized structures. The system used here essentially follows the "ecomorphological" system of Balon (1975a), who based his system on the ideas of the Russian ichthyologist S. G. Kryzhanovsky. In this section we will describe (where possible), in general terms, the courtship and spawning behavior, the parental behavior, and the behavioral and morphological adaptations of embryos and larvae of fishes in the reproductive groupings ("Guilds" of Balon [1975a]) listed in Table 9-1.

Nonguarders are fishes that do not protect their eggs and young once spawning has been completed. They fall into two basic groups, those that simply scatter their eggs in the environment (open substrate spawners) and those that hide the eggs as part of the spawning behavior (brood hiders). The open substrate spawners by and large spawn in groups, without elaborate courtship behavior or specialized reproduction structures. Often the spawning groups are quite large, with males outnumbering the females. The spawning behavior is very difficult to describe precisely because typically all that can be observed is a swirling mass of fish.

Pelagic spawners spawn in open water, often near the surface. Many such spawners are schooling fishes, such as tuna (Scombridae), sardines (*Sardinops*), and whitefish (*Coregonus*), that spawn in open waters. Many river-dwelling anadromous fishes, such as shads of the genus *Alosa,* are also pelagic spawners, often seeking out areas where current conditions are most favorable for successful spawning. Although pelagic spawning is most often associated with pelagic fishes, many benthic fishes temporarily rise off the bottom to spawn. This is particularly true of fishes associated with coral reefs, such as wrasses (Labridae) and parrotfishes (Scaridae). On the reefs the density of predatory fishes is so high that the eggs and young presumably have a greater chance of survival in the open water than on the reef. However, one of the main functions of pelagic spawning seems to be to assure that the young

TABLE 9-1
A Classification of Reproductive Strategies

I. Nonguarders of eggs and young
   A. Open substrate spawners
      1. Pelagic spawners (pelagophils)
      2. Benthic spawners
         a. Spawners on coarse bottoms (rocks, gravel, etc.)
            (1) Pelagic free embryo and larvae (lithopelagophils)
            (2) Benthic free embryo and larvae (lithophils)
         b. Spawners on plants
            (1) Nonobligatory (phytolithophils)
            (2) Obligatory (phytophils)
         c. Spawners on sandy bottoms (psammonophils)
   B. Brood hiders
      1. Benthic spawners (lithophils)
      2. Cave spawners (speleophils)
      3. Spawners on invertebrates (ostracophils)
      4. Beach spawners (aero-psammonophils)
      5. Annual fishes (xerophils)

II. Guarders
   A. Substratum choosers
      1. Rock spawners (lithophils)
      2. Plant spawners (phytophils)
      3. Terrestrial spawners (aerophils)
      4. Pelagic spawners (pelagophils)
   B. Nest spawners
      1. Rock and gravel nesters (lithophils)
      2. Sand nesters (psammonophils)
      3. Plant material nesters
         a. Gluemakers (ariadnophils)
         b. Nongluemakers (phytophils)
      4. Bubble nesters (aphrophils)
      5. Hole nesters (speleophils)
      6. Miscellaneous materials nesters (polyphils)
      7. Anemone nesters (actinariophils)

III. Bearers
   A. External bearers
      1. Transfer brooders
      2. Forehead brooders
      3. Mouth brooders
      4. Gill-chamber brooders
      5. Skin brooders
      6. Pouch brooders
   B. Internal bearers
      1. Ovi-ovoviviparous fishes
      2. Ovoviviparous fishes
      3. Viviparous fishes

Source: After Balon (1975). Names in brackets are the special terminology of Balon.

become widely dispersed by water currents. Indeed, most pelagic spawners have wide distributions, as reflected in the amazing uniformity of the reef fish fauna of the Indian and Pacific oceans. Most of these fishes, if not pelagic spawners, have pelagic larvae.

In order to become widely dispersed, the eggs, embryos, and larvae of pelagic spawners have to be buoyant; and buoyancy is achieved either through the presence of oil globules or through high water content. One of the problems with this strategy, however, is that the mortality of eggs and young is extremely high, either because they are carried to unfavorable areas or because they are eaten by pelagic predators. To compensate, females have extremely high fecundities and spawning periods are often protracted, since all the eggs can rarely be released in a single spawning act. The shortest spawning periods are found in temperate zone pelagic fishes, since optimal conditions for embryo and larval survival are likely to be highly seasonal. In pelagic spawners associated with tropical reefs, spawning may be a nearly daily activity for months, with each female producing a small number of eggs each day. In these fishes, the breeding behavior may be extremely complex and variable. Indeed, some of the most complex mating systems known are found in such fishes (see Chapter 34), involving territoriality, harems, leks, and sex changing.

Benthic spawners are of three basic types, those that spawn on gravel or rocks, those that spawn on aquatic plants, and those that spawn on sand. Such fishes are typically mass spawners, without elaborate courtship rituals. Very often when spawning is observed, there is one female closely followed by several males who fertilize the eggs as the female releases them. The eggs and embryos are either adhesive and stick to whatever surface on which they are laid, are laid in long strings which are wrapped around objects, or drop into interstices and cracks where they take on water, swelling enough to wedge themselves in place. Benthic spawning fishes that choose gravel or rocks are typically stream-dwelling fishes, such as suckers (Catostomidae), minnows (Cyprinidae), or intertidal fishes, since these are habitats where these substrates are often dominant. However, many fishes also migrate to these areas for spawning. The free embryos and larvae of these fishes may be either pelagic or benthic. Those that are pelagic (such as those of sturgeons [Acipenseridae] or smelt [Osmeridae]) become active or buoyant immediately after "hatching," whereas those that are benthic stay close to the spawning area until they can swim freely. In streams there are a few species of fishes that scatter their eggs on sandy bottoms or on the roots of plants adjacent to such areas. One such species is the eulachon (*Thaleichthys pacificus*), an anadromous smelt that has small embryos that are anchored to the bottom on a short stalk. This presumably reduces the probability of being buried by slight shifts in the sand and keeps the embryos in well-oxygenated water until the pelagic embryos hatch. In lakes or shallow ocean waters, plants are often important substrates for the adhesive embryos of benthic spawners. Some fishes always spawn on such plants. For example, carp (*Cyprinus carpio*), pikes (*Esox*), and buffalofishes (*Ictiobus*) generally spawn only on vegetation that is flooded by high water in the spring. If such material is not available, spawning usually does not take place or is much less successful. Once the embryos hatch, the young remain among the plants; many of them have adhesive organs on their heads so they can stick to the stems of the plants.

Brood hiders are fishes that hide their eggs in one way or another but do not show any parental care beyond spawning. A majority of these species are benthic spawners that build nests in which the eggs are buried. The females of salmon and trout, for example, excavate redds (see Chapter 19) by digging with their tails. The redds are constructed prior to spawning and are defended by both sexes from other members of the same species. The most vigorous defenders, however, are the brightly colored males. Once the eggs are laid, fertilized, and buried (by the female), the nest site is abandoned, although Pacific salmon (*Oncorhynchus*) may spend their final days on the site. This may prevent, at least temporarily, other salmon from using the same site and thereby digging up the embryos already buried. Many minnows (Cyprinidae) build nests as well, although a number of species build piles of stones rather than depressions. The males of these species also defend the nest sites and have well-developed tubercles on the head and body to assist them in doing this. The eggs of benthic brood hiders are often larger than those of fishes that do not hide the embryos, since they are more likely to survive. The larger size may also provide the large surface area necessary for respiration in a buried embryo. In salmonids, the embryos with large yolk sacs remain in the gravel long after hatching, emerging as small, active fish (alevins). In this way they manage to avoid the enormously high mortality of the larval period found in fish with pelagic young.

While most brood hiders use burying techniques such as those of salmon and minnows, a number of other methods have evolved as well. Some cave fishes lay large, adhesive eggs in crevices, so the embryos cannot be cannibalized or eaten by other predators in the food-short environment of caves (see Chapter 31). A number of fishes lay their eggs in the gill cavities of hard-shelled invertebrates, where the embryos receive both protection and oxygen. Perhaps the best-known example of this is the bitterling (Cyprinidae, *Rhodeus sericeus*), which deposits eggs, by means of long ovipositor, in the gills of unionid clams. While the embryos may be a burden to the clams, the clams in turn burden the fish with their own larvae (glochidia), which attach to the gills of the fish. A more one-sided relationship is found in the snailfishes (Cyclopteridae), many of which lay eggs in the gill cavities of crabs and may actually cause the host's gills to collapse (Peden and Corbett 1973).

While the preceding methods of brood hiding seem to have evolved largely as a way of protecting the embryos from predators, at least one group of brood hiders, the annual fishes of the family Cyprinodontidae, bury their embryos in the mud of pond bottoms as a way of maintaining populations in ponds that dry up every year. The embryos remain in a state of arrested development in the mud (which may dry out completely), only to hatch when the rains fill the ponds again (see Chapter 22).

Guarders go a step further in their reproductive behavior than the brood hiders, since they not only protect the eggs while spawning but also guard the embryos until they hatch and frequently through the larval stages as well. Because tending the eggs usually means being tied to a specific location in which the eggs are laid, territoriality (often implying competition for egg-laying sites) and elaborate courtship behavior are the usual state of affairs among the fishes of this group. Except among the cichlids, the embryos are almost always guarded by males, who not only protect them against predators (including other members of the same species) but typically keep oxygen levels high around the embryos by fanning currents of water across them and keep the embryo mass free of dead embryos and debris. The amount of time spent guarding can range from a few days to over four months (Antarctic plunderfish [*Harpagifer bispinis*]). Guarding species can be broken into two groups, those that do not build nests (substratum choosers) and those that do. The differences between substratum choosers that merely clean off a suitable area of bottom and fish that build slightly more elaborate structures, however, are often slight.

Substratum choosers do not build nests, but the males do typically clean the spawning substratum before enticing a female to spawn there. There are four basic types of substratum choosers, rock spawners, plant spawners, terrestrial spawners, and pelagic spawners (Balon 1975a). Rock spawners, such as the lumpsucker (*Cyclopterus lumpus*) and many gobies (Gobiidae), clean off the surface of a flat rock upon which the eggs are laid and then defended. Even more unusual are terrestrial spawners, since the only examples known are the spraying characins (*Copeina*). These small fishes manage to spawn on the underside of overhanging leaves or rocks. To accomplish this, a pair of characins leap backwards together out of the water, pressing their bellies to the overhanging material and spawning. The embryos adhere to the substrate, and the male keeps them damp by splashing water on them until they hatch in three days or so. Such embryos not only are relatively free from predation but have plenty of oxygen, often in short supply in tropical waters. Low dissolved oxygen in the water seems to be one the the principal reasons all members of the air-breathing families Anabantidae (climbing gouramis), Helostomatidae (kissing gourami), and Channidae (snakeheads) have evolved embryos which float at the surface of the water, where oxygen levels are highest. The embryos contain oil droplets for flotation, and the floating clusters are guarded.

Nest spawners construct some sort of structure, cavity, or pit in which the eggs are laid and fertilized and the embryos defended. The young are often defended in the nest as well, and in some species the parents even herd schools of young around for a period of time. Pit nests can be made of a wide variety of material, but most common are nests of gravel and rock. Such nests are typically shallow depressions that are carefully constructed and tended by territorial males. Most sunfishes and black basses (Centrarchidae) construct nests of this sort, often in colonies. The males defend the embryos and young until the young become too active to be kept in the nest. In some cichlids, such as *Tilapia zilli*, eggs are laid and incubated in one nest depression but the young are tended (by both parents) in one or more additional depressions constructed nearby. A few species construct nests in sandy bottoms. Either the eggs and embryos in such nests have special adaptations to reduce the possibility of being smothered, such as being semibuoyant, or the parent fish must spend considerable time handling them (as in *Cichlasoma nicaraguense*). In areas where bottoms are muddy, nest building fishes commonly built nests of plant material. Usually plant nesting fishes construct loose aggregations of material in which the eggs are laid. However, the African electric fish (*Gymnarchus niloticus*) constructs a floating "cave" of plant material in which the eggs are laid and defended. A special type of plant nest builders are those that use a kidney secretion to glue the pieces of plant together to form a tight nest. The main examples of this type of nesting known are the sticklebacks (Gasterosteidae), in which the male builds a tube, usually attached to rooted plants, or placed in a small pit. By means of a complicated courtship ritual (the famous zig-zag pattern so well studied by N. Tinbergen and other ethologists) a female is enticed into a nest, where she deposits some eggs after being nudged by the male. After the eggs are laid, he chases the female out and fertilizes them. This process is repeated several times, until there are enough embryos in the nest, at which time the male begins to incubate them by fanning currents of water across them. After the embryos hatch, the male guards the young for several days, first in the nest and then in a school outside the nest.

Another group of fishes with well-studied nesting behavior are the gouramis (Belontiidae), especially the Siamese fighting fish (*Betta splendens*), since these fishes build bubble nests. The eggs and embryos of these fishes, like those in the closely related Anabantidae and Helostomatidae (discussed in the previous section), are buoyant and are often laid in clusters at the surface of the water or picked up and spat there by the males. The gouramis place these embryos in a floating nest of frothy bubbles built by the male, who secretes a substance to make the bubbles last. In some species the embryos may not be buoyant and the bubble nests are built on the bottom or attached to aquatic plants.

Perhaps the most common type of nest among fishes are nests in caves, cavities, or burrows. Such nests are characteristic of such abundant families as the Gobiidae and Cottidae, of such inhabitants of the intertidal region as the Stichaeidae and Pholidae, and of many members of the freshwater families Cyprinidae, Ictaluridae, and Percidae. For stream-dwelling fishes, the typical cave nest is the underside of a flat rock in midstream, where there is plenty of current to keep the water well oxygenated. Sculpins (Cottidae) and many darters (Percidae) deposit their eggs in clusters on the roofs of such shelters and guard the embryos until they hatch. In quieter water, minnows such as the fathead minnow (*Pimephales promelas*) will lay their eggs on the underside of a log or board, in an area that has been cleaned off by the male. Spawning males develop a thick, horny pad on their heads which is used for rubbing algae and other material off the spawning surface. Many large catfishes (*Ictalurus*) lay their eggs in cavities ranging from hollow logs, to old muskrat burrows, to oil drums, where the embryos are guarded by the males. These catfishes also guard schools of the young for one or more weeks after they emerge from the nest. Many gobies construct burrows in soft bottoms with two or more openings or use those of invertebrates, in which the eggs are laid and fertilized. The embryos are on stalks, presumably to intercept oxygen in the water flowing through the burrow during tidal fluxes. Perhaps the most extreme adaptations to burrow spawning low-oxygen conditions are found in the South American lungfish (*Lepidosiren paradoxa*). This species constructs a long burrow in swamps in which the water is nearly without oxygen. To provide the needed oxygen, the pelvic fins of the brooding male are highly vascular and capable of releasing oxygen into the water by the embryos.

In contrast to the commonness of the use of holes for protecting the embryos and young, only one group, the anemone fishes (Pomacentridae: *Amphiprion*) is known to co-opt the defenses of an invertebrate to protect its eggs. These fishes lay their eggs at the base of a sea anemone, to which the fishes are acclimated. The embryos are constantly tended until they hatch and do not seem to be affected by being touched by the tentacles of the anemone. The free embryos leave the anemone after hatching, however, and are planktonic for a while before each settles down on an anemone of its own (Allen 1972).

Bearers are fishes that carry their embryos (and sometimes their young as well) around with them, either externally or internally. Fishes that carry their embryos externally have developed a wide variety of ways of doing so, ranging from short-term attachment of embryos to the fish until a suitable place to put them is found (transfer brooders) to the carrying of embryos and young in special pouches. **Transfer brooders** are known mainly in a few families of South American catfishes and in a few cyprinodontoid fishes such as the medaka (*Oryzias latipes*).

In the medaka a cluster of embryos remains attached to the belly of the female until it is deposited on a plant or the embryos hatch. In **forehead brooders** the embryos are placed in a depression on the forehead of the males, where they are held in place by threads attached to an overhanging hooklike structure. This peculiar method of incubation is practiced only by two species of nurseryfishes (Kurtidae: *Kurtus*). A much commoner type of brooder is the **mouth brooder,** which is found in families as diverse as the sea catfishes (Ariidae), cichlids (Cichlidae), cardinal fishes (Apogonidae), and bonytongues (Osteoglossidae). Mouth brooders carry the large, yolky embryos about until they hatch and typically carry the free embryos about as well. Even after the young become active, they usually are closely associated with the parent fish for a period of time and may flee back into the mouth cavity when threatened. In cichlids it is usually the female that carries the embryos (although both sexes may participate in some species), which she picks up quickly after spawning. **Gill chamber brooders** are an extreme form of mouth brooders and are found only in the North American cave fishes, Amblyopsidae. The advantages of this form of brooding are not known.

Skin brooders, in which the eggs are attached to the belly of a parent, are known mainly from the South American catfish families Aspredinidae and Loricariidae and from pipefishes (Syngnathidae). In the catfishes the females develop a layer of spongy skin on the belly to which the eggs stick after being fertilized. Each egg is eventually surrounded by a vascularized tissue on a stalk that grows from the brood skin. Presumably, the stalk functions like a placenta. A similar situation exists in some species of pipefish, only the males do the brooding rather than the females. After the eggs are fertilized, the female places the embryos on the male. Herald (1959) points out that there is a continuum of forms in the Syngnathidae starting with skin-brooding pipefishes, progressing through pipefishes with open brood pouches on their bellies, and ending with seahorses, which have closed pouches with only one opening. Seahorses are the best known of **pouch brooders,** although many pipefishes and some catfishes (in the same families as the skin brooders) are pouch brooders as well. In seahorses, after an extended courtship period, the female deposits eggs in the pouch (marsupium) of the male, by means of a penislike oviduct. The eggs are fertilized as they enter the marsupium, and anywhere from 25 to 150 embryos may be incubated. After hatching, the free embryos are carried in the pouch until they are capable of fairly active swimming, at which time they are expelled by the brooding male.

Internal bearers have many similarities to pouch brooders, although females always carry the embryos and/or young and fertilization is internal. There are a wide variety of arrangements for caring for the embryos in this group, ranging from embryo laying following internal fertilization (ovi-ovoviviparity), to internal incubation of embryos

120

with no nutrients provided by the mother (ovoviviparity), to internal incubation with nutrients provided by the mother (viviparity). Internal bearers typically produce only a small number of large, active young, a strategy characteristic of all Chondrichthyes and of certain bony fish families such as the Poeciliidae and Embiotocidae. There seems to be no strong correlation between internal bearing and the elaborateness of the courtship behavior. In guppies and other poeciliids, courtship behavior is barely noticeable and the most important trait of males that successfully copulate with females seems to be persistence (although in fact there are subtle interactions among competing males and other courtship-related behaviors). In contrast, some surfperches (Embiotocidae) have fairly elaborate courtship behavior, with males establishing breeding territories to attract passing females.

Ovi-ovoviviparity is considered to be the first evolutionary step towards true "live-bearing." It is perhaps best developed in some sharks and rays, in which many species, following internal fertilization and a number of weeks of incubation, lay a few large embryos, each covered with a horny capsule (see Chapter 14). Among teleosts, ovi-ovoviviparous fishes typically lay their embryos immediately after fertilization. Curiously, some of the most elaborate copulatory organs are known from the fishes that use this strategy: the complicated priapium on the throat of the males of the Phallostethidae and Neostethidae (see Chapter 22), and the hollow tube in the anal fin of the butterfly fish (*Pantodon buchholzi*). In the Poeciliidae, one of the most complicated intromittent organs known for the family (very long, with two thornlike prongs at the tip) is present in one embryo-laying member, *Tomeurus gracilis*.

Ovoviviparity is best known from squaliform sharks (Chapter 14) and from the coelacanth (*Latimeria chalumnae*, Chapter 15). In these fishes, large active young are born after the yolk sac has been absorbed. Among teleosts, rockfish (*Sebastes*) and Baikal sculpins (Comephoridae) give birth to a large number of feeble larvae. This is in marked contrast to most other "live-bearing" fishes, and, like their oviparous relatives, these fishes have no special structures for internal fertilization.

Viviparity is the main reproductive method used by the families Goodeidae, Anablepidae, Jenynsiidae, Poeciliidae, Embiotocidae, and Carcharinidae, as well as a few members of other families. These fishes have various ways of providing nutrients to the developing embryos. The biggest variety is found in the sharks (see Chapter 14), but the teleosts also show a considerable variety of methods. In the surfperches the young develop in the ovary of the mother and obtain nutrients through the close contact of the extra-large fins with the ovarian wall. The embryos of goodeids develop placentalike growths (trophotaeniae) from the anal region. Most poeciliid embryos have highly vascular pericardial tissue that loops around the neck and is in close contact with the ovarian wall of the mother. The number of young produced by each female is small, although in poeciliids several broods in different stages of development may be carried at once, so production of young may be nearly continuous when conditions are favorable.

Developmental Adaptations

It should be obvious from the previous section that the adaptations of the eggs, embryos, larvae, and juveniles of a fish species reflect the reproductive behavior and ecology of the parent. Only recently have these often remarkable developmental adaptations gotten the attention they deserve (e.g., Blaxter 1974; Russell 1976; Braum 1978; Balon 1980). In describing these adaptations, it is useful to divide the life history of a fish into the five major developmental periods of Balon (1975b): embryonic, larval, juvenile, adult, and senescent periods. For convenience these periods can be further divided into more or less arbitrary developmental phases. It should be noted that Balon developed this classification scheme both to provide some consistent terminology for the enormously confusing literature on fish development and to support the saltational theory of development (Balon 1979, 1980). According to this theory, development proceeds gradually through each period until a point is reached when a rather abrupt change in habits is possible, such as the change from an embryo which cannot capture food to a larva which can. The change is accompanied by further, rather rapid changes in morphology and physiology. Once a new developmental threshold is reached through this process, development proceeds gradually again. The contrasting theory of development is that the process is continuous and gradual, so that all designated periods or phases are arbitrary.

Embryonic period. This is the period in which the developing individual is entirely dependent on nutrition provided by the mother, either by means of yolk from the egg, by a direct placentalike connection (in viviparous fishes), or by some compromise between the two methods. The period begins at fertilization or, in unisexual fishes, at whatever event triggers cell division. The period can be usefully divided into three phases: cleavage egg, embryo, and free embryo (eleutheroembryo of Balon, 1975b). The *cleavage phase* is the interval between the first cell division and the appearance of recognizable predecessors of the organ systems, but especially the neural plate. The *embryonic phase* is the interval in which the embryo becomes recognizable as a vertebrate, as the major organ systems begin to appear. It ends at hatching. Although hatching is a major, recognizable event in the life of a fish (at least from our perspective), the exact state of development an embryo may be in at hatching not only varies among species but may vary within a species, depending on environmental conditions. In any case, once the embryo is free of the egg membranes, the *free embryo phase* begins. During this phase, the embryo ceases to be curled up, becomes increasingly fishlike, continues to rely on its yolk or mother for nutrition, and usually remains in the same environment it was in for the previous two stages. This phase may range from very lengthy (e.g., in salmon embryos in the spawning beds) to nonexistent (in the annual cyprinodont fishes with their rapid life cycles).

Larval period.   The beginning of the larval period is signified by the appearance of the ability to capture food organisms.   During this period special larval structures may develop, often related to respiration.   The period ends when the axial skeleton is formed and the embryonic median fin-fold is gone (Fig. 9.2).   In marine fishes the period is often lengthy, lasting from one to two weeks (sardines, rockfishes, etc.) to many months (anguillid eels).   For those fishes with pelagic larvae (and free embryos), it is often the major period of dispersal, as well as the period of highest mortality, because of the vulnerability of the larvae to predation and starvation (see Chapter 35). In freshwater fishes pelagic larvae are present mainly in lake- or river-dwelling forms, such as sunfishes (*Lepomis*), pike-perches (*Stizostedion*), and whitefishes (*Coregonus*), but are absent from most stream-dwelling forms.   Such forms typically have benthic larvae (Cottidae, many Cyprinidae) that exist only for short periods and often live in heavy cover, such as flooded beds of vegetation.   In live-bearing fishes, the larval period may be absent or very short (and internal).   The elimination or reduction of the larval stage is usually a reflection of the reproductive "strategy" of having a comparatively small number of young that start out life as large, active individuals.   In salmon and trout, the alevins that emerge from the gravel and begin feeding seem to be vestigial larvae because while they possess many larval characteristics, they are more like true juvenile fishes in their overall appearance and behavior (Balon 1980).

Juvenile period.   Although the change from larva to juvenile may involve a dramatic metamorphosis, as in the transformation of the leptocephalus larva of an eel to an elver, usually the change is more subtle.   The period begins when the organ systems are fully formed, or nearly so.   Juveniles are recognizable by the presence of fully formed fins as well; by appearance they are miniature adults, although they often possess distinctive color patterns that reflect the distinct habitats they typically occupy.   The juvenile period lasts until the gonads become mature and is usually the period of most rapid growth in the life of a fish.

Adult period.   Once the gonads are mature, a fish is an adult. The onset of the period is reflected in spawning behavior and often in the development of reproductive structures and color pattern.

Senescent period.   Few fish reach this period of "old age," when growth has virtually stopped and the gonads are degenerate and usually not producing gametes.   While the period may last for years in sturgeon, it only lasts for a few days in Pacific salmon.

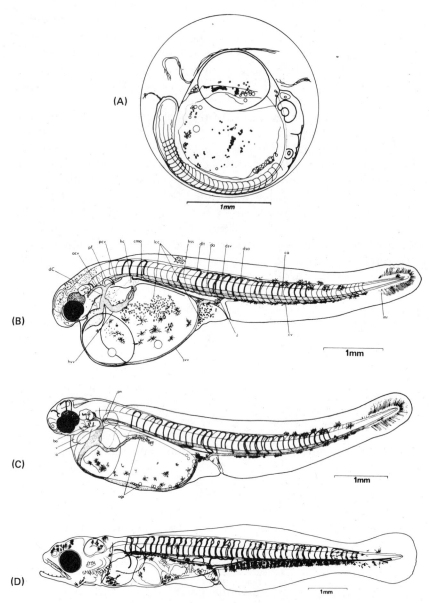

FIGURE 9.2 Some stages in the development of the walleye (*Stizostedion vitreum*). (A) Embryo at age 3 days, 50 minutes. (B) Embryo at 6 days, 18 hours, which has been removed from the egg membranes to show structures (*acv* anterior cardinal vein, *ca* caudal artery, *cv* caudal vein, *da* dorsal aorta, *dC* duct of Cuvier, *dlt* dorsal longitudinal trunk of the segmental muscles, *dsv* dorsal segmental vein, *dsa* dorsal segmental artery, *hc* hepatic capillaries, *hss* horizontal skeletogenous septum, *hvv* hepatic vitelline vein, *il* intestinal loop of caudal vein, *lcc* large clear cells, *mr* mesenchyme rays, *pcv* posterior cardinal vein, *pf* pectoral fin bud, *svv* subintestinal vitelline vein). (C) Embryo at 8 days, 1 hour, immediately after hatching. (D) Larva at 17½ days. (From McElman and Balon, 1979.)

Physiological Adaptations   The complex behavioral adaptations that fishes have evolved to insure reproductive success are obviously of little use if reproduction takes place at a time when environmental conditions are unfavorable for the survival of the young. Thus, the reproductive cycles of fishes are closely tied to environmental changes, particularly seasonal changes in light and temperature. These two factors are often most important because they can act, directly or through sense organs, on glands that produce hormones, which in turn produce the appropriate physiological or behavioral responses. This can be demonstrated by examining the reproductive cycle of the longjaw mudsucker (*Gillichthys mirabilis*) in San Francisco Bay, California (DeVlaming, 1972a, b, c).

In the mudsucker the testes and ovaries develop between late September and mid-November, although ovarian development typically continues through early December (Fig. 9.3). Spawning occurs from December to June, with each individual spawning more than once. Gonads of both sexes regress abruptly in July and remain regressed through August and September. Laboratory studies show temperature to be the primary environmental factor regulating the reproductive cycle in the mudsucker, although changing photoperiods also play a role. For example, temperatures of less than 20°C are required for gonadal development under any experimental light regime. However, at

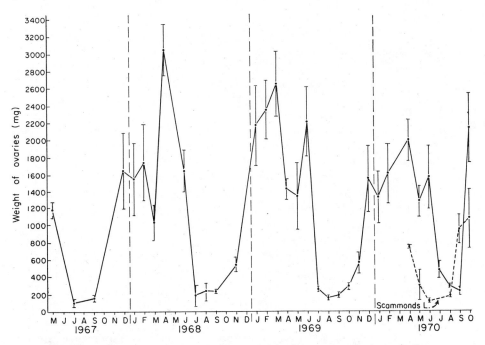

FIGURE 9.3 Seasonal variation in ovarian weight (mean ± standard error) of the Alviso population (solid line) and Scammonds Lagoon population (broken line) of *Gillichthys mirabilis*. (From DeVlaming, *Copeia*, 1972a.)

low temperatures, short photoperiods (equivalent to those of late autumn) accelerate gonadal development. Further, the continuous production of eggs and sperm that characterizes wild fish during their protracted spawning period can be maintained in the laboratory only if temperatures are kept below 20°C. Likewise, temperatures above 24°C (even for only 7.5 hours a day) cause the testes to regress, regardless of photoperiod, by blocking the transformation of spermatogonia to spermatocytes. In females temperatures of only 22°C are required to cause regression of the ovaries, through inhibition of formation of the vitelline membrane (vitellogenesis). These processes appear to be controlled by the action of temperature on gonadotropic hormone production by the pituitary gland. Thus, surgical removal of the anterior portion of the pituitary gland (neurohypophysis) inhibits the formation of sperm cells in male mudsuckers and blocks vitellogenesis in females. Not surprisingly, gonadal development in mudsuckers can also be stimulated regardless of temperature, by the injection of pituitary gonotropins. In other fishes the sequence of events is generally similar to that of the mudsucker, although often the increasing photoperiods of spring are the major environmental factor stimulating gonadotropin production by the pituitary. In the threespine stickleback (*Gasterosteus aculeatus*), for example, the development of the gonads and movement to spawning areas is largely a response to increasing light, although actual spawning does not take place until appropriate temperatures are reached in the water.

The responsiveness of the reproductive cycle of fishes to changes in temperature and photoperiod, as well as to injections of hormones, has been taken advantage of by fish culturists to get spawning to occur at times convenient to culture operations. In trout hatcheries, trout of several different strains may be raised, each with a different response to the hatchery light cycle, so eggs will be produced over a long period of time and the production of "catchable" size trout can be nearly continuous. Both carp (*Cyprinus carpio*) and channel catfish (*Ictalurus punctatus*) are today routinely injected with pituitary extracts to induce spawning on a prescribed schedule. While most fishes can be induced to spawn with pituitary extracts from other fishes or even mammals, carp are extremely selective and respond only to the extract from carp.

When the gonadtropic hormones stimulate the gonads to develop, they also stimulate the gonads to produce gonadal steroid hormones, which stimulate reproductive behavior and the development of secondary (nongonadal) sexual characteristics. In males the production of nuptial colors, breeding tubercles, and other secondary sexual characteristics is stimulated by androgens produced in the testes (or cells adjacent to them).

It should be pointed out here that while temperature and/or photoperiod are typically responsible for the initiation of gonadal development, ovulation, sperm maturation, and spawning often depend on other factors as well, such as pheromones, visual, auditory, or tactile stimuli (by the opposite sex), presence of suitable substrate for spawning, increasing (or decreasing) stream flows, and the absence of inhibitory chemicals, particularly metabolites of the same species. Thus Chen and Martinich (1975) found that zebrafish (*Brachydanio rerio*) would ovulate in response to an apparent male pheromone and that ovulation was inhibited by metabolite accumulation in aquaria. For spawning to occur in most fishes, not only do the environmental conditions have to be satisfactory but the behavioral cues of the opposite sex have to be correct. If conditions are not right for spawning, most fish will resorb the gonadal material, thereby conserving energy and increasing the probability of survival until the next spawning time.

Energetic Adaptations   It should be obvious from the previous sections that fishes invest a great deal of energy in reproduction, both in behavior and in the production of gonadal tissue. Indeed, the life history strategies of fish can be viewed as balancing the amount of energy put into reproduction with that put into growth and metabolism (Fisher 1930, Williams 1966). Among fish species (and even within species) there is enormous variation in the amount of energy invested in reproduction in a year, as well as in the amount of energy invested in the various aspects of reproduction, such as spawning migrations, courtship behavior, parental care, and egg and sperm production. There are many factors contributing to this variation, and in this section we will examine some of the more general factors: (1) reproductive effort; (2) age of onset of reproduction; (3) fecundity; (4) survivorship rates; and (5) frequency of reproduction.

Reproductive effort is a measure of the amount of energy (or time) invested in the production of offspring. A rough index of this, at least among fishes that do not provide any parental care, is the Gonadal-Somatic Index (GSI), which is equal to the amount of gonadal tissue (measured in calories or grams) divided by the amount of somatic and gonadal tissue. When this index is calculated for males and females of the same species, it quickly becomes obvious that females have much more energy invested in gonadal tissue than males (which explains in part the general reluctance of females to mate, as they have much more to lose if a wrong choice is made). Gonadal investment is most nearly equal in fishes that are pelagic spawners, since the females have tiny eggs and the males have to produce enormous quantities of sperm to assure fertilization. Even in these fishes, however, the gonadal investment of females is several times that of males. Differences in gonadal investment between the sexes may be partially evened out by the greater investment on the part of males in reproductive structures (breeding tubercles, etc.) and in reproductive behavior, such as courtship and territoriality. The investment of energy in reproductive behavior and in species-specific color patterns and breeding structures can be interpreted as a way in which both males and females are assured that their reproductive effort is not wasted by matings with closely related species. For example, in Mexico there are a number of female "species" of poeciliids in which the females must mate with males of bisexual species in order for ovulation to occur, although the male does not fertilize the eggs. It has been found that the males that do most of the mating are "excess" males that have been excluded from mating with females of their own species by the aggressive behavior of dominant males. When densities of the bisexual species are low, the dominance hierarchies do not develop and there are few males available to the unisexual species for mating (see Chapter 22). This example points out another way in which the reproductive effort between the sexes is equalized: the fact that in many species many of the males are excluded from mating. Mortality of males is also often higher than that of females because of their conspicuousness, as the result of color patterns or behavior, during the spawning season. Among most species, the oldest and largest members are females.

The territorial behavior of many fishes, such as the sunfishes (Centrarchidae) and the sticklebacks (Gasterosteidae), combined with external fertilization of the eggs, in a sense predisposes the males for parental care, as a way of further protecting their investment in the zygotes. The fact that parental care in fishes is generally performed by the males (including those of nonterritorial species such as pipefishes and seahorses) indicates that this is another way of equalizing the energetic investments of the sexes in reproduction. Parental care in such fishes is apparently more "cost effective" than merely increasing the output of the gonads!

The age of onset of reproduction is another factor which varies with sex, since males typically mature at a smaller size and younger age than females. For both sexes, however, the age at first reproduction depends in good part on the nature of the environment in which the population of concern lives, as well as the nature of the population itself. Where the environment is favorable for growth and favors high adult survival, fishes will tend to delay reproduction, while if conditions are unfavorable so that growth and adult survival are low, reproduction tends to take place at a younger age (see Stearns [1976] for a discussion of the theory behind this statement). For example, in Europe there are two distinct forms of the brown trout (*Salmo trutta*) whose life history tactics reflect the environments in which they live (Alm 1949). The lake-dwelling form inhabits a fairly stable and productive environment and so grows to a large size and spawns first when 5 to 7 years old. The stream-dwelling form, in contrast, lives in a much less stable and productive environment and so grows more slowly and matures in 3 to 5 years. On an energetic basis, it appears that in a more stable environment natural selection favors females that delay reproduction in order to invest their energy in producing large numbers of large eggs, since egg size and number tend to increase with size of the female, while in a more unstable environment natural selection favors females that reproduce as quickly as possible, since the probability of survival from one year to the next is low.

The nature of the population to which a female belongs also influences the age of reproduction. Females which belong to an expanding population tend to reproduce at an earlier age than those in more stable populations. Part of the reason for this is that expanding populations tend to be in favorable environments, so that a larger size can be achieved at a younger age. Natural selection may also favor, in this situation, females who can fill the "empty" space most quickly with the most young, especially if juvenile mortality is exceptionally low. One of the impacts commercial fishing can have on fish populations is to put them in a perpetually expanding state, since a typical fishery removes both a large number of fish and the larger individuals. Thus, the fishery tends to reduce intraspecific competition, increasing growth rates, and also favors females that reproduce at a young age and small size.

Fecundity is the most common measure of reproductive potential in fishes because it is a relatively easy measure to make; it is the number of eggs in the ovaries of a female fish. In general, fecundity increases with the size of the female, with the relationship:

$$F = aL^b$$

where F = fecundity, L = fish length, and a and b are constants derived from the data (Bagenal 1978). With this relationship, larger fish produce considerably more eggs than smaller fish, both absolutely and relative to body size (number of eggs per gram body weight). Since larger fish often produce larger eggs as well, this means that the energetic investment in reproduction tends to be higher in the larger members of a species; smaller members tend to invest more in growth (particularly in the first year or so of life).

While the above relationship seems to hold true for many species (but especially for species that produce large numbers of eggs and spawn just once each year), there are many factors which complicate the interpretation of fecundity data, especially in relation to the investment of energy. Some of these complications are (1) the relationship between fecundity and fertility; (2) the fecundities of multiple spawners; (3) the fecundities of viviparous species and those with parental care; (4) the relationship between fecundity and egg size; (5) the relationship between population density and fecundity; and (6) the impact of environmental factors on fecundity (Bagenal 1978).

Fertility contrasts with fecundity in that it is the actual number of young produced rather than the number of eggs. Since in terms of measuring reproductive success, it is the number of young produced that really counts, fertility should be a better measure than fecundity. Unfortunately, it is extremely hard to measure, since young fishes typically disperse immediately after hatching. For many species, however, fecundity is probably a fairly close approximation of fertility. This is especially true of viviparous fishes. In many other species the relationship between fecundity and fertility is not clear, because many eggs may be laid but not fertilized or eggs may be developed in the ovary but then resorbed. In some populations the resorbed eggs may exceed 50% of those produced. In fishes which spawn repeatedly over long periods of time, there may be eggs in the ovary in several stages of development, and it is very difficult to determine the contribution of the immature eggs to the season's spawning. In fishes with parental care the relationship between fecundity and fertility is obscured by the limitations placed on the parents by the number of young for which they can effectively care. Thus in mouthbrooding cichlids, the fecundity is often considerably higher than the number of embryos capable of being brooded (Welcomme 1967), although this discrepancy is reduced somewhat by the larger eggs of mouthbrooders (in contrast to nest brooders) and by the failure of one ovary to develop in some species.

Parental care is just one of a number of factors that seems to be related to egg size. Most important of these factors is size of the female, since egg size does generally increase with the size of the parent. The advantage of larger eggs seems to lie in the greater ability of larger young to survive. As Svardson (1949) pointed out, each population of fish seems to achieve a balance between egg size and number that produces the greatest number of young. Rounsefell (1957) found that within the Salmonidae, river spawners produce larger eggs than lake spawners and that, in anadromous forms, species with the longest freshwater stages produce the largest eggs, demonstrating fine evolutionary "tuning" to environmental factors.

Although the evolutionary adjustment of fecundity to environmental conditions is important, equally important is the ability of fishes to adjust egg production on an annual basis in relation to environmental variation. Usually, this adjustment seems to be related to food supply. When food is plentiful, there is plenty of energy available for investment in reproduction, beyond what is required for maintenance and growth. As a result, well-fed fish produce more and, frequently, larger eggs. Wooten (1973) found that threespine sticklebacks (*Gasterosteus aculeatus*) were exceptionally fecund in food-rich environments. A female in such situations could produce two to three times her weight in eggs over a season, despite the limitations placed on egg production by the abilities of the males to care for the eggs and young. High availability of food leading to high fecundities is often related to the lack of intense intraspecific competition. Thus, when population levels are low, reproductive success is likely to increase, whereas when they are high, it is likely to decrease, providing an effective feedback mechanism for density-dependent population regulation (see Chapter 35 for an example of this). This mechanism also allows fish to adjust their populations to other unfavorable conditions that reduce the availability of food, such as unfavorable water temperatures and oxygen levels.

Survivorship rates are inversely related to fecundity, since fishes with high fecundities have very high death rates, especially through the free embryo and larval stages. Indeed, much research on commercially important fishes with pelagic larvae has focused in recent years on factors affecting larval survival, because it has been recognized that a very small increase or decrease in the survival rate of the larvae can have enormous impact on the size of the adult population of which they will be part (see Chapter 35). In these fishes any individual larva has a very low probability of survival. At the opposite extreme, viviparous fishes, such as the poeciliids, surfperches, and many sharks, produce a small number of young that have a fairly high probability of surviving to adulthood. Curiously, it is likely, if all appropriate measurements could be made, that the amount of parental investment per successful offspring is about equal in the two groups, or at least show equal variability. What are the advantages of these two divergent reproductive strategies if the energetic investment is about the same? Williams (1975) argues that highly fecund fishes are capable of making rapid genetic adjustments to environmental change, because even with such high mortality rates, larval deaths are not entirely random, so the survivors are likely to be particularly "fit" for the particular set of local or short-term environmental conditions that exist. In addition, highly fecund fishes are capable of rapidly adjusting their populations to environmental changes. For example, under favorable conditions that increase larval survival rates, even a small number of adults can produce a large number of successful offspring. Alternatively, under unfavorable conditions, only a small number of fish will survive the larval stages regardless of the number of spawning adults. Essentially in such fishes, the number of young surviving to adulthood is independent of the number of parents. This strategy is likely to be characteristic of fishes that live in environments where food availability fluctuates in an unpredictable fashion from year to year and in which competition is usually not a major problem. It is termed r-selection by ecological theorists (see Stearns [1976] or any recent ecology text).

In contrast, viviparous (or low-fecundity) fishes are not as capable of responding genetically to environmental change, although the large, adultlike young have (in theory) much greater capacities as individuals of adjusting to environmental changes than do small larvae. As a result, the population sizes are likely to be much more constant through time. This strategy, called K-selection by ecological theorists, is usually presumed to be characteristic of species living in fairly predictable environments, where inter- and intraspecific competition is keen. Unfortunately for the theory of r- and K-selection, viviparous fishes, such as the poeciliids, are frequently found in highly unpredictable environments (see Chapter 22). Obviously, many factors influence the type of reproductive strategy besides environmental predictability, and in fact most fishes have fecundities (and consequently strategies) that place them in an intermediate position between these two polar strategies.

The **frequency of reproduction** is another characteristic of fish life history strategies that appears to reflect the predictability of the environment in which the fishes live. The two basic strategies here are semelparity and iteroparity. **Semelparity** is "big bang" reproduction, where the adults spawn and die (as among Pacific salmon), while **iteroparity** is repeated reproduction (characteristic of most fishes). The predominance of iteroparity among vertebrates bothered ecologists such as Cole (1954) because, in theory, iteroparity does not provide much of a gain in the intrinsic rate of population increase. Energetically, semelparity would seem advantageous because semelparous organisms can invest the maximum amount of energy in reproduction and not have to keep any in reserve for postreproductive survival. However, Murphy (1968) suggested that the reasons for the commoness of iteroparity lie in the fact that most environments are unpredictable enough so that there is no guarantee that young in any particular spawn will survive to adulthood. If conditions are favorable, a semelparous fish may have very high reproductive success, but if they are unfavorable, it may lose out completely. Thus, most fishes adopt a "bet-hedging" strategy of not putting all their energy into one spawn.

A study which demonstrates very nicely the advantages of iteroparity and semelparity is that of Leggett and Carscadden (1978) on American shad (*Alosa sapidissima*). They examined the reproductive strategies of this anadromous species in rivers of the Atlantic coast of North America, from Florida to New Brunswick, and found that the degree of iteroparity increased with the latitude of the river; Florida populations are entirely semelparous, while those in New Brunswick are 55% to 77% iteroparous, with intermediate populations having intermediate values for the frequency of repeat spawners. In addition, the fecundity of the northern populations is lower than that of the southern populations. The northern shad essentially devote less of their energy to reproduciion than the southern shad, so they will have more in reserve for postspawning survival. The differences in strategy seem to be the result of differences in environment; the northern rivers are a harsher and more variable environment for the eggs and larvae, while the southern rivers are more benign.

It should be obvious from this discussion of reproductive strategies that each species, and each population, of fish has its own complex suite of adaptations that together allow it to achieve reproductive success in what presumably is an energetically efficient manner, in an ever-changing environment.

Supplemental Readings   Bagenal 1978; Balon 1975a, b, 1979, 1980; Breder and Rosen 1966; DeVlaming 1972a, b, c; McElman and Balon 1979; Stearns 1976.

ααααααααααααααααααααααααααααααααααααααααααααααααααααααααααααααααααααααααααα

Sensory Perception

Fishes sense the world around them in a diversity of ways. While most fish have the "terrestrial" senses of sight, hearing, smell, and taste that we can comprehend from our own experience, they also possess sensory means for detecting stimuli such as water particle displacement and electrical currents, for which we have little empathy. Such modes take advantage of the physical and chemical properties of water and work in conjunction with the more "conventional" sensory modes. In this chapter, therefore, aspects of chemoreception (smell and taste), mechanoreception (hearing, orientation, and lateral-line detection of water disturbances), electroreception, and vision are covered.

Chemoreception   Odors and tastes are quite distinguishable to the great majority of terrestrial animals; olfactory organs, stimulated by airborne molecules, are more sensitive and chemical-specific than gustatory organs, which are generally stimulated by contact with dilute solutions. In fish, both types of organs are sensitive to "contact" stimuli of chemicals dissolved in water. Besides differences in sensitivity, the two sensory systems are also distinguished by the location of the sensory receptors. Olfactory organs reside in special pits, while gustatory receptors are often more dispersed on external surfaces or in the mouth.

OLFACTION   In fishes the olfactory organs are still the more sensitive of the two means of chemoreception and, therefore, the more useful for more dilute (e.g., distant) odors. The olfactory receptors are usually located in olfactory pits, which have incurrent and excurrent channels (nares) divided by a flap of skin. Water is induced to flow through olfactory pits by movements of cilia within the pit, by the muscular

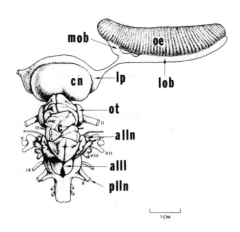

FIGURE 10.1 Dorsal view of the brain of a sphyrnid shark known as the bonnet-head shark (*Sphyrna tiburo*): *alll* anterior lateral-line lobe, *alln* anterior lateral-line nerve, *cn* central nucleus, *lob* lateral division of the olfactory bulb, *lp* lateral pallium, *mob* medial division of the olfactory bulb, *oe* olfactory epithelium (organ), *ot* optic tectum, *plln* posterior lateral-line nerve, *II* optic nerve, *III* oculomotor nerve, *V* trigeminal nerve, *VII* facial nerve, *VIII* statoacoustic nerve, *IX* glossopharyngeal nerve, *X* vagal nerve. (From Northcutt, 1978.)

movement of the branchial pump, by swimming, or by a combination of these. Odors are perceived when the dissolved chemical makes contact with the olfactory rosette, a multifolded epithelium rich in receptor cells, located in the olfactory pit (Fig. 10.1). Fishes relying heavily on olfactory cues have elongated rosettes with many receptor cells located in elongate olfactory pits. In anguillid eels such elongate olfactory rosettes can detect certain chemicals such as B-phenylethanol in concentrations of 1×10^{-13} M (Teichmann 1962)! Seasonal variations in sensitivity suggest that cyclical hormone action may influence the threshold level of detection.

Olfactory stimuli are communicated to the olfactory lobe of the brain via the first cranial nerve (Fig. 10.1). Species which rely heavily on olfactory information, such as anguillid eels, moray eels, and sharks, display oversized olfactory lobes. A few fishes, such as some of the puffers (Tetraodontidae), have greatly reduced lobes consistent with the evolutionary loss of the olfactory organs and pits. These puffers probably rely entirely on sight for feeding.

Olfactory cues have been shown to be of importance to salmon in locating their natal stream, once they are in the vicinity of the river mouth. Thus, salmon are thought to be imprinted with odors as pre-smolts and smolts as they migrate down rivers and streams to a larger body of water where they spend the majority of their adult life (Chapter 19). Bodznik (1978) recorded sensory responses from the olfactory lobes of sockeye salmon (*Oncorhynchus nerka*) and found that the inorganic ion calcium could be used as an upstream odorant cue substance.

CHEMORECEPTION **135**

Studies on nurse sharks (Orectolobidae) show a distinct gradient-searching activity (klinotaxis) for food detection. By detection of a stronger chemical concentration in the olfactory rosette on one side of its head, the shark turns in that direction. Thus, tacking motions through the odorant field lead the shark to the odor source. Experimentally plugging the water channels on one side of its head will produce a continuous circling in the opposite direction. The extremely wide head of the hammerhead shark, *Sphyrna*, should be particularly useful in locating odor sources when only dilute concentrations are detectable because of the increased separation of the nares. Particular amines and amino acids attract teleosts as well as elasmobranchs. Sutterlin (1975) found glycine and alanine to be especially attractive to winter flounder (*Pseudopleuronectes americanus*), while alanine and methionine attracted Atlantic silversides (*Menidia menidia*) most effectively.

TASTE   Taste or gustatory chemoreception is generally a "close-range" sense in fishes, especially useful in the identification of both food and noxious substances. Whereas the olfactory receptors are localized in the nares, taste buds are commonly located on several exterior surfaces of the fish besides in the mouth. Bottom fishes, such as catfish, have considerable numbers of taste receptors on their skin, fins and barbels. The high gustatory sensitivity of the barbels extends the usefulness of these chemoreceptors a reasonable distance from the fish, presumably to aid in finding food in murky water. A similar "distant touch" sense might be inferred from the presence of taste buds on the free pelvic fin rays of some codfishes and *Trichogaster trichopterus*. Other structures bearing recognizable taste buds include the well-developed lips of some minnows (Cyprinidae) and the suckers (Catostomidae). Suckers may have 41 to 57 taste buds in a 1.3 mm² field (Miller and Evans 1965). Taste buds have also been described on the palatal organs in the buccal cavities of various cyprinids, catostomids, cobitids, and salmonids as well as on the gill rakers and arches, primarily in freshwater fishes (Kapoor et al. 1975).

Whereas the cutaneous taste buds are innervated by branches of the facial (cranial nerve VII) nerve (Fig. 10.1), the sensory signals from the "internal" taste buds (e.g., those in the pharyngeal cavity and palate) are transmitted to the glossopharyngeal (IX) and vagus (X) nerves. In species having a palatal organ, the total number of taste buds is considerably augmented and the terminal centers in the visceral sensory column of the medulla are correspondingly enlarged as "vagal lobes" (Kapoor et al. 1975). Just as the olfactory lobes of the brain are grossly enlarged in fishes relying heavily on olfactory sensory information (e.g., Atlantic eels, sharks), the facial and/or vagal lobes of the medulla display a marked enlargement in species which find food by taste. For example, the vagal lobes are larger than the remainder of the brain in suckers, reflecting the large number of taste buds found on the palatal organs and their

136

"mouth-tasting" behavior (Miller and Evans 1965). These correlations between brain morphology and feeding habits have prompted researchers to categorize teleostean taxa into one of (usually) three overlapping groups: (1) fishes that feed by sight and taste and show prominent optic lobes, facial lobes, and relatively large vagal lobes; (2) those which detect food using barbels and have enlarged facial lobes with less prominent vagal lobes; and (3) sight-feeding species possessing well-developed optic lobes and poorly-developed facial and vagal lobes (Khanna and Singh 1966).

The functional importance of taste receptors to catfishes has been demonstrated by the fact that surgical removal or sectioning of optic and olfactory senses does not prevent catfish from swimming to a food source in still water. When taste reception is surgically blocked on one side of the catfish, it continually circles toward the side of intact reception until, eventually, the food is found. Thus, the bilateral taste receptors in *Ictalurus* function much as the sensitive olfactory system does in some other fishes to indicate the directionality of a food source. Further, surgical removal of the facial lobes of the medulla prevented catfish from locating and ingesting food. In contrast, removal of the vagal lobes did not inhibit the finding of food or taking it into its mouth, but prevented swallowing, which is controlled via the glossopharyngeal and vagus nerves (Atema 1971). Interestingly, sharks and rays show no sensory elaboration (including enlarged medullary lobes) for taste functions (Kapoor et al. 1975). Elasmobranchs rely primarily on olfaction, vision, and electroreception to locate their food.

Acoustico-Lateralis System   The acoustico-lateralis system of fishes senses sounds, vibrations and other displacements of water in their environment. It has two main components, the inner ear and the neuromast/lateral line system. Besides sound detection, the fish inner ear functions to orient or "balance" the animal in three-dimensional space, giving it a feeling of the direction in which gravity is acting even when suspended in lightless, pelagic habitats. In this section, hearing will be considered first, followed by aspects of spatial equilibrium and balance and a discussion of the lateral line system.

HEARING   The nature of sound transmission in water has had an important influence on the evolution of hearing in fishes. Because of its greater density, water is a much more efficient conductor of sound pressure waves than is air. Therefore, sounds will carry much further and travel 4.8 times as fast under water. Sound consists of extremely small fluid motions (vibrations) which have a discernible *particle displacement* component close to the sound source ("near field") as well as a *sound pressure* component which persists through the more extensive "far field." The extent of the near field increases at lower sound frequencies.

For example, at 100 Hz, the near field extends to approximately 2.3 m from the source of the sound (Popper and Fay 1977). Within the near field, vibrations are detected in comparatively direct fashion by both teleosts and elasmobranchs, via the inner ear and/or the lateral line.

Structure of the inner ear. Figure 10.2a and b show diagrammatic representations of teleostean inner ears. The dorsal part (pars superior) includes three semicircular canals (through the horizontal, lateral, and longitudinal planes) with their respective ampullae (fluid inertia sensing chambers). The utriculus with its utricular otolith (ear stone) completes the pars superior, which mainly functions as an equilibrium system and gravity detector. The ventral part (pars inferior) consists of the sacculus and lagena, which also contain otoliths and functions primarily in sound detection. As sound vibrations (e.g., in the near field) impinge on a fish, the whole fish moves to and fro with the particle displacement of the water. The inertia of the comparatively dense otoliths (approximately three times the total fish density) in their chambers causes the otoliths to lag somewhat behind the movements of the fish. The otoliths are suspended in fluid and surrounded by ciliary bundles emanating from sensory hair cells. This layer of hair cells constitutes a sensory epithelium (macula) in each chamber. Thus, the differential amplitude and phase motions of the otolith with respect to its chamber cause the otolith to bend some of these cilia mechanically. Bending the cilia causes the sensitive hair cellular membranes to deform, thereby stimulating neural transmissions to the auditory center of the brain, where they are processed and comprise the sense of "hearing."

At higher frequencies the amplitude of "fish displacement" de-

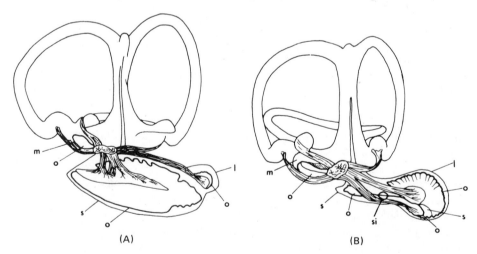

(A)   (B)

FIGURE 10.2 Drawing of a medial view of the inner ear of (A) *Luciopera sandra* Cuv., and (B) *Cyprinus idus* L., modified from drawings by Retzius. Only the auditory portions of the ear are labeled. The nerves shown in both figures are the auditory portions of the eighth nerve. *l* Lagena, *m* utriculus, *o* otolith of each otolithic organ, *s* sacculus, *si* transverse canal. (From Popper and Fay, 1973.)

creases and more sound energy is needed for otolithic stimulation. The sensitivity of hearing in the far field is increased by anatomical devices which can transform sound pressure into displacement movements so as to provide a movement differential between the sacculus/lagena and their respective otoliths. The gas bubble in the swimbladder provides this acoustical transformation in many bony fishes. Because the gas is far more compressible than water, it pulsates when exposed to sound. The pulsating surface of the swimbladder acts to vibrate the tissues of the fish surrounding it. This provides the necessary particle movement for otolithic/auditory nervous stimulation, especially in species having a close association of the swimbladder and the auditory apparatus (pars inferior). Among three species of squirrelfishes (Holocentridae) the species having the shortest distance between swimbladder and inner ear also had the most sensitive (lowest intensity threshold) hearing. Certain squirrelfishes, along with the tarpon (Elopidae), featherbacks (Notopteridae), deep sea cods (Moridae), and sea breams (Sparidae), all have a forked, forward extension of the swimbladder ending close to the ear. Herrings (Clupeidae) and mormyrids feature a similar swimbladder extension which actually enters the cranial auditory capsule and lies close to the inner ear.

Minnows, catfishes, and other ostariophysan teleosts connect the auditory system to the swimbladder with a chain of small bones called Weberian ossicles. The ossicles connect the pulsating swimbladder wall (tunica interna) with a Y-shaped lymph sinus (sinus impar), which abuts the lymph-filled transverse canal joining the sacculi of the right and left ears (Fig. 10.3). In studies on the goldfish (*Carassius auratus*), deflation of the swimbladder significantly decreased the hearing sensitivity at frequencies above 150 Hz. Swimbladder deflation of another ostariophysid (*Ictalurus*) revealed an even greater loss of "high-frequency" sensitivity, whereas the same procedure on the perciform *Tilapia*, which

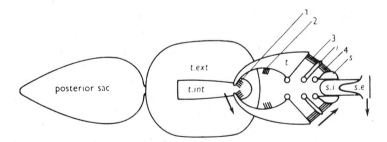

FIGURE 10.3 Diagrammatic dorsal view of the swimbladder and Weberian apparatus of a typical member of the Cyprinidae. The anterior parts (right) are drawn to a larger scale than the posterior ones. Arrows indicate movements resulting from enlargement of the swimbladder. The axes about which the ossicles pivot are indicated by circles. *t.ext.* tunica externa, *t.int.* tunica interna seen through the slit in the tunica externa, *1,2,3,4* ligaments, *t* tripus, *i* intercalarium, *s* scaphium, *s.i.* sinus impar, *s.e.* sinus endolymphaticus. (From Alexander, 1966.)

lacks Weberian ossicles and a close swimbladder–ear connection, had no significant effect on its already poor sense of hearing.

Sharks, skates, and rays also show evidence of "hearing" sounds or vibrations, especially at lower frequencies. Sharks seem especially attracted to *irregularly* pulsed sounds, perhaps signaling a crippled prey. However, they seem to have little sensitivity to high-frequency sounds. This low frequency range correlates well with near-field displacement hearing and the fact that elasmobranchs have no swimbladders which may act as a sound pressure transducer. For example, the auditory sensitivity of the horn shark (*Heterodontus fancisci*) is maximal at 40 Hz.

Many shark species also show an ability to directionally locate pulsed, low-frequency sounds from as far as 100 m, which is well into the far field (Popper and Fay 1977). It is possible that the taut skin over the parietal fossae of the shark's ears serves in "drumlike" fashion to induce fluid movements on the canal-based sensory organ, the macula neglecta. The functional similarities between this auditory system and the tympanic membrane and associated structures of higher vertebrates are striking (Myrberg 1978). Presumably, the differences in amplitude or time of the sounds received at the right and left ears give the shark a general direction to the source of the sound.

Because of the vertically oriented axis of the macula neglecta in sharks, sound "bounced" off the surface of water bodies may also be useful in determining direction. In this case, the air–water interface would mimic the far-field sound transduction of the swimbladder wall in some teleosts. Thus, it is possible that sharks (and other fishes) may increase their auditory sensitivity and directionality by swimming just below the water surface (Popper and Fay 1977).

EQUILIBRIUM AND BALANCE   The dorsal part (pars superior) of the inner ear is concerned with spatial equilibrium and balance in fishes. The utriculus connects to three semicircular canals in teleosts and elasmobranch fishes (Fig. 10.2a, b). Lampreys have only two such canals, and hagfish make do with one. The three canals (also termed the labyrinth) in jawed fishes are filled with lymph (endolymph) and function to inform the fish as to angular accelerations through space. Because the three canals are more or less aligned in the horizontal, vertical, and lateral planes, changes in pitch (head up or down), yaw (head from side to side), roll (rotation about the head-to-tail axis), straight-line acceleration or deceleration, or any combination of these are detectable. Each canal has an ampulla (bulbous area) containing a sensory hair cell area and a gelatinous cupula attached to the hair cell cilia. The cupula extends into the canal path, partially blocking the flow of endolymph. Angular accelerations, either from swimming/turning movements of the fish or from water currents moving the fish, are detected from the endolymph lagging behind the movements of the labyrinth. The appropriate cupula(e) are bent by the pressure of the endolymph, thereby stimulating the hair cells. Thus, the sensory hair cell system as a mechanoreceptor parallels that of the hearing and lateral line systems. Changes in the pattern of the continuous trains of nervous impulses from the hair cells to the balance/equilibrium center in the medulla provoke the appropriate motor responses by the fish such as eye movements to maintain a stable visual field and fin movements to restore body equilibrium. Even at rest in quiet water, some fish, such as northern pike (*Esox lucius*), constantly make pectoral fin movements to maintain balance. This species, among others, has denser tissues in the dorsal part of its body (bone, muscle) than in the ventral part (swimbladder, viscera). Thus, its center of gravity (balance point) is dorsal to its roll axis (midline through body profile), and the fish is always tending to roll to one side or the other to reach stability—ventral side up!

LATERAL LINE   The lateral line of fishes provides a *ferntastsinn* or "distant touch" sense (Dijkgraaf 1962). By means of mechanoreceptors, similar to those in the auditory and equilibrium systems, water movements around the fish can be detected. The receptors are called neuromasts, and each consists of individual hair cells with an attached cupula (Fig. 10.4). Water movements bend the protruding cupula, which stimulates the hair cell by bending the attached cilia (sense hairs). All of the fishes, including hagfishes and lampreys, have at least some free (individual) neuromasts on the body surface or at the bottom of shal-

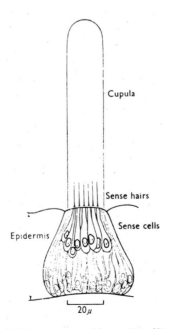

FIGURE 10.4 Superficial neuromast of bony fish (*Phoxinus*). Characteristic features are the bottle-shaped sense cells, each bearing a hair, and the jellylike cupula ensheathing the hairs. (From Dijkgraaf, 1962.)

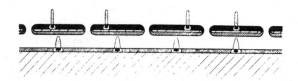

FIGURE 10.5 Longitudinal lateral-line canal section. Black denotes epidermis; spacious striation denotes subepidermal tissues; dots denote cupulae. (From Dijkgraaf, 1962.)

low pits or grooves (Dijkgraaf 1962). Most teleosts and elasmobranchs have also developed lateral line canals, in which the neuromasts lie between canal pores which open to the environment (Fig. 10.5). The cupulae of the canal neuromasts are sensitive to movements of the watery, endolymph fluid through the canal. Like the auditory and equilibrium hair cells, the neuromasts continually send neural impulses to the brain, even when "undisturbed." As in the sensory cells of the auditory and equilibrium systems, the neural impulse frequency is increased as the cupulae are flexed in one direction and decreased when flexed in the other direction. Thus, the pattern of impulses from the free or canal neuromasts imparts a direction to the disturbance. Most of the lateral line organs of the head region are innervated by sensory fibers of the lateralis anterior root of cranial nerve VII (facialis). The remaining organs of the system are innervated by the lateralis posterior root of the vagus (X). The fibers of both roots unite with those of the labyrinth nerve (VIII) in the acoustic tubercle of the medulla oblongata.

The lateral line system is developed and used in various ways by fishes exhibiting different modes of life. For example, the roach (*Rutilus*) and the stone loach (*Noemacheilus*), which inhabit streams, both have extensive canal neuromast systems. In contrast, another loach that lives in still water has no canals (Alexander 1967). In general, more active fishes have a greater percentage of canal neuromasts compared with free neuromasts. Presumably, the canals offer some "protection" from the continuous stimulation of water rushing past the laterally located neuromasts. Thus, the canal-based receptors can still function to detect weak local water displacements during rapid swimming (Dijkgraaf 1962). Figure 10.6 shows a dorsal displacement of the lateral line in the region of the pectoral fins in two species where this fin may drive water against the canal during locomotion. In these cases a straighter lateral line would generate more "noise" from locomotion alone and provide less sensitivity to external water disturbances. Similarly, lateral line placements on the dorsal side of the demersal stargazer (Fig. 10.6c) and the ventral side of the flying fish (Fig. 10.6d) show selection toward the direction where water movements would be critical for survival.

Parts of the lateral line system are often specialized for detecting prey. Surface-oriented fishes such as killifish (*Fundulus*) sense surface

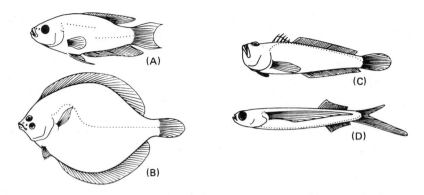

FIGURE 10.6 Secondary displacement of lateral line on trunk in connection with dorsal shift of pectoral fin [(A) *Macropodus viridi-auratus*; (B) *Pseudorhombus sp.*] or as an adaptation to special modes of living [(C) *Uranoscopus scaber*; (D) *Exocoetus volitans*]. (From Dijkgraaf, 1962.)

ripples from struggling insects by using the short canal neuromast system on the flattened dorsal surface of their heads. Blind cavefish, such as *Typhlichthys osborni*, have rows of free neuromasts on the head which stand out in ridges, presumably to aid the cavefish in locating food so precisely that it can be ingested without sight (see Chapter 31). The deepsea gulper eel (*Eurypharynx*) features groups of neuromasts on the ends of stalks projecting from its body, which would aid lightless detection of prey (Marshall 1966).

Neuromast function can also be useful to fish for stimuli other than localized water disturbances from distant objects. As fish swim, they "push" some water in front of their heads, as a boat creates a bow wave. The amount of water pushed or displaced depends on the size of the fish and the shape of the head. These forward displacements of water rebound from objects in front of the swimming fish. The rebounds or increases in resistance in front of the fish are apparently sensed by the neuromasts on the head, allowing avoidance of the obstacle. Fish with very sensitive cephalic neuromast systems seem to be especially skilled in object avoidance. Hahn (1960) found that blind cavefish could navigate better through a barrier of thick, fixed rods than thin ones when placed equal distances apart. Presumably, this system also accounts for the avoidance of transparent aquarium walls when naive fish are first introduced into an aquarium, even in total darkness. Experiments with adult saith (*Pollachius virens*) fitted with opaque eye covers showed that schooling behavior continued when these fish were placed among non-blinded individuals as long as their lateral line remained intact. Five blinded saith having their lateral lines cut at the operculum failed to school at all (Pitcher et al. 1976). In addition, near-field sounds are detected by lateral line neuromasts at frequencies up to 200 Hz because of the accompanying water displacements. On the other hand, sensitivity to temperature changes or physical touches stem from general cutaneous endings of spinal nerves, not from lateral line receptors. Trained minnows (*Phoxinus*) could not distinguish between warm and cold jets of water from a pipette located posterior to the point where the spinal cord was sectioned, even though the water movements (of either temperature) were detected by the lateral line neuromasts.

Electroreception The primary function of the external pit organs of teleosts is the reception of minute electrical currents in the water. These pit organs open to the surrounding water via canals filled with an electrically conductive gel. The freshwater examples, including the Gymnotoidei, the catfishes, and the Mormyriformes, have very short canals (300 μm). In contrast, the marine catfish (*Plotosus*) has longer canals resembling similar structures found in marine elasmobranchs called ampullae of Lorenzini, which range from 5 mm to 160 mm in length. The longer ducts in the marine species compared with those living in freshwater environments are related to the electrical conductivity differences between the environments compared with those of the skin and body tissues. Specifically, the relatively low resistivity of the skin and the somewhat greater resistivity of the internal tissues compared with the sea-water environment make the marine animal quite transparent to external voltage gradients. In contrast, freshwater fishes have relatively good conducting tissues compared with their environment. However, their skin has high electrical resistance, causing large voltage drops compared with the other tissues. Thus, freshwater fish electroreceptors need be only skin deep to sample a maximum change in potential. In both cases the gel-filled canals terminate at sensory cells in the more bulbous pit portion of the organ.

An array of electroreceptors (Fig. 10.7) capable of detecting weak electrical currents can be very helpful to a fish in perceiving aspects of its environment. For example, sensitivity to the electrical phenomena

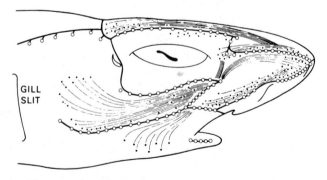

FIGURE 10.7 Location of sense organs on the head of the dogfish (*Scyliorhinus*). Openings of the ampullae of Lorenzini are shown by black dots. The open circles show the pores of the lateral line system and the black lines its location. (From Dijkgraaf and Kalmijn, 1963.)

generated by the movement through the earth's magnetic force field, that resulting from the depolarization and repolarizations of a contracting muscle, or even the electrical transmissions from a conspecific individual may have adaptive value. Lissman (1963) described both electrical reception and transmission used by the mormyrid and gymnotid fishes to probe their turbid African and South American stream environments (see Chapter 11). The rigid body posture of these electric fishes, with locomotion generated by undulation of the long anal (gymnotid) or dorsal (mormyrid) fins, may make the electrolocation process easier (Alexander 1967). Body undulations would continually change the distances and orientations among the electric organs and receptors, complicating the processing of the electroreception information.

Kalmijn (1971) demonstrated that predaceous marine elasmobranchs can locate prey by electroreception alone. For example, the dogfish shark (*Scyliorhinus canicula*) can locate a flounder buried in sediment, even when concealed by an electrically conductive agar plate. The dogfish was not attracted to buried chopped fish or to live flounder covered by an electrically insulating sheet of polyethylene. Conclusively, the shark tenaciously dug out two electrodes emitting a biological-strength electrical current, which were buried in sediment. Nighttime field studies showed that smooth dogfish (*Mustelus canis*) also responded more strongly to short-term electrical rather than olfactory stimulation. As an applied use of this information, the U.S. Navy's antishark screen (a large polyvinyl bag suspended from an inflatable collar) provides good electrical as well as visual and olfactory insulation for a mariner with skin cuts in shark-infested waters (Kalmijn 1978a).

Any electrical conductor moving through a magnetic field induces an electrical field through the conductor. Thus, a fish having dorsally and ventrally located electroreceptors and swimming across the earth's north–south magnetic field should be able to detect the induced electrical currents (Fig. 10.8). These induced currents are of sufficient strength for detection by sharks swimming as slowly as 2 cm/sec, proving the

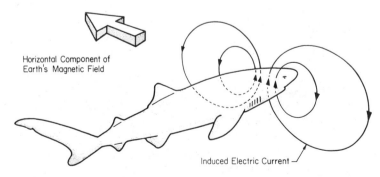

FIGURE 10.8 A shark swimming through the earth's magnetic field induces electric fields that provide the animal with the physical basis of an electromagnetic compass sense. (From Kalmijn, 1974.)

feasibility of an electromagnetic compass sense (Kalmijn 1978b). When the eastbound shark depicted in Fig. 10.8 turns to the north or south, the potentials vanish. Turns toward the west induce potentials of the opposite polarity.

Vision   The eye of a fish is the primary receptor site of light from its surroundings. It is worth noting as well that the pineal organ is also sensitive to light in some fishes and appears to have importance in the control of circadian rhythmicity (Kavaliers 1979). The eyes of all vertebrates have many similarities. A notable feature of the "typical" teleost eye is the cornea of constant thickness (Fig. 10.9). This cornea imposes no optical alterations (convergence or divergence) on incoming light. Thus, all of the focusing of light occurs at the spherical lens, which has the highest effective refractive index (1.65) among the vertebrates (Marshall 1966). As in other vertebrate eyes, the lens consists of water and structural proteins. High concentrations of soluble protein in the lens confer the high refractive index.

The teleost eye lens protrudes through the pupilar opening in the iris, and the eye bulges from the body surface. Therefore, the field of view includes a considerable arc forward, continuing laterally to almost directly behind the fish. The alternating head movements of anguilliform

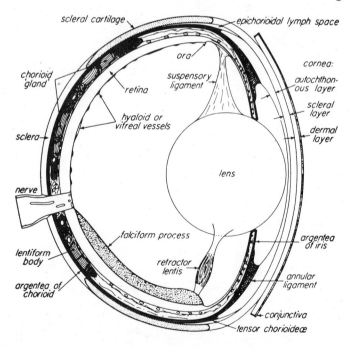

FIGURE 10.9 Diagrammatic vertical section of a typical teleost eye. Not all structures shown are present in every teleost eye; for example, hyaloid vessels are not present in conjunction with a falciform process. (From Walls, 1942.)

or subcarangiform swimmers with coordinated eye movements (Harris 1965) tends to eliminate the blind spot to the rear. Light focused by the lens is projected in the appropriate pattern of light, shade, and (often) color on the retina, the light-sensitive cell layer in the eye. Because the spherical lens is eccentrically located in the elliptical eye of teleosts, the lens-retinal distance varies, determining relatively near-field (close-up) vision in front of the fish and comparatively far-field vision to the side. Presumably this "near-sightedness" to the front coupled with the binocular depth-perception capabilities allow fish to seize their prey accurately, avoid obstacles, and so on.

The lens of elasmobranchs, on the other hand, is slightly flattened on the optical axis. Most elasmobranchs have a unique ability to dilate and constrict the pupil of the eye, comprising another mechanism to regulate incoming light levels, although some deepsea sharks have fixed pupils (Kuchnow 1971). The constricted, light-adapted pupil takes the shape of a pinhole in the blacktip shark (*Carcharhinus limatus*), a vertical slit in the lemon shark (*Negaprion brevirostris*), a horizontal slit in the bonnethead shark (*Sphyrna tiburo*), and an oblique slit in the nurse shark (*Ginglystoma cirratum*). The sawfish (*Pristis*) and ray (*Raja*), among others, have an *operculum pupillare* or opaque projection which descends ventrally to shield part of the pupillary opening. In contrast, the nictitating membrane (semiopaque eyelid) present in some sharks probably functions more to protect the eye than to reduce incoming light levels (Gruber 1977).

Adjustments in focus for near or far vision (optical accommodation) are accomplished by movement of the lens without changing its shape by muscles within the eye. The specific muscles within the eye which are responsible for these movements differ in lampreys, elasmobranchs, and teleosts. For example, in teleosts the lens is pulled inwards by a retractor muscle (Fig. 10.9), while in elasmobranch fishes it is pulled outwards by a protractor muscle. The four-eye fish (*Anableps*) displays an aspherical lens and two-part retina as structural adaptations associated with its life at the air–water interface. The lens thickness differences allow for the density differences of the two media.

The retina is made up of a dense packing of (often) both rod and cone cells for discrimination of light images. Incoming light must penetrate a clear layer of nerve cells and fibers to reach the photochemically active tips of the rods and cones (Fig. 10.9). The closer spacing of the rods and the connection of many rods to one neural fiber allows for reasonably fine image definition of "lightness and darkness," especially in dim light. The more widely spaced cone cells are each connected to an individual nerve fiber and provide vision of higher resolution as well as in color, but only in reasonably brightly lit surroundings (Marshall 1966). Gruber et al. (1975a) measured a rod:cone cell ratio of approximately 10:1 in the retinas of four species of requiem sharks (Carcharhinidae) and about 6:1 in three species of the more active mackerel sharks

(Lamnidae). As light strikes the rods or cones, it is absorbed by the light-sensitive pigment (e.g., rhodopsin, porphyropsin) in the cell. Visual pigments are organic dyes consisting of an opsin protein complexed onto a short-chain prosthetic or chromophore molecule (e.g., retinal) related to Vitamin A (Gruber and Cohen 1978). These pigments are located in the photoreception area of the retina, giving it its characteristic purple or pink coloration. For example, rhodopsin constitutes up to 35% of the dry weight of the rod outer segments. The pigments reversibly bleach out when exposed to light, and each has a characteristic absorption spectrum. The maximum absorption of "typical" shallow-water dogfish sharks (*Squalus*), skates (*Raja*), and rays (Myliobatidae) visual pigments occurs at wavelengths around 500 nm, which is typical for rhodopsin (Gruber and Cohen 1978). Denton and Warren (1956) reported high densities of a golden-colored pigment ("chrysopsin") in the retinas of three teleosts living below 500 m depth. As one would predict from the spectral shift in light penetrating to deeper strata, the absorbance maximum of chrysopsin is shifted toward the blue (shorter-wavelength) end of the spectrum by about 20 nm. Parallel evolution of "deepwater" visual pigments is found among three elasmobranch species (caught at 1150 m) containing pigments which absorb maximally from 472 nm to 484 nm (Denton and Shaw 1963). In all cases, pigmental absorption of light stimulates the retinal cells to send impulses via the optic nerve (Fig. 10.9) to the optic lobe on the same side of the brain. The reception and integration of the visual image in the brain would then provoke the "appropriate" motor response (e.g., to the muscles and/or fins).

The choroid coat underlies the retinal layer and primarily functions to supply nutrients and oxygen to the retina with its high metabolic demand. Most teleosts possess a pigmented, choroid projection into the posterior portion of the interior of the eye called the falciform process (Fig. 10.9). The falciform process is highly vascularized and probably serves a nutritive function (Munz 1971). In addition, a choroid gland (or rete) is present in most teleosts (and the bowfin [*Amia*]) behind the retina. The countercurrent arrangement of blood vessels of the choroid rete makes it eminently suited for oxygen delivery to the retina, in similar fashion to the rete mirabile of physoclistous swimbladders (Chapter 3). Wittenberg and Haedrich (1974) described the presence and relative size of choroid retia in several species of North Atlantic fishes. Invariably, the fishes which rely heavily on sight such as bluefish (*Pomatomus saltatrix*), have the best-developed choroid retia. Presumably, local acidification of the blood in the rete drives oxygen off the hemoglobin via the Root shift, much as in the swimbladder rete (Chapter 3). Hayden et al. (1975) attributed the significant Root shift in the swimbladderless winter flounder to choroid rete function in this demersal sight feeder. Wittenberg and Wittenberg (1962) measured the partial pressure of oxygen (P_{O_2}) in the vitreous humour of living marine fishes. Those species having the best-developed choroid rete also had the highest vitreous P_{O_2} (250 mm Hg to 820 mm Hg). Teleosts with smaller retia had lower P_{O_2} values (20 mm Hg to 210 mm Hg), while elasmobranchs and those teleosts that lacked the choroid rete had the lowest P_{O_2} values (10 mm Hg to 20 mm Hg).

The choroid layer of elasmobranch fishes also contains the tapetum lucidum or reflecting layer. It is the reflecting layer that produces eyeshine when a direct beam of light is trained on the eye, especially under darkened conditions. Many teleosts have tapeta lucida also, but most are located in the retinal pigment epithelium (Nicol and Zyznar 1973). The reflecting material of the tapetum varies among the fishes. Guanine crystals comprise the primary reflecting substance in the bigeye (*Priacanthus arenatus*), the bream (*Abramis brama*), the bay anchovy (*Anchoa mitchilli*), and all of the elasmobranchs investigated. A lipid reflecting substance is found in at least six teleost families, yellow "melanoid" substances occur in gars (Lepisosteidae) and catfishes, and a pteridine is found in the gizzard shad (*Dorosoma cepedianum*) (Zyznar and Nicol 1973).

In all cases, the tapetal layer functions to increase the visual sensitivity of retinal pigments by shining most of the transmitted light back through the retina. The arrangement of choroidal tapetal plates reflects light back in the same direction from which it first stimulates the retina, preserving image clarity. Whereas most benthic and deepsea elasmobranchs have tapeta lucida which function continuously, pelagic species from well-lit waters can cover the reflecting layers by moving dark pigment between the tapetal plates. Occlusion of the reflecting layer prevents "overloading" of the retinal pigments under brightly lit conditions. With the onset of darkness, the occluded tapetum becomes completely shiny after one hour. Gruber and Cohen (1978) point out that the light reflection from elasmobranch tapeta approaches 90% at certain wavelengths. This layer gives elasmobranchs a light sensitivity approximately equal to that of sympatric teleosts (without tapeta), which typically have twice the concentration of visual pigment per unit area of retinal surface.

The pineal gland, dorsally located on the brain, also has light sensitivity. Gruber et al. (1975b) showed that the chondrocranium of three sharks (*Negaprion, Carcharhinus,* and *Mustelus*) is modified for light transmission in that seven times more light impinged on the pineal receptors than on surrounding areas of the brain. Hamasaki and Streck (1971) found evidence that the pineal of *Scyliorhinus* responds to changes in illumination approximating 4×10^{-6} lumens/m^2, which is far below the intensity of moonlight at the water surface. Thus the pineal may function as an ultra sensitive light sensor closely connected to the brain and be used to cue the fish's behavior to changes in light intensity on a daily and seasonal basis.

Supplemental Readings

Alexander 1966, 1967; Dijkgraaf 1962; Gruber and Cohen 1978; Kalmijn 1978; Marshall 1966; Munz 1971; Myrberg 1978; Nicol and Zyznar 1973; Northcutt 1978; Popper and Fay 1977.

ααααααααααααααααααααααααααααααααααααααααααααααααααααααααααααααααα
~~~~~~

Behavior and Communication

The anatomical and physiological characteristics of a fish are best understood when explained in relation to their effect on its behavior. Thus, much of the space in the chapters of the major fish groups (13 through 23) is spent describing behavior patterns. Similarly, descriptions of fish behavior are important to the chapters on ecology (27 through 37) because ecology is the study of organism–environment interactions and the most conspicuous manifestation of these interactions is behavior, particularly behavioral change in response to environmental change. For this chapter it is convenient to divide the subject of behavior into seven categories (which are not necessarily mutually exclusive): (1) migratory behavior; (2) schooling behavior; (3) feeding behavior; (4) aggressive behavior; (5) resting behavior; (6) reproductive behavior; and (7) interspecific interactions. Reproductive behavior is covered in Chapter 9, and interspecific interactions, which include predator-prey, mimicry, and symbiotic relationships, are covered in the ecology chapters; thus, only the first five areas will be discussed in this chapter.

Because so much behavior involves interactions with other fish of the same or different species, it is important to understand how fishes communicate. Therefore, the latter half of this chapter will be devoted to communication using visual, auditory, chemical, tactile, and electrical signals.

Migratory Behavior   Mass movements of fish from one place to another, on a regular basis, are common. Such migratory behavior can range in occurrence from seasonal to daily. The daily migrations are typically for feeding and/or predator avoidance (see Chapters 27 and 36), so only less frequent patterns will be discussed here.

The seasonal migrations of fishes are often quite spectacular. Tuna, salmon, and eels, for example, may migrate thousands of kilometers in relatively short periods of time, often arriving within a relatively narrow time span at a fairly specific locality. Two questions will be addressed here: "Why do they do it?" and "How do they do it?"

Why fish migrate is a fascinating question because in many cases the energetic investment in migration is quite high and often migrating fishes do not feed. The European eels that migrate to the Sargasso Sea near Bermuda cease feeding once they enter salt water (Chapter 27), as do salmonids once they enter fresh water, some to swim hundreds of kilometers upstream. Most such migrations are for spawning, allowing the eggs to be laid in places favorable for their development and for the survival of the newly hatched larval stages (which typically have the highest mortality rates of any life history stage). As Harden-Jones (1968) points out, many such migrations have a triangular pattern. The adults swim against a current (ocean or stream) to the spawning grounds; the currents then carry the helpless young to favorable feeding areas; once the young reach a certain size and are active swimmers, they migrate to the adult feeding grounds. This pattern has several advantages: (1) it greatly increases the probability of the larval stages finding their way to the proper habitats; (2) it reduces the likelihood of intraspecific competition for food among different age classes, a problem most likely to affect plankton-feeding fishes such as herring; and (3) it reduces the probability of cannibalism.

The use of migration to separate life history stages is characteristic not only of diadromous fishes such as salmon and eels but also of pelagic fishes such as herring and sardines (see Chapter 35), of many freshwater fishes, and of many marine benthic fishes. River- and lake-dwelling fishes often migrate up into small tributary streams to spawn in riffle areas. The young may then use the small streams as nursery areas, before moving down to the adult habitat. Many lake-dwelling species migrate only as far as suitable spawning grounds in shallow waters of the lake itself. In fishes such as the sunfishes (*Lepomis*) and crappie (*Pomoxis*) the young become pelagic after hatching and drift about in the surface waters for several weeks before settling down to the bottom and then moving inshore, where they school in large numbers in shallow weedy areas or other protected habitats. A similar pattern may be found in marine benthic species, such as winter flounder (*Pseudopleuronectes americanus*) and various rockfishes (*Sebastes*).

While perhaps a majority of fish migrations are related to reproduction and the separation of the life history stages, many are also in response to changing environmental conditions, particularly temperature, and the movements and abundance of food organisms. The seasonal movements of albacore (*Thunnus alalunga*), for example, appear to follow the development of the 14°C isotherm in the north Pacific. In herring (*Clupea harengus*) the northward movement in spring in the

North Sea is related to the warmth of the inflowing Atlantic waters; the warmer the water, the greater the blooms of plankton upon which the herring feed. Increasingly, knowledge of the responses of migratory fish to temperature, salinity, and other oceanographic conditions is being used to predict how good fishing is likely to be in a given area, sometimes several months in advance.

One factor that greatly increases the predictability of the migrations of many fishes is their ability to find their way back to a "home" area, particularly a spawning area. Homing has been well documented in nonmigratory as well as migratory fishes. Many tidepool fishes, for example, can find their way back to their home pool, using olfactory and visual clues, after being displaced several hundred meters (Green 1971; Khoo 1974). The most studied of homing fishes, however, have been the Pacific salmon (*Oncorhynchus*) because they have been shown to return with an amazing degree of accuracy to the stream and area in which they were spawned, after wandering for several years and thousands of kilometers through the Pacific Ocean. A. D. Hasler and his students have shown rather conclusively that the precision of homing is due to the ability of the salmon to recognize the distinctive odor of their home stream, and that they become imprinted on this odor as they transform into smolts, just prior to their outward migration (Hasler and Scholz 1978). Not only are migrating salmon capable of recognizing the odor of their home stream, but they also recognize, and use as navigational cues, the odors of other streams they pass on their way up the main rivers. Furthermore, there is evidence that salmon may also respond to chemicals (pheromones) given off by conspecifics (Dizon et al. 1973) and are able to discriminate between water that contains fish from the same population and that from other populations. Such abilities can permit a great deal of precision in homing. Mechanisms other fishes use for the precise location of home areas have not been as well studied, but besides odor, it is likely that topographic cues, currents, and salinity and temperature gradients are important.

The recognition that migratory fishes can home precisely has led to the widespread acceptance of the idea that they can also navigate precisely over long distances. This has resulted in an extensive search for mechanisms of orientation. The most likely mechanisms proposed have been (1) orientation to gradients of temperature, salinity, and chemicals; (2) sun orientation; (3) orientation to polarized light; and (4) orientation to geomagnetic and geoelectric fields (Leggett 1977).

As the previous discussion has indicated, fish can detect gradients in the water and do orient to them, often timing migrations on the basis of seasonal changes in such factors as temperature and salinity. However, such phenomena fluctuate from year to year and frequently cover wide areas, and thus they seem to be poor candidates as cues for the precise nature of the homing observed. It is possible that migrating salmon may be able to detect sequential changes in the chemical content of the oceanic water masses they move through, much as they detect changes in the streams they pass through, but direct evidence for this is limited. In contrast, there is a great deal of evidence that fish can navigate by orienting to the position of the sun. The first strong evidence of sun orientation was provided by Hasler et al. (1958), who tied small floats onto white bass (*Morone chrysops*) and noted that on sunny days bass displaced from their spawning grounds had a strong directional bias when released, while on cloudy days such bias was lacking. Other studies have demonstrated that, in the laboratory at least, many fish not only are capable of finding compass directions by using the sun but also can adjust their orientation to compensate for the daily changes in angle of the sun's azimuth (Leggett 1977). Unfortunately, evidence that fishes in the wild use the sun compass for navigation is limited. Indeed, for both salmon and American shad (*Alosa sapidissima*), correctly oriented migrants have been observed both at night and on cloudy days.

Another type of sun orientation is the use of polarized light, particularly during dawn and dusk when polarization is the strongest. Although it has been demonstrated that some fish can orient to polarized light (Waterman and Forward 1972), its use as a migrational cue has not been established. Evidence is somewhat stronger that migratory fish can detect and orient to the earth's magnetic fields. These fields are weak but can be detected by many migratory fishes, particularly when additional electric fields are generated by the movement of oceanic currents through them. The strongest evidence for the use of geomagnetic fields for navigation is for eels (*Anguilla*), which migrate long distances in deep water, have an extreme sensitivity to the fields, and have different directional responses to them, depending on their developmental stage (Leggett 1977).

In the search for precise mechanisms of fish orientation, many bits of evidence suggesting that the migrations are not always that accurate were overlooked. Tagged salmon frequently show up in the wrong streams many miles distant from their home streams. Tagging studies of various migratory fishes frequently note that dispersal from the tagging site is essentially random in direction, even though a majority of the marked fish do end up in the home area. Furthermore, in orientation experiments, outright "mistakes" by fish are common and the overall orientation of fish to the factor being tested (e.g., sun azimuth) tends to be rather general and not exact. In fact, Saila (1961) was able to demonstrate that the homing of winter flounder to inshore spawning areas could be explained largely on the basis of random search movements of fish that will not go deeper than 40 m. A majority of these fish will find the coastline during the spawning period and then subsequently find their way to the spawning area partially through random searching and partly through the use of environmental cues, such as topography and water chemistry. Similarly, salmon do not need highly precise navigational abilities to reach a general area of coastline that contains their spawning stream. All they need is some cue that gets them swimming in the general direction. Patten (1964) points out that this does not have to be done by one specific mechanism but could be the result of multiple cues, such as food availability, currents, and temperature and chemical gradients, as well as more predictable cues such as sun direction and geomagnetic fields. By using a combination of cues, most of the fish can reach their home region and, once there, use more precise mechanisms, particularly olfaction, to find the home stream.

Schooling

Schooling is perhaps the most spectacular and fascinating social behavior pattern possessed by fish. A school often seems to have a mind of its own, moving in a coordinated fashion, through complicated maneuvers with its members precisely spaced within it. Schooling is also of interest because of its prevalence; Shaw (1978) estimated that 25% of all fishes school throughout their lives and that about half of all fishes spend at least part of their lives in schools. Most of the important commercial fish species also school, and their schooling behavior greatly increases their vulnerability to capture in large numbers.

Although no one would argue that the highly organized, rapidly swimming aggregations of pelagic fishes such as tuna and herring are schools, there has been considerable debate as to how to classify less organized aggregations of fish (Radakov 1972). The most workable definition seems to be that of Shaw (1970, 1978), who defines a school as a group of fish that are mutually attracted to each other. Usually the members of a school are about the same size. This definition eliminates from consideration aggregations of fish created by the attractiveness of some feature of the environment, such as a reef. Within this definition, schools can be viewed as either polarized or nonpolarized. A polarized school is one in which each fish has a rather precise orientation to other fish in the school, while a nonpolarized school is one in which the fish have a more or less random orientation to each other. These distinctions are not rigid, however, because a single school may change from one state to another, depending on whether its members are traveling, feeding, resting, or avoiding predators (Fig. 11.1). The shape of a school can also vary widely. Traveling schools, for example, range in shape from long, thin lines, to ovals and squares, to more amoeboid shapes. However, fast-moving traveling schools most typically assume a wedge shape, while feeding schools are usually more or less circular. The sizes of schools show tremendous variability, even within species. In many species, the largest schools form during migrations, when smaller schools join together. Radakov (1972) mentions "chains" of schools of migrating mullet (*Mugil*) over 100 km long in the Caspian Sea! In the north Atlantic, herring schools are sometimes encountered in the winter that occupy 279 million m^3 to 4580 million m^3, with densities of 0.5 fish per m^3 to 1.0 fish per m^3 (Radakov 1972).

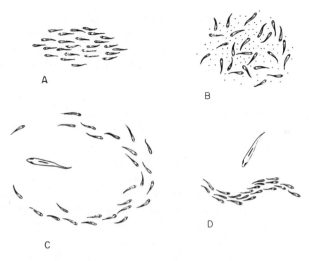

FIGURE 11.1 Common patterns of schooling: (A) traveling; (B) planktivores feeding; (C) encirclement of a predator; and (D) streaming school avoiding predator. (After Radakov, 1962.)

How do fish school? Obviously, the precise structure and movements of polarized schools require precise sensory contacts among the individuals within the schools. The fact that most schools break up at night indicates that vision is the main sensory link. Many laboratory experiments with temporarily blinded fish also demonstrate the importance of vision. Shaw (1978) has proposed one way that vision can be used to maintain the regular spacing noted in schools is through the "optomotor reaction." This is the response fish have when placed in a container around which alternating vertical black and white stripes are rotating. The fish "stops" the motion of the stripes by fixing on one stripe and swimming at the same speed at which it is rotating. This response is quite useful to schooling fish, because position in a school can be maintained by visually fixing on the sides of neighboring fish, especially on the conspicuous dark lateral stripe possessed by so many schooling fishes.

The importance of vision in schooling does not mean that other senses are not important as well. Because the lateral line system is so sensitive to water movement, it is quite likely that fish use the regular turbulence created by neighboring fish as another cue to help maintain spacing. It is also possible that pheromones or sounds may play a role in schooling, although there is no direct evidence for either one.

Why do fish school? There appear to be a number of advantages to schooling which may be acting simultaneously: (1) increased hydrodynamic efficiency; (2) reduced risk of predation; (3) increased efficiency of food finding; and (4) increased reproductive success.

The best evidence that schooling increases the efficiency of the

CH. 11 BEHAVIOR AND COMMUNICATION

swimming of its members is the position of the fishes in a school relative to one another. Typically, each fish is not directly behind the closest fish in front of it but at a diagonal to it. In addition, each fish is separated from its nearest neighbor by one half to one body length. Weihs (1973) points out that this is just the pattern you would expect if each fish was getting a small boost from the vortices created by the tail movements of the fish in front of it; if it was swimming directly behind the fish in front, it would actually have to swim against the current created by the other fish. Another possible advantage of swimming in the vortices of other fish is that they may contain small amounts of slime produced by the fish, which can in fact reduce the resistance of the water flowing along the fish (drag). Breder (1976) has shown that the introduction of small amounts of artificial slime into water can greatly increase the swimming speed of a fish without increasing its energy output. For a fish to take advantage of swimming vortices, the correct distance from the preceding fish has to be carefully maintained. Similarly, by maintaining its distance from its lateral companions at less than one body length, a fish may be able to increase the efficiency of the shoving motion of its tail against the water (Weihs 1973). Despite these compelling observations, in experimental tanks, where careful measurements can be made, fish do not necessarily swim in the hydrodynamically correct positions (Partridge and Pitcher 1979).

While the hydrodynamic advantages of schooling have only recently been recognized, its advantages for reducing the effectiveness of attacks of predators have long been part of the lore of ichthyology. Many workers have observed that schooling fish tend to get eaten mostly when they have been separated from the school and that many of the attack strategies of predators can be best interpreted as efforts to break up the schools so individuals can be picked off (e.g., Major 1978). Most small schooling fish are silvery, and it is difficult for a visually oriented predator to pick an individual out of a mass of twisting, flashing fish and then to have enough time to "fix" on that prey and grab it before it disappears into the school. Schooling fish that are captured are individuals that have become separated from the main school somehow (Major 1978). Thus, when a predator approaches, a school initially typically bunches up into a tight, weaving mass. One of the reasons that attacks on schooling fish are often more successful at dawn or dusk than during the day is presumably the reduced effectiveness of flashing scales in confusing the predators. Schooling fishes also confound their predators by complicated maneuvering. One common maneuver is for the school to divide in two, turning away from the predator in two directions and finally joining again behind it. The effect of this is constantly to leave the predator isolated in a large, empty pocket in the school, from which it is very difficult to attack effectively because its every movement can be closely monitored by individuals in the school. Indeed, one of the general advantages of being in a school is presumably being accompanied by a large number of eyes that make it virtually impossible for a predator to approach during the day without being detected. The compactness of schools compared to dispersed populations of fish may also simply decrease the probability of an individual encountering a predator. When predators do attack, large shools are particularly advantageous because of the reduced probability of any one individual being eaten. In any one attack, a smaller percentage of a large school will be eaten than of a small school (Major 1978).

Despite the many antipredator advantages of schools, schooling fishes are still the favorite prey of most pelagic predators, and many effective hunting strategies have been evolved to overcome the defenses of the school. One strategy is simply to attack at low light levels when the schools are more dispersed and the predators are more difficult to spot. Another strategy is to swim along with the school and grab fish that make defensive errors and become separated from it or that are sick or injured. Perhaps most effective, however, is to adopt schooling itself as an attack strategy. When a school of jacks (Carangidae) or tuna (Scombridae) attacks a school of herring, the school cannot respond as effectively as to a single predator, and many individuals become separated from the mass in the confusion and are eaten. Schools of small fish can be devastated when a school of predators drives them to the surface of the water and then flocks of seabirds dive down on them from above. Schooling by the predators may also increase the probability of their detecting a school of prey, just as schooling in plankton-feeding fishes may increase the probability of detection of patches of plankton. However, for planktivores, this advantage may be partially compensated for by having to share the patch with many other fish; fish in the rear of a school in particular are likely to encounter much lower densities of plankton than those in the front. On the other hand, Robertson et al. (1976) have observed that on reefs, parrotfish (Scaridae) are able to overcome the aggressive defenses of territorial damselfishes (Pomacentridae) only by moving into a territory as a school. This enables them to browse on the algae patches defended by the damselfish.

Although the predator–prey interactions seem to be the most important reasons for the development of schooling, it cannot be denied that when spawning time comes around, little energy has to be expended in finding a mate (except in species in which the sexes school separately).

Feeding Behavior   The feeding behavior of fish is as diverse as their morphology, which more often than not reflects their general method of feeding (Chapter 2). It is important to note, however, that while most fish are specialized in their feeding to a greater or lesser degree, their actual diet at any given time depends on the availability of both typical and atypical food items, as well as on the presence of potentially competing fish species (Ivlev 1961). When a major hatch of mayflies occurs in a lake, for example, almost every fish large enough to capture them will do so, although normally mayflies would be taken mainly by fishes with adaptations for surface feeding (e.g., Moyle 1973). Similarly, fishes that normally filter-feed on plankton will on occasion selectively feed by "picking" large individual zooplankters, including larval fish. Rainbow trout (*Salmo gairdneri*) usually feed on drifting organisms in streams (Chapter 28) but may become benthic feeders when drift is hard to see, even though this mode of feeding is generally less efficient (Tippets and Moyle 1978). Other fishes may regularly switch between two or more modes of feeding, depending on the abundances of different kinds of prey. Bay gobies (*Lepidogobius lepidus*), for example, will hop up from the bottom to seize swimming prey or bite the substrate to obtain benthic prey, especially polychaete worms (Grossman et al. 1980). Obviously, the feeding behavior of fishes is influenced by many factors, including characteristics of the environment, the predators, and the prey.

In an effort to understand just how and why predators select their prey, a general theory of optimal foraging has been developed (Pyke et al. 1977; Krebs 1978). The basic idea behind this theory is that natural selection will favor predators that maximize the efficiency of their capture of prey. Thus, the feeding "strategy" adopted by a fish at any time should be one that allows it to take in the most or highest quality food with the least amount of effort (energy expenditure). Because the principal ways a predator expends energy in feeding are in searching for and pursuing prey, handling the prey, and then digesting it, an optimal foraging strategy should balance these factors in such a way that the total energy expenditure is minimized, even if the cost of one of the factors is higher than it could be. For example, it does not "pay" a carnivorous bass to browse on algae, even though the algae might be very easy to find and handle, because the fish would presumably expend more energy passing it through the gut than it could extract from it. On the other hand, it may pay the bass quite well to select slender, soft-rayed minnows over deep-bodied, spiny sunfish because the handling time is likely to be considerably less. Similarly, the bass is most likely to select for larger minnows over smaller ones, because the search time per gram of fish ingested will be less.

Although, as the above example indicates, the morphological characteristics of the prey can greatly influence prey selection, the most important factors are usually size and availability. For example, in aquaria bluegill (*Lepomis macrochirus*) will select all size classes of *Daphnia* equally, if all are present at low densities; they simply grab the prey as they encounter them. However, if the densities of all sizes of *Daphnia* are greatly increased, the fish will select only the largest sizes (Werner and Hall 1974). An interpretation of such an experiment is that when food is scarce, a fish will capture any prey item for which there is likely to be a net gain of energy for the fish, no matter how small, while when food is abundant, the fish will select the prey that produce the most energy for the least amount of effort (resulting in more energy available for growth and reproduction). However, Ringler (1979) noted that brown trout (*Salmo trutta*) in stream aquaria continued to take small amounts of small "suboptimal" prey long after preferred, larger prey became abundant. These fish would even abandon, for short periods of time, areas where prey were most abundant to check out other areas. While such behavior kept the trout from completely optimizing their diets in the aquaria, in the wild it would be highly adaptive because prey size, availability, and location are likely to fluctuate considerably. Another possible explanation for the continued ingestion of small prey is that when they are close to a feeding fish, they *appear* to be larger than a much larger organism some distance away and so will be selected on the basis of apparent, rather than actual, size (O'Brien et al. 1976). However, fish do show considerable ability to learn the "real" characteristics of their prey, and trout will begin the pursuit of larger prey at greater distances away than they will for smaller prey (Ringler 1979).

One of the problems with optimal foraging theory is that it is difficult to test the hypotheses generated by the theory in wild populations of fish because the number of factors influencing the choice of prey is likely to be large and variable, as are the kinds of prey consumed. Sculpins in streams, for example, apparently choose prey not only on the basis of size and abundance but on the basis of activity pattern (both time of day and amount of activity), how hard-shelled they are, their microhabitat, and, perhaps, their caloric content (Li and Moyle 1976). An additional complicating factor is that fish may have individual preferences. Bryan and Larkin (1972) found that individual trout in the same stream seemed to have distinct preferences for prey types, so that trout of the same size feeding in the same general area might be selecting different items.

Of course, an optimal foraging strategy for a fish may include other factors besides maximizing the energy obtained per prey item, most importantly, avoiding predators. Thus an optimal strategy for a small, crevice-dwelling bottom fish might be to minimize the time spent foraging, in order to minimize exposure to predation. Such a fish could presumably obtain more food by foraging more continuously but would increase its own probability of being eaten as it spent more time away from cover. An optimal foraging strategy here would balance energy gains against survival probabilities.

Aggressive Behavior   Aggressive interactions among fish are frequently observed, particularly in aquaria. In form, such interactions range from direct charges of one individual at another, which may result in bites or fights, to elaborate ritualistic displays involving modified swimming, flaring of gill covers and fins, and changes in color, to barely detectable movements. The best known aggressive interactions among fishes are those related to reproduction and the defense of breeding territories because they are part of elaborate sets of conspicuous, ritualized behavior (Chapter 9). Just as important to many fishes, but much less conspicuous, is aggressive behavior associated with the defense of food and space (cover). Trout and juvenile salmon, for example, frequently defend feeding territories in streams. Such territories generally center around a rock or some other object that shelters the fish from the currents but provides a good view of food organisms drifting downstream. Proximity of the territory to cover, for protection from predators, may also be important. The most frequently observed form of territory defense is the "nip," where a defending fish charges an intruder and attempts to nip its caudal peduncle or side. When the intruder is the same size or smaller than the defender, it usually flees quickly. Occasionally, an intruder will not flee at once, and more elaborate displays result, most conspicuously lateral displays, where the two fish swim side by side in a rigid fashion, with opercula and fins flared. Three factors seem to be of greatest importance in deciding which fish wins a bout: prior residency, size, and results of previous encounters. A fish which already lives in a territory is likely to defeat an intruder unless that intruder is considerably larger than the defender. The displacement of small fish by larger fish can result in frequent shifts in the patterns of territories in trout and salmon streams, because larger fish also require larger territories. In trout, several fish of different sizes may coexist in the same area, with the larger fish being dominant over the smaller fish but not driving them away (T. Jenkins 1969). Such dominance hierarchies presumably exist in part because the smaller trout feed on smaller prey, and so are not competing too much with the larger trout for food, and because the smaller trout may actually help the larger trout defend the area against other intruders.

It has been implied in the above discussion that aggressive behavior has an adaptive significance. The gain in food availability is assumed to offset the costs of patrolling a territory and chasing away intruders. Thus, in the tide-flat-dwelling bay goby (*Lepidogobius lepidus*) winners of aggressive encounters are able to consume more food than losers under conditions of artificial food shortage (Grossman 1979). Likewise, in reef-dwelling damselfishes, the density of filamentous algae, upon which they feed, is much higher in the territories than outside of them. Further discussions of the ecological significance of aggressive behavior can be found in Chapters 27, 28, and 34.

Resting Behavior

Although it is not often acknowledged in studies of fish behavior, most fishes spend a good part of each 24-hour period in an inactive state. On coral reefs there are marked differences between the day and night fish faunas, in large part because day-active fishes hide in crevices and caves in the reef at night, where they rest quietly, while night-active fishes are inactive in the crevices during the day (Chapter 34). Many species even change color patterns when at rest. In freshwater lakes many fish become pale at night and rest quietly on the bottom, under logs, or on beds of aquatic weeds. Often such fish are so torpid that a scuba diver can swim up to one and touch it, something that would be impossible to do during the day (Emery 1973). Some pelagic fishes, such as tuna, that must swim to keep water moving across the gills are presumably active all night long, but other pelagic fishes, such as herring, tend to remain in a quiescent state in the water column. The polarized school of the day becomes unpolarized at night, but the members remain close enough to each other so that the polarized school can re-form as soon as there is enough light. The inactivity of many fish at night is presumably an energy-conserving measure.

Communication

VISUAL SIGNALS   For most fish, vision is the most important sense for finding food and for communicating with other fish. Thus, it is not surprising to find that there is an enormous variety of visual signals among fish, from subtle movements of the body and fins to bright colors arranged in elaborate patterns. Because colors and color patterns are so important for visual communication, this section will discuss (1) how they are produced by fish; (2) their general significance; and (3) the specific significance of some of the most common types of color patterns.

Colors in fish are of two basic types, pigments (biochromes) and structural colors. **Pigments** are colored compounds that are located primarily in chromatophores, cells located mainly in the dermis of the skin (but also in the epidermis, in the peritoneum, in the eyes, and in the various organs). Chromatophores are highly irregular in shape but usually appear as central core giving out many branched processes. This shape permits the rapid color changes frequently observed in fish; when the pigment granules are concentrated in the center portion, the overall appearance of the fish will be paler than when the granules are dispersed through the branches. The hues change through the combined action of chromatophores containing pigments of different colors overlying one another or by the internal changes of chromatophores containing more than one pigment.

The internal control of the chromatophores, and consequently color patterns, is complex, involving both hormones and nerves. As might be expected, the initiation of a color change usually comes from visual cues. A flounder placed with its head on one background and its body on another will have a body color matching that of the background around the head. Likewise, body coloration can be experimentally altered by fitting colored transparent eye lenses or by changing the intensity of illumination. Visual stimuli are carried to the chromatophores by sympathetic nerves, by special hormones secreted by the pituitary, or by both. The method used depends on the type of chromatophore and on the species of fish. Nonvisual cues may also cause color changes, as indicated by the sensitivity of the nerves associated with chromatophores to such substances as adrenalin (epinephrine) and acetylcholine. Adrenalin and its relatives cause pigment granules in the chromatophore to aggregate, rapidly making the fish lighter in color, while acetylcholine will make them disperse slowly. Thus, fish that are frightened may undergo rapid color changes and then slowly revert back to their original colors when the danger is past.

There are many different kinds of pigments found in fishes (Fox 1978), but the most frequently encountered types are carotenoids, melanins, and purines. Carotenoid pigments are those responsible for the bright reds and yellows frequently seen in fishes, and greens as well, when yellow carotenoids overlie a blue structural color. Melanins are mainly dark red, brown, and black and form the background coloration of most fishes. Purines (mostly guanine in fishes) are crystalline substances that perhaps should not be classified as pigments because they are colorless and are often nonmotile in the chromatophores. However, they have the peculiar reflective qualities that produce the silvery sheen of pelagic fishes and the iridescent colors of many reef and freshwater tropical fishes. In fact, most of the **structural colors** of fishes (colors produced by light reflecting from structures rather than by pigments) are caused by light reflecting from purine crystals located in special chromatophores. The silvery color of pelagic fishes, for example, is created by the stratum argenteum, a sheet made up of layers of guanine-containing cells (iridophores) that is capable of reflecting most of the light that hits it. Because the light is scattered as it is reflected, it appears silvery; if the crystals or iridophores are aligned in such a way that the light waves are reflected back in parallel, iridescent colors are created.

What is the adaptive significance of the complex color patterns of fishes? Color patterns in general seem to have three main purposes: thermoregulation, intraspecific communication, and evasion of predators (Endler 1978). The role of color patterns in fishes in thermoregulation is not known, but it is not likely to be great, given the closeness of fish body temperatures to environmental temperatures. Nevertheless, the importance of color patterns, but particularly countershading (dark above, light below), in the thermoregulation of terrestrial animals indicates that thermoregulation cannot be dismissed entirely as a function of coloration in fishes (Hamilton 1973). However, most color patterns of fishes, if they can be explained at all, can be viewed as compromises between the "need" to communicate with other members of the species and the "need" to avoid being eaten. The former "need" will favor bright, distinctive, and conspicuous coloration, while the latter will favor cryptic coloration. The fact that a particular color or color pattern may be either quite conspicuous or quite cryptic depending on such factors as background colors, water clarity, and visual capabilities of the predators means that the significance of color patterns must be interpreted

FIGURE 11.2 Color patterns of tilapia (*Sarotherodon mossambica*): (1) neutral pattern; (2) male territorial pattern; (3) aggression pattern; (4) arousal pattern; (5) female spawning pattern; (6) female brooding pattern; (7) frightened juvenile; (8) and (9) frightened adult. The arrows show probable direction of change of color pattern. (From Lanzing and Bower, 1974.)

carefully. Interpretation of the significance of color patterns is also complicated by the ability of many fishes to change colors, often quite rapidly in response to changing conditions, but particularly in relation to reproduction (Fig. 11.2). The compromising, multipurpose nature of color patterns in fishes can be best demonstrated by examining some of the more common patterns in fishes: (1) red coloration; (2) poster colors; (3) disruptive coloration; (4) countershading; (5) eye ornamentation; (6) eye spots; (7) lateral stripes; and (8) polychromatism.

Red coloration. The wavelengths in the red region of the spectrum are the first to be filtered out as light passes through water, yet bright red fishes are common. Fishes that are solid red in color are generally either nocturnal (such as the cardinal fishes [Apogonidae] or the squirrel fishes [Holocentridae]) or live at moderate depths (such as many rockfishes [*Sebastes*]). In both situations red light is virtually absent from the water, so the fish are in fact cryptically colored. Red is also a cryptic color in tidepool fishes because many of them are found in close association with red algae. Many shallow-water fishes, however, do have red bands and other markings that seem to make them quite conspicuous. Such coloration is particularly common in the spawning males of freshwater fishes, such as minnows of genus *Notropis* and *Chrosomus*, most suckers (Catostomidae), many salmon and trout, and sticklebacks (*Gasterosteus*). It can be argued that red is a good compromise color for spawning fish because it is highly visible at short distances, important for males trying to attract females for spawning, yet is likely to be difficult to see laterally for any distance, especially if the water is turbid or shaded. The importance of hiding even small patches of red color that do not function in communication is demonstrated by white sturgeon (*Acipenser transmontanus*), which have a small dorsal portion of their gill exposed. While the covered part of the gill is red, the exposed portion is darkly pigmented, like the skin of the sturgeon (Burggren 1978).

Poster colors is the name given by Konrad Lorenz to the bright, complex color patterns so characteristic of coral reef fishes because he thought their primary function was advertisement of territory ownership. The most conspicuous, and most studied, of the poster-colored fishes are the butterfly fishes (Chaetodontidae), which are typically yellow or white, with dark, contrasting stripes and other markings. For many reef fishes the bright colors may indeed be important for advertising territories, but it is now apparent that that is only one of a number of possible functions (Ehrlich et al. 1977). Many highly colored reef fishes are not territorial, while many territorial fishes, such as some damselfishes (Pomacentridae), are rather plain in color. For more gregarious species, the bright colors may serve to keep foraging individuals in contact with each other. Ehrlich et al. (1977) noted that when a pair of butterfly fish become separated, one of them may rise off the bottom in a brief display that helps to bring the two together again. Coloration may also be closely tied to sex and courtship; the complex polymorphic patterns of wrasses (Labridae) and parrotfishes (Scaridae), for example, reflect sex, status, and maturity.

Still other possible functions of poster colors lie in the realm of predator avoidance. Often fishes with bright colors can hide very effectively in the reef, partly because the reef itself is quite colorful and partly because the patterns may be disruptive in nature (see next section). In fact, it may be the patterns and not the colors that are most important for concealment because being invisible to reef predators is most important when light levels are low and colors hard to see (Chapter 34). Thus the patterns could serve different purposes at different light levels. Brightly colored fishes may also be able to escape predators through the "flash effect," whereby a predator is confused when a fish approached from the side suddenly turns and "disappears" because only the narrowest profile is visible. On the other hand, bright colors may actually function to announce a fish's presence to a predator because the fish is too poisonous or spiny to be worth pursuing. Indeed, the spiny nature of butterfly fishes is thought to account at least partially for their rarity in the stomachs of predatory reef fishes.

Disruptive coloration consists of colors and patterns that break up the outline of fish, thereby making them less visible. Thus fishes that associate with beds of aquatic plants, such as sunfishes (*Lepomis*) and many cichlids, often have on their sides vertical bars that help them to blend in with the vertical pattern of the plants. Part of the effect of such patterns may be "flicker fusion" in the predator (Endler 1978), whereby the rapid movement of the vertical bars on the side of the fish across a field of vertical bars (plant stems) may cause them all to blend together in the eyes of the predator, much like motion picture film. The intriguing aspect of flicker fusion as camouflage is that it may permit a fish to have a color pattern that is conspicuous at rest but confusing when the fish is swimming rapidly. Many of the bright but irregular patterns of coral reef fishes or freshwater fishes of the tropics may function in this way, because they are often associated with irregular, dappled backgrounds.

The real masters at matching their backgrounds, however, are slow-moving bottom fishes, such as sculpins (Cottidae), darters (Percidae), flounders, and blennies. Flounders are famous for their ability to match their background, even to the point of coloring themselves in a fair imitation of a checkerboard when placed on one in the laboratory. Other fishes may break up their outlines by having cirri and other irregular growths that resemble seaweed, especially on the head.

Countershading is the commonest way fish disguise themselves. Being dark on top helps to hide them from predators attacking from above, while being light on the bottom helps them to blend in better with the light streaming down from above. Its effectiveness in concealing a fish can be demonstrated simply by turning a countershaded fish upside down in the water and noting how conspicuous it becomes. On the other hand, Hamilton (1973) warns that countershading may have other functions as well. He suggests, for example, that countershading in butterfly fishes may enhance their ability to signal each other because countershading may be nearly eliminated in intraspecific encounters, increasing the conspicuousness of the fish.

Eye ornamentation. The eye in fish, being naturally conspicuous, seems to be a focus for both the attacks of predators and for intraspecific communication. Thus there are two trends in eye ornamentation: to disguise the eye and to emphasize it. Disguising the eye is accomplished in a variety of ways, such as minimizing the contrast between the iris and pupil and then surrounding the eye with a matching background, having a line run through the eye that matches the pupil, and having a field of spots surround the eye of a size similar to the pupil. Eye lines are the most common form of eye disguise, and Barlow (1972) notes that such lines tend to be vertical on deep-bodied species but horizontal on slender-bodied species, so that they are consistent with body patterns. Although disguising the eye is a common practice, particularly in reef fishes, much more common is emphasizing the eye with a striking pattern around it or with bright colors in the eye itself. In Caribbean reef fishes, a majority of the species have eyes with conspicuous coloration, mostly black, blue, and yellow (Thresher 1977). Usually, the dark pupil is emphasized by a light-colored iris and often with some supplementary markings, such as eye rings, as well. Presumably such conspicuous eyes have developed in reef fishes because of the ease with which they can find cover during the day, when such eyes would be most conspicuous, and because of their general importance for intraspecific signaling.

Eye spots. Among the commonest marking on the bodies of fish are single spots about the size of the pupil of the eye and often surrounded by light-colored pigmentation for emphasis. Such eye spots are most commonly located at the base of the caudal peduncle. They are found most often in the juveniles of tropical characins, cyprinids, and cichlids but many other small fishes have them as well (such as all the juveniles of the endemic cyprinids of California). Although it is possible that such spots may function as orientation marks for fishes in a school, their principal function seems to be to confuse predators into aiming attacks at the caudal area rather than the head, giving the fish greater opportunities to escape (McPhail 1977a). In some species, eye spots serve as recognition signals that inhibit cannibalism of juveniles by adults. In the poeciliid fish *Neoheterandria formosa* the midlateral spot that apparently serves such a function is retained in the adults as well and used as an appeasement signal during courtship (McPhail 1977b).

Lateral stripes, typically a single midlateral band, are best developed in schooling fishes, where they seem to serve the dual function of keeping school members properly oriented to each other and of confusing predators. Presumably the latter aim is achieved by the effect of visual fusion of the stripes of members of the school, increasing the difficulty of picking out individuals.

Polychromatism. Nowhere is the conflict between the need to be cryptically colored to avoid predators and the need to be bright to attract mates more apparent than in fishes that are polychromatic, with different patterns predominating in different populations depending on the degree of predation. In the midas cichlid (*Cichlasoma citrinellum*) gold morphs are dominant over plainer morphs, particularly in contests over food (Barlow 1973), yet the failure of the gold morphs to "take over" their habitats in the wild presumably reflects their greater vulnerability to predation. In the annual killifish (*Nothobranchius guntheri*) brightly colored morphs are dominant over dull morphs and so have greater reproductive opportunities early in the season. However, they gradually are picked off by predators, giving the dull morphs greater reproductive opportunities later in the season (Haas 1976a, b).

Special patterns.   Besides general patterns, such as those just discussed, many species have special color patterns that fit their own particular lifestyles. The males of some cichlids (*Haplochromis*) have circles on their anal fins that resemble eggs; these are displayed just after a female has laid some eggs and taken them into her mouth. When she tries to pick up the dummy eggs as well, the male releases sperm and the eggs in the mouth are fertilized. On coral reefs, there are many fishes with special color patterns, such as the bright colors of cleaner fishes that advertise their presence to fish wanting to be "cleaned" and the patterns of fishes that mimic other fishes or invertebrates (Chapter 34). In the deep sea, photophore patterns play much the same roles as color patterns in lighted environments (Chapter 36).

AUDITORY SIGNALS   The use of sound for communication among fish is common but far from universal, although the hearing of fish is usually fairly keen (Chapter 10). In some species, however, the sounds produced can be very loud and continuous and be fundamental to their way of life, especially during reproduction, when courtship "singing" may occur. Fish produce sounds in three main ways: by stridulation of bones, by vibration of the swimbladder, and incidental to other activities. The stridulation of bones produces mainly low-frequency sounds, but this method is the most common means of deliberate sound production, presumably because it often requires little modification of existing structures. Thus some fishes can communicate just by grinding the pharyngeal or jaw teeth together in a regular fashion. Some filefishes (Balistidae) even have special ridges on the backs of their front teeth that are used for sound production. Another common stridulatory mechanism is to rub the specially roughened base of a fin spine (usually pectoral spines) against its socket. Sea catfishes (Ariidae) are particularly well known for their use of this mechanism. Many, perhaps most, stridulatory sounds are amplified by the fish's swimbladder, and often there are muscular connections between the sound-producing structure and the swimbladder. Tilapia (*Sarotherodon mossambica*), for example, have sound-transmitting muscles that run from their pharyngeal teeth to the swimbladder.

In fishes with the most complex auditory signals, it is usually the swimbladder itself that serves as the sound-producing organ. There are many ways this is done, often involving major modification of the swimbladder, but the basic means is to vibrate the swimbladder either by moving special muscles attached to it or by rubbing it with adjacent structures. The special musculature may either be muscles that insert on the swimbladder and originate on the skull or vertebral column or musculature intrinsic to the swimbladder itself. In the former case, the sound produced by the muscles depends on their tension and rate of vibration. This mechanism is found in the noisier members of many families of spiny-rayed fishes and in some catfishes. The loudest and most elaborate sounds, however, seem to be made by fishes with intrinsic swimbladder musculature for sound production, such as the toadfishes (Batrachoididae), searobins (Triglidae), and gunnards (Dactyolpteridae), although the drums (Sciaenidae) get their name and sound-producing reputation by vibrating muscles in the body walls next to the swimbladder.

Deliberate sounds are important in communication, but the most common sounds of fishes are those made incidental to other activities. Thus, the swimming movements of a school may create detectable sounds, as do feeding activities such as the crushing of hard-shelled prey. The leaping of fish from the water and the consequent splash may create a sound that will carry long distances. Whether or not most of these sounds have communication functions is not known, but they may be important in many species for keeping individuals in contact with one another when vision is limited.

Compared to the sounds of many terrestrial animals, the sounds produced by fish are not particularly elaborate. In general, fish have only limited abilities to make and detect sounds of different frequencies, perhaps the most important means of varying sound patterns in mammals and birds. Nevertheless, sounds produced by fish can be varied by changes in loudness (amplitude), duration, repetition rate, and number of pulses within a signal (Fine et al. 1977). The loudest calls produced by fishes seem to be those associated with agonistic behavior, especially territorial defense, and with stress conditions that produce warning calls. Anemone fish (*Amphiprion*) have an extremely loud call that is used in defense of an anemone against conspecifics, but a much quieter call is associated with close encounters and fighting between two fish. The calls of anemone fish can also be distinguished on the basis of their duration; the more intense a threat, the longer a call will last. The repetition rate of a signal and the number of pulses within it (i.e., its complexity) may also increase with the intensity of the interaction. In drums (Sciaenidae) the drumming sounds are produced when the fish are in schools and increase in intensity during certain times of the day. As the intensity of the drumming increases, the length of each call increases as well, as does its frequency of repetition. Such variation in calls may also serve to keep closely related species reproductively isolated from each other. For example, Gerald (1971) found that the courtship grunts of six species of sunfish (*Lepomis*) could be distinguished from each other on the basis of duration and number of pulses per second.

As is true of visual signals, the usefulness of auditory signals is limited by the likelihood that they will attract predators as well as conspecifics. The larger marine predators, such as seals, porpoises, and large species of cod, possess keen low-frequency hearing that enables them to detect both deliberate and incidental sounds made by their prey. Among the codfishes and their relatives it is mainly the largest species that have the ability to produce sounds for communication, presumably because they are less susceptible to predation than smaller species (Hawkins and Rasmussen 1978).

CHEMICAL SIGNALS   As the discussion of the use of odors as migrational cues indicates, most fish have a well-developed sense of smell. Thus it is not surprising to find that chemicals produced by fish even in very small amounts are often important in intraspecific communication, especially in fish that do not have keen eyesight (such as the catfishes). The chemical nature of most of the substances used in communication by fishes is not known, but it is likely that many of them are produced specifically for that purpose. This is particularly true of compounds that when released into the water produce an immediate and fairly specific reaction in other fish of the same species (pheromones). The general areas in which pheromones have their most important uses are in reproductive behavior, individual recognition, and predator avoidance.

For reproductive behavior, pheromones are often important for recognition of both sex and sexual condition and may be necessary for the release of certain behavior patterns. In the frillfin goby (*Bathygobius soporator*), for example, a pheromone produced by the ovary will elicit courtship behavior in males, even in the absence of any females (Tavolga 1956). Similarly, blind gobies (*Typhlogobius californiensis*) react very differently to the invasion of their burrows by conspecifics depending on their sex; gobies of the same sex produce aggressive behavior, whereas those of the opposite sex produce more passive behavior. It has been demonstrated that this sexual recognition is accomplished largely through the detection of pheromones (MacGintie 1939).

In some species of fish, odors may be used not only to determine sex but also to identify individuals. In yellow bullheads (*Ictalurus natalis*) individuals recognize each other by odors and also associate the odors with rank in social hierarchies. Thus, a subordinate fish will avoid an area of an aquarium into which the water from the tank of a dominant fish has been introduced, even though the dominant fish is not present (Bardach and Todd 1970). Some cichlids can identify their own young on the basis of odor as well, at least during the three weeks or so when parental care is necessary (McKaye and Barlow 1976).

Predator avoidance by means of chemical signals is accomplished through the use of fear scents or *Schreckstoff*. These compounds are present in epidermal cells and are released into the water when the skin is broken. When the compound is detected, other fish of the same (or closely related) species immediately adopt some sort of predator avoidance behavior, such as diving into the vegetation, bunching up as a school, or becoming motionless. This ability is known mainly from fishes of the superorder Ostariophysi, although a few other fishes may possess it as well. Presumably, fear scents not only enhance the ability of the fishes to avoid predators (especially in turbid environments) but also inhibit cannibalism.

ELECTRICAL SIGNALS   Every time a muscle contracts, it gives off a small electrical discharge. Water containing dissolved minerals is a good conductor of electricity. These two facts together mean that electricity is a means of communication readily available to aquatic organisms. Thus, its use for communication has evolved independently in six groups of fishes (Rajidae, Torpedinidae, Mormyriformes, Gymnotoidei, Malapteruridae, and Uranoscopidae). Of these fishes, the mormyrids and the gymnotoids, both inhabitants of turbid tropical freshwaters (Chapters 18, 20), are most dependent on electricity for intraspecific signaling. The signals produced by the electric organs of these fishes can be modified in complex ways, by varying such factors as discharge frequency, wave form, and the times between discharges. As a consequence, electrical discharges can have all the functions visual and auditory signals have in other fishes, including courtship, agonistic behavior, and individual recognition.

Supplemental Readings   Endler 1978; Fine et al. 1977; Harden-Jones 1968; Krebs and Davies 1978; Leggett 1977; Radakov 1972; Shaw 1978.

PART III

The Fishes

ααααααααααααααααααααααααααααααααααααααααααααααααααααααααααααααααααααααααααα
~~~~~~

Evolution

The evolutionary history of fishes is a complex and fascinating topic that is just beginning to be well understood. However, the frequent lack of a good fossil record for critical periods of fish evolution, coupled with the diversity and specialized nature of both modern and fossil fish groups, makes controversies over relationships among the groups common. Even as the fossil record becomes better known, the controversies continue and increase, for as the paleontologist Alfred S. Romer has noted, the increasing knowledge of fossil forms often leads to a "triumphant loss of clarity." Partly for this reason, recent studies of the evolutionary relationships among fishes have relied heavily on comparisons among living forms and the use of analytical techniques (such as Hennig's cladistics) that produce less ambiguous results than the more arbitrary methods of the past (Patterson 1977). However, the results of the new inquiries into the evolutionary relationships of fishes still produce many contradictions. Thus, the relationships expressed here should be regarded as tentative and are necessarily over-simplified.

The chordate ancestors of fish and, of course, of vertebrates in general were presumably sessile forms that had free-swimming larvae for dispersal. The basic vertebrate organization gradually evolved as the larval stage became more active, perhaps as a means to increase the probability of the larvae landing on a suitable site for the adult stage. Eventually, however, larvae capable of reproduction evolved (neoteny), and finally, the sessile adult stage was lost altogether. One of the interesting, if actually unresolvable, controversies in fish evolution is whether these first steps took place in salt water or in fresh water. The marine origin theory (currently the most popular) holds that the typical vertebrate organization developed as neotenous larvae assumed a more and more pelagic existence in the oceans. The freshwater origin theory holds that the vertebrate organization developed in larvae of chordates that had invaded freshwater streams. Presumably, an evolutionary premium would be placed on a fishlike larva that could actively avoid being swept away by the currents. The actual evolutionary events may have taken place in both environments, with the early stages taking place in the sea and the later ones in fresh water.

Ostracoderms One of the main supports for the freshwater origin theory has been that the first known vertebrates, the ostracoderms (class Agnatha[1]), are largely known from freshwater deposits. However, the earliest known fossils of this group are pieces of broken bony armor from Upper Cambrian (490 million years B.P.) deposits that are marine in origin (Repetski 1978). Such fossils are also known from a number of marine Ordovician deposits. The first complete ostracoderm fossils are not found until the next period, the Silurian, which is well represented by freshwater deposits. By the time these fossils were laid down, extensive adaptive radiation had taken place and the four major ostracoderm orders currently recognized had evolved.

Considering the fact that the ostracoderms were the dominant vertebrates for the Silurian and part of the Devonian periods, roughly 80 million to 100 million years, it is not surprising that they were quite diverse. At the same time, they all had a basic body plan that seems to have limited their ability to become as ecologically diverse as later fish groups, which may explain in part why they eventually became extinct. The ostracoderms were characterized by the lack of jaws, the lack of paired fins, the presence of bony armor, an internal cartilaginous skeleton, and a heterocercal tail. In addition, most of them were quite small, less than 15 cm long. The overall body structure of the ostracoderms indicates that they were bottom dwellers that probably lived by sucking up organic ooze and small invertebrates. Their gills, which were quite large, presumably served as food filters as well as respiratory organs much like those of the primitive chordate, amphioxus. It may also be presumed that the ostracoderms moved about much as tadpoles do, since they lacked the control of movement granted by paired fins. Many of the later ostracoderms developed bony, finlike structures behind the gill openings that undoubtedly increased their stability and maneuverability. However, the habits of these advanced forms are a bit of a mystery because most of them also had reverse heterocercal tails (Fig. 12.1). Such a tail would tend to push the animals off the bottom. Perhaps such forms moved about by continual leaping off the bottom.

---

[1]The Agnatha were formerly divided into the Cyclostomata (living forms) and the ostracoderms, a system which has proved to be too artificial to be of value. The term "ostracoderm" (meaning shell-skinned) is still used, however, as a handy way of referring to the ancient armored agnathans.

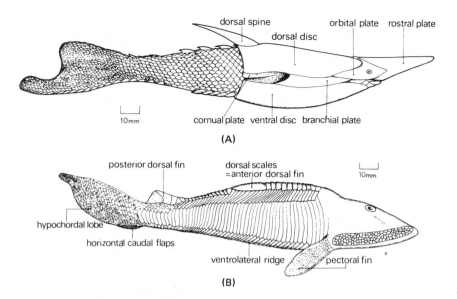

FIGURE 12.1 Ostracoderms: (A) *Pteropsis rostrata* (Pteraspidiformes); and (B) *Hemicyclaspis murchisoni* (Cephalaspidiformes). (From Moy-Thomas and Miles, 1971.)

The armor is one of the most interesting features of the ostracoderms because it represents the first true bone. It is generally assumed that the bony armor evolved for protection against predators, although its use as an osmotic barrier in freshwater forms and as a phosphate storage mechanism have also been suggested (Halstead 1968).

Thanks to the work of E. A. Stensio and his students, who carefully sectioned and analyzed numerous ostracoderm fossils, many other details of ostracoderm structure are also known, including a surprising amount about the structure of the nervous system. As a result of these studies, the ostracoderms can be divided into four distinct orders: Anaspidiformes, Cephalaspidiformes, Pteraspidiformes, and Thelodontiformes. The present-day lampreys (Petromyzoniformes) are apparently most closely related to the first two ostracoderm orders, whereas the hagfishes (Myxiniformes) are apparently most closely related to the last two. The lampreys are also an ancient group in their own right. Fossil lampreys remarkably similar to modern forms have been found in deposits from the Pennsylvanian period. Thus, it seems quite likely that the ostracoderms did give rise to the modern agnathans. It is unlikely, however, that they played any direct ancestral role in the history of the rest of the vertebrates; they seem to have diverged early from a common stock.

Placoderms

The first major group of fishes to appear after the ostracoderms was the placoderms (class Placodermi, meaning plate-skinned). Another group, the

Acanthodii, actually appeared earlier in the fossil record and are important as the earliest known jawed fishes. However, they remained a minor element of the fish fauna for millions of years. The placoderms, in contrast, dominated the seas of the late Devonian period and died out completely in the Mississippian period. They were a highly diverse group of fishes, often very bizarre in appearance. Because of their diversity, they may in fact be an artificial assemblage of fishes based on an inadequate fossil record. However, most of them have the following characteristics: a covering of dermal bony plates, an internal bony skeleton, paired fins, jaws, and a dorsoventrally compressed body (Fig. 12.2).

The development of this combination of characteristics permitted the placoderms to achieve a much greater ecological diversity than the ostracoderms. Indeed, the jaws, paired fins, and internal bony skeleton are characteristics fundamental to the bony fishes that eventually re-

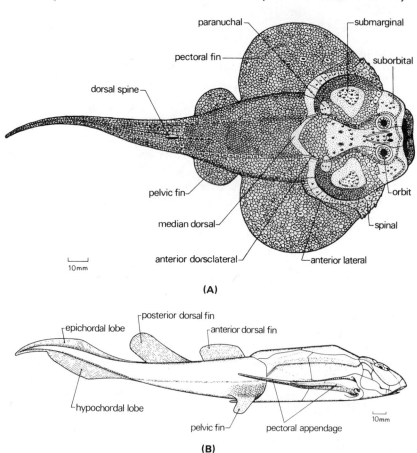

FIGURE 12.2 Placoderms: (A) *Gemuendina,* dorsal view (Rhenaniformes); and (B) *Bothriolepis* (Antiarchiformes). (From Moy-Thomas and Miles, 1971.)

CH. 12 EVOLUTION

placed them. At the same time, their bony armor, flattened bodies, and other specializations seem to have pretty much limited them to the role of bottom dwellers (with a few exceptions). Their success as bottom dwellers was considerable, and this is perhaps best attributed to the development of jaws (from the first gill arch), which enabled them to become predators. During their Devonian heyday, large jawed predators such as *Dunkleosteus* achieved lengths of 10 m or more. Curiously enough, the failure of the placoderms to evolve more advanced types of jaw suspension and true teeth, both characteristics of the Osteichythyes and Chondrichthyes, may have been partially responsible for their replacement by these two groups.

What is the significance of the placoderms in the evolution of modern fishes? No satisfactory answer to this question yet exists. They appear in the fossil record at a time when we would expect to find ancestors of the modern groups, yet they are so bizarre and specialized that it hardly seems possible they could have served as such ancestors. The major placoderm groups hardly even seem related to each other. As A. S. Romer (1966) indicated, it would make things much easier for students of fish evolution if the placoderms had never existed. There is some evidence, however, that the placoderms are related to the Chondrichthyes (Moy-Thomas and Miles 1971). If so, the two groups should be treated together under the heading (class or superclass) Elasmobranchiomorphi.

Acanthodians

The so-called spiny sharks (Acanthodii) are the oldest known jawed vertebrates (Silurian, about 440 million years B.P.), so they have long excited the interests of students of vertebrate evolution. Despite their early appearance in the fossil record, they were somewhat specialized forms. They were small (less than 20 cm long) with large eyes and flexible, streamlined bodies covered with bony, scalelike plates. However, their most distinctive feature was the rows of ventral paired fins, one row on each side and each fin preceded by a stout spine (Fig. 12.3). The number of fins in a row was variable, and the presence of the row is frequently

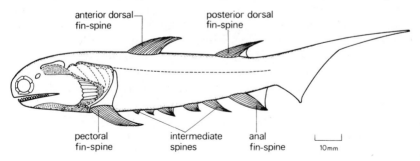

anterior dorsal fin-spine   posterior dorsal fin-spine

pectoral fin-spine   intermediate spines   anal fin-spine   10mm

FIGURE 12.3 Typical acanthodian, *Climatius reticulatus.* (From Moy-Thomas and Miles, 1971.)

cited as evidence of the fin-fold theory of the origin of paired fins (and limbs). The acanthodian fins would represent an intermediate stage between the primitive lateral folds that evolved as stabilizers on the presumably tadpolelike early fishes and the modern paired fins. Despite the presence of such "ancestral" characteristics, the acanthodians were successful occupiers of a presumably minnowlike niche in fresh water well into the Permian period, long after the much more abundant placoderms had become extinct.

The systematic position of the acanthodians, in relation to other fish groups, has been a subject of some controversy. Early workers usually placed them in with the placoderms, as just one more peculiar group, or considered them to be somehow related to the Chondrichthyes. In the 1960s and early 1970s, however, the Acanthodii became widely accepted as aberrant offshoots of the early Osteichthyes (e.g., Romer 1966; Moy-Thomas and Miles 1971), partly because their internal skeleton is partially ossified. However, recent work indicates that the true relationship of the acanthodians does seem to lie with the Chondrichthyes. Jarvik (1977) points out that they have a surprising number of anatomical similarities to modern sharks. These include similarities in dentition, the basically subterminal mouth (as opposed to the basically terminal mouth of osteichthyan fishes), similarities in the structure and suspension of the jaws and in the structure and position of the gill arches, similarities in the structure of the pectoral and caudal fins, scales, teeth, and spines that resemble those of sharks, and numerous similarities in the position of major nerves and blood vessels. Jarvik (1977) also points out that sharks pass through an embryonic stage in which they possess ventrolateral finfolds similar to those of acanthodians. From this evidence it seems likely that the acanthodians are a peculiar early offshoot of the same evolutionary line that gave rise to the sharks and should be treated as a subclass of the Chondrichthyes.

Chondrichthyes

The cartilaginous fishes (class Chondrichthyes) are an easier group to define than the Osteichthyes, partly because there are only 600 to 700 species and partly because the fossil groups (with a few exceptions) are so poorly known that the characteristics of the living forms suffice for the entire class. The group can be distinguished by the following features: skeleton, teeth, fins, lack of a swimbladder, spiral valve intestine, internal fertilization, and osmoregulation through the use of urea. The skeleton is always cartilaginous, although the cartilage may be calcified, giving it the appearance of bone. These characteristics are described in detail in Chapter 14. Internal fertilization is present in all modern forms, so the males all have claspers. However, well-preserved sharks from upper Devonian deposits lack claspers (e.g., *Cladoselache*).

The Chondrichthyes are the last major group of fishes to appear in the fossil record, and most deposits from which they are known are marine. This is in marked contrast to the bony fishes, which accomplished much of their early evolution in fresh water. Because the cartilaginous fishes appear considerably later in the fossil record than the placoderms and because certain placoderm groups do seem to have some characteristics in common with the Chondrichthyes, it is possible that the cartilaginous fishes were derived from the placoderms. If this is the case, then the cartilaginous fishes are derived from forms with bony skeletons. Within the Chondrichthyes there are two distinct evolutionary lines, going back independently perhaps as far as the placoderms: the subclass Elasmobranchi (sharks and rays) and the subclass Holocephali (chimaera).

Elasmobranchs   The elasmobranchs have been important predators in the oceans ever since the first sharklike forms appeared in the middle Devonian. Unfortunately, their lack of a bony skeleton means that good fossils are rare, although teeth and spines are often abundant as fossils. They seem to have achieved a successful combination of characteristics early in their evolution, and the greatest deviation from the basic body plan occurred when the skates and rays (superorder Batoidea) appeared in the Jurassic period. The characteristics that distinguish the elasmobranchs are: five to seven gill openings, plus a spiracle (secondarily lost in some forms); placoid scales; upper jaw not fused to cranium but attached with either amphistylic or hyostylic suspension (usually the latter in modern forms, which permits a large gape); and teeth numerous. With a few exceptions, elasmobranchs are top-level carnivores that are not particularly dependent on sight for prey capture (in contrast to most bony fishes).

The evolution of elasmobranchs is difficult to discuss, since it requires that leaps of imagination be made between the few well-preserved fossil forms and modern forms. The overall trend, however, is toward modest improvements of the basic Devonian shark design, with numerous side excursions into bottom-dwelling, invertebrate-feeding forms. The Devonian cladoselachian sharks (superorder Cladoselachimorpha, order Cladoselachiformes) were primitive in that they lacked claspers, had an elongate skull, had amphistylic jaw suspension, lacked an anal fin, and had broad-based, triangular, paired fins (Fig. 12.4). These early sharks had sharp, multicusped teeth (termed cladodont) and were undoubtedly predators on other fishes. However, as cephalopods and other molluscs radiated in the seas of the Carboniferous period (340 million to 280 million years B.P.), forms with flat, pavementlike teeth for crushing hard-shelled invertebrates became common. During the Permian period, the cladoselachians were replaced by the hybodont sharks (superorder Selachimorpha, order Hybodontiformes), which are considered to be ancestral to the modern sharks, skates, and rays. The hybodont sharks seem to have been adapted for feeding primarily on large, active invertebrates (e.g., squid), since they had sharp teeth for

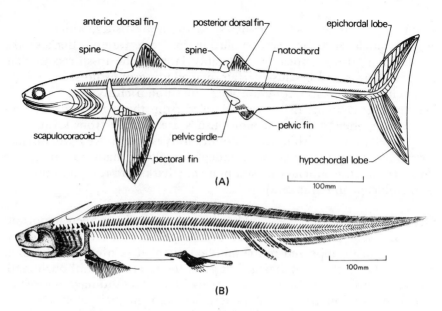

anterior dorsal fin
posterior dorsal fin
epichordal lobe
spine
spine
notochord
scapulocoracoid
pelvic girdle
pelvic fin
pectoral fin
hypochordal lobe
100mm
(A)

100mm
(B)

FIGURE 12.4 Devonian Chondrichthyes: (A) *Cladoselache;* and (B) *Xenacanthus,* a freshwater form. (From Moy-Thomas and Miles, 1971.)

biting in the front of their jaws but blunt teeth for crushing in the rear. During the Jurassic period (180 million to 130 million years B.P.), the hybodonts apparently gave rise to the modern lines of elasmobranchs: the three lines of sharks largely adapted for preying on bony fishes, albeit with many exceptions to this rule, and the skates and rays (Batoidea), which are largely adapted for feeding on benthic invertebrates (also with many exceptions!). It should be emphasized, however, that ideas concerning the relationships of modern elasmobranchs are in a state of flux.

Chimaeras

The Chimaeras (subclass Holocephali, order Chimaeriformes) are a strange group of bottom-dwelling, invertebrate-feeding fishes that have been present in small numbers apparently since the upper Devonian period. Among their more distinctive characteristics are: an operculum that covers four gill openings, no spiracle, an upper jaw fused to the skull, teeth consisting only of a few large, flat plates, no scales, and males with a clasper on the head, in addition to ones on the pelvic fins. Early "chimaeras" are known only from teeth, so their inclusion in the Holocephali is problematical. Modern-type chimaeras first appear in the Jurassic period.

Osteichthyes

The bony fishes (class Osteichthyes) are a large, diverse group, with a fairly rich fossil record. For this reason, they are a hard group to define precisely.

CH. 12 EVOLUTION

There is no one feature which distinguishes them, but rather a common structural pattern, combined with the absence of the features characterizing the Chondrichthyes and Agnatha. The most distinctive elements of the osteichthyan structural pattern are the presence of lungs, bone, scales, and lepidotrichia.

Lungs (represented as swimbladders in "derived" forms) are an ancestral characteristic of bony fishes that presumably indicates that the early steps of bony fish evolution took place in the fresh waters of a tropical region, where the ability to breathe air would be decidedly advantageous (as it still is) as protection against periods of stagnation. The history of the development of the lungs into a swimbladder that acts primarily as a hydrostatic organ is an interesting one, since it reflects the overall structural changes that have taken place in the course of bony fish evolution. The first lungs were probably ventral outpouchings of the gut that evolved in fishes that had originally increased their survival rates in stagnant waters by swallowing bubbles of air and exchanging oxygen and carbon dioxide through the gut. Ventral lungs still characterize the South American and African lungfishes (Lepidosirenidae) and tetrapods. However, such lungs present problems to fish that swim about actively, since a pocket of air under the gut tends to make a fish top-heavy and subject to rolling over. The primitive solution to this problem seems to have been the development of a dorsal lung with a ventral opening. This situation is still found in the Australian lungfish (*Neoceratodus*). The next step, found in most modern bony fishes, is to have a dorsal "lung" with a dorsal connection. Such swimbladders function primarily as hydrostatic organs. In many advanced forms, the connection to the gut is lost altogether and gases enter and leave the swimbladder entirely through the circulatory system. In addition, a number of teleosts have lost the swimbladder as well, largely as an adaptation to a bottom-dwelling existence.

Bone, or at least some ossification, is present in most Osteichthyes, but it may be secondarily lost in a few forms such as the sturgeons and paddlefishes (Chondrostei) and the lungfishes (Dipneusti). The skeletal structure of the head, although quite variable, also seems to have a general osteichthyan pattern, particularly in relation to the importance of dermal bone in making up the skull and jaws. **Scales** can also be considered dermal bone. In more primitive fishes, particularly fossil forms, scales (of several different types) have a distinct bony layer and a very solid-appearing construction. Scales, like bone and swimbladder, may be secondarily lost in some groups of fishes. **Lepidotrichia,** like scales, are of dermal origin. They form the soft rays of the fins and are segmented.

True bony fishes appear suddenly and well diversified in the fossil record of the middle Devonian period. Most of these early bony fish are from freshwater deposits, a good indication that bony fishes in general originally evolved in fresh water. The three major subclasses of the class Osteichthyes appear in the fossil record nearly simultaneously: Dipneusti (lungfishes), Crossopterygii (fringe-finned fishes), and Actinopterygii (ray-finned fishes). A fourth subclass, the Brachiopterygii, is represented only by the Polypteridae (bichirs and reedfish), a modern family of uncertain affinities, but probably closest to the primitive actinopterygians. The Dipneusti and Crossopterygii are frequently placed together in the Sarcopterygii (lobe-finned fishes).

Lungfishes   The lungfishes (subclass Dipneusti) have been a very conservative group in their evolution and have never achieved much diversity of form. However, their evolutionary history is well known because they have lived throughout their history in fresh waters prone to stagnation and drying up and hence conducive to the making of fossils. On the basis of these fossils, the amount of change from the earliest known forms to the present-day forms has been plotted (Fig. 12.5). Lungfish evolution seems to have been most rapid early in their history, but the rate of change has been extremely slow for the past 200 million years or so. This change in lungfish over their history has largely been one of reduction, e.g., reduction in the amount of bone, loss of various hard layers from the scales, reduction in the number of skull bones, loss of the separation between the dorsal, caudal, and anal fins. Besides lungs and a largely cartilaginous skeleton, modern lungfishes are characterized by internal nostrils, platelike teeth, and a spiral valve intestine. Because they do seem to represent an intermediate condition between "true" fishes and amphibians, lungfishes were often considered to be ancestral to the tetrapods. The lungfishes are so specialized, however, that this seems very unlikely. Instead, they are just a moderately successful group of freshwater fishes with a long independent evolutionary history.

Crossopterygians   The fringe-finned fishes (subclass Crossopterygii) were the dominant predators of the fresh waters of the Devonian period. This group seems to have two distinct evolutionary lines, the rhipidistians (superorder Osteolepimorpha) and the coelacanths (superorder Coelacanthamorpha). The rhipidistians are of special interest to students of vertebrate evolution because they are intermediate in many ways between the first amphibians (Labyrinthodontia) and fish. Indeed, some authorities prefer to place the rhipidistians and the labyrinthodont amphibians together in one group. The most dramatic characteristics that link the crossopterygians and the early amphibians are the lobed fins, means of jaw suspension, and the structure of the teeth (Fig. 12.6). The fins are lobed because they contain a series of bony elements that link them to the pelvic and pectoral girdles, much like tetrapod legs. The jaw suspension, like that of tetrapods, is autostylic, and the jaw connects directly to the brain case. The teeth have the complex foldings of the enamel—visible as grooves on the outside of each tooth—that are also found in labyrinthodont

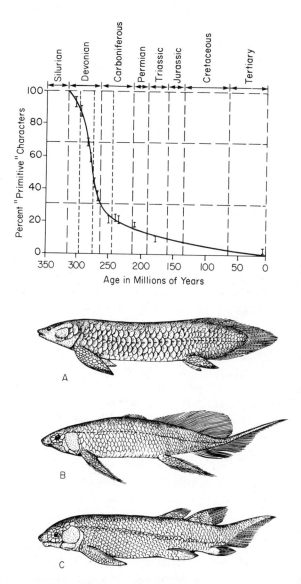

FIGURE 12.5 Rate of evolutionary change in lungfishes, from primitive characteristics (defined as those possessed by the Devonian genus *Dipnorhynchus*) to advanced characteristics (those of the modern genus *Protopterus*). (After Westoll, 1949.) The lungfishes illustrated are: (A) *Neoceratodus* (recent); (B) *Scanmenacia* (late Devonian); and (C) *Dipterus* (middle Devonian).

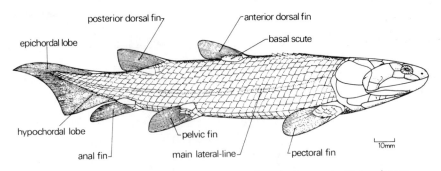

FIGURE 12.6 A rhipidistian crossopterygian, *Osteolepis macrolepidotus.* (From Moy-Thomas and Miles, 1971.)

("labyrinth tooth") amphibians. A very distinctive characteristic of fossil crossopterygians is the presence of cosmine, a complex tissue making up much of their external covering, including the scales. The three layers of the cosmine are penetrated by a system of canals which open to the surface through pores. It has been proposed that this canal system served for electroreception (Thomson 1977). Thomson has also proposed that an important function of cosmine was to store minerals and other nutrients, since it is frequently found partially resorbed. The early crossopterygians were mostly armored, air-breathing predators of tropical freshwater environments. The rhipidistians became extinct by the lower Permian period, replaced by the amphibians to which they gave rise. The coelacanths pursued a more typically fishlike mode of existence as marine, bottom-oriented predators. They evolved a three-lobed tail (diphycercal) with the vertebral column entering the middle lobe. This tail is essentially homocercal in function and, when coupled with the large swimbladder, presumably permitted a free-swimming existence. They completely disappeared from the fossil record during the Cretaceous period. It was thus a major ichthyological event when in 1938 coelacanths (*Latimeria chalumnae*) were discovered to be still living in the deep waters off the African coast, in the Indian Ocean (see Chapter 15).

Ray-Finned Fishes

The subclass Actinopterygii contains most of the bony fish species that exist today. However, when they first appeared in the fossil record, in Devonian freshwater deposits, they were uncommon. By the beginning of the Mississippian (Carboniferous) period some 340 million years ago, they had become the dominant freshwater fishes and had begun their invasion of the seas. The history of this group is one of constant change, with continuous "improvements" being made on the basic fish design, culminating in the modern teleosts. Because of their enormous diversity and change through time, it is difficult to define the Actinopterygii precisely, although, by and large, they have bone-based scales, fins that are attached to the body by the fin rays (rather than with a fleshy lobe), branchiostegal rays, and no internal nostrils. The Actinopterygii can be divided into three infraclasses; Chondrostei, Holostei, and Teleostei. There is considerable diversity of structure within each infraclass, and some fossil groups are intermediate in structure, so the infraclasses are not tightly defined but can be looked upon as representing a common level of organization.

CHONDROSTEANS   The Chondrostei are the original ray-finned fishes, achieving their greatest abundance and diversity in the Mississippian and Pennsylvanian periods. The most important order within this group is the Palaeonisciformes, because the most primitive and most numerous forms are placed within it and because its members probably gave rise to most of the holosteans. All modern chondrosteans (25 species) belong to the order Acipenseriformes, with its two highly specialized families, Acipenseridae (sturgeons) and Polyodontidae (paddlefishes) (see Chapter 16).

The ancient chondrosteans developed many of the body shapes, and presumably ways of living, that also characterize the more "derived" groups (Fig. 12.7). However, they also have many structural features

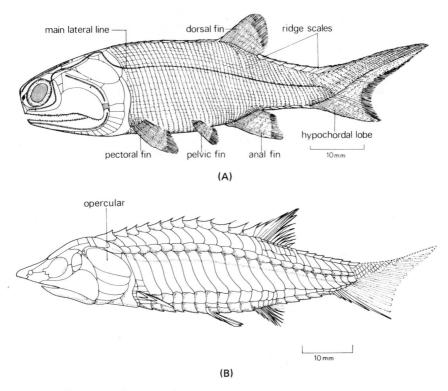

(A)

(B)

FIGURE 12.7   Fossil Chondrostei: (A) *Moythomasia* (Devonian); and (B) *Phanerorhynchus* (Pennsylvanian). (From Moy-Thomas and Miles, 1971.)

considered to be ancestral because the fishes that replaced the chondro-steans had either lost or modified them. Among these features are (1) heavy ganoid scales (so called because the outer enamel layer is made up of a distinct substance, ganoine); (2) presence of a spiracle; (3) hetero-cercal tail; and (4) a cranium consisting of three strongly fused units of bone. In more derived fishes the structure of the skull is more complex and flexible, especially in relation to the jaws.

HOLOSTEANS   Just where the infraclass Chondrostei ends and that of the Holostei begins is difficult to say. There are a number of groups that are treated by some experts as chondrosteans and by others as holosteans. Romer (1966) solves this problem in part by referring to such forms informally as subholosteans. A similar problem exists in separating the primitive teleosts from the advanced holosteans. This has caused some recent students of fish interrelationships to put holosteans and teleosts together in one infraclass, the Neopterygii (Patterson 1973), and others to erect another infraclass (Halecostomi) for the intermediate forms (Nelson 1976). To complicate matters further, it appears that the two living groups of holosteans, the gars (Semionotiformes, Lepisosteidae) and the bowfin (Amiiformes, Amiidae), are the result of independent evolutionary lines going back to the chondrosteans. These two groups are the only remnants of the fish group that dominated the seas and fresh waters through most of the Triassic, Jurassic, and lower Cretaceous periods (Fig. 12.8). In this long period a wide variety of forms developed, approaching the teleosts in the diversity of body shapes. The inter-mediate nature of the holosteans is reflected in their distinguishing characteristics:

1. The tail is heterocercal in internal structure, but the upper and lower lobes are nearly symmetrical, often giving the impression externally that the tail is homocercal.
2. The scales have lost the layer of dentine found in most chondrosteans, and the ganoine layer may be lost as well in some ad-vanced forms.
3. There is a marked reduction in the number of fin rays, usually to correspond to the number of internal skeletal elements. This results in greater control over fin movements.
4. The spiracle is absent.
5. There has been considerable modification of the structure of the skull and jaws, in the direction of teleost flexibility, to permit a greater diversity of feeding methods.

TELEOSTS   Unlike the holosteans, which seem to have multiple origins within the chondrosteans, the Teleostei seem to be derived from one advanced holostean group, the Pholidophoriformes. This group appears to be closely related to the Leptolepiformes, a generalized fossil group

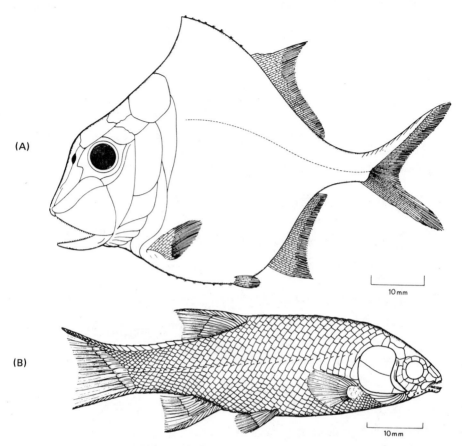

FIGURE 12.8 Jurassic holosteans: (A) *Platysomus;* and (B) *Acentrophorus.* (From Moy-Thomas and Miles, 1971.)

(Triassic to Cretaceous) usually placed in the teleosts on the basis of their homocercal tail. From either the pholidophorids or the leptolepids, four distinct lines of teleosts seem to have developed (Fig. 12.9). The first line consists (in the modern fauna, at least) solely of the two very distinctive and peculiar freshwater orders Osteoglossiformes (bony-tongues) and Mormyriformes (African electric fishes). The osteoglossids are an ancient group and consequently important to the study of fish zoogeography. The second line includes three rather disparate orders: Elopiformes (tarpons), Anguilliformes (eels), and Notacanthiformes (spiny eels). The third line consists of the highly specialized (for plankton feeding) Clupeiformes. The fourth line (Euteleostei) is the main line of teleost evolution, containing everything not placed in the first three divisions. The superorder Protacanthopterygii (pikes, trouts, galaxiids, etc.) is considered to contain the most generalized (primitive) members of this division, while the superorder Acanthopterygii (perches, etc.) is con-

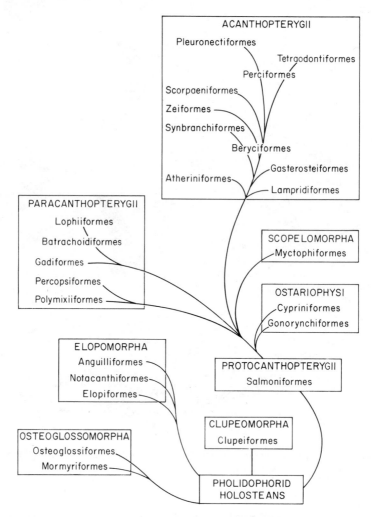

FIGURE 12.9 Probable phylogenetic relationships of major teleost groups, greatly modified from Greenwood et al. (1966), Rosen (1973), and Patterson (1977).

sidered to contain the most advanced members on the basis of structure and behavior. Successful offshoots of the main line of evolution are the superorders Ostariophysi (minnows, catfishes, etc.), Scopelomorpha (miscellaneous deepsea forms), and Paracanthopterygii (codfishes, anglerfishes, etc.). The Ostariophysi may actually be a fourth, distinct line of teleost evolution, independent from the Protacanthopterygii. It should be emphasized that the interrelationships of the major teleost groups are still a matter of considerable debate, stimulated initially by the provisional classification system of Greenwood et al. (1966) and continued in such papers as Rosen (1973), Patterson and Rosen (1977), and Patterson (1977).

Despite the presence of these distinct evolutionary lines within the teleosts, the modern teleosts are a fairly cohesive group with a number of distinctive characteristics:

1. The tail is homocercal.
2. The scales, referred to as bony-ridge scales, are made up of two thin layers of unmineralized bone and lack ganoine.
3. The vertebrae are completely ossified and reduced in number from the holosteans. Because of their structure, they are lighter and stronger as well.
4. The swimbladder is reduced in size and functions primarily as a hydrostatic organ.
5. The skull is highly modified and variable in structure. The number of bones in the lower jaw is reduced, and the premaxilla tends to be the principal bone of the upper jaw.
6. The fins are highly maneuverable, giving teleosts good control over their movements.
7. The body shape is amazing in its variety, and a large number of the species are quite small (less than 30 cm long), enabling the teleosts to occupy niches and habitats not previously available to fishes.

Overall, the trend in teleost evolution, as well as actinopterygian evolution in general, has been toward fish capable of rapid and complex movements, with an efficient respiratory system, and capable of utilizing a wide variety of food resources.

Structural Changes in Actinopterygians

Scales. The general trend in scales has been a reduction in heaviness and complexity, along with an increase in flexibility. The heavy scales of chondrosteans must have served as a moderately flexible suit of armor. Such armor was a definite improvement over the solid sheets of bone used by the placoderms but still a heavy burden to carry around. It is probably significant that the surviving chondrosteans (sturgeons and paddlefishes) have no scales at all over most of their bodies. The typical holostean scale, as found on modern gars, still had three layers, but the general trend in the group was to reduce the heaviness of these layers. This culminated in the thin, two-layered, bony-ridge scale of the teleosts, which is light and flexible. Many teleosts have gone a step further and eliminated scales altogether.

Branchiostegal rays. In fossil chondrosteans the floor of the branchial cavity is rather rigid, so water had to move across the gills by movements of the operculum, through the spiracle, or by simply being rammed across during swimming. The branchiostegal rays developed from bones in the floor of the branchial cavity. This increased the efficiency of active pumping of water across the gills. The efficiency of the two-pump respiratory system is further increased by the modification of one branchiostegal ray on each side to become part of the gill cover, as the interopercular bone. This bone, a definitive feature of holosteans and teleosts, increased the size of the opercular cavity and hence the amount of water that can flow across the gills. A secondary, but equally important, function of the branchiostegal rays has been to permit the development of the feeding methods based on suction rather than grabbing. Thus, the evolution of branchiostegal rays has been an important factor in the development of teleost diversity. Within the holosteans and teleosts there is a general trend toward decreasing the number of branchiostegal rays, although a reverse trend is present in some groups.

Swimbladder. Presumably, the swimbladder in the earliest actinopterygians functioned primarily as a lung, as it did for other bony fish groups. The general trend in actinopterygian evolution has been to increase the importance of the swimbladder's hydrostatic function and to decrease its importance in respiration. In most "ancestral" teleosts the swimbladder is still connected to the gut by a tube, but the tube functions primarily as a means for regulating the volume of gas in the bladder necessary for adjustments of buoyancy. In derived teleosts and in deepsea forms, even this connection is lost. In teleosts the swimbladder is also reduced in size. A final trend in swimbladder evolution is for it to assume other functions in addition to being a hydrostatic organ. In many teleosts it serves as an amplifier of sound waves for hearing, and in a number of derived teleosts it is used for sound production as well. So specialized has the swimbladder become for nonrespiratory functions that most teleosts adapted for surviving in stagnant waters have developed other means for breathing air.

Jaws. In the course of actinopterygian evolution the jaws changed from being rigid, toothed structures adapted for biting and grabbing to much more flexible structures, often without teeth, adapted for feeding by a wide variety of methods. This is best illustrated by following the changes in the two principal bones of the upper jaw, the maxilla and premaxilla. In chondrosteans these bones are firmly united to the skull. The maxilla is the main bone of the upper jaw and possesses many sharp teeth. In holosteans and some primitive teleosts, the maxilla is reduced in size and is firmly attached to the skull only by its anterior portions. The premaxilla is greatly increased in size, and both bones still carry teeth. This arrangement developed in conjunction with branchiostegal rays and seems to be an intermediate step in the development of suction feeding. In most derived teleosts, the premaxilla is the dominant bone of the upper jaw and is largely free of strong attachments to other bones, so it can be easily extended. The maxilla in these fishes has become a sort of lever to increase the protrusibility of the premaxilla. The maxilla is usually without teeth, and they are frequently absent from the premaxilla as well. One of the results of having this type of mouth structure is that biting and chewing have to take place at some location other than the rim of the mouth. Thus, predatory fish with protrusible pre-maxillae more often than not have pharyngeal teeth for this purpose. The flexible mouth also permits other types of feeding specializations to develop, such as plankton straining. In this case the O-shaped mouth opening is very efficient because it provides the maximum opening with the minimum perimeter. (The mouth opening of fish that feed by biting tends to be elliptical.) It should be noted, however, that suction feeding is most characteristic of the smaller invertebrate-feeding teleosts and that large piscivorous forms tend to have a firm biting mouth with teeth.

Tail.   The original actinopterygian tail was heterocercal, but there seems to have been an inexorable trend in actinopterygian evolution toward the symmetrical, homocercal tail. Even in holosteans, which by and large have a tail that is structurally heterocercal, the tail is often externally symmetrical. The development of the homocercal tail is presumably related in large part to the development of the swimbladder and neutral buoyancy, which eliminate the need for a heterocercal tail to provide lift. The homocercal tail is also advantageous for fast-swimming, pelagic forms (because it delivers uniform thrust) and for small, maneuverable forms that require a tail in which each ray can be controlled, for precise movements.

Fins.   Two of the most important trends in fin structure have been the addition of spines and the changes in the positions of the pelvic and pectoral fins. True spines are characteristic of advanced teleosts. Spines are antipredator devices that are usually best developed in fishes that cannot rely on speed to escape from their predators. Their development followed the loss of heavy bony scales and coincided with changes in the relative positions of the pelvic and pectoral fins. Basically, in advanced teleosts the pelvic fins are located immediately below, or even slightly anterior to, the pectoral fins, whereas in most other actinopterygians the pelvic fins are well behind the pectorals. The anterior positioning of the pelvic fins is associated with an increase in the maneuverability of the fish, since they are used for assisting the pectoral fins in controlling movement, rather than functioning primarily as stabilizers. The anterior positioning of the pelvic fins is also associated with the development of deep-bodied forms, since even in deep-bodied chondrosteans and holosteans the pelvic fins occupied a more anterior position than they did in elongate forms.

Supplemental Readings   Greenwood et al. 1966; Halstead 1968; Jarvik 1977; Moy-Thomas and Miles 1971; Nelson 1976; Orvig 1968; Robertson 1957; Romer 1966; Schaeffer 1967; Thomson 1969, 1972; Westoll 1949.

CHAPTER 13

Lampreys and Hagfishes

Superclass Agnatha
Class Cephalaspidimorpha
  Order Petromyzoniformes (lampreys)
    Families Petromyzonidae, Geotriidae, Mordaciidae
Class Pteraspidomorpha
  Order Myxiniformes (hagfishes)
    Families Myxinidae, Eptatretidae

The lampreys and hagfishes, being agnathans, are not really fish. Nevertheless, ichthyologists have gladly adopted them for study because they are aquatic vertebrates that typically occur in association with true fish, often preying or scavenging on them as well. In addition, they are fascinating creatures in their own right. Although superficially similar, the two main groups of living agnathans, lampreys and hagfishes, are in fact extremely different (Table 13-1). The main characteristics they have in common, besides eel-like bodies, are the general agnathan traits such as absence of jaws, absence of paired fins, and cartilaginous skeletons. Despite their primitive structural features, lampreys and hagfishes are both highly successful groups that are more abundant than most people realize.

Lampreys   Lampreys have acquired an evil reputation in modern times because some species feed on fishes also favored by humans, especially salmon and trout. Their habit of latching on to the sides of fish and sucking their blood and other body juices has caused them to be placed in the "nasty creature" category, along with vampires and leeches. This is despite the fact that their prey often survives the attack, which is not

194

TABLE 13-1
Characteristics of Adult Lampreys and Hagfishes

Characteristics	Lampreys	Hagfishes
Dorsal fins	One or two; well developed in adult	None or only a trace
Pre-anal fin	Absent	Present
Eyes	Moderately developed	Highly degenerate
Oculomotor muscles in eye	Present	Absent
Oral disc	Present	Absent
Teeth	On both tongue and disc	On tongue plus one on "palate"
Barbels	Absent	Present
Intestine	Ciliated	Unciliated
Spiral fold of intestine	Present	Absent
Buccal glands	Present	Absent
Nasohypophysial opening	On top of head	In front of head
Nasohypophysial sac	Not opening into pharynx	Opening into pharynx
Number of gills	Always 7	5 to 14
External gill openings	7, close to head	1 or 5 to 14, remote from head
Internal gills opening	Into a single suboesophageal tube communicating with oral cavity	Separately and directly into pharynx
Gill pouches	Ectodermal origin	Endodermal origin
Skull	Mostly cartilaginous with incomplete roof	Roof entirely membranous and feebly developed
Branchial skeleton	A conspicuous basketwork	Rudimentary
Neural arches	Present but rudimentary	Lacking
Dorsal and ventral roots of spinal nerves	Distinct	United
Ductus Cuvieri of heart	Left one obliterated	Right one obliterated
Kidney	Mesonephros	Pronephros anteriorly, mesonephros posteriorly
Eggs	Small, unkeratinized, and without hooks	Very large, keratinized, and with hooks
Segmentation	Holoblastic	Meroblastic

Source: With permission from C. L. Hubbs and I. C. Potter (1971), Distribution, phylogeny and taxonomy, in M. W. Hardisty and I. C. Potter, eds., *The Biology of Lampreys.* Copyright by Academic Press, Inc. (London) Ltd.

true of the prey of more conventional predators, and that they have some value as a gourmet food item themselves.[1] Lampreys are also useful as experimental animals, but particularly for neurobiological studies (Rovainen 1979).

Structure. The most distinctive feature of adult lampreys is their oral disc, with its numerous toothlike plates of keratin that cover the disc and tongue in species-specific patterns (Fig. 13.1a). These plates are used for grasping the prey and rasping the hole through which the fluids and tissues are sucked. Other features of lampreys (Table 13-1), particularly the large eyes and gills that do not require the intake of water through the mouth, also reflect the efficient means by which lampreys have been able to take advantage of the abundant fishes that replaced their ostracoderm ancestors. The sexes of spawning lampreys may be distinguished by the presence of an anal fin (ventral fin fold) on the female and of a penislike structure (genital papilla) on the male.

The larval lamprey (ammocoetes), in contrast to the adult, is adapted for living a secretive life buried in the mud of river backwaters, where it filter-feeds on algae and detritus. Structurally, the ammocoetes is the most ancestral living vertebrate and is so different from the adult that the two were not connected until 1856. The eyes of ammocoetes are located beneath the skin of the head and are barely functional. In fact, the most important light-sensing organs are photosensitive cells in the tail. The fins are also barely visible and consist mostly of a low dorsal fold with a notch in the end to form the caudal fin. The most conspicuous feature of the ammocoetes is the expanded pharynx, which is used for both respiration and feeding. Water is drawn into the pharynx by the movements of a special muscular structure (velum) in the anterior portion and by expansion and contaction of the posterior portion (branchial cavity). The water departs through seven gill slits on each side. In gill filaments and in the walls of the pharynx are goblet cells that secrete mucus. The mucus traps the particulate matter drawn into the pharynx and is swallowed in a continuous stream. Some mucus is also secreted to help stabilize the walls of the burrows in which the ammocoetes live.

Distribution. Of the approximately 40 species of lamprey, four are known from temperate areas of the southern hemisphere, in South America, New Zealand, and Australia (families Geotriidae with one species and Mordaciidae with three species). The rest of the lampreys are placed in the family Petromyzonidae and are found in coastal drainages throughout the northern hemisphere.

Life history. One of the most fascinating aspects of lamprey biology is the presence of two distinct life history patterns. The most notorious lamprey species are those that migrate as adults to the ocean

---

[1] It should be noted, however, that Henry I of England died after overindulging himself with a dish of cooked lampreys.

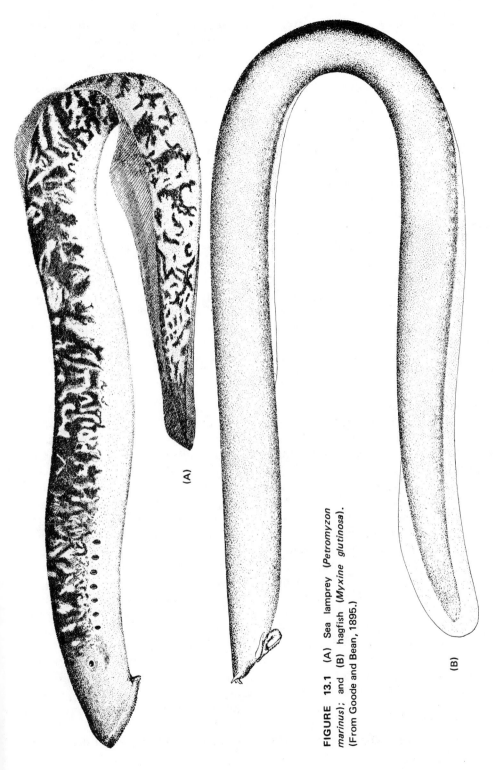

(A)

(B)

FIGURE 13.1 (A) Sea lamprey (Petromyzon marinus); and (B) hagfish (Myxine glutinosa). (From Goode and Bean, 1895.)

or large bodies of fresh water, where they prey on fishes. Many of these predatory forms have given rise to nonmigratory "satellite species" that do not feed as adults (Vladykov and Kott 1979). The nonpredatory adults have poorly developed teeth, are small in size (usually less than 20 cm total length), and often inhabit small streams or streams located a great distance from the ocean or other sources of large fish. The adult stage generally lasts less than 6 months. Predatory species are most abundant as spawners in short coastal streams, but they may migrate as much as 250 km to 300 km up large streams. The adult stage of these species may last up to 2 years, although 6 months to 8 months of this time may be taken up with migrations, during which they do not feed. When feeding, they prey on a wide variety of fishes, concentrating on larger species. Vision seems to be the sense most involved in prey location, although there is some evidence that smell may be used as well. The lampreys grow rapidly on their diet of fish. Species that spend the predatory stage in the ocean reach a total length of 30 cm to 80 cm; those that spend this stage in fresh water seldom exceed 30 cm. The differences in sizes achieved by adults with different life history strategies is well illustrated by the lampreys of the Klamath River in Oregon and California. The anadromous Pacific lamprey (*Entosphenus tridentata*) may reach lengths of 60 cm to 70 cm in this river. However, a landlocked version (*E. similis*), which preys on fishes in the lakes and reservoirs of the upper river, typically reaches only 20 cm to 30 cm. The two nonpredaceous species recently described from this area seldom exceed 20 cm as adults. There is an interesting exception to this size rule, however. *E. minima*, known only from Miller Lake in the Klamath drainage of Oregon, was a predatory species (it is now extinct) that was similar in size to the nonpredatory forms.

Regardless of the size and feeding habits of the adults, the life cycle of lampreys from the time of spawning, through the ammocoetes stage, and through the period of metamorphosis varies little from species to species. The spawning adults generally choose a shallow, gravel-bottomed riffle as a spawning site, and spawning takes place in the late winter or early spring. The males tend to arrive first at the spawning site, and each begins to construct a nest depression by latching onto the larger stones in the site and pulling them downstream. Apparently attracted by olfactory cues released by the male, one or more females move into the nest site and help with nest construction. Spawning of each pair takes place repeatedly over a week or more. The eggs fall into the interstices of the gravel and then adhere to the gravel. The number of eggs per female varies with the species. The females of the anadromous sea lamprey (*Petromyzon marinus*) contain 124,000 to 260,000 eggs, whereas most of the females of nonpredatory lampreys only contain 1000 to 2000 eggs.

Newly hatched ammocoetes swim out of the nest and drift with the currents until they are swept into an area with a muddy bottom. They burrow into the mud and feed with only their oral hoods sticking out above the surface. The currents created by their feeding apparatus bring a steady stream of diatoms, desmids, detritus, and small invertebrates to the animal, although local depletions of digestible material apparently cause the ammocoetes to change positions frequently. This stage usually lasts 3 years to 5 years, and the ammocoetes may grow to a total length in excess of 10 cm.

Lampreys as predators. Under normal conditions, lampreys are "prudent" predators that do not seriously deplete the populations of their prey species. In some instances, prey species may have a very high incidence of scars from lamprey attacks. Such scars indicate that at least some (and perhaps most) of the fish lampreys attack survive the experience. The attacks may seriously reduce the growth of the prey, but at least it is capable of reproducing itself. The outstanding exception to this general set of circumstances was the near-extinction of many fish populations following the invasion of the Great Lakes by sea lamprey. The lamprey moved into Lake Ontario about 1890 and into Lake Erie, via the Welland Canal, about 1921. By 1936 they were established in Lakes Huron and Michigan, and 10 years later they were established in Lake Superior. Following the invasion of each lake, the populations of the large fish species, such as lake trout, burbot, and lake whitefish, collapsed, as did the fisheries for them. The only exception to this was Lake Erie, which is too warm for the lampreys and has few streams suitable for spawning. An intensive research program following the disaster made the life cycle of the sea lamprey one of the best known of any aquatic vertebrate (Applegate 1950) and eventually resulted in the development of a poison that is rather specific for ammocoetes. Through the use of this lampricide and other control measures, the lamprey populations have been knocked down, and most of the prey species have recovering populations. However, the lamprey will never be eradicated from the Great Lakes, so continued control measures will be required to maintain the fish populations in them. It is interesting to note that in Cayuga Lake, New York, the sea lamprey manages to coexist with many of the same species that were depleted by lamprey predation in the Great Lakes. This seems to be a situation where predator and prey occurred together naturally and have coadapted so that both survive. Given enough time, presumably the same thing would happen to the Great Lakes! It is also worth noting that the control programs in Great Lakes' streams may be having a severely detrimental effect on the native nonpredaceous lampreys, which are also killed by the lampricide.

Hagfishes   Besides being eel-like agnathans, one of the main characteristics hagfishes have in common with lampreys is that they are not loved by fishermen.

They live in part by scavenging dead and dying fishes, so it is not uncommon for marine commercial fishermen who use set-lines or gill nets to find fish in their nets that have been burrowed into by hagfish and may in fact still contain one or more of them. As if this were not enough, once on deck the hagfish secrete incredible amounts of slime that sticks to both deck and fishermen (the stem *myxin* even means slime). However, they are a comparatively minor nuisance and more than make up for it by their value as objects of study for biologists.

Structure. Hagfish are remarkable for their lack of striking external features (Fig. 13.1b). Linnaeus even classified them as worms! The most conspicuous structures are the three pairs of barbels around the nostrils and mouth, which are used as tactile organs. The single nostril connects to the pharynx and functions as the water intake for both respiration and the sense of smell. The eyes are rudimentary, visible mainly as shallow depressions on the top of the head. The ventral mouth is somewhat inconspicuous but contains a tongue with four rows of keratinized "teeth." These teeth work against each other and a cartilaginous dental plate to form a jawlike structure that is capable of tearing out pieces of flesh from a dead fish. Along the sides of the body are 1 to 14 gill openings and a long series of pores that are the openings for the slime glands.

Life history. Approximately 30 to 35 species of hagfishes are known, all of them marine. Most are found in water deeper than 25 m, at temperatures of less than 13°C, which means they are largely confined to temperate seas. Members of the family Myxinidae are generally found in association with muddy bottoms, into which they burrow and search for soft-bodied invertebrates as food. Members of the family Eptatretidae, the common forms off the west coast of North America, seem to be less inclined to burrow and are often associated with rocky bottoms. Although they prey extensively on invertebrates, hagfish apparently are also important scavengers on the ocean floor.

Hagfish are unknown from the stomachs of predatory fish. It appears that their main defense mechanism is their mucus, with which they can coat themselves in large quantities quite quickly. The mucus may also be used to coat dead fish and other "carrion" they encounter on the bottom, thereby making it unpalatable to other scavengers such as rattails. In order to clear their gill openings and body surface of a heavy load of mucus, hagfish have developed the remarkable ability to tie themselves in a knot, which passes down the body, pushing the mucus away. The knotting behavior is also useful in giving hagfish extra leverage when taking a bite out of a large fish and perhaps in escaping capture by predators as well.

Little is known about reproduction in hagfish, except that each female lays only a small number (20 to 30) of large (2 cm to 3 cm), leathery eggs. The eggs have small hooklike structures on their ends for attaching to the bottom and to each other. When the young hatch from the eggs, they are essentially miniature adults, so they do not undergo the dramatic metamorphosis of lampreys.

Supplemental Readings

Applegate 1950; Brodal and Fange 1963; Hardisty and Potter 1971; Jensen 1966; Vladykov and Kott 1979.

αααααααααααααααααααααααααααααααααααααααααααααααααααααααααααααααααα
~~~~~~

Sharks, Skates, and Ratfishes

Class Chondrichthyes
Subclass Elasmobranchi
  Superorder Galeomorphi
    Order Heterodontiformes
      Family Heterodontidae (horn sharks)
    Order Lamniformes
      Families Ondontaspidae (sand tigers), Lamnidae (thresher, basking, and mackerel sharks)
    Order Orectolobiformes
      Families Rhincodontidae (whale sharks), Orectolobidae (nurse sharks).
    Order Carcharhiniformes
      Families Scyliorhinidae (cat sharks), Carcharhinidae (requiem sharks), Sphyrnidae (hammerhead sharks)
  Superorder Squatinomorphi
    Order Squatiniformes
      Family Squatinidae (angel shark)
  Superorder Squalomorphi
    Order Hexanchiformes
      Families Chlamydoselachii (frill sharks), Hexanchidae (cow sharks)
    Order Squaliformes
      Families Squalidae (dogfish sharks), Echinorhinidae (bramble sharks)
    Order Pristiophoriformes
      Family Pristiophoridae (saw sharks)
  Superorder Batoidea
    Order Rajiformes
      Families Rhinobatidae (guitarfishes), Rajidae (skates)
    Order Pristiformes
      Family Pristidae (sawfishes)
    Order Torpediniformes
      Family Torpedinidae (electric rays)
    Order Myliobatiformes
      Families Dasayatidae (sting rays), Potamotrygonidae (river sting rays), Myliobatidae (eagle rays), Mobulidae (manta and devil rays)

Subclass Holocephali
    Order Chimaeriformes
        Families Callorhynchidae (plownose chimaeras), Chimaeridae (shortnose chimaeras), Rhinochimaeridae (longnose chimaeras)

Physiology   The cartilaginous fishes have long been held in low esteem by humans. As a group, they are generally considered to be vicious, inedible, and primitive. With a few notable exceptions, however, most members of this surprisingly diverse class possess none of these attributes. The common application of the word primitive to the group is particularly inappropriate because they are as specialized in their own way as are the teleosts among the bony fishes. The Chondrichthyes *are* less diverse than the teleosts, in the sense of having fewer species, and most of the species are predators on large invertebrates and fish, so the extreme diversity in ways of making a living is also lacking. As predators, their success is undisputed. This success seems to be due to the particular combination of adaptive characteristics that distinguishes them from the bony fishes, including their solutions to the structural and physiological problems of (1) buoyancy; (2) respiration; (3) external covering; (4) feeding; (5) movement; (6) sensory systems; (7) osmoregulation; and (8) reproduction.

    Buoyancy. One of the major adaptive problems that the ancestors of modern fish groups had to "solve" in order to achieve a higher degree of ecological diversity was how to get off the bottom and stay there without burning excessive amounts of energy. The ideal is to achieve neutral buoyancy, which many bony fishes have accomplished with a swimbladder. This particular solution does not seem to have been available to the Chondrichthyes, and this may be one of the main reasons why they never managed to occupy the niches typically occupied by small teleosts. One of the chondrichthyan solutions to the buoyancy problem was simply never to leave the bottom; a substantial number of modern forms are bottom-dwelling (e.g., skates and rays) or bottom-oriented. Even these forms possess a feature that significantly reduces their average density: the cartilaginous skeleton. Other elasmobranchs benefit from the presence of huge livers and/or hydrodynamic lifts while swimming, which also helps to keep them off the bottom (Chapter 3).

    Respiration. Perhaps the most distinctive feature of the chondrichthyan respiratory system is the presence of the spiracles, immediately preceding the principal gill openings on each side. They are used for drawing water into the gill chambers and may consequently be greatly reduced or absent in pelagic sharks that "ram" the water across the gills while swimming. In pelagic sharks, however, the spiracles may be important for supplying oxygen to the eyes. In contrast, in skates, rays, and other bottom-dwelling forms the spiracles are extremely important for respiration, since they are located on the top of the head and thus can be used to draw water into the gill chambers while the fish is lying motionless on the bottom waiting to ambush prey or avoiding predators.

External covering. All members of the Chondrichthyes have placoid scales in one form or another on the outside of their bodies. In skates and rays they are typically found only as a few rows of large denticles on the back, sometimes modified into spines (as in the stingray). In sharks the skin is filled with tiny, overlapping placoid scales, giving it a sandpaperlike feel. These scales form a lightweight, protective coat over the sides that may be particularly important in increasing hydrodynamic efficiency. It is interesting to note that placoid scales are characteristic of the oldest known sharks, yet it took the bony fishes several hundred million years to develop a covering of scales of their own (ctenoid scales) that apparently work as well as placoid scales.

Feeding. Most members of the Chondrichthyes are specialized predators, and their dentition reflects this. Sharks that prey on large fish and marine mammals have triangular, bladelike teeth with which they can grab their prey and saw or snap off large chunks. The jaws of some such sharks can exert biting pressures in excess of 2800 kg/cm^3. Sharks that swallow their prey whole, usually fish, have teeth that come to a long, thin point, for simply holding onto the prey so it can be swallowed. Skates and rays tend to have flattened, pavementlike teeth for crushing hard-shelled invertebrates. Some sharks, such as the horn sharks (Heterodontidae), have pointed teeth in front for grasping the prey but crushing teeth in the back of the jaw. Each species of Chondrichthyes has distinctive teeth that reflect, in subtle ways, the way it makes a living. Despite their variety, however, all these teeth are really just modified placoid scales, and like the scales, they are continually being shed and replaced.

Aside from the teeth, the main reason sharks can ingest large prey is that their jaw suspension is hyostylic in most forms, which allows the gape to be maximized. The jaws are also rather loosely attached to the cranium. This is particularly important to the skates and rays, since they have the ability actually to protrude the jaws a short distance for picking or pulling organisms off the bottom.

Once the prey is ingested, it quickly reaches the large stomach, where the initial stages of digestion take place. From the stomach the food passes to the spiral valve intestine, a distinctive feature often considered to be primitive (presumably because only the most ancestral bony fishes possess one). In fact, the spiral valve is a remarkably efficient way to increase the digestive surface area without increasing the length of the intestine.

Movement. How sharks and skates swim has already been discussed (Chapter 2), but it is worth emphasizing that the characteristic heterocercal tail of modern sharks is a complex organ that serves the fish well for propulsion, steering, and hydrodynamic stability. Some pelagic sharks (*Isurus, Lamna*) have countercurrent exchangers in their circulatory system that permit them to be "warmblooded" and increase the efficiency of their swimming (Chapter 3).

Sensory systems. The cartilaginous fishes have a number of remarkably well-developed sensory systems which act in concert to help them locate prey (among other things). Probably the first sensory cues they pick up when in the search of prey are either odor, particularly from injured prey, or low-frequency sounds. The well-developed olfactory organs attest to the keenness of their sense of smell. Low-frequency vibrations and turbulence created by struggling fish or even fish swimming in schools may also be detected at a distance, either with the inner ear (vibrations) or with the lateralis system (turbulence). At closer range, vision comes into play. Contrary to much of the literature on elasmobranchs, their visual systems are well developed and used both during the day and during times when light levels are low (Gruber 1977). When sharks are almost ready to seize their prey, nictitating membranes may cover the eyes, and other sensory systems take over. One of these is the electroreception system, which can detect the tiny electrical fields created by muscular movement. The ampullae of Lorenzini, located on the snout, may function in the latter capacity, as do sensory receptors on the lower jaw. The ampullae may also play a role in intraspecific communication, since many elasmobranchs, particularly among the skates and rays, possess weak electrical organs.

Osmoregulation. The osmoregulatory system of the Chondrichthyes is extremely efficient. The concentration of solutes in the body is actually close to or higher than that of seawater largely due to the retention of nontoxic nitrogenous wastes, mostly urea and trimethylamine oxide, to which the gills are nearly impermeable. The rectal gland is used primarily for the excretion of sodium and chloride ions, while the kidney excretes divalent ions (Chapter 6).

Reproduction. It is likely that the osmoregulatory and reproductive systems of Chondrichthyes evolved simultaneously, since the long gestation periods of the embryos, either in egg cases or in the body cavities of the females, would hardly be possible without the ability of the embryos to withstand high concentrations of their own waste products. In some sharks the embryos may be carried for nearly two years, although the concentration of urea around the embryos is periodically reduced by the ability of the female to flush the "uterus" with sea water.

The cartilaginous fishes, unlike most bony fishes, expend most of the energy used for reproduction in producing a relatively small number of large, active young. They have a remarkable variety of ways of doing this, from oviparity to ovoviviparity, to viviparity, and all stages inbetween. Oviparous forms lay large eggs covered with tough, leathery cases. Many of the cases have tendrils at the corners, apparently for attachment to seaweeds (Fig. 14.1). Those of skates (Rajidae) are fre-

FIGURE 14.1 Egg capsule of a swell shark (*Cephaloscyllium ventriosum*) showing embryo inside. (After Springer, 1979.)

quently washed up on beaches as "mermaids purses." The eggs of the horn shark (Heterodontidae) are surrounded by a spiral shelf, which presumably helps to keep the eggs from sinking by imparting a spin to them. Ovoviviparous forms also produce eggs, but the shells are thin and the eggs are retained in the uterus of the female. The shell soon disappears, and the young are retained in the uterus until fully developed. Like the young of oviparous forms, these young obtain most of their nutrition from a yolk sac, although in a few sharks some nutrition apparently is obtained as well from a nutrient-rich solution surrounding the young. In a few other sharks, such as the sand tiger (*Ondontaspis taurus*), the first young to "hatch" in each of the two oviducts proceed to eat the other embryos in the oviduct with them (oophagy). The mother shark continues to produce unfertilized eggs for the nutrition of the two young, which are born at large sizes (90 cm or so). The nutrition of the embryos of viviparous forms is by a placentalike arrangement, including an umbilical cord. This type of reproduction is characteristic of the families Carcharhinidae (requiem sharks) and Sphyrnidae (hammerhead sharks).

Diversity While the preceding discussion indicates that the Chondrichthyes are a cohesive group taxonomically in that they share a common structural pattern, examination of the adaptations of the various groups within the Chondrichthyes demonstrates their diversity. The major taxonomic groups used in this section are those of Compagno (1973, 1977), since his detailed anatomical studies (especially of jaw suspension, head musculature, and chondrocranial structure) demonstrate that the diversification of the Chondrichthyes has been proceeding for a long time.

Galeomorph sharks. The shark superorder Galeomorphi contains not only the sharks with the classic body shape that usually comes to mind at the word "shark" but also many of the sharks that diverge markedly from this shape (Fig. 14.2). The "typical" sharks are mostly in the families Lamnidae (mackerel sharks) and Carcharhinidae (requiem sharks). These sharks are mostly large, pelagic forms, with bladelike teeth. They are efficient predators on large fish, cephalopods, and marine mammals and are also responsible for most attacks on humans. The sharks that perhaps most deserve the reputation of man-eater are the great white shark (Lamnidae, *Carcharodon carcharias*), the shortfin mako shark (Lamnidae, *Isurus oxyrinchus*), and the tiger shark (Carcharhinidae, *Galeocerdo cuvieri*), although almost any shark will attack a human if provoked. It is worth noting that recent studies of shark behavior (e.g., Johnson and Nelson 1973) indicate that many attacks on humans may not be feeding attacks but defensive attacks on swimmers behaving (often unknowingly) in a way the shark interprets as threatening. Such attacks are preceded by a ritualized display.

Two sharks in this superorder definitely not capable of biting

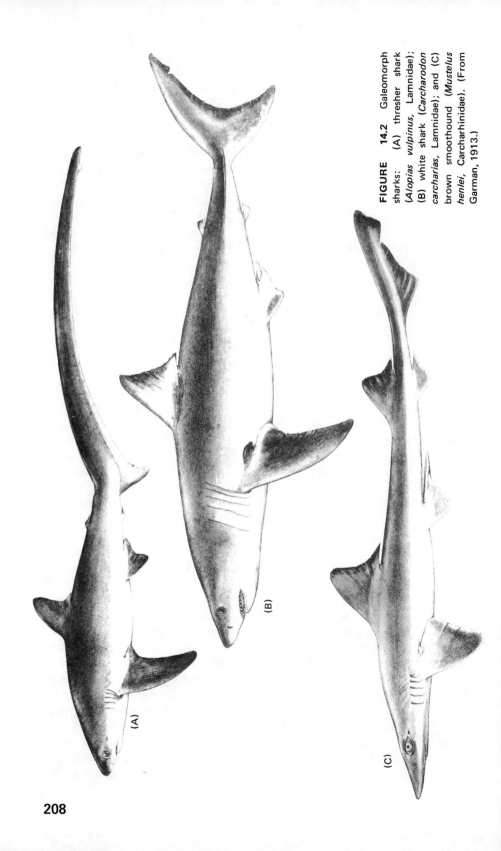

FIGURE 14.2 Galeomorph sharks: (A) thresher shark (*Alopias vulpinus*, Lamnidae); (B) white shark (*Carcharodon carcharias*, Lamnidae); and (C) brown smoothhound (*Mustelus henlei*, Carcharhinidae). (From Garman, 1913.)

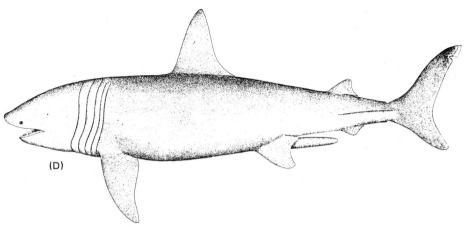

FIGURE 14.2 (continued) Galeomorph shark: (D) basking shark (*Cetorhinus maximus,* Lamnidae). (From Jordan and Evermann, 1900.)

attacks on humans are the whale shark (Rhincodontidae, *Rhincodon typus*) and the basking shark (Lamnidae, *Cetorhinus maximus*), although male whale sharks apparently mistake boats on occasion for competitors and ram them! The whale shark, which may reach lengths of 18 m, is the world's largest fish, while the basking shark runs a close second, with lengths approaching 14 m. Whale and basking sharks are only distantly related to each other and have independently evolved mechanisms for straining plankton. Both have fine, elongate gill rakers for the straining, but those of the basking shark have developed from placoid scales, while those of the whale shark are cartilaginous rods with spongy material between that acts as a filter. The gill rakers of the basking shark are shed in the fall and regrown in the spring, and the sharks, at least in the North Sea, become inactive during the winter, when plankton populations are low.

Some of the most peculiar sharks in this superorder are the thresher sharks (Lamnidae, *Alopias* spp.), with their extraordinarily long upper lobe of the caudal fin. The long lobe seems to be used for herding fish schools into tight balls, making them easier to attack. However, Budker (1971) questions the completeness of this explanation, noting that other sharks can accomplish such herding without an elongate tail and that the peculiar shape of the tail must decrease the swimming ability of the sharks.

The horn sharks (Heterodontidae) are often considered to be one of the most ancestral groups of living elasmobranchs. However, as Compagno (1973) points out, they seem to have as many derived as ancestral characteristics and so are best treated as part of the galeomorph sharks. Since they are rather sluggish, shallow-water bottom dwellers, horn sharks are comparatively easy to study. Consequently, the life history of *Heterodontus portusjacksoni* is among the best known of any shark (McLaughlin and O'Gower 1971).

Angel shark. The angel sharks (Squatinidae, *Squatina* spp.) appear to be intermediates between sharks and rays (Fig. 14.3). They are flattened like rays, yet the large pectoral fins are not attached to the head. They have large spiracles on top of the head, yet the five gill openings are as much lateral as ventral and the mouth is terminal rather than ventral. Like rays, they lack anal fins and have two small dorsal fins on the caudal region of the body. In most other details, however, they bear little resemblance to the rays, have many characteristics in common with both the squalomorph and galeomorph sharks, as well as many characteristics of their own. Because of their distinctiveness, Compagno (1973) places the angel sharks in their own superorder (Squatinomorpha), although other authorities have usually placed them in with the squalomorph sharks, the group with which they have the most in common. Angel sharks have spikelike teeth and feed mostly on bottom-dwelling animals.

Squalomorph sharks. The three orders in the superorder Squalomorphi superficially differ considerably from each other (Fig. 14.3), but they are best treated together because of considerable similarities in the structure of the chondrocranium (skull). The order Hexanchiformes contains only about six species of peculiar sharks with six or seven gill openings that are largely inhabitants of deep water. The frill shark (Chlamydoselachidae, *Chlamydoselachus anguineus*) has an eel-like body. The first gill extends across the throat, from one side to the other. This shark is usually considered to be related to the ancient cladodont sharks, but Compagno (1973) argues that the similarities to the ancient sharks are only superficial and that in most respects the frill shark is a modern form. The cow sharks (Hexanchidae) are a group of rather flabby, bottom-oriented sharks with weak jaws and small teeth. They apparently live mostly by scavenging.

The sharks of the order Squaliformes are abundant and widely distributed. All have two dorsal fins, and many have spines preceding one or both fins. Although one of the sleeper sharks (Squalidae, *Somniosus microcephalus*) may exceed 6 m in length, most of the squaliform sharks seldom exceed 2 m in length. In fact, the smallest sharks known are from this order. The tsuranagakobitozame[1] (Squalidae, *Squaloides laticaudus*) is mature at 11 cm to 15 cm. A number of other species are also mature at less than 50 cm. All of these small sharks are apparently mesopelagic in habitat (see Chapter 33), and some are luminescent with photophores (Hubbs et al. 1967). There is some evidence that at least one of them (*Isistius brasiliensis*) may mimic the squid which they prey upon. This mimicry may also allow them to cut out small, round pieces of flesh from larger fishes, porpoises, and whales which mistake the sharks for prey. The evidence for this is the peculiar mouth and dentition of these sharks, a body shape that would

---

[1] A Japanese name meaning "dwarf shark with a long face" (Lineaweaver and Backus 1969).

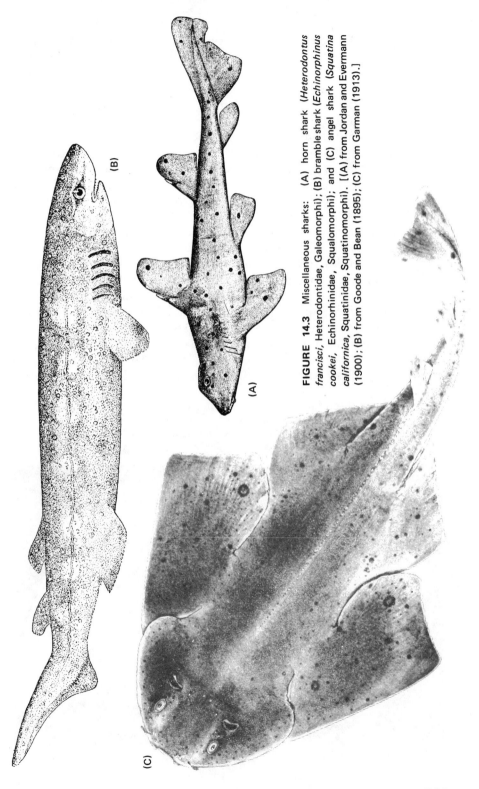

FIGURE 14.3 Miscellaneous sharks: (A) horn shark (*Heterodontus francisci*, Heterodontidae, Galeomorphi); (B) bramble shark (*Echinorhinus cookei*, Echinorhinidae, Squalomorphi); and (C) angel shark (*Squatina californica*, Squatinidae, Squatinomorphi). [(A) from Jordan and Evermann (1900); (B) from Goode and Bean (1895); (C) from Garman (1913).]

seem to preclude the capture of fast-swimming prey (Fig. 14.4), and the commonness of the peculiar crater wounds on large fish and cetaceans (Jones 1971). As more has become known about these remarkable fish, they have acquired the name of "cookie-cutter sharks."

Perhaps the best known and most abundant squaliform shark is the spiny dogfish (Squalidae, *Squalus acanthias*), which commonly inhabits anatomy and ichthyology teaching laboratories. They are also found worldwide in temperate to subpolar waters, mostly along coastlines. They form huge schools which contain both sexes when the dogfish are immature but only one sex or the other when they are mature (Jensen 1966). They may migrate considerable distances. A dogfish tagged off Washington has been caught off Japan, while one tagged off Newfoundland was subsequently caught in the North Sea (Templeman 1976). In many parts of the world they are an important commercial fish, but off North America they are still considered to be mostly a nuisance that preys on more valuable fish. In contrast to the abundant dogfish, bramble sharks (Echinorhinidae, *Echinorhinus* spp.) are considered to be uncommon, although this is probably mostly a reflection of their deepwater habitat. Despite their rather weak jaws and teeth, they are bottom-oriented predators that apparently feed by suction. Their rather flabby bodies are covered with a scattering of spinelike denticles. Another squalomorph family with modified external

FIGURE 14.4 Cookie-cutter sharks: (A) *Isistius plutodus;* and (B) *I. brasiliensis.* These small sharks grab onto the side of a larger fish, hold on with their strong suctional lips, and then cut along a cookie-shaped plug of flesh with their lower teeth. (Photo by L. J. V. Compagno.)

(A)   (B)

denticles is the Pristiophoridae, the saw sharks. These fish have teeth attached to their snout, which is extended as a long, flat blade. In this respect they are like the true sawfishes (superorder Batoidea, family Pristidae), but the peculiar snout seems to have evolved independently in the two groups. In the saw sharks the teeth on the blade are unequal in size and are rather weakly attached, while in the sawfishes the teeth are all about the same size and are firmly held by sockets. Both forms, however, have flattened heads, although the gill openings are lateral on the saw sharks and ventral on the sawfishes. It is nevertheless worth noting that the saw sharks seem to have more characters in common with the Batoidea than any other sharks, which may indicate their common ancestry. In both saw sharks and sawfishes the "saw" is used for slashing through schools of fish, after which they return to devour the pieces and incapacitated fishes.

Skates and rays. The members of the superorder Batoidea are primarily adapted for bottom living, although a number of forms have developed the ability to "fly" through the water with their enlarged pectoral fins and have become nektonic. Even the bottom-dwelling forms are surprisingly diverse, although all members of the superorder are characterized by ventral gill openings, enlarged pectoral fins that attach to the side of the head, no anal fin, eyes and spiracles located on the top of the head, and pavementlike teeth (Fig. 14.5). The most speciose of the Batoidea are the skates (family Rajidae), which are often extremely abundant, especially in water less than 1000 m deep. The tail of skates is very slender, usually without a caudal fin, but containing weak electric organs. It is common to find several morphologically similar species of skates, especially of the genus *Raja*, occurring together. Recent studies indicate that these species segregate by subtle ecological factors such as temperature and depth preferences, and by feeding habits, reflected in specialized dentition. Skates are the only family of batoids that lay eggs; all the rest are ovoviviparous. Closely related to the skates are the guitarfishes (family Rhinobatidae), which have a sharklike body. Most of the guitarfishes are small, shallow-water feeders on small crustaceans, although one species may exceed 3 m in length.

Perhaps the most remarkable of the batoids are the electric rays (family Torpedinidae), which can deliver as much as 200 V from the electric organs in their heads. Although electric rays are rather flabby, they use electric discharges to stun the active fish which make up most of their prey (Bray and Hixon 1978). The eyes of all electric rays are quite small, however, and a number of species are blind, so it is quite possible that they also use electricity for navigation. Another group of rays with formidable weapons are the stingrays (Dasyatidae and Potamotrygonidae). The sting is a spine modified from a placoid scale with a venom gland at its base. The spine is whipped about most effectively by the tail and, since stingrays feed mostly on crustaceans

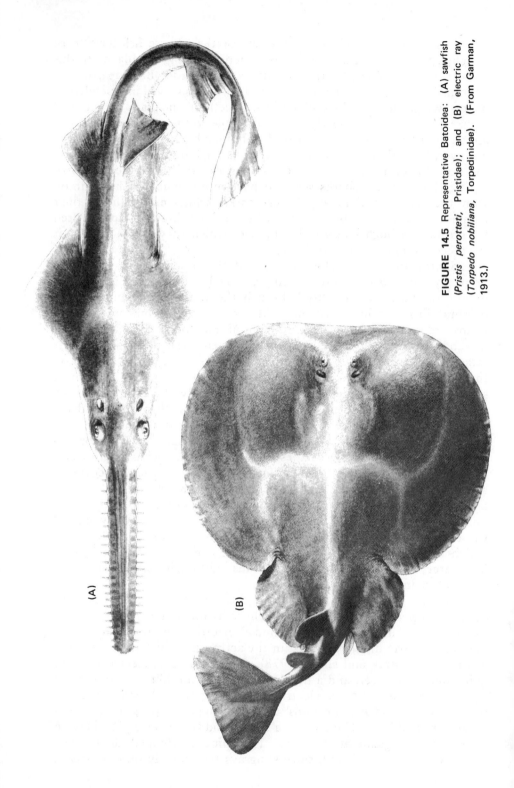

(A)

(B)

FIGURE 14.5 Representative Batoidea: (A) sawfish (*Pristis perotteti*, Pristidae); and (B) electric ray (*Torpedo nobiliana*, Torpedinidae). (From Garman, 1913.)

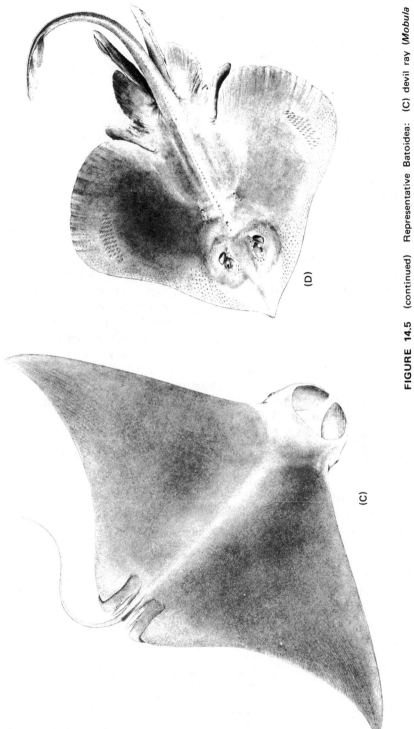

(D)

(C)

FIGURE 14.5 (continued) Representative Batoidea: (C) devil ray (*Mobula hypostoma*, Mobulidae); and (D) smooth skate (*Raja senta*, Rajidae). (From Garman, 1913.)

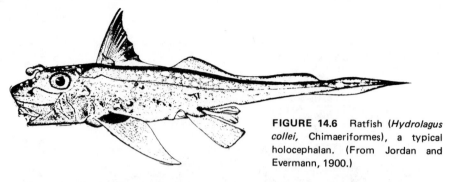

FIGURE 14.6 Ratfish (*Hydrolagus collei*, Chimaeriformes), a typical holocephalan. (From Jordan and Evermann, 1900.)

and other invertebrates, it must be used solely for defense against large predators. The Dasayatidae are the common saltwater stingrays, whereas the Potamotrygonidae are found exclusively in rivers of South America and, possibly, southeastern Asia.

The eagle rays (Myliobatidae) are closely related to the stingrays and, in fact, a number of species have venomous spines. The eagle rays fly through the water in schools, flapping their powerful pectoral fins. They have powerful jaws and teeth for crushing molluscs and appear to move around in search of concentrations of invertebrates. This is in marked contrast to rays like the round stingray (Dasayatidae, *Urolophus halleri*), which tend to remain in the same locale for long periods of time (Babel 1967). A group of rays very similar in habits to the eagle rays are the manta and devil rays (Mobulidae), which swim in the manner of eagle rays but are adapted for plankton feeding. The mobulids are distinguished by large, scooplike appendages on the head that direct the plankton into the mouth. Like whale and basking sharks, mobulid rays have fine gill rakers for straining out the plankton. The mantas are also the largest of the batoids, some achieving a pectoral fin span in excess of 6 m and weights over 1360 kg.

Chimaeras. The chimaeras (subclass Holocephali) have had a long evolutionary history independent of the elasmobranchs, and their anatomy reflects it (see Chapter 12). The chimaeras are commonly known as ratfishes because of their long, slender tail (Fig. 14.6). This body shape is convergent to that of teleosts (e.g., Macrouridae) that also live on the bottom in deep water. There are only about 25 species of chimaeras, most of them in the family Chimaeridae. All apparently feed on bottom-dwelling crustaceans and molluscs and consequently have well-developed, pavementlike teeth for crushing. For defense, they all have a spine in front of the dorsal fin with an associated venom gland. All lay eggs with leathery coverings.

Supplemental Readings

Bigelow and Schroeder 1948; Budker 1971; Compagno 1973; Gilbert, Mathewson, and Rall 1967; Herald 1961; Lineaweaver and Backus 1969; Moss 1977; Northcutt 1977; Ronsivalli 1978; Springer and Gilbert 1976.

ααααααααααααααααααααααααααααααααααααααααααααααααααααααααααααααααααα
~~~~~~

Lobefinned Fishes

Subclass **Dipneusti**
Order Ceratodiformes
  Family Ceratodidae (Australian lungfishes)
Order Lepidosireniformes
  Family Lepidosirenidae (South American and African lungfishes)
Subclass **Crossopterygii**
Order Coelacanthiformes
  Family Latimeriidae (coelacanth)
Subclass **Brachiopterygii**
Order Polypteriformes
  Family Polypteridae (bichirs)

    The three subclasses of fishes discussed in this chapter are sometimes placed together in one subclass (Sarcopterygii) to separate them from the ray-finned fishes (Actinopterygii). However, the three groups seem to represent long independent evolutionary lines (Chapter 12) and so are best treated separately. The Brachiopterygii in particular seem to have affinities to the primitive ray-finned fishes. Aside from a number of "primitive" features, such as the spiral valve intestine, the main feature uniting the three groups is lobed fins (Fig. 15.1). These fins are supported internally by skeletal elements which attach to a pectoral and/or pelvic girdle. They are homologous to tetrapod limbs.

Lungfishes   Modern lungfishes fall into two distinct families, the Ceratodidae of Australia and the Lepidosirenidae of Africa and South America. The Australian lungfish (*Neoceratodus forsteri*) bears the greatest resemblance to fossil forms, with its flipperlike fins, large scales, unpaired lung, and compressed body. In contrast, the South American (*Lepidosiren paradoxa*) and

FIGURE 15.1 A bichir (*Polypterus*) as an example of a lobe-finned fish. (After Boulenger, 1907.)

African (*Protopterus*, four species) lungfishes have fins that are reduced to filaments, small scales, paired lungs, and eellike bodies. The Australian lungfish is relatively rare, confined to the Mary and Burnett Rivers of Queensland. These rivers have low flows in the summer, and the lungfish live in the deep pools that remain. Although their lung is functional in a limited way, even during the dry season the Australian lungfish seems to rely primarily on gill respiration. The lung supplements the gills during times of stress. The South American and African lungfishes live in swamps that are likely to dry up, and they breathe air to survive. As the waters recede in their swamps, they dig burrows in the mud in which they can survive until the rains come. The African lungfishes undergo true aestivation, which includes drastic metabolic changes. They line their burrows with a heavy coating of mucus, which dries to form a hard, impermeable cocoon. Each burrow is connected to the surface by a narrow tube plugged with mud except for a small hole. When the rains come, the plug dissolves, water enters the lung of the fish, and it awakens by coughing.

While aestivating, the oxygen consumption of the lungfish is reduced to extraordinarily low levels and what metabolic energy is needed is derived entirely from the utilization of protein. The aestivating lungfish live by metabolizing their own muscles. During this process, carbohydrate (glycogen) reserves actually build up and are consequently available for immediate use when the lungfish emerges from the cocoon. Another substance that builds up during aestivation is urea (Chapter 7). Urea may build up in tissues to seven times its normal level, far beyond the levels toxic to most other bony fishes. Once the lungfish leave the cocoon, the urea is rapidly excreted and ammonia becomes the main nitrogenous waste product.

The Lepidosirenidae all hollow out nests in mud banks or bottoms. The female then lays the eggs in the nest, and the male guards them. The newly hatched lungfish resemble salamander tadpoles in that they have external gills. Such gills, as well as the nesting behavior, are not characteristic of Australian lungfish, which lay their eggs on aquatic plants.

All lungfishes have dermal tooth plates. These tend to be flattened in fossil forms, apparently for crushing and grinding, but are more bladelike in living lungfishes. The South American and Australian lungfishes are omnivorous, and plant material is an important part of the diet; the African lungfishes are more carnivorous, preying on molluscs, crustaceans, and fish. On this diet, some species may exceed 2 m in length, although fish longer than 1 m are seldom encountered.

Coelacanth Probably no single event in the history of ichthyology has received more public attention than the discovery of the coelacanth (*Latimeria chalumnae*) in 1938. The discovery excited the public imagination because the coelacanth is large (up to 2 m long), is from deep water, was previously known only from fossils (the most recent being about 70 million years old), and would supposedly reveal much about the evolutionary transition between fish and tetrapods. The coelacanth brought instant fame to the South African ichthyologist J. L. B. Smith, who described it, and a certain celebrity, in scientific circles anyway, to Ms. M. Courtney-Latimer (hence *Latimeria*). Ms. Latimer was the curator of a small local museum who recognized the significance of the fish brought to her by a local fisherman, and so notified Smith. Unfortunately, the fish was stuffed and mounted for display by the time Smith was able to examine it, so he could only describe the external anatomy. A second specimen was not obtained until 1952. It had been caught nearly 3000 km north of the first collection locality, in the deep trenches around the Comoro Islands. All subsequent specimens have come from this area, where it is common enough so that the local fishermen have a name for it (gombessa). Since 1952 considerable research has been conducted on the coelacanth, although new discoveries about its biology are still being made. For example, the fact that the coelacanth is ovoviviparous (i.e., retains the eggs in the body cavity where the young hatch and develop) was only discovered in 1975 (C. L. Smith et al. 1975).

Little is known about the ecology of coelacanths, aside from the observations that they live on the bottom, on reefs and sea mounts, at depths between 70 m and 600 m and feed on fish and squid. McCosker (1979) speculates that they behave much like "large, reef-associated piscivorous groupers." Certainly this way of life seems to be reflected in their anatomy and physiology. Presumably they rest on the bottom on their lobed fins and use them to "walk" or lunge forward when ambushing prey. The skeletons of the paired fins articulate with the pelvic and pectoral girdles, making such movement possible. The entire skeleton is made up of both bone and cartilage, although the vertebral column is essentially notochord constricted by cartilaginous neural and haemal arches (this is true of lungfishes as well). The fin "spines" are also cartilaginous and are hollow as well, hence the name coelacanth (*coel*, "hollow," *acanth*, "spine"). However, there is bone present in the large, highly modified cosmoid scales which cover the body. The skull and jaws are also partially bony and are well suited for an ambush feeder that swallows its prey whole. Unlike other living fishes, the coelacanth has an intracranial joint that allows the cranium to flex dorsally when the jaws are opened. In addition, the gape of the mouth is very wide and the head is capable of being moved somewhat independently from the trunk (Thomson 1969, 1973).

One of the more fascinating aspects of coelacanth biology is the similarity of physiology and soft anatomy between *Latimeria* and the Chondrichthyes. Most striking is the coelacanth osmoregulatory strategy, which consists of being nearly iso-osmotic with sea water by maintaining high concentrations of urea in the blood (Chapter 6). The structure of the pituitary gland also bears a great resemblance to that of the Chondrichthyes. The similarities in soft anatomy between coelacanths and elasmobranchs has led Lagios (1979) to conclude that coelacanths are more closely related to the Chondrichthyes than to the Osteichtl yes. This conclusion has been disputed by Compagno (1979) and others, who point out the many basic similarities between coelacanths and bony fishes in skeletal structure, as well as the presence of such bony fish characters as endoskeletal bone, bony scales, and a swimbladder. Regardless of their true relationships, it is obvious that the coelacanths have a long independent evolutionary history that has made them very peculiar but fascinating fishes.

Bichirs

The Polypteriformes are usually placed with the Actinopterygii, as an offshoot of the ancient paleoniscid chondrosteans. Although it seems likely that they do have affinities to the chondrosteans (Schaeffer 1973), arguments can also be made for including them with the lungfishes and crossopterygians (Nelson 1969). Regardless of their relationships with other groups, they obviously have had a long independent evolutionary history, so it seems safest to treat them as a separate subclass, Brachiopterygii (Jessen 1973).

Superficially, the characteristic of the bichirs that links them with the lungfishes and coelacanth is the lobed pectoral fins, although the supporting skeletal structure is so distinctive that it probably developed independently. In common with the chondrosteans, bichirs possess ganoid scales. In common with both groups, bichirs possess such "ancestral" features as a spiral valve intestine, paired lungs (attached ventrally, with the right lung larger), heterocercal tails, and spiracles. In most features, however, they are distinct. The body is elongate or eel-like, and although covered with heavy scales, quite flexible. The dorsal fin consists of a series of 5 to 18 separate finlets, each supported by a single spine. They normally respire with the gills, supplementing them with the lungs. The lungs can be filled by drawing air through the spiracle, allowing the fish to breathe by protruding only a small part of its head out of the water.

Most of the features of the bichirs are adaptations for predatory living in the tropical swamps and rivers of Africa, where oxygen levels in the water may be quite low. Even the larvae reflect this, since they have external gills. There are 10 species of bichirs (*Polypterus*) and one of reedfish (*Calamoichthys calabaricus*) in the family Polypteridae. The reedfish is very eel-like and lacks pelvic fins.

Supplemental Readings

Bjerring 1973; Herald 1961; Jessen 1973; Mc-Cosker and Lagios 1979; Millot 1955; G. J. Nelson 1969; Schaeffer 1973; J. L. B. Smith 1956; Thomson 1969, 1973.

ααααααααααααααααααααααααααααααααααααααααααααααααααααααααααααααααα
~~~~~~

Chondrosteans
and Holosteans

Subclass Actinopterygii
Infraclass Chondrostei
  Order Acipenseriformes
    Families Acipenseridae (sturgeons), Polyodontidae (paddle fishes)
Infraclass Holostei
  Order Semionotiformes
    Family Lepisosteidae (gars)
  Order Amiiformes
    Family Amiidae (bowfin)

    The Chondrostei and the Holostei were both, in turn, the dominant bony fishes in both fresh and salt water (Chapter 13) but were replaced by their descendents, the Teleostei. Today only about 33 species in both groups combined still exist, entirely in the fresh waters of Eurasia and North and Central America. The forms that have managed to coexist with the teleosts are highly specialized as large bottom feeders (sturgeons), large plankton feeders (paddlefishes), or as predators capable of living in oxygen-deficient waters (gars and bowfin).

Chondrostei   As the name "Chondrostei" implies, all
                       sturgeons and paddlefishes have a largely
cartilaginous skeleton. They also have a heterocercal tail, a spiral valve intestine, an upper jaw that does not articulate with the cranium, only one branchiostegal ray, fin rays that are more numerous than the supporting basal elements, and a notochord that persists in the adults. Otherwise, the two families of Chondrosteans are quite different from each other and probably are products of long separate evolutionary lines.
    The sturgeons are distinguished by five rows of bony scutes on the body that represent the remnants of ganoid scales and by a highly

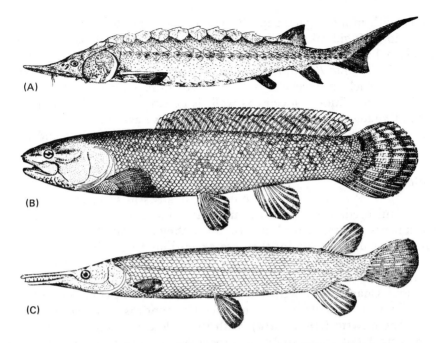

FIGURE 16.1 (A) Sturgeon (Chondrostei, *Acipenser*); (B) bowfish (Holostei, *Amia*); and (C) gar (Holostei, *Lepisosteus*). (From Jordan and Evermann, 1900.)

protrusible, bottom-oriented mouth which is preceded by four barbels. Teeth are absent in adults. As their morphology indicates (Fig. 16.1), sturgeons feed on the bottom by sucking up organisms detected by their highly sensitive barbels. Although various types of garbage found in their stomachs indicate that they feed in part by scavenging, most of their diet is benthic invertebrates, with fish becoming increasingly important as the sturgeon grows larger. Most fish eaten are probably captured at night, when it is difficult for the prey to avoid a large sturgeon, even though the sturgeon are somewhat sluggish. The shovelnosed sturgeons (*Scaphirhynchus*) may use their flat snouts for stirring up the bottom to expose the invertebrates on which they feed.

Sturgeons are the largest fish found in fresh water, although the largest species are in fact anadromous. The beluga sturgeon (*Huso huso*), the main source of true Russian caviar, has been found to achieve a length of 8.5 m and a weight of nearly 1300 kg. In North America there are apparently authentic records of white sturgeon (*Acipenser transmontanus*) growing to about 4 m and weights of 590 kg.

The paddlefishes possess a long, paddlelike snout, whose function is still not known, although it does hold a few small barbels and other sensory endings. Their skin is smooth and scaleless, except for a small patch on the caudal peduncle. Like most sturgeons, they possess a small spiracle, which is covered with a greatly elongated operculum. Paddlefish feed on zooplankton, which they capture by swimming through the water with mouth agape and filtering out the plankton with their many fine, elongate gill rakers. There are two species of paddlefish. *Polyodon spathula* lives in the Mississippi River system and achieves lengths of about 2 m, while *Psephurus gladius* lives in the Yangtze River of China and may reach in excess of 5 m. The North American paddlefish (and probably the Chinese species as well) is declining in numbers thanks to habitat changes and overexploitation. It does have considerable potential for aquaculture, however, because of its feeding habits and rapid growth rate.

Holostei

The bowfin and the gars, although the only holosteans still surviving, are highly successful predators on teleosts and may achieve pest status in some environments disturbed by humans. Since they are found throughout the Mississippi drainage basin, they are exceptions to the general rule that air-breathing fishes are confined to tropical environments. Aside from their general way of making a living and the general holostean characteristics (see Chapter 12), gars and bowfin have little in common and presumably were even derived from different chondrostean ancestors.

The bowfin (*Amia calva*), with its cycloid scales and functionally homocercal tail (structurally heterocercal), is somewhat similar in appearance to some "ancestral" teleosts. However, its many sharp teeth, 10 to 13 branchiostegal rays, vestigial spiral valve intestine, stout body, solid jaws and head, and large lung also make it seem distinctly archaic. One of its distinguishing features is the bony gular plate under the lower jaws. Like teleosts, the bowfin has vertebrae that are concave at both ends (amphicoelous). The large lung is definitely advantageous to the bowfin in the warm summer waters in which it normally occurs. It is not an obligate air breather, but once the water temperatures exceed about 10°C, it supplements oxygen obtained through the gills with that absorbed through the lung. The rate of air breathing increases with increasing temperature (Horn and Riggs 1973). On occasion, bowfin can apparently survive entirely by air breathing while lying torpid in muddy burrows during periods of drought. There is some evidence that during such periods they, like lungfish, may actually metabolize muscle rather than fat. Although they cannot accumulate urea in their body tissues, they can reduce water demand by excreting urea and uric acid (Thomson 1969).

Gars are among the most distinctive of freshwater fishes. Their cylindrical bodies are covered with hard, nonoverlapping, diamond-shaped ganoid scales, and their hard, bony heads have long snouts with sharp, conspicuous teeth. The long body and snout, coupled with the placement of the dorsal and anal fins near the tail, make gars superb lie-in-wait predators. Passing fish are seized sideways during a sudden dash from ambush by the gar, held firmly with the teeth, and eventually turned around and swallowed whole. The heavy armor that gars carry with them as protection against predators is made possible by large swimbladders, which make gars neutrally buoyant. The swimbladders are also used for air breathing. Like bowfin, gars are not obligate air breathers but become increasingly dependent on the lung for oxygen as water temperatures increase and the dissolved oxygen in the water decreases (Renfro and Hill 1970). Aside from the large, well-vascularized swimbladders, the most distinctive internal features of gars are the spiral valve intestine and the vertebral column with opisthocoelous vertebra; each vertebral centrum has a convex anterior surface and a concave posterior surface.

Although gars do not build nests, the eggs and probably the sac-fry are protected from predators by being toxic. The eggs are laid on aquatic vegetation, to which they adhere. The young cling to the stems with an adhesive disc on the head until the yolk sac is absorbed and they can swim actively. Most of the seven species of gar reach a maximum length of 1 m to 2 m, although the alligator gar (*Lepisosteus spatula*) can exceed 3 m.

Supplemental Readings   Herald 1961; Moyle 1976a; Pflieger 1975; Renfro and Hill 1970; Scott and Crossman 1973; Thomson 1969.

αααααααααακαααααααααααααααααααααααααααααααααααααααααααααααααααααααααα
~~~~~~

𝕳erring, 𝕵arpons, and 𝕰els

Subclass **Actinopterygii**
Infraclass Teleostei
  Division Taenopaedia
    Superorder Clupeomorpha
      Order Clupeiformes
        Families Denticipitidae (denticle herring), Clupeidae (herrings), Engraulidae (anchovies), Chirocentridae (wolf herring)
      Superorder Elopomorpha
        Order Elopiformes
          Families Elopidae (tenpounders), Megalopidae (tarpons), Albulidae (bonefishes)
        Order Anguilliformes
          Families Anguillidae (freshwater eels), Heterenchelyidae, Moringuidae (spaghetti eels), Nemichthyidae (snipe eels), Cyemidae, Xenocongridae (false morays), Myrocongridae, Muraenidae (moray eels), Synaphobranchidae (cutthroat eels), Simenchelyidae (snubnose eel), Dysommidae (arrowhead eels), Macrocephenchelyidae, Colocongridae, Congridae (conger eels), Muraenesocidae (pike eels), Nettastomidae (duckbill eels), Serrivomeridae (sawpalate eels), Ophichthidae (snake eels), Derichthyidae (longneck eels), Saccopharyngidae (swallowers), Eurypharyngidae (gulpers), Monognathidae
        Order Notacanthiformes
          Families Halosauridae (halosaurs), Lipogenyidae, Notacanthidae (spiny eels)

The four orders treated in this chapter do not fit together comfortably. Other classification systems may have them widely separated. As Nelson (1976) points out, how each order is placed in a classification scheme of the teleosts depends in part on what principles of classification are followed. If a "vertical" system is used, as is done here, generalized forms and their more specialized (presumed) descendents are placed together. If a "horizontal" system is used, as in Gosline (1971), ancestral groups may be placed together but the major offshoots of each ancestral line are placed in separate groups.

FIGURE 17.1 Leptocephalus larvae of an eel.

The Clupeiformes are placed here because of their superficial resemblances to the Elopiformes, although the resemblances are probably more a reflection of convergent adaptations to pelagic living than of common ancestry. Both groups have had long independent evolutionary histories. The link of the Elopiformes to the Anguilliformes and Notacanthiformes is somewhat stronger (hence the Elopomorpha), since they all have leptocephalus larvae (Greenwood et al. 1966). These planktonic larvae are thin, transparent, and leaflike, drifting passively with currents (Fig. 17.1). Despite this seemingly basic link between the groups, the classification system used here is far from being universally accepted by experts in groups. For example, Greenwood (1977) presents a convincing analysis that erects a separate superorder (Anguillomorpha) for the eels. Within this superorder are two orders, the Anguilliformes and the Albuliformes. The latter order contains not only the families placed under the Notacanthiformes here but also the bonefishes (Albulidae), which superficially resemble tarpons much more than eels!

Clupeiformes
The herrings and their kin form one of the most well-defined teleost orders. All are adapted for living in well-lighted surface waters, where most species school and feed on plankton. Their most conspicuous adaptations for this way of life are silvery scales, a compressed, often keeled, body, a flexible mouth, and fine gill rakers. The silvery scales and compressed body function in reducing the visibility of the fish, since the scales scatter the light coming from above, while the compressed body reduces the profile visible from below. The mouth and gill raker structure are used for plankton feeding. More definitive are their skeletal characteristics, the structure of the lateral line system, and the connection of the swimbladder with the inner ear by means of a narrow diverticulum of the bladder. The latter structure apparently improves the ability of the fish to hear high-frequency sounds (Alexander 1967). Most clupeiform fishes belong to the families Clupeidae and Engraulidae. The family Denticipitidae contains a single, rather peculiar-looking freshwater species in Nigeria, and the family Chirocentridae contains a single predacious marine species, with large teeth.

   Clupeidae. The herrings (*Clupea*), shads (*Alosa*), gizzard shads (*Dorosoma*), sardines (*Sardinops*), menhaden (*Brevoortia*), and other clupeid fishes (about 180 species) can be readily recognized by their keeled (sawtooth) bellies and silvery, deciduous scales (Fig. 17.2b). They play key roles in many food webs because of their abundance and their ability to feed on both zooplankton and phytoplankton. They

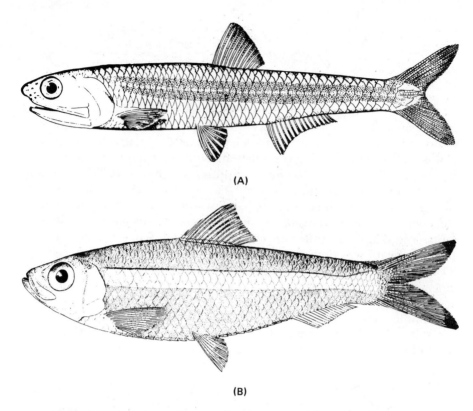

FIGURE 17.2 Clupeiform fishes: (A) anchovy (*Stolephorus,* Engraulidae); and (B) sardine (*Sardinella,* Clupeidae). [(A) from Jordan and Evermann (1895-1900); (B) from Jordan (1895).]

tend to concentrate in coastal waters, in areas of upwelling, so they have long been important to humans, either as the object of commercial fisheries or as food for predacious fishes harvested by humans. Since they often have boom-or-bust population cycles, especially when under pressure from commercial fisheries (see Chapter 35), they may have considerable impact on human affairs. In the fourteenth century the power of the Hanseatic League declined when the herring populations in the Baltic Sea, upon which the League depended for a steady source of fish for trade, collapsed.

While clupeids are usually thought of as marine fishes, many species are abundant in inland lakes and seas, and still others are anadromous. In North America the freshwater species (especially the gizzard shads) are valued mostly as forage for game fishes, and for this purpose they have been planted in lakes and reservoirs far outside their native ranges, with mixed results. In such situations they frequently have population explosions, taking advantage of the lightly exploited zooplankton populations. They also typically become important prey of the game fishes, and growth rates of the game species may increase dramatically.

Unfortunately, the introduced shad are often too successful and, through competition for zooplankton, may decrease the growth and survival rates of juvenile game fishes (which typically feed on zooplankton) and of native planktivorous fishes.

Like the freshwater clupeids, anadromous clupeids are found in many parts of the world: Shad (*Alosa*) are characteristic of coastal streams flowing north into the Black and Caspian Seas, and hilsa (*Hilsa kelee*) spawn in streams that flow into the Indian Ocean, from China to Africa. These fishes typically move upstream during periods of high water to spawn. Following spawning, the embryos and/or larvae are quickly washed downstream, and the young live initially in estuaries or nutrient-rich coastal waters. It is worth noting that spawning migrations are characteristic of clupeids in general. Most marine species congregate for spawning in areas away from the adult feeding grounds. Herrings (*Clupea*) seek inshore areas with submerged plants or rocks to which they can attach their eggs; gizzard shads (*Dorosoma*) move to the upper ends of reservoirs, where the inflowing currents will keep their embryos suspended.

Engraulidae. The 110 or so species of anchovies can be distinguished from clupeids by their overhanging snout and long upper jaw, which extends behind the eye (Fig. 17.2a). As a consequence of this mouth structure, anchovies can open their mouths to an incredible extent, producing a round opening that is efficient for filter feeding on plankton. The actual filtering apparatus is the 50 or more gill rakers on the first gill arch. Anchovies are usually small (less than 15 cm), translucent fish that inhabit inshore areas of the oceans where plankton densities are high, although a few tropical species inhabit fresh water. Many anchovies are important commercial species, and their populations, like those of the clupeids, may fluctuate considerably in response to changing oceanographic conditions.

Elopiformes

This order contains 11 species (in three families) that resemble large, predaceous herrings (Fig. 17.3). Although these fishes have many primitive charac-

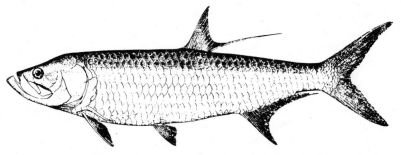

FIGURE 17.3 An elopiform fish, the tarpon (*Megalops,* Elopidae). (From Jordan and Evermann, 1895-1900.)

teristics (e.g., cycloid scales, gular plate, generalized body shape), they are in fact very difficult to relate to any other group of teleosts. While the presence of leptocephalus larvae seems to link them with the eels, the larvae are quite distinctive. Elopiform larvae have a forked tail and a distinct dorsal fin, while eel larvae have a rounded "tail" that merges with an elongate dorsal fin. The members of this order are all shallow-water tropical or subtropical marine forms that occasionally enter fresh or brackish water. Although not esteemed for eating, species such as the Atlantic tarpon (*Tarpon atlanticus*), the bonefish (*Albula vulpes*), and the tenpounder (*Elops saurus*) are favorite sport fishes because of the spectacular, leaping fights they put on once hooked.

Anguilliformes   The diversity of eels is not widely appreciated. Their public "image" has been formed largely by the culinary and sporting qualities of freshwater eels and by lurid descriptions of fierce moray eels attacking divers on coral reefs. Their image is not helped by the fact that most species are quite secretive in their habits, many are quite rare (or at least are found in habitats that are difficult to sample), and superficially there is not much variation in eel morphology. Nevertheless, there are 600+ species of eels, belonging to 22 families. These species are found in a wide variety of habitats, from freshwater lakes and streams, to coral reefs, to the deep sea, although most eels live in shallow tropical or subtropical marine habitats, where they inhabit rocky or coralline crevices or burrows in soft bottoms. An idea of the diversity of eels can be obtained by briefly examining five of the families: Anguillidae, Muraenidae, Congridae, Ophichthidae, and Saccopharyngidae (Fig. 17.4).

   Anguillidae. Although there are only 15 species in this family, it is the best known of the various eel families because most of the species live in fresh water and spawn in the ocean. They are "typical" eels, however, in that each has a wedge-shaped head with a "hard" mouth that lacks the maxilla and premaxilla and an elongate body with dorsal, caudal, and anal fins that merge into one another. Pelvic fins are lacking, and the cycloid scales are deeply imbedded in the skin. The gill openings are far back on the head and are covered with a small, flexible operculum. The branchial cavity is quite large, so the eels breathe mostly by "swallowing" water and moving it past the gills in pulses. All of these features make eels admirably suited for living secretive lives in crevices or burrows or among stalks of aquatic plants in which it can seek out equally secretive prey or ambush fishes that pass by.

   In the eastern United States the American eel (*Anguilla rostrata*) is an important (if declining) predator in many lakes and streams, and the closely related *A. anguilla* plays a similar role in European waters. After spending 6 to 12 years in these habitats and growing to lengths of 35 cm to 150 cm, both species transform from being cryptically colored green and yellow to being silvery. The silver eels then migrate out to sea and

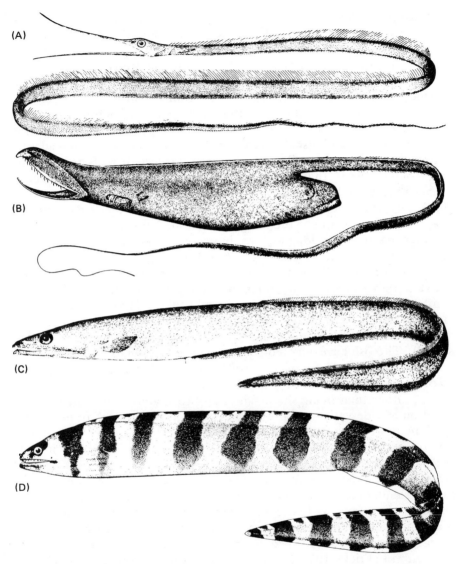

FIGURE 17.4 Representative anguilliform fishes: (A) snipe eel (*Nemichthys*, Nemichthyidae); (B) gulper eel (*Eupharynx*, Eurypharyngidae); (C) cutthroat eel (*Synaphobranchus*, Synaphobranchidae); and (D) moray eel (*Gymnothorax*, Muraenidae). [(A), (B), and (C) from Goode and Bean (1895); (D) from Jordan and Evermann (1895-1900).]

then apparently seek deepwater currents, with which they swim to their spawning grounds in the Sargasso Sea, a distance as much as 5600 km. Once there, they apparently spawn at great depths and die after spawning. The spawning grounds of the eels were located by Johannes Schmidt (1922) by plotting the distribution of leptocephalus larvae by size on a map of the Atlantic. The smallest larvae were found in the vicinity of the Sargasso Sea. To reach Europe, the larvae must drift with the currents about three years; to reach North America, about one year. Once the leptocephali reach coastal waters, they metamorphose into elvers, which proceed to migrate into streams and estuaries.

Muraenidae. Moray eels are efficient predators of fish and invertebrates of reefs and rocky shores in tropical and temperate regions. They lack both paired fins and scales and have hard, pointed heads with many teeth, small, round gill openings, and a posterior set of nostrils set high on the head, usually between the small eyes. With such adaptations, they penetrate easily into the deep crevices of reefs to consume night-active fishes that are in hiding during the day and day-active fishes that are in hiding during the night (see Chapter 34). Most species have daggerlike teeth for grabbing their prey, but some (e.g., *Echidna*) have flattened teeth for breaking up hard-shelled invertebrates. Some morays may grow as long as 3 m, but most do not exceed 1 m. Their colors range from drab yellow-green to bright yellow or red with spots or rings of white. While many morays are considered to be dangerous because they can give severe bites to an unwary diver, they are probably most dangerous as a cause of ciguatera fish poisoning. The flesh of tropical species of morays can become poisonous when they consume other fishes that have fed on the algae that produce the toxins (Halstead 1967). The fish have adapted to the toxins, but humans have not!

Congridae. Most of the 100+ species of conger eels resemble moray eels, except that they usually possess pectoral fins and that their teeth, rather than being sharp fangs, are stout and cone-shaped. They feed on a wide variety of prey, but mostly invertebrates. In temperate regions most conger eels are associated with shallow, rocky areas, but in tropical areas many of them instead construct burrows in soft bottoms. Most remarkable of the latter eels are the garden eels (*Gorgasia, Heteroconger, Nystachtichthys,* and *Taenioconger*). Garden eels are small, slender eels with moderately large eyes, rounded heads, and small mouths that form colonies on sandy bottoms in areas of moderate currents. Each eel constructs a burrow from which it can extend its long (to 1 m) body and feed during the day on zooplankton carried by the current (Fricke 1970). When all the eels in a colony are feeding and waving about in the current, the colony has more the appearance of a field of seagrass than an aggregation of fish.

Ophichthidae. The family of snake and worm eels is the largest in the Anguilliformes, with about 270 species. Most are found in shallow water in tropical and subtropical areas, are small in size (less than 1 m), and are brightly colored. Despite their abundance, bright colors and habitat, they are rarely seen and are difficult to collect because they burrow into soft bottoms and are active mostly at night. Unlike the garden eels, they do not have permanent burrows but use them for a day and then abandon them. The "true" snake eels (subfamily Ophichthinae) have a spikelike tail which lacks a caudal fin, with which they can quickly penetrate sand and mud bottoms. The worm eels (subfamily Echelinae) possess a caudal fin but are mostly found in soft mud bottoms. When in their burrows, snake and worm eels leave just their heads exposed. Consequently, they have exceptionally well-developed branchial pumping apparatus for moving water across the gills, and both sets of nostrils are located on the tip of the snout.

Saccopharyngidae. The swallower eels and their relatives the gulper eels (Eurypharyngidae) are deepsea eels that are so bizarre in their anatomy that some early ichthyologists questioned whether or not they were even bony fishes. Among other things, they lack opercular bones, branchiostegal rays, scales, pelvic fins, ribs, pyloric ceca, the swimbladder, and, usually, the caudal fin. What structures they do possess are highly modified for the role these eels play as predators that are capable of swallowing prey larger than themselves. The mouth and pharynx are extremely large and distensible, with small teeth for holding onto the prey. The gill openings are small and placed far back on the body, closer to the anus than to the tip of the snout in the gulpers, while the tiny eyes are set near the tip of the snout. These fishes are among the largest (or at least the longest, reaching 60 cm to 180 cm) bathypelagic fishes, but their watery flesh and poorly developed fins indicate that they do not actively pursue prey but hang suspended in the water column waiting for their prey to come to them. It seems likely that they attract their prey by using a light-producing organ at the tip of the tail. At present four species of swallower eels and one species of gulper eel are recognized. In addition, there are three species of small, gulper-type eels that are placed in a separate family (Monognathidae) because they lack an upper jaw and pectoral fins. However, the systematics of these three families are likely to change, since each species is known from only a small number of specimens.

Notacanthiformes   The halosaurs and spiny eels consist of 24 species in three families (Fig. 17.5). All are eel-like inhabitants of the floor of the oceans, in deep water. Their subterminal mouths and body structure indicate that they probably make a living by pulling small invertebrates out of muddy bottoms. Although similar to eels in many respects, they differ from them in many important characteristics, such as the presence of both pelvic and pec-

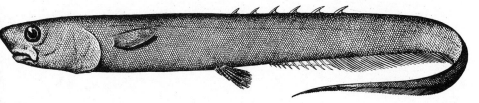

FIGURE 17.5   A notacanthiform eel: spiny eel (*Notacanthus*, Notacanthidae). (From Goode and Bean, 1895.)

toral fins, the flexible jaw structure, and the elongate anal fin, which merges with the caudal fins (if one is present). The dorsal fin is short or consists of a series of spines (Notacanthidae). One curious aspect of this group is that the leptocephalus larvae may be quite large (up to 180 cm) but then metamorphose into much smaller juveniles (D. G. Smith 1970).

Supplemental Readings   Gosline 1971; Herald 1961; Nelson 1976; Sinha and Jones 1975; Tesch 1977; Wheeler 1975.

ααααααααααααααααααααααααααααααααααααααααααααααααααααααααααααααααααα
~~~~~~

Osteoglossids

Infraclass Teleostei
Division Archaeophylaces
  Superorder Osteoglossomorpha
    Order Osteoglossiformes
      Families Hiodontidae (mooneyes), Notopteridae (knifefishes), Osteoglossidae (bonytongues), Pantodontidae (butterfly fish)
    Order Mormyriformes
      Families Mormyridae (mormyrids), Gymnarchidae

The osteoglossids are an unusual group of about 116+ species of freshwater fishes, most of which (100+ species) are in one African family, the Mormyridae. The rest of the species are scattered about the continents and are generally considered to be relicts of a once much more abundant group. Although the fossil record is scanty, osteoglossids may have been a dominant element in the freshwater fauna of the world before the emergence of the ostariophysan fishes. The relationships of the osteoglossids to other fish groups are poorly understood, presumably because they are such an ancient group. Their osteology is quite distinctive and ties the members of the Osteoglossomorpha together, if somewhat tenuously. Most osteoglossids have most of their teeth located on the tongue (*osteo*, "bony"; *glossid*, "tongue") and on the roof of the mouth (or the parasphenoid). They also have a caudal fin with 16 or fewer rays (most bony fishes have more), no intermuscular bones on the back (epipleurals), cycloid scales with ornate microsculpturing, and an intestine that curls around to the left side of the esophagous rather than to the right as in most other bony fishes (Nelson 1976). Curiously (and unlike other fishes), they lack an apparatus for actively pumping water over the olfactory epithelium.

Osteoglossiformes   This order contains just 15 odd, relict species, with two species in North America, three in South America, four in Africa, four in Asia, and two in Australia. The fact that representatives of the family Osteoglossidae appear in South America, Africa, Southeast Asia, and Australia is frequently cited as evidence for continental drift (see Chapter 24).

Hiodontidae.   The two species in this family, the mooneye (*Hiodon tergisus*) and the goldeye (*H. alosoides*), are the most "normal"-looking fish in their entire superorder, since they superficially resemble shad (Fig. 18.1a). Their most distinctive external features are their large eyes, which have bright gold irises in the goldeye and gold-silver irises in the mooneye. The gold color in both species is apparently from a tapetum lucidum which increases their ability to see at low light levels (see Chapter 10). Goldeye are known to feed mostly at night and to have only rods in their retinas (no cones). The goldeye and mooneye are found in the backwaters of the larger rivers and lakes throughout the Mississippi drainage system. They are also found in the Hudson Bay drainages and Arctic drainages (goldeye only) of Canada, where the goldeye is abundant enough to be an important commercial species. Both species are carnivorous, taking a wide variety of prey, but they are largely piscivorous as adults (Scott and Crossman 1973).

Notopteridae.   The six species of knifefish have long, strongly compressed bodies that taper to a point. They swim mainly through the rhythmic movements of the long anal fin, which extends from just behind the head to the tiny caudal fin, which it joins. They appear to be able to swim equally well forwards or backwards. The dorsal fin (absent from one species) is small and featherlike, so these fishes are commonly called featherbacks. The swimbladder is connected to the gut and is used for air breathing by these fishes. Thus, the knifefishes are extremely well adapted for living among submerged and emergent vegetation in stagnant backwaters and ponds of tropical Asia and Africa. They generally remain quietly in cover during the day but come out to prey on invertebrates and small fish in the evening. The larger species, which may approach 1 m in length, are favored food fishes in Southeast Asia.

Osteoglossidae.   The seven (possibly eight) species in this family are large fishes that have heavy, elongate bodies covered with large scales (Fig. 18.1b). The dorsal and anal fins are long and placed on the rear half of the body. All apparently can breathe air by using their lunglike swimbladders. Most of the species make their living as predators in tropical rivers. The arapaima (*Arapaima gigas*) of the Amazon River is one of the largest freshwater fish species, regularly reaching lengths between 2 m and 3 m and reportedly growing as large as 4.5 m. The silvery arawana (*Osteoglossum bicirrosum*) occurs with the arapaima but only reaches lengths of about 1 m. It is characterized by two chin barbels and a remarkably large, angled mouth, with which it can capture oth-

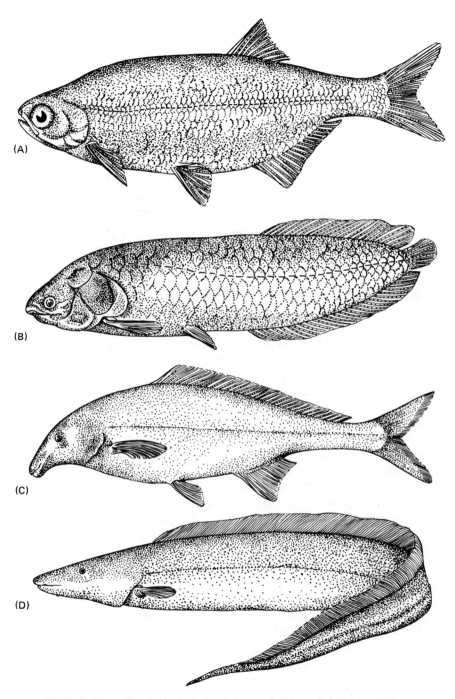

FIGURE 18.1 Representative osteoglossomorph fishes: (A) Goldeye (*Hiodon*, Hiodontidae); (B) African bony-tongue (*Heterotis*, Osteoglossidae); (C) elephant fish (*Mormyrus*, Mormyridae); and (D) electric fish (*Gymnarchus*, Gymnarchidae), [(A) from Jordan and Evermann (1900); (B), (C), and (D) after Boulenger (1907).]

er fishes and small animals that fall into the water from the overhanging vegetation. It incubates its young in a special pouch in its mouth, as does its close relatives the barramundis (*Scleropages*) of Australia and Asia. The only member of the Osteoglossidae that is not predatory is *Heterotis niloticus* of western Africa. This large fish (to 1 m) has its fourth gill arch modified into a spiral-shaped filtering apparatus. This organ secretes mucus in which phytoplankton and small bits of organic matter are trapped and then swallowed. *Heterotis* also builds large, mud-walled nests in which its large eggs are laid. The young have external gills.

Pantodontidae. The single species in this family, the butterfly fish (*Pantodon bucholzi*), is a small (10 cm), surface-feeding fish of central Africa. It is most remarkable for its specialized paired fins. The pectoral fins are large and capable of being used for gliding short distances after the fish leaps out of the water, while the pelvic fins have elongated rays upon which the fish can "stand" in shallow water.

Mormyriformes

The order Mormyriformes consists of two families, the Mormyridae (100+ species; Fig. 18.1c) and the Gymnarchidae (containing just *Gymnarchus niloticus*; Fig. 18.1d). Both families are adaptable for nocturnal living in the muddy rivers and lakes of Africa and are quite abundant in many areas. They have also successfully adapted to the reservoirs that now exist on many African rivers and contribute significantly to the reservoir fisheries. One of the principal reasons for the success of this group seems to be their use of electric organs to find their way about, to detect prey, and to communicate with each other. Weak electric signals are produced by modified muscles in the caudal peduncle, and an electrical field is set up around each fish. Anything which disrupts the field can be detected and identified with a surprising (to us) degree of precision. The electric signals can be modified by the fish to communicate with other fish by changing the shape of the field, the form of the waves, the discharge frequencies, the timing of the discharges, and the pattern of stopping and starting the discharges (Hopkins 1974). Thus the electric signals can be used in courtship, aggressive behavior, and other intraspecific encounters. Since each species has its own set of electrical patterns, recognition and avoidance of other species is also possible. Apparently the acute discrimination between different types of electrical signals of which mormyrids are capable requires an extremely well-developed nervous system. The cerebellum, in particular, is so large that, relative to body size, it is roughly the same size as that of humans. The complexity of the mormyrid brain is also reflected in their complex behavior patterns. Aquarists have long admired mormyrids for their learning abilities and the fact that many species engage in apparent play behavior, usually considered to be a sign of intelligence. The "play" usually consists of batting around a small object with the head.

The morphology of mormyriform fishes reflects the importance of electricity as a sensory modality. In both families the eyes are small and the skin thick. All species usually swim slowly, with their bodies rigid, presumably to avoid distorting the electrical field they are generating. *Gymnarchus* does this by propelling itself with its long dorsal fin; by passing waves down this fin it can move either forwards or backwards. With its long, eel-like body (no anal, caudal, or pelvic fins) and large electrical organs, *Gymnarchus* has exceptionally well-developed electrical sensory abilities and so has been one of the most studied of electrical fishes. In contrast to *Gymnarchus,* members of the family Mormyridae maintain a rigid body by relying primarily on the tail for propulsion. As a consequence the tail is often deeply forked and the caudal peduncle very narrow, somewhat reminiscent of the arrangement in tunas.

Another peculiar feature of the Mormyridae is that many of the species have proboscislike snouts. These species presumably feed by probing in the bottom mud for small invertebrates. Species without the protruding snout usually feed on plankton or small fish. *Gymnarchus* is entirely piscivorous as an adult.

It is worth noting that despite the importance of the electrical system in mormyrids, they also possess a well-developed sense of hearing, which depends on the swimbladder for amplifying sound (Werns and Howland 1976). The swimbladder is quite small and located mostly in the head region, where it is in contact with the inner ear.

Supplemental Readings   Bullock 1973; Herald 1961; Hopkins 1974; Lissman 1963; Nelson 1976; Sterba 1959.

ααααααααααααααααααααααααααααααααααααααααααααααααααααααααααααααααααααα
~~~~~~

Salmonids

Infraclass Teleostei
Division Euteleostei
 Superorder Protacanthopterygii
  Order Salmoniformes
   Suborder Esocoidei
    Families Esocidae (pikes), Umbridae (mudminnows), Lepidogalaxiidae
   Suborder Salmonoidei
    Families Salmonidae (salmon, trout, whitefish), Retropinnidae (New Zealand smelts), Aplochitonidae (southern smelts), Galaxiidae (bullies), Osmeridae (smelts), Plecoglossidae (ayu), Salangidae (oriental icefishes)
   Suborder Argentinoidei
    Families Argentinidae (argentines), Bathylagidae (deepsea smelts), Opisthoproctidae (barreleyes), Alepocephalidae (slickheads), Searsididae (tubeshoulders)
   Suborder Stomiatoidei
    Families Gonstomatidae (bristlemouths), Sternoptychidae (marine hatchetfishes), Chauliodontidae (viperfishes), Stomiatidae (scaly dragonfishes), Astronesthidae (snaggletooths), Melanostomidatidae (scaleless black dragonfishes), Malacosteidae (loosejaws), Idiacanthidae (black dragonfishes)

The order Salmoniformes is now considered to be the ancestral group from which the "higher" teleosts (discussed in the next four chapters) evolved (see Chapter 12). The order as constituted here contains 500 to 520 species divided up into four suborders, with each suborder representing a distinct, and ancient, phyletic line. The Salmoniformes are characterized in a large part by the absence of characteristics that define the more derivative orders. They lack spines, but most possess an adipose fin. Their pelvic fins are abdominal in position and widely separated from the pectoral fins (the pelvic and pectoral girdles are not connected), which are placed low on the body. The scales are cycloid, and the upper jaw contains both the maxilla and the premaxilla, the latter not protractile. The swimbladder is connected to the gut with a duct.

240

Esocoidei   This suborder contains just eleven species, all freshwater: five species of pike (Esocidae), five species of mudminnow (Umbridae), and the peculiar *Lepidogalaxias salamandroides* (Lepidogalaxidae) (Rosen 1974). The pikes and mudminnows are characteristic of North America and northern Eurasia, while *Lepidogalaxias* is confined to western Australia. The body morphology of all the species is that of the lie-in-wait predator, with dorsal and anal fins placed far back on the body, about equal in size, and aligned with each other. The adipose fin is lacking, as are pyloric ceca, teeth on the maxillary bone, and the mesocoracoid bone in the shoulder girdle.

The pikes, with their elongate snouts and forked tails, are classic lie-in-wait predators and are important piscivores in weedy lakes and other slow-moving bodies of water. In North America and Europe they are favorite sport fishes, especially the circumpolar northern pike (*Esox lucius*), which may reach 24 kg to 26 kg (1.3 m) and the muskellunge (*E. masquinongy*) of eastern North America, which may reach 32 kg (1.6 m). Pike generally capture their prey with a sudden rush from cover. They grab the prey sideways, impaling it on sharp teeth before retreating to cover to turn the prey around and swallow it head first. Pike require flooded vegetation for spawning and nursery areas for the young, so stabilization of lake levels and stream flows by humans is frequently detrimental to their populations.

In contrast to the pikes, the mudminnows are all small, rarely reaching 20 cm, and have blunt snouts and rounded tails. However, all are voracious lie-in-wait predators on invertebrates. They are most characteristic of weedy ponds, lakes, and backwaters, where temperatures may be very warm and oxygen levels low. At least one species (*Umbra limi*) has limited abilities to breathe air (Scott and Crossman 1973). The mudminnows are of particular interest to zoogeographers because they are obligatory freshwater fishes with a distinct family distribution pattern. The three species of *Umbra* are found in Atlantic coast drainages of North America, the Mississippi River system, and Europe, respectively; *Novumbra hubbsi* (Olympic mudminnow) is confined to the Olympic peninsula of Washington; and *Dallia pectoralis* (Alaska blackfish) is widely distributed in arctic North America and Siberia (see Chapter 24). Blackfish are extraordinarily abundant in some arctic lakes and ponds and have been used by the native peoples for food for themselves and their dogs.

Salmonoidei   The 150 or so species in this suborder are for the most part freshwater or diadromous, with the exception of a few marine smelts (Osmeridae). They are also largely inhabitants of temperate waters, with the exception of some tropical oriental icefishes (Salangidae) and one species of Galaxiidae. Three of the families (Retropinnidae, Aplochitonidae, and Galaxiidae) are confined to the Southern Hemisphere, and the rest are native only to the Northern Hemisphere (although the Salmonidae have been widely introduced on the southern continents). It is difficult to characterize this suborder morphologically because there are few distinctive characteristics possessed by all the families, yet the families are all linked together by shared characteristics. For example, all except the Galaxiidae possess adipose fins, but the galaxiids are closely tied to the Aplochitonidae by osteological features. Regardless of their interrelationships, most members of this suborder are tasty, and many are among the world's most sought-after food fishes.

Salmonidae.   Salmonids are the dominant fishes in the cold-water streams and lakes of North America and Eurasia, where they support major sport and commercial fisheries. Because of the favor they find with anglers and their ease of propagation, salmonids now dominate the cold fresh waters of the Southern Hemisphere as well. A member of the family is readily recognized by its streamlined body, forked tail, adipose fin, axillary process by the pelvic fins, and large number of pyloric ceca (11 to 210) and branchiostegal rays (7 to 20) (Fig. 19.1a, b). Most species grow to at least 20+ cm, and the largest species is the chinook salmon (*Oncorhynchus tshawytscha*), which may grow nearly 1.5 m long (57 kg).

The Salmonidae can be divided up into three readily recognizable groups, usually treated as subfamilies (but often as families): the Salmoninae (salmon and trout), the Coregoninae (whitefishes), and the Thymallinae (graylings). Salmon and trout have fine scales (more than 110 in the lateral line), a short dorsal fin, and teeth on the maxillary bone of the upper jaw. Whitefishes have coarse scales (fewer than 110 along the lateral line), a short dorsal fin, and no teeth on the maxillary bone. Graylings have moderately large scales (70 to 110 in the lateral line), a long, saillike dorsal fin, and teeth on the maxillary bone. Among these three groups about 70 species are currently recognized, but many of the species are controversial. For example, the rainbow trout (*Salmo gairdneri*) is usually considered to be distinct from the cutthroat trout (*S. clarki*), and indeed, where the two species occur together naturally in coastal streams, they seem to be reproductively isolated from each other. However, when rainbow trout are introduced into cutthroat trout streams of the interior basins of western North America, hybrid swarms often result, usually to the detriment of the cutthroat trout phenotype. On the other hand, many northern lakes contain several distinct populations of whitefish (*Coregonus*) that are ecologically and reproductively isolated from each other yet are all assigned to just one species.

Presumably, the abundance of small fish in the ocean is one of the principal reasons anadromy has developed in salmon and trout. In the ocean such fish grow extremely rapidly and can consequently produce more (and larger) eggs than fish that spend their entire life cycle in fresh water. A 500-g rainbow trout that has lived in a stream for four years

CH. 19 SALMONIDS

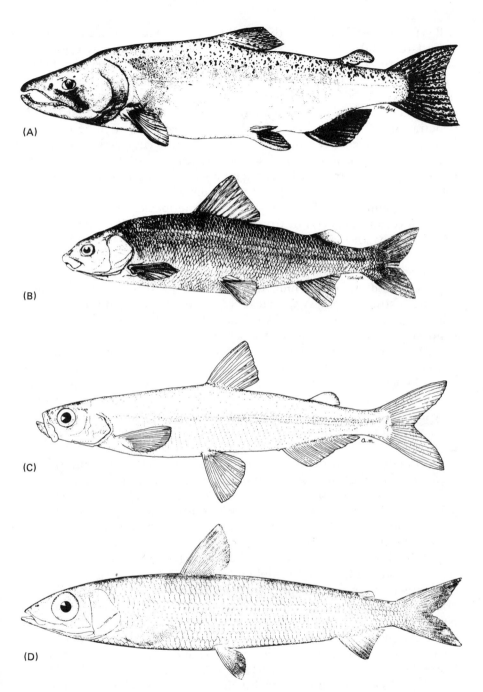

FIGURE 19.1 Representative salmonoid fishes: (A) chinook salmon (*Oncorhynchus tshawytscha,* 64 cm, Salmonidae); (B) mountain whitefish (*Prosopium williamsoni,* 28 cm, Salmonidae); (C) delta smelt (*Hypomesus transpacificus,* 8 cm, Osmeridae); and (D) Atlantic argentine (*Argentina silus,* 36 cm, Argentinidae). [(A), (B), and (C) from Moyle (1976a); (D) from Goode and Bean (1895).]

will typically produce fewer than 1000 eggs, whereas a 4-kg anadromous trout (steelhead) of the same age will produce 4000 or more eggs. The advantage of continuing to use streams for spawning is presumably the protection they afford the embryos and young from marine predators, including other salmon and trout. The embryos are particularly well protected, since they are buried in riffles, in gravel beds that permit penetration of oxygen-rich water but few predators. By the time the young fish have emerged from the gravel, they are large in size (for newly hatched fish) and quite active, so they are capable of avoiding most invertebrate predators and of feeding on a wide range of prey items themselves. Despite the advantages of anadromy, it is a highly variable trait among the salmonids. It is obligatory in some species of Pacific salmon, optional for most species of trout, and not present at all in some species of char, most notably the lake char (*Salvelinus namaycush*). Most species of whitefish and grayling are not anadromous.

While anadromy is not a universal feature of the salmonids, most species do undertake spawning migrations and possess a series of distinctive life history stages. A special set of terminology has arisen in association with these stages, thanks to the interest of them by salmon and trout anglers. The eggs are laid in a depression dug in the gravel, called a *redd*. The egg develops into *alevins* or sac fry, small fish which still possess a yolk sac. As the yolk sac is absorbed and the alevins emerge from the gravel, they become *fry*. The small, active fry develop a series of bars on their sides (parr marks) and are then called *parr,* a stage which may last a few months or years. Stream-dwelling trout frequently retain the parr marks throughout their life. In anadromous populations parr transform into silvery *smolts* and migrate to the sea. Since the parr-smolt transformation is in preparation for a dramatic change in habitat, it includes profound changes in morphology, physiology, and behavior (Hoar 1976). In the ocean (or large lakes) the smolts gradually become mature adults and return to their home streams for spawning. Some males, called *jacks* or *grilse*, return to spawn at an early age and small size. Spawned-out fish are termed *kelts*.

Galaxiidae. The galaxiids or bullies, together with the related families Aplochitonidae and Retropinnidae, are a fascinating group to zoogeographers because of their occurrence in fresh water on all the southern continents except Antarctica. They are found in Australia, Tasmania, New Zealand, southern South America (including Tierra del Fuego and other islands), South Africa, and New Caledonia. Most of these areas have endemic genera and species, but one species, *Galaxias maculatus*, is present in all regions where galaxiids are found except South Africa. Rosen (1974) indicates that the distribution pattern of the galaxiids can be explained by the former connection of the continents and their subsequent separation through the processes of continental drift (see Chapter 24). On the other hand, McDowall and Robertson (1975) argue that the distribution of *G. maculatus* can be at least partially explained by the fact that larvae of this species are planktonic and marine and are capable of being carried to distant shores by oceanic currents.

Despite their far-flung distribution pattern, galaxiids are a readily recognizable group. They are small (usually less than 15 cm), elongate fishes that lack an adipose fin but have a dorsal fin placed far back on the body, above the anal fin. The caudal fin is usually rounded, the pectoral fins large, and the pelvic fins small or absent in some species. Scales and maxillary teeth are lacking. Most of the 50 or so species spend their entire life cycle in fresh water, but a few spawn in estuaries and have marine larvae. *G. maculatus* seems to move downstream to spawn in response to lunar cycles, since it lays its eggs among grasses flooded by high spring tides. When the tides ebb, the eggs are stranded among the grasses but hatch when the next high tide covers the grasses, about two weeks later (McDowall and Whitaker 1975). In the streams, bullies are the approximate ecological equivalents of salmonids in the Northern Hemisphere.

Osmeridae. The smelt family contains only about 10 species, but these species are characteristic of the coastal areas of the northern halves of North America and Eurasia. Some species are entirely marine (although confined to inshore areas), some are entirely fresh or brackish water dwellers, and some are anadromous. All make excellent eating, but only about half the species are regularly sought as food fishes. Smelt are generally small in size (usually less than 20 cm, but some species may reach 40 cm), but they are still voracious pelagic carnivores, consuming both zooplankton and small fish. The mouth is well equipped with small teeth, including those on the maxilla and premaxilla. As in salmonids, the adipose fin is present, but in contrast to them, the axillary process on the pelvic fin is absent and the number of pyloric ceca is 0 to 11 (Fig. 19.1c). Smelt are silvery in color and, as McAllister (1963) notes, have "a curious cucumber odor," although this odor has also been characterized as that of putrid cucumbers (McPhail and Lindsey 1970). Smelts generally seek out gravelly areas for spawning, either beaches or riffles, and lay adhesive demersal eggs. It is typically when they aggregate for spawning that they are most vulnerable to capture.

Argentinoidei   The 109 or so species, from five families, in this suborder are all small, deepsea, smeltlike fishes with large or tubular eyes. They are either silvery in color (Argentinidae, Bathylagidae, Opisthoproctidae) or black (Alepocephalidae, Searsiidae). Many lack the adipose fin, and only a few have photophores. However, they all possess an epibranchial (crumenal) organ for grinding up small prey. This organ consists of a small diverticulum located just behind the fourth gill arch, into which the gill rakers from both sides can fit, interdigitating with one another to break up the food particles.

One of the more peculiar adaptations present in some members of this suborder, including the eleven known species of barreleyes or spook-fishes (Opisthoproctidae), is tubular eyes. Such eyes are pointed upwards and contain exceptionally large numbers of rods. The fishes that possess such eyes are apparently capable of binocular vision under extremely low light conditions. Fishes that possess them typically prey on small, active invertebrates toward the lower limits of light penetration; the upward-pointing eyes enable them to locate prey silhouetted against the light above.

Most species within this suborder are known only from a few specimens, although some species are common enough to be part of the diets of epipelagic predatory fishes that descend into deeper waters to feed.

Stomiatoidei

The Stomiatoidei have a mixture of an-cestral and derived teleost characteristics and seem to have had a long independent evolutionary history. They probably do not belong in the Salmoniformes at all (Rosen 1973). They have been left in the Salmoniformes following Nelson (1976), mostly as a matter of convenience but also because their relationships to other euteleostean groups are unclear.

The stomiatoids are mostly tropical, deepsea fishes with photo-phores and large mouths with teeth on both the maxilla and premaxilla (Fig. 19.2). Many species have an adipose fin. The scales, if present, are cycloid. Most species are black in color, although a few are silvery. The group includes the most abundant fishes in the world (Gonosto-matidae), as well as some of the most fearsome-looking small predators (Chauliodontidae).

Gonostomatidae. The bristlemouths (or lightfishes) are extraor-dinarily abundant in many parts of the world's oceans; members of the genus *Cyclothone* are probably more numerous than any other fishes. However, all the 60 or so species are also quite small (most are less than 5 cm long). Bristlemouths have large, horizontal mouths with numerous small teeth, typical of fish that feed on large prey, yet they also have fine gill rakers, typical of fish that feed on small prey (Fig. 19.2a). This arrangement may partially explain their success, since it enables them to feed on whatever prey comes along, regardless of size. The bodies of bristlemouths are elongate and somewhat rounded.

Sternoptychidae. In many areas of the oceans, the marine hatchet-fishes (27+ species) are second in abundance only to the bristlemouths. These small (to 10 cm) fishes are indeed hatchet-shaped, with deep, extremely compressed bodies (Fig. 19.2d). Not only does the belly taper to a thin edge, but the top of each fish has a "blade" made of fused pterygiophores. The sides of the body are silvery and contain numerous large photophores. The eyes and mouth are all turned upwards and the eyes of some species are tubular. These features are all indicative of the fact that most species of hatchetfish move up and down the water

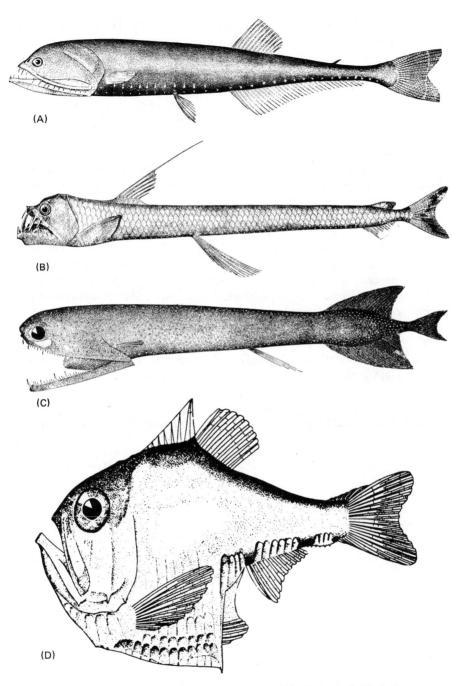

FIGURE 19.2 Representative deepsea salmonoids: (A) bristlemouth (*Cyclothone elongata,* 8 cm, Gonostomatidae); (B) viperfish (*Chauliodus sloani,* 35 cm, Chaulidontidae); (C) loosejaw (*Malacosteus niger,* 12 cm; Malacosteidae); and (D) hatchetfish (*Argyropelecus olfersi,* 3 cm, Sternoptychidae). [(A), (B), and (C) from Goode and Bean (1895); (D) from Jordan and Evermann (1900).]

column, preying on copepods and other migrating zooplankters. The slender profile of these fish when seen from above or below, coupled with the light-scattering abilities of their silvery sides and, perhaps, their photophores, serves to conceal them from both predators and prey.

Piscivorous families. The remaining stomiatoid fishes belong to six families that are largely piscivorous, including species that can capture prey larger than themselves. The viperfishes (Chauliodontidae, six species) have extraordinary fanglike teeth and an ability to swing open their mouths to swallow very large prey (see Chapter 36). The scaly dragonfishes (Melanostomiatidae, 90+ species) and loosejaws (Malacosteidae, 10 species) are all widespread families of elongate lie-in-wait deep-sea predators, black in color with rows of tiny photophores. Their jaws are large with many sharp teeth, and most species possess a long chin barbel with a luminescent "lure" at the end, presumably for attracting prey. The maximum size of these fishes is 10 cm to 25 cm. The black dragonfishes (Idiacanthidae, three species) are similar in many respects to the preceding families, except that their bodies are nearly eellike, with elongate dorsal fins. The black dragonfishes also possess extremely peculiar larvae that are colorless and have eyes on the tips of long stalks. Although these fishes can achieve lengths between 35 cm and 40 cm (but only 25 g to 30 g by weight), it is only the females that reach such sizes. The males are much smaller and apparently serve only for reproduction, since they lack teeth, the chin barbel, and a functional digestive tract!

Supplemental Readings   Fitch and Lavenberg 1968; Gosline 1971; Hart 1973; Herald 1961; Marshall 1966; McAllister 1963; Moyle 1976a; Nelson 1976; Nikolsky 1954; Rosen 1973, 1974; Scott and Crossman 1973; Wheeler 1975.

ααααααααααααααααααααααααααααααααααααααααααααααααααααααααααααααααααααααααα
~~~~~~

Minnows, Characins, and Catfishes

Infraclass Teleostei
Division Euteleostei
  Superorder Ostariophysi
    Order Gonorynchiformes
      Families Chanidae (milkfish), Kneriidae, Phractolaemidae, Gonorynchidae (mousefish)
    Order Cypriniformes
      Suborder Characoidei
        Superfamily Characoidea
          Families Characidae (characins), Erythrinidae, Ctenolucidae (pike characins), Hepsetidae (Kafue pike), Cynodontidae, Lebiasinidae (pencilfishes), Parodontidae, Gasteropelecidae (freshwater hatchetfishes), Prochilodontidae, Curimatidae, Anostomidae (headstanders), Hemiodontidae, Chilodontidae, Distichodontidae, Citharinidae, Icthyboridae (African pike characins)
        Superfamily Gymnotoidea
          Families Gymnotidae (knife eels), Electrophoridae (electric eels), Apteronotidae, Rhamphichthyidae (knifefishes)
      Suborder Cyprinoidei
        Superfamily Cyprinoidea
          Families Cyprinidae (minnows or carps), Catostomidae (suckers)
        Superfamily Cobitoidea
          Families Cobitidae (loaches), Gyrinocheilidae (suckerbelly loaches), Psilorhynchidae, Homalopteridae (hillstream loaches)
      Suborder Siluroidei
        Families Diplomystidae, Ictaluridae (North American catfishes), Bagridae, Cranoglanididae, Siluridae (Eurasian catfishes), Schilbeidae, Pangasiidae, Amblycipitidae (Asiatic torrent catfishes), Amphiliidae, Akysidae (stream catfishes), Sisoridae, Clariidae (air-breathing catfishes) Heteropneustidae (airsac catfishes), Chacidae (squarehead catfish), Olyridae, Malapteruridae (electric catfishes), Mochokidae (upside-down catfishes), Ariidae (sea catfishes), Doradidae (thorny catfishes), Auchenipteridae, Aspredinidae (Banjo catfishes). Plotosidae (eel catfishes), Pimelodidae (longwhisker catfishes), Ageneiosidae (barbel-less catfishes), Hypophthalmidae (loweye catfishes), Helogeneidae, Cetopsidae (whale catfishes), Trichomycteridae (parasitic catfishes), Callichthyidae (armored catfishes), Loricariidae (armored catfishes), Astroblepidae (South American torrent catfishes).

249

The superorder Ostariophysi contains between 5000 and 6000 species, over one-quarter of the known fish species. More important, nearly three-fourths of all freshwater fish species belong in this superorder. They are the dominant freshwater fishes on all continents except Australia and Antarctica. As might be expected with such a large group of fishes, much controversy surrounds the higher taxonomic categories. Prior to Greenwood et al. (1966), the Ostariophysi did not include the Gonorynchiformes but only the fishes placed here under the Cypriniformes. This is because the order Cypriniformes is the most cohesive of all the major teleost taxa; its members are easily recognized by a number of distinctive features. The Gonorynchiformes lack most of these distinctive features, but the members of this order have enough in common with the cypriniform fishes to be considered derivatives of the forerunners of Cypriniformes (Rosen and Greenwood 1970). The characteristics used to link the two orders are similarities in the skeletal structure of the vertebral column, tail, and jaws, the structure of the swimbladder, the presence of histologically distinctive breeding tubercles, and the presence of fright substances (*Schreckstoff*). Schreckstoff is released into the water when a fish is injured and causes a fright reaction in members of the same or closely related species.

Gonorynchiformes There are only four families and about 16 species in this order, most of them small freshwater fishes. Aside from the various family specializations, they are not a particularly distinctive group. They have small, usually toothless mouths and epibranchial organs (modified gillrakers) for breaking up the particles of food they ingest. Their first three vertebrae are modified in such a way as to suggest the condition that permitted the development of the distinctive Weberian ossicles of the Cypriniformes.

The best-known member of the Gonorynchiformes is the milkfish (*Chanos chanos*), the sole member of the family Chanidae (Fig. 20.1a). This is a marine and brackish-water species that is one of the most important food fishes of southeast Asia. The adults are large (to 1.8 m), active fish, with silvery sides and deeply forked tails. They feed mostly on planktonic algae. They are extremely tolerant of a wide range of temperature and salinity, and so are successfully raised in brackish and freshwater ponds. The fish used for pond culture are collected as fry in estuaries and other inshore areas used.

The gonorynchiform family with the most species (12) is the Kneriidae, a group of small, loachlike freshwater fishes of Africa. These fishes are well adapted for living in swift streams, having fine (or no) scales, subterminal and protractile mouths, elongate bodies, and large pectoral fins that when placed together can form a sucker to enable the fish to cling to rocks in strong currents. Some species are also air breathers, which enables them to survive in stagnant pools. The remaining two gonorynchiform families contain just one species each. *Phractolaemus*

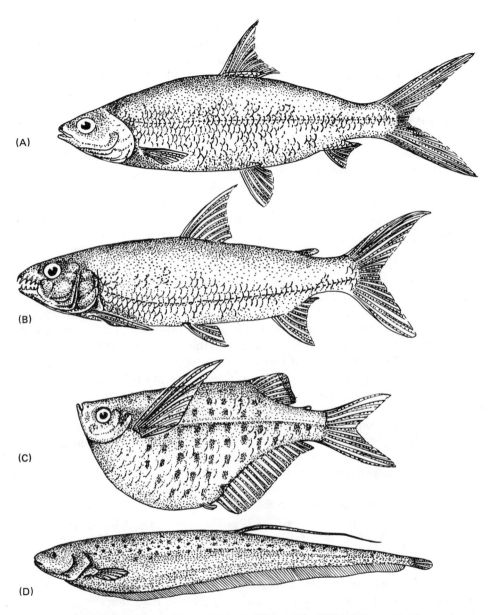

(A)

(B)

(C)

(D)

FIGURE 20.1 Representative ostariophysan fishes: (A) milkfish (*Chanos,* Chanidae, Gonorynchiformes); (B) characin (*Astyanax,* Characidae, Cypriniformes); (C) freshwater hatchetfish (*Gasteropelecus,* Gasteropelecidae); and (D) electric knifefish (*Sternarchus,* Apteronotidae, Gymnotoidea).

ansorgei is a small, air-breathing (through the swimbladder) inhabitant of backwaters of the Nile River. The mousefish (*Gonorynchus gonorynchus*) is a widely distributed Indo-Pacific marine species that inhabits sandy-bottomed areas, burrowing into the sand with its eel-like (and brightly colored) body.

Cypriniformes   The composition of the Cypriniformes varies considerably among fish classification schemes. In schemes which exclude the Gonorynchiformes from the Ostariophysi, it either is the only ostariophysan order or shares this position with the catfishes (Siluriformes). In the latter case the order Cypriniformes is considered to have two main divisions, the characins and the cyprinids. However, Roberts (1969) argues that the three groups represent three independent evolutionary lines from a characinlike ancestor. He therefore treated the three groups as suborders of the Cypriniformes, a scheme also used here.

Although the order Cypriniformes contains 5000 to 6000 species with a wide variety of morphological adaptations, they are united by a number of distinctive skeletal features. Most obvious of these features is the Weberian apparatus. This is a chain of bones that connects the swimbladder to the inner ear, giving the fishes a sensitive sound reception system similar in function to that of the inner ear in mammals. The connecting bones are modified portions of the first four or more vertebrae. Other distinctive morphological features include a protractile upper jaw (except in most characins), abdominal pelvic fins, and pharyngeal teeth. These features are important components of the complex of cypriniform adaptations that has made this group so successful in fresh water. The acute sense of hearing from the Weberian apparatus is presumably particularly useful in turbid water or at night, when most catfishes are active. The pharyngeal teeth permit the separation of the grabbing and chewing functions of the mouth, important for fish that feed mostly on active prey. The many specializations in pharyngeal dentition present in the Cypriniformes, from molariform grinding teeth, to comblike teeth for breaking up fine materials, to sharp teeth for piercing prey, have undoubtedly contributed to the success of these fish much in the same way that the specialized jaw teeth of mammals have contributed to their success on land.

Other cypriniform features that seem to be particularly important contributors to their success are their fear scent, their generally small size, and their reproductive strategies. Like the keen sense of hearing, the fear scents of cypriniform fishes are likely to be particularly useful under conditions, common in fresh water, where a predator is hard to see. Once the scent has been released, the fish may flee the area, hide, or school more closely even though the predator is not visible, so any additional attacks by the predator are likely to be less successful. The use of fear scents by these fishes is a reflection of the fact that most of the species are highly social and school during at least one stage of their life history. It also reflects the fact that most cypriniform fishes are quite small, even as adults, and so are seldom at the top of local food chains. There are a number of cypriniform species that reach 1 m to 2 m in length, but they are decidedly a small part of the total. Most of these large forms are either piscivores or detritivore/herbivores. Small size seems to be advantageous for feeding on the myriad of small aquatic invertebrates, as well as on the terrestrial invertebrates that fall into the water. Small size is also advantageous for the occupation of the numerous microhabitats in fresh water, such as between rocks in fast streams or among the aquatic vegetation in lakes, or for the occupation of small or intermittent waterways, where low oxygen levels and shallow water are likely to discriminate against large fish. Yet another advantage of small size lies in the ability of the fish to reach maturity quickly. Freshwater environments, but particularly streams, fluctuate from season to season and from year to year; wet years and droughts may alternate with one another on an irregular basis. Thus the availability of conditions necessary for successful reproduction may vary considerably from year to year and from place to place. Mobile, small fish with early maturity can quickly take advantage of favorable conditions and flood the environment with young and so maintain large populations as long as the favorable conditions exist.

Characoidei

This suborder has two main divisions, the charcins (superfamily Characoidea), with 1100+ species, and the South American electric fishes (superfamily Gymnotoidea), with 40 to 50 species. The former group contains an enormous variety of fishes, but their morphology is rather generalized ("primitive"), while the latter fishes are highly specialized derivatives of the characins.

CHARACOIDEA The characins are confined to South and Central America (900 to 1000+ species) and to Africa (150 to 200 species), with the exception of the Mexican tetra (*Astyanax fasciatus*), which has managed to invade North America. In South America, characins, together with catfishes, totally dominate the freshwater fish fauna. Although the many species possess a wide array of specialized features, as a group they are readily recognizable. In the past this has resulted in all species being placed in just one family, the Characidae. However, recent workers have split up this group in recognition of its diversity, but the 16 families listed here are by no means stable entities. They are bound to change in number and composition as our understanding of the characoid fishes increases.

The characins are characterized by the following features: Most are diurnal predators, with large eyes (absent in some cave-dwelling forms), no barbels, and numerous teeth set in the jaws. They tend to be small, bright (often silvery) in color, and have fusiform or laterally compressed bodies that are completely covered with cycloid scales. Most possess an adipose fin, a short dorsal fin located midway on the body, abdominal pelvic fins, and a caudal fin with 19 principal rays.

Characidae. This is the largest and most varied of the characin families. Its members are found in Africa, South and Central America, and North America (Mexican tetra). The South American and African characins are usually placed in separate subfamilies. The family Characidae essentially contains the various characins that lack the specializations used to characterize the other fifteen families (Fig. 20.1b). All have good sets of jaw teeth, and most are predatory.

Other families. The 15 other characin families are small groups of rather specialized species. Three of the families (Ctenoluciidae, Hepsetidae, Ichthyboridae) contain fishes with pikelike morphologies; most are lie-in-wait predators on other fishes, although some ichthyborids (e.g., *Phago*) have peculiar, beaklike snouts that enable them to pluck scales and pieces of fin from other fishes. The members of two other families (Erythrinidae, Cynodontidae) are also largely piscivorous as adults. In contrast, members of the South American family Prochilodontidae are deep-bodied, bottom-feeding fishes of moderate size with subterminal, suckerlike mouths. Members of two African families (Distichodontidae, Citharinidae) are somewhat similar, although they are more adapted for picking invertebrates from the bottom than for sucking up algae, ooze, and small invertebrates.

GYMNOTOIDEA   The 40 to 50 species of gymnotoids are found entirely in the fresh waters of South America, where they presumably evolved from the characins. All have electric organs and, as a result, they are remarkably similar to the mormyrids of Africa, although they evolved independently (Fig. 20.1c). The electric organs are used for navigation and detection and capture of prey organisms, at night or in murky water. The distinctive morphology of the gymnotoids can largely be explained as an accommodation to the efficient use of the electric organs. Their bodies are eellike, and much of the muscle mass has been converted to electric organs, so they can create large electric fields around them. Because of the large electric organs and the need to keep the body fairly rigid to create a uniform electric field, the fish propel themselves, slowly and gracefully, through wavelike movements of their long (140+ rays) anal fin. Using this fin, they can move either forwards or backwards. Each individual fin ray actually moves in a circular pattern, made possible by the way they connect to the internal supporting bony element (basal pterygiophore). Other fins on the gymnotoids are minimal; the pelvics are absent, the caudal absent or very small, the pectorals small, and the dorsal absent or reduced to a few filaments. The viscera of the gymnotoids are confined to a relatively small anterior part of the body. The gills are small with small openings, reflecting both the leisurely activity patterns of the gymnotoids and the ability of many of them to breathe air. The dependence on electric organs for sensory input is indicated by the small eyes of gymnotoids, although some species of knifefishes (Rhamphichthyidae) have an attenuated, fingerlike caudal region that apparently enables them to feel their way into protective cover, which they frequently enter backwards.

Perhaps the best known of the gymnotoids is the electric eel (*Electrophorus electricus*), the only member of the family Electrophoridae. It inhabits the backwaters and shallow streams of the Amazon region of South America. About half the body musculature of this fish has been converted into electric organs, which together can produce 350 V to 650 V, depending on the length of the fish, although the amperage is low (less than 1 A). These extraordinary electrical powers are used both for defense and for stunning the fish the eel feeds on. The eels also have two other, much smaller sets of electrical organs, one of which is used for navigation.

Cyprinoidei   This suborder contains the Cyprinidae and specialized cyprinid derivatives: the Catostomidae and the four families of cobitoid fishes. Together, these fishes dominate the fresh waters (but especially streams) of North America and Eurasia and, to a lesser extent, Africa. The nearly 2000 species in the suborder are diverse in their external appearances, but all possess protractile mouths without teeth (most possess pharyngeal teeth). Their heads are scaleless, and with the exception of a few cobitids, all lack an adipose fin.

Cyprinidae. The minnow or carp family is the largest family of fishes, with over 1600 species. Remarkably, considering the number of species involved, cyprinids all have body plans that are mainly variations on the "classic" fish theme, with fusiform to moderately deep bodies, large eyes, conspicuous scales, abdominal pelvic fins, and small, terminal or subterminal mouths (Fig. 20.2a). As might be expected from such a body plan, most are diurnal predators on small invertebrates, although some are also piscivorous and others feed on algae, higher plants, and organic ooze. They are distinguished from other members of the suborder by their pharyngeal teeth (one to three rows, but always fewer than eight teeth per row) and thin lips (upper jaw usually bordered only by the premaxilla). Although most have only soft rays in the fins, rays that have been modified into spines are present in some forms, most notably common carp (*Cyprinus carpio*), goldfish (*Carassius auratus*), and North American spinedaces (*Lepidomeda, Meda, Plagopterus*).

In North America there are about 200 species of cyprinids, over half of them small, silvery "shiners" of the genus *Notropis*. The *Notropis* species are often the most abundant, or at least the most conspicuous, fishes in small streams and lakes of eastern North America, where they form large schools in shallow water. Bright breeding colors, nuptial tubercles, and some type of nest building are characteristic of many North American cyprinids, so for a few weeks each year they can rival their tropical relatives in beauty. A number of these cyprinids have developed the curious habit of using nests of other fishes, mostly those of larger cyprinid species or centrarchid basses, for spawning. Nests of fallfish (*Semotilus corporalis*) and hornyhead chubs (*Hybopsis*

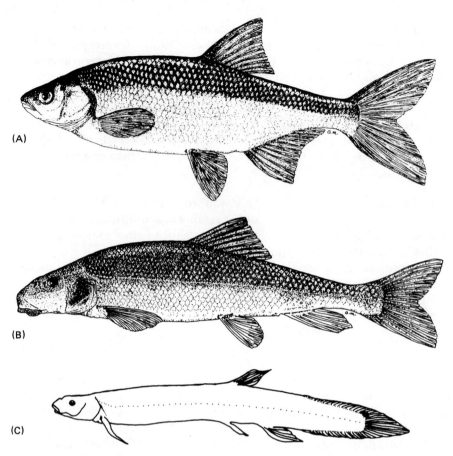

FIGURE 20.2 Representative cyprinoid fishes: (A) hitch (*Lavinia,* Cyprinidae);
(B) sucker (*Catostomus,* Catostomidae); and (C) loach (*Misgurnus,* Cobitidae).
(From Moyle, 1976a.)

micropogon) may be used for spawning simultaneously by as many as
three species of small cyprinids, resulting in numerous hybrids among
the species.

In eastern North America a large majority of the cyprinids have a
maximum length of less than 10 cm, although some *Hybopsis* may reach
25 cm to 30 cm. In the major drainages of western North America,
however, a majority of the species are large, commonly exceeding 25
cm as adults. Largest of these western species are the four piscivorous
squawfishes (*Ptychocheilus*). The Colorado squawfish (*P. lucius*), now
an endangered species, is reported to have reached nearly 2 m in length
and a weight of 45 kg. Perhaps these pikelike cyprinids evolved in western
rivers because the true pikes (Esocidae) and centrarchid basses, the main
large piscivores of the Mississippi and associated drainages, were absent.
The streams of California's great Central Valley originally were home to
eight species of cyprinids, six of which grew to large sizes. The two small

species of minnow present are extraordinarily tolerant of adverse conditions. One of them, the speckled dace (*Rhinichthys osculus*), is successful throughout the West in environments ranging from desert springs to trout streams. It is one of the most widely distributed cyprinids in North America.

Despite their diversity, North American cyprinids are all usually placed in just one subfamily (Leuciscinae), which is the most generalized of the five subfamilies recognized by Gosline (1978). This subfamily is also well represented in northern Eurasia, providing evidence that it was the dominant cyprinid group on the ancient continent of Laurasia, before it split into North America and Eurasia (see Chapter 24). Subsequently, southeast Asia is generally considered to have become the center of cyprinid evolution because the cyprinids are extraordinarily numerous and diverse in southeastern Asia and the Indian subcontinent. Most African cyprinids belong to genera also found in Asia and are apparently derived from them. The Asiatic genera with the most species are *Rasbora* and *Barbus*. The majority of these species are the small, bright, colorful, and highly active forms favored by aquarists, although some species of *Barbus* grow quite large. One of the largest is the mahseer (*B. tor*) of India, which may reach a length of 2 m. Many other Eurasian cyprinids also grow to respectable sizes and are important sport and commercial fishes. In Europe large cyprinids such as the barbels (*Barbus* spp.), tench (*Tinca tinca*), nase (*Chondrosteus nase*), roach (*Rutilus rutilus*), bream (*Abramis brama*), orfe (*Leuciscus idus*), and common carp are much sought after by anglers, often in catch-and-release fishing contests. Because of their ability to grow rapidly to harvestable sizes in ponds, on diets of organic ooze, plants, and small invertebrates, a number of the Asiatic carps, such as common carp, grass carp (*Ctenopharyngodon idella*), and silver carp (*Hypophthalmichthys molitrix*), are among the most important aquaculture animals in the world.

Catostomidae. The suckers are a small (55 to 60 species) but very successful family of fishes (Fig. 20.2b). Throughout North America they are among the most abundant fishes, particularly in streams and rivers. Their success can be attributed to the tolerance most species have of a wide variety of environmental conditions and to their feeding habits. Most species are bottom browsers, sucking up organic ooze, algae, and small invertebrates through their subterminal mouths with fleshy lips. The food ingested is then broken up by comblike pharyngeal teeth (one row of 16 or more teeth) and digested in a long, winding intestine. A majority of the suckers are moderate-sized (40 cm to 80 cm), streamlined forms belonging to the genera *Catostomus* and *Moxostoma*. Although often found in lakes and reservoirs, species of these genera are most characteristic of streams.

One group of *Catostomus* species (subgenus *Pantosteus*) has become specialized for scraping algae and invertebrates from rocks in the swift mountain streams of western North America; they are small in size and have a cartilaginous plate on the inside edge of the upper jaw that functions as a scraper. Other species of suckers have become adapted for life in large, fast-moving rivers. Most extreme in this regard are the razorback sucker (*Xyrauchen texanus*) of the Colorado River and *Myxocyprinus asiaticus* of the Yangtse River in China. Both have backs that rise steeply behind the head to form an inverted keel. Water flowing past this keel apparently pushes the fish against the bottom, allowing it to feed and move in swift water. An evolutionary trend in suckers in the opposite direction is toward lake living. Suckers adapted for living in quiet water (mostly *Carpoides, Ictiobus,* and *Chasmistes*) are large, deep-bodied forms. While many of these forms are still bottom feeders, a number have developed terminal mouths and fine gill rakers that enable them to feed on plankton.

Cobitoidea. This superfamily contains four families of small fishes largely adapted for living in the streams of Eurasia. The loaches (Cobitidae, 150 to 160 species) are the largest and most widespread of these families. The loaches are most diverse in southeast Asia, but the spined loach (*Cobitis taenia*) has managed to invade North Africa and the Japanese weatherfish (*Misgurnus anguillicaudatus*) has become established through introductions in both California and Michigan. Most loaches are small (to 30 cm) fishes that range in body shape from wormlike to chunky (with a flattened belly). All have subterminal mouths with three or more pairs of barbels (Fig. 20.2c). As might be expected, most are secretive bottom dwellers that feed on small invertebrates and plant matter. The Psilorhynchidae (two species), Gyrinocheilidae (three species), and Homalopteridae (90 species) are apparently cobitid derivatives that are adapted for life in fast-flowing streams in southeast Asia. Some of the species are small, dacelike fish with subterminal mouths and large pectoral fins that actively forage among the rocks. Others are highly specialized for browsing on algae growing on rocks in torrential streams. The suckerbelly loaches (Gyrinocheilidae) hold on to the rocks with their fleshy lips and scrape off algae with rasplike ridges on the inside margin of the lips. Since such an arrangement precludes bringing in water through the mouth for respiration, they have developed a special opening above the regular opercular opening for inhaling water into the pharynx, to then be pumped over the gills with rapid beats of the operculum. The homalopterids also have a ventral sucking disc, but it is created by the pelvic and pectoral fins joining on a flattened belly, so the fish can inhale water through the mouth.

Siluroidei
The catfishes are one of the most distinctive groups of fishes. While their Weberian apparatus and fear scents link them to the characoid and cyprinoid fishes, their distinctive morphology is also indicative of a long independent evolutionary history. In general, it appears that the catfishes have diversified for being active after dark or in turbid water, thereby reducing

interactions with the vision-oriented cyprinoids and characoids. This diversification has produced over 2000 species of catfish, about 1200 of which reside in South America. Although any group of fishes with so many species is bound to have its share of bizarre forms, most catfishes are readily recognizable by their whiskery snout, containing one to four pairs of barbels (invariably one of the pairs is supported by the maxilla), small eyes, head that is usually flattened, adipose fin, and streamlined body that is either without scales or covered with heavy, bony plates. Most also have a stout spine leading each pectoral and dorsal fin. Many species have venom glands associated with the spines. Although catfishes are readily recognizable on the basis of their external anatomy, their most definitive features, which separate them from the cyprinoids and characoids, are osteological:

1. They lack the parietal, symplectic, intercalar, and interopercular bones in the skull and intermuscular bones in the body. The latter feature makes them especially desirable as food fish, in contrast to the carps.
2. The premaxilla is usually covered with small teeth, but they are absent from the maxilla, which is reduced to a rod to support the barbels. The only exception to this is found in *Diplomystes,* a South American genus considered to be the most ancestral of all catfishes.
3. Teeth are usually present on the vomer.
4. The Weberian apparatus is generally more complex than that of the characoids and cyprinoids and always involves five vertebrae.

Most catfishes are small in size, reaching 10 cm to 30 cm, although a number of species can exceed 1 m in length. Probably the largest is the wels (*Silurus glanis*) of Europe, which may reach 5 m and 300+ kg. In contrast, many members of the South American family Trichomycteridae attain lengths of only 2 cm to 3 cm. The larger catfishes are much favored as food fishes, while many of the smaller forms are popular as aquarium fishes.

The systematics of the catfishes are just beginning to be understood. While the 31 families used here (following Greenwood et al. [1966] and Nelson [1976]) are, for the most part, widely accepted, there is no widespread agreement as to how the families relate to each other. The problem of determining interrelationships among the families is somewhat simplified by the fact that each continent has been an independent center of catfish radiation, so most families are confined to just one continent. Thus, South America has 13 families of its own, Eurasia 10, Africa three, and North America one. Three other families are found in both Eurasia and Africa, while the remaining two (Ariidae and Plotosidae) are mostly marine. The 14 species of catfish found in the fresh waters of Australia are members of the two marine families.

Ictaluridae. The North American catfish family (referred to in much of the older literature as the Ameiuridae) contains about 40 species

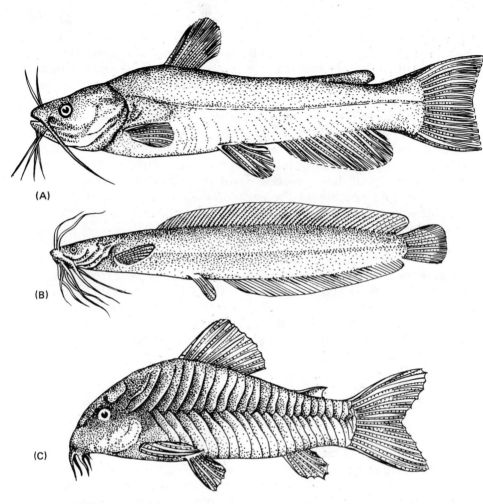

FIGURE 20.3 Representative siluroid fishes: (A) bullhead (*Ictalurus,* Ictaluridae); (B) air-breathing catfish (*Clarius,* Clariidae); and (C) armored catfish (*Callichthys,* Callichthyidae).

of rather unspecialized catfishes (Fig. 20.3a). All are scaleless and dark in color (except for cave forms), with large, flattened heads that support eight barbels (two on the snout, two on the maxillae, and four on the chin). These catfishes can be divided into three distinct groups: the large species sought by anglers (*Ictalurus* and *Pylodictis*), the small, secretive madtoms (*Noturus*), and the blind cave catfishes (*Satan, Trogloglanis, Prietella*). The first group of catfishes were originally native to warm waters east of the Rocky Mountains, with the exception of one species in Mexico. Thanks to their popularity as food fishes, they have been spread by humans to suitable waters throughout western North America. The madtoms are a widely distributed but poorly known group of 25 to 30 species of small (less than 10 cm) catfishes. Most live in small to moderate-sized streams, where they hide under rocks, logs, and trash (such as old automobile parts and beer cans) during the day, coming out to forage on invertebrates at night. Besides their secretive habits, their main protection against predators seems to be stout spines, whose effectiveness is increased by the mild venom associated with them. Like all members of the Ictaluridae, madtoms exhibit a high degree of parental care, building nests and then guarding the eggs and young. The madtoms probably gave rise to the three known species of cave catfishes, all of which are small, white, blind, and known from only a few specimens (see Chapter 31).

Clariidae.   The air-breathing catfishes are perhaps the most widely distributed catfish family, occurring in a wide range of habitats from South Africa through most of Africa and the southern half of Asia over to Java and the Phillipine Islands. A majority of the 100+ species belong in the genus *Clarias*. Their bodies are rather elongate (some species are re-markably eellike), their heads flattened with four pairs of long barbels, and their dorsal and anal fins long (Fig. 20.3b). The adipose fin is frequently absent. Their most distinctive feature, however, is the air-breathing organ made up of modified gill filaments on particular gill arches. These gill filaments are supported by a treelike structure with a cartilaginous "trunk" so they do not collapse (as do normal gill filaments) when ex-posed to air (Chapter 4). The posterior portion of the gills is normal and can be used for aquatic respiration, although most species of clariids seem to depend at least partially on aerial respiration.   Surprisingly, many clariids are found in large lakes and rivers, where oxygen levels are normally high. A number of such species support important fisheries. However, many other species are found in low-oxygen waters, and some are capable of moving for short distances across land to colonize new areas. The latter forms "walk" on the tips of their stout pectoral spines by using them as pivots as they shove themselves along by flexing their bodies. The species best known for this activity is the so-called walking catfish (*Clarias batrachus*), which has become established, presumably by escapees from aquaria and tropical fish farms, in such places as Guam, Hawaii, and Florida. In Florida it is considered to be a real pest because it has spread rapidly, to the detriment of populations of more desirable fishes, despite periodic die-offs caused by cold weather (Courtney et al. 1974).

Other Eurasian and African families.   Throughout much of Africa and southern and eastern Asia (to Japan), the "typical" catfishes belong to the family Bagridae. Ecologically, morphologically, and economically they are similar to the ictalurid catfishes of North America. In Europe and northern Asia, the "typical" catfish role is played by members of the family Siluridae. However, members of this family diverge markedly from the classic catfish shape of the bagrids by having a long anal fin, short (or no) dorsal fin, no adipose fin, strongly compressed trunk, and, for catfish, large eyes. Alexander (1966) interprets these features and others as being adaptations for a more pelagic mode of existence than is true of most catfishes. The small glass catfishes (*Cryptopterus*) are in fact completely pelagic, as evidenced by their diurnal activity and semi-transparency, which should offer them camouflage in open waters. The 40 or so species of the African and Indian family Schilbeidae have a morphology similar to the silurids, including "glass catfish" species (*Physailia*). The remaining families in this group have various specializations. For example, five families (Amblycipitidae, Amphiliidae, Akysidae, Olyridae, Sisoridae) contain mostly small species adapted for life in fast-moving streams, the Heteropneustidae have lunglike extensions of the gill cavity they use for air breathing, and the electric catfishes (Malapteruridae) have powerful electric organs they use for stunning prey.

South American catfishes. The 13 families and 1200+ species of catfish in South America rival the characins in their diversity (Fig. 20.3c). Over a third of the species belong in the family Loricariidae, a group of heavily armored, attenuated catfishes. Most are adapted for scraping or sucking algae from the bottom in streams and can use their suckerlike mouths for holding onto rocks in fast water. Two other families of armored catfishes are the Callichthyidae and the Doradidae. Members of both families tend to be moderately deep-bodied (but flattened ventrally) and protected with large, bony plates and spines. The callichthyids are characteristic of waters that frequently become stagnant and so swallow bubbles of air, which is absorbed in a highly vascularized portion of the hind gut. Like the clariid catfishes of Africa and Asia, many of these catfishes are capable of moving overland on their stout pectoral spines.

The remaining families of South American catfishes all have smooth bodies. The Pimelodidae fill the "typical" catfish role, being widely distributed (including Cuba), abundant (250 to 300 species), and large enough to support fisheries for them. However, the bodies of pimelodids tend to be much more flattened than those of the ictalurid and bagrid catfishes, and they possess extremely long barbels (three pairs). Eight other families of smooth catfishes are mostly distinguished by their minor morphological variations on the typical catfish theme. The most deviant of the smooth catfish families is the Trichomycteridae, which make up 150 to 200 species of small, elongate catfishes that lack the adipose fin. Many of them seem to be parasitic on other fishes, entering their gill cavities and feeding on gill filaments and blood. Still other species apparently hide themselves in sand, mud, or leaf litter and snatch scales from passing fishes.

Marine catfishes. The only families in the Cypriniformes whose member species are primarily found in salt water are the Ariidae (sea catfishes) and the Plotosidae (catfish eels). The sea catfishes are unspecialized-looking catfishes found in tropical and subtropical waters over much of the world but particularly in estuarine waters. On the east coast of the United States, the gafftopsail catfish (*Bagre marinus*), so named because of its large dorsal fin, and the sea catfish (*Arius felis*) are common fishes that move in and out of the estuaries on a seasonal basis. They swim about, feeding on benthic invertebrates, in noisy schools, the noises being created by the clicking of pectoral spines and the vibration of the swim-bladder. The males of these two species, as well as of other species in the family, incubate the eggs in their mouths.

The plotosid catfishes look as if they have the head of a catfish welded onto the body of a stout eel. They are widely distributed in the Indian and eastern Pacific Oceans, where a number of the species have colonized the fresh waters of Australia and other islands.

Supplemental Readings   Alexander 1966a, b; Herald 1961; Moyle 1976a; Pflieger 1975; Sterba 1959; Wheeler 1975.

CHAPTER 21

ααααααααααααααααααααααααααααααααααααααααααααααααααααααααααααααααααααααααα
~~~~~~

Lantern Fishes, Codfishes, and Deepsea Predators

Infraclass Teleostei
Division Euteleostei
Superorder Scopelomorpha
Order Myctophiformes
Families Aulopodidae, Synodontidae (lizardfishes), Giganturidae (telescope fishes), Rosauridae, Chlorophthalmidae (greeneyes and spiderfishes), Scopelosauridae (paperbones), Myctophidae (lanternfishes), Neoscopelidae (blackchins), Paralepididae (barracudinas), Omosudidae, Alepisauridae (lancetfishes), Anotopteridae (daggertooth), Evermannellidae (sabertooth fishes), Scopelarchidae (pearleyes).
Superorder Paracanthopterygii
Order Polymixiiformes
Family Polymixiidae (beardfishes)
Order Percopsiformes
Families Percopsidae (troutperches), Aphredoderidae (pirate perch), Amblyopsidae (cavefishes).
Order Gadiformes
Families Muraenolepidae, Moridae (flatnose cods), Melanonidae, Bregmacerotidae (codlets), Gadidae (cods), Merlucciidae (merluccid hakes), Macrouridae (grenadiers), Ophidiidae (brotulas and cuskeels), Carapidae (pearlfishes), Zoarcidae (eelpouts).
Order Batrachoidiformes
Family Batrachoididae (toadfishes)
Order Lophiiformes
Families Lophiidae (goosefishes), Brachionichthyidae (warty anglers), Antennariidae (frogfishes), Chaunacidae (sea toads), Ogcocephalidae (batfishes), Caulophrynidae (fanfins), Melanocetidae (black devils), Diceratiidae, Himantolophidae (football fishes), Oneirodidae (dreamers), Gigantactinidae (whipnoses), Neoceratiidae, Centrophrynidae (deepsea anglerfish), Ceratiidae (sea devils), Linophrynidae (netdevils).

This chapter discusses two important lines of teleost evolution that have diverged from the "main" line leading to the acanthopterygian fishes. Most of the species in these two superorders are specialized for life in the deep sea or in other unusual habitats and so are also

264

discussed in some detail when their habitats are discussed (see especially Chapters 31 and 36).

Myctophiformes The myctophiform fishes are, in many respects, similar to the salmoniform fishes, and the two groups have been lumped together in the Salmoniformes (Greenwood et al. 1966). Both groups have many "ancestral" features, such as soft-rayed fins, the presence (usually) of an adipose fin, abdominal pelvic fins, and various skeletal features, but the Myctophiformes also differ from the Salmoniformes in many important respects, such as the exclusion of the maxillary bone from the gape of the mouth (although the upper jaw is not protrusible) and the presence of the physoclistic (closed) swimbladder (Gosline 1971). The order as constituted here contains 14 families with 400+ species, most of which inhabit deepsea environments where they prey on fishes and invertebrates. The diversity of the group is reflected in the fact that seven of the families contain less than 10 species each. As a consequence of this diversity, Rosen (1973) suggests that this order as presented here is really made up of two only distantly related evolutionary lines, the Myctophiformes (containing only the Myctophidae and Neoscopelidae) and the Aulopiformes (containing the other 12 families listed above).

Myctophidae. About 60% (240) of the species of myctophiform fishes are lanternfishes, including 100 species in the genus *Diaphus* (Nafpaktitis 1978). They are a remarkably abundant group that can be found in all the oceans of the world. Most live between 200 m and 1000 m deep in the open ocean, but some have been observed at depths greater than 2000 m and others may be found at the surface at night. They are often an important part of the deep scattering layer, so called because sound produced by sonar units of ships bounces off the thousands of swimbladders in a school, at times giving the impression of a false bottom (e.g., Backus et al. 1968). The lanternfishes are small, with blunt heads, large eyes, and rows of photophores on the body and head (Fig. 21.1c). The photophore patterns are different for each species, and they are also different for the sexes of each species (which led some early investigators to describe the males and females as separate species). It is not unusual for several species of lanternfishes to be caught together in sampling devices. How they manage to coexist is an interesting question, since most are generalists in their feeding, apparently taking whatever prey of suitable size are available (Tyler and Pearcy 1975). It is possible that there is some segregation by depth preferences and by patterns of vertical migration.

Synodontidae. This family contains three distinct subfamilies of fishes, often listed as families: the lizardfishes (Synodontinae), the deepsea lizardfishes (Bathysaurinae), and the Bombay ducks (Harpadontinae) (Sulak 1977). The 34 or so species of lizardfishes contradict most of the generalities made previously about the ecology of myctoph-

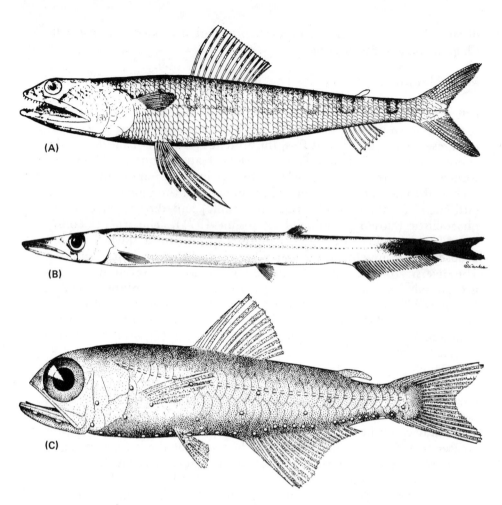

FIGURE 21.1 Myctophiform fishes: (A) lizardfish (*Synodus,* Synodontidae); (B) barracudina (*Lestidium,* Paralepididae); and (C) lanternfish (*Myctophum,* Myctophidae). (From Jordan and Evermann, 1895, 1900.)

iform fishes, since they are moderate-sized (25 cm to 50 cm) benthic fishes found mainly in shallow water of tropical and subtropical areas. A few species also penetrate temperate areas, such *Synodus foetens* of the Atlantic Coast of the United States (to Cape Cod) and *S. lucioceps* of the southern California coastline. The lizardfishes have a vaguely lizardlike appearance, with their flattened bony heads, large scales on the body and head, and large mouths in pointed snouts (Fig. 21.1a). The mouth contains numerous long, pointed teeth useful for holding onto the prey they ambush. Lizardfishes conceal themselves by resting quietly on their large pelvic fins on rocky bottoms or coral reefs or by partially covering themselves with sand in soft bottomed areas. The deepsea lizardfishes have the same basic morphology but are nearly transparent, while the Bombay ducks have taken the morphology to another extreme and are adapted for pelagic life in shallow water.

Chloropthalmidae. Members of this family resemble lizardfishes in general morphology, but all occupy deepwater environments. Within the family there are two basic groups, the greeneyes (Chloropthalminae) and the spiderfishes and grideye fishes (Ipnopinae). The greeneyes have exceptionally large eyes of a pale green color, which permit them to see in the dim light that exists just above the bottom at the edge of the continental shelf. There they feed on small, pelagic invertebrates. In deeper water the spiderfishes (*Bathypterois,* 18 species) play a similar role, except that they "stand" on the bottom with the extraordinarily long rays on their pelvic and caudal fins (see Fig. 36.2). These fishes have tiny eyes, and it seems likely that they detect their prey with the long, independent rays of their pectoral fins (Sulak 1977). Several other genera (*Ipnops, Bathymicrops, Bathytyphlops*) are similar but lack the elongate fin rays. These fishes feed on benthic invertebrates. In *Ipnops* the eyes have been modified into large, lensless light receptors on the top of an extremely flattened head. How these function is not known.

Alepisauroid fishes. The six families discussed here apparently represent a distinct line of myctophiform evolution in the direction of slender-bodied mesopelagic predators. The 50+ species of barracudinas (Paralepididae) look like miniature barracudas, complete with sharp teeth (Fig. 21.1b). They have large eyes but no swimbladder. Barracudinas, although typically less than 15 cm long, seem to be very important in marine food chains, since they prey on smaller deepsea fishes and are themselves extensively preyed upon by such predators as salmon, tuna, and swordfish. The daggertooth (*Anopterus pharao,* the only member of its family) is similar to the barracudinas, except that the jaws are enlarged, with numerous bladelike teeth. Extremely large jaws and teeth are also characteristic of the Omosudidae (one species), Evermannellidae (six species), and Scopelarchidae (18 species), although these fishes are less elongate than the members of the previous two families and their heads are blunt rather than pointed. The evermannellids (sabertooth fishes) are capable of swallowing fishes larger than themselves. Both the sabertooth fishes and the pearleyes (Scopelarchidae) have telescopic eyes that point upwards, enabling them to see their prey from below. While these fishes are spectacular predators, they are less than 50 cm long and rarely receive much public attention. This is not true, however, of the lancetfishes (Alepisauridae), which may exceed 2 m in length and occasionally wash up on beaches. Besides having long fangs and elongate bodies, these fishes have an enormous, saillike dorsal fin. They seem to be among the largest fishes that spend full time in the mesopelagic region of the world's oceans, feeding on all the other fishes present. A number of rare deepsea fishes are known mainly from specimens obtained from lancetfish stomachs.

Paracanthopterygii   The paracanthopterygians are a major evolutionary line of predominantly marine fishes (900 to 1000 species) that possess many "ancestral" osteological and myological features but also possess many of the derived features of the Acanthopterygii (Rosen 1973). Among the derived features that characterize most (but not necessarily all) species are (1) an elaborate and protractile premaxilla; (2) spines on the dorsal, anal, and pelvic fins; (3) reduced numbers of pelvic and caudal fin rays; (4) ctenoid scales; and (5) pelvic fins in the thoracic or jugular position.

POLYMIXIIFORMES   This order contains just one living family (Polymixiidae) with three species of beardfishes (Fig. 21.2b), although a number of fossil forms are also known. The beardfishes are abundant at depths between 180 m and 640 m in the tropical and subtropical regions of the Atlantic, Pacific, and Indian Oceans. Their large eyes and

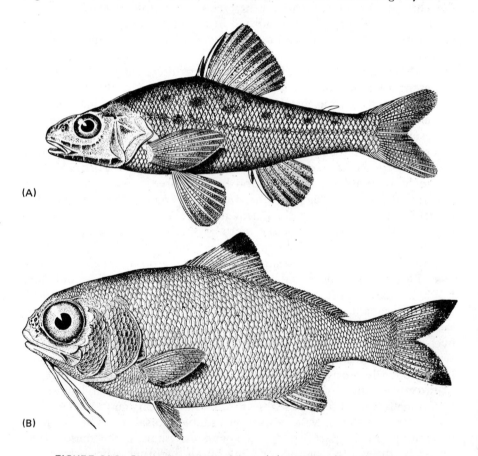

(A)

(B)

FIGURE 21.2 Paracanthopterygian fishes: (A) sandroller (*Percopsis,* Percopsidae); and (B) beardfish (*Polymixis,* Polymixiidae). [(A) from Jordan and Evermann (1900); and (B) from Goode and Bean (1895).]

long chin barbels indicate that they are bottom-oriented predators. They are deep-bodied fishes that possess all the conspicuous derived features listed above for the Paracanthopterygii. Because of these features, as well as other anatomical details, they are often placed in the Beryciformes, an "ancestral" order of the Acanthopterygii. In many respects they appear to be intermediate in their characteristics between the Paracanthopterygii and Acanthopterygii, so their final placement will depend on future research on the interrelationships between the two superorders.

PERCOPSIFORMES   This order contains just three families and eight species of peculiar North American freshwater fishes, all small (less than 15 cm) in size. The species have an interesting mixture of ancestral and derived characteristics. The premaxilla forms the entire margin of the upper jaw but is not protractile. The pelvic fins (if present) are "subthoracic" in position in that they are located close to the pectorals but slightly behind them. Spines are weakly developed and present only in the dorsal fin. Scales are either ctenoid or cycloid.

The two species of trout perches (Percopsidae, Fig. 21.2a), with their adipose fins, ctenoid scales, and weak dorsal, pelvic, and anal fin spines look like a cross between trout and perch. The pirateperch (*Aphredoderus sayanus*), the sole member of the Aphredoderidae, is more perchlike with its ctenoid scales, spines in the dorsal and anal fins, subthoracic pelvic fins, and most distinctively, its anus in its throat. In contrast to the pirate perch, the five or so species of Amblyopsidae have cycloid scales, spines on the anal and dorsal fins (optional), and no pelvic fins (except in one species). They are adapted for living in the caves and springs of the limestone regions of the southeastern United States (Chapter 31).

GADIFORMES   This order contains between 650 and 700 bottom-oriented marine fishes, some of which play major ecological roles in their respective communities (but particularly in the benthic communities of deep water). A number of the codfishes and hakes are among the most important commercial fishes. Gadiform fishes typically have elongate bodies (often tapering to a point at the tail) with long dorsal and anal fins. It is not unusual for these fins to be broken up into two or three sections (especially the dorsal fins). The pelvic fins are either thoracic or jugular in position or absent. With the exception of the Macrouridae, all have small, cycloid scales. Since they are predators on fishes and invertebrates, most have large, terminal or subterminal mouths, many with barbels.

Gadidae.   The cod family contains only about 55 species, but most of them are large and edible and so have long played an important economic and nutritional role for Western peoples. The Atlantic cod (*Gadus morhua*) has been particularly important because of its size, abundance, and ease of capture. At least 100 years before the landing of the *Mayflower* in Massachusetts, European fishermen (but particularly the Portuguese) were capturing cod by hook and line off the coast of North America and landing in Newfoundland to dry and salt their catches. The importance of the cod fisheries to the early development of America is indicated by the fact that since 1784 the effigy of a cod has been prominently displayed in the Massachusetts statehouse.

The Gadidae are characterized by having their caudal fin separate from the dorsal and anal fins, with the dorsal fin divided into two or three sections. None of the fins have spines, the swimbladder is physoclistous, and a chin barbel is usually present. As might be expected from their morphology, the cods are bottom-oriented species, feeding on such animals as crabs, fish, and molluscs. Some species make extensive seasonal migrations for spawning and feeding. Besides the "true" cods (*Gadus*), the commercially important members of this family are the haddock (*Melanogrammus aegelfinus*), pollock (*Pollachius, Theragra*), and hake (*Phycis, Urophycis*). In the Arctic, some cold-adapted species of cod (*Arctogadus, Boreogadus*) are the dominant predators (see Chapter 37) and have some importance as commercial fishes in the Soviet Union. One species of cod, the burbot (*Lota lota*), is confined to cold freshwater lakes and rivers of North America and Eurasia. It is a good food fish but is harvested mainly in the Soviet Union.

Merlucciidae.   The merluccid hakes are often placed in the Gadidae but differ from them by having one or two dorsal fins, one anal fin, no chin barbel, and spines on the first dorsal fin (Fig. 21.3a). A few species have a long, pointed tail in which the anal, caudal, and dorsal fins are united. All have terminal mouths with sharp teeth, indicative of their tendency to be piscivorous. The true hakes (*Merluccius*, 7 to 12 species) are found at moderate depths over much of the world, near coastlines. Although their flesh is not as prized as that of the cods, the hakes now rank among the most important commercial fishes of the world because of their abundance and ease of capture with trawls. The only other species in this family besides the merluccid hakes are about six species of small deepwater hakes (e.g., *Steindachneria*) that resemble grenadiers (Marcrouridae), a family in which they are sometimes placed.

Moridae (Eretmophoridae).   The flatnose cods are moderate-sized (50 cm to 70 cm) deepsea forms that are apparently very abundant on the upper continental slope throughout the Atlantic, Pacific, and Indian Oceans. The 70 or so species resemble hake in many respects but can be distinguished from them by their pointed snouts, which are quite flat over the mouth, and by their swimbladders, which connect to the inner ear. Two closely related species of *Antimora* are abundant off the Atlantic and Pacific coasts of North America.

Macrouridae and Ophidiidae.   The fishes in these two families are, with the exception of a few brotulas (Ophidiidae), elongate forms with pointed tails and joined dorsal, caudal, and anal fins (Fig. 21.3b, c). The

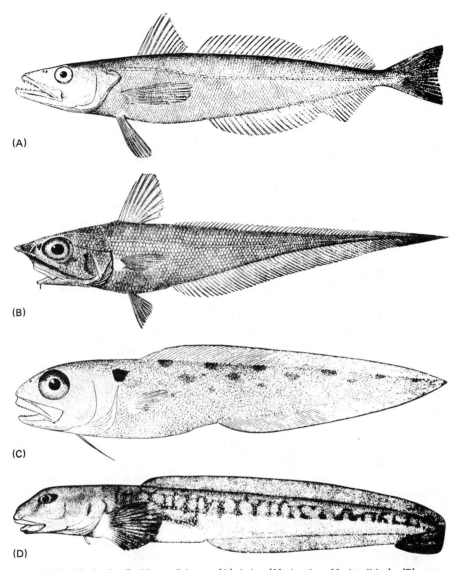

(A)

(B)

(C)

(D)

FIGURE 21.3 Gadiform fishes: (A) hake (*Merluccius,* Merlucciidae); (B) grenadier (*Coelorhynchus,* Macrouridae); (C) cusk-eel (*Otophidium,* Ophidiidae); and (D) eelpout (*Lycodes,* Zoarchidae). (From Goode and Bean, 1895.)

grenadiers (Macrouridae, 250+ species) and the brotulas (150+ species) are probably the most abundant fishes on the continental slope, and brotulas have been recorded as deep as 7.6 km, the maximum for any fish. When cameras are set over a can of bait on the ocean floor in deep water, these fishes are typically the first to appear, often in large numbers. Most forage on benthic invertebrates or scavenge. It has been hypothesized that their predation has a profound effect on the distribution and abundance of the deepsea benthos (see Chapter 36). The various species in the two groups show a wide variety of adaptations to the deepsea environment. Eyes range from being large and functional to practically nonexistent. Photophores may be present or absent. The swimbladder is well developed in most species but reduced in some, as is the skeleton and body musculature. Although the family Macrouridae has the most species, the family Ophidiidae seems to show the greatest range of morphologies and habitats. For example, some brotulas are inhabitants of fresh water in caves of Cuba and the Bahamas. The family Ophidiidae also contains 35 or more species of cuskeels, small (usually) eel-like fishes that burrow into soft bottoms, usually on the continental shelf. Although the grenadiers and the ophidiids are superficially somewhat similar, they differ in such features as chin barbels (Macrouridae only), pelvic fins (reduced or absent in the Ophidiidae), and dorsal spines (may be present in the grenadiers). The many differences between the Ophidiidae and other codlike fishes has prompted Cohen and Nielsen (1978) to place them, along with the Carapidae, in their own order (Ophidiiformes). Also placed in this order are two families of viviparous species, the Bythitidae (removed from the Ophidiidae) and the curious Aphyonidae (removed from the Ophidiidae).

Carapidae.   The 25 to 30 species of pearlfishes are worth mentioning mostly because many of them live in close association with such invertebrates as sea cucumbers, clams, sea urchins, and starfish (Trott and Trott 1972). The relationships with the invertebrates range from commensalism to parasitism. In the latter case, certain species live inside the body cavity of sea cucumbers, where they feed on the internal organs. Pearlfish are small (to 30 cm) with elongate, slender bodies that taper to a fine point. The pelvic, caudal, and sometimes the pectoral fins are absent, and scales are small or absent. This morphology allows a pearlfish to back into the body cavity of its host species through the mouth or anus. Besides the peculiar way of life of the adults, pearlfishes are also noted for their complex life cycle. They pass through two larval stages, a vexillifer stage, which is planktonic, and a tenuis stage, which is benthic. The larval forms are different enough from the parents so that the first ones known were described as distinct species.

Zoarcidae.   The eelpouts are another group of elongate fishes with large heads, pointed tails, and small or absent pelvic fins (Fig. 21.3d). Most are less than 30 cm long, but at least one species may reach 1m. Although they lack fin spines, many classification systems put the eelpouts in the Perciformes on the basis of their similarities (perhaps convergent) with the blennies. There are at least 65 species of eelpout, a number of them common in deepwater environments, as well as in the Arctic and Antarctic.

Batracoidiformes

This order contains just the toadfish family (Batrachoididae), which contains only about 55 species. What the order lacks in species it makes up for in conspicuousness, since toadfishes are commonly encountered in shallow marine waters, especially off North America. As the common name suggests, the toadfishes have a flat, toadlike head, with protruding, dorsally located eyes and a large mouth. The body is squat, drab in color, and usually without scales. The pelvic fins are jugular in position, and spines are present in the dorsal fin. In some South American forms the spines are hollow and associated with venom glands. Perhaps the best known toadfish is the oyster toadfish (*Opsanus tau*), which can make incredibly loud sounds by vibrating its swimbladder and has the habit of laying its eggs (which it defends vigorously) in old cans and other trash. Midshipmen (*Porichthys*) are also well-known members of this family, since they are one of the few inshore fishes that have numerous photophores.

Lophiiformes   All the 200 to 250 members of this order are called anglerfishes, because most possess a fishing pole (illicium) on the head, complete with an artificial lure (esca). The illicium and esca develop from the first ray of the spinous dorsal fin. Anglerfishes are inactive forms with large heads and mouths, cryptic coloration, scales small or absent, small gills, jugular pelvic fins (if present), no ribs, and physoclistic swimbladders (Fig. 21.4). The anglerfishes fall into two ecological groups: (1) those that live on the bottom or attached to drifting seaweed, usually in shallow water (families Lophiidae, Brachionichthyidae, Antennariidae, Chaunacidae, Ogcocephalidae); and (2) those that live in the Bathypelagic Zone (suborder Ceratoidei, the remaining 10 families). The fishes in the first group lie hidden on the bottom and wave the illicium and esca around to attract potential prey. The esca mimics particular types of organisms; at least one species of anglerfish (*Antennarius* sp.) has an esca that looks remarkably like a small fish (Pietsch and Grobecker 1978). Most species in the latter four families of the first group have muscular pectoral fins that look like arms and are used either for "walking" across the bottom or for clinging onto floating seaweed. Most of the shallow-water anglerfishes are small in size, but some goosefishes (Lophiidae) may reach 1.3 m in length and a weight of nearly 32 kg. Despite their ugly appearance, such fish are quite edible.

While the shallow-water anglerfishes are extremely peculiar in appearance, many of the deepsea anglers can only be described as bizarre. They are, by and large, small, soft-bodied forms without scales or pelvic fins but with large mouths and teeth, dark-colored bodies, and a variety of illicia and esca. However, the fishing organs are present only on females; the males exist primarily for reproduction and in many species are actually parasites attached to the females (see Chapter 36 for a discussion of reproductive strategies). As in the shallow-water forms, the esca seems to mimic other organisms to attract them to the anglerfish. Since most potential prey organisms in the deep sea are luminous, the esca contains a light organ, in which light is produced by symbiotic

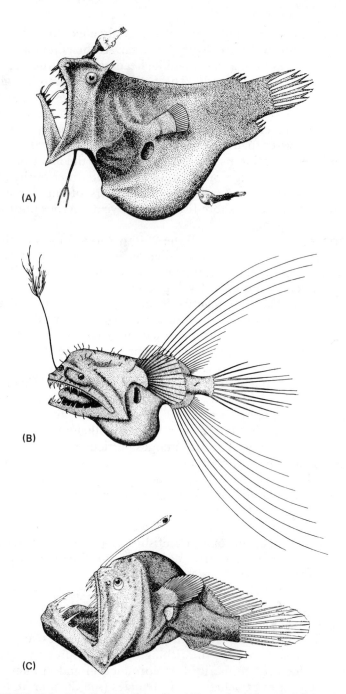

FIGURE 21.4 Deepsea anglerfishes (Lophiiformes): (A) netdevil (*Linophryne,* Linophrynidae); (B) fanfin anglerfish (*Caulophryne,* Caulophrynidae); and (C) black devil (*Melanocetus,* Melanocetidae). Life size of these fish is 5 cm to 10 cm. Note the parasitic male attached to the fish in (A). (From Regan and Trewavas, 1932.)

bacteria (O'Day 1974). This light attracts not only prey but also (because the esca is different for each species of anglerfish) males. As might be expected of an organ that is so important for both prey capture and reproduction and that is so likely to become damaged by animals attracted to it, the illicium is apparently capable of regeneration (Pietsch 1974). In addition to the esca, some deepsea anglerfishes (e.g., *Linophryne*) have barbels that also produce light. Curiously, these barbels do not contain light-producing bacteria but have an intrinsic light-producing system (Hansen and Herring 1977).

Supplemental Readings   Fitch and Lavenberg 1968; Gosline 1971; Hart 1973; Herald 1961; Nikolsky 1954; Wheeler 1975.

αααααααααααααααααααααααααααααααααααααααααααααααααααααααααααααααααααααααααα
~~~~~~

𝓕𝓵𝔂𝓲𝓷𝓰 𝓕𝓲𝓼𝓱𝓮𝓼, 𝓚𝓲𝓵𝓵𝓲𝓯𝓲𝓼𝓱𝓮𝓼, 𝓪𝓷𝓭 𝓢𝓲𝓵𝓿𝓮𝓻𝓼𝓲𝓭𝓮𝓼

Infraclass Teleostei
Division Euteleostei
  Superorder Acanthopterygii
    Series Atherinomorpha
      Order Atheriniformes
        Suborder Exocoetoidei
          Families Exocoetidae (flying fishes and halfbeaks), Belonidae (needlefishes), Scomberesocidae (sauries)
        Suborder Cyprinodontoidei
          Families Oryziatidae (medakas), Adrianichthyidae, Horaichthyidae, Cyprinodontidae (killifishes), Poeciliidae (livebearers), Goodeidae, Anablepidae (four-eyed fishes), Jenynsiidae
        Suborder Atherinoidei
          Families Melanotaeniidae (rainbow fishes), Atherinidae (silversides), Isonidae (surf sardines), Neostethidae, Phallostethidae

The Atheriniformes have a checkered systematic history. The classification scheme presented here is basically that of Rosen (1964), who pointed out the structural similarities between the three rather disparate groups listed above as suborders. The features used to link the three groups are largely osteological, such as the absence of spines or serrations on the opercular bones, the rarity of ctenoid scales, the lack of an orbitosphenoid bone, and the connection of the pectoral girdle to the skull with Baudelot's ligament. Prior to Rosen (1964) the suborders had been treated as unrelated orders with various positions in the euteleostean family tree. Gosline (1971) expresses the opinion that the apparent similarities among the three groups are the result of convergent adaptations to living at the water's surface, so that the older systems are probably valid. However, Rosen's system does seem to have gained wide acceptance, perhaps in part because it is a convenient way of disposing of three groups that otherwise do not fit comfortably into most classification schemes.

276

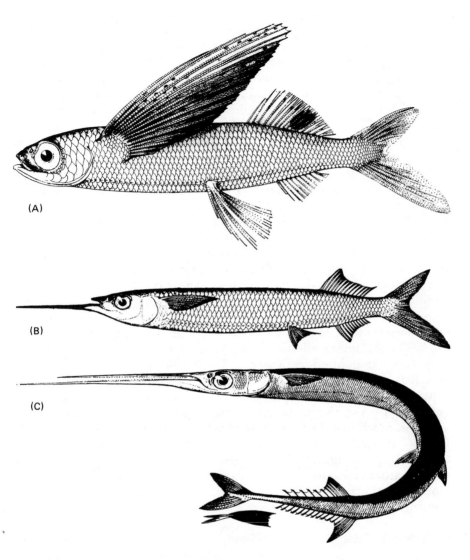

FIGURE 22.1 Exocoetoid fishes: (A) flying fish (*Cypselurus*, Exocoetidae); (B) halfbeak (*Hemirhampus*, Exocoetidae); and (C) needlefish (*Belone*, Belonidae). (From Jordan and Evermann, 1900.)

Exocoetoidei   The flying fishes (Exocoetidae, about 50 species), halfbeaks (Exocoetidae[1], 60+ species), needlefishes (Belonidae, 25 to 30 species), and sauries (Scomberesocidae, four species) are small to moderate-sized epipelagic fishes that are often placed by themselves in the order Beloniformes (Fig. 22.1). Most are marine, but a few halfbeaks and needlefishes also live in fresh water. The four families are all characterized by having the single dorsal

---

[1] The halfbeaks are often treated as a separate family, Hemiramphidae.

and anal fins about equal in size and located close to the tail. The pelvics are abdominal in position, and none of the fins have spines. The lateral line is well developed and low on the body, which is typically long and narrow. The members of the three families can be readily distinguished by their unique specializations. The flying fishes have long pectoral fins which they use for gliding after they jump out of the water. The length of the glide is increased by sculling motions of the lower lobe of the tail, which is larger and longer than the upper lobe. Some species have enlarged pelvic fins as well, which assist in the gliding. The "flying" of these fish appears to have developed as a means of escaping predators; larger individuals can gain nearly a meter of altitude and glide as far as 100 m, although most flights are lower and shorter. Adult flying fish have blunt snouts and small, unspecialized mouths. However, the juveniles of some species have elongated lower jaws such as those possessed by halfbeaks. The fact that some halfbeaks also have enlarged pectoral fins for making longer leaps from the water further indicates the close relationship between the two groups. The elongate lower jaw of the halfbeaks apparently functions in directing small, surface-oriented zooplankters into the mouth of the fish, since halfbeaks capture such prey while swimming in schools close to the surface of water. In contrast to the halfbeaks, the needlefishes and sauries prey on small fishes, as their long jaws with pointed teeth attest. The needlefishes are elongate fishes that look like unarmored gars, while the sauries are even more terete. Both groups are speedy epipelagic fishes. The speed of the sauries is enhanced by the five to seven finlets behind both the dorsal and the anal fins, much like those possessed by tunas. Despite their speed, these fishes (but particularly the sauries) are important prey for larger predators, such as the tunas and swordfishes. One reason for this, perhaps, is that the stocks of sauries in many parts of the oceans are relatively unexploited by humans because of their difficulty of capture. This situation is changing rapidly.

Cyprinodontoidei   Throughout the tropical and temperate world, wherever there is water too saline, too warm, too small, too isolated, or too extreme in its fluctuations in quality for most fishes, chances are reasonably good that it will be inhabited by one or more cyprinodontoid species. By and large they are small (less than 15 cm) omnivores, although many species are such efficient predators on insects that they are used for mosquito control, while other species are capable of digesting bluegreen algae. Morphologically, they are surface-oriented, with upturned mouths, large eyes, flattened heads, and dorsal fins placed far back on the body (Fig. 22.2a, b). This morphology, besides allowing them to take advantage of the abundance of food in the surface layers, enables them to pump the thin oxygen-rich layer of water at the air-water interface across the gills, an ability especially useful for life in warm stagnant waters. As a result of their surface

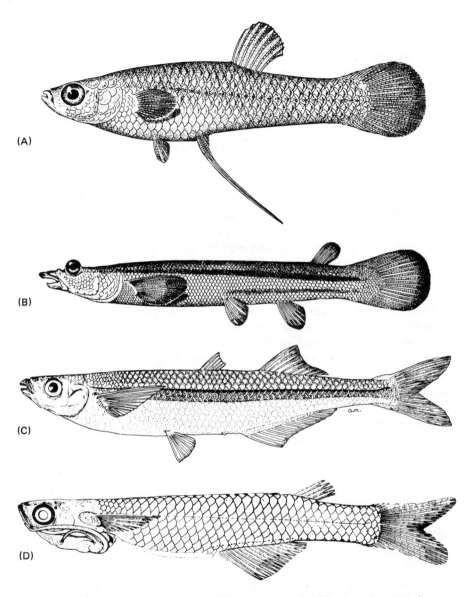

FIGURE 22.2 Atheriniform fishes: (A) male mosquitofish (*Gambusia,* Poeciliidae);
(B) four-eyed fish (*Anableps,* Anablepidae); (C) topsmelt (*Atherinops,* Atherini-
dae); and (D) *Ceratostethus* male (Phallostethidae). [(A) and (B) from Jordan and
Evermann (1900); (C) from Moyle (1976a); (D) from Roberts (1971).]

orientation, these fishes are frequently called topminnows. They are
distinguished from similar true minnows (Cyprinidae) by the presence
of small teeth in the jaws (and hence "tooth-carp" is another name for
the group). The pelvic fins are reduced or absent in many species, and
fin spines are absent. Scales are generally cycloid, although the males of a

few species develop ctenoid scales. The lateral line is usually well developed on the head but absent from the body, the nostrils have double openings, and the upper jaw is bordered by a protractile premaxilla.

Cyprinodontidae. The 300+ species of killifishes are scattered throughout South America, North America (into southeastern Canada), southern Eurasia, and Africa, including Madagascar. Morphologically, the killifishes are the least specialized of the cyprinodontoid fishes, and most other families in the group are defined according to how they diverge from the standard killifish pattern. Many of them are brightly colored and are favored as aquarium fishes. All lay eggs, and many exhibit territorial behavior at breeding time. However, at least one species (*Rivulus marmoratus*) is a self-fertilizing hermaphrodite (Harrington 1961).

Killifishes are successful in a wide range of habitats. Perhaps the best known killifishes are those that occur in desert springs (Chapter 31) and coastal habitats, such as salt marshes and mangrove swamps (Chapter 33). Other habitats of special interest are temporary ponds, Lake Titicaca, and lakes and streams of North America. Ponds in tropical areas in both Africa and South America which dry up each year often contain annual cyprinodonts, mostly of the genera *Cynolebias* and *Nothobranchius*. These fish complete their life cycles in a year. Eggs are deposited in the mud of the pond bottoms where they can survive after the pond dries up. When the rains come again, the eggs hatch quickly, and the pond is soon populated with fish again. At least one species, *Nothobranchius guentheri,* grows from egg to spawning adult in four weeks, the fastest such growth known in fishes (Haas 1976a, b). If temporary ponds are an unexpected habitat for fish in general, Lake Titicaca, a large (8100 km^2), cool ($11°C$ to $16°C$) lake located high (3803 m) in the Andes Mountains, is an unexpected habitat to be dominated by cyprinodonts. Of the 20 or so species known to be native to the lake, 19 are cyprinodonts of the genus *Orestias* and one is a catfish, *Trichomycterus rivulatus* (Richerson et al. 1977). The *Orestias* species radiated in the absence of competition, have taken the basic cyprinodont morphology to its limits, resulting in a rather peculiar-looking array of piscivores, planktivores, insectivores, grazers, etc.

The tendency of killifishes to inhabit extreme or isolated environments has resulted in many species becoming extinct, threatened with extinction, or greatly reduced in numbers, despite their hardiness. This is largely because exotic predators or competitors have been introduced into some habitats and because coastal habitats, such as salt marshes and lagoons, have been drained and/or polluted. The killifishes have yet to produce a species that can live permanently out of the water!

Poeciliidae. The 150 or so species of livebearers differ from the killifishes mainly in their method of reproduction (viviparity) and in the structures associated with reproduction. The anal fin of the male, together with its internal supports of bone, muscle, and cartilage, is highly modified into a copulatory organ, the gonopodium. The structure of the gonopodium forms the basis of poeciliid classification (Rosen and Bailey 1963). The livebearers are small; most rarely exceed 10 cm in length, and some species have a maximum length of only 2 cm to 3 cm. They are found in warm water at low elevations from northeastern Argentina to the southeastern United States, and in the West Indies as well. They are most numerous in Central America, perhaps because this region is so unstable geologically. Poeciliids in general are well suited for maintaining populations in such areas because:

1. They have a broad tolerance of extremes in temperature, salinity, and dissolved oxygen.
2. They are small in size, so a large population can exist in a small area.
3. They will eat whatever food is available.
4. Their method of reproduction frees them from the need to have special substrates for spawning and assures high survival of the young, even under adverse conditions.
5. Their quick attainment of maturity results in a high reproductive rate that can produce rapid population expansion under favorable conditions.

These same factors help to explain the success of livebearers such as guppies (*Poecilia reticulata*), mollies (*Poecilia* spp.), and swordtails (*Xiphophorus* spp.) as aquarium fishes, as well as the ability of guppies to establish populations in sewage treatment plants (into which they are frequently flushed by aquarists tired of their prolific charges!).

The above factors are also important reasons why the mosquitofish (*Gambusia affinis*) has proved to be such a successful mosquito-control agent, resulting in its being introduced into warm waters throughout the world (Fig. 22.2a). Although native only to the southeastern United States, it is today probably the most widely distributed species of freshwater fish in the world, beating out such perennial favorites for this honor as rainbow trout (*Salmo gairdneri*), largemouth bass (*Micropterus salmoides*), Mozambique tilapia (*Sarotherodon mossambica*), and grass carp (*Ctenopharyngodon idella*). In the process of becoming established around the world, the mosquitofish has probably displaced native cyprinodonts in many areas, although this has been documented mainly in the American Southwest (Minckley and Deacon 1968). Their success as mosquito-control agents has also led to reduced consideration, in many parts of the world, of native fishes that might be equally useful in mosquito control (such as annual cyprinodonts).

While the success of the mosquitofish has been spectacular, some of the most fascinating success stories among fishes are those of the all-female "species" of *Poecilia* and *Poeciliopsis* in Mexico. The first of these forms to be discovered was the Amazon molly (*Poecilia formosa*), which is abundant in streams of northeastern Mexico and northern

Texas (Hubbs and Hubbs 1932). Studies eventually revealed that the Amazon molly is a sexual parasite on two other species: *P. mexicana* and *P. latipinna*, from which it probably originally was derived as a hybrid. The sperm from males of the host species is required to activate the development of the eggs of the Amazon molly, but union of the male and female chromosomes does not occur, so only genetically uniform females are produced (gynogenesis). In *Poeciliopsis*, successful all-female "species" are produced by a process called hybridogenesis (Schultz 1971). In this case, the mating between the female and the host male results in fertilization of the egg, and a true hybrid is formed. However, during oogenesis in the hybrid females, the chromosomes contributed by the host male are lost in meiosis, so that only the female genes are passed on to the next generation. The result is a self-perpetuating strain of all female fish. To make matters even more complicated, some unisexual populations of *Poeciliopsis* exist that are actually trihybrids (Vrijenhoek and Schultz 1974). The trihybrids apparently result from hybridogenetic females mating with males from a third species, resulting initially in fish that are hybrids in fact between the original maternal species and the new species. However, in this new hybrid some chromosomal reassortment takes place, resulting in eggs containing at least some genetic material from the third species. The new hybrid females then mate with the males that produced the original hybridogenetic fish, resulting in female progeny with characteristics of all three of the original species (Vrijenhoek and Schultz 1974).

One of the interesting questions posed by the unisexual "species" is, why are they so successful? There is little question that they are indeed successful; they are widespread and typically more abundant in most localities than the parent species. This is attributed to a combination of factors such as: (1) the heterosis (hybrid vigor) exhibited by the hybrids (e.g., larger size, higher survival rates); (2) the increased reproductive potential of an all-female population; and (3) the ability of the "species" to thrive in intermediate or changing environments (Schultz 1971, Moore 1976). However, these factors offer only a partial explanation, since the unisexual "species" have two other problems to overcome: the low genetic variability expected in the absence of genetic recombination, and the continued dependence of the unisexual fishes on bisexual males for reproduction. The first problem is minimized by the fact that the unisexual populations have apparently arisen repeatedly, so that each "species" in fact represents many different clones, each with a different origin. When individuals from two clones coexist, they may segregate ecologically from one another (reflected in dentition and feeding behavior), as well as from the parent bisexual species (Vrijenhoek 1978). The continued dependence of the unisexual fishes on the bisexual males is a problem because the unisexual fishes cannot afford to be so successful in their competitive interactions with the bisexual fishes that they eliminate them. In addition, there are obviously strong selection pressures on the host species to develop mechanisms for not wasting reproductive effort on the parasitic unisexual fishes. Fortunately for the unisexual forms, the males of the bisexual species have strong dominance hierarchies in which the dominant males prevent subordinate males from mating with correct females. The subordinate males then apparently mate with the unisexual females. If the densities of the bisexual species are too low, this hierarchy apparently does not develop and all males mate with the correct females (Schultz 1971). This in turn presumably causes a drop in the number of the competitively superior unisexual fishes, allowing the populations of the bisexual species to build up again.

Other families. The seven remaining families of cyprinodontiform fishes contain few species but a number of interesting adaptations. The medakas (Oryziatidae, seven species) of southeast Asia are often placed in the Cyprinodontidae, but the premaxilla is not protrusible and teeth are lacking on the vomer. The Adrianichthyidae, with three species confined to the Celebes Island, have an enormously elongated and flattened snout set over a large mouth. Little is known about how these structures are used. The Horaichthyidae contains just one species, which looks remarkably like a poeciliid, including the presence of a gonopodium on the males, but it apparently evolved independently, in India. The Goodeidae (35 species) are a family of livebearers largely confined to the Rio Lerma basin in the highlands of Central Mexico, where the various species are specialized for a wide variety of niches (Fitzsimmons 1972). The male copulatory organ is a muscular "pseudophallus," since the anal fin is only slightly modified (Nelson 1975). The embryos obtain nutriments from a placentalike affair called atrophotaenia. The Jenynsiidae are another small family (three species) of South American livebearers that are distinguished from the poeciliids by the presence of a tubular gonopodium. The four-eyed fishes (Anablepidae, three species) also have a tubular gonopodium, but they are distinguished by their remarkable eyes, each of which is divided into two parts with separate corneas and retinas (Fig. 22.2b). With this system they can see simultaneously both above the water and beneath it. These fishes forage in shallow water in both freshwater and marine environments.

Atherinoidei   The 200+ species of atherinoid fishes are mostly elongate species, with terminal mouths, large eyes, and two dorsal fins. The first dorsal fin is made up of weak spines, and a similar spine usually precedes the anal fin as well. The lateral line is weak or absent, while deciduous cycloid scales are present. About 150 of the species are silversides (Atherinidae), slender, silvery fishes with abdominal pelvic fins and large scales (Fig. 22.2c). Silversides are often extremely abundant in inshore regions of freshwater lakes, estuaries, and various shallow marine environments. They are schooling, diurnal planktivores. Perhaps the most famous of the atherinids is the grunion (*Leuresthes tenuis*), which deposits its eggs in the sands of the beaches of southern California during high spring tides (see Chapter 33). In lakes, silversides are frequently important forage fishes for predatory game fishes. This and their supposed potential for control of nuisance insects have resulted in one species, the Mississippi silverside (*Menidia audens*), being introduced into lakes and reservoirs in California, Oklahoma, and elsewhere. Such introductions often seem to create more problems than they solve (Moyle 1976a).

The atherinids have apparently given rise to two families of moderately deep-bodied forms, the rainbow fishes (Melanotaeniidae) and the surf sardines (Isonidae). The rainbow fishes (19 species) are small, attractive fishes with compressed bodies and subthoracic pelvic fins. They are confined to the fresh waters of Australia and New Guinea. The surf sardines (six species) look like a cross between a silversides and a herring, since they possess a silversides body that has been deepened, with a keel added. Although they are frequently found in the surf, their habits and habitats are similar to those of the atherinids. They can be found, often in large numbers, along the continents that border the Indian and southern Pacific Oceans.

The remaining two families, Neostethidae (16 species) and Phallostethidae (three species) are rather peculiar freshwater fishes residing in southeast Asia. They are small, elongate, translucent fishes distinguished by an extremely complex copulatory organ (priapium) located on the throat of the males, which also serves as the exit for excretory products (Fig. 22.2d).

Supplemental Readings   Gosline 1971; Herald 1961; Moyle 1976a; Nelson 1976; Rosen 1964; Rosen and Bailey 1963; Sterba 1959; Wheeler 1975.

ααααααααααααααααααααααααααααααααααααααααααααααααααααααααααααααααααααα
~~~~~~

Ruling Perches

Subclass Actinopterygii
Infraclass Teleostei
  Division Eutelostei
    Superorder Acanthopterygii
      Series Percomorpha
        Order Lampridiformes
          Families Lampridae (opah), Veliferidae, Lophotidae (crestfishes), Trachipteridae (ribbonfishes), Regalecidae (oarfishes), Stylephoridae (tube-eye), Ateleopodidae, Mirapinnidae (hairyfish), Eutaeniophoridae (tapetails), Megalomycteridae (largenoses)
        Order Beryciformes
          Families Stephanoberycidae (pricklefishes), Melamphaeidae (bigscales), Gibberichthyidae (gibberfish), Trachichthyidae (slimeheads), Diretmidae, Korsogasteridae, Anoplogasteridae (fangtooth), Berycidae (alfonsinos), Monocentridae (pinecone fishes), Anomalopidae (lanterneyes), Holocentridae (squirrelfishes), Rondeletiidae (redmouth whalefishes), Barbourisiidae, Cetomimidae (flabby whalefishes)
        Order Zeiformes
          Families Parazenidae (parazen), Macrurocyttidae, Zeidae (dories), Oreosomatidae (oreos), Grammicolepidae, Caproidae (boarfishes)
        Order Gasterosteiformes
          Families Aulorhynchidae (tubesnouts), Hypoptychidae (sandeel), Gasterosteidae (sticklebacks), Indostomidae, Pegasidae (seamoths), Solenostomidae (ghost pipefishes), Syngnathidae (pipefishes and seahorses), Macrorhamphosidae (snipefishes), Centriscidae (shrimpfishes), Aulostomidae (trumpetfishes), Fistulariidae (cornetfishes)
        Order Synbranchiformes
          Family Synbranchidae (swamp eels)
        Order Scorpaeniformes
          Families Scorpaenidae (rockfishes), Triglidae (searobins), Caracanthidae (orbicular velvetfishes), Aploactinidae (velvetfishes), Pataecidae (prowfishes), Anoplopomatidae (sablefishes), Hexagrammidae (greenlings), Zaniolepididae (combfishes), Platycephalidae (flatheads), Hoplichthyidae (ghost flatheads), Congiopodidae (pigfishes), Icelidae (Arctic sculpins), Cottidae (sculpins), Cottocomephoridae

(Baikal sculpins), Comephoridae (Baikal oilfishes), Normanichthyidae, Cottunculidae, Psychrolutidae, Agonidae (poachers), Cyclopteridae (lumpsuckers and snailfishes)

Order Dactylopteriformes
Family Dactylopteridae (flying gurnards)
Order Perciformes
Suborder Percoidei
Families Centropomidae (snooks), Percichthyidae (temperate basses), Serranidae (sea basses), Grammistidae (soapfishes), Pseudochromidae (dottybacks), Pseudogrammidae, Grammidae (basslets), Plesiopidae (roundheads), Pseudoplesiopidae, Anisochromidae, Acanthoclinidae, Glaucosomidae, Theraponidae (tigerperches), Banjosidae, Kuhliidae (aholeholes), Centrarchidae (sunfishes), Priacanthidae (bigeyes), Apogonidae (cardinal fishes), Acropomatidae, Percidae (perches), Sillaginidae (smelt-whitings), Branchiostegidae (tilefishes), Labracoglossidae, Lactariidae (false trevallies), Pomatomidae (bluefishes), Rachycentridae (cobia), Echeneidae (remoras), Carangidae (jacks), Coryphaenidae (dolphins), Formionidae, Menidae (moonfish), Leiognathidae (ponyfishes), Bramidae (pomfrets), Caristiidae (manefishes), Arripidae (Australian salmon), Emmelichthyidae (bonnetmouths), Lutjanidae (snappers), Nemipteridae (threadfin breams), Lobotidae (triple tails), Gerreidae (mojarras), Pomadasyidae (grunts), Lethrinidae (emperors), Pentapodidae (large-eye breams), Sparidae (porgies), Sciaenidae (croakers), Mullidae (goatfishes), Monodactylidae (moonfishes), Pempheridae (sweepers), Leptobramidae (beachsalmon), Bathyclupeidae, Toxotidae (archerfishes), Coracinidae (galjoens), Kyphosidae (seachubs), Ephippidae (spadefishes), Scatophagidae (scats), Rhinoprenidae (threadfin scat), Chaetodontidae (butterflyfishes), Enoplosidae, Pentacerotidae (boarfishes), Nandidae (leaffishes), Oplegnathidae (knifejaws), Embiotocidae (surfperches), Cichlidae (cichlids), Pomacentridae (damselfishes), Gadopsidae (Australian blackfish), Cirrhitidae (hawkfishes), Chironemidae (kelpfishes), Aplodactylidae, Cheilodactylidae (morwongs), Latridae (trumpeters), Owstoniidae, Cepolidae (bandfishes)
Suborder Mugiloidei
Family Mugilidae (mullets)
Suborder Sphyraenoidei
Family Sphyraenidae (barracudas)
Suborder Polynemoidei
Family Polynemidae (threadfins)
Suborder Labroidei
Families Labridae (wrasses), Odacidae, Scaridae (parrotfishes)
Suborder Trachinoidei
Families Trichodontidae (sandfishes), Opisthognathidae (jawfishes), Champsodontidae, Chiasmodontidae (swallowers), Bathymasteridae (ronquils), Percophididae, Mugiloididae (sandperches), Trichonotidae (sanddivers), Cheimarrhichthyidae, Creediidae, Limnichthyidae, Oxudercidae, Trachinidae (weaverfishes), Uranoscopidae (stargazers), Leptoscopidae, Dactyloscopidae (sand stargazers)
Suborder Notothenioidei
Families Bovichthyidae, Nototheniidae (cod icefishes), Harpagiferidae (plunder fishes), Bathydraconidae (antarctic dragonfishes), Channichthyidae (crocodile icefishes)
Suborder Blennioidei
Families Xenocephalidae (armored blenny), Congrogadidae (eelblennies), Notograptidae, Peronedysiidae, Ophiclinidae (snakeblennies),Tripterygiidae (threefin blennies), Clinidae (clinids), Chaenopsidae (pike blennies), Blenniidae (combtooth blennies), Stichaeidae (pricklebacks), Cryptacanthodidae (wrymouths), Pholidae (gunnels), Anarhichadidae (wolffishes), Ptilichthyidae (quillfish), Zaproridae (prowfish), Scytalinidae (graveldiver), Alabetidae (single slit eels)

Suborder Icosteoidei
    Family Icosteidae (ragfish)
Suborder Schindlerioidei
    Family Schindleriidae
Suborder Ammodytoidei
    Family Ammodytidae (sandlances)
Suborder Gobioidei
    Families Eleotridae (sleepers), Gobiidae (gobies), Rhyacichthyidae (loach gobies), Kraemeriidae (sand gobies), Gobioididae (eel gobies), Trypauchenidae (burrowing gobies), Microdemidae (wormfishes)
Suborder Kurtoidei
    Family Kurtidae (nurseryfishes)
Suborder Acanthuroidei
    Families Acanthuridae (surgeonfishes), Siganidae (rabbitfishes)
Suborder Scombroidei
    Families Gempylidae (snake mackerels), Trichiuridae (cutlass fishes), Scombridae (mackerels and tunas), Xiphiidae (swordfish), Luvaridae (luvar), Istiophoridae (billfishes)
Suborder Stromateoidei
    Families Amarsipidae, Centrolophidae (medusafishes), Nomeidae (driftfishes), Ariommidae, Tetragonuridae (squaretails), Stromateidae (butterfishes)
Suborder Anabantoidei
    Families Anabantidae (climbing gouramies), Belontiidae (gouramis), Helostomatidae (kissing gourami), Osphronemidae (giant gourami)
Suborder Luciocephaloidei
    Family Luciocephalidae (pikehead)
Suborder Channoidei
    Family Channidae (snakeheads)
Suborder Mastacembeloidei
    Family Mastacembelidae (spiny eels), Chaudhuriidae
Order Gobiesociformes
    Families Gobiesocidae (clingfishes), Callionymidae (dragonets), Draconettidae
Order Pleuronectiformes
    Families Psettodidae, Citharidae, Bothidae (lefteye flounders), Pleuronectidae (righteye flounders), Soleidae (soles), Cynoglossidae (tonguefishes)
Order Tetraodontiformes
    Families Triacanthodidae (spikefishes), Triacanthidae (triplespines), Balistidae (triggerfishes), Ostraciontidae (boxfishes), Triodontidae (threetooth puffers), Tetraodontidae (puffers), Diodontidae (porcupinefishes), Molidae (ocean sunfishes).

The percomorph fishes are an immensely variable and successful group, making up about half of all known fish species. Representatives can be found in most major habitat types, and their food and feeding mechanisms are as varied as the group itself. Despite this variability, most members are easy to place in this series because of their common structural plan. One reason for the structural similarities is that, while there are species that live in habitats as diverse as the deep sea and swift streams, most live either in shallow-water marine habitats or in lakes, especially in tropical regions. Most also live in, on, or in close association with the bottom. The general percomorph plan includes (1) variable body shape, with pelvic fins (if present) thoracic or jugular in position and pectoral fins placed high on the body; (2) fin spines present; (3) protractile premaxilla; (4) upper and lower sets of pharyngeal teeth; (5) swimbladder physoclistous (or absent); (6) pelvic fins usually with one spine and five rays each, caudal fin usually with 15 branched rays, and spinal column usually with 24 vertebrate; (7) small spines usually on bones of head and/or operculum; (8) pleural ribs but no intermuscular bones, (9) absence (usually) of specializations common in other major groups, such as photophores, otophysic connections (e.g., Weberian apparatus of Ostariophysi) and viviparity; (10) ctenoid scales (usually); and (11) well-developed eyes.

The above mosaic of characteristics (and others) have made the percomorph fishes successful because they have been modified, in concert with one another, into an extraordinary array of specializations. A majority of these specializations are those that allow the fishes to take advantage of the complexity of benthic inshore habitats in both salt and fresh water. They fall into three general categories: predator avoidance, feeding, and behavior, especially reproductive behavior.

Perhaps the single most important percomorph characteristic that has reduced predation pressure is the presence of spines. Spines increase the effective diameter of small fish and thereby increase the size of predator necessary to prey upon them. Big predators are fewer than small predators, and even they are likely to prefer prey in which the edible body size is close to the effective diameter for swallowing. Spines thus give fish the type of protection otherwise available mainly through the use of heavy armor, which greatly reduces mobility. With spines a fish can afford to be small, slow-moving, and day-active and have a body shape advantageous for something other than a speedy escape from predators. Protection from predators is also given by the maneuverability of percomorph fishes, which results from the placement of the paired fins and the fine control they possess over buoyancy. They can turn quickly, dive into cover, and, in some species, swim backwards if necessary. It is worth noting here that, contrary to the above discussion, many percomorph fishes have abandoned both stout spines and swimbladders (and, in many cases, pelvic fins) in favor of a completely benthic existence in which small size, cryptic coloration, secretive habits, and unusual body shapes offer protection from predation (e.g., blennies, flounders, sculpins).

Both the cryptic benthic forms and the more conventional percomorph fishes have a wide array of feeding specializations. Most of these are designed for capturing small invertebrates, but specializations exist for feeding on everything from organic ooze to plant material to large fish. As is true of the cypriniform fishes, these specializations are made possible by the combination of a flexible mouth for sucking in or grabbing prey and pharyngeal dentition for breaking up, grinding, or holding it. The acute vision of most percomorph fishes (the result of the tight pattern of cones in the retina) allows, in addition, precise location of prey (Marshall 1971).

As might be expected of fish that exhibit such varied and complex feeding habits, their behavior in general is quite complex. Many are highly social, exhibiting either schooling or territorial behavior. In addition, many interact symbiotically with other organisms. To accomplish these various inter- and intraspecific interactions, the percomorph fishes have developed a variety of means of communication, including rapid color changes, sound production, and stereotyped movements (fin and body language). The ability of the percomorph fishes to develop complex behavior patterns has presumably contributed to their success by increasing the number of "niches" open to them and by helping the species to maintain their integrity.

Since the series Percomorpha contains 10 orders, 230 families, and roughly 10,000 species, only the largest or most representative families in each order will be discussed in this chapter. Most of the families not discussed are small and poorly known (although they do invariably have fascinating specialized features of their own!).

Lampridiformes   This order contains a bizarre mixture of large, often brightly colored, pelagic fishes. Most species apparently live at depths between 100 m and 1000 m and so are rarely seen, despite broad, often worldwide, distribution patterns. Their diversity of form is indicated by the fact that 10 families are recognized, but only about 35 species! Most of these species lack many of the "typical" percomorph characteristics, such as spines and ctenoid scales. The mouth is highly protrusible, since not only the premaxilla but also the maxilla is protractile. Protrusibility is especially characteristic of the tube-eye (*Stylephorus chordatus*), which has a membranous pouch connecting the mouth to the cranium. The pouch can be expanded to a volume nearly 38 times that of the closed buccal cavity, creating the tremendous suction pressure for drawing in planktonic organisms (Pietsch 1978b). All have an elongate dorsal fin. In body shape they range from extremely deep-bodied (Lampridae, Veliferidae) to extremely elongate (Lophotidae, Regalecidae). Most spectacular of the deep-bodied forms is the opah, the sole member of the family Lampridae. Not only is it large (to 1.5 m), disc-shaped, and deeply compressed, but it is brilliantly colored: The body is dark blue on top, shading to a silver-flecked green and iridescent purple on the sides, and then to pink on the belly; the fins and jaws are vermillion. How these colors function is not known, since the opah is found mostly below 100 m, where it feeds on other fish, squid, octopus, and crustaceans. In marked contrast to the opah are the two species of oarfish (Regalecidae). These fishes are extremely attenuated, reaching lengths of 8 m, and have the anterior rays of the dorsal fin modified into a peculiar red "cockscomb" over the head and the pelvic rays into long filaments. Their mouth and eyes are quite small, and they seem to feed mainly on pelagic crustaceans. Apparently, they normally maintain themselves in the water column in a vertical position, which enables them to see their prey silhouetted against the downstreaming light (Pietsch 1978b). Because oarfish are only rarely seen on the surface, the appearance of a "monster" oarfish in a coastal area is likely to arouse a considerable amount of attention.

Beryciformes   The fishes in this order are a mixed bag of spiny-rayed fishes that share a number of primitive osteological features (e.g., presence of the orbitospenoid bone and more than five rays in the pelvic fins). Many of the 14 families and 150 or so species are poorly known, so it is quite likely that the Beryciformes is not a natural grouping and may be split up as more is learned about its members. Some of the families are well represented in fossil deposits of the Cretaceous period, and during the later portions of that period they may have played the dominant role in inshore waters now played by perciform fishes. Today the beryciform fishes are either found in various deepsea habitats or are night-active inshore forms. The deepsea forms are mostly small and chunky, with large (or no) scales and, usually, conspicuous spines on the body and/or fins. A few species have photophores. The deepsea species make up all the beryciform families except the Holocentridae and a few species in the Trachichthyidae, Anomalopidae, and Berycidae, which live in shallow water. The latter fishes are characterized by large eyes, bright red coloration, and rather conventional perchlike bodies. The squirrelfishes (Holocentridae, 70+ species) are the largest and most widely distributed family in the order, found throughout the tropical and subtropical marine regions (Fig. 23.1b). Most species inhabit coral reefs or shallow rocky areas in which they hide during the day, coming out at night, often in amazing numbers, to feed on zooplankton in the water column. As a group, they are rather noisy fish, communicating with each other with a variety of clicks, croaks, and grunts. Some species of lanterneye fishes (Anomalopidae) are also active at night over reefs. These fish have a large light-emitting organ beneath each eye, which apparently functions in enabling the fish to see prey, in confusing predators (it can be quickly covered with a lid), and in intraspecific communication (Morin et al. 1975).

Zeiformes   The zeiform fishes are a curious mixture of six families and 50 species. Most live in the deep sea, but a number of the better-known forms occur at only moderate depths, in midwater, and may actually support small fisheries. Most zeiform fishes have deep, compressed bodies with ctenoid scales and a few well-developed fin spines. Their heads are large, with extremely distensible jaws, which enable them to capture the fishes and large crustaceans on which they feed. Most possess a row of scutes on the ventral half of the body at one stage or another of their life history. Anatom-

290

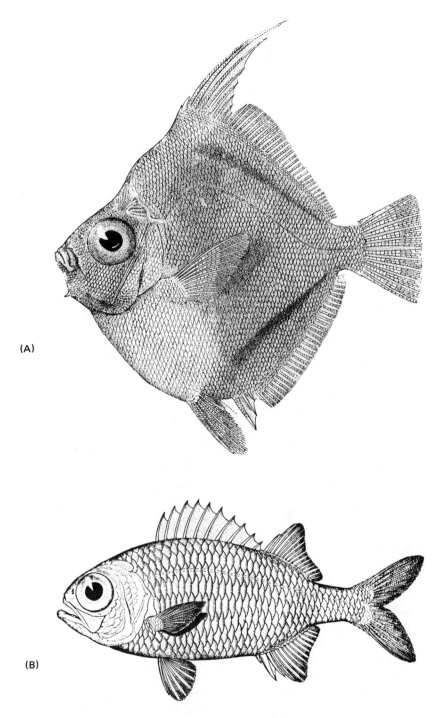

(A)

(B)

FIGURE 23.1 Percomorph fishes with ancestral characteristics: (A) boarfish (*Antigonia,* Zeiformes); (B) squirrelfish (*Myripristis,* Beryciformes). (From Jordan and Evermann, 1900.)

ically, these fishes are a mixture of ancestral, derived, and specialized percomorph features, so they are usually linked with the Beryciformes.

Perhaps the best-known fishes in this order are the dories (Zeidae), which are readily recognized by the large, upward-angled mouth, silvery color, and long filaments on the dorsal fin (Fig. 23.1a).

Gasterosteiformes

This order is small (210+ species) but contains some of the most unusual and best-known teleost fishes, such as the seahorses, pipefishes, and sticklebacks. It is divided into two suborders, which are so different from each other that they are often treated as separate orders: the Gasterosteoidei (Aulorhynchidae, Hypoptychidae, Gasterosteidae and, probably, Indostomidae) and the Syngnathoidei (the remaining seven families). The two groups are treated together here, following the suggestion of Pietsch (1978), who has demonstrated that the seamoths (Pegasidae) are intermediate in structure between the two groups. Previously, the seamoths had been placed in an order by themselves. The problem with defining this order, even with the seamoths included, is that there are few anatomical features possessed by all members, since each group has its own bizarre specializations. However, there is enough overlap between groups to link all the families listed, although the development of these characteristics shows considerable variation, as the following accounts should demonstrate.

Gasterosteidae. The sticklebacks are the one family in this order with body shapes approaching that of "normal" fish (Fig. 23.2a). They are small fishes that live in either fresh or salt water (or both) and are found throughout the Northern Hemisphere, usually in close association with coastlines. They are readily recognized by the presence of 3 to 16 isolated spines on the back that precede the dorsal fin, large eyes, small, upturned mouths, and narrow caudal peduncles. Most possess a row of bony plates on each side. Sticklebacks are territorial nest builders, and their elaborate reproductive behavior is perhaps the best documented of any animal species (see Wooton 1976), thanks to their abundance in the wild and the ease with which they reproduce under artificial conditions. Their physiology (mostly as related to reproduction) has also been well documented. Only eight species of stickleback are usually recognized, but two of these "species," the threespine stickleback (*Gasterosteus aculeatus*) and the ninespine stickleback (*Pungitius pungitius*), are in fact complexes of hundreds of divergent populations. Each of these populations may have many of the characteristics of a "good" species, reflecting the ability of sticklebacks to adapt to local conditions, such as food supply, substrates, and abundance of predators. This nightmare for traditional taxonomists has been a dream for students of evolution and genetics, providing many fascinating insights into general problems in these fields (see Chapter 26).

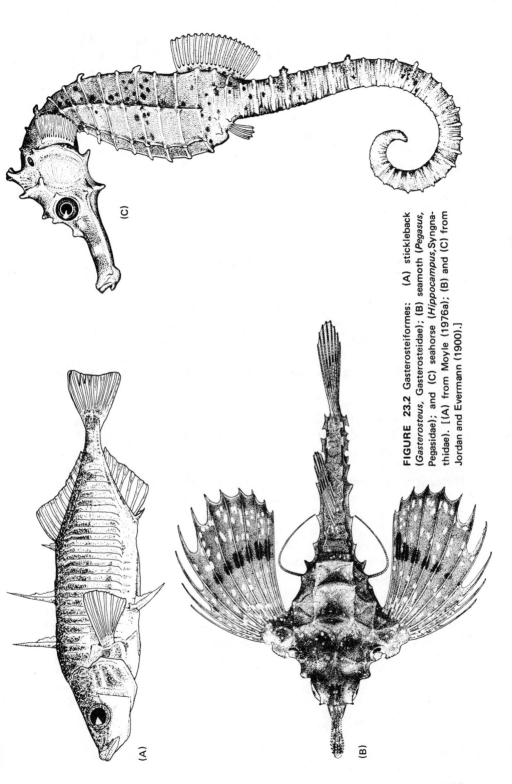

FIGURE 23.2 Gasterosteiformes: (A) stickleback (*Gasterosteus*, Gasterosteidae); (B) seamoth (*Pegasus*, Pegasidae); and (C) seahorse (*Hippocampus*,Syngnathidae). [(A) from Moyle (1976a); (B) and (C) from Jordan and Evermann (1900).]

Pegasidae. The seamoths have excited the interest of biologists ever since the first dried specimens were imported to Europe from China by early explorers. They are small (to 15 cm) marine fishes that are completely encased in bony plates and have winglike pectoral fins and long, bony snouts (Fig. 23.2b). The mouth, rather than being at the end of the snout, is underneath it and is a uniquely complicated structure that can be folded when not in use into a cavity beneath the snout. When the fish is feeding, the mouth unfolds, and the buccal cavity expands, creating a powerful suction device (Pietsch 1978a).

Syngnathidae. The pipefishes (150+ species) and seahorses (25+ species) are a family that has sacrificed streamlining and speed for armor, cryptic coloration, and secretive behavior. They are nevertheless very successful and are found in shallow marine waters the world over and occasionally in fresh water as well. All are long and thin, are encased in bony rings, have tubelike snouts with the mouth at the end, and lack pelvic fins (Fig. 23.2c). Pipefishes propel themselves with their tails, and seahorses employ the dorsal and pectoral fins, having converted the caudal peduncle into a prehensile organ for holding onto plant stems. Seahorses consequently swim upright in a very slow and unfishlike manner. To compensate in part for their slow swimming, the tubelike mouth of syngnathids allows them to suck in small crustaceans from some distance, after locating the prey precisely with their apparently binocular vision.

One of the most fascinating aspects of syngnathid biology is the means by which they care for the eggs and young. Each male seahorse has a sealed brood pouch on the underside of the tail with a tiny opening on the top. The female lays her eggs in this brood pouch, where they are incubated and hatched. The young are expelled once they are capable of swimming on their own. In the pipefishes there are brood pouches as well, but they are open down the middle or sealed with overlapping flaps. In the most primitive species the brood pouch is completely lacking, and the female merely attaches the eggs to a bare spot on the belly of the male (Herald 1959, 1961).

Aulostomidae and Fistularidae. The trumpetfishes (four species) and cornetfishes (four species) are long (0.8 m to 1.8 m), extremely slender fishes generally associated with tropical reefs. The snout is especially long but tipped with a surprisingly large mouth, which enables them to capture other fishes. As their body shape and fin placement indicate, they are lie-in-wait predators that conceal themselves either by hanging in the water column above the reef, by hanging close to the reef itself (often at an angle to it), or by associating closely with large browsing fish (e.g., parrotfishes).

Synbranchiformes   According to Rosen and Greenwood (1976), there is just one family (Synbranchidae) and 15 species in this order. However, the swamp eels enjoy a wide distribution in the fresh and brackish waters of tropical Africa, Asia, Australia, and South America. Like the "true" eels (Anguilliformes), the swamp eels have a distinct lack of external features, so that identification of species is difficult. Pectoral fins are present only in the larval stages, pelvic fins are absent, dorsal and anal fins are reduced to small folds, without rays, in the caudal region, and the caudal fin is reduced or absent. Scales are absent or confined to the caudal region. The eyes are small or absent in cave-dwelling species. The gill membranes are united and continuous, so there is only one, continuous ventral gill opening. The gills themselves are often quite small, because swamp eels are capable of breathing air, either through a vascularized portion of the hindgut, through the vascularized lining of the gill pouch, or through a pair of lunglike sacs off the gill pouch. Some species are capable of moving across land for short distances, while others may burrow into the mud and survive even if the covering water evaporates. Where found, swamp eels are important nocturnal predators on small fishes and are often large enough (to 1.5 m) and abundant enough to support fisheries for them.

Scorpaeniformes   With over 1000 species in 21 families, the Scorpaeniformes is one of the largest teleost orders. Most members of the order are bottom-oriented and so possess large, rounded pectoral fins, large heads, rounded caudal fins, and bodies and heads with many spines and/or bony plates. All possess a suborbital stay on each cheek, a ridge of bone that runs across the operculum. As a result, the Scorpaeniformes are frequently referred to as the mail-cheeked fishes. Most members of this group are found in marine environments at depths of less than 100 m, but a number of species are freshwater forms.

Scorpaenidae. The rockfishes and scorpionfishes, with over 350 species, are the largest family in the order. They are mostly found in the Indian and Pacific Oceans; only about 60 species are known from the Atlantic. Off the Pacific coast of North America alone there are over 55 species of *Sebastes,* many of them morphologically similar to each other and found together, apparently in mixed aggregations. This complex of species presents some interesting problems in evolution and ecology. One way the species do segregate is by depth, and those found in the deepest water are typically bright red or orange in color, since at that depth such coloration serves as camouflage. However, the color patterns of many inshore forms are also quite bright; this may serve to advertise that they possess toxic spines in the dorsal, anal, and pelvic fins. The spines not only are toxic but also stout and numerous so that, when combined with the spines on head and operculum, they give the fishes a very prickly appearance. These fishes have large heads, large mouths and eyes, and stout, laterally compressed bodies with large pectoral fins (Fig. 23.3a). Scales are either absent or very fine and ctenoid.

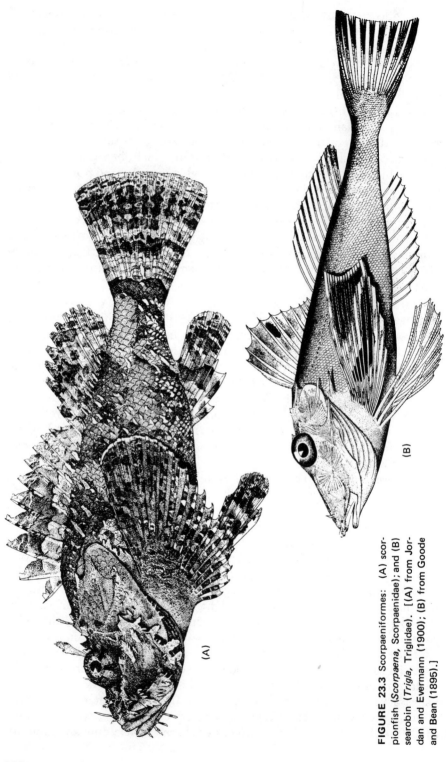

FIGURE 23.3 Scorpaeniformes: (A) scorpionfish (*Scorpaena*, Scorpaenidae); and (B) searobin (*Trigla*, Triglidae). [(A) from Jordan and Evermann (1900); (B) from Goode and Bean (1895).]

(A)

(B)

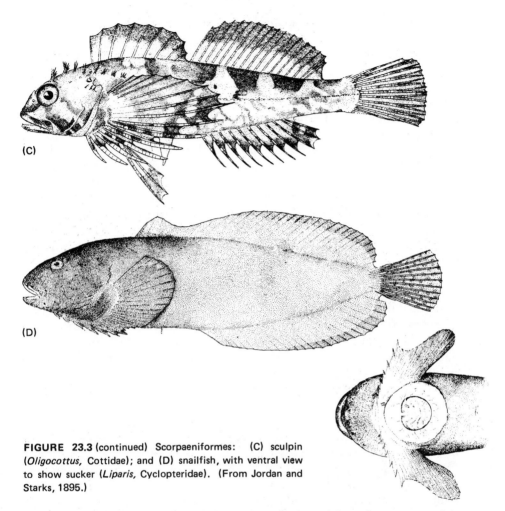

FIGURE 23.3 (continued) Scorpaeniformes: (C) sculpin (*Oligocottus,* Cottidae); and (D) snailfish, with ventral view to show sucker (*Liparis,* Cyclopteridae). (From Jordan and Starks, 1895.)

Most scorpaenids are bottom-oriented predators, although many species enter the water column after schools of fish and squid. Many species also enter the water column to mate and to give birth to their young. Despite the fact that most are livebearers, they have not sacrificed much in the way of total egg production; the eggs are tiny and retained in the body cavity after fertilization, but the larvae are released immediately after hatching. Thus, a 45-cm Pacific ocean perch (*Sebastes alutus*) may give birth to over 300,000 young. This same fish is likely to be 15 to 20 years old. Such slow growth is fairly typical of scorpaenids and is one reason that the commercially important species, such as Pacific ocean perch and Atlantic redfish (*S. marinus*), have been so easy to over-exploit. Both species were once enormously abundant in their respective northern oceans but now support only modest fisheries.

While scorpaenids are generally known as rockfishes in northern waters, where they support valuable sport and commercial fisheries, in tropical waters they are usually known as scorpionfishes because of the extreme toxicity of the spines of some species. Most spectacular are the turkeyfishes and tigerfishes of coral reefs (*Pterois* spp.), which have bright bodies crossed with white and black stripes that extend onto the extremely long rays of the pectoral and dorsal fins. These species are toxic and act as if they are well aware of the fact; they cruise the reefs during the day and have been known to swim aggressively toward human swimmers, toxic spines angled forwards. In contrast to the turkeyfishes, the stonefishes (*Synanceia*) are rather dull in color. They sit quietly on reefs and are extremely well camouflaged. However, they possess the most deadly fish venom known. It is a neurotoxin that can actually be injected by a stonefish into the foot of a hapless wader by means of hypodermiclike venom glands at the base of hollow dorsal spines.

Triglidae. The searobins or gurnards (85+ species) are a widely distributed group of marine fishes adapted for living on soft ocean bottoms at moderate depths. Typically, they are red in color, with large eyes set toward the top of a head covered with heavy, bony plates (Fig. 23.3b). The body may be covered with such plates as well. The mouth is subterminal and quite protrusible. The benthic invertebrates on which searobins feed are apparently located in part through the use of two or three fingerlike, independent rays that are part of each pectoral fin. These rays are used to probe the bottom and also to rest on. The swimbladder of searobins is large and muscular and is used for sound production. They are perhaps the noisiest fishes on the Atlantic coast of North America.

Cottidae. The sculpins are a large (300+ species) family of bottom-dwelling fishes. With the exception of about five species, all are confined to the marine coastal waters and fresh waters of the Northern Hemisphere. They are characterized by a broad, flattened head that usually has conspicuous spines and large, dorsal eyes, a smooth body (scales embedded, absent, or modified into tiny prickles), lack of a swimbladder, and large pectoral fins (Fig. 23.3c). Most are small, the largest species being the cabezon (*Scorpaenichthys marmoratus*). This fish reaches lengths of 75 cm to 80 cm off the California coast and is highly regarded as a food fish despite the greenish color of its flesh. Many species of sculpin live in turbulent water, such as that found in the intertidal zone of oceans, in swift streams, or in the wave zone of lakes. They maintain themselves in these habitats by hiding beneath objects or by taking advantage of their negative buoyancy and hydrodynamic body shape. Presumably, when their pectoral fins are spread out and the fish face into a current, the current will flow over them, actually pressing them to the bottom.

Perhaps the best known members of this family are the freshwater sculpins of the genus *Cottus,* called bullheads in Europe. They inhabit cold-water streams and lakes and consequently are frequently accused of competing with or preying on trout and salmon, charges that are usually not justified (Moyle 1977). Like other members of the family, however, they are efficient predators on active benthic invertebrates.

Two other scorpaeniform families that are largely confined to fresh water, the Cottocomephoridae (24 species) and the Comephoridae (2 species), are apparently derived from cottid ancestors. With the exception of a few species of Cottocomephoridae, they are confined to ancient Lake Baikal in the Soviet Union. They have radiated into a number of unsculpinlike niches, including that of pelagic planktivores. Some species are important as commercial fishes and as food for various endemic predators, such as the Baikal seal.

Agonidae. The poachers and alligator fishes make up a curious family of about 50 species with a bipolar distribution pattern. However, most of the species occur in the northern Pacific. They are small (25 cm to 30 cm), elongate fishes that are covered with bony plates, so that many species look somewhat like a cross between a sculpin and a pipefish. They are bottom dwellers and are frequently common in shallow marine waters, but their biology is poorly known.

Cyclopteridae. This family contains three rather different groups, generally treated as subfamilies (or as families): the lumpsuckers (Cyclopterinae, 26+ species), the snailfishes (Liparinae, 110 to 120 species), and the peculiar semipelagic *Rhodichthys* of the North Atlantic. The lumpfishes are found in the temperate and arctic portions of the northern hemisphere, while the snailfishes have a bipolar distribution pattern. All members of this family tend to have rather flabby bodies, which range in shape from globular in the lumpsuckers to more elongate in the snailfishes (Fig. 23.3d). The pelvic fins are modified into a large sucking disc (or absent altogether), and the gill openings are small, both features indicative of the inactive life these fishes live. The lumpsuckers, especially *Cyclopterus lumpus*, are found attached to the bottom and to drifting objects but are often caught in midwater as well. Despite their repulsive appearance, created by their lumpy build, complete with wartlike tubercles, lumpsuckers are favored foodfishes (they reach 60+ cm) not only of humans but of sperm whales, seals, and sleeper sharks. The eggs are frequently sold as lumpfish caviar.

The snailfishes are somewhat more fishlike in appearance than the lumpsuckers, but their skin is without scales and jellylike in texture. They favor cold waters and are common in both the Arctic and the Antarctic, as well as in deep water (up to 3 km to 4 km). Some species lay their eggs in the gill cavities of crabs and other crustaceans.

Dactylopteriformes Superficially, the four species of flying gurnards (Dactylopteridae) that make up this order resemble searobins (Triglidae). Like the searobins, they have an armored head with large, dorsal eyes, bony plates on the body, large pectoral fins with free inner rays that can be used to "walk" over the bottom, and the ability to make loud sounds (Fig. 23.4a). The flying

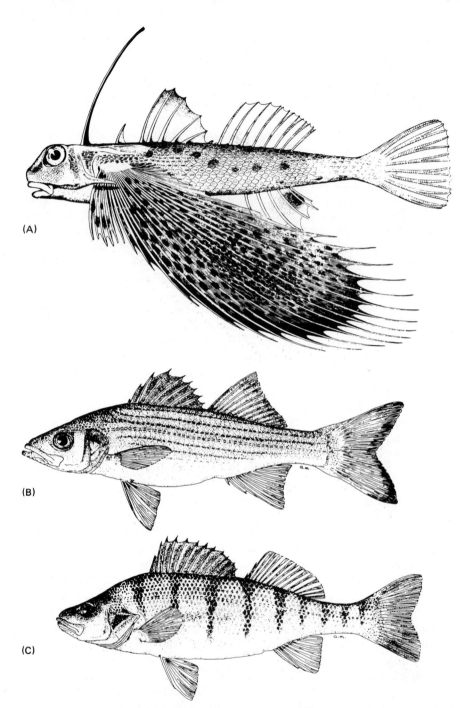

FIGURE 23.4 (A) Dactylopteriformes: flying gurnard (*Dactyloptera,* Dactylopteridae). Perciformes, Percoidei: (B) striped bass (*Morone,* Percichthyidae); and (C) yellow perch (*Perca,* Percidae). [(A) from Jordan and Evermann (1895-1900); (B) and (C) from Moyle (1976a).]

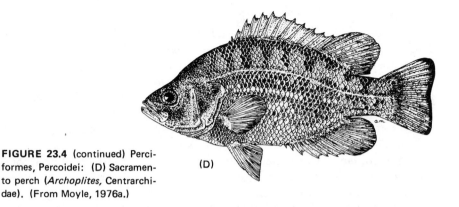

FIGURE 23.4 (continued) Perciformes, Percoidei: (D) Sacramento perch (*Archoplites,* Centrarchidae). (From Moyle, 1976a.)

(D)

gurnards show their independent evolution from the searobins by the
"primitive" arrangement of the pectoral fins, by the production of sound
using hyomandibular stridulations rather than by "twanging" the swimbladder, and by the presence of two long, free spines just before the
dorsal fin. Although the large pectorals have given rise to the supposi-
tion that these small fish (30 cm to 40 cm) can fly, it appears that pectorals are used mainly to frighten potential predators. When a gurnard is
startled, the brightly patterned pectorals are flashed open, presumably
startling the predator.

Perciformes   The Perciformes, with nearly 7000 species, is the largest order of vertebrates.
They are extremely diverse, but most species are adapted for life as
predators in the shallow or surface waters of the oceans or for life in
lakes. Despite the enormous diversity of fishes within this order, they
form a fairly cohesive group taxonomically, in part because aberrant
forms tend to be placed in their own small orders. Perciform fishes have
the following characteristics: (1) spines present; (2) dorsal fins either
double or made up of two distinct parts, the lead part spiny; (3) adipose
fin never present; (4) pelvic fins thoracic or jugular in position, or absent; (5) pelvic fins with one spine and five or less rays; (6) pectoral
fins on side of body, with a vertical insertion; (7) principal caudal fin
rays fewer than 17; (8) scales ctenoid or absent (but cycloid in a few
forms); (9) premaxilla the only bone bordering the upper jaw; (10) orbitosphenoid, mesocoracoid, and intermuscular bones absent; and
(11) swimbladder physoclistous or absent.

Within the Perciformes, general lines of evolution are indicated
by the 18 suborders, although nearly 60% of the species are in the suborder Percoidei and nearly 40% are found in just five families (Gobiidae,
Cichlidae, Labridae, Serranidae, and Blenniidae). In contrast, many of
the 148 families recognized here contain fewer than 20 species, as do
seven of the suborders.

Percoidei   This suborder, with nearly 4000 species, contains the bulk of the perciform fishes. The percoid fishes by and large have the classical perciform appearance: body deep to moderately elongate, two dorsal fins, large mouth and eyes, and thoracic pelvic fins. Most are inshore, diurnal (or crepuscular) predators, and those of any size are usually harvested by humans for food. Some of the most popular saltwater and freshwater game fishes, such as striped bass, snook, bluefish, jacks, snappers, croakers, barracudas, perches, and sunfishes belong to this suborder.

Serranidae.   Until the revision of Gosline (1966), the family Serranidae was a "wastebasket" for lower percoids; and rather poorly defined. Gosline removed many fishes from the family, leaving it with about 370 species. Most serranids are large, piscivorous fishes associated with tropical reefs and inshore environments; a few are found in inshore temperate areas, and still others are found in fresh water. They can be distinguished from other generalized lower percoids by (1) presence of three spines on the opercle; (2) complete lateral line; (3) rounded caudal fin (rarely forked); (4) no scaly process in the axillae of the pelvic fins; and (5) scales well developed, usually ctenoid but occasionally cycloid. Many species are hermaphroditic, a trait first noticed by Aristotle around 300 B.C. Most hermaphrodites in this family are female when small and convert to males when large, although there are records in some species of male and female gonads developing simultaneously.

Percichthyidae.   The temperate basses are a group of about 40 species of marine and freshwater piscivores that Gosline (1966) separated out from the Serranidae. While the two families have numerous osteological differences, the temperate basses can be best told from the sea basses by the presence of only two spines on the opercle, a tail that is usually forked, and the absence of hermaphroditism (Fig. 23.4b). Most of the species are freshwater or estuarine and are important elements of the faunas of North America, South America, Australia, and Asia. In North America the four species found in fresh water are all members of the genus *Morone* and are much sought after as sport and commercial fishes.

Centrarchidae.   The sunfishes are a family of 30 freshwater species that are native only to North America. They are most characteristic of warm-water lakes and sluggish streams. Since the black basses (*Micropterus*), sunfishes (*Lepomis*), and crappies (*Pomoxis*) are very popular sport fishes, many populations have been established far outside their native ranges. The largemouth bass (*M. salmoides*), in particular, has become established in ponds and lakes throughout the world. In a number of localities, such as Lake Atitlan, Guatemala, the establishment of largemouth bass has been responsible for the disasterous decline of native fishes and fisheries. In the Central Valley of California introduction of various centrarchids from the eastern United States was accompanied by the near disappearance of the one native centrarchid, the Sacramento perch (*Archoplites interruptus*), from its native habitats.

The centrarchids are considered to be lower percoids and are related to the percichthyids and serranids, from which they differ in a number of minor osteological features and from which they can be distinguished by the absence of a well-developed pseudobranch (small gill-like structure) on the inside of each operculum. Otherwise, they are recognizable as fishes that are deep-bodied (or moderately deep-bodied), with the spinous and soft dorsal fins joined together and with moderately forked tails (Fig. 23.4d).

Apogonidae. The cardinal fishes are the percoid equivalent of the beryciform squirrelfishes, but they are usually smaller (5 cm to 15 cm as adults) and possess two short and well-separated dorsal fins. Like the squirrelfishes, most are red in color, have large eyes, and are active mainly at night. A majority of the 170 or so species are associated with tropical reefs, where they hide in crevices and caves (often with squirrelfishes) during the day and emerge in large schools to feed on plankton at night. A few species have managed to invade the freshwater streams and mangrove swamps of Pacific islands, while a few others inhabit deep (to 1200 m) water (e.g., *Epigonus telescopus* of the Atlantic Ocean). They are unusual among coral reef fishes in that many, perhaps most, of them are mouthbrooders.

Percidae. This family is found in fresh waters throughout the Northern Hemisphere, but about 90% of the 130+ species are found in North America east of the Rocky Mountains. The reason for this is the presence of the darters (*Etheostoma, Percina, Ammocrypta*) in the streams and lakes. These are small, bottom-dwelling fishes, elongate, with small mouths and conspicuous eyes, and with the swimbladder reduced or absent. Although they are secretive fishes that pick small invertebrates from the bottom, many are brightly colored, especially when spawning. In small, warm streams darters are usually second in abundance only to cyprinids. Aside from the darters, the percids contain two other groups of fishes: the perches (e.g., *Perca*) and the pike-perches (e.g., *Stizostedion*). Both groups have generalized percid bodies and fins (Fig. 23.4c). They are largely inhabitants of lakes and large rivers and are highly prized food fishes in both Eurasia and North America. The most favored of these fishes in North America is the walleye (*S. vitreum*), a species which prefers deep, cool water and has large, reflective eyes for capturing other fishes in dim light.

Echeneidae. The remoras or sharksuckers are such specialized fishes that Gosline (1971) placed them in a separate order, although in many respects they are rather similar to the cobia (Rachycentridae: *Rachycentrus canadum*), a large percoid predator. The specializations of the seven to eight species of remora center around the remarkable sucking disc they possess on top of their heads. This disc is formed from the spiny dorsal fin and contains 10 to 28 slatlike transverse ridges, which are modified spines. When a remora presses this disc against a large fish, turtle, or whale, the ridges are erected to create a powerful suction and the remora becomes very difficult to dislodge. The disc is fused to the upper jaw and consequently forms part of the snout, beyond which projects the lower jaw. The body of remoras is smooth (small, cycloid scales) and fusiform, and the fishes are good swimmers, but their dependence on rides from other fishes is indicated by the absence of a swimbladder. The exact nature of the relationship between remoras and their hosts is still a subject of debate. Some remoras will pick parasites and diseased tissues from their hosts, but it is unlikely that such activity compensates for the energy expended by the host to carry one or more remoras. On the other hand, the remoras get a free ride, enjoy the protection of a large fish, and probably make short forays away from their host to capture small fishes.

Carangidae. Although the body shapes of the 200+ species of jacks and pompanos range from torpedolike to nearly platelike, all are fast-swimming predators. This is reflected in their deeply forked tails and narrow caudal peduncles, the fine, cycloid scales (often absent or modified into scutes along the lateral line), the deeply sloping heads (with large eyes and mouth), and the laterally compressed bodies. Carangids range in color from silvery to metallic blue or green to bright yellow or gold. Adult size ranges from about 25 cm to 2 m. Most jacks are schooling fishes that feed by making rapid, slashing attacks at schools of smaller fishes, especially herrings and anchovies.

Lutjanidae. The snappers are among the most important food fishes in tropical or subtropical waters. There is nothing remarkable about their morphology, which may in part explain their success (200 to 300 species), since they are generalized, bottom-oriented predators. The typical snapper is heavy-bodied, with a continuous dorsal fin, slightly forked tail, fully scaled body, and triangular head with a large mouth located at the base of the triangle. The mouth is protractile and equipped with many teeth, including some large canine teeth. Most are brightly colored, ranging from bright red to yellow to iridescent blue, often with contrasting stripes and bars. Most species are associated with tropical reefs, submerged banks, or inshore areas. They have also shown themselves to be quite adaptable; the red snapper (*Lutjanus campechanus*), an important commercial species off the Florida coast and in the Gulf of Mexico, is one of the more abundant fishes around oil platforms, shipwrecks, and artificial reefs.

Sciaenidae. The croakers or drums are another group of bottom-oriented invertebrate crunchers. Despite many similarities, they can be told from the previous three families by their divided dorsal fins (united in the others), rounded or truncated caudal fin (rather than forked or straight), and two anal spines (rather than three). In addition, many possess one or more chin barbels. Internally, croakers are notable for their multibranched swimbladder and huge otoliths. Both features are presumably related to the fact that croakers produce loud sounds, especially during spawning season, by vibrating muscles associated with the swimbladder. Since the 150 to 200 species are often inhabitants of turbid estuaries, bays, and rivers, it is quite possible that their elaborate sound-producing and receiving systems may assist them in finding their way about. The well-developed lateral line (extending into the rays of the tail) is also indicative of their murky habitats. In North America there are about 34 species of croakers, many of them important as sport and commercial fishes. One species, the freshwater drum (*Aplodinotus grunniens*), is an important commercial species throughout much of the Mississippi River drainage, whereas the rest are usually associated with estuaries and warm, shallow waters (see Chapter 32).

Chaetodontidae. It is unusual to see a photographic view of a reef that does not include at least one individual of the 200 or so species of butterflyfishes or angelfishes. They are all extremely colorful, with striking patterns of stripes and spots on multihued backgrounds of colors that include most of the visible spectrum. However, yellow does seem to be the most common color. The spectacular patterns are made even more noticeable by the constant activity of these fishes during the day. There are also large surface areas, relative to the volume of the fish, on which to display the colors and patterns, since butterflyfishes are thin in cross section but nearly circular in side view, with large dorsal and anal fins.

Butterflyfishes and angelfishes are remarkable not only for their coloration but for their feeding specializations. Most have small, protractile mouths with many tiny teeth. Different species are specialized for feeding on invertebrates at different depths in crevices, as indicated by the length of the snout. Others specialize on prey types such as zooplankton, coral polyps, sponges, and polychaete worms, since each food type requires particular morphological and behavioral specializations to be fed upon efficiently.

Embiotocidae. The surfperches form a small (23 species) but abundant family that is found only along the northern Pacific coasts of North America and Asia. One species, the tule perch (*Hysterocarpus traski*), is confined to fresh water, in California. Externally, they are not particularly remarkable, being moderately deep-bodied percoid fishes, with cycloid scales and small mouths that are handy for picking up small invertebrates (DeMartini 1969). However, when discovered in the early 1800s, they greatly aroused the interests of biologists, including Louis Agassiz, because they are viviparous. The young develop in uteruslike sacs in the ovary and obtain most of their nutrition from the body fluids of the mother. This is possible because the dorsal, pelvic, and anal fins of the embryo are greatly enlarged, highly vascularized and in close contact with the tissues of the mother, allowing transfer of nutrients to take place. When born, the young are 3 cm to 5 cm long, and they may become sexually mature a few weeks after birth.

Cichlidae. The cichlids are over 700 species of fresh-water and brackish-water fishes inhabiting Africa, South America, Central America and parts of Asia and North America. Their most amazing characteristic is their tendency to form flocks of extremely specialized species in large lakes, especially in Africa; Lakes Malawi, Victoria, and Tanganyika contain among them about 500 endemic species of cichlids (Fryer and Iles 1972).

A major factor that promotes speciation in the cichlids is that most species have a strong orientation in their feeding toward the bottom, a heterogeneous environment with a wide variety of invertebrates and plants to feed on. The tendency in lake-dwelling cichlids is to specialize in feeding on just one type of food, such as filamentous algae growing on rocks or fly larvae living in sand (see Chapter 30). According to Liem (1974), the extraordinary ability of the cichlids to specialize is the result of the unique and complex structure of the pharyngeal "jaw" apparatus, which permits efficient grinding and chewing of food ingested, using highly specialized teeth. The pharyngeal jaws free the jaws of the mouth to develop specializations just for food gathering, such as long, forceps-like teeth for picking up small invertebrates from plants or pulling scales from other fish.

As might be expected of substrate-feeding fishes, most cichlids are deep-bodied, with large, spiny fins, rounded tails, protractile mouths, and well-developed eyes. Many are brightly colored, although many also have color patterns to match the substrate. Many of the more colorful forms, such as discus fishes (*Symphysodon*), angelfishes (*Pterophyllum*), South American cichlids (*Cichlasoma*), and jewelfishes (*Haplochromis*), are favorite aquarium fishes, a preference increased by the ease with which they breed in captivity.

Pomacentridae. The damselfishes are another group of conspicuous diurnal fishes characteristic of tropical reefs. Their conspicuousness stems not just from bright color patterns, for many are in fact rather plain, but from their abundance and activity. Many of the 230 or so species in the family actively defend territories on reefs not only against members of the same species but against many other species as well (see Chapter 34). The functions of the territories are multiple, but one of the most important appears to be in providing food for the fish, since the defended areas typically have much heavier growths of algae than undefended areas and the main food of many damselfishes is filamentous algae. Damselfishes that do not defend territories fall mostly into two general categories: schooling fishes that feed on plankton above the reef and fishes that are commensal with anemones and coral. The plankton-feeding forms are similar in body shape to the territorial forms, since both types seem to represent a compromise between the

306

convenience of being deep-bodied for hovering and picking out small food items and having the ability to flee quickly to cover when a predatory fish approaches. The latter "need" places a limit on just how deep-bodied they become and results in a forked tail. The plankton-feeding and territorial forms also have large eyes and small, protractile mouths, although the teeth of the territorial forms (e.g., *Pomacentrus*) are incisorlike, for nipping off pieces of algae, whereas the teeth of the plankton feeders (*Chromis*) are conical or villiform, for holding onto small prey. The group of 30+ species of damselfishes that live in close association with anemones and corals are generally small, brightly colored forms, many (*Amphiprion*) with rounded tails. These fishes actually live among the tentacles of the invertebrates and have a mucus layer that seems to inhibit the anemones from stinging them.

Mugiloidei The mullets (Mugilidae) are the sole family in this suborder, according to Greenwood et al. (1966), but they have been lumped with many other groups in the past, especially the next two suborders and assorted families in the Atheriniformes. The 70+ species of mullets are readily recognizable, with their thick yet streamlined bodies, forked tails, hard angled mouths, large, cycloid or faintly ctenoid scales, subabdominal pelvic fins, and two widely separated dorsal fins, the first containing just four spines (Fig. 23.5a). The streamlined body of the mullets is necessary both to avoid the numerous predators that attack their schools in the shallow inshore waters they inhabit and to speed them along their way in their spawning migrations, many of which closely follow coastlines. The main reason the mullets favor the inshore environment is for feeding, since they subsist largely on organic detritus and small algae cells. This material is scooped up by the fish when they swim at an angle to the bottom, running their mouth through the sediment. The larger particles are retained by their fine gillrakers and then ground up in their gizzardlike stomachs. Digestion takes place in an extraordinarily long intestine (5 to 8 times the body length), which is necessary because much of the material ingested is sand and other indigestible matter.

Sphyraenoidei The barracudas (Sphyraenidae), the only fishes in this suborder, are on the opposite end of the trophic spectrum from the mullets, yet the two groups exhibit enough anatomical similarities so that they should perhaps be placed in the same suborder, along with the Polynemidae. They are fearsome predators on other fishes, with elongate, pikelike bodies, protruding lower jaws, formidable pointed teeth in the jaws, two widely separated dorsal fins, forked tails, and tiny or nonexistent gill rakers. Curiously, the barracudas have lost the protractile upper jaw so characteristic of teleosts and have instead a solidly fused unit to support a biting mouth, much like more ancestral bony fishes. Their body plan

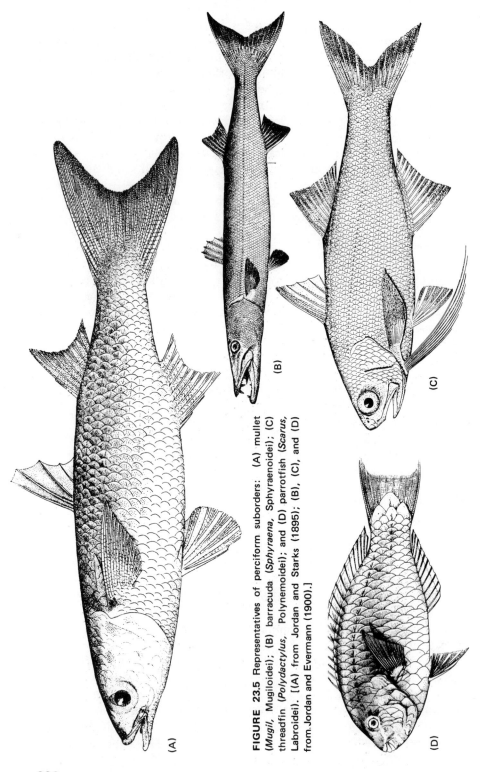

FIGURE 23.5 Representatives of perciform suborders: (A) mullet (*Mugil*, Mugiloidei); (B) barracuda (*Sphyraena*, Sphyraenoidei); (C) threadfin (*Polydactylus*, Polynemoidei); and (D) parrotfish (*Scarus*, Labroidei). [(A) from Jordan and Starks (1895); (B), (C), and (D) from Jordan and Evermann (1900).]

(A)

(B)

(C)

(D)

is an interesting compromise between that of the lie-in-wait predator and that of an active predator (Fig. 23.5b). Barracudas swim about actively in clear water, often in schools, searching for prey. Their narrow head-on profile and silvery color reduce their visibility to the prey, and their long caudal region, with matching dorsal and anal fins, allows them to put on a quick burst of speed to close the gap between them and the prey before it can flee. This strategy is particularly effective when light levels are low. The great barracuda (*Sphyraena barracuda*) of the Atlantic may reach lengths of nearly 2 m and has been known to attack divers, but such attacks are rare and virtually unknown in the other 17 species. However, they are excellent food fishes and favored sport fishes.

Polynemoidei   This suborder also has but one small (35 species) family (Polynemidae) of unusual fishes, the threadfins. They are somewhat mulletlike in appearance (and sometimes called bastard mullets), but the snout is pointed, overhanging the large mouth, the eyes are quite large, and four to seven of the pectoral fin rays are detached from the rest of the fin and used for probing the bottom (Fig. 23.5c). They feed on benthic invertebrates and fishes. Some species reach 1 m to 2 m in length and are important food fishes that can be captured in tropical bays and estuaries.

Labroidei   The suborder Labroidei contains but three families, but two of them (Labridae, Scaridae) contain large numbers of species that are especially important on tropical reefs. The third family (Odacidae) contains just eight species that seem to be intermediate in many respects between the other two families.

Labridae. With 400 to 500 species, this is one of the largest perciform families. Although there is considerable variation in body shape among the wrasses, most can be quickly recognized by (1) the pointed snout; (2) the small to moderate-sized mouth containing conspicuous, outward-pointing teeth; and (3) the solid, semicylindrical body with its cycloid scales, long dorsal fin, and square or slightly rounded tail. Most are less than 12 cm long, but members of the genus *Cheilinus* may reach 3 m. Whether they occur in tropical or temperate regions, wrasses are usually brightly colored, diurnal fishes that live by picking up small invertebrates. At night many species bury themselves in the sand (Herald 1961). Perhaps the best-known trait of wrasses is that many of them are cleaner fishes that pick parasites from other fishes. Such fishes are usually solitary or live in pairs and may behave very aggressively toward other wrasses. Most noncleaner wrasses behave in a similar manner, although a few species, especially wrasses that inhabit temperate regions, are schooling fishes. On the Atlantic coast of North America two such species are the cunner (*Tautogolabrus adspersus*) and the tautog (*Tautoga onitis*), both of which have some value as commercial and sport fish. The mating systems of wrasses can be extremely complicated, much like those discussed below for the Scaridae (Warner and Robertson 1978).

Scaridae. The 60 to 80 species of parrotfishes look like larger, heavy-bodied wrasses that have their jaw teeth fused into a solid, parrotlike beak. They also have heavy pharyngeal teeth consisting of solid units of bone (Fig. 23.5d). These structures permit the parrotfishes to scrape algae and invertebrates from the hard surfaces of the reef and then to crush the material ingested. They move about the reefs in conspicuous small schools during the day and hide in caves and crevices at night. A few species can secrete a mucus cocoon about themselves when at rest, presumably to foil night-feeding predators such as moray eels. Perhaps the most remarkable feature of the parrotfishes, however, is their color patterns, which change dramatically with age and sex (which may also change), reflecting extremely complicated mating systems. Robertson and Warner (1978) recognize three basic color phases in parrotfishes: a *juvenile* phase, an *initial* phase (characteristic of young adults), and a *terminal* phase (characteristic of large, dominant males). Depending on the species, males and females may or may not have different color patterns and color patterns may or may not be reversible. To complicate matters further, parrotfish populations may contain two types of patterns of sexual development: fishes that have their sex genetically fixed (*gonochorists*) and fishes that can change sex from female to male (*protogynous hermaphrodites*). In many species much of the mating is controlled by large, terminal-phase males (which are often protogynous hermaphrodites) who defend permanent territories, each containing a harem of females. In these situations the smaller, initial-phase males manage to spawn largely by *sneaking* and *streaking* (Robertson and Warner 1978). Sneaking occurs when a small male manages to get a member of a harem to spawn with it within the territory of the terminal male; streaking occurs when a male dashes into a territory and spawns with a female just as the terminal male is also spawning. Not all species have permanent territories; some resort instead to either group spawning or lek spawning. In the latter case, the terminal males defend territories only temporarily and mate with females, singly or in groups, that enter the territory. The preceding discussion only partially reflects the complexity and variety of mating systems in the Scaridae (and the Labridae as well).

Trachinoidei   This suborder includes perhaps 200 species, divided among 16 families. Most are bottom-dwelling predators with: (1) flattened heads containing dorsal eyes and large, usually upward-pointing mouths; (2) enlarged pectoral fins (pelvics in the Champsodontidae); and (3) long dorsal and anal fins. The main exception to this general description are the swal-

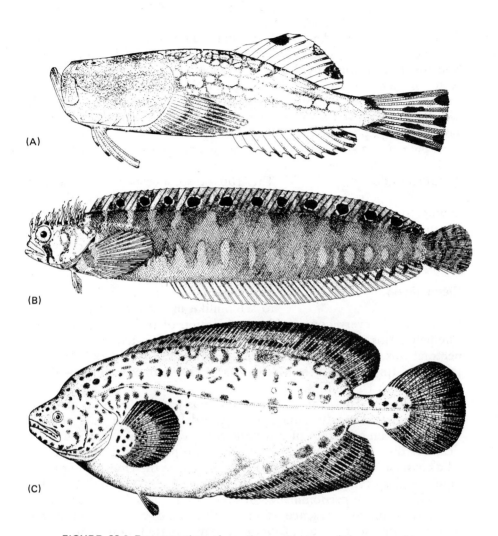

(A)

(B)

(C)

FIGURE 23.6 Representatives of perciform suborders: (A) stargazer (*Astro-scopus,* Trachinoidei); (B) mosshead warbonnet (*Chirolophis,* Stichaeidae, Blennoidei); and (C) ragfish (*Icosteus,* Icosteoidei). [(A) and (D) from Jordan and Evermann (1900); (B) from Jordan and Starks (1895); (C) from Goode and Bean (1895).]

lowers (Chiasmodontidae), deepsea midwater predators that perhaps do not belong in this suborder. Members of the more typical familes may spend much of their time buried in sand, in shallow marine environments, waiting for prey to come by. Besides mouths handy for engulfing prey and secretive behavior patterns, there are a number of special adaptations in the families of this suborder, associated with bottom living. The weaver fishes (Trachinidae) and the stargazers (Uranoscopidae) have poisonous spines that can inflict painful injuries on waders and other predators (Fig. 23.6a). The stargazers have, in addition, electric organs, formed from modified eye muscles, that they probably use for detection of prey. However, some species can deliver up to 50 V, so they may also function in stunning their prey. When buried, stargazers can inhale water through their nostrils, which open into the branchial cavity. Some species also have a wormlike lure growing from the floor of the mouth, which can be moved about to attract prey. Yet another adaptation for bottom living, possessed by the sand stargazers (Dactyloscopidae), is to have the eyes on stalks, so they will project above the buried fish.

Notothenioidei

The 100 or so species of notothenioid fishes are the dominant fishes of the Antarctic, although a few species are also found along the coasts of southern South America, Australia, and New Zealand. The remarkable morphological and physiological adaptations of these fishes are discussed in Chapter 37.

Blennioidei

The blennioid fishes range from eel-like to sculpinlike in their body shapes and include nearly every conceivable combination of these two conditions. The pelvic fins are either absent or small and are located in front of the pectoral fins. Most have long dorsal and anal fins, which are fused with the caudal fin in eel-like forms (Fig. 23.6b). The suborder contains about 650 species in 15 families.

Clinidae. The clinids are an enormously variable group of about 175 species that mostly inhabit the intertidal zone. They are perhaps the most common group of intertidal fishes of Australia and South Africa, but they are not unusual elsewhere (but particularly along the Pacific coast of North America). Many species have the elongate body and blunt head so typical of blennies, but they are distinguished from the Blenniidae by the predominance of spines in the dorsal fin (many more than rays) and the presence of patches of fixed, conical teeth in the mouth. Some species (e.g., *Gibbonsia*) have pointed snouts and laterally compressed heads and bodies. Most species have small, cycloid scales, although scales are absent from some species. Their reproductive habits vary considerably; a number of species are viviparous, so the males have intromittent organs. Some of the most distinctive of the clinids are the fringeheads (*Neoclinus*) of the California coast, 20-cm-long blennylike fishes with long, fleshy cirri over the eyes and extraordinarily large mouths.

Blenniidae. Combtooth blennies are an important part of the rocky inshore marine fauna over much of the world, but especially in tropical and subtropical regions. The common name stems from the numerous closely packed teeth present on their jaws, although a few species also possess daggerlike teeth on each side of the lower jaw. Most of the 275 to 300 species have blunt heads, usually topped by cirri, and moderately long, scaleless bodies with dorsal fins containing more rays than spines. Many species have pelagic larvae or postlarvae, so they can quickly colonize disturbed areas of coastline, such as new breakwaters. Wherever they are, blennies tend to be secretive in their behavior but eclectic in feeding, consuming both invertebrates and algae. One of the more famous exceptions to this characterization of the blennies is the sabertooth blenny (*Aspidontus taeniatus*), which mimics cleaner wrasses so that it can sneak up on unsuspecting fishes in order to take bites out of their fins and tails. As the name implies, these are among the blennies that have large jaw teeth; the large teeth are not used for feeding, however, but for aggressive displays to members of the same species (Ehrlich 1975).

Icosteoidei   There is but one family (Icosteidae) and one species in this suborder. The ragfish (*Icosteus aenigmaticus*) of the deep waters off the Pacific coast of North America is well described by its scientific name, which means "puzzling fish with soft bones." The adults can exceed 2 m in length and are extremely flabby, with a largely cartilaginous skeleton and no spines, scales, or pelvic fins. The body shape of the adult is somewhat troutlike, with a blunt head, forked tail, and chocolate brown color. The juvenile fish, in contrast, are deep-bodied, with rounded tails, pelvic fins, and a blotched brown and yellow color pattern (Fig. 23.6c). It is not surprising, therefore, to find that the juveniles were originally described as a different genus and species from the adults.

Schindlerioidei   The two species of *Schindleria* (Schindleriidae) that make up this suborder are very peculiar indeed and of uncertain systematic affinities. They are tiny (2 cm to 3 cm) surface-dwelling fishes of the tropical Pacific. They would be classified as larvae with adults unknown except that they become sexually mature. Like larval fishes, they are elongate and transparent and have a poorly developed skeleton, except for the bones of the jaw, which bear fine teeth. They are extremely abundant in many areas, especially around Hawaii.

Ammodytoidei   The sandlances (Ammodytidae, 12 species) are small, schooling fishes that are abundant enough in inshore waters of the Northern Hemisphere to be of major importance in marine food chains leading to larger, commercially exploited fishes. They are elongate, rarely exceeding 30 cm, with deeply forked tails, long dorsal fins (without spines), reduced or absent pelvic fins, cycloid scales, and no swimbladder (Fig. 23.7a). Their heads are pointed with projecting lower jaws. The latter characteristic is apparently an adaptation that allows them to burrow quickly, head first,

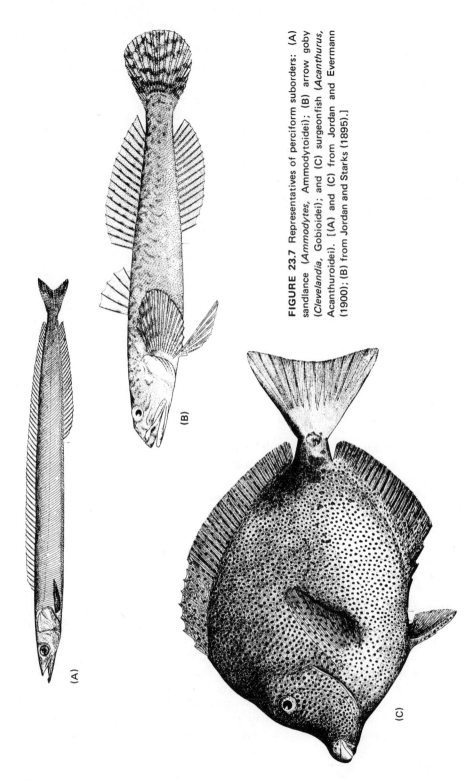

FIGURE 23.7 Representatives of perciform suborders: (A) sandlance (*Ammodytes*, Ammodytoidei); (B) arrow goby (*Clevelandia*, Gobioidei); and (C) surgeonfish (*Acanthurus*, Acanthuroidei). [(A) and (C) from Jordan and Evermann (1900); (B) from Jordan and Starks (1895).]

(A)

(B)

(C)

into sand when attacked by predators. Despite this important defense mechanism, shimmering schools of sandlances are frequently found off-shore feeding on zooplankton.

Gobioidei   The gobioid fishes form a quite distinctive group of bottom dwellers, on the basis of both osteology (Gosline 1971) and external morphology, and so perhaps should be given the status of a separate order. They usually lack both lateral line and swimbladder, have gill membranes that are joined to the isthmus (i.e., have opercula that are not free at the bottom), have a short, spiny dorsal fin (1 to 8 spines), and have pelvic fins that either are united to form a sucking disc or at least are close together. This suborder contains over a 1000 species in seven families, but a recent, comprehensive systematic treatment of them is lacking.

Gobiidae.   The gobies are the largest family of primarily marine fishes and second only to the cyprinids in total number of species (800+). They are found worldwide in both fresh and salt water, with the bulk of the species associated with shallow tropical and subtropical environments. Despite their wide distribution and richness of species, the gobies are a readily recognizable group (Fig. 23.7b). They are characterized by: (1) a sucking disc created by the pelvic fins; (2) two dorsal fins, the first consisting of 2 to 8 soft spines; (3) a rounded caudal fin; (4) a blunt head dominated by relatively large eyes; (5) visible scales, either cycloid or ctenoid; and (6) small size (few reach 20 cm, and most are shorter than 10 cm). Their success seems to be best explained by their remarkable ability to adapt to habitats or microhabitats inaccessible to most other fishes, such as: (1) cracks and crevices in coral reefs; (2) burrows of invertebrates; (3) mudflats; (4) mangrove swamps; (5) fresh water on oceanic islands; and (6) inland seas and estuaries.

The cracks and crevices of coral reefs, and other inshore habitats, provide homes for perhaps a majority of goby species. Many of these gobies are very small and brightly colored and live symbiotically with other reef animals. Some species are found only in the "chimneys" of sponges, others in the arms of branched corals. While these are probably commensal relationships, some gobies associated with sea urchins appear to behave as parasites, since they browse on the tube feet of the urchins (Teylaud 1971). In Atlantic reefs, gobies of the genus *Gobisoma* leave their crevices to pick ectoparasites from other fishes.

When gobies are found on soft bottoms, they typically live in the burrows of invertebrates, ranging from polychaete worms to shrimp to clams. On tideflats some gobies manage to survive by breathing air and "walking" across the mud. The longjaw mudsucker (*Gillichthys mirabilis*) absorbs oxygen from the air in its large and highly vascularized mouth cavity. It is also capable of making "sojourns" from one muddy pool to another (Todd 1968). However, the most extreme examples of a goby adapted to the terrestrial environment are the mudskippers

(*Periopthalamus*), which inhabit the mangrove swamps and mudflats of the tropical Indian Ocean. These fishes actually climb out of the water, along mangrove roots, etc., seeking terrestrial insects. They "walk" on their pectoral fins, propelled in part by the tail, and breathe air trapped in highly vascular opercular cavities.

Another characteristic of the mudskippers is their tolerance of low salinities. Indeed, this seems to be a characteristic of the family, since gobies have invaded freshwater habitats throughout the world but particularly on oceanic islands and in Asia. On the islands, they are frequently the principal native freshwater fishes, although many of them return to the sea to spawn. These island gobies include the world's smallest vertebrate *Pandaka pygmaea* of Luzon (Phillipines), which is mature at 6 mm to 12 mm. In Asia gobies are common in inland waters from estuaries to rivers to brackish inland seas. In the Black and Caspian Seas they are abundant enough to be exploited commercially, despite their small size.

Kurtoidei

Only two species (*Kurtus,* Kurtidae) are placed in this suborder, both of them rather peculiar but abundant fishes of the estuaries and streams of southeast Asia, New Guinea, and northern Australia. They are unmistakable fishes with their deep, compressed bodies, long anal fins, deeply forked tails, small, cycloid scales, large, upward-oriented mouths, and, most of all, depressed foreheads topped by a hooklike structure of modified dorsal fin spines. The latter feature is found only on males and is used to carry eggs. This has earned them the names of nurseryfishes or humpheads.

Acanthuroidei

Although this suborder is small, it contains some of the most conspicuous and colorful fishes on tropical reefs: the surgeonfishes and moorish idols (Acanthuridae, 75 to 80 species) and the rabbitfishes (Siganidae, 10 species). Surgeonfishes are deep-bodied fishes of moderate size (20 cm to 30 cm) that are extremely compressed laterally. They tend to have beaklike snouts with small mouths and incisorlike teeth that are used for scraping algae from rocks and coral (Fig. 23.7c). Their name comes from the scalpel-like spines they possess on the caudal peduncle, which generally point forward when erected. A few species which engage in picking ectoparasites off other fishes are called doctorfishes. Moorish idols (*Zanclus*) resemble surgeonfishes in body shape and mouth structure but lack the "scalpels" on the tail. They are readily recognized by their strong black-and-white striped pattern and symmetrical dorsal and anal fins. In fact, moorish idols are probably the most familiar of all reef fishes, since stylized versions of them are standard decorations on shower curtains, tiles, towels, bathroom wallpaper, and other water-related items.

Scombroidei   The scombroid fishes are only about 100 species distributed among six families, but these species are usually characterized by superlatives for their value as food fishes, for their speed, for their voraciousness as predators, for their long migrations, for the sport they provide anglers, and for their peculiarities of anatomy and physiology.

Scombridae. There are only 40 to 50 species of mackerels and tunas, and they make up less than 10% of the total catch by weight of marine fishes. However, their monetary value is extremely high because of the favor they find as food fish, particularly with Americans and Europeans. Tuna and mackerel are the top carnivores of the Epipelagic Zone of tropical and subtropical seas. Their prey consists of small schooling fishes and squid, which they locate and capture through high-speed swimming, also in schools. Most of the features that thus characterize the scombrids are adaptations for fast and continuous swimming. Their bodies are beautifully streamlined: spindle-shaped and oval to round in cross section (Fig. 23.8a). The skin is smooth, with tiny, cycloid scales, and tends to be shades of iridescent blue or green on top of the fish, countershading to silver and white below. The first dorsal fin, while made up of stout spines, depresses into a groove on the back while the fish is swimming rapidly. The soft dorsal and anal fins are short, identical in shape and size, and located opposite one another, just in front of rows of small finlets that run down the caudal peduncle to the tail. The tail fin is deeply forked to lunate in construction (high aspect ratio) and provides the tremendous thrust needed to maintain high speeds. The caudal peduncle is very narrow and contains mainly the bony keel on each side (created by the flattening of the caudal vertebrate) and the tendons running to the tail from both red and white muscle. Since the tendons run over the keel, the keel apparently acts as a pulley, to increase the amount of pull exerted by the muscles (Marshall 1971). In many species the swimbladder is reduced or absent, enabling them to move throughout the water column in search of deep-water as well as surface prey.

The respiratory pump system tends to be reduced because constant rapid swimming forces plenty of water across the gills. In the larger scombrids (*Thunnus,* etc.) the circulatory system has been modified with countercurrent exchangers in order to reduce loss of the heat generated by the tremendous muscular activity. This in turn increases the efficiency of the muscle. For information on scombrid ecology, see Chapter 35.

Xiphiidae and Istiophoridae. These two families contain the 11 species of billfishes that roam the surface waters of tropical and subtropical seas. The family Xiphiidae consists solely of the swordfish (*Xiphias gladius*), and the Istiophoridae consists of the sailfishes (*Istophorus,* two species), spearfishes (*Tetrapturus,* six species), and marlins (*Makaira,* two species). The two families, while superficially similar,

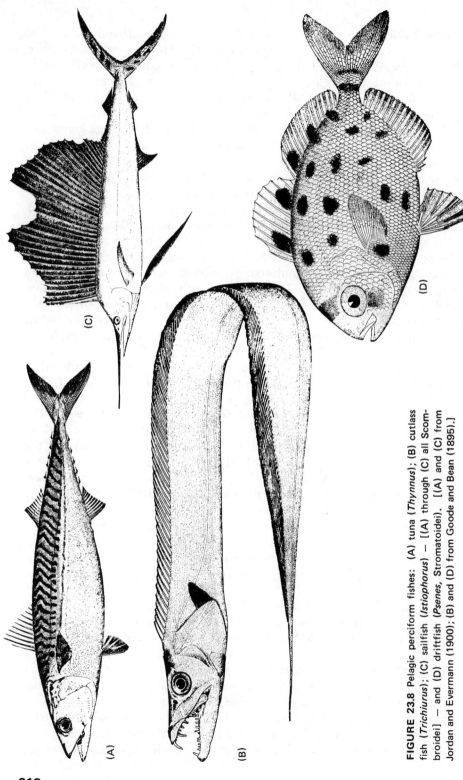

FIGURE 23.8 Pelagic perciform fishes: (A) tuna (*Thynnus*); (B) cutlass fish (*Trichiurus*); (C) sailfish (*Istiophorus*) — [(A) through (C) all Scombroidei] — and (D) driftfish (*Psenes*, Stromatoidei). [(A) and (C) from Jordan and Evermann (1900); (B) and (D) from Goode and Bean (1895).]

differ in many details (Fig. 23.8c). The sword of the swordfish is flat and, at its maximum extent, is about one third the length of the fish (which may reach 4.5 m). The sword of istiophorids is rounded in cross section and is generally less than one quarter the total length (up to 4 m). In addition, in contrast to the istiophorids, swordfish lack pelvic fins, teeth, and, in the adult, scales. The caudal peduncle has but one keel on each side, in contrast to the two possessed by the istiophorids. Billfishes capture other fishes for food by swimming through schools and slashing the bill back and forth, stunning or injuring the prey in the process. Swordfishes apparently can also spear large fishes with their snouts (Gordon 1977).

Stromateoidei

In this curious group of six families and 60+ species, the juveniles are mostly better known than the adults. The reason for this is that, with the exception of the members of the Ariommidae (which are bottom-oriented deepsea fishes), juvenile stromateoid fishes are associated with jellyfishes or drifting objects in the epipelagic region. The juveniles found with jellyfishes swim among the tentacles, dodging the stinging nematocysts, to which they are *not* immune. With this association they obtain not only protection from large piscine predators but food as well, since they nibble on the tentacles. These juveniles, in contrast to the adults, have a well-developed swimbladder and a color pattern of vertical stripes. The rather drab and unremarkable-looking adults (Fig. 23.8d) are mostly also pelagic and may compensate in part for the reduced or absent swimbladder by having a high lipid content of the body and by reducing the firmness of muscle and bone. However, exceptions to this are the 13 species of deep-bodied, iridescent butterfishes (Stromateidae), which do have a high lipid content but are nevertheless negatively buoyant. The butterfishes are active inshore species that apparently move freely up and down the water column feeding on coelenterate medusae, ctenophores, and other soft-bodied animals. Like other stromateoid fishes, which also feed on such organisms, they possess tooth-covered pharyngeal sacs, just behind the last gill arch.

Anabantoidei

The gouramies are a group of four closely related freshwater families well known to aquarists through such species as the climbing gourami (Anabantidae: *Anabas testudineus*), the Siamese fighting fish (Belontiidae: *Betta splendens*), the kissing gourami (Helostomatidae: *Helostoma temmincki*), and the giant gourami (Osphronemidae: *Osphromenus goramy*). The 70+ species in these families are mostly small (less than 10 cm), surface-oriented fishes, with moderately deep bodies, rounded tails, and long anal fins (Fig. 23.9a). Internally, they have two particularly distinctive features: a long body cavity, so that the swimbladder extends into the caudal region, and labyrinth (suprabranchial) organs.

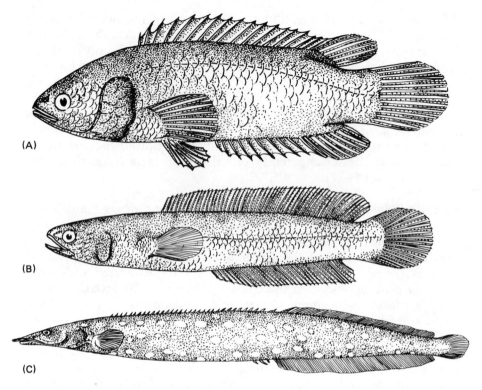

FIGURE 23.9 Representatives of tropical freshwater perciform suborders: (A) climbing perch (*Anabas,* Anabantoidei); (B) snakehead (*Channus,* Channoidei); and (C) spiny eel (*Mastacembelus,* Mastacembeloidei).

The labyrinth organs permit the gouramis to breathe air. They are made up of elaborately folded layers of highly vascularized skin that cover modified lamellae from the first functional gill arch. The organs occupy much of the gill chamber, as well as an extra chamber on its roof. The gills have become reduced in size as a consequence, and gouramis suffocate if deprived of access to the surface. Gouramis breathe by swallowing bubbles of air, holding them in the labyrinth organs for extended periods of time, and then forcing them out through the gill covers. The air bubbles taken in by the gouramis are also important for hearing and reproduction. When in the chambers of the labyrinth organ, the air bubbles are right next to the sides of the cranium containing the inner ear. In gouramis, membranous "windows" are present at this point, so vibrations picked up by the air bubbles are easily transmitted to the inner ears (Alexander 1967). For reproduction, male gouramis expel air bubbles through their mouths and build a bubble nest on the surface of the water, into which eggs are laid by the female and subsequently tended by the male. The bubble nests and labyrinth organs of the gouramis are obviously adaptations for life in the stagnant waters of tropical Asia and Africa in which they live.

Luciocephaloidei	The pikehead (*Luciocephalus pulcher*), the sole species in this suborder, resembles the gouramis in that it has labyrinth organ for air breathing, but it seems to have evolved independently (Liem 1963). Otherwise, the pikehead diverges from the gouramis in many respects, such as the absence of spines in the dorsal and anal fins, the absence of a swimbladder, and the extraordinarily protrusible mouth, which can be greatly extended as a tube for sucking in prey. The body of the pikehead is cigarlike in both shape and size, reaching a maximum length of 18 cm. It feeds on invertebrates and small fish in streams of southeast Asia.

Channoidei	The 11 known species of snakeheads (Channidae) are famous for their voraciousness as predators. For this purpose they have a large mouth with an underslung, well-toothed jaw, large eyes, and a thick, elongate body with long dorsal and anal fins (Fig. 23.9b). Like the gouramis with which they typically occur, snakeheads have a labyrinth organ in the gill chamber, but it is quite different in structure from that of the gouramis. Other adaptations for life in stagnant waters possessed by snakeheads are eggs which float (by means of oil droplets) at the surface, where they are guarded by the males, and the ability of some species to move overland by "swimming" in an eel-like fashion.

Mastacembeloidei	The spiny eels (Mastacembelidae, 50 species) are freshwater fishes of tropical Africa and Asia. They are distinguished by their eel-like bodies, which lack pelvic fins and have soft dorsal and anal fins placed far back on the body, often joining with the tail (Fig. 23.9c). Each soft dorsal is preceded by a row of stout, isolated spines which can inflict painful wounds on any fisherman unfortunate enough to grab one around the middle. Their most peculiar feature is their pointed snout, which has a fleshy appendage at the end. The appendage has three lobes, the two side lobes containing the anterior nostrils. The appendage is apparently used for finding invertebrates on and in the soft bottoms of the backwaters commonly inhabited by these eels. The only other family in this suborder (Chaudhuriidae) contains just one species, which lacks the appendage on the snout, the dorsal spines, and scales as well (present on spiny eels).

Gobiesociformes	This order consists of three families (140 to 150 species) of small, bottom-dwelling, shallow-water marine fishes that seem to be derived from the notothenioid fishes (Gosline 1971). They are without scales or swimbladders but have flattened heads, enlarged pectorals, rounded tails, and spiny opercular bones. The clingfishes (Gobiesocidae, 100+ species) are small,

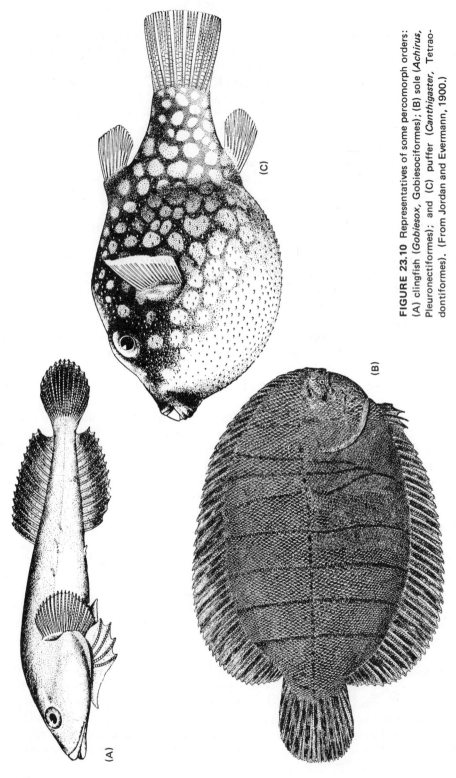

FIGURE 23.10 Representatives of some percomorph orders: (A) clingfish (*Gobiesox*, Gobiesociformes); (B) sole (*Achirus*, Pleuronectiformes); and (C) puffer (*Canthigaster*, Tetraodontiformes). (From Jordan and Evermann, 1900.)

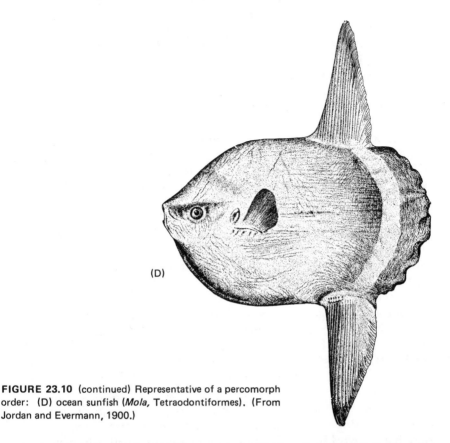

(D)

FIGURE 23.10 (continued) Representative of a percomorph order: (D) ocean sunfish (*Mola,* Tetraodontiformes). (From Jordan and Evermann, 1900.)

often tiny (less than 7 cm) fishes recognizable by their broad, flat heads, smooth, often jellylike, bodies, and pelvic fins that are modified into a sucking disc (Fig. 23.10a). The sucking disc is used for holding onto rocks in areas subject to strong tidal currents or for clinging to the sides of rocks or seaweed stalks. They can be separated from the gobies, which also possess a sucking disc, by the absence of spines in the dorsal and anal fins. In contrast, the dragonets (Callionymidae, 40 species; Draconettidae, 4 species) have well-developed spines but lack the sucking disc. The principal opening of the operculae on dragonets is a nearly dorsal notch, which permits the fish to remain partially buried on the bottom but still capable of taking in water for respiration. A number of dragonets are covered with evil-smelling mucus, which apparently decreases their desirability to predators. They are best known, however, for the brightness of the males in contrast to the females and the readiness with which they court and spawn in aquaria.

Pleuronectiformes   There are few problems in recognizing a member of the flatfish order, since it is the only group of fishes in which the adults are not bilaterally symmetrical. One side of the body is white and eyeless, while the other side is dark colored and has both eyes (Fig. 23.10b). The flatfish lie on the bottom with the pale side down and the dark side up. Since they are very flat, secretive in their behavior, and able to change color to match the substrate, flatfishes are masters at hiding from both predators and prey. Most flatfishes remain close to the bottom even while swimming, which is accomplished by undulating motions of the body; presumably the efficiency of this type of swimming is improved by the long dorsal and anal fins, which together with the caudal fins may nearly completely encircle the body. These fins are usually without spines and very flexible. As might be expected in such fishes, the swimbladder is absent and the body cavity is very small.

One of the most fascinating aspects of flatfish biology is the change that takes place as the pelagic, bilaterally symmetrical larvae become benthic, asymmetrical juveniles (Fig. 23.11). The most visible parts of this process are the change in pigmentation patterns and the migration of one eye across the top of the head to its final resting place close to the other eye. Of course, this involves not only the movement of the eye but also changes in nerves, blood vessels, skull bones, and muscles. One of the features used to distinguish various flatfish groups is whether or not they have both eyes on the left or right side of the body. Left-eyed flatfishes rest on the right side of the body, and vice versa. Some species, however, such as the starry flounder (*Platichthys stellatus*), have both right- and left-sided forms. Flatfishes are found mostly on soft bottoms of continental shelves, although a few species inhabit the continental slope and others may invade fresh water. On the shelves they have a worldwide distribution and are abundant, often supporting important fisheries. The large number of flatfish species (520+) means that many species coexist with each other. Ecological segregation is reflected in differential depth distributions (see Chapter 33) and in different feeding habits, as reflected in the structure of the mouth and pharyngeal teeth. Piscivorous species, such as halibut (*Hippoglossus*), have large, symmetrical mouths, lined with tiny teeth for grasping, and sharply pointed pharyngeal teeth. Species which feed by taking chunks out of the siphons of clams and other buried invertebrates have asymmetrical mouths (favoring the down side) with chisellike teeth for biting and molariform pharyngeal teeth for grinding (Alexander 1967).

Tetraodontiformes

If degree of alteration of the basic perciform body plan is the key to determining how "derived" a fish group is, then this order includes the most derived of all teleosts. While perhaps the best indications of this are found internally, in the modifications of the skeleton (they lack, for example, parietals, nasals, infraorbitals, and lower ribs), the tetraodontiform fishes are also visibly different from other fishes. To begin with, they come in a variety of body shapes that are the antithesis of the fusiform bodies

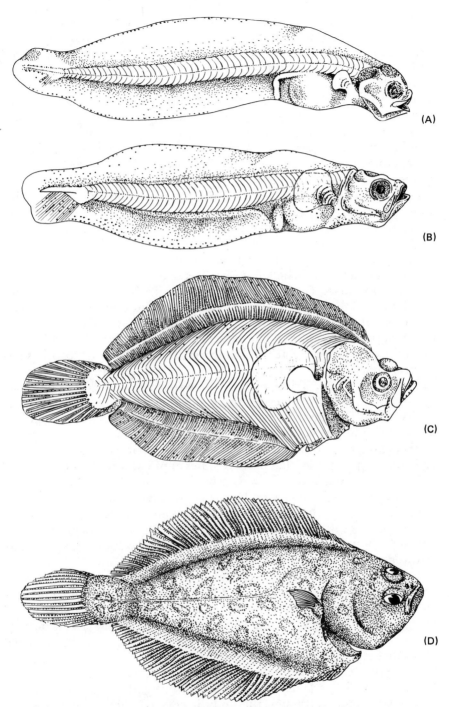

(A)

(B)

(C)

(D)

FIGURE 23.11 Metamorphosis of halibut (*Hippoglossus stenopleois*) from a pelagic larva to a bottom fish. Note the migration of the eye from one side to the other. (After Thompson and Van Cleve, 1936.)

of "typical" fish, ranging from globular to triangular to extremely compressed. All are slow swimmers, propelled either by a rounded caudal fin, by sculling with the pectoral fins, or by movements of the dorsal and anal fins, which are typically symmetrical and placed far back on the body. Presumably because of the vulnerability of such fishes to predators, most possess some form of protection such as inflatable, spine-covered bodies, body armor (often of scales), stout fin spines that can be locked erect, tough, leathery skin, and/or poisonous flesh. Gill openings are small, usually just holes on the side of the fish, in front of the pectoral fins. The food of tetraodontiform fishes is mostly invertebrates that attempt to avoid being eaten by having heavy shells or other armor. As a result, the fish have stout teeth in the jaw, or toothlike bones fused into a beak. The maxillae and premaxillae also fused to each other. This hard jaw is powered by large muscles. The pharyngeal teeth are also stout and provide additional crushing abilities. Most of the 320 or so species in this order are associated with coral reefs, which are dominated by hard-shelled invertebrates.

Triodontidae, Tetraodontidae, Diodontidae. The 150 or so species in these three families have the outer bones of the jaws modified into strong, beaklike structures for shearing off corals and other such invertebrates (Fig. 23.10c). The beaks are divided by sutures, which give them the appearance of teeth. However, the number of "teeth" is distinctive and is handy for distinguishing the three families: Diodontidae means two-toothed, Triodontidae, three-toothed, and Tetraodontidae, four-toothed. For protection these slow-moving fishes rely on their ability to puff themselves up and on their toxicity. In order to inflate themselves the puffers and porcupine fishes suck water into a ventral diverticulum of the stomach. This greatly increases their diameter, especially in the species that possess spines or prickles on the sides. Fishes unfortunate enough to be caught by humans will inflate themselves with air. The toxin possessed by many of these fishes, called tetrodotoxin, is found mostly in the internal organs and can be fatal to humans. This has not kept the puffers from being a favored fish (fugu) in Japan, although they must be cleaned by licensed cooks. Presumably the risk involved in eating fugu enhances the flavor.

Molidae. The three species of molas are unlike any other members of the order. They are adapted for life as sluggish pelagic predators on jellyfish or other large invertebrates that come close enough to be sucked in. While they possess the fused "teeth" in the jaws typical of the order, in most respects they are unique. They are large, flattened fishes that lack a caudal peduncle but do have a fin of sorts running along the posterior edge of the body, immediately behind the tall, short-based dorsal and anal fins (Fig. 23.10d). Pelvic fins and swimbladder are absent, as are spines, although the body is covered with a tough leathery skin. Two of the species (*Mola mola* and *Masturus lanceolatus*) may reach 4 m in length and weigh 1500 kg. Since such large fish are typi-

326

cally found on the surface (and are often called, as a result, ocean sunfish), they can be a hazard at times to boats. The molas are considered to be the most fecund of all vertebrates, producing upwards of 30 million eggs. They are not considered to be especially edible, since the flesh is flabby and parasite-ridden.

Supplemental Readings

Alexander 1967; Bigelow and Schroeder 1953; Fitch and Lavenberg 1968; Gordon 1977; Gosline 1971; Hart 1973; Herald 1961; Leim and Scott 1966; Lindberg 1971; Marshall 1971; Nelson 1976; Nikolsky 1954; Sterba 1959; Wheeler 1975.

PART IV

Zoogeography

ααααααααααααααααααααααααααααααααααααααααααααααααααααααααααααααααα
~~~~~~

Zoogeography of Freshwater Fishes

The study of fish zoogeography is alternately one of the most fascinating and one of most frustrating areas of ichthyology. It is fascinating because the explanation of the world patterns of fish distribution requires putting together knowledge from many other areas of ichthyology, such as ecology, physiology, systematics, and paleontology, as well as from other disciplines such as geology and biogeography. It is frustrating, however, because so much of our knowledge of these areas is nonexistent, fragmented, or incomplete, so that any attempt to explain fish distribution patterns, particularly over large areas, is bound to contain gaps that have to be bridged with guesswork. Nevertheless, the recent acceptance of continental drift as a concept that explains many perplexing geological problems has led to the solution of many zoogeographic puzzles, so that worldwide patterns of fish distribution have become much easier to understand. This has been particularly true for freshwater fishes. Therefore, this chapter will summarize the broad zoogeographic patterns of freshwater fishes by describing (1) the basic zoogeographic types of freshwater fishes; (2) the fish faunas and drainage patterns of the major continental areas; and (3) the zoogeographic history of primary freshwater fishes, especially the Ostariophysi.

Zoogeographic Types

There are two basic types of fishes found in fresh water, euryhaline marine fishes and obligatory freshwater fishes. Euryhaline marine fishes are those that are primarily marine but are capable of entering fresh water for extended periods of time and so are frequently characteristic of the lower reaches of coastal streams. Most commonly, it is juveniles that inhabit fresh water, perhaps to avoid predation, but adult forms, such as the large bull sharks (*Carcharinus leucus*) and sawfishes (*Pristis* spp.) that move in and out of Lake Nicaragua, are important in some areas. Euryhaline marine forms are generally most important in freshwater systems where the obligatory freshwater fish fauna is not well developed.

Obligatory freshwater fishes are those that must spend at least part of their life cycle in freshwater. For zoogeographic studies, two basic types can be recognized, freshwater dispersants and saltwater dispersants. **Freshwater dispersants** belong to fish families whose members by and large are incapable of traveling for long distances through salt water. The distribution patterns of these families are best explained through the use of overland (freshwater) routes of dispersal and through plate tectonics (Rosen 1974). Freshwater dispersants include the primary and secondary freshwater fishes of Myers (1951). As D. E. Rosen (1974, 1975a) points out, the distribution patterns of most secondary freshwater fishes (fishes characteristic of fresh water but with distribution patterns seeming to indicate saltwater dispersal) can often be better explained on the basis of continental drift than on the basis of long-distance movements through salt water. In addition, many primary freshwater fishes (those supposedly incapable of entering salt water) have been shown to be tolerant of a wide range of salinities. Typical examples of freshwater dispersants include most of the Ostariophysi (minnows, catfishes, characoids, etc.) and families such as the Esocidae (pikes), Percidae (freshwater perches), Mormyridae (African electric fishes), Poeciliidae (livebearers), Lepisosteidae (gars), and Cichlidae (cichlids). Freshwater dispersants dominate the fresh waters of most of the world (Fig. 24.1).

Saltwater dispersants are those fishes whose distribution patterns can be explained in a large part by movements through salt water. Even in this group, however, there are many families whose broad distribution patterns in freshwater environments are related to continental movements. Saltwater dispersant fishes are of two basic types: diadromous fishes and freshwater representatives of marine families. Diadromous fishes are those that regularly move between fresh water and salt water, spending different parts of their life cycle in each environment. Anadromous fishes are those that spend the adult phase of their life cycles in salt water (or large bodies of fresh water) but move up streams and rivers to spawn (for example, Pacific salmon [*Oncorhynchus* spp.]). Catadromous fishes, such as the eels of the family Anguillidae and some bullies of the family Galaxiidae (Fig. 24.1), spend most of their life in fresh water but spawn in salt water. Catadromy is much less common than anadromy. Diadromous fishes are frequently important members of the faunas of coastal streams, especially if the region is geologically young. In most areas where they occur, diadromous species have given rise to numerous nonmigratory forms, which if isolated from the parent stock may evolve into distinct species. This has happened repeatedly in families such as the Galaxiidae, Salmonidae (Fig. 24.1), and Petromyzonidae (lampreys).

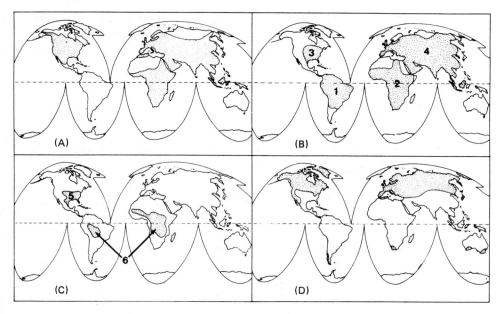

FIGURE 24.1 Representative distribution patterns of freshwater fish families: (A) distribution of the Cyprinidae, a widely distributed family of freshwater dispersants that is absent from South America and Australia; (B) distribution of four families of freshwater dispersants largely confined to one continent (1 — Gymnotidae, 2 — Mormyridae, 3 — Centrarchidae, and 4 — Cobitidae); (C) distribution of two ancient families of freshwater dispersant fishes (5 — Lepisosteidae, and 6 — Lepidosirenidae); and (D) distribution of two saltwater dispersant families, Salmonidae (Northern Hemisphere) and Galaxiidae (Southern Hemisphere). (From Rosen, 1975a.)

If a region lacks a well-developed fish fauna of freshwater dispersants, it is quite likely that the fauna will be made up of a mixture of diadromous species and species that are otherwise representative of marine families. A good example of the latter group are the sculpins of the genus *Cottus* (Cottidae), which have a circumarctic distribution, mostly in streams dominated by salmonids. However, it should be noted that some of these marine-derived species are quite successful members of well-developed freshwater fish faunas, such as the many freshwater herrings (Clupeidae) and freshwater puffers (Tetraodontidae).

It should be emphasized that this classification system of zoogeographic types is quite arbitrary and is set up mostly as a means of simplifying the explanation of general patterns of fish distribution. It is intended to be applied mostly at the family level even though some species within each family may not fit the family category well. For example, the Galaxiidae (bullies), although containing a number of diadromous species, have a broad distribution pattern (Fig 24.1) that seems to reflect more the ancient connections of the southern continents to each other than the ability of the diadromous species to disperse through the ocean (Rosen 1974). However, on the southern continents, local distribution patterns of Galaxiidae may be explained at least partially by saltwater dispersal.

Zoogeographic Regions   For the study of fish zoogeography, it is convenient to divide the world up into six zoogeographic regions (Darlington 1952): (1) the African Region, consisting of the entire African continent; (2) the Neotropical Region, consisting of South and Central America; and (3) the Oriental Region, which includes the Indian subcontinent, southeast Asia, Indonesia, and the Phillipines; (4) the Palaearctic Region, which includes Europe and Asia north of the Himalaya Mountains and the Yangtze River; (5) the Nearctic Region, which is North America down to central Mexico; and (6) the Australian Region, which consists of Australia, New Zealand, New Guinea, Bali, and the many smaller islands in the same region. Each of these regions has distinctive elements of its fish fauna that reflect its isolation from (as well as its connections to) the other regions.

African Region   The African Region possesses an extremely diverse fish fauna and is of special interest to students of fish evolution and zoogeography because of its wealth of ancient forms, such as lungfishes (Lepidosirenidae), bichirs (Polypteridae), and osteoglossids (five families). The region contains at least 2000 species of freshwater fishes, belonging to about 280 genera and 47 families (Lowe-McConnell 1975; Roberts 1975). Over 95% of the species belong to freshwater dispersant families, mostly (43%) ostariophysans (about 300 cyprinid species, 190 characoid species, and 365 catfish species). The ostariophysans belong to 15 families which include seven endemic families and two families of marine catfishes. One or another of the remaining six families is found in all other zoogeographic regions, except Australia.

The nonostariophysan freshwater fishes belong to a variety of endemic and nonendemic families. One of the most numerous (100+ species) of the endemic families is the Mormyridae, a group related to the ancient osteoglossids but possessing many unusual adaptations, including electric organs, for living in muddy tropical waters. Another endemic family of interest is the Polypteridae (bichirs and reedfish, 11 species), which seem to be related to the fossil paleoniscid fishes that gave rise to the dominant bony fishes of today (Actinopterygii). The nonostariophysan, nonendemic families are shared with a number of other zoogeographic regions. They include Lepidosirenidae (lungfishes, shared with South America), Osteoglossidae (bony-tongues, with South America and Australia), Anabantidae and Mastacembelidae (gouramis and spiny eels, respectively, both with the Oriental Region), and Cichlidae and Cyprinodontidae (cichlids and killifishes, respectively, with South America, North America, and the Oriental Region).

An interesting, if minor, component of the African freshwater fish fauna is the freshwater representatives of marine families, such as Tetraodontidae (puffer fishes), Syngnathidae (pipefishes), Mugilidae (mullets), Clupeidae (herrings) and Centropomidae (snooks). The latter family is important ecologically because the nine freshwater species in Africa, including the Nile perch (*Lates niloticus*), are important predators in many lakes and rivers.

One of the curious aspects of the African freshwater fish fauna is that the dominant groups each tend to be characteristic of a broad habitat type (Roberts 1975). Thus the cichlids (600+ species) exist mostly as members of the spectacular species flocks that characterize the great rift lakes. The characoid fishes (families Hepsetidae, Characidae, Distichodontidae, and Ichthyboridae) are found almost exclusively in sluggish lowland streams, as are most mormyrids. A number of minor families that have air-breathing abilities (e.g., Lepidosirenidae, Polypteridae) are also confined to the lowland habitats. The cyprinids are most characteristic of flowing waters of middle to high elevations. The catfishes are found in most habitats, although with different types of specializations for the different environments. Their success is presumably largely due to their nocturnal activity patterns, because most of the other large families (except the mormyrids) are diurnal.

Africa contains an extraordinary mixture of endemic and non-endemic families of different ages of origin because it has been a rather stable tropical land mass with at least intermittent connections with the other continents. These families have produced a large number of endemic species because Africa contains a number of ancient, isolated drainage basins. The region can thus be divided up into at least 11 ichthyological provinces, each with its characteristic fish fauna (Roberts 1975).

Neotropical Region   The Neotropical Region has two distinct zoogeographic subregions, mainland South America and Central America. The fish faunas of the two subregions reflect the fact that South America was isolated from the other continents for a long period of time while Central America is of geologically recent origin.

The diversity of South America's fish fauna is just beginning to be fully appreciated. It has the most species of obligatory freshwater fish of any continent (2600 to 2800 or more), many of them undescribed. One of the most striking aspects of the South American fish fauna is the complete absence of the family Cyprinidae, which dominates the freshwater fish fauna in all other zoogeographic regions except the Australian region. Instead, the dominant fishes are characins (suborder Characoidei, 16 families, 15 of them endemic, with about 1500 species) and catfishes (suborder Siluroidei, 14 endemic families, with about 1100 species). The characins show an extraordinary variety of ecological and morphological adaptations, yet the basic similarities in the body plans of the many forms seem to reflect a rather limited common ancestry. Only the family Characidae occurs outside South America, in Africa. The most divergent fishes of this group are of the superfamily Gymnotidae, four families of electric fishes that are strikingly convergent on the unrelated mormyrids of Africa. The South American catfishes are as diverse as the characins and include the most "ancestral" family (Diplomystidae) of the order, as well as three families distinguished by the presence of bony plates on their bodies (Doradidae, Callichthyidae, and Loricariidae).

In contrast to Africa, nonostariophysan freshwater fishes are a relatively minor component (about 10%) of the South American fish fauna, although they often play important roles in South American lakes and streams. Cichlids (Cichlidae, 100 to 150 species) are widespread in South American streams, while killifishes (60+ species) are most abundant in habitats (such as stagnant backwaters) not utilized by larger fishes. In Lake Titicaca, a species flock of about 18 endemic killifishes is present. The killifishes have also given rise to three other South American families, Anablepidae (four-eyed fishes, three species), Jenynsiidae (Jenynsiids, three species) and Poeciliidae (livebearers, about 15 species in South America). The two most ancient families of freshwater fishes present in South America are probably the Lepidosirenidae (lungfishes, one species), and the Osteoglossidae (bony-tongues, two species). Both families also have representatives in Africa, and osteoglossids occur in Australia as well.

The final elements of the South American fish fauna are fishes of marine origin and diadromous fishes. The lower Amazon alone has 20 to 30 endemic freshwater representatives of marine families and about an equal number of euryhaline marine species. Among the freshwater species are members of the families Potamotrygonidae (freshwater stingrays, found also in the Mekong River is Asia and, apparently, the Niger River in Africa), Soleidae (soles), Clupeidae (herrings), Engraulidae (anchovies), and Sciaenidae (drums). The diadromous species are confined to coastal Chile, Patagonia, Tierra del Fuego, and the Falkland Islands. The families involved include two of lampreys (Geotriidae and Mordaciidae), the Galaxiidae (bullies), and the Aplochitonidae (southern smelts). These families are also characteristic of the Australian Region. The family Galaxiidae is found in southern Africa as well.

South America can be divided into eight provinces characterized by distinctive fish faunas (Gery 1969). However, because many of the major geological features of South America are comparatively recent in origin (e.g., the Andes Mountains) and because connections between drainage systems are common, the regions share many species and genera.

Another portion of the Neotropical Region with a fish fauna resembling that of South America is Central America. However, the Central American fish fauna (which includes species in part of Cuba and other Antillean islands) also shows affinities to that of North America and has many unique characteristics of its own. The distributional history of the fishes of the region is confusing because the geological history of the region is extraordinarily complex (Rosen 1975b). Miller (1966) lists 456 species from the fresh waters of mainland Central America. Of these, 201 (60%) are freshwater dispersants, 31 (7%) are freshwater representatives of marine families, and the rest (33%) are euryhaline marine fishes. Most species in the latter group are only sporadic in their occurrence in the lower reaches of the streams. In contrast to both North and South America, only 38% of the freshwater dispersant species are ostariophysans. Most of these are found in the southernmost part of Central America and belong to families and species found otherwise only in South America. However, many species are endemic, with highly localized distribution patterns. In the northern part of Central America three of the ostariophysan species belong to the North American families Ictaluridae (catfishes) and Catostomidae (suckers), but even here most of the few ostariophysans present have South American affinities (e.g., Pimelodidae, Characidae). However, the ostariophysans do show a high degree of endemism, indicating long isolation from South America.

The most curious aspect of the Central American fish fauna is not the ostariophysan element but the fact that it is dominated by cichlids (Cichlidae, 82+ species), livebearers (Poeciliidae, 58+ species), and killifishes (Cyprinodontidae, 22+ species). The "classic" explanation for this phenomenon is that these fishes colonized Central America by moving through salt water and were able to diversify in the area because of the absence of the ostariophysans, which presumably were competitively superior. However, as Rosen (1975b) points out, land, either as part of the two continents or as islands, has been present in the Central American Subregion continuously since the late Mesozoic. It is therefore likely that ostariophysans have been there at least as long as the dominant nonostariophysan families. The success of the cichlids, livebearers, and killifishes is most likely related to adaptations that have enabled them to survive in an area that is geologically very unstable. These adaptations include an ability to live under fluctuating temperature and salinity regimes, live-bearing (Poeciliidae), and small body sizes, which permit large populations to live in small, isolated streams and lakes. In addition, the success of the cichlids is at least partially related to their ability to do well in lakes. For example, the species "flocks" of the great lakes of Central America have many similarities to the species "flocks" of the great lakes of Africa, representing similar phenomena of speciation.

Oriental Region   The Oriental Region has three subregions: the Peninsular India Subregion (including Sri Lanka), the Southeast Asian Mainland Subregion, and the Southeast Asian Islands Subregion, principally Sumatra, Java, Borneo, and Mindanao. Although the subregions have distinctive aspects to their fish faunas, they have more in common than differences. In particular, they are all dominated by cyprinids and, to a lesser extent, by catfishes, especially of the families Bagridae and Clariidae.

Peninsular India, according to the continental drift theory, was an independent island continent for perhaps 100 million years before it collided with Asia, creating the Himalaya Mountains. It is somewhat surprising, therefore, to find that its freshwater fish fauna contains no truly ancient forms but is instead made up mostly of advanced ostariophysans of Asiatic or recent African origin. Fossil evidence indicates that the original fish fauna must have been overwhelmed by the advanced ostariophysans once invasion routes were open, a decline that may have been hastened by the climatic change that presumably took place as the Himalaya Mountains rose. There are over 700 species of freshwater dispersant fishes, from 27 families, known from Peninsular India (Jayaram 1974). Of these, 373 (53%) belong to the family Cyprinidae and 176 species (25%) belong to 12 families of catfishes. Since the presence of endemic genera is usually indicative of long isolation from surrounding areas, it is significant that there are no endemic genera of cyprinids or catfishes in Peninsular India. The genera present are found either in southeast Asia, in Africa, or in both (Menon 1973). Those shared with Africa are also found in southwest Asia (the Middle East). Other ostariophysan families found in India are the Cobitidae (loaches, also found in the Palearctic Region), the Homalopteridae (hillstream fishes, Oriental Region only) and the Psilorhynchidae (Oriental Region only). The nonostariophysan freshwater fish families found here include the Channidae (snakeheads), Mastacembelidae (spiny eels), Anabantidae (climbing gouramis), Belontiidae (gouramis), Notopteridae (knife-fishes), Cichlidae, Cyprinodontidae (killifishes), Nandidae (leaf-fishes), and Synbranchidae (synbranchid eels). All of these families have representatives in Africa as well as elsewhere in the Oriental Region. The Notopteridae are particularly noteworthy, since they are highly specialized members of the order Osteoglossiformes, members of which are usually regarded as relict species. Saltwater dispersant fishes play a relatively small role in the fresh waters of Peninsular India, presumably because of the dominance of the ostariophysans.

The **Southeast Asian Mainland** is poorly understood ichthyologically. However, an idea of the composition of the fish fauna of this area can be gotten by analyzing the fish fauna of Thailand (Smith 1945). Of the 549 fish species listed for Thailand, from 48 families, 72% are from freshwater dispersant families, principally Cyprinidae (39%) and various catfish families (18%). The representatives of marine families

338   CH. 24 ZOOGEOGRAPHY OF FRESHWATER FISHES

found in Thailand's fresh waters are mostly gobylike fishes of the families Gobiidae (gobies) and Eleotridae (sleepers). The only three representatives of apparently ancient fish families found here are two species of Notopteridae and one of Osteoglossidae (both families in the Osteoglossiformes).

In the **Southeast Asian Islands** the large islands (Sumatra, Java, Borneo) have fish faunas very similar to that of the mainland. These islands all protrude from a shallow continental shelf area that was dry during much of the Pleistocene, thanks to lower sea levels. At that time, most of the river systems of the islands and those of the mainland drained into a large central system, giving the fishes ready access to all the areas. Thus, Borneo alone has at least 300 freshwater dispersant species and Java has at least 100 (Myers 1951).

Palaearctic Region   The Palaearctic Region consists of all of Eurasia not included in the Oriental Region. Berg (1949) divides the area into six subregions, but a general idea of the composition of the fish fauna of this region can be obtained by examining the combined faunas of the Soviet Union and Europe (Berg 1949; Muus 1967). In this broad area 36 families of fish with about 420 species are found in fresh water. Species from 12 families of freshwater dispersants make up 53% of the fauna, mostly Cyprinidae (minnows, 37%) and Cobitidae (loaches, 8%). The Ostariophysi are otherwise represented in the area by only 10 catfishes from three families (Siluridae, Bagridae, and Sisoridae) and one sucker (Catostomidae). The sucker is a recent invader from North America, although the loaches and silurid and sisorid catfishes apparently evolved in Asia. Other freshwater dispersants found in the area are the Percidae, Channidae, Cyprinodontidae, Esocidae, and Umbridae, all except the Channidae found in North America as well. Anadromous fishes make up 17% of the total fauna, representing six families (but principally the Salmonidae, 11%). However, anadromous species are most important in the arctic drainages, where they make up about 51% of the fishes, as opposed to 30% for freshwater dispersants. Freshwater representatives of eight marine families make up another 11% of the total fauna, if the two endemic families of "sculpins" from Lake Baikal, the Cottocomephoridae (about 24 species) and Comephoridae (2 species), are counted here. These families might better be listed as freshwater dispersants. The remaining 18% of the fish fauna of this region consists of euryhaline marine species, from 13 families but mostly the Gobiidae (gobies, 11%).

Nearctic Region   The Nearctic Region consists of North America down to the southern edge of the Mexican plateau (Fig. 24.2). It can be divided into three ichthyological subregions: (1) the Arctic–Atlantic Subregion, consisting of all drainages into the Arctic and Atlantic Oceans, as well as the Gulf of

FIGURE 24.2 Zoogeographic subdivisions, for fishes, of North America: (I) Arctic–Atlantic Subregion; (II) Pacific Subregion; (III) Mexican Transition Subregion; (IA) Mississippi Province; (IB) Rio Grande Province; (IC) Atlantic Coast Province; (ID) Great Lakes–St. Lawrence Province; (IE) Hudson Bay Province; (IF) Arctic Province; (IIA) Alaska Coastal Province; (IIB) Columbia Province; (IIC) Great Basin Province; (IID) Klamath Province; (IIE) Sacramento Province; (IIF) Colorado Province; and (IIG) South Coastal Province.

Mexico down to the Rio Panuco; (2) the Pacific Subregion, consisting of all drainages along the Pacific coast down to the Mexican border (including Baja California, but excluding the Yukon River drainage in Alaska), and all interior drainages west of the Rocky Mountains; and (3) the Mexican Transition Subregion, consisting of most of Mexico except the upper Gulf of Mexico drainages, down to the imperceptible upper limits of Central America.

The fish faunas of the Pacific and Arctic–Atlantic Subregions are well known, since they are also the fish faunas of Canada and the United States (Bailey et al. 1970). Together, their fresh waters contain about 700 species of fish. Freshwater dispersant fishes from 18 families make up about 77% of this fauna, although most of the species are from the families Cyprinidae (minnows, 29%), Percidae (perches and darters, 17%), Cyprinodontidae (6%), Catostomidae (suckers, 2%), Ictaluridae (North American catfishes, 5%), and Centrarchidae (sunfishes, 4%). Another 11% of the fishes belong to diadromous families, principally the Salmonidae (salmon, trout, and whitefishes, 6%) and Petromyzonidae (lampreys, 3%). Freshwater representatives of marine families, including the Cottidae (sculpins, 4%), make up only 6% of this fauna, while an additional 6% is contributed by euryhaline marine species from 18 families.

The **Arctic–Atlantic Subregion** is the largest and most speciose of the Nearctic subregions. It can be divided into six ichthyological provinces that largely reflect the major drainage systems: (1) Mississippi; (2) Rio Grande; (3) Atlantic coast; (4) Great Lakes–St. Lawrence; (5) Hudson Bay; and (6) Arctic.

The **Mississippi Province** consists of all of the United States and Canada presently drained by the great Mississippi–Missouri River system, as well as all the many Atlantic and Gulf coast drainages south of the St. Lawrence River and east of the Rio Grande. A number of tributary systems have large numbers of endemic forms (e.g., the Tennessee and Cumberland Rivers) and so should, perhaps, be treated as separate provinces.

The Mississippi Province, partly because of these partially isolated tributaries, is by far the richest in North America in obligatory freshwater species, with about 280 to 300. Freshwater dispersants make up about 88% of these species, predominantly Cyprinidae (30%), Percidae (26%), Centrarchidae (7%), Catostomidae (9%), and Ictaluridae (5%). Diadromous fishes (7%) and freshwater representatives of marine families (5%) are poorly represented. In addition, a small number of euryhaline marine forms occur in the Mississippi Delta area. As the high percentage of freshwater dispersants attests, the Mississippi–Missouri drainage system is an ancient one. It is uniquely important in North America as a center of fish evolution, as a refuge during times of glaciation from which species have been able to reoccupy waters they were forced to vacate by the advance of the glaciers, and as a refuge for representatives of past fish faunas. Its role in the development of the North American fish fauna is indicated by the fact that the families Centrarchidae, Percidae (Etheostominae), Ictaluridae, and Esocidae are most abundant and diverse in its waters, as are cyprinids of the large genus *Notropis*. Its role as a glacial refuge is indicated by the fact that most of the species found in the Great Lakes–St. Lawrence, Hudson Bay, and Arctic Provinces, once largely covered by ice sheets, are also characteristic of the northern parts of the Mississippi Province. Its role as a refuge, however, has not been confined to just the Pleistocene period, since it still is a refuge for many relict Chondrostei, Holostei, and Teleostei. The Chondrosteans consist of three species of sturgeons (Acipenseridae), including two species in the endemic genus *Scaphirhynchus,* and one species of paddlefish (Polyodontidae). Only one other species of paddlefish exists, in the Yangtze River of China, while the closest relatives of the *Scaphirhynchus* sturgeons live in the Palaearctic Region. The holosteans are represented by six species of gar (Lepisosteidae) and by the bowfin (Amiidae). Aside from one additional species of gar found in Central America, these holosteans are the only representatives on earth today of the fishes that were dominant during most of the Mesozoic period. Among the relict teleosts are the mooneye and goldeye (*Hiodon*, family Hiodontidae, order Osteoglossiformes), a mud minnow (*Umbra*, family Umbridae, with single species in some Atlantic drainages, in Washington [*Novumbra*], in Alaska and Siberia [*Dallia*], and in Europe), a sucker (*Cycleptus,* which seems to be closest to the relict sucker *Myxocyprinus* of the Yangtze River system in China), and the peculiar families Percopsidae (trout-perches), Amblyopsidae (cavefishes), and Aphredoderidae (pirate perch), which are confined to North America.

The **Rio Grande Province** is essentially the Rio Grande River and its tributaries in Texas, Mexico, and New Mexico. About 75 species of obligatory freshwater fishes are found in the province, about one-third of them cyprinids. Of these species 20% to 25% are considered to be endemic, and many of the other species are assigned to endemic subspecies. While the fish fauna is similar in most respects to that of the Mississippi Province, it also contains a single species of characin (Mexican tetra [*Astyanax mexicanus*]) and of cichlid (Rio Grande perch [*Cichlasoma cyanoguttatum*]) whose closest relatives are in the Mexican Transition Subregion.

The **Atlantic Coast Province** is an artificial assemblage of independent drainage systems that flow into the Atlantic Ocean or the Gulf of Mexico, from Maine on the north to the gulf streams of Florida on the south. It should probably be subdivided into subprovinces, since the fish faunas at the two ends of the province bear little resemblance to each other. However, the changes in the fish fauna are gradual, so the faunas of adjacent streams are very similar. Endemic forms exist in many streams, especially in those draining the southern Appalachians, but all the streams have faunas that show strong ties to that of the Mississippi River system. In the northern third of this province the streams are dominated by anadromous fishes and by minnows and suckers that can colonize new waters through headwater connections (e.g., blacknose dace [*Rhinichthys atratulus*], creek chub [*Semotilus atromaculatus*], and white sucker [*Catostomus commersoni*]). In the middle third there are many ancient drainage systems with former connections to the Mississippi drainage, through the low ridges of the Appalachian Mountains. The streams in this region often have endemic species among the many they contain. In the region bounded by the Potomac River on the north and the Pee Dee River in the south, there are 94 species of fish spending at least part of their life cycle in fresh water, including 11 species endemic to just one drainage (Jenkins et al. 1972). Of the 94 species, six belong to diadromous families, five are freshwater representatives of marine families, leaving 87% of the fishes as freshwater dispersants. However, the marine element becomes more prevalent as one moves south and as the fauna becomes less rich.

The **Great Lakes–St. Lawrence Province** has had major connections to the Mississippi River system in the late Pleistocene, so it is not surprising to find that its fauna is essentially that of the northern part of the Mississippi Province. Most of it was glaciated at one time or another during the Pleistocene. It is treated as a separate province here because it is a distinct large drainage system and because the Great Lakes do (or did) have a number of endemic forms, such as the members of the whitefish (*Coregonus*) species complex, the siscowet lake trout (*Salvelinus namaycush siscowet*), and the blue walleye (*Stizostedion vitreum glaucum*). Of the 162 native obligatory freshwater fishes listed for the province by Hubbs and Lagler (1964), 77% belong to freshwater dispersant families (30% Cyprinidae), 16% to diadromous families, and 7% to marine families.

The **Hudson Bay Province** includes most of central Canada and the portion of the United States drained by the Red River of the North. Although all its waters drain into Hudson Bay, its fish fauna shows strong affinities with that of the Mississippi Basin, particularly in its freshwater dispersants. Of the 85 native species listed for this drainage (Scott and Crossman 1973), 70% belong to freshwater dispersant families (29% Cyprinidae), 18% to diadromous, and 12% to marine. These figures are deceptive, however, since most of the freshwater dispersant fishes occur in the southern edges of the basin. The more northern lakes and streams are dominated by salmonids, cottids, and a few cold-hardy cyprinids, catostomids, esocids, and percids.

The **Arctic Province** includes all those streams of Canada and Alaska that flow into the Arctic Ocean, up to and including the Yukon River drainage. There are 56 species of obligatory freshwater fish native to this region (McPhail and Lindsey 1970). Of these, 48% belong to diadromous families, 41% to freshwater dispersant families, and 6% to marine families. As in the Hudson Bay Province, most of the primary fishes occur in the southern edge of the province. These species have invaded from both the Mississippi Province and the Pacific Subregion. The salmonids found in this province are also characteristic of both areas. There are no unique forms, although the inconnu (*Stenodus leucichthys*), the Arctic cisco (*Coregonus autumnalis*), the arctic lamprey (*Lampetra japonica*), the least cisco (*C. sardinella*) are otherwise found only in Siberia. This province should thus be regarded as a region transitional between the Palaearctic and Nearctic Regions, as well as between the Pacific and Arctic–Atlantic Subregions.

The **Pacific Subregion** contains many fewer species than the Arctic–Atlantic Subregion because it is smaller in size and, more importantly, because much of it is arid or semiarid. However, the fish faunas of its seven provinces are much more distinct from each other than are the faunas of the provinces of the Arctic–Atlantic Subregion. The presence of mountain ranges and deserts in the subregion has created many barriers to fish movements, resulting in many fish species that are endemic to small regions. Many of these species appear to be relicts of the Nearctic fish fauna that partly gave rise to, and were displaced by, the dominant fishes of the Arctic–Atlantic Subregion. The zoogeographic provinces of the Pacific Subregion are: (1) Alaska Coastal; (2) Columbia; (3) Great Basin; (4) Klamath; (5) Sacramento; (6) Colorado; and (7) South Coastal.

The **Alaska Coastal Province** consists of all the minor coastal drainages from the Aleutian peninsula down to the Canadian border of the Alaskan panhandle. Only 34 freshwater species are found in this province (excluding euryhaline marine forms), 79% of them in diadromous families, 12% in marine families, and 8% in freshwater dispersant families. The three freshwater dispersant species (*Esox lucius, Catostomus catostomus,* and *Dallia pectoralis*) are also found in Siberia.

The **Columbia Province** includes the great Columbia River drainage, which penetrates into the interior as far as Montana and Idaho, and its associated coastal drainages of British Columbia, Washington, and Oregon. It contains the greatest number (51) of species of obligatory freshwater fishes of the provinces of the Pacific Subregion. Only 37% of these are freshwater dispersant fishes (25% Cyprinidae), but these are the most distinctive elements of the fauna, since 58% of these species are endemic to the province (Miller 1958). They include a relict mudminnow (Umbridae) and a trout-perch (Percopsidae). Of the remaining species, 43% are from diadromous families (24% from the Salmonidae alone) and the rest are freshwater representatives of marine families, especially the Cottidae (sculpins, 16%).

The **Great Basin Province**, the site of the classic studies of fish zoogeography and speciation by R. R. Miller and C. L. Hubbs, is a collection of internal drainage systems roughly bounded by the Sierra Nevada Mountains on the west and south, by the Wasatch Mountains on the east, and the Columbia plateau on the north. All the basins within the area are quite arid, although they were filled with large lakes during various periods of the Pleistocene. Consequently, there is a high degree of endemism in the desert basins, but the species also tend to show a common faunal ancestry. The basins with the most fish species within the Great Basin are Death Valley (11 species), the Lahontan System (which includes Lakes Tahoe and Pyramid, about 10 species), and the Bonneville System (including Bear and Utah Lakes, about 22 species). The Great Basin Province contains a total of about 50 species. The exact number is uncertain, since there are a number of undescribed and/or controversial species present. Nearly 60% of the species are either cyprinids or catostomids, although eight species of killifish (Cyprinodontidae) make up most of the Death Valley fish fauna and there are four species of whitefish (*Coregonus,* Salmonidae) in Bear Lake, Utah. About 80% of the species found in the Great Basin are endemic to it (Miller 1958).

The **Klamath Province,** consisting of the Klamath and Rogue drainages on the California–Oregon border, contains about 30 obligatory freshwater fishes, with only eight freshwater dispersant species (three cyprinids, five suckers). It is characterized instead by its representatives of diadromous families (53% of fishes, including four lampreys and eight salmonids) and its six species of sculpin (Cottidae). Thirty-seven percent of the species are endemic to the system, including all the suckers.

The **Sacramento Province** contains most of the water that flows in California, since it is dominated by the great Sacramento–San Joaquin drainage system. It also includes numerous coastal drainage systems from Monterey Bay north to the mouth of the Klamath River. It contains at least 43 native obligatory freshwater species, of which 42% are endemic (Moyle 1976a). Among the endemic forms are a unique complex of 10 minnow species and the Sacramento perch (*Archoplites interruptus*), the only centrarchid native west of the Rocky Mountains, and the most archaic member of the family. Only 28% of its obligatory freshwater fishes are freshwater dispersant species, while 47% of the fishes belong to anadromous families and the rest are all freshwater representatives of marine families. Of particular interest is the tule perch (*Hysterocarpus traski*), the only freshwater species in the marine family Embiotocidae (surf perches).

The **Colorado Province** is drained by the Colorado River system. This province is home mostly to freshwater dispersant fishes, which make up about 73% of its about 30 obligatory freshwater species. Among these fishes are six species of the endemic cyprinid group of spinedaces (Plagopterini), at least three species in a complex of the cyprinid genus *Gila* that lives in the main Colorado River, and the Gila topminnow (Poeciliidae, *Poecilopsis occidentalis*), which apparently entered the system from the Yaqui River of Mexico (Miller 1958). The rest are either representative of anadromous families (17%) or of marine families (10%).

The **South Coastal Province** is an artificial collection of small coastal drainage systems that enter the ocean between Monterey Bay on the north and the tip of Baja California on the south. Only 13 species of obligatory freshwater fishes are found in this region, three of them freshwater dispersants. The latter three species (two minnows and a sucker) are native only to the streams of the Los Angeles Basin.

The **Mexican Transition Subregion** has a fish fauna that is derived from both the Arctic–Atlantic and Pacific Subregions, as well as from Central America. The provinces of this subregion are somewhat indefinite, mostly as a result of our state of the knowledge of the fauna, but it is worth noting that: (1) the arid interior region contains many spring environments with endemic complexes of killifishes (Cyprinodontidae) and cichlids (Cichlidae); (2) the Pacific coastal streams contain complexes of livebearer "species" (Poeciliidae) with some of the most unusual sexual systems known among vertebrates; and (3) the Rio Yaqui system of northwestern Mexico contains a true "transitional" fauna. Miller (1958) lists 31 species for this river, including 16 freshwater dispersant forms and a number of forms derived from tropical marine families. Among the freshwater dispersants are seven species apparently derived from species in the Rio Grande drainage (including an ictalurid catfish and cyprinids of the genus *Notropis*), three species closely related to species in the Colorado River system, and four species (including a cichlid and two livebearers) showing affinities to the Central American fish fauna.

Australian Region

The Australian Region has long been cut off from the major evolutionary events taking place in the other continents. This is reflected dramatically in its fish fauna, which contains only two species of freshwater dispersants, both of ancient lineage: the Australian lungfish (*Neoceratodus forsteri,* family Ceratodidae) and the barramundi (*Scleropages leichardti,* family Osteoglossidae). The rest of its somewhat impoverished fish fauna is made up of representatives of diadromous or marine families. The Australian Region can be divided into three subregions in terms of its fish fauna: Australia (including Tasmania), New Zealand, and New Guinea, including nearby islands.

Australia contains 130 to 166 native species that spend all or most of their life cycles in fresh water, plus about 50 species of marine fishes found occasionally in fresh water (Lake 1971). The fishes perhaps most characteristic of its lakes and rivers are diadromous fishes or their freshwater derivatives: Mordaciidae and Geotriidae (lampreys, three species), Anguillidae (eels, four species), Galaxiidae (bullies, 26 species), Retropinnidae (New Zealand smelts, three species), and Aplochitonidae (southern smelts, one species). There are also about 37 families of marine fishes that have freshwater representatives in Australia. Of particular interest are the marine catfishes (Ariidae and Plostosidae, 14 species), gobies (Gobiidae, 28 species), Melanotaeniidae (rainbow fishes, six species), silversides (Atherinidae, 12 species), tigerperches (Theraponidae, 19 species), snooks (Centropomidae, nine species), aholeholes (Kuhliidae, seven species), and sea basses (Serranidae, seven species). Members of the latter four families are the typical perciform predators of Australia's lakes and rivers. Despite its apparently recent marine origin, the freshwater fish fauna does show a certain amount of endemism, enabling Lake (1971) to divide Australia up into 15 fish provinces. Fish species are most numerous, not surprisingly, in coastal areas where rainfall is highest and so the most permanent water exists. It is worth noting that 17 species manage to exist in the largely intermittent waters of the Lake Eyre Province of the interior but that only 27 species inhabit the extensive Murray-Darling Province of southern Australia.

New Zealand has long been isolated from other land masses, even Australia, so its 27 recognized freshwater species are wholly of marine or diadromous origin (McDowall and Whitaker, 1975). Most abundant are species from the diadromous families: Geotriidae (lampreys, one species), Retropinnidae (New Zealand smelts, two species?), Aplochitonidae (southern smelts, one species, now extinct), Galaxiidae (bullies, 13 species), and Anguillidae (eels, two species). Despite their ability to enter salt water, it is quite possible that ancestral fishes in the first four families were already present in New Zealand when it separated from Antarctica in the late Cretaceous period. Marine families with freshwater representatives are Pleuronectidae (flounders, one species), Eleotridae (sleepers, six species), and Mugiloididae (sandperches, one species). All but four of the species found in New Zealand are endemic to it, although only two of the genera are, and none of the families.

In contrast to New Zealand, the fish fauna of New Guinea is very similar to that of Australia, so that it might better be treated as a province of Australia rather than a subregion. New Guinea is divided in half by a mountain range, and the fish fauna reflects this division. The fauna of the southern half is nearly identical with that of northern Australia, while that of the northern half has a large number of species of its own (Whitley 1959).

Continental Drift and the Distribution of Freshwater Fishes   The advances in geophysics that have lead to the acceptance of the theory of plate tectonics and continental drift in recent years have permitted the solution of many perplexing zoogeographic problems. However, many of the families and species distribution patterns are still puzzling and await solution. Therefore, the following discussion, based in part on the papers of Cracraft (1974) and of Novacek and Marshall (1976), should be considered to be hypothetical.

About 200 million years ago, during the Triassic period, the continents were united as one land mass, Pangaea (Fig. 24.3). The freshwater fish fauna at this time was presumably made up of a mixture of chondrostean fishes (represented today by the paddlefishes and sturgeons),

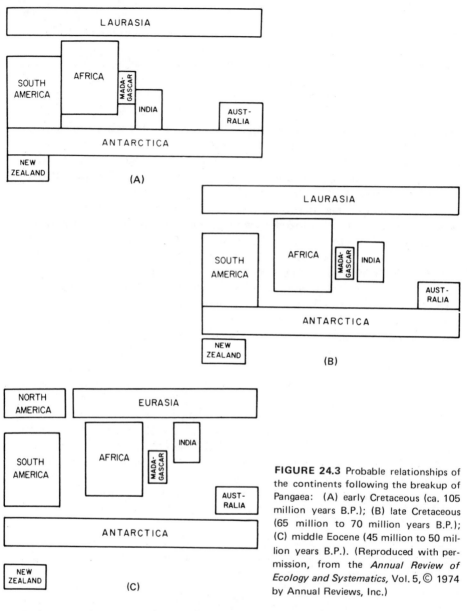

FIGURE 24.3 Probable relationships of the continents following the breakup of Pangaea: (A) early Cretaceous (ca. 105 million years B.P.); (B) late Cretaceous (65 million to 70 million years B.P.); (C) middle Eocene (45 million to 50 million years B.P.). (Reproduced with permission, from the *Annual Review of Ecology and Systematics,* Vol. 5, © 1974 by Annual Reviews, Inc.)

holostean fishes (represented today by bowfin [*Amia calva*], and the gars), lungfish, and crossopterygians. It is also possible that some early teleosts were present at this time, represented today by the osteoglossids, although teleost radiation is usually considered to have taken place in the Cretaceous. By the end of the Triassic (180 million years B.P.), Pangaea had split into two continents: Laurasia (the future North America and Eurasia), and Gondwanaland (the future South America, Africa, Antarctica, India, and Australia). In both areas the Pangaean fish fauna probably remained dominant until the Cretaceous period, when various modern freshwater fish groups started to develop. The modern descendants of the first of these groups to develop in Laurasia are the Esocidae (pikes), Umbridae (mudminnows), and Salmonidae (salmon and trout), as well as the exclusively North American families Percopsidae (trout-perches), Aphredoderidae (pirate perch), and Amblyopsidae (cavefishes). However, most of whatever distinctive teleost fauna developed in Laurasia appears to have been swamped by the ostariophysans invading from Gondwanaland and by the perciform groups that evolved somewhat later.

The Ostariophysi seem to have developed in Gondwanaland in the early Cretaceous, as the African and South American plates were well on their way to separation. Antarctica, Australia, India, and Madagascar had separated from Gondwanaland soon after Laurasia split off and so played no role in the early development of the Ostariophysi. Because the most ancestral-like ostariophysans are known from South America, it is likely that the early stages of their evolution took place on the South American half of Gondwanaland (but see Briggs [1979] for an alternate point of view). The early ostariophysan stock split initially into the characoids (Characoidei) and the catfishes (Siluroidei). Representatives of both lines managed to invade western Africa before the two continents finally separated, in the middle Cretaceous. South America then became an island continent, and its characoid fishes and catfishes diversified enormously into numerous endemic families. Africa, in contrast, made contact with the Eurasian portion of Laurasia at about the end of the Cretaceous period, permitting ostariophysans to enter Laurasia. Then, in the early Paleocene, the family Cyprinidae evolved, presumably from the characoid fishes, either in North Africa or in Europe. This family, together with the catfishes, spread throughout Laurasia and most of Africa. However, the advanced characins that had evolved in Africa managed to hold their own and diversify, as did the African catfishes, mormyrids, and other endemic groups.

During the early Cenozoic period, as the North American and Eurasian continents gradually separated from each other, the modern representatives of the holarctic fish fauna developed and spread: Cyprinidae, Catostomidae (suckers), and Percidae (perches).

Following (and during) the final separation of North America and Eurasia, endemic groups of fishes developed on both continents. In North America, the sunfishes (Centrarchidae), the catfishes (Ictaluridae), and the darters (subfamily Etheostominae of the Percidae) evolved. In Asia the advanced subfamilies of cyprinids developed, probably in the Oriental Region, along with the Cobitidae (loaches), Siluridae, and other ostariophysan families with more restricted distributions. Many of the families of freshwater dispersants endemic to Asia are found only in the Oriental Region, which gradually became separated from the rest of Asia following the rise of the Himalaya Mountains, which in turn seems to have been related to the collision of India with Asia in the late Eocene.

The Oriental fauna subsequently invaded India, replacing whatever indigenous families were present. There appear to have been some exchanges of fishes with Africa somewhat later, indicated by the broad distributional patterns of catfishes of the families Bagridae and Clariidae and perciform families like the Channidae and Mastacembelidae. In more recent times, the Cobitidae have managed to invade northern Africa and have a very limited distribution there.

Supplemental Readings

Banarescu 1975; Berg 1949; Briggs 1979; Bussing 1976; Cracraft 1974; Croizat 1958; Darlington 1957; Greenwood 1976; Hubbs and Lagler 1964; Jayaram 1974; Jenkins, Lachner, and Schwartz 1972; Knapp 1953; Kozhov 1963; Lake 1971; Lowe-McConnell 1975; McDowell and Whitaker 1975; Menon 1973; Miller 1958, 1966; Moyle 1976b; Munro 1967; Muus 1967; Myers 1938, 1951; Nelson 1976; Nichols 1943; Novacek and Marshall 1976; Rosen 1974, 1975b; Scott and Crossman 1973; Whitley 1959.

ααααααααααααααααααααααααααααααααααααααααααααααααααααααααααααααααααααααααααα
~~~~~~

Zoogeography of Marine Fishes

The zoogeography of marine fishes is much less well understood than that of freshwater fishes. Not only are there many more fishes spread over a much greater area, but there are fewer dramatic, seemingly permanent barriers to movement, such as mountain ranges, than are found on land. The distribution patterns of freshwater fishes can be broadly related to plate tectonics (continental drift) and drainage systems. For marine fishes, broad distribution patterns seem to be related in a good part to oceanographic features and to the positions of the continents. Because of the latter aspect (most marine fishes are shallow-water species), continental drift has undoubtedly played an important role in the distribution and evolution of marine fishes, but this role is poorly understood and so is rarely considered in what analyses exist of their distribution patterns (but see Rosen 1975b). Thus most discussions of marine zoogeography are largely descriptive in nature, dividing the marine world up into zoogeographic regions whose boundaries are often rather vague. Such boundaries are typically regions where oceanographic conditions, and consequently the fish fauna, change rather rapidly as the result of current patterns or the position of continental shelves and islands. Rarely are such boundaries complete barriers to fish movement, however, nor are they necessarily permanent features, so the designated zoogeographic regions are likely to be even more arbitrary than those found in fresh water. The two principal works in English on marine zoogeography are Ekman (1953) and Briggs (1974), and this chapter is based on these books. Unfortunately, neither work gives much attention to the role of plate tectonics in determining the distribution of marine life (see Hubbs 1974 and Rosen 1975a). This chapter will nevertheless briefly describe the major zoogeographic regions of the world ocean and discuss the kinds of fishes that occur in them. Following Briggs

351

(1974), we will first discuss the fishes of the continental shelves and ocean reefs, and then the fishes of the open sea and the deep sea.

Continental Shelves

The distribution of fishes on continental shelves can be related not only to the presence of continents and islands and the extent of the shelf surrounding them, but to annual temperature regimes and oceanic currents (Fig. 25.1). On the basis of temperature regimes it is possible to divide up the shelves into a wide tropical region around the equator, northern and southern temperate regions, and two polar regions. There are, of course, broad transition areas between adjacent regions, but particularly between the tropical and temperate waters (which, as a consequence, are frequently divided into warm temperate waters and cold temperate waters).

TROPICAL REGIONS   Nearly 40% of all known fish species occur in the shallow waters of the tropics. Most of these are associated with coral reefs (Chapter 34). Largely on the basis of the reef fishes, the tropical oceans can be divided into four large regions: (1) the Indo-Pacific Region; (2) the Eastern Pacific Region; (3) the Western Atlantic Region; and (4) the Eastern Atlantic Region. The regions are separated from one another either by continents or by vast areas of open ocean that are nearly impassable to shallow-water fishes. The northern and southern boundaries of these regions are roughly the 20°C isotherm for the coldest month of the year.

The **Indo-Pacific Region** contains by far the most diverse fish fauna of the four regions, presumably because the sheer size of the region has provided many opportunities for speciation. Most of the fishes belong to the same families that are characteristic of the other three regions as well, such as Muraenidae, Holocentridae, Scorpaenidae, Serranidae, Apogonidae, Carangidae, Lutjanidae, Mullidae, Chaetodontidae, Pomacentridae, Labridae, Scaridae, Blenniidae, Acanthuridae, and Tetraodontidae. However, a few small families are endemic to the region (Pegasidae, Silliginidae, Kraemeriidae, Siganidae, Plesiopidae). Despite the size of the region, the presence of many wide-ranging species (most have pelagic larvae) makes it fairly homogeneous. However, within the region there are areas with fish faunas distinctive enough so that Briggs (1974) has divided the region up into provinces. Four of these provinces are associated with groups of isolated oceanic islands (Lord Howe-Norfork, Hawaiian, Easter, and Marquesas) that have a fairly high degree of endemism in the fishes (20% to 40%), although this may only reflect the lack of study of many intervening island areas and the confused state of the taxonomy of many of the families. Other provinces that have been designated are sections of the coastline containing endemic species, but because the continental shelf in this region is essentially continuous from Australia, to the Malay Peninsula, to India, and down along the east coast of Africa (including Madagascar and the Commorro Islands)

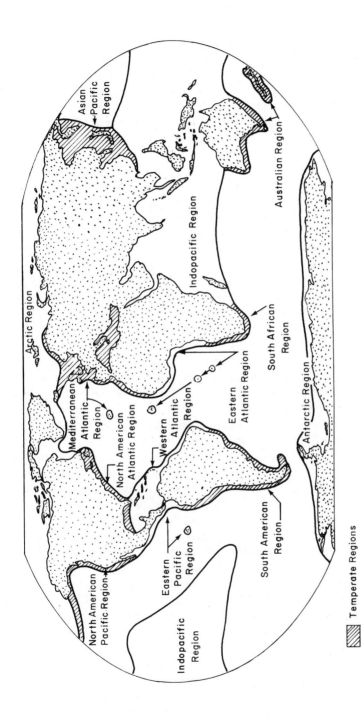

FIGURE 25.1 Major zoogeographic regions associated with continental shelves and islands. Boundaries between regions are not firm but are wide, shift seasonally, and contain elements from both adjoining faunas.

▨ Temperate Regions

353

to South Africa, much of the fish fauna is continuous as well. However, it should be pointed out that the fish fauna of the African coast is by no means identical with that of the Malay Peninsula, although there are no really abrupt breaks to separate one fauna from the other. Despite the lack of distinctness, there are two areas along this vast stretch of coast that are worth mentioning separately, the triangle bounded by the Phillipines, the Malay Peninsula and New Guinea, and the Red Sea.

The above "triangle" was recognized by Ekman (1953) as the Indo-Malayan Region because of the extraordinary richness of its fauna. Although there are few species unique to this area, the total number of species is higher than in any similar-sized area of the world, and many families seem to have the most representatives here. The Red Sea is of special interest partially because it is a semiisolated part of the region without a particularly high number of endemics (10% to 15% of the fish fauna) and partially because it is a participant in a great zoogeographic experiment. The other participant is the Mediterranean Sea, which has been connected to the Red Sea by the Suez Canal since 1869. The high salinity of the Bitter Lakes area of the canal originally was a barrier to the movement of fish between the two basins, but at the present time the salinity of the entire canal is close to that of the water at both ends (about 41 ppt). It is thus possible for fishes to move through the canal in either direction, although the length (160 km) of the canal, combined with its soft bottom and turbidity, undoubtedly have acted as a selective filter of species. The fish faunas of the two basins are quite distinct, that of the eastern Mediterranean being largely (250 of 290 species) the temperate fish fauna of the rest of the Mediterranean, while that of the Red Sea is the typical diverse Indo-Pacific fauna. As a result of the canal, at least 36 species of Red Sea fishes have immigrated to the Mediterranean Sea, where some of them have become established in very large numbers (Ben-Tuvia 1966, 1978). Only three fish species from the Mediterranean have managed to move into the Red Sea, although all three appear to be well established there (Ben-Tuvia 1978).

This mostly one-way dispersal seems to be related to the "poverty" of the Mediterranean fauna as compared to the Red Sea fauna, combined with the presumption that the temperate nature of the eastern Mediterranean fauna means they are less well adapted to tropical conditions and thus unable to compete successfully with Red Sea fishes (Ben-Tuvia 1966; Aron and Smith 1971). It has also been speculated that the surface currents of the canal may favor movement into the Mediterranean Sea of larval fishes (Norman and Greenwood 1975).

The **Eastern Pacific Region** is often referred to as the Panamanian Region, since the Pacific coast of Panama is central to a region that extends from Bahia Magdalena near the tip of Baja California (but including the Gulf of California as well) down to the Gulf of Guayquil on the coast of South America. The southern boundary of this region is only about $3°$ of latitude from the equator because the cold Humboldt Current from the Antarctic keeps tropical conditions at bay (most of the time). The northern boundary is not very definite, since there is considerable mixing of "temperate" and "tropical" species along the coasts of Baja California and southern California and in the Gulf of California. The Eastern Pacific Region is separated from the Indo-Pacific Region by a wide stretch of deep water and from the Western Atlantic Region by the isthmus of Panama. Most of the 800+ species therefore are confined to the region, although there are about 62 species in common with the Indo-Pacific Region and at least 12 in common with the Western Atlantic (Briggs 1974). Prior to the final closing of the Panamanian isthmus in the late Oligocene or early Miocene, the eastern Pacific and the western Atlantic had a common fish fauna (Rosen 1975b).

There are few offshore islands in the Eastern Pacific Region, but they include the fascinating Galapagos. The fish fauna is fairly rich (223 species according to Walker [1966]), with 23% of the species endemic, 54% found along the coast of Central America, and 12% of Indo-Pacific origin. The importance of Eastern Pacific Region fishes around the islands give support to the contention of Rosen (1975b) that the Galapagos have had connections to the mainland in the past.

The **Western Atlantic Region** includes the Atlantic and Gulf coasts of Central America and southern Mexico, the coast of South America to Cape Frio, the multitudinous islands of the West Indies, Bermuda, and the tip of Florida. Much of the fish fauna is associated with coral reefs and so is similar to the fish faunas of coral reefs elsewhere, at least superficially. It is interesting to note the many subtle differences that do exist, however. For example, in the Indo-Pacific Region the principal cleaner fishes are wrasses (Labridae), while in the Western Atlantic Region they are gobies (Gobiidae). Within the region, the species are mostly widely distributed, although there is enough endemism in some areas for Briggs (1974) to divide the region into provinces. However, three areas of particular interest to fish zoogeographers are not provinces as such: Bermuda, the Brazilian Coast, and the Panamanian coast.

Bermuda is a cluster of about 360 small islands that is of interest because it is the northernmost (32° latitude) bastion of tropical fishes. The tropical nature of its fauna is maintained by the warm Gulf Stream flowing up from Florida and the Gulf of Mexico. The Gulf Stream also helps to maintain a genetic connection of the fishes to their counterparts in the Caribbean, despite a separation of over 1400 km. Bermuda is a fairly ancient group of islands, but its fauna shows little sign of differentiation, presumably not only because of the present influence of the Gulf Stream but also because of its lack of influence during the Pleistocene (11,000 years B.P.), when presumably most of the tropical fauna of Bermuda disappeared as a result of lower water temperatures (Briggs 1974).

Along the coast of Brazil, the shallow-water coral reef fauna is missing for nearly 2900 km because of the influence of the Amazon,

Orinoco, and other rivers which decrease salinity, increase turbidity, and deposit large amounts of silt over a large area. In this stretch, typical reef fishes are replaced by fishes more characteristic of soft bottoms, such as sea catfishes (Ariidae) and croakers (Sciaenidae). The shallow-water reef fauna resumes as the influence of the rivers diminishes. This separation has resulted in a certain amount of endemism in the south Brazilian fauna, but the endemism seems to be most characteristic of shallow-water forms, since deep-water reefs are apparently still present along the entire coast. It is assumed that prior to the rise of the Andes, the influence of the rivers was not as strong in Atlantic coastal waters, so that shallow-water reefs could exist all along the coast (Briggs 1974).

The Panamanian coast is of interest not because the fauna is particularly unique, but because the proposed construction of the sea-level Panama Canal may create another giant zoogeographic experiment. Recent changes in world politics make this an increasingly unlikely event, but the discussion surrounding the proposal has provoked some interesting zoogeographic arguments. The present canal fairly effectively excludes the transfer of marine fishes between the two oceans because of the presence of a large freshwater lake (Gatun) in its center. Even so, 10 species of fish have managed to make it through in one direction or the other, although only one species (a goby, *Gobiosoma hildebrandi*) appears to have actually established populations on both sides (McCosker and Dawson 1975).

The **Eastern Atlantic Region** consists of the continental shelf along the west coast of Africa from Cape Verde to central Angola in the south, plus a few islands off the coast (Cape Verde Islands, St. Helena, Ascension). The northern boundary is rather arbitrary, but it does mark a region south of which temperate fishes are rare. It is the smallest and most isolated of the tropical regions and contains the fewest fish species. Presumably, one of the reasons for the comparative lack of faunal richness is the near absence of coral reefs. Briggs (1974) lists 434 shore fishes from the region, compared to 900 on the opposite side of the Atlantic. The main affinities of the fishes are to those of the Western Atlantic Region. Not only are there about 120 species in common, but many of the genera are the same as well. About 40% of the species are endemic, however, reflecting the area's isolation. Presumably, the Eastern and Western Atlantic Regions had a common fauna at the time Africa and South America were in the process of drifting apart and a much smaller Proto-Atlantic Ocean existed, which was less of a barrier to movement than the present ocean. However, one of the fascinating aspects of the Eastern Atlantic fish fauna is that it also includes about 32 species also found in the Indo-Pacific Region. Sixteen of these are found in all four regions, eight are also found in the western Atlantic, four are solely West African, and four are found only around the island of St. Helena. Presumably, such fishes have made it around the Cape of Good Hope at one time or another; the presence of four such species at

St. Helena is particularly indicative of this. The fish fauna of this island, although not rich (55 species), is curious for other reasons as well. It consists of a mixture of endemic species (18, including six shared with Ascension Island), circumtropical species, and species from all four major tropical regions (Briggs 1974). This fauna reflects the island's Miocene (?) origin as a volcano plus its strategic position in the central southern Atlantic where it can intercept fishes coming from various directions. The fish fauna of St. Helena points out nicely the interconnectedness of the fauna of the four regions. They share most of their families, many of their genera, and even a few species. The similarities of the faunas reflects largely the closeness of the continents during the time the tropical fish fauna was evolving; the differences reflect the considerable isolation of the faunas that now exists and has for some time, as well as the limited dispersal abilities of most of the fishes.

NORTH TEMPERATE REGIONS   Although the North Temperate Regions of the Atlantic and Pacific Oceans are marked on maps and generally broken up into a number of provinces or subregions, boundaries between them and the Arctic Region on the north and the Tropical Regions on the south are very hard to fix. The reason for this is that the change from one fauna to the next is rather gradual and the ranges of many species fluctuate from year to year depending on the vagaries of coastal currents. Some coastal features, such as Point Conception of the California coast, do mark rather sharp changes in the fish fauna, yet even in such situations there are typically more similarities than differences on the two sides of the boundary. However, distinctive faunas of temperate-water fishes do exist along long stretches of coast on both sides of the Atlantic and both sides of the Pacific. These four areas will therefore be treated as separate zoogeographic regions: (1) the Mediterranean–Atlantic Region; (2) the North American Atlantic Region; (3) the North American Pacific Region; and (4) the Asian–Pacific Region.

The **Mediterranean–Atlantic Region** consists of the Atlantic coast of Europe and North Africa, together with the Mediterranean, Black, and Caspian Seas. In the north it merges with the Arctic Region, while in the south it merges with the tropical Eastern Atlantic Region. Because the Gulf Stream swings south along the coast of Europe, forming the North Atlantic Current, comparatively warm water is usually present as far north as the British Isles. As a result, representatives of "tropical" families such as the Gobiidae (gobies), Labridae (wrasses), Mugilidae (mullets), Sparidae (porgies), Mullidae (goatfishes), and Scaridae (parrot-fishes) are common in the more southern portions of this region, including the Mediterranean Sea (Lythgoe and Lythgoe 1971). However, representatives of typically cold-water marine families, such as Gadidae (cods), Agonidae (poachers), Cottidae (sculpins), Pleuronectidae (right-eye flounders), and Cyclopteridae (snailfishes), are common throughout much of the region. Although many of the fish species and genera found in this region are endemic, none of the families are. Many of the species characteristic of the more northern areas are shared with the Arctic Region and the North American Atlantic Region, while a number of the southern species occur in tropical areas on both sides of the Atlantic. Although the gradual faunal changes characteristic of this region make provinces difficult to establish firmly, it is worth examining some of the more isolated components of the region: the Mediterranean Sea, the Black Sea, and the Baltic Sea.

The *Mediterranean Sea,* despite its apparent isolation, contains a fauna of 540 fish species that differs little from that of the Atlantic coasts of northern Africa and southern Europe. Indeed, 35% of the fish species found north of the Arctic Circle in Europe are also found in the Mediterranean (Lythgoe and Lythgoe 1971). However, the Mediterranean does possess a number of local endemic fishes, especially in the families Blenniidae, Gobiidae, and Labridae, as well as a distinctly tropical fauna in the eastern portion, a fauna currently being augmented by Red Sea fishes emigrating through the Suez Canal. The *Black Sea* has a complex history of connections with the Mediterranean and Caspian Seas, presumably with considerable fluctuations in salinity. At present its narrow connection with the Mediterranean, coupled with freshwater inflow from the Danube and other large rivers, gives it a salinity of 17 ppt to 18 ppt over much of its surface. This fish fauna (140 species) is mostly a depauperate Mediterranean fauna, with a few (33) endemic species and a few species (mostly gobies) shared with the Caspian Sea. The *Baltic Sea* is of interest because it is the largest estuary in the world, with salinities that gradually increase from the upper to the lower end. The salinity gradient, the shallowness of the sea, and the extreme temperature fluctuations it experiences greatly limit the Baltic Sea's capacity to support a diverse fish fauna, although it does contain a mixture of freshwater and marine species. The marine fishes are the same as those found in the North Atlantic, although some (such as the cod [*Gadus morhua*]) are considered to have distinct Baltic "races."

The **North American Atlantic Region** consists of the Atlantic coast of North America (excluding the tip of Florida with its distinctly tropical fauna) and the northern Gulf of Mexico. Because of the presence of "tropical" fishes from the Caribbean along the Gulf and southern Atlantic coasts, there have been many attempts to subdivide this region (Briggs 1974), but general lack of agreement among workers with different animal groups indicates the gradual nature of the change along the coasts. Usually, however, a boundary of some sort is made in the Cape Hatteras (North Carolina) area because the Gulf Stream tends to swing away from the coast in this area, permitting the cooler waters from the north to have greater influence. However, seasonal temperature fluctuations and vagaries in the flow of the Gulf Stream make even this boundary a tenuous one at best, especially for mobile fishes. Thus, the region between Cape Hatteras and Cape Cod contains many typically "southern" species in the summer, when water temperatures are high, but in the winter the dominant species are typical fishes of northern waters. These northern fishes include representatives of the same families as are found off northern Europe, such as the Gadidae (cods), Pleuronectidae (right-eye flounders), Cottidae (sculpins), Cyclopteridae (snail fishes), and Stichaeidae (pricklebacks), as well as diadromous members of the Anguillidae, Clupeidae, and Salmonidae. The fishes more characteristic of southern (warmer) waters include members of such families as Sciaendae (croakers), Sparidae (porgies), Serranidae (sea basses), Pomadasyidae (grunts) and Labridae (wrasses). However, even these families are widely distributed up and down the Atlantic coast, with some species more characteristic of northern than southern faunas. One of the factors complicating any discussion of the distributional patterns is the general decrease in the number of species toward the north. Thus, there are about 375 to 400 species along the gulf coast of Texas, perhaps 250 along the coast of South Carolina, 200 to 250 in the area south of Cape Cod, about 225 (130 shore fishes) in the Gulf of Maine, 61 along the Labrador coast, and 34 from Greenland (Briggs 1974). The figures for the middle three localities are somewhat deceptive, since 50% to 60% of the species recorded are warm-water species of sporadic or rare occurrence.

The **North American Pacific Region** extends along the Pacific coast from Baja California north to the end of the Aleutian Island chain. As in the North American Atlantic Region, there is a very gradual change from a tropical fauna, to a mixed tropical–temperate fauna, to a largely temperate fauna, to a mixed temperate–artic fauna. The region is extremely rich in fishes. At its southern end, most of the 800 or so species known from the Gulf of California (Thomson et al. 1979) can be expected at one time or another (although only about 220 have been recorded so far), but especially in years when the California current is not flowing strongly, so that the cool water from the Gulf of Alaska does not extend so far south. For the California coast, Miller and Lea (1972) list 554 species of which 439 should perhaps be considered continental shelf species. Along the Pacific coast of Canada, 325 species are known, of which perhaps 40 species belong in deepsea or pelagic regions rather than inshore. Further north the fauna merges with that of the Arctic Region and to the west with the Asian–Pacific Region. Briggs (1974) divides the region up into a number of provinces, but as Hubbs (1974) and Horn and Allen (1978) point out, there is so much intermixing of the northern and southern elements and so much year-to-year variation in distribution patterns that such provinces have limited usefulness.

However, there are many fascinating aspects of this fauna. It is extremely diverse, with 144 families being represented off California alone. Several of these families are found only in this region and in the Asian–Pacific Region, most prominently the Embiotocidae (viviparous perches, 23 species), Hexagrammidae (greenlings, 11 species), and

Anoplopomatidae (sablefish and skilfish). A number of other families have attained great diversity here, such as the Scorpaenidae, with 55 species in the genus *Sebastes* alone, the Salmonidae, which includes five species of Pacific salmon (*Oncorhynchus*), the Cottidae, with about 60 species, the Pleuronectidae, with 20 to 25 species, the Agonidae, with 20 to 25 species, and numerous species in various blennioid families (Stichaeidae, Blenniidae, Clinidae, etc.). Most of the species belonging to these families in the North American Pacific Region are endemic to the region, although there are many closely related species in the Asian-Pacific Region and a few species, such as the starry flounder (*Platichthys stellatus*), with wide distributions in both regions.

The **Asian-Pacific Region** extends roughly from Hong Kong north past the Kamchatka Peninsula. These boundaries are very arbitrary, however, since the warm Kuroshio Current brings a large number of Indo-Pacific Region species north to Japan, occasionally as far as the island of Hokkaido. Hong Kong marks the southern limit of many temperate species. However, the fishes of the coast of China (up to the Yellow Sea), of Formosa, and of southern Japan are predominantly tropical. For example, only 10% of the 924 species known from the southern Japanese island of Shikoku are found in northern Japan as well, although another 29% are more or less endemic to the area and many of the tropical species do not occur on a regular basis (Kamohara 1964). The Yellow Sea, although at about the same latitude as Shikoku, contains a more characteristically cool-water fauna, because the sea is not heavily influenced by the Kuroshio Current. Thus the main resident fishes are about 40 to 50 species of typical northern Pacific fishes (Cottidae, Hexagrammidae, Pleuronectidae, etc.), although at least 174 tropical species make sporadic appearances there (Briggs 1974). Further to the north, the fauna of the Okhotsk Sea is very similar to that of Canada and Alaska in terms of families and genera present (Schmidt 1950). Only a few of the 300 or so species in the Okhotsk Sea are shared with the North American Pacific Region. It is interesting to note also differences in the number of species in the dominant families. The sculpins (Cottidae), greenlings (Hexagrammidae), and right-eye flounders (Pleuronectidae) have about the same number of species on both sides, but there are only one species of surfperch (Embiotocidae) and six species of rockfish (*Sebastes*). On the other hand, eelpouts (Zoarcidae, about 35 species) and lumpsuckers (Cyclopteridae, 50 to 60 species) are very abundant. The entire northern Pacific coast of Asia is also considered to have been an important center of salmonid evolution, since not only do all five "North American" species of Pacific salmon (*Oncorhynchus*) occur here but three purely Asiatic species do as well.

To the north, the fauna of this region merges with that of the Arctic Region in the Bering Sea. Presumably, the Bering Sea serves as something of a barrier for exchange of inshore species between North America and Asia because of its essentially arctic temperature regime, although it has also apparently been dry when sea levels were lower during the Pleistocene.

ARCTIC REGION   The Arctic Region includes all the Arctic Ocean, the waters around Greenland, and the Bering Sea. The fishes are discussed in some detail in Chapter 37 and so will only be briefly mentioned here. There are probably fewer than 110 species that occur in the Arctic on a regular basis, most of them cold-tolerant species that also occur in the northern Atlantic or Pacific, in such families as the Cottidae, Cyclopteridae, Zoarcidae, and Pleuronectidae. About one half of the arctic species are largely confined to the Arctic Region, and most of these species are circumpolar, providing connecting links to the faunas of the northern Atlantic and northern Pacific.

SOUTH TEMPERATE REGIONS   Only three South Temperate Regions will be considered here: South American, South African, and Australian. Briggs (1974) and others tend to divide up these regions into provinces, mostly on the basis of differences in the faunas of the coasts that border on different oceans and Antarctic waters. However, despite differences in the faunas of the various coasts of the three continents, there is a great deal of faunal interconnectedness on each continent, making it possible to treat each as a unit. There are also many similarities in the faunas of the three continents, presumably the result of their connections by ocean currents and by their ancient existence as just one continent.

The **South American Region** extends from the coast of Peru around the tip of South America to about Rio de Janeiro on the Brazilian coast. The northern ends of this region merge gradually with the tropical faunas of their respective coasts, while the fauna of the tip of South America shows strong affinities to that of the Antarctic. The strong prevailing winds along the west coast are responsible for the far northward extent of this region along the coast; they also create immense upwelling along the coasts of Peru and Chile, making the anchoveta (*Engraulis ringens*) the most abundant harvestable fish in the world (see Chapter 35). Although many purely tropical fish families are represented along the west coast of South America, especially in the more northern areas, families typical of the southern areas of the North Temperate Regions are also abundant here: Engraulidae (anchovies), Clupeidae (herrings), Serranidae (sea basses), Carangidae (jacks), Pomadasyidae (grunts), Sciaenidae (croakers), and Scorpaenidae (rockfishes) (Hildebrand 1946). On the more southern portions of the coast, families such as the Gadidae (cods), Zoarcidae (eelpouts), Bovichthyidae, and Nototheniidae (plunderfishes) become well represented. There are a few small, peculiar families, such as the Normanichthyidae (with a single species apparently related to the Cottidae), the Aplodactylidae (otherwise found only in the Australian Region), the Cottunculidae (cottidlike fishes with species in the North Temperate Regions as well as the South African Region), Cheilodactylidae (found in the three South Temperate Regions and in the Asian Pacific Region), Latridae (otherwise known only from the Australian Region), and Congiopodidae (scorpaeniform fishes confined to the three regions and the Antarctic). The Cheilodactylidae and the Congiopodidae are found on the Pacific coast portion of this region as well, although the nature of the Pacific fauna is too poorly known to determine its complete similarity to the Atlantic fauna. The fish fauna of the tip of South America and Tierra del Fuego contains many notothenioid fishes, many of them endemic, and so bears a great resemblance to that of the Antarctic Region.

South African Region. Because of the combination of its more northward location and the presence of warm currents (the South Equatorial Current on the Pacific side, the Agulhas Current around the Cape of Good Hope, and the Benguela Current on the Atlantic Coast), the South African Region lacks most of the cold-water fish families characteristic of the South American Region, such as the Nototheniidae, Bovichthyidae (except one island species), Cyclopteridae, and Zoarcidae (Smith 1949). However, species in the latter two families do occur in deep water off the South African coast. Most of the region's fishes belong to widespread tropical families, although there are a number of endemic species, especially in the families Clinidae ("klipfishes," the most species-rich [28+] inshore family), Gobiidae, Blenniidae, Gobiesocidae, and Batrachoididae (Smith 1949). This region shares a number of distinct families with the Australian Region, such as the Pentacerotidae, Oplegnathidae (found also off Japan, Hawaii, and the Galapagos Islands!), Congiopodidae (racehorses), and Callorhynchidae (plownose chimaeras). The latter two families are also found in South America. However, many of the species and genera are endemic to the region, reflecting its long isolation.

Australian Region. Warm currents from the Indian and Pacific Oceans moderate the water temperatures along the southern half of Australia, from Shark Bay on the west to about Hervy Bay on the east, so that it is inhabited by a temperate fish fauna with a strong tropical element. Around Tasmania and the southern tip of Australia, as well as around much of New Zealand, the tropical element tends to drop out, and a more cold-water element comes in. Southern Australia, New Zealand, and small islands around New Zealand constitute the Australian Region. Along the coast of southern Australia, the pattern of fish distribution is indicated by the work of Scott (1962) on the fishes of the southern edge of the continent. He found that 101 of the 253 species discussed were characteristic of the entire Australian Region (and many lived in the Indo-Pacific Tropical Region as well). Another 114 species were endemic to the region between Shark Bay and Tasmania, although 72 of these species were not found in the colder waters around Tasmania. Thirty-eight species have a break in their distribution created by the cold water around the tip of Australia. This break has apparently also resulted in the evolution of a number of pairs of species, one on each side of the cold-water area. The exact composition of the fish fauna of Tasmania itself is poorly known, but besides the previously mentioned widely distributed species that occur here, there are a number of endemic forms, especially in the families Rajidae, Clinidae, Bovichthyidae, and Ostraciodontidae (Briggs 1974). Curiously enough, the fish fauna of Tasmania bears many resemblances to that of southern New Zealand, including the presence of the notothenioid fish family, Bovichthyidae. The fauna of northern New Zealand is more like that of southeastern Australia, with only about one fourth of the species being endemic.

ANTARCTIC REGION   The Antarctic Region, thanks to the stability of the antarctic convergence, is one of the most isolated marine regions. Most of the species are endemic and belong to four families in the suborder Notothenioidei (see Chapter 37). The remaining fishes are divided up among five families, one of which (Muraenolepididae) is an Antarctic family with representation on the tip of South America and two of which (Cyclopteridae and Zoarcidae) are widely distributed cold-water families also present in the Arctic.

Unlike the Arctic Region, however, the Antarctic Region does not connect the faunas of the surrounding continents, since it shares few species with them. Nevertheless, the fact that the South Temperate Regions share most of their fish families, many of their genera, and even a few species is a strong indication of their past connection as Gondwanaland. Presumably the more temperate elements died out in the Antarctic Region as the continent "drifted" into its present position while the cold-adapted notothenioid fishes (represented in the South Temperate Regions by the Bovichthyidae) speciated.

There have been many attempts made to divide the Antarctic Region into provinces, but as more and more collections are made, distributions of "provincial" forms are expanded and provincial borders become harder to justify.

Pelagic Regions   The Mesopelagic Zone and the offshore portions of the Epipelagic Zone (see Chapters 35 and 36) are inhabited by fishes that are, for the most part, not bound to the continents. Many of these species have a worldwide distribution (though many do not), yet they are still restricted in their distribution. Since the distribution patterns of species from many groups, vertebrate and invertebrate, that inhabit the open ocean often coincide, it is possible to divide the world ocean into pelagic regions. The boundaries between the regions are areas where oceanographic conditions, but particularly temperature, change more rapidly over wide areas than elsewhere in the ocean. Such regions of change, while they tend to fluctuate with season, are often coincident with isotherms and thus have latitudinal limits. For mesopelagic fishes, temperature boundaries may be less important determinants of distribution patterns than the location of oxygen minimum layers or regions of low productivity (e.g., see Johnson and Glodek 1975). Even so, mesopelagic regions are usually largely coincident with epipelagic regions. Most of the regions used here are widely recognized (Parin 1968; McGowan 1974; Briggs 1974; Backus et al. 1977): Arctic, Subarctic, North Temperate, North Subtropical, Tropical, South Subtropical, South Temperate, and Antarctic (Fig. 25.2).

The **Arctic Region** seems to contain no true pelagic fishes, although the cods of the genera *Arctogadus* and *Boreogadus* are associated with pack ice on a regular basis. Mesopelagic fishes are apparently of only irregular occurrence (Backus et al. 1977).

The **Subarctic Region** is, roughly, the area between the Arctic Region and the 8°C to 10°C isotherm. Its fish fauna differs considerably in the Atlantic and Pacific Oceans. In the Pacific, the dominant epipelagic piscivores are Pacific salmon (*Oncorhynchus* spp.), with a few odd forms such as pomfret (Bramidae: *Brama japonica*), skilfish (Anoplopomatidae: *Erilepis zonifer*), and the ragfish (Icosteidae: *Icosteus aenigmaticus*) joining in. When temperatures warm up a bit in the summer, many large predatory fishes from the North Subtropical Region may move into this region. This movement is perhaps even more marked in the Atlantic than the Pacific because of the lack of a well-developed endemic epipelagic fish fauna, although Atlantic salmon (*Salmo salar*) and pomfret (*Brama brama*) are widely distributed in the region. Backus et al. (1978) note that the mesopelagic community in this region is dominated by just one species of myctophid, *Benthosoma glaciale*.

The **North Temperate Region** is bordered on the south by the 14°C to 16°C isotherm. The dominant epipelagic fishes are such fish as tuna (*Thunnus alalunga*, Pacific; *T. thynnus*, Atlantic), swordfish (*Xiphia gladiator*), basking shark (*Cetorhinus maximus*), sauries (Scomberesociade), and opah (*Lampris regius*). They are joined in the summer months by many species, but especially scombrids, from the North Subtropical Region.

The **North Subtropical Region** and its counterpart to the south, the **South Subtropical Region**, are bounded by the 14°C to 16°C isotherm on one side and the 18°C to 20°C isotherm on the other. These regions are characterized by tunas, sauries, flying fish (especially *Hirundichthys rondeletii*), louvar (*Luvarus imperialis*), and marlins (*Tetrapturus*). In the Atlantic, Backus et al. (1977) note that 13 species of mesopelagic myctophids have their center of abundance in the two subtropical regions, and that 11 of these species are present in the two regions but missing from the Tropical Region in between. A similar antitropical pattern with many of the same species presumably exists in the Pacific as well. A unique feature of the North Subtropical Zone of the Atlantic is the Sargasso Sea, with its distinctive set of fishes associated with drifting *Sargassum* weed (Chapter 35). In both oceans during the sum-

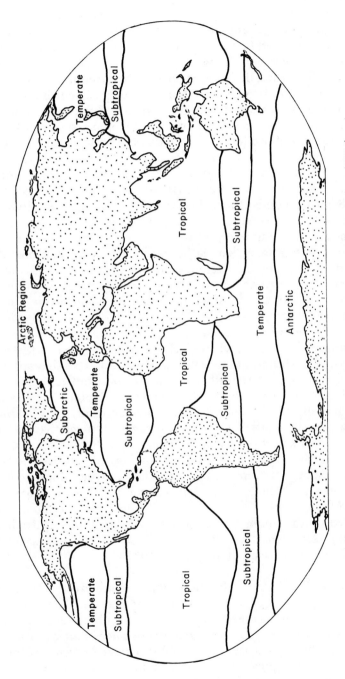

FIGURE 25.2 Major zoogeographic regions for pelagic fishes. [Based on Briggs (1974) and Backus et al. (1977).]

mer, virtually all the epipelagic fishes characteristic of the Tropical Region occur here as well.

The **Tropical Region** consists of a broad, worldwide belt of equatorial water that rarely drops below 20°C. Its limits in the various oceans correspond roughly to the limits of the tropical shelf regions. Much of the epipelagic fish fauna of this region has a worldwide distribution, although distinct differences do exist between the faunas of the Atlantic and Pacific/Indian Oceans. Since the epipelagic fishes do move into the subtropical regions during the summer, this region is perhaps better defined by the absence of many subtropical species of fishes than by its year-round residents. The characteristic species of the region are tropical flying fishes (such as *Exocoetus volitans* and *Hirundichthys speculiger*), scombrids (such as skipjack, *Katsuwomus pelamis*), tropical pelagic sharks, and various billfishes (Istiophoridae). The mesopelagic fish fauna is most abundant and diverse in this region, especially in the Pacific and Indian Oceans, and although the distribution patterns of most species are not completely known, it appears that many species of lanternfishes (Myctophidae), hatchetfishes (Sternoptychidae), and others are confined to the Tropical Region. Many of these species also appear to be endemic to one or the other of the oceans or areas with distinct oceanographic conditions, but at least as many have worldwide distribution patterns.

The **South Temperate Region** is marked on the north by the 14°C to 15°C summer isotherm (subtropical convergence) and in the south by the 3°C to 5°C isotherm (antarctic convergence). Its fish fauna is not as well studied as that of the other pelagic regions, but it shares many species and genera with the North Temperate Region. The lamnid sharks, the basking shark, sauries, pomfrets, scombrids, etc., belong to the same or closely related species. This region is a relatively narrow one and so shares many fishes with the Subtropical Region seasonally.

The **Antarctic Region** consists of the shallow waters that circle the antarctic continent. It is remarkable for its lack of true epipelagic fishes, except for a few coast-bound forms such as the antarctic herring (Nototheniidae: *Pleurogramma antarcticum*). The mesopelagic fauna is better developed, with a number of species in the families Myctophidae, Bathylagidae, Gonstomatidae, Paralepidae, and Scopelarchidae being largely confined to the region (Andriashev 1962).

Deepsea Regions

In the deep sea there are two ecological groups of fishes that tend to be confined to zoogeographic regions, the bathypelagic fishes and the deepsea benthic fishes. For both groups, a factor of great importance in their distribution patterns is that the greatest number of individuals and species are located in tropical and subtropical areas and that in all areas where they are found their abundance tends to be greatest near the continents. By and large, the bathypelagic fishes tend to be located in regions approximately equivalent to those described for epipelagic fishes. However, there are relatively few species with worldwide distribution patterns; most tend to be associated with specific ocean basins or water masses with distinctive salinities, temperatures, and dissolved oxygen levels. Genera nevertheless do tend to be widespread (e.g., see Pietsch 1974), and many cases of apparent endemism may be the result of the scarcity of bathypelagic samples (especially of rare species) or of the need for more complete taxonomic studies.

For the benthic species, those that inhabit the upper continental slope tend to fall into zoogeographic patterns like those for fishes of the continental shelf, although the greater uniformity of temperatures at great depths tends to make the fishes even less respectful of zoogeographic boundaries. In deeper water the dominant fish families are the Ophidiidae and Macrouridae, but in more polar waters the Zoarcidae and Cyclopteridae are usually more common. Despite their commonness, however, most species in these families are confined to single ocean basins; undersea mountain ranges and trenches seem to be barriers to dispersal. A few species do seem to have wide distributions, however. For example, the flatnose cod (*Antimora rostrata*) is found in deep water in the Atlantic, Pacific, and Indian Oceans (although the populations are often listed as separate species). In the deepwater family Chlorophthalmidae, there are 18 species of spider fishes (*Bathypterois*). Most of the species have fairly restricted distributions, but one, *B. atricolor,* is found in the tropical and subtropical regions throughout the world, except for the northeastern Atlantic (Sulak 1977). As the result of such distribution patterns, the distribution patterns of deepsea fishes can either be related to those of the pelagic regions (by using distributional patterns of families and genera) or be divided up on a basin-by-basin basis, using the distributional patterns of species.

Antitropical Distribution Patterns   One of the recurring patterns in marine zoogeography is the presence of species, genera, and families that are absent from the tropics but present in regions on both sides. These antitropical (or bipolar) patterns have been noted in such diverse families as hagfishes (Myxinidae), eelpouts (Zoarcidae), snailfishes (Cyclopteridae), and cods (Gadidae), in genera such as *Clupea* (herrings), *Engraulis* (anchovies), *Merluccius* (hakes), *Raja* (skates), and *Squalus* (dogfish sharks), and in species such as Atlantic pomfret (*Brama brama*), flying fishes (*Hirundichthys speculiger* and *Exocoetus volitans*), basking shark (*Cetorhinus maximus*), saury (*Scomberesox saurus*), and lanternfishes (e.g., *Loweina interrupta* and *Lampanyctus pusillus*). Almost all species with antitropical distributions are pelagic, so it is likely that their distribution patterns are the result of movements across the tropical regions. However, many of the families or genera are bottom-oriented or shallow-water forms, which are not likely to move over long distances as pelagic forms. Further, the general lack of antitropical species of this sort indicates that the events leading to the present distribution pattern were fairly ancient.

Four theories have been advanced to explain the antitropical distribution patterns: (1) lower sea temperatures in the tropics in the past may have permitted the passage of cool-water fishes; (2) the cool-water fishes may have moved through deep water of suitable temperatures, thus avoiding the warm surface waters; (3) the fishes with antitropical distributions may once have been present in the tropics as well but were displaced through competition with more advanced groups; and (4) the distribution pattern may be the result of continental drift. The first theory, although having been favored by many zoogeographers (e.g., Hubbs 1974), seems to have little evidence to support it, since it would require a worldwide decline in sea temperatures that would presumably have had a disastrous impact on the tropical faunas. The second theory may explain the patterns of some antitropical genera of the subtropical and temperate regions, but it is applied with difficulty to explain the presence of families such as the Zoarcidae and Cyclopteridae at the two poles (Ekman 1953). The difficulty arises from the very lack of family representatives in the deep waters of intermediate regions, since presumably, if such water was suitable for migration, it should also be suitable as a permanent place to live. The third theory is favored by Briggs (1974), although there is little direct evidence to support such drastic effects of competitive interactions among species that presumably coevolved. If there were once species of eelpouts and snailfishes adapted to oceanographic conditions of the tropics, it is not unreasonable to expect relict populations in a few localities. As indicated at the beginning of this chapter, the role of continental drift in determining the present distribution of marine fishes is poorly understood. It seems very likely, however, given the fact that families such as the Zoarcidae and Cyclopteridae are closely tied to continents, that it will prove to be of major importance and help to explain many of the distributional anomalies that now exist. Applying what has been learned about plate tectonics and sea floor spreading to the distribution of marine organisms is therefore one of the major challenges of the marine zoogeographer.

Supplemental Readings   Backus et al. 1977; Briggs 1974; Ekman 1953; McGowan 1974; Parin 1968; Schmidt 1950.

ααααααααααααααααααααααααααααααααααααααααααααααααααααααααααααααααα
~~~~~~

Taxonomy and Speciation

For as long as humans have had language, they probably have tried to create some order out of the complexity of nature by naming animals and plants. In societies prior to our own, the "folk taxonomies" that developed contained 250 to 800 kinds of animals (Raven et al. 1971). Most of these kinds would probably be recognized today as species or genera. In the fifteenth century the invention of printing and the beginnings of world exploration by Europeans made the expansion of taxonomy both possible and inevitable. A number of attempts at classification of animals were subsequently made, but all were limited in scope until Linnaeus introduced his binomial system of nomenclature in the eighteenth century. Linnaeus recognized species as being the basic unit of nature. Each species was considered to be an immutable entity, descended, presumably, from the original pair created by God. This meant that it was necessary to describe only one individual to describe an entire species. While this practice worked most of the time, Linnaeus and his successors did encounter natural variation within species and were forced to recognize "varieties." Today, taxonomists recognize and try to account for the tremendous amount of variation that usually exists within each species, yet the basic Procrustean bed upon which this variation is placed is still the Linnaean system of binomial nomenclature. It is used because it is a very convenient and comprehensible way of labeling the kaleidoscopic population phenomena we now understand species to be.[1] Actually,

---

[1] A good modern definition of a species is that of Dobzhansky et al. (1977): "Mendelian populations, or arrays of Mendelian populations, between which the gene exchange is limited or prevented by reproductive isolating mechanisms" (p. 171). A perhaps more inclusive definition, however, is that of Wiley (1978): "A species is a lineage of ancestral descendant populations which maintains its identity from other such lineages and which has its own evolutionary tendencies and historical fate" (p. 18).

the Linnaean system seems to be at its best when applied to vertebrates, although it increasingly appears to be totally inadequate for the 10 million or so species of plants and invertebrates, most of them still undescribed (Raven et al. 1971). Even for vertebrates, and particularly for fishes, there are many problems associated with attempts to pigeon-hole all forms into Linnaean species. These problems are the subject of this chapter, which will deal first with traditional fish taxonomy and its names and methodology, and then with the speciation of fishes.

Taxonomy

Taxonomy is the science (some would say, the art) of classification of organisms. Taxonomists are concerned not only with the description of new forms (mostly species) but also with the placing of each form within a taxo-nomic system that shows its relationships to other forms. Taxonomic systems are hierarchical: Individuals are grouped into populations (called subspecies if geographically isolated and morphologically different from other similar populations), populations into species, species into genera, genera into families, and so on up to the kingdom Animalia. Today, such systems are supposed to reflect phylogeny; species belonging to the same genus presumably had a common ancestral population in the not too distant geological past and so share more characteristics with each other than with species of different genera placed in the same family. A similar relationship exists among families within orders, among orders within superorders, among superorders within classes, and so on. The understanding of such relationships permits phylogenetic trees, such as those in Chapters 1 and 12, to be constructed. However, the further one proceeds down such a tree, away from species, the more arbitrary the divisions become. Each point of branching is largely the result of decisions by taxonomists to designate a certain degree of differentiation (usually carefully defined) as the point where branching occurs, despite that such differentiation takes place very gradually over long periods of time (but see Balon 1980) and that intermediate forms between two taxa may exist, either in the modern fauna or in the fossil record. Because of the arbitrary nature of the branchings and the even more arbitrary ranks assigned the branchings, it is not surprising to find that there is considerable controversy as to what constitutes many taxa, especially at the higher levels. Various attempts have been made to find ways to make the decisions less arbitrary, one of the latest being the cladistics of Hennig (1966), which has proven to be particularly useful to ichthyologists (Nelson 1972a). Hennig's methods have been vigorously attacked by other systematists (see, for example, Mayr 1976 and Szalay 1977), and the result has been a general reexamination of phylogenetic relationships, especially among fishes. This controversy will not be discussed here, but anyone interested in taxonomy should examine at least the above works or read discussions of the ideas in such general works as Dobzhansky et al. (1977).

NAMES OF FISHES   Each species of fish has a scientific (binomial) name and, usually, a common name as well. Examination of the origins and meanings of the names is fascinating because it can reveal not only something about the species but also about the people who named them.

Common names are highly variable, changing from language to language and, within a country, from region to region. For example, *Oncorhynchus tshawytscha* is known as king salmon, chinook salmon, tyee, and quinnaut salmon depending on where you happen to catch one. In North America many common names are anglicized versions of Indian names: chinook, crappie, sockeye. However, most are descriptive of the fish itself or of the region in which it is found: Mississippi silverside, bluegill, redear sunfish, golden shiner, sarcastic fringehead. Many of the descriptive names have been tacked onto the names of similar fishes that occur in Great Britain: speckled dace, creek chub, yellow perch, rainbow trout, Pacific sardine. One of the oddest names is Dolly Varden (*Salvelinus malma*), which is the name of a dowdy character in Charles Dickens' novel *Barnaby Rudge.* In the 1870s there was a popular fishery for Dolly Varden (then known as calico trout) in the McCloud River, California, and the fishermen started calling it Dolly Varden after a bright fabric popular in women's dresses at the time (which was named for the Dickens character). The famed ichthyologist David S. Jordan started using the name, and it soon became widespread (Moyle 1976a). In North America the American Fisheries Society initiated a highly successful effort to standardize the common names of fishes and publishes a list that is updated every ten years (Bailey et al. 1970).

Scientific names of fishes have two purposes: to provide names that will be recognized all over the world and to provide names that say something about the relationships of the species to each other. Each name has two parts: the genus name, which is always capitalized, and the trivial name (species epithet), which is not capitalized. The two names *together* constitute the species name (i.e., *Salmo trutta* is the species name, *not* just *trutta*). The meanings of scientific names of fishes fall into seven basic categories: descriptive names, place names, names of people, Latinized common names, whimsical names, and nonsense names.

A majority of scientific names have important characteristics of the species encoded in them. For example, the Sacramento blackfish is *Orthodon microlepidotus,* meaning "straight tooth" (referring to the pharyngeal teeth) and "small scale" (referring to the 90 to 105 scales in the lateral line). Similarly, the logperch is *Percina caprodes,* meaning "small perch" and "piglike" (referring to its blunt snout). Some of the older names have perpetuated taxonomic errors: The genus name *Micropterus* means "small fin" because the specimen used by Lacépède for his species description had a deformed dorsal fin which was divided into two parts, one of them very small; *Notropis* means "keeled back" because the minnows used by Rafinesque to erect this genus were partially dried out, creating a false keel on their backs.

Two other common types of scientific names are those after places and people. For example, *Gibbonsia montereyensis* is named after Dr. W. P. Gibbons, an early California naturalist, and Monterey Bay, where the species (crevice kelpfish) is common. Usually, the individuals whose names the fish bear are either prominent ichthyologists or individuals associated with the discovery of the species. Especially influential ichthyologists such as C. L. Hubbs and D. S. Jordan have numerous species and even families and genera named for them (*Jordanella, Carlhubbsia*).

Less common than the above three types of names are those that are Latinized versions of vernacular names and those that are whimsical or nonsense names. Among the best known names in the vernacular category are the trivial names given by the German naturalist J. J. Walbaum to the Pacific salmons. These names are his versions of the names used by the natives of the Kamchatka Peninsula of Russia: *Oncorhynchus* (meaning hooked snout) *tshawytscha, nerka, gorbuscha, keta, kisutch.* Whimsical names include *Satan* for a cave-dwelling catfish genus and *Gambusia* for the small mosquitofish. *Gambusia* is derived from a Cuban vernacular term, used by fishermen in the time of the naturalist Poey, to indicate they had caught nothing ("I fished for gambusinos today"). Nonsense names, or at least names of which no one can currently make sense, include *Lucania* and *Morone.*

TAXONOMIC METHODS   When a new species is described, a *holotype* is designated. True to the Linnaean concept of species, a holotype is a single fish that represents the entire species (and is consequently stored in a special vault in a major museum!). Modern taxonomists, in recognition of variation, usually also designate a number of *paratypes,* additional fish used in the species description and often distributed to museums other than the one possessing the holotype. Sometimes the describer of a species does not designate a holotype or paratype, so all the fish used in the description are labeled as *syntypes* or *cotypes.* If necessary, a single specimen may be designated by someone else to function as a holotype but is termed a *lectotype.* While such specimens are important for defining species, even more important are careful and comparative descriptions published in widely circulated and carefully reviewed scientific journals. This was not always the case. Nineteenth-century ichthyologists such as Charles Girard or David S. Jordan and their coworkers described large numbers of species from diverse groups in papers that devoted only a short paragraph to each species. Since many of these descriptions were incomplete, modern workers have found the old holotypes (if they still exist) invaluable for determining what name belongs to what species and for revising various taxa. Although modern taxonomists must be much more thorough than their

CH. 26 TAXONOMY AND SPECIATION

predecessors, they also have better tools available to them. Foremost among these tools is the computer, which permits complex multivariate analyses of large amounts of data. Of course, an analysis can only be as good as the data used (the Garbage In–Garbage Out Rule), and modern taxonomists gather these data using both old and new techniques: (1) morphometric measurements and ratios; (2) meristic counts; (3) anatomical characteristics; (4) color patterns; (5) karyotypes; (6) electrophoresis; and (7) tests of reproductive isolation.

Morphometric measurements are any standard measurements that can be made on a fish, such as standard length, snout length, length of longest ray on the dorsal fin, or depth of caudal peduncle. The best instructions for making these measurements are found in Hubbs and Lagler (1964). Since these measurements change as a fish grows, they are usually expressed as ratios to standard length (or some other measurement that is easily made). Even such ratios, however, are most useful if comparisons are made between samples of fish of approximately the same size and sex, since the growth of a fish is not always proportional in all directions, and sexual dimorphism is common among fishes (but often not obvious). Comparisons of ratios also present some statistical difficulties (Atchley et al. 1976). Thus morphometric measurements, while vital for describing fish species, are by themselves of limited usefulness.

Meristic counts are generally considered to be the most reliable taxonomic characteristics because most are easy to make. Meristic counts include anything on a fish that can be counted, such as vertebrae, fin rays and spines, scale rows, pyloric ceca, and lateral line pores. Since there is often considerable variation in these characteristics within a species, it is important to make the counts on enough individuals so means, ranges, and standard errors can be determined, especially if the fishes involved are to be compared with other populations. It should be pointed out that one of the biggest sources of variation in meristic counts is human error, especially on small fish. Such error is reduced if standard methods, such as those in Hubbs and Lagler (1964), are used. Another source of variation is the conditions under which larval fish develop. Any factor, such as temperature, dissolved oxygen concentration, salinity, or food availability, that affects larval growth is likely to affect meristic characters (Barlow 1961; Lindsey and Harrington 1972; Johnson and Barnett 1975).

Anatomical characteristics are hard to quantify but are nevertheless important for species descriptions. They include such things as shape, completeness, and position of the lateral line, position and size of internal organs, special anatomical features (such as air-breathing and electric organs), secondary sexual characteristics (such as breeding tubercles on males), and the shapes, sizes, positions, and interrelationships of bones and muscles. Most of these are yes–no characteristics; either a fish has them or it does not. As a consequence they can be definitive characteristics, useful for separating not only species but also higher taxa. However, even these characteristics are not always absolute, since occasionally individuals of a species are found that possess characteristics supposedly definitive for another, closely related species. Thus, basibranchial teeth, usually a reliable feature for separating cutthroat trout from rainbow trout, are rarely found in "good" rainbow trout and are occasionally absent from "good" cutthroat trout.

Color patterns are perhaps the most variable characteristics of species, since they may change with age, time of day, or the environment in which a fish is found. Nevertheless, they should be an important part of every species description, since color patterns are species specific, reflecting such aspects of its biology as habitat, reproductive condition, sex, and methods of communicating with conspecifics (Chapter 11). The main problem with using color as a taxonomic tool is that it tends to fade in preservatives and descriptions of living fish tend to be highly subjective.

Karyotypes are descriptions of the number and morphology of chromosomes. The number of chromosomes per cell seems to be a rather conservative characteristic and so may be used as an indicator of the closeness of species interrelationships within families. The number and position of arms of chromosomes is even more conservative than chromosome number and is often equally useful in taxonomic studies. Thus, in the course of an evolutionary change, two one-armed (acrocentric) chromosomes may fuse into a single two-armed (metacentric) chromosome, decreasing the chromosome number but not the number of arms. This is called Robertsonian fusion. Fission of chromosomes, increasing their number, may also occur very rarely. Another way chromosome number may increase is through polyploidy, which is the result of the failure of an entire set of chromosome pairs in a diploid cell to separate. The production of diploid gametes by this method is infrequent, but common enough so that triploid and tetraploid individuals may result (Ohno 1974). Triploidy has been shown to be of significance in the origin of certain unisexual "species" of poeciliid fishes in Mexico (Thibault 1978; see also Chapter 22). Tetraploidy, if the reasoning of Ohno (1974) is correct, may have been very important in the evolution of species and hence an important taxonomic indicator. For example, carp, goldfish, and barbel all have approximately double the number of chromosome arms of other cyprinids, as do all members of the derivative family Catostomidae (Uyeno and Smith 1972, Ohno 1974), indicating that tetraploidy may have played an important role in the early evolution of these successful species. Similarly, salmon, trout, whitefish, and graylings (Salmonidae) all have double the number of chromosome arms of the smelts (Osmeridae), a more ancestral member of the order Salmoniformes. The usefulness of karyotypes in salmonid taxonomy is discussed by Behnke (1970).

Another useful technique, related to karyotyping, is the measurement of the amount of DNA per cell. Curiously, within phylogenetic lines, the amount of DNA tends to decrease from more generalized to more specialized species (Hinegardner and Rosen 1972). This is thought to be the result of the loss of "extra" DNA by forms that have achieved their success through extreme specialization. In contrast, more generalized species have populations that are continually adapting to local conditions and retain DNA that can be subjected to the selection process.

Electrophoresis is a technique useful for evaluating the protein (mostly enzyme) similarities of species. In this technique a tissue sample is treated mechanically to disrupt the membrane structure of the cells, thereby releasing water-soluble protein. The resulting solution is placed in a gel, usually made of starch or agar, which is then subjected to an electric current. Each protein migrates in response to the current at a rate that depends on its molecular size and electric charge. The proteins can then be identified, and the genetic similarity of individuals and species can be compared by noting the presence and absence of proteins as well as differences in their position in the gels. A slight difference in the molecular structure of a protein can result in its having a different net charge and hence a different position in the gel. The number of such differences encountered between two samples is considered to be an index of genetic similarity and, if the samples involve different species, of the closeness of their evolutionary relationship (Fig. 26.1). Electrophoresis has proved to be particularly valuable for examining the genetic variation *within* populations. Its use in taxonomy has really just begun, and so far most studies in which it has been used have largely confirmed conclusions reached by more traditional methods. However, often the results are used effectively to quantify relationships in a way difficult with other methods (e.g., Ferris and Whitt 1978). Despite the enthusiasm with which electrophoresis has been used for taxonomic and evolutionary studies, it has a serious weakness in that proteins can differ from each other in structure and still appear the same on the gels (Johnson 1977). The reason for this is that proteins may change in shape and other properties without necessarily changing their net charge. Thus much of the variation between samples may not be detectable by standard electrophoretic techniques. More sophisticated techniques may uncover much of this "hidden" variability (Johnson 1977), but when the complexity of the electrophoretic process is greatly increased, its attractiveness as a handy taxonomic tool is greatly decreased.

REPRODUCTIVE ISOLATION   Reproductive isolation is central to most modern definitions of species, yet only rarely are tests of its existence part of a species description. Usually it is inferred, either from the geographic isolation of the species in question or from reasoning (in a somewhat circular manner) that a population that is morphologically

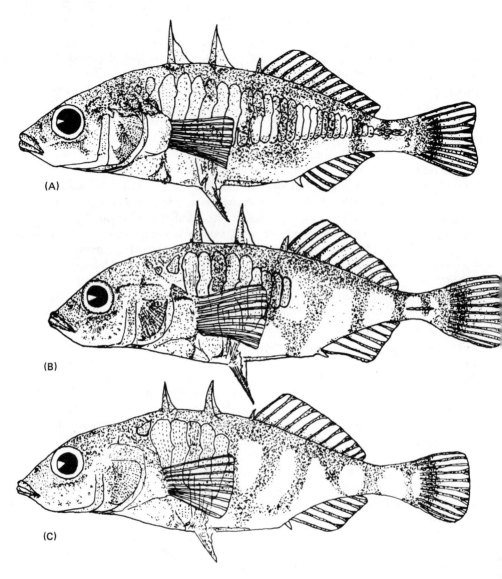

FIGURE 26.1 Threespine sticklebacks from the Pajaro River drainage, California, with (A) high, (B) intermediate, and (C) low counts of lateral bony plates. (Drawing by J. J. Smith.)

distinct from other populations must be reproductively isolated from them.[2] In order to see whether reproductive isolation in fact exists, many possibilities must be examined, including (1) geographic isolation; (2) habitat isolation; (3) temporal isolation; (4) ethological isolation; (5) gametic isolation; and (6) hybridization.

---

[2] However, Endler (1977) argues that complete isolation may not be necessary.

Geographic isolation is the most frequently cited evidence of reproductive isolation, and distribution maps are consequently important parts of most modern descriptions of fish species. Obviously, two populations of fish separated by a range of mountains will not be able to exchange genes. However, the geographic isolation that we observe may be very recent in origin and temporary in nature; streams erode mountain ridges, ocean currents change their flow patterns, and earthquakes cause major alterations of land and seascapes. Early taxonomists often described similar fishes in separate drainage systems as distinct species on the basis of minor morphological differences mostly because the forms were physically isolated from one another. Many of these forms are now recognized as being, at best, subspecies. Thus geographic isolation by itself is of little value as a test for species. In fact, the most reliable criteria are those that follow, since they apply when two populations are in contact with each other.

Habitat isolation occurs when two forms are found in the same geographic area but rarely meet because of different habitat preferences (which often reflect, in fishes, physiological differences). Thus, in California, hitch (*Lavinia exilicauda*) and California roach (*L. symmetricus*) are interfertile yet rarely hybridize because hitch prefer rivers and lakes, while roach prefer small streams (Avise et al. 1975). Similarly, one of the arguments for maintaining cutthroat trout (*Salmo clarki*) and rainbow trout (*S. gairdneri*) as separate species, even though they freely hybridize in interior basins (into which rainbow trout have been introduced), is that in coastal streams (where the species occur together naturally) cutthroat trout are found mainly in small tributary streams while the rainbow trout are found more in the larger main streams (Hartman and Gill 1968).

Temporal isolation occurs when two populations use the same habitat or area but rarely come in contact either because they are present at different times of the year or because they spawn at different times. It is not unusual for coastal streams to support several distinct populations of anadromous salmon, trout, or shad of the same species with each population maintaining its genetic integrity by spawning at a different time of year or by spawning in different years. For example, pink salmon (*Oncorhynchus gorbuscha*) have a two-year life cycle, so the fish present in streams during even and odd years are isolated from each other and consequently differ from each other genetically (Aspinwall 1974). Such populations can be distinguished from each other biochemically or morphologically and, given the right conditions, could presumably evolve into distinct species.

Ethological isolation occurs when two similar forms occur together but do not properly respond to each other's behavioral signals, especially in sexual behavior, and so remain unable to mate and hence reproductively isolated. It is likely that in areas where "flocks" of species of the same genus occur together, such as in the cichlid fishes of tropical lakes or the darters of North American streams, species-specific behavior patterns may be the principal means by which the species maintain their identities.

Gametic isolation, the situation in which mating between two species occurs but fertilization does not, seems rare in fishes, although it is a means by which all female "species" of poeciliid fishes are maintained (see Chapter 22). However, its apparent rarity may be mostly a function of its difficulty to document.

Hybridization between recognized taxa is very common in fishes, especially freshwater fishes (Hubbs 1955; Schwartz 1972). However, the mere fact that members of two species can mate with each other and produce offspring does not mean they belong to the same population or even that they are not reproductively isolated from each other. The important test of the significance of hybridization between two populations is whether or not under *natural conditions* significant gene flow between them occurs, resulting in introgression of characters and, eventually, a continuum of forms from one population to the next. Many species of fishes will freely interbreed in captivity, producing fertile hybrids that will backcross with either parent species; many varieties of aquarium fishes are the result of such hybridization between species. Some of the best examples of this are in swordtails (Poeciliidae: *Xiphophorus*), which rarely, if ever, hybridize in the wild. Even when hybridization between fish species does occur in the wild, reproductive isolation is usually maintained because the hybrids either are unviable, are sterile, or have low survival and/or fertility.

Hybrids are considered to be unviable if they invariably die before reaching sexual maturity. Since most hybrid fish collected in the wild at least seem capable of attaining sexual maturity, examples of hybrid unviability come mostly from laboratory studies. It has been demonstrated, for example, that most crosses between genera in the family Centrarchidae are unviable because the zygotes usually fail to develop normally (Hester 1970).

Hybrid sterility, in which the hybrids develop to adulthood but prove to be sterile, seems to be fairly common in fishes. Among the best known examples are crosses among species of the genus *Lepomis* (Centrarchidae), especially the bluegill-green sunfish cross (*L. macrochirus* X *cyanellus*). This hybrid is common where the two species occur together and results mostly from male green sunfish sneaking into bluegill nests and releasing sperm when a pair of bluegill is spawning. The hybrids that result are all male and exhibit hybrid vigor (heterosis) in that they typically grow faster than either parent species. During the spawning season they build nests and defend them with great vigor, dominating the nonhybrid fish. However, such fish are sterile, so no introgression occurs between the two species.

Hybrids that are fertile typically have low survival rates and poor success at reproduction. The reasons for this are complex but are presumably related in part to their intermediate nature. In most cases the two parent species have a competitive advantage over the hybrids in occupying their respective niches. Hybrids are likely to be successful only when environmental conditions are intermediate. Thus, hybrids between two darters (*Percina*) are abundant only in stretches of stream that have been altered by humans, creating an intermediate type of habitat (Loos and Woolcott 1969). A similar situation exists naturally in the Pajaro River of California, where California roach and hitch hybridize in some areas. There is even evidence of introgression within the hybrid zones, yet outside the zones the two species maintain their genetic identities (Avise et al. 1975).

In situations such as those mentioned in the preceding paragraph, hybridization seems to be the result of deliberate matings between members of two species. However, it is much more common among fishes for the matings to be accidental, the result of sex products becoming mixed when two species spawn in the same area at the same time. For example, Tsai and Zeisel (1969) found that hybrids among three species of cyprinids were common in a small stream because all three species spawned simultaneously on the gravel nest mound of yet another species.

Speciation

The preceding discussion on reproductive isolation and hybridization indicates how fish species maintain their identities. An equally interesting question is, How did the various species evolve? This is a surprisingly difficult question to answer, since how and when speciation occurred usually has to be inferred from taxonomic data, distribution patterns, and the fossil record. In most cases it is assumed that the factor most important for species formation is geographic isolation of a population from related populations for a long period of time. In isolation, different selection pressures, combined with intrinsic factors such as size and makeup of the gene pool of the isolated population, result in divergence. A population that had its origin in a small number of individuals that had become isolated from the main population may show differences that result from the unique genetic makeup of the "founding" organisms. (This is called the founder effect.) Given sufficient time, this divergence will continue until the population is able to retain its genetic identity even after it comes into contact again with other, similarly derived populations, even if some hybridization occurs. For example, Nelson (1968) found that two species of suckers, *Catostomus macrocheilus* and *C. commersoni,* evolved from a common ancestral population during the Pleistocene, after advancing glaciers isolated one portion of the population in the Columbia River drainage and the other in the eastern United States. In recent years *C. commersoni* has, by natural means, entered the range of *C. macrocheilus.* The two species hybridize, but there appears to be little gene flow between them, even though they are ecologically and reproductively still quite similar. In situations such as the above, given enough time and continued lack of backcrossing, the two species can be expected to continue to diverge ecologically in the region of overlap, exaggerating whatever adaptive differences in morphology and behavior now exist (*character displacement*). Character displacement over long periods of time is presumably one of the main reasons for the extraordinary number of specializations observed in the cichlid fishes of the ancient rift lakes of Africa (see Chapter 30). These cichlids are bottom-oriented, have complicated courtship rituals, and have a high degree of parental care. The young seem to become imprinted on the habitat of their parents and so do not enter unfamiliar habitats. Thus a long stretch of sandy beach or swamp between two rocky points may serve as an effective barrier to gene exchange between closely related populations confined to the points (Fryer and Iles 1972). On the rare occasions when fish from one point (probably a female carrying young in her mouth) manage to make it to another point, long-term persistence of their gene pool presumably depends upon further specialization through character displacement. Although this scenario of character displacement in cichlid fishes is a very attractive one, it should be pointed out that other hypotheses, such as character divergence before sympatry, may also explain the facts both here and in other situations in which character displacement is invoked as a cause of observed differences between species. As Grant (1972) points out, unequivocal examples of character displacement are very rare, despite the wide acceptance of the phenomenon as an important evolutionary process. However, Bell (1976b) does demonstrate that it can indeed occur in fishes.

One of the interesting questions associated with allopatric (geographic) speciation is how long a population must be isolated physically before it achieves species status. This depends on many factors, such as the kind of fish, the nature of the environment, the number of generations per year, and the conservatism of the taxonomist who has described the species. One of the shortest times on record seems to be the less than 4000 years it has been estimated that the Cottonball Marsh pupfish (*Cyprinodon milleri*) has been isolated from the Salt Creek pupfish (*C. salinus*) in Death Valley. Similarly, Moodie and Reimchen (1976) indicate that populations of sticklebacks (*Gasterosteus*) on islands off the British Columbia coast have diverged to the species level in 8000 to 10,000 years. More usual estimates for the amount of time required for adaptive differentiation of fish to have reached the species level are between 100,000 and several million years (e.g., Avise et al. 1975).

While allopatric speciation offers the best explanation for most speciation events that have been studied, there are some examples that do not fit the model well and so are candidates for sympatric speciation. Sympatric speciation occurs when two forms diverge without geographic isolation. Perhaps the best (but highly unusual) examples of sympatric speciation in fishes occur in the formation of unisexual species of poeciliids through hybridization of two or three bisexual species (see Chapter 22). This type of speciation can even be repeated using laboratory populations of the bisexual species (Schultz 1973). Whether or not sympatric speciation can occur in more normal situations is not really known, although it is tempting to postulate such a mechanism for some groups of fishes, especially marine species, in which geographic isolation is difficult to visualize. For example, 55 species of rockfishes (*Sebastes*) occur off the Pacific coast of North America, most with wide distributions. It is difficult to imagine how these species could have evolved under geographic isolation, unless conditions along the coast were once drastically different than they are today. Lebedev (1969) has speculated that distinct taxa of herrings (Clupeidae) may evolve sympatrically because of the need for all fishes in the same school to be of the same size. Populations with slightly different breeding times could maintain their identities because fishes spawned at different times would be too small or too large to school with each other. Such size-specific schools could presumably maintain their identities throughout the lives of the member fishes and would also spawn together (if the time of reproduction was an inherited trait). If such a system was maintained over a number of generations, distinct taxa could evolve. A perhaps more plausible computer simulation of sympatric speciation is provided by Endler (1977).

Threespine Stickleback: Problem in Taxonomy and Speciation

The threespine stickleback (*Gasterosteus aculeatus*) is found in coastal streams, lakes, bays, and estuaries throughout much of Eurasia and North America, being absent only from some arctic regions. A number of distinct forms of threespine stickleback have long been recognized, usually as subspecies but occasionally as species. Along the Pacific coast of North America, the complexity of interrelationships among the forms was not really realized until D. W. Hagen (1967) published his classic study of isolating mechanisms in the stickleback populations of a small stream in British Columbia. This study spawned a large number of related followup papers by many people, reviewed by Wooten (1977) and Bell (1976a).

Hagen found that two distinct populations of stickleback existed in his stream. One was a resident upstream population of small, bottom-feeding sticklebacks that were characterized by having (among other things) a low number (three to seven) of bony plates on their sides (Fig. 26.1). The other was an anadromous population that spawned in the lower reaches of the stream, showed a number of morphological adaptations for plankton feeding, and had a high number of plates (30 to 35) on each side. The two populations were separated by several miles of fast water in which no sticklebacks occurred. Just above the areas used by the anadromous populations was a region of stream intermediate in many of its characteristics between the upstream region and reaches below it. This region was occupied by an inbreeding population of sticklebacks that were hybrids between the two populations. Hagen demonstrated effectively that there was no gene flow between the hybrids and the anadromous sticklebacks and that the upstream and anadromous populations were reproductively isolated from each other not only physically but in their time of spawning. Later, Hay and McPhail (1975) also demonstrated that some behavioral isolating mechanisms were also present. On the basis of his remarkably complete evidence, Hagen concluded that the two populations represented distinct species, using a biological definition similar to the one presented earlier in this chapter. He labeled the upstream (freshwater) form *G. aculeatus* and the anadromous form *G. trachurus,* following the taxonomic designations of European workers.

Hagen's conclusions were attacked by Miller and Hubbs (1969), not only on the designation of the two forms as species but also on the nomenclature used to designate the species. In the first case, they pointed out that there are many stickleback populations on the Pacific coast that do appear to be intermediate between the low-plate-count freshwater form and the high-plate-count anadromous form and that these populations appear to have arisen as the result of introgression (followed by intergradation) of the two types of fish. As a consequence, they argued that the two forms should only be recognized as subspecies, and that the Pacific freshwater forms were distinct from the European freshwater forms as well. They therefore proposed that *G. aculeatus aculeatus* should be used for the anadromous form and *G. a. microcephalus* for the low-plated freshwater form. In addition, they recognized *G. a. williamsoni* for a form without plates found in southern California.

Hagen and McPhail (1970) countered the arguments of Miller and Hubbs on a number of grounds, including some methodological ones, and proposed an alternate hypothesis to explain the variability observed, the local selection hypothesis. This hypothesis states that the low-plated freshwater populations are not all derived from a common low-plated ancestor but evolved repeatedly from anadromous forms in response to local conditions. This hypothesis has subsequently received strong support from many other studies (summarized in Bell 1976a) that show that: (1) there are many highly divergent freshwater populations of sticklebacks that appear to have evolved independently (e.g., populations with black rather than red breeding colors, populations with no plates and reduced spines and girdles as well); and (2) there is strong evidence that many of these characteristics have evolved in response to predation. In British Columbia forms with few or no lateral plates and weak spines occur in lakes where predatory fishes are rare or absent, while forms with about seven plates per side and strong spines occur where predators of fish are abundant. Curiously enough, the selective advantage given seven-plated sticklebacks in the face of heavy predation appears not to be the result of the protection offered by the plates but rather to some behavioral differences associated with the seven-plate phenotype.

One of the factors that makes the repeated evolution of distinctive stickleback populations likely is that fossil evidence indicates that three-spine sticklebacks have been present on the Pacific coast for at least 10 million years (Bell 1976a). There have thus been many opportunities for repeated invasions of coastal streams and for the isolation and subsequent divergent evolution of small populations to occur. However, as Bell (1976a) points out, none of these distinct populations has been able to invade other areas extensively and then live in sympatry with previously established populations of sticklebacks (as two distinct coexisting species), although there are a few highly localized such instances.

It should be obvious that the "species" we currently recognize as the threespine stickleback is a collection of dynamic populations, each capable of responding rapidly, in an evolutionary sense, to changing local conditions. A number of these populations fit all the criteria for biological species, but others do not, even though they may be distinctive in some ways. As Bell (1976a) states, "the threespine stickleback appears to be a superspecies composed of semispecies some of which are polytypic and polymorphic but all of which form a cohesive taxonomic unit" (p. 211). Unfortunately, this concept of the threespine stickleback does not mesh well with Linnaean nomenclature. To give separate names to all the distinctive populations would be most confusing, since many are similar to each other, even if they did evolve independently. To give one species or subspecies name to all the freshwater forms would also be confusing, since such a name would only obscure the large differences that do exist among many of the populations. The safest course of action therefore seems to be to recognize most forms as just part of the *Gasterosteus aculeatus* "complex" but, for convenience, to give subspecies names to the few local populations that can be readily distinguished from all other such populations.

Supplemental Readings   Bell 1976a; Dobzhansky et al. 1977; Hubbs and Lagler 1958; Mayr 1963, 1976.

PART V

Ecology

ααααααααααααααααααααααααααααααααααααααααααααααααααααααααααααααααααααααααααααααα
~~~~~~

Introduction to Ecology

Fish are found in an extraordinary variety of habitats, yet each species has rather limited habitat requirements. Thus, each of the major habitat types listed in Table 27-1 largely contains species that are not found in the other major habitat types, and each can be further subdivided into many more specific habitats with distinct physical, chemical, and biological characteristics. Such habitats contain distinct, if often widely overlapping, fish faunas. Each of the fish species that make up a fauna associated with a particular habitat generally responds to the main features of the habitat in a different way than the other species (i.e., occupies its own niche). Although at any given time a fish is responding simultaneously to a variety of physical, chemical, and biological factors in its environment, often just one or two factors are of overwhelming importance in determining just why it is found where it is. Similarly, the overall distribution pattern of a particular species may be largely determined by its response to one particular factor, such as temperature. The ways in which fish respond to dominant biological factors is the subject of this chapter; the influence of physical and chemical characteristics are explained in the chapters on form and function (Chapters 2-10) as well as in the subsequent chapters dealing with ecology (Chapters 28-37), which describe the complex fish–environment interactions in the major habitat types.

While physical and chemical factors often have an obvious impact on the distribution and ecology of fish, biological factors are usually equally important, if harder to understand because of their subtlety or complexity. For convenience, the biological factors can be divided into interspecific and intraspecific interactions. The interspecific interactions can be further divided into: (1) predator–prey relationships; (2) competition; and (3) symbiosis.

387

TABLE 27-1
General Types of Aquatic Habitats Containing Fish

I. Inland waters	II. Oceanic waters
A. Lakes	A. Coastal habitats
1. Temperate and arctic	1. Rocky intertidal zone
a. Natural	2. Exposed beaches
b. Reservoirs	3. Mudflats
2. Tropical	4. Salt marshes
a. Natural	5. Seagrass flats
b. Reservoirs	6. Mangrove swamps
	7. Kelp beds
B. Streams	8. Nearshore rocky bottoms
1. Cold-water	9. Nearshore soft bottoms
2. Temperate warm-water	10. Miscellaneous minor systems
3. Tropical	a. Tidal inlets
	b. Bluegreen algal mats
C. Special habitats	c. Hypersaline lagoons
1. Desert waters	d. Salt ponds
2. Caves	e. Others
3. Inland seas	
	B. Tropical reefs
D. Estuaries	
	C. Epipelagic zone
	D. Deepsea habitats
	1. Mesopelagic Zone
	2. Bathypelagic Zone
	3. Deepsea Benthic Zone
	E. Polar habitats
	1. Arctic
	2. Antarctic

Predator–Prey Relationships

With few exceptions fish are simultaneously predator and prey, especially if humans are counted as predators. Relatively few species of fish are herbivores or detritivores, and even these species typically are predators on invertebrates during their early life history stages. As a result of their dual predator–prey role, fishes have evolved a wide array of feeding and defense mechanisms, from the strong beak and spiny covering of porcupinefishes (Tetraodontidae), to the sharp teeth and sleek bodies of barracudas (Sphyraenidae), to the pharyngeal teeth and fear scents of minnows (Cyprinidae), to the fine gill rakers and schooling behavior of herrings (Clupeidae). Such adaptations are a reflection of the coevolution of predators and prey through time. Defense mechanisms evolve presumably because they confer a reproductive advantage on the possessors, at least until their predators evolve the means to overcome the defense. While predators and prey obviously coexist, the predator–prey relationships are not necessarily stable and even minor environmental changes (especially those created by humans) may result in gross imbalances. Thus the study of predator–

prey relationships in fishes is of interest not only to theoretical ecologists but to biologists interested in managing fisheries either by creating imbalances deliberately or by trying to retain stable predator–prey relationships in a system. The former course would be taken if removing a predator species would leave more of its prey for humans to harvest, the latter course if both predators and prey are harvested. Understanding predator–prey relationships is also important for understanding the impact of introductions of exotic fishes into various types of ecosystems.

One of the major questions in ecology (and fisheries biology) is, Do predators control populations of their prey? When an exotic predaceous fish is introduced into a new ecosystem, the answer is often a dramatic yes, at least initially. When peacock bass (*Cichla ocellaris*) were introduced into Lake Gatun, Panama, they nearly eradicated seven species of native fishes from the lake through predation (Zaret and Paine 1973). Introduced fishes may also have a serious impact on invertebrate populations, particularly zooplankton. When planktivorous fish are introduced into a lake that lacked them previously, they may almost eliminate the larger species of zooplankton and cause small species to become dominant (Brooks and Dodson 1965). For example, the introduction of alewife (*Alosa pseudoharengus*) into Lake Michigan resulted in the near disappearance of two large species of zooplankton, the decline of five other species, and an increase in ten species of small zooplankters (Wells 1970). In contrast to the above examples, the impact of predators on prey populations is much more subtle when the two have evolved together in the same system, especially if the system is a complex one. On coral reefs, it is unlikely that the elimination of one or two species of fish-eating predators would result in a population explosion of any of the prey species, either because food and space are the main limiting factors for the prey or because other predators would move in. Even comparatively simple and variable systems, such as trout and salmon streams, seem surprisingly well "buffered" from letting either predators or prey get out of hand. Although sculpins (*Cottus*) may prey on salmon and trout eggs and fry, they will not have much impact on the salmonid populations unless the sculpin populations are abnormally high and/or the salmonid populations are abnormally low (Moyle 1977). In many streams, salmon may actually control sculpin populations because the adults dig up the riffles while spawning and cause drastic reductions in the populations of invertebrates that serve as prey for sculpins most of the year.

In some situations, a prey population may control those of a predator rather than the reverse. In a pond, for example, bluegill (*Lepomis macrochirus*) may keep the population of the piscivorous largemouth bass (*Micropterus salmoides*) small by preempting limited nesting sites and by preying on the bass eggs in the nest. This situation is particularly likely to develop if fishermen have removed the largest bass from the pond. Despite examples such as this, most predator populations seem to fluctuate independently of that of any one prey species, since they are usually capable of switching prey when the population of one gets too low. Although examples of predators controlling prey populations are common, even these may be more the exception than the rule. For most fishes, predator–prey interactions are just one factor out of many that regulates their distribution and abundance.

Competition

Competition is "the demand, typically at the same time, of more than one organism for the same resources of the environment in excess of immediate supply" (Larkin 1956). It is generally assumed that as a result of competition, two species with identical ecological requirements will not be able to coexist. If two species whose ecological requirements are similar but not identical come in contact, the differences between the two species will become emphasized in such a way that the resource under dispute will be divided between them. Selection pressure may then cause the species to diverge permanently from each other through behavioral, morphological, and physiological specializations (*character displacement*). An extreme result of this process is the many highly specialized fishes found in the ancient rift lakes of Africa (Chapter 30). At the opposite end of the spectrum are the species of trout characteristic of the streams and lakes of recently glaciated areas, which have a behavioral plasticity that allows them to segregate quickly from other species of trout, as well as other kinds of fishes that they come in contact with (Chapter 28). Because competition is such an ephemeral phenomenon, it is difficult to study and difficult to demonstrate. This does not prevent it from frequently being invoked (usually without evidence) to explain patterns of distribution and abundance of many fish species, particularly if the species are economically important and are declining while less valuable species are on the increase.

Some of the best examples of distribution patterns that are most easily explained as the result of competition followed by species segregation occur in mountain lakes, with trout. Nilsson (1963) has found that arctic char (*Salvelinus alpinus*) and brown trout (*Salmo trutta*) in Swedish lakes will occupy both inshore and offshore habitats and feed on everything from zooplankton to benthic and terrestrial insects when either one of the species is the sole fish occupant of a lake. However, when the two species occur together, the trout are mostly found close to shore, associated with the bottom, where they feed on both benthic and terrestrial insects. The char, on the other hand, are almost entirely found out in the open waters of the lake, where they feed on zooplankton. In aquaria the trout have proven to be more aggressive than the char and will consistently dominate the char. In a lake this behavior presumably keeps the char out of the inshore areas. The competition in this case is for the limited, but productive, inshore space, and segregation results directly from the behavioral interactions of the two morphologically similar salmonids. However, it should be pointed out that there are minor morphological differences between the species that also have some bearing on the results of their interactions. Arctic char, for example, have more and longer gill rakers than brown trout, which should give them an advantage in feeding on zooplankton. Given enough time, the differences between the two species where sympatric should become even greater, thereby increasing the efficiency of utilization of the limited resources present and reducing interactions between species.

As the above example indicates, a number of behavioral mechanisms may be acting simultaneously to enable fishes to avoid competition by segregating ecologically. Some of the most important of these mechanisms are (1) differential exploitation; (2) aggressive behavior; (3) predation; (4) habitat interference; (5) habitat imprinting; and (6) fugitive species. **Differential exploitation** of the resources available in a given environment is perhaps the most important mechanism (Nilsson 1967). Thus, when brown bullhead (*Ictalurus nebulosus*), a bottom-adapted species, and the deep-bodied pumpkinseed (*Lepomis gibbosus*) are kept in separate aquaria, they both show a strong preference for benthic insect larvae over *Daphnia*, a large zooplankter. However, when kept together in an aquaria, the pumpkinseed switch to *Daphnia*, presumably because the bullhead is able to exploit the insects at a very rapid rate but is unable to feed effectively on the zooplankton (Ivlev 1961).

Interspecific **aggressive behavior**, especially when expressed as territoriality, may be one of the most important mechanisms that initially forces two similar species into different habitats, as is demonstrated by the interactions of brown trout and arctic char.

As the previous section on predator–prey relationships indicated, **predation** is a complex phenomenon. In some situations it has been demonstrated that a predator may increase the number of species in an area by keeping the numbers of an otherwise dominant species low. However, this has not been conclusively demonstrated for any situation involving fish. On the other hand, there is some evidence that when fishing (a form of predation) removes large trout from a stream, large minnows and suckers that are normally kept out by the trout through aggressive behavior and predation may become abundant.

Habitat interference occurs when the activities of one species change a habitat in such a way that the populations of potentially competing species are reduced or excluded. One of the reasons for the success of the carp (*Cyprinus carpio*) in shallow lakes seems to be that while feeding it roots up the bottom and thereby greatly increases the turbidity of the lake. High turbidity effectively excludes some ecologically similar species such as buffalo fishes (*Ictiobus*) as well as many predatory species.

Habitat imprinting is a poorly understood phenomenon that may permit species, or even morphs of the same species, to coexist with a minimum of interaction. The basic idea is that young fish become imprinted on the particular type of habitat with which they are first associated and thereafter choose that habitat type over others that might be equally suitable. For example, juveniles of the reef fish *Dascyllus aruanus* will selectively choose, in an experimental situation, the type of coral from which they had originally been collected (Sale 1971). It has been hypothesized that one of the factors accounting for the extraordinary diversity of cichlid fishes in the rift lakes of Africa is that, because of the high degree of parental care, the juvenile cichlids become imprinted on the specific habitat of their parents, permitting divergence to occur over even minor habitat differences. In contrast to fishes that might rely on habitat imprinting, **fugitive species** are unspecialized forms that are capable of utilizing a resource that is temporarily unexploited because the habitat is newly created or because some disaster has befallen the original possessors. Thus the bay blenny (*Hypsoblennius gentilis*) manages to coexist with two similar species by having larvae that disperse quickly and early in the season to settle in a new area before it is colonized by the other species (Stephens et al. 1970). In a Minnesota lake, common shiners (*Notropis cornutus*) seem to become abundant only when the mimic shiner (*Notropis volucellus*) has a major reproductive failure (Moyle 1973).

It should be emphasized that usually no one factor by itself is responsible for the pattern of species segregation observed in any association of fishes. This is well illustrated by the studies of P. A. Larkin and his students on Paul Lake, B.C., which show how competitive and predator-prey relationships interact to produce an observed community structure. Paul Lake was originally occupied only by rainbow trout, although redside shiner (*Richardsonius balteatus*) was introduced into the lake in 1945 (Johannes and Larkin 1961). Prior to the introduction of the shiner, the trout fry lived in the shallow waters of the lake, where they fed primarily on amphipods, small crustaceans associated with the beds of aquatic plants. The adult trout lived mostly in the open waters of the lake, feeding on surface insects and zooplankton. They seldom grew any larger than 40 cm. Immediately following the introduction of the shiners (apparently by fishermen) and their subsequent population explosion, it was found that both shiners and trout fry were feeding mostly on amphipods. However, the shiners were more efficient at feeding on the amphipods because they could penetrate the plant beds to get them, while the trout generally had to wait for the amphipods to emerge from the plants. By 1960 the amphipod population had been so depleted by the shiners that they were no longer a major item in the diet of either shiners or trout. Instead, the two species had segregated, with the trout fry feeding mostly on aquatic and terrestrial insects and the shiners feeding mostly on zooplankton. Since the shiners had also moved out into the open waters of the lake, they came in contact with the larger rainbow trout. The trout avoided competing for the zooplankton with the shiners by preying on the shiners themselves. As a result of these interactions, the overall biomass of fish in the lake was probably higher, although the biomass of rainbow trout was lower than previously. However, the rainbow trout were able to grow to larger sizes because of the availability of shiners as forage.

Symbiosis

Symbiosis means simply "living together," so virtually all interactions among species could fall under this heading, including competition and predation. However, symbiosis is usually considered to include just three special types of interactions (mutualism, commensalism, and parasitism), so these will be the only topics considered here. Mimicry is another special type of symbiosis, but since examples in fishes come primarily from coral reefs, it will be discussed in Chapter 34.

Mutualism. Perhaps the most common instances of mutualism among fishes, where two or more species form a close association for their mutual benefit, are schools involving more than one species. In streams and lakes of eastern North America, for example, it is common to find several species of minnows, especially of the genus *Notropis,* schooling together. Presumably, such behavior confers on all the species the advantages large schools give, advantages none of them could achieve individually (Barlow 1974; Morse 1977). Another common type of mutualistic behavior is cleaning, where one species feeds on the external parasites and diseased tissues of other species. Both the cleaner and the fish being cleaned have special behavior patterns that accompany the interactions. Cleaning behavior has been observed in many species of fish, including freshwater fishes (Spall 1970; Able 1976), but it has been most intensively studied in the cleaning wrasses (Labridae) of the Indo-Pacific Region, which make their living largely as cleaners. Typically, a cleaner wrasse has a station on a reef over which it displays its often brilliant color patterns. Large fish approaching the station to be cleaned assume a special relaxed posture and permit the cleaner wrass to move over their bodies and even to enter their mouth cavities. Only rarely is a cleaner wrass eaten. Although the advantages to both parties of cleaning behavior seem to be obvious, Losey (1978) points out that the relationship between the cleaner and the cleanee are not as clear-cut as once thought. When levels of parasitic infections are high, the fishes being cleaned may gain from the cleaning, but usually the level of infection is low, whether or not cleaner fishes are available. Often, the main food of cleaner fishes is mucus, pieces of fin, and other healthy tissues, as well as eggs of reef fishes, making the cleaners more parasites than mutualists. It appears that a fish being cleaned tolerates the attentions of the cleaner because it has a positive response to the tactile stimulation provided by the cleaner. This response appears to have evolved for other purposes and is taken advantage of by cleaners (Gorlick et al. 1978). In a sense, the cleaner is a vice of the cleanee!

Clearer examples (perhaps) of mutualism are the interactions between certain species of burrow-dwelling shrimp and small gobies

(Gobiidae). The shrimp construct burrows inhabited by both species, so the goby gains a home by being associated with the shrimp. The shrimp gains by remaining in contact with the goby when at the mouth of the burrow or foraging nearby, since the goby, with its superior vision, can warn the shrimp of approaching predators. It appears that a special series of signals between goby and shrimp have developed to enhance this relationship.

Commensalism. While the above goby–shrimp relationship is mutualistic, there are many other instances of gobies using the burrows of invertebrates in which the invertebrate gains nothing from the relationship (but is not harmed either). These are examples of commensalism. The remoras (Echeneidae) are a whole family of fishes adapted for commensal living with large fishes, particularly sharks. Each remora possesses a large sucker on the top of its head with which it attaches to a host, who carries it to new sources of food. While the presence of remoras may have a negative impact on the hydrodynamics of their hosts, they may also benefit them by keeping them clear of parasites.

Parasitism. Although most fishes carry a variety of parasites with them, clear examples of fish acting as parasites are few. The pearlfishes (Carapidae) are one such example. These small, elongate fishes live in association with sea cucumbers (Holothuria) and actually enter the gut through the anus. Once inside, they may penetrate into the body cavity of the host and feed on the gonads. The sea cucumbers usually survive the experience, although their reproduction may be interfered with (Marshall 1966). In fresh water many of the small South American catfishes in the family Trichomycteridae are apparently parasites on other fish. They enter the gill cavities, attach themselves with the spines on their opercula, and feed on gill filaments and blood. One species, *Vandellia cirrhosa,* is famous for entering, presumably by mistake, the urogenital openings of swimming humans, with painful results for both species. While the above examples fit most definitions of parasitism, there are many others that fall into the grey area between parasitism and predation, mostly because the predator (parasite) is small and does not usually kill its larger prey (host). In this area are: (1) the many species of tropical fish that feed largely by removing scales from other fish; (2) predatory fishes that mimic harmless or beneficial species, such as the sabertooth blenny (*Aspidontus taeniatus*), which imitates cleaner wrasses but takes painful bites out of the fins of waiting fish rather than cleaning or nibbling them; and (3) lampreys, which attach temporarily to the sides of fish and suck blood and other bodily fluids.

Intraspecific Interactions

The interactions between members of the same species are similar in many respects to those between different species, but more mutualistic arrangements are present (Chapter 11). However, since most intraspecific interactions presumably enhance the chances that the particular set of genes possessed by each individual is passed to the next generation, intense intraspecific competition and predation are also more the rule than the exception. Thus, the territorial behavior that causes salmonid species to segregate is even more important to each species as a way of dividing the limited space available for feeding and reproduction within the population. In streams trout that cannot find a suitable space to establish themselves either must colonize new areas (which they can do quite rapidly) or be eaten by predators.

In some species, but especially pelagic ones such as sardines and herrings, intraspecific competition is one of the main mechanisms that regulates population size. If numbers of a species are high, the food resources become diminished and the ability of each individual to produce eggs or sperm becomes reduced, resulting in fewer young and a smaller population in the following years. In the absence of severe environmental fluctuations, intraspecific competition (feedback) alone in such species will produce regular population oscillations.

Cannibalism is a form of predation that is surprisingly common in fishes and may be quite advantageous if the probability of eating one's own offspring is low and if habitat available for the young is limited. It may also be advantageous if the young are superabundant and adult predation does not affect their annual survival rate. In the Sacramento–San Joaquin estuary of California, one of the main foods of adult striped bass (*Morone saxatilis*) is young-of-year bass, which in turn are effective predators on the opossum shrimp (*Neomysis*), the most abundant invertebrate in the system. These shrimp are too small for large bass to feed on efficiently. Despite the cannibalism, there appears to be no relationship between the abundance of adult bass and the success of each year's class of bass.

While intraspecific competition and predation are common, the life history strategies of many fishes result in spatial segregation of adults and young, so that neither type of interaction is likely to occur. Thus, many species of fish, such as salmon and herring, have breeding grounds that are far removed from the adult feeding areas. Many marine and lake-dwelling fishes have planktonic larvae that spend the most vulnerable stages of their lives in a food-rich environment that is often quite different from that of the adults.

Supplemental Readings   Blaxter 1970; Brett 1970; Cushing 1968; Gibson 1969; Helfman 1978; Hynes 1970; Ivlev 1961; Larkin 1956; Marshall 1966; Nikolsky 1963; Nilsson 1967; Remane and Schlieper 1971; Rounsefell 1975; Weatherley 1972.

CHAPTER **28**

ααααααααααααααααααααααααααααααααααααααααααααααααααααααααααααααααααα
~~~~~~

Temperate Streams

The streams of temperate North America and Eurasia are among the better-understood environments fish inhabit because of their accessibility, diversity, and, most important, the fact they contain many of the favorite species of sport fishes. Unfortunately for the fishes, however, these streams are also among the most manipulated of aquatic habitats, being dammed, diverted, polluted, channelized or otherwise altered for the supposed good of humankind. Despite the radical changes in the amount and quality of water flowing through temperate streams, there have been few extinctions of temperate stream fish species, although local faunal depletions are common (e.g., Smith and Powell 1971). The reason for this is that most temperate stream fishes are adapted for living in an environment that fluctuates, often considerably, on a daily and seasonal basis. Climatic changes that result in droughts, floods, and ice ages create long-term fluctuations in the environment that also have had to be survived. Thus most temperate stream fishes can maintain populations under a wide variety of physical and chemical conditions, are capable of successfully interacting with a wide variety of other fish species, and are quick to colonize new areas of suitable habitat. Under normal conditions, however, each species tends to be found in a rather specific microhabitat as part of a distinct faunal assemblage. The purpose of this chapter, therefore, is to describe how important environmental factors affect the distribution of stream fishes and how the fish interact with each other to form the assemblages typical of zoogeographic regions and habitat types.

396

Factors That Affect
Distribution
It is convenient to divide the factors that affect the distribution of stream fishes into four categories, physical, chemical, biological, and zoogeographic, although the distribution pattern of any one species is caused by an interaction of factors from all four categories.

PHYSICAL FACTORS   In the study of stream fishes, four complex factors have proven to be most useful in predicting patterns of distribution and abundance: temperature regime, gradient, stream order, and fluctuations in flow.   North American fishery managers have long recognized the importance of temperature in fish distribution and have divided the fluvial world into warm-water streams and cold-water streams. Warm-water streams have temperatures that exceed 24°C to 26°C for extended periods of time and are characterized by smallmouth bass, green sunfish, catfish, and a diversity of small fishes, especially cyprinids and darters (Percidae), while coldwater streams seldom exceed 24°C to 26°C and are characterized by trout and sculpins. It is worth noting that many of the "problem" streams of fishery managers are streams that do not fit well into either category and consequently may not provide good fishing for any of the "approved" game fish. Management problems also arise when flows of cold water are reduced by human activities, even if the temperature regime is relatively unchanged. This is because, while the downstream limits of trout are usually temperature-related, the upstream limits of many "warm-water" fishes, such as squawfish (*Ptychocheilus*) and suckers (*Catostomus*), may be limited more by other factors, particularly water velocity. Even in the face of presumed competition from such fishes, trout may still maintain the upper hand as long as the water temperatures remain cold. At low temperatures, trout have comparatively high standard metabolic rates and tend to be more active and are therefore able to utilize the food resources more effectively than most other species.

Even in streams that are clearly "warm-water" or "cold-water," there are considerable differences in the temperature tolerances and preferences of the species present. Brown trout (*Salmo trutta*), at least in Colorado, are usually found in streams that exceed 13°C for extended periods of time (Vincent and Miller 1969), while brook trout (*Salvelinus fontinalis*) are rarely successful in such waters, especially when other species of trout are present. On the other hand, some warmwater species, such as the Rio Grande perch (*Cichlasoma cyanogutattus*), cannot survive temperatures lower than 14°C to 18°C (Deacon and Minckley 1974). In some species the temperature tolerances of different life history stages may be different. In speckled dace (*Rhinichthys osculus*) the young can survive in water 2°C warmer than the maximum adults can tolerate, which may permit them to survive periods of extreme low water in their streams (John 1964).

While temperature is of great importance in determining the broad distributional patterns of stream fishes, gradient (the number of meters of drop per kilometer of stream) is much more likely to be important in any particular stream. This is because gradient has a profound influence on water velocity, bottom type, and on the number and size of pools. Where gradients are high, the current speed tends to be high (and, likewise, water flow, which also takes into account water volume), the bottom is predominantly bedrock, boulders, and cobbles, and deep, quiet pools tend to be few. More often than not, water temperatures are also cool, the water is saturated with oxygen, and the dominant fishes are trout. At the opposite end of the spectrum are the sluggish, muddy-bottomed reaches of low-gradient streams, which are characterized by deep-bodied fishes. In general, the higher the gradient, the lower the habitat diversity, and, consequently, the fewer species of fish. The size and depth of pools is particularly important in this regard (Sheldon 1968). When a stream section is channelized, the overall gradient may remain the same but large pools are eliminated. As a result, the numbers and biomass of fish are greatly decreased. The number and relative abundance of species is usually reduced as well. Thus, when sections of a stream in northern California were channelized, dace (*Rhinichthys*) and sculpin (*Cottus*) became dominant, while populations of two species of trout (*Salmo*) became greatly reduced and the Modoc sucker (*Catostomus microps*, a threatened species) nearly disappeared altogether (Moyle 1976b).

Both gradient and water temperature contribute to the impact of the third "factor," stream order, which is a means of classifying streams according to a complex of physical factors. Stream systems can be "ordered" according to their pattern of branching. The headwater streams are first-order streams and unite to form second-order streams, which in turn unite to form third-order streams, and so on until the main river is reached. In most systems first-order streams are the smallest, coldest, and highest-gradient streams, and they generally contain the fewest species of fish. As the stream order increases, habitat diversity, stream size, turbidity, and temperatures usually increase as well, while gradient and environmental fluctuations usually decrease. As a consequence, the number of species tends to increase with stream order. Thus, in eastern Kentucky, Kuehne (1962) found that first-, second-, third-, and fourth-order streams contained, respectively, one, 12, 20, and 27 species of fish. In most instances, as stream order increases, species are added but few drop out. The ones that *do* drop out are either fishes adapted to cold water, such as brook trout (*Salvelinus fontinalis*) and sculpins (*Cottus*), or species that are adapted for surviving in intermittent headwater streams, such as the fathead minnow (*Pimephales promelas*) or the California roach (*Lavinia symmetricus*). The latter species are capable of surviving under harsh physical and chemical conditions but tend to be eliminated from complex fish communities by predation or

TABLE 28-1
**Occurrence (X) of Fish Species in the First-, Second-, and Third-Order
Portions of Clemons Fork, Kentucky**

Species	Food[a]	Order		
		First	Second	Third
Semotilus atromaculatus	T	X	X	X
Campostoma anomalum	A		X	X
Etheostoma sagitta	I		X	X
Etheostoma nigrum	I		X	X
Etheostoma flabellare	I		X	X
Etheostoma caeruleum	I		X	X
Hypentelium nigricans	I		X	X
Catostomus commersoni	A		X	X
Ericymba buccata	I			X
Notropis ardens	T			X
Notropis chrysocephalus	T			X
Pimephales notatus	D			X
Ambloplites rupestris	V			X
Lepomis megalotis	V			X
Micropterus dolomieui	V			X

[a]The principal food type of each species is indicated by the letters as follows. T — terrestrial insects; A — algae; I — aquatic invertebrates; D — detritus; V — vertebrates, principally fish.
Source: After Lotrich (1973).

competition. In some systems the number of species actually decreases in the highest-order streams, usually because of pollution, water removal by humans, or floods (e.g., Whiteside and McNatt [1972]).

As might be expected, the trophic structure of the fish community in a stream system changes with the order. In first-order streams the dominant fishes are usually feeding largely either on insects that drop into the water from the overhanging vegetation (e.g., brook trout, creek chub [*Semotilus atromaculatus*]) or on detritus (California roach, fathead minnow). In higher-order streams predators on aquatic insects are added and, gradually, piscivores, herbivores, and other specialists (Table 28-1).

One factor which may greatly modify the usefulness of the preceding three physical factors as predictors of distributional patterns is fluctuation in flow, either annually or over a longer period. Severe floods or extreme low flows eliminate or reduce populations of some fishes from sections of stream where they would be expected to occur, while long periods of moderate fluctuations in flow may allow species normally found only in high-order streams to invade those of lower orders. The actual extirpation of a species from an area by a flood is a relatively rare event, since most adult fishes native to a stream system seem to be able to find refuge during floods. It is worth noting that a tremendous flood in the Salt River, Arizona, virtually eliminated the exotic fishes present, while the native suckers (*Catostomus* spp.) survived in numbers (Deacon and Minckley 1974). Floods may also modify fish populations by affecting reproductive success. In Sagehen Creek, California, fall floods may destroy most of the recently spawned eggs of brook trout. In the absence of competition from young brook trout, survival of young rainbow trout, which are spawned in the spring, increases, and rainbow trout become the most abundant trout in the stream. Spring floods have just the opposite effect, favoring survival of brook trout (Seegrist and Gard 1972). Although floods have many negative effects on stream fishes, many species actually require them for reproduction, since they spawn on flooded vegetation and use flooded areas as nursery grounds for their young (Starrett 1951). The actual amount of high water is crucial, however, since either too much or too little may result in low reproductive success.

Although the local elimination of a species by floods is unusual, elimination by low flows, whether caused by drought or by human diversion of water, is fairly common. Smith (1971) lists 12 species whose range in Illinois has been greatly reduced by long-term droughts. If a stream has not dried up completely, fishes may be eliminated by their inability to tolerate high temperatures, low oxygen levels, or even heavy growth of aquatic plants created by the low water. When more favorable conditions return to the stream, the "normal" fish fauna returns gradually. The order of appearance of the species depends on their relative abilities to colonize new waters or to withstand extreme conditions (Larimore et al. 1959). Examples of rapid colonizers are red shiner (*Notropis lutrensis*), fathead minnow (*Pimephales promelas*), Rio Grande killifish (*Fundulus zebrinus*), mosquitofish (*Gambusia affinis*) and green sunfish (*Lepomis cyanellus*). In some desert streams in Arizona the dominant species may change depending on the amount of water flowing. During wet years the speckled dace and other species flourish, but during dry years the longfin dace (*Agosia chrysogaster*) may be the only fish found in abundance (Deacon and Minckley 1974).

CHEMICAL FACTORS   Because they flow over varied substrates, streams tend to be well buffered chemically and well oxygenated. It is consequently difficult to find strong correlations betweeen chemical factors and fish distribution patterns, except under extreme conditions (e.g., drought) or where streams have been heavily polluted by humans. Thus acid waters draining mines and roadfills are a major limiting factor of stream fishes in the southeastern United States (e.g., Huckabee et al. 1975; Davis 1973), affecting fish through a combination of low pH and heavy metal and sulphide poisoning. In Oklahoma there is a definite group of fishes that is associated with moderately saline streams. This group is likely to increase in abundance if the pollution of streams by brine from oil-drilling operations continues (Stevenson et al. 1974). The potentially lethal effect of such highly alkaline water was demonstrated in the late 1800s when a large amount of alkali water in the Gila River in Arizona spilled over a dam, entered the Colorado River, and caused a major fish kill (Deacon and Minckley 1974). Many of the chemicals that may limit fish distribution in both acid and saline waters are present in sewage (e.g., heavy metals, chlorine), and as a result, many fish species may be absent from the immediate vicinity of sewage outfalls (Tsai 1973). Equally important, however, is the depletion of oxygen in the water caused by decay of the organic matter in sewage. This favors species, such as carp, that are tolerant of low oxygen levels and generally decreases the number of species in an area.

BIOLOGICAL FACTORS   Temperate stream fishes are, for the most part, members of complex communities. Yet, because the physical environment fluctuates so much, the particular set of organisms any species interacts with is likely to vary considerably from place to place within the species range, from year to year and even from season to season. As a result, most species are quite flexible in their interactions with other organisms, particularly other fishes, although the morphological, physiological, and behavioral characteristics of each species place definite limits on these interactions. The distribution of stream fishes may thus be limited by predator–prey, competitive, and symbiotic interactions, as well as by the different requirements of various stages in their life histories (intraspecific interactions).

Predator–prey interactions. As predators, the distribution of stream fishes is definitely limited by the distributions of potential prey organisms. Piscivorous fishes, for example, occur mainly in higher-order streams where there is a variety of prey available in abundance. However, there are few instances where it can be shown that the distribution of a stream fish species is severely limited by its predators, although predation is probably the ultimate cause of death of most stream fishes under natural conditions. The clearest examples of distribution of species being limited by predators occur where native fishes are eliminated by exotic predators, such as the elimination of California roach from some streams by green sunfish (Moyle 1976a). The best examples of predators limiting the numbers of a prey species come from studies of salmon streams, where it has been found that the number of young salmon can be increased considerably in some instances by reducing populations of mergansers, kingfishers, Dolly Varden char (*Salvelinus malma*), and other predators. Predacious fish also may limit the number of aquatic insects in a section of stream.

Competitive interactions. Studies of the ecology of temperate stream fishes have revealed that there is a remarkable degree of segregation among the species, despite the fact that the exact species composition of a stream is likely to vary from year to year or season to season and also be somewhat different from other nearby streams. Most temperate stream fishes must have a considerable degree of behavioral plasticity that allows them to interact successfully with a variety of other species, minimizing competition for food and space. The "plasticity" of each species, however, does have distinct limits, which are imposed by its morphology, physiology, and total behavioral repertoire.

Much of the ecological segregation observed among temperate stream fishes is the result of differences in the morphology of the species. For example, a typical North American cold-water stream may contain four species of fish: trout (*Salmo* or *Salvelinus*), dace (*Rhinichthys*), sculpin (*Cottus*), and sucker (*Catostomus*) (Fig. 28.1). Body shape alone indicates that the trout is a fast-swimming predator, the sucker a bottom-oriented suction feeder, the sculpin a bottom-dwelling ambush feeder on large invertebrates, and the dace an active, bottom-oriented browser on small organisms. In warm-water streams, such as the creek in Ontario studied by Keast (1966), the number of species tends to be much higher and morphological differences among the species tend not to be as sharp, but such differences nevertheless account for much of the segregation observed.

Another way habitat differences among similar species can often be explained is on the basis of differences among the species in their physiological responses to physical and chemical conditions. For example, in the foothill streams of California, hardhead (*Mylopharodon conocephalus*, a large cyprinid) and rainbow trout show strong habitat segregation despite many similarities in feeding habits and behavior. One of the main differences between the species seems to be that the higher metabolic rates and superior swimming abilities of the trout enable them to live successfully in fast-flowing water, where food is most abundant, while the more sluggish hardhead are largely confined to pools (Alley 1976).

Although physiological differences among species can often explain habitat differences, behavioral differences that result in differences in feeding habits and microhabitats are probably the most important mechanisms of segregation among species that regularly occur together. Such species may segregate according to where in the water column they take their food, the time of day they feed, the type of food eaten, and the size of food items taken. There may also be seasonal changes in distribution that reduce competition. Some of the best examples of these rather subtle kinds of segregation occur among the small, silvery minnows of the genus *Notropis*, which contains over 100 species. The species are all quite similar to one another and typically two or more species are found together, in different combinations. In a Wisconsin stream, Mendelson (1975) found that four species of *Notropis* minimized competition for food by feeding at different places in the water column, in slightly different microhabitats (e.g., head of pool vs. bottom of pool), on different types of food (drifting or bottom-dwelling organisms), and on different sizes of food. The difference

402 CH. 28 TEMPERATE STREAMS

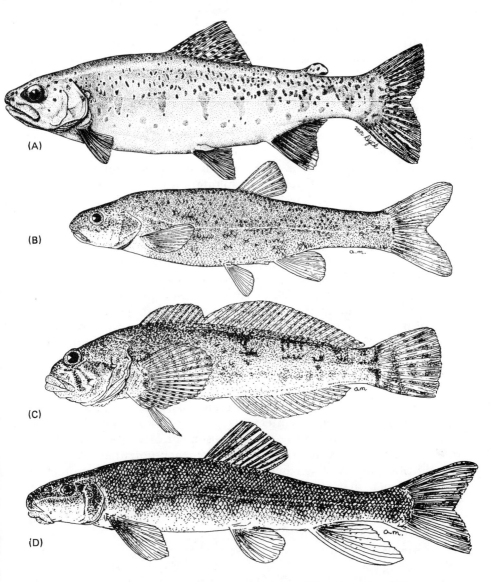

FIGURE 28.1 Typical fishes of cold-water streams of North America: (A) trout (*Salmo*); (B) dace (*Rhinichthys*); (C) sculpin (*Cottus*); and (D) sucker (*Catostomus*). (From Moyle, 1976a.)

between any two species in any one of the above categories is not sharp, but the overall differences in all four categories result in apparent subdivision of the food and spatial resources available.

Among the most interesting but least understood aspects of stream fish ecology are the exact behavioral mechanisms that result in the observed segregation. It appears that the two main mechanisms are aggressive behavior and differential exploitation (see Chapter 27). There are many examples of the use of **aggressive behavior** by salmon and trout to keep out potential competitors. Juvenile Atlantic salmon (*Salmo salar*) will defend territories against minnows and suckers as well as other salmon (Symons 1976). Interactions between juvenile coho salmon (*Oncorhynchus kisutch*) and rainbow trout in some streams force the coho into the pools while the trout defend territories in the riffles (Hartman 1965). In other streams, coho may be the dominant fish, forcing other species of salmon into less desirable habitats (Stein et al. 1972). Such aggressive interactions, although common in salmonids, seem to be unusual in other families of stream fishes, suggesting that **differential exploitation** is the main mechanism that segregates similar species in streams. Presumably, the many species of *Notropis* have broader feeding habits and occupy a wider range of microhabitats when by themselves than when they occur with other species of the genus. Just how each species specializes in the presence of another would depend on slight differences in body morphology (e.g., subterminal vs. terminal mouths) that give each species advantages in exploiting slightly different parts of the environment.

Symbiotic interactions. Clear examples of parasitism, commensalism or mutualism as important determinants of the structure of stream fish communities are hard to find, although parasitic infestations of native stream fishes in the western United States by exotic parasites brought in with exotic fishes have been given some blame for the decline of the native fish faunas (e.g., Wilson et al. 1966; Vanicek and Kramer 1969). In the Pit River system of California, the presence of *Ceratomyxa shasta*, an infectious protozoan to which the native trouts are resistant, has made the establishment of exotic trout strains difficult, indicating that disease does have some potential for limiting fish distribution. At the other end of the symbiotic spectrum, there is some evidence that the multispecies schools of minnows frequently encountered in streams may function to give protection from predators for all species, while still permitting members to retain their feeding specializations (Mendelson 1975).

Intraspecific interactions. In streams it is common for the young to be ecologically distinct from the adults. Many stream fishes make spawning migrations up small tributary streams, where the young may spend the first year or so of their lives without having to compete with the adults for food and space. Sculpins (*Cottus*) in coastal streams may actually make downstream migrations in order to spawn near estuaries, where the young may live for a period of time. In situations where the juveniles and the adults occur together there is frequently microhabitat segregation or segregation by feeding habits. Gee and Northcote (1963) found that the young of two species of dace (*Rhinichthys*) schooled together in shallow water where water temperatures were high and small food organisms abundant but that, as they matured, the two species moved into different habitats, one into pools and one into riffles. In the foothill streams of California, the juvenile squawfish feed on insects, while the adults feed largely on fish. Among trout, which consume a wide variety of organisms, the segregation among different-sized individuals of the same species is largely on the basis of size of the food items taken. Juvenile trout typically have large numbers of small fly and mayfly larvae in their stomachs, while the adults will contain large stoneflies and caddisflies. This difference in food is presumably one of the main reasons that large trout will typically tolerate the presence of smaller trout in their feeding territories, although one of the main functions of the feeding territories is to reduce the amount of competition for food among members of the same species.

Zoogeographic factors. One of the factors complicating any study of a local stream fauna is the presence of zoogeographic barriers that prevent fish from moving up into habitats that would probably be suitable for them. While sections of stream with different temperatures, salinities, or flow may act as barriers to some specialized species, usually the barriers are waterfalls or at least high-gradient areas. For example, St. Anthony Falls in Minnesota has acted as a major barrier for fishes to the upper Mississippi River (Eddy et al. 1963). In the Pit River system of California, Pit Falls and the high-gradient canyon below it have kept the deep-bodied fishes of the Sacramento Valley from invading valley habitat above the falls. One such species, the tule perch (*Hysterocarpus traski*), actually occurs in the Pit River all the way up to the falls. The turbulent water of the canyon also seems to act as a barrier to the downstream movement of the rough sculpin (*Cottus asperrimus*), which requires a smooth-flowing "run" type of environment. However, the construction of dams on the river has created more habitat suitable for the sculpin, so it has extended its range downstream in recent years (Daniels and Moyle 1978).

Zonation

Despite the fact that the distribution patterns of fish species are determined largely by the interactions between the fish and various physical and chemical factors, in most regions there are a number of species that all respond to these factors in a similar fashion. Groups of such species tend to occur together in particular stream environments, forming recognizable associations. Since such associations of species tend to succeed one another as the stream environment changes from high-gradient headwaters to the low-gradient river on the valley floor, they and the physical environment they typify are together called *fish zones*. Generally, the species found together in a fish zone complement one another ecologically, thereby minimizing competition and presumably maximizing the utilization of the resources present. It should be emphasized, however, that the fish zones are not sharply distinct from one another but rather blend into one another as the environment changes. Indeed, many fish species may typify several zones, since frequently downstream zones are created mainly by the addition of species to those characteristic of upstream zones. For example, in most temperate stream systems, the uppermost waters are dominated by trout and are referred to as the Trout Zone. However, trout typically also occur in one or more downstream zones, usually becoming less and less abundant relative to other species as one moves downstream. In some streams, the downstream change in the fish fauna is so gradual that clearly recognizable fish zones cannot be distinguished. Nevertheless, in many streams zones can be recognized, and to do so greatly facilitates the descriptions of regional or local fish faunas. Three fish zonation schemes will be described here: for central Europe, for the San Joaquin River system of California, and for Brier Creek in Oklahoma.

Central Europe. Four fish zones have been recognized for this region, all strongly related to gradient (Huet 1959). The *Trout Zone* occurs in swift, cold, high-gradient headwaters and is dominated by brown trout. The *Grayling Zone* still contains brown trout in some numbers but contains grayling (*Thymallus thymallus*) and a few cyprinids adapted for living in fast water as well. This zone occurs in mid-elevation streams with lower gradients than in the Trout Zone, slightly warmer water, more flow, and larger pools. The *Barbel Zone* occurs in stream sections where slower currents and more water permit greater habitat diversity, as well as conditions particularly suitable for cyprinids that prefer flowing water, barbel (*Barbus barbus*), chub (*Squalius cephalus*), and nace (*Chondrostoma nasus*). These fishes resemble in morphology and feeding habits the suckers (Catostomidae) and large cyprinids (e.g., *Semotilus*) of North American streams. The Barbel Zone often contains a few trout and grayling in the riffles and a few deep-bodied cyprinids in the pools. The *Bream Zone* is found on the valley floor in large, sluggish streams. The fish fauna is quite diverse but is dominated by such deep-bodied cyprinids as bream (*Abramis brama*), tench (*Tinca tinca*), and carp (*Cyprinus carpio*). Large carnivorous fishes are also present here: pike (*Esox lucius*), perch (*Perca fluviatilus*), and eel (*Anguilla anguilla*).

San Joaquin River System. The three zones recognized for this system are rather sharply delineated compared to the fish zones in most other areas of North America. The main reason for this is that the environment changes sharply from cold, precipitous streams in the Sierra Nevada Mountains, to warm foothill streams of moderate gradient, to the meandering, sluggish river on the floor of the San Joaquin Valley (Moyle and Nichols 1974). The cold, high-gradient streams of the *Trout Zone* originally contained rainbow trout only in the lowest part. The zone was extended throughout the high mountain areas by the planting not only of rainbow trout but also of brown trout, brook trout, and golden trout (*Salmo aguabonita*). The *Sucker-squawfish-roach Zone* contains two distinct fish associations. California roach are present by themselves, or with low numbers of juveniles of other minnows and suckers, in the small, intermittent tributaries to the larger

406

streams. The larger streams are dominated by Sacramento squawfish and Sacramento sucker (*Catostomus occidentalis*) and, in some streams, hardhead. This zone is found in the warm foothill streams and, as a consequence, has been much disrupted by the construction of dams in the zone. The *Deep-Bodied Fishes Zone* occurs in the warm, turbid waters of the valley floor. It was orginally dominated by four large native minnow species adapted for quiet water and the piscivorous Sacramento perch (*Archoplites interruptus*). These fishes are now either extinct or rare in the zone and have been replaced by exotic quiet-water fishes, including three species of sunfish (*Lepomis*), largemouth bass (*Micropterus*), four species of catfish (*Ictalurus*), and carp. Despite the changes in the fish fauna caused by humans, the body shapes of the fishes in each of the three zones are remarkably similar to the body shapes of fishes found in the Trout, Barbel, and Bream Zones of Europe.

Brier Creek, Oklahoma. Where fish faunas are more complex and gradients less sharp than in Europe or California, fish zones are harder to define, especially on a regional basis. In Oklahoma two broad distributional studies (Stevenson et al. 1974; Echelle and Schnell 1976) found complex associations between groups of fish species and groups of environmental variables, but these are difficult to map out as zones. However, an intensive study of one creek revealed definable zones (Smith and Powell 1971). The *Headwater Zone* is found where the gradient is comparatively high for the region (but low compared to the Trout Zones of other areas). The stream here is intermittent, with mud, sand, or gravel bottom, high turbidity, and warm summer temperatures. The fishes present are all capable of living under severe environmental conditions. In the most ephemeral parts of the zone, the two dominant species (fathead minnow and green sunfish) are good colonizers. In more permanent parts, the dominant fishes are a catfish (*Ictalurus melas*), a sunfish (*Lepomis humilis*), and a deep-bodied minnow (*Notropis lutrensis*). All are more or less omnivorous. The *Midstream Zone* contains 19 to 21 species that require more permanent conditions than found in the Headwater Zone. The habitat is much more diverse in this zone, and the fishes fall into two general assemblages, one associated with riffles and one associated with pools. The species present are mostly small: minnows, darters, killifishes, catfishes, and sunfishes, although two species of piscivorous bass are also present, as are a few large carp and suckers. The species represent a wide range of body types and feeding habits. The *Downstream Zone* occurs where the water is deep and sluggish and contains 28 fish species generally associated with lakes or large rivers, such as plankton-feeding shad (*Dorosoma*) and silversides (*Menidia audens*) and the deep-bodied predators, white crappie (*Pomoxis annularis*) and white bass (*Morone chrysops*).

General Zones. Despite species differences in the zones in different regions, the zones often have much in common in terms of environmental factors and fish morphology. Three general types of zones can therefore be recognized in most stream systems: an erosional zone, an intermediate zone, and a depositional zone (Cummins 1972). *Erosional zones* occur in high-gradient regions and are characterized by rocky bottoms and swift, usually cold water. Long riffles and small pools are the main habitat types. The fishes of the erosional zones tend to be streamlined, active forms, such as trout, or small, bottom-dwelling forms, such as sculpins and dace. In regions where gradients in head-water streams are not particularly high, such as the central United States, the classic cold-water erosional zone may be replaced by zones dominated by warm-water fishes adapted for fluctuating or extreme conditions, such as are found in the headwaters of Brier Creek or in streams that drain swamps. *Intermediate zones* characterize the long middle reaches of tributary streams. They typically have moderate gradients, warm water, and about equal amounts of shallow riffles, deep rock-bottomed or mud-bottomed pools, and runs that undercut the banks. They also merge imperceptibly with the erosional zones above and the depositional zones below and may be subdivided into two or more fish zones. In North America the typical fishes of the intermediate zones are minnows (Cyprinidae), suckers (Catostomidae), centrarchids (especially smallmouth bass, *Micropterus dolomieui*), darters (Etheostominae), and small catfishes of the genus *Noturus*. None of these forms is particularly deep-bodied, and many specialize in particular habitats within the zone. *Depositional zones* occur in the warm, turbid, and sluggish lower reaches of stream systems where bottoms are muddy and beds of aquatic plants common. A wide variety of fishes occur here, but most typical are deep-bodied forms, such as those adapted for bottom feeding (e.g., carpsuckers, *Carpiodes*), picking up small invertebrates from plants (e.g., sunfish, *Lepomis*), plankton feeding (shads, *Dorosoma*) or predation (basses, *Micropterus* and *Morone*). The assemblages of fishes are nearly the same as those found in lakes in the regions. Where a river runs into the sea, the depositional zone will merge gradually with an estuarine zone that contains a mixture of euryhaline freshwater and saltwater fishes (see Chapter 32).

As a final point, it should be reemphasized that fish zones are as much descriptive tools of fish biologists as they are real entities. They typically merge into one another very gradually and, in low-gradient areas, one "zone" may occupy many miles of stream. In some streams no zones may exist because the distributional patterns of the fishes present do not coincide enough to form easily identified associations of species. It is also not uncommon for the sequence of zones described to be absent because the lower reaches of a stream have a higher gradient than the upper reaches (e.g., Hocutt and Stauffer 1975) or because high-gradient stretches are interspersed with low-gradient stretches (e.g., Barber and Minckley 1966).

Supplemental Readings

Allen 1969; Deacon and Minckley 1974; Huet 1959; Hynes 1970; Jones 1964; Keast 1966; Mendelson 1975; Moyle 1976a, b; Moyle and Li 1979; Northcote 1969; Oglesby et al. 1972; Sheldon 1968; Whitton 1975.

ααααααααααααααααααααααααααααααααααααααααααααααααααααααααααααααααααααα
~~~~~~

Temperate Lakes and Reservoirs

On the geological time scale, most lakes and reservoirs of North America and Eurasia are ephemeral, with ages ranging from fifty to several thousand years. They disappear as they fill up with sediment, dry up with changes in climate, or are covered by advancing continental glaciers. They are also created rather easily, as water collecting in depressions and holes left by various natural processes, such as the retreat of glaciers, earthquakes, and floods, and as oxbows left behind by meandering rivers. In recent years humans have been creating lakes by the thousands by impounding rivers. In North America alone, there are now over 1500 reservoirs with a surface area of 200 hectares or greater and countless smaller ones. In view of the impermanence of lakes, it is not surprising to find that there are comparatively few species of fish in the north temperate and arctic regions that are adapted only for life in lakes. Instead, most lake fishes are the same as those found in nearby streams, especially large rivers. Many lake populations have made modest behavioral, physiological, and morphological adaptations to the lake environment and a number of species are most abundant in lakes, yet most of them still must rely on streams for dispersal and long-term survival as species. The main exceptions to this rule are fishes that occur in very large lakes, such as the species complexes of salmonids found in the Great Lakes and the unique fish fauna of Lake Baikal in the Soviet Union, which is not only one of the largest lakes in the world but also one of the oldest (Kozhov 1963).

Despite this general lack of fish species highly specialized for lake living, lakes have many special characteristics that restrict the distribution of fishes within and among them. The effects of physical, chemical, temporal, biological, and zoogeographical factors, and their

410

interactions, on fishes result in distinctive regional fish faunas as well as resource partitioning by the fishes of the ecological resources of each lake.

Physical Factors The principal physical factors that affect the distribution and abundance of fishes in lakes are temperature, light, water movement, water level fluctuations, size (surface area and depth), and substrate.

Temperature. Fishery managers have long recognized that the basic fish fauna of a lake is determined in large part by temperature and have, as a consequence, tended to divide lakes into three basic types: (1) cold-water lakes, in which the dominant sport or commercial fishes are salmonids; (2) warm-water lakes, in which the dominant sport or commercial fishes are centrarchids (black basses and sunfishes), percids (perch and walleye), esocids (pike), and percichthyids (white, yellow, and striped basses); and (3) two-story lakes, with warm-water fishes in the warm upper layer (epilimnion) and cold-water fishes in the deep water (hypolimnion). There are, of course, many lakes which do not fit nicely into any of the three categories, but the system does demonstrate that in lakes, as in streams, temperature is a major determinant of distribution patterns. The presence of the two-story lake category indicates that temperature also is important in determining distribution patterns within lakes, at least during the summer months. When the thermocline forms in the spring in such lakes, separating the epilimnion from the hypolimnion, the species quickly segregate by temperature preferences. Even in lakes that do not categorize easily, temperature may be one of the main determinants of distribution. For example, in Lake Michigan, in which temperatures below the thermocline are 4°C to 7°C, bloater (*Coregonus hoyi*) are most abundant at 6°C to 10°C, smelt (*Osmerus mordax*) at 6°C to 14°C, spottail shiner (*Notropis hudsonius*) at 13°C to 22+°C, trout-perch (*Percopsis omiscomaycus*) at 10°C to 16°C, yellow perch (*Perca flavescens*) at 11°C to 22+C, slimy sculpin (*Cottus cognatus*) at 4°C to 6°C, fourhorn sculpin (*Myoxocephalus quadricornus*) at 4°C to 4.5°C, and alewife (*Alosa pseudoharengus*) at 8°C to 22°C (Wells 1968). The wide temperature range tolerated by the alewife is of particular interest because it is a recently introduced species that has had a highly disruptive influence on the native fish fauna, which apparently segregated in part by temperature.

It is worth noting that the number of species, the standing crop (biomass per square meter), and the growth rates of fish in cold-water lakes tend to be considerably less than those of fish in warm-water lakes. However, temperature is just one of a number of factors (e.g., growing season, nutrient availability) that may cause this.

Light. Light has many rather subtle effects on fish distribution patterns within and between lakes. Most warm-water lakes are rather turbid, so the typical deepwater fishes are species that do not have to rely on vision for prey capture, such as catfish, carp, and suckers. In such lakes, most aquatic plant growth is also in shallow water. Since beds of aquatic plants increase both habitat diversity and abundance of invertebrates, fish species and numbers tend to be highest in shallow water. Pelagic plankton-feeding fishes also tend to concentrate in well-lighted waters, where their prey is most visible. For example, in highly turbid Clear Lake, California, the Mississippi silverside (*Menidia audens*) is found almost exclusively in the upper meter of the water column. In contrast, in lakes that are fairly clear, including most cold-water lakes, both vision-oriented predators (e.g., lake trout [*Salvelinus namaycush*]) and plankton feeders (e.g., whitefishes [*Coregonus* spp.]) are found at considerable depths. One predatory species that is successful in both turbid and clear lakes is the walleye (*Stizostedion vitreum*), which has exceptionally large eyes equipped with a light-gathering layer, the tapetum lucidum. In turbid lakes the walleye tends to feed during the day, while in clear lakes its feeding tends to be crepuscular (Ryder 1977).

The activity patterns of most other lake fishes are also affected by light. Vision-oriented predators are most active during the day, often with peaks of feeding in the early morning and evening when invertebrates become more available: Zooplankton are moving upwards, benthic insects start to become active, and flights of terrestrial and aquatic insect adults increase. Dawn and dusk are also the times when piscivorous fishes move into shallow water, attracted by the feeding activities of the smaller fishes and the fact that they are less visible themselves at low light intensities. After dark most day-active fishes lie quietly on the bottom, beneath submerged objects, or among aquatic plants, although some species, such as the sunfishes (*Lepomis* spp.), may remain in slowly circling schools. Night-active fishes, particularly catfish and suckers, then move into shallow water to forage. Because summer temperatures in shallow water are often considerably cooler at night, fishes found only below the thermocline during the day may move inshore to forage in the evening.

Water movements. Steady, predictable currents, such as those existing in the oceans, seldom exist in natural lakes, yet the movement of water by winds can have considerable impact on fish distribution within a lake. A series of days with wind from one direction can cause zooplankton to concentrate along the lee shore. This may result in a concentration of zooplankton-feeding fishes as well. The distribution of larval fishes that drift in the surface waters of a lake may be quite patchy because of temporary gyres and currents created by winds, although these same currents also concentrate the zooplankton on which the larval fish feed. On the other hand, the discharge of water from reservoirs at critical times of the year may result in substantial losses of planktonic larvae, which in turn will greatly affect the number of adult fishes of certain species (Walburg 1971). As these examples indicate, reservoirs frequently have conditions that are intermediate between those found in rivers and those in natural lakes, since the demand for the water they store is likely to cause detectable currents at both their upper and their lower ends. Consequently, the fish fauna at the upper end of a reservoir may be somewhat different from that found in the more lakelike middle areas. In many North American reservoirs, smallmouth bass (*Micropterus dolomieui*) tend to be most abundant at the upper ends of the reservoirs and largemouth bass (*M. salmoides*) most abundant elsewhere. Although such current-related patterns of distribution are most characteristic of reservoirs, more subtle versions can be found in natural lakes. Most natural lakes do have definite inlets and outlets, which create a general, if barely detectable, pattern of flow through the lake. Usually, such patterns are too slight to affect fish distribution within the lake. However, in Lake Memphremagog, on the border of Quebec and Vermont, such flow results in a gradual decrease in the amount of nutrients from the inlet end of the lake to the outlet end and, consequently, in the abundance and diversity of fish species (Gascon and Leggett 1977).

Water level fluctuations are primarily a problem to fishes in reservoirs and lakes with regulated water levels. Rapid drops in water level may expose the nests of spawning centrachids, especially largemouth bass, and rapid rises in water level may cover the nests with a depth of water intolerable to the spawning fish. Such fluctuations also prevent the establishment of plants such as cattails and willows along the reservoir edges. In natural lakes, flooded shoreline marshes are important spring spawning sites for fish such as northern pike (*Esox lucius*). Later in the year, the emergent vegetation serves as cover for the young of many species, such as largemouth bass and carp. Drops in water level may also create barriers to spawning for lake-dwelling species that spawn in streams. In Pyramid Lake, Nevada, the near extinction of the cui-ui (*Chasmistes cujus*) and the extinction of Lahontan cutthroat trout (*Salmo clarki henshawi*) were largely caused by reduced flows into the lake from the Truckee River, which had been diverted for irrigation. The drop in lake level exposed an extensive, shallow delta that was impassable to the spawning fish.

Size. There are three aspects of lake size that particularly affect both the number of species and total fish production in lakes: surface area, mean depth, and shoreline length. The relationship of surface area to number of species is not a strong one because so many other factors, especially zoogeographic factors, can affect the number of species. However, in general, the greater the surface area, the more species are likely to be present (Barbour and Brown 1974), although Carlander (1955) could find no relationship between surface area and standing crop of fishes. One of the factors which obscure the relationship between surface area and fish numbers is that there is a fairly strong negative relationship between mean depth and species number, as well as standing crop (Carlander 1955; Ryder 1965; Jenkins 1967). Deep water in lakes is often cold, poorly lighted, and poorly oxygenated and hence supports few fish. The length of shoreline has the opposite effect of depth; usually, the more shoreline, the more species. All three of these size variables indicate one thing: within a zoogeographic region, as habitat variety increases, so does the number of species and the standing crop of fishes. Overall, the greatest variety of habitat suitable for fish is likely to occur in a large, shallow lake with many bays and other irregularities in its shoreline.

Substrate. Although it is quite difficult to relate the overall distribution pattern of any lake-dwelling species to the presence of a particular kind of substrate, substrate nevertheless does have a strong influence on fish distribution within a lake, especially for spawning. For example, spawning sunfishes and black basses (Centrarchidae) require areas soft enough for digging a nest depression but firm enough so that the eggs will not be smothered in mud. Sculpins and bluntnose minnows (*Pimephales notatus*) lay eggs on the underside of overhanging rocks or logs. Perch (*Perca flavescens*) and many minnows scatter adhesive eggs over beds of aquatic plants. Lake trout (*Salvelinus namaycush*) lay their eggs in deep water among concentrations of boulders. The importance of substrate for lake trout spawning is well illustrated by the fact that in Cayuga Lake, New York, the trout populations have to be artificially maintained by planting because their main spawning ground was silted over by soil carried into the lake by a nearby inlet (Young and Oglesby 1972).

Even when not spawning, most lake fishes show some preference for a general type of substrate. Particularly attractive to many fishes are beds of aquatic plants which contain abundant food and cover. Such beds are most often located on soft, usually muddy, bottoms. Other species are associated mainly with rocky bottoms. Thus, in many lakes of eastern North America, sculpins (*Cottus*) and some darters (*Etheostoma*) are found mainly in rocky inshore areas. The cover provided by submerged objects, such as fallen trees and old boats, are also very attractive to fishes, including many important game fishes (catfishes, black basses, sunfishes, etc.). This fact is being taken advantage of today by fishery managers who construct artificial reefs on sandy or muddy-bottomed areas with little natural relief in order to improve fishing (Johnson and Stein 1979). Another type of cover that is often attractive to lake fishes is shade created by overhanging trees, bushes, piers, and anchored boats. Although fishes hovering in the shade may seem to be in a rather exposed position, they are in fact harder for predators to see and at the same time it is easier for them to see predators approaching through sunlit areas (Helfman 1981).

Chemical Factors

Gases. The only gas dissolved in lake water that exerts a major direct effect on fish distribution is oxygen, although carbon dioxide is indirectly important to fish through the carbonate–bicarbonate cycle and the relationship of this cycle to primary production (see Wetzel 1975). Primary production is, in fact, the main source of oxygen in lakes, although the action of wind and waves is an important secondary source. The absence of these two sources of oxygen, combined with the removal of oxygen through decay of organic matter, is the reason that major fish kills may occur in shallow ice-covered lakes in the winter.

Because some species (e.g., carp) have a much higher tolerance for low oxygen levels than other species (e.g., northern pike), the composition of the fish fauna of many lakes in the midwestern United States is in part determined by dissolved oxygen levels in winter, when they are lowest (Moyle and Clothier 1959). Similarly, the absence of trout from the deep water of many "two-story" lakes is due to low oxygen levels in the hypolimnion. Despite dramatic examples such as these, the influence of oxygen on fish distribution in and between lakes is quite subtle and closely bound to temperature effects.

Ions. The influence of dissolved ions on the distribution of lake-dwelling fishes is complex, since the concentrations of the various ions in a lake affect not only the fish but also every other organism present. Moreover, the chemistry of a lake's water is related to that of the surrounding rocks, soils, and plant communities, and so broad relationships between fish distribution and lake chemistry may be partly the result of zoogeographic coincidence. However, zoogeography usually does not go very far in explaining the high correlations often found between patterns of fish distribution and production, and water chemistry patterns (expressed as pH), nutrient concentrations, or some measure of total dissolved inorganic and organic salts (e.g., salinity, total dissolved solids, conductivity, alkalinity).

Lakes with pH values above 8.5 or below 5 support only a few rather tolerant fish species or, if the values are extreme, none at all. Most lake fishes are capable of living within the pH range of 5 to 8.5, so pH measurements in lakes normally say little about the fish populations present, although alkaline lakes do have higher fish production than acidic lakes. Fish production in turn is determined through food chains by primary production, which is limited by the availability of nutrients, particularly phosphorus and nitrogen. Thus, the fertilization of oligotrophic lakes in British Columbia and Alaska has been found to increase the growth and survival of juvenile sockeye salmon (*Oncorhynchus nerka*) by increasing the supply of zooplankton upon which the salmon feed. It is worth noting here that unexploited oligotrophic lakes may support surprisingly high standing crops of fish (usually salmonids) despite low nutrient levels. Most of the fish biomass is tied up in large, old, slow-growing adults. Johnson (1976) compares such populations to "climax" communities of plants, since almost all the energy derived from primary production goes into maintenance and reproduction rather than growth.

The complexity of the interactions between dissolved salts, nutrients, and fish distribution and production are well illustrated by the broad distributional patterns of the four major fish associations found in Minnesota lakes (Fig. 29.1). Not only can presence or absence of the fish associations be related to water chemistry, but they can also be related to the surrounding plant communities and, to a lesser extent, climatic variables such as temperature. Because the relationship between distributional patterns and water chemistry is complex and is influenced by various physical factors as well, the morphoedaphic index was developed by Ryder (1965). This is a ratio between one of the most useful (if crude) chemical measurements, total dissolved solids, and one of the most useful physical measurements, mean depth. Within a region there may be a strong correlation between fish production and the index (Ryder 1965), although the relationship is not necessarily linear (Jenkins 1968).

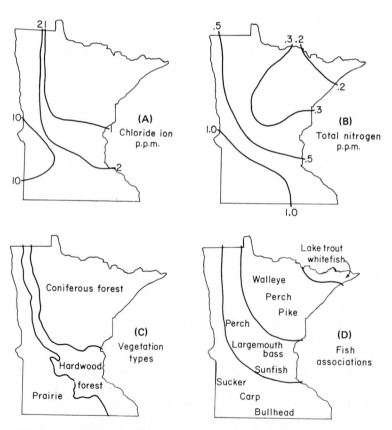

FIGURE 29.1 Generalized clines of salinity (as measured by chlorinity), dissolved nutrients (as indicated by total nitrogen), and vegetation types in relation to major fish associations in Minnesota lakes. (From Moyle, 1956.)

Temporal Factors
The composition of the fish fauna of most lakes is rarely constant. It is likely to change as a lake ages, as the climate fluctuates from year to year, and as the abundance of species changes from season to season.

Long-term changes in the fish faunas of lakes are poorly documented, although they are inevitable as the chemistry of lakes change with the accumulation of nutrients and other ions from the surrounding land, and as the physical environment changes with the accumulation of sediments. A gradual addition of species is also likely as species enter lakes through outlets or inlets. Actually, the types of changes likely to occur naturally in lakes can be understood, more or less, through the study of lakes that have been strongly affected by humans through "cultural eutrophication" and the introduction of exotic species. For example, there are many lakes in North America and Europe close to urban areas that formerly were dominated by salmonids. Under the influence of increased nutrients, species introductions, and overexploitation, they have become dominated by cyprinids and perch (*Perca*), with an overall increase in fish biomass (Loftus and Regier 1972).

Reservoirs provide another general example of the changes that can take place in the fish fauna of a lake through time, although it seems unlikely that the typical sequence of events observed in reservoirs happens in many natural lakes, even on a more expanded time scale. For the first few years, fish populations and species numbers are high in reservoirs, because both the lacustrine species planted by humans and the riverine species already present grow rapidly in the new environment. Reproduction may also be good initially because spawning areas are not yet silted over and because water level fluctuations are minor. As the reservoir ages and extreme fluctuations become the rule, the total fish biomass declines, as does the number of abundant species, particularly riverine species. The species that remain abundant are those that (1) are long-lived, so that one successful spawn will sustain their populations over a long period (e.g., carp); (2) migrate upstream to spawn (e.g., sauger [*Stizostedion canadense*], many suckers of the genus *Catostomus*); (3) spawn pelagically (e.g., freshwater drum [*Aplodinotus grunniens*], shad [*Dorosoma* spp.]); or (4) spawn in water deep enough not to be affected by the fluctuations (e.g., channel catfish [*Ictalurus punctatus*]). Habitat of the larval fishes is also important, since pelagic larvae may be washed downstream. Unfortunately, as far as fishermen are concerned, the species that are most likely to decline from lack of reproductive success are predatory gamefishes. Angling pressure and lack of suitable prey may also contribute to the decline of these species.

Climatic fluctuations are likely to cause fluctuations in the composition of a lake's fish fauna mainly as a result of their effect on water temperatures and lake levels. Most fishes have a limited range of temperatures at which they will spawn. If these temperatures are not reached, spawning will not occur, or if they are reached late in the season, the eggs and larvae may have to face larger populations of small predatory fishes. In either case reproductive failure is likely, and the species, or at least the year class, is likely to be less abundant in future years. Reproductive failure is also likely in drought years for species that require flooded vegetation for spawning or emergent plants as cover for their young. The reproductive failure of one species may also affect the abundance of other species. In Oneida Lake, New York, young yellow perch are the principal prey of walleye. When the perch have poor reproductive success, walleye predation on their own young increases, resulting in a less abundant year class of walleye (Forney 1974). On the other hand, reproductive failure of one species may increase survival of species whose populations are being suppressed by competition or predation. For example, the opportunistic common shiner (*Notropis cornutus*) seems to become most abundant in small Midwestern lakes when more specialized species of *Notropis* have reduced populations. As a result of such interactions, the overall composition of a lake's fish fauna may show considerable year-to-year variation.

Seasonal changes in the fish fauna of lakes are related to a combination of reproductive and seasonal movements. The major fish species in lakes tend to reproduce at different times, and this results in a definite succession of planktonic larvae in the open waters of lakes in the summer (e.g., Amundsrud et al. 1974), as well as a succession of abundance of juvenile fishes in the inshore areas. Many adult and juvenile fishes make decided seasonal migrations to different depths or parts of lakes, resulting in a seasonally changing species composition in some habitats, particularly inshore areas (e.g., Wells 1968). The ability of the alewife to move to different habitats as the seasons change has enabled it to disrupt the less migratory, more stationary inshore and deepwater communities of Lake Michigan (Smith 1970).

Biological Factors   Like the fishes found in streams, lake-dwelling fishes in temperate regions are quite flexible in their living arrangements with other species of animals and plants, particularly other fishes. These arrangements are best examined under the general heading of predator–prey relationships, competitive interactions, and symbiotic interactions.

Predator–prey relationships.   Predation by fish is a major factor influencing the composition of the biotic communities of lakes, from plants through invertebrates to fish. Grazing and rooting about by fish, particularly carp, can greatly influence the amount and species of aquatic plants growing on lake bottoms, as well as the species and numbers of invertebrates associated with the plants (Straskraba 1965). Most fish that browse on invertebrates associated with aquatic plants or the bottom are selective as to what species they prey on, and such selective predation will greatly affect the composition of the invertebrate community (e.g., Stein et al. 1975). The impact of such selective predation on the zooplankton community of lakes is even more pronounced, or at least better understood. In lakes without specialized planktivores, the dominant zooplankters tend to be large species, such as *Daphnia pulex*. In lakes with such planktivores, the dominant species are much smaller, may have protective spines, or may have smaller eyes, making them less visible (Brooks 1968; Zaret 1972). The impact of fish on zooplankton has been demonstrated repeatedly when zooplanktivorous fish have been introduced into lakes. For example, the development of alewife populations in Lake Michigan resulted in declines in the populations of seven species of large zooplankters, including the near disappearance of two species, and increases in the numbers of 10 small species (Wells 1970).

Predation also has a major impact on the structure of fish communities and populations in lakes. Occasionally, the introduction of a new predator into a lake can drastically reduce the populations of many of the fishes present, as the impact of the sea lamprey on the larger fishes of the Great Lakes so graphically illustrates. Interestingly enough, as the large predatory fishes of the Great Lakes declined, populations of fish species that were too small to be preyed on by the lampreys increased greatly, presumably as a result of the absence of predation and competition from the larger fish (Smith 1968) (Fig. 29.2). The complexity of predator–prey interactions in lakes is well illustrated by the long-term studies of pike (*Esox lucius*), perch (*Perca fluviatilis*), and char (*Salvelinus willughbii*) in Lake Windermere, England (Le Cren et al. 1972). Prior to 1941, large pike apparently kept char numbers down by preying on the adults as they moved inshore to spawn. Although perch were the main food of the pike for the rest of the year, the number of adult pike was apparently too low to be able to limit the perch population size. Between 1941 and 1964, adult perch were removed from the lake by intensive fishing, but the perch populations failed to recover when the fishing was stopped. The reason for this apparently was that an experimental pike fishery had removed most pike larger than 55 cm from the lake from 1944 onwards, resulting in optimum conditions for the growth and survival of small pike. The abundant small pike feed on small prey, particularly young perch, making it difficult for the perch populations to build up again to their former levels. Meanwhile, in the absence of predation from large pike, char numbers increased.

As the preceding examples indicate, there are many ways predators and prey can affect each other's populations in lakes. Under more or less stable environmental conditions, self-regulating predator–prey systems can theoretically develop. Steady "cropping" of a prey species by a predator will reduce intraspecific competition and consequently

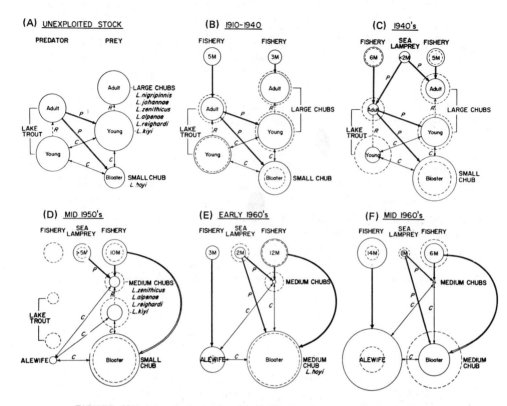

FIGURE 29.2 Interrelations of major deepwater fishes of Lake Michigan: (A) before exploitation; (B) during moderate exploitation; (C) during the period of increasing sea lamprey abundance; (D) during the peak of sea lamprey abundance, when large fish became rare and small chubs increased in numbers and in size; (E) during the period when bloaters were at their peak abundance and the alewife was just becoming established; (F) during the period of maximum abundance of the alewife. The nature of the interactions is indicated by *P* for predation, *C* for competition, and *R* for recruitment. (From Smith, 1968.)

increase growth rates of the prey. Such rapid growth may increase the reproductive potential of the prey by allowing the prey to mature at an earlier age and by increasing egg production, since the increase in fecundity of fishes tends to have an exponential relationship to length. If the increased reproduction by the prey results in a "surplus" of prey, two things may happen simultaneously: The predator population may increase, and intraspecific competition among the prey may increase, resulting in slower growth and lower reproduction. These two factors will cause a rapid decline in the population of the prey, followed by a decline in the predator population, to the former lower level of both species. The cycle then repeats itself. While this system may in fact operate in lakes, it is likely to be highly modified by the fact that predators will switch prey and that reproduction and growth are also likely to be affected by changing environmental conditions. There is evidence that in some lakes used by sockeye salmon as nurseries, the feedback scheme described above plays a major role in determining the abundance of adult salmon (Hartman and Burgner 1972). However, in salmon nursery lakes in which there are a number of alternate prey species for the predators, the system may not work because the alternate prey either serve to maintain high populations of predators or, alternately, serve as buffer species that reduce predation on the young salmon.

Regardless of its effect on community structure in lakes, predation is probably the single biggest source of natural mortality of fishes. The ultimate effect of most physical and chemical changes in a lake is to change the relative vulnerability to predation of the species present. Thus year class failures of largemouth bass and other species may be due on occasion to falling water levels that force young fish to leave the protection of emergent vegetation, making them more vulnerable to predation. When environmental conditions result in unsuccessful spawning of a normally abundant species, predators may switch to feeding more heavily on their own young, thus reducing their own populations. Predation may also determine the ultimate result of competitive interactions between and within species, since individuals displaced as the result of competition are likely to be consumed by predators.

Competitive interactions. Fish in lakes, like those in streams, show a remarkable degree of ecological segregation. Although the segregation can be explained in part by differences in body morphology, the coexistence of similar, closely related species in lakes is common. Fish populations in lakes are probably more constant in general than those in streams, but there is nevertheless considerable year-to-year and season-to-season variation in species composition. In addition, food and habitat (e.g., aquatic plant beds) show considerable variation in availability from season to season. All these factors indicate that competitive interactions are likely to be important in the shaping of fish communities in lakes. As the studies of trout and char in Scandinavian lakes show, such interactions can be expressed as direct aggression of one species on another, resulting in the domination of the preferred habitat by the most aggressive species. However, differential exploitation of resources as a cause of observed ecological differences is probably more common. For example, when pumpkinseed (*Lepomis gibbosus*), bluegill (*L. macrochirus*), and green sunfish (*L. cyanellus*) occur together, they are found in different habitats and feed on different kinds and sizes of invertebrates. However, if the other species are absent, the "niche" of any of the species will expand to include at least partially the habitat and food that would otherwise be utilized by the other two species (Werner and Hall 1976). The least change in niche occurs with the green sunfish, which feeds on large invertebrates among the aquatic plants. Green sunfish apparently protect these resources from the other species in part by aggressive behavior and in part by more efficient foraging for the prey. As a result of the interactions, bluegill and pumpkinseed prey on smaller organisms, pumpkinseed become more bottom-oriented, favoring molluscs as food, and bluegill become more oriented toward the water column and zooplankton. It is worth noting that in the spring, when food is most abundant and fish populations are lower, there is more overlap in food and habitat than in the fall, when resources are likely to be depleted (Seaburg and Moyle 1964). Another consequence of abundant food is the likelihood that more species will be utilizing it. For example, in Lake Memphremagog the small, bottom-feeding cyprinodont *Fundulus diaphanus* is found mainly in areas where benthic insects are abundant. In other areas it is apparently excluded by other bottom-feeding species (Gascon and Leggett 1977).

In reservoirs, the effects of competitive interactions among species normally are minimized by the extreme fluctuations in the physical environment. The main exception to this occurs among the plankton-feeding fishes, in part because zooplankton populations are less likely to be affected by fluctuations in water level than benthic invertebrates. When a planktivore, such as threadfish shad (*Dorosoma petenense*), is introduced into a reservoir that has lacked such a species, it will reduce the zooplankton populations and consequently the populations of bluegill, largemouth bass, and other fishes that have early life history stages dependent on abundant zooplankton for survival (von Geldern and Mitchell 1975).

Symbiotic interactions. Examples of symbiosis affecting fish communities in lakes are few, although this may be in part because they have not been looked for. It *is* common to find different species schooling with each other, presumably forming mutualistic or commensal associations. In Long Lake, Minnesota, small groups of blunt-nose minnows (*Pimephales notatus*) were found in shallow water, outside weed beds, only when they were in association with large schools of mimic shiners (*Notropis volucellus*). In the mixed schools the minnows were found below the main school of shiners, feeding on the bottom, while the shiners were feeding in midwater (Moyle 1973). Presumably, the minnows could take advantage of the protection from predators afforded by the large school of shiners to feed in habitat otherwise too hazardous for them.

Zoogeographic Factors   Barriers to fish dispersal are major determinants of the fish faunas of lakes, as the presence of zoogeographic regions alone (Chapter 24) shows. The closer a lake is (or was) to a major river system, the more species are likely to be present. Lakes with long stretches of stream, especially high-gradient stretches, between them and a major river or other lakes are likely to contain only the same fishes found in headwater streams or derivatives of them, such as trout, suckers, dace, and chubs. Indeed, most of the lakes of the high mountains in the West were without fish until trout and other species were planted by humans. In remote lakes already containing fishes, the fact that a number of new species can be added indicates the importance of barriers in limiting fish faunas. For example, Clear Lake, California, originally contained 12 native fish species. Between 1880 and the present, 15 exotic species were added to the fauna and three of the native species became extinct, leaving 24 species total. Although it can be argued that the present fish fauna is unstable, with a number of further extinctions likely, the ultimate fish fauna will undoubtedly contain more than 12 species (Moyle 1976a).

Fish Zones

The designation of fish zones in lakes is likely to be even more arbitrary than for streams, because lake fishes are comparatively free to move from one zone to another. Fish zones in lakes are also likely to be highly seasonal, being best developed in the summer. However, fish species in lakes do tend to sort themselves out along environmental gradients during the summer months, when most individual and population growth occurs. As a result, distinct clusters of species tend to be associated with the broad habitat types within lakes, and these associations can be described as fish zones. Within each fish zone the species further tend to segregate by microhabitat and food preferences. As examples of these patterns, the zones in three types of lakes will be described here: (1) a small, "two-story" lake (Long Lake); (2) a large, cold-water lake (Lake Tahoe); and (3) warm-water reservoirs.

Long Lake, located in north central Minnesota, is somewhat unusual for its bathtublike morphology (deep and steep-sided) and for its clarity (Moyle 1969, 1973). However, these same factors, result in sharp environmental gradients and easily observable fish zones. The nineteen species of fish that are common in the lake are typical of small lakes in areas subjected to Pleistocene glaciation, and the patterns of segregation observed are also typical of such lakes (e.g., Keast 1965; Werner et al. 1977; Gascon and Leggett 1977). Four zones were recognizable in the lake: (1) Shallow-Water Zone; (2) Aquatic Plant Zone; (3) Deep-Water Zone; and (4) Open-Water Zone (Fig. 29.3).

The Shallow-Water Zone occurs in water less than 1 m deep and is strongly influenced by wave action. Aquatic plants are thinly distributed, and cobbles are the main substrate close to shore. The most conspicuous fish in the zone are schools of mimic shiners, which feed in midwater and surface areas. Bluntnose minnows and common shiners are often associated with these schools as well. On the bottom are Iowa darters (*Etheostoma exile*) and, beneath cobbles, mottled sculpin (*Cottus bairdi*). The main resident predators are green sunfish, found associated with whatever cover (logs, etc.) the zone affords,

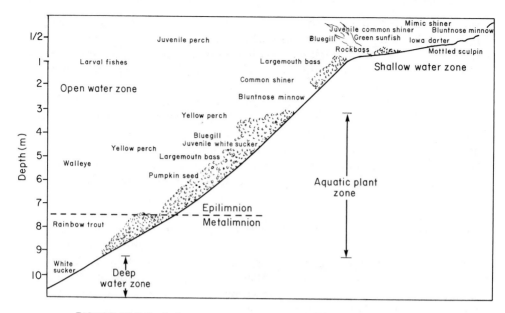

FIGURE 29.3 Typical summer locations during the day in a Minnesota lake of common fish species. (From Moyle, 1969.)

although piscivorous largemouth bass and walleye move into the zone to forage at dusk.

The Aquatic Plant Zone is characterized by dense beds of mixed species of aquatic plants, between 1 m and 9 m deep. The beds are thickest and most diverse at depths between 2 m and 3 m, and populations of the six species most abundant in the zone are also highest here. Bluntnose minnows are found in the clearings in the plant beds, where they feed on detritus, diatoms, and small benthic invertebrates. In contrast, large common shiners and yellow perch are typically associated with clumps of aquatic plants that grow higher than the main mass of vegetation. Both species are opportunistic foragers, with the perch consuming large invertebrates and small fish. Rockbass (*Ambloplites rupestris*) are the main ambush predators on large prey in this zone and are consequently associated with logs, large rocks, and other cover in the shallower areas. Largemouth bass are roving predators on crayfish and fish. Bluegill and pumpkinseed are perhaps the most morphologically similar species in the zone, and both do feed by picking invertebrates from the aquatic plants. However, the pumpkinseed feed largely on snails, whereas the bluegill feed on aquatic insects.

The Deep-Water Zone is found below the lower limits of the aquatic plant beds and below the epilimnion. It is thus cold, dark, and silt-bottomed. Only two species, johnny darter (*E. nigrum*) and white sucker (*Catostomus commersoni*), are regularly found here. The darter feeds on small benthic invertebrates, while the sucker consumes detritus as well and may move into shallow water to forage at night. Rainbow trout are also present in this zone, although their population is maintained by stocking.

The Open-Water Zone, away from the influence of the bottom, is characterized by large schools of juvenile perch and by all size classes of walleye. The walleye generally move inshore to feed in the evening. During the summer there is undoubtedly also a succession of larval fishes, each species occupying the zone on a temporary basis.

Lake Tahoe is a large (surface area 304 km^2), deep (mean depth 313 m), and clear (the bottom is visible at 20 m to 30 m) mountain lake on the California–Nevada border. The six native fish species now characteristic of the lake are also found in the local streams. Originally, the main piscivore in the lake was the Lahontan cutthroat trout (*Salmo clarki henshawi*), but it has now been replaced by lake trout (*Salvelinus namaycush*), rainbow trout (*Salmo gairdneri*), and brown trout. In addition, kokanee salmon (*Oncorhynchus nerka*) have been added to the fauna. The lake can be divided into three broadly overlapping zones: (1) the Shallow Water Zone; (2) the Deep-Water Benthic Zone; and (3) the Midwater Zone. The locations of the zones and the species associated with each one are shown in Fig. 29.4.

Warm-water reservoirs. There are now more surface acres of water in reservoirs in the United States than there are surface acres of natural lakes excluding the Great Lakes (Hall 1971). Most of these reservoirs are dominated by fishes characteristic of warm-water lakes. However, many are stratified and many, particularly in the western United States, are dominated by cold-water fishes. Warm-water reservoirs throughout the United States are remarkably similar in their fish faunas because the extreme fluctuations in water levels and other factors select for the success of certain species and because the reservoirs are always planted with the preferred species of game fishes. The main variations in the fish faunas of the reservoirs are the result of the persistence of species native to the river impounded. Although the fluctuating conditions assure that almost any species found in a reservoir can be collected at one time or another at almost any location in the reservoir, each species is generally most characteristic of one of three zones: (1) Inshore Zone; (2) Open-Water Zone, and (3) Deep-Water Benthic Zone.

The **Inshore Zone** is associated with the sides of the reservoirs. Fish are most abundant where the bottoms are soft and the water is less than 3 m deep, but adults of the larger species are also commonly associated with steep, rocky areas. The typical species of this zone are sunfishes (*Lepomis*), especially bluegill, black basses (*Micropterus*), bullheads (*Ictalurus*), crappie (*Pomoxis*), carp, carpsuckers (*Carpiodes*), buffalofishes (*Ictiobus*), shiners (*Notropis* or the golden shiner [*Notemigonus chrysoleucus*]), and silversides (Atherinidae). The exact composition of the inshore fauna will depend on the particular reservoir, the location within the reservoir, and time of day. Carp, carpsuckers,

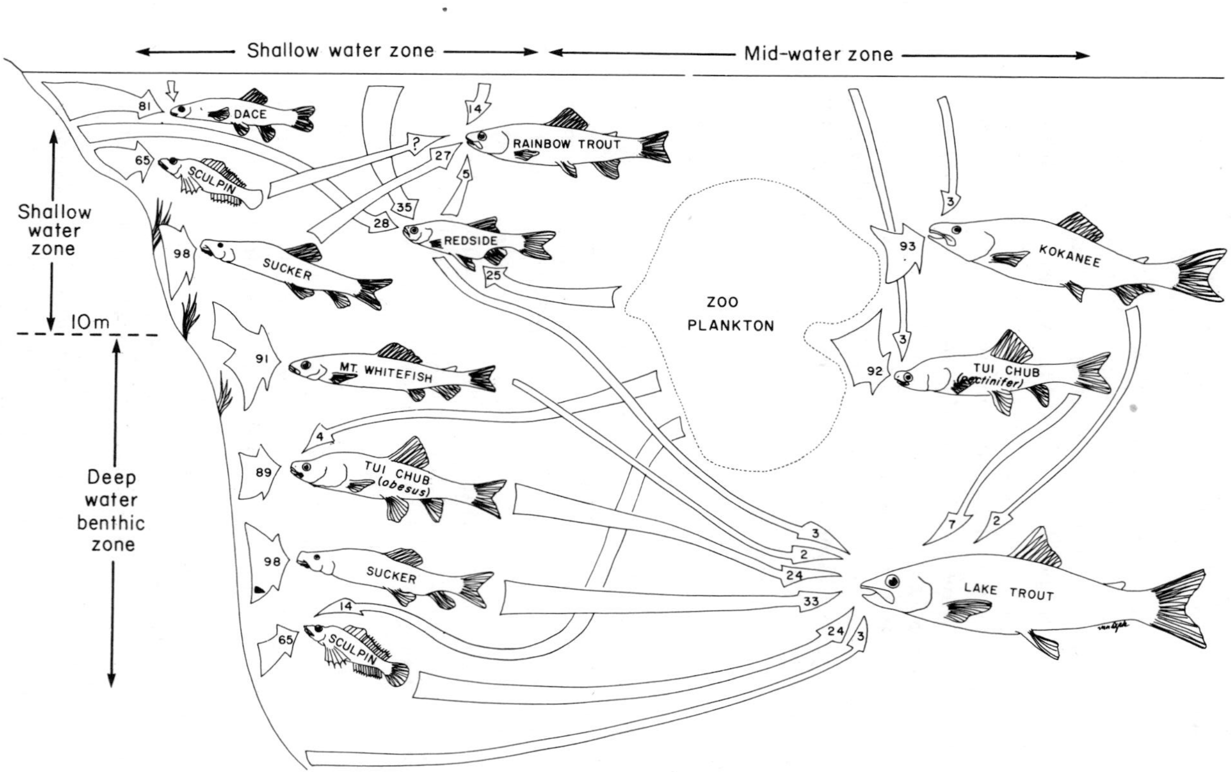

FIGURE 29.4 Zones and feeding relationships of Lake Tahoe fishes. The numbers represent the percentage of diet by volume of the most important food items for each species. The major food categories are benthic organisms, flying insects, zooplankton, and fish. Note that there are two forms of tui chub (*Gila bicolor*) in the lake, a bottom-feeding form (*obesus*) and a zooplankton-feeding form (*pectinifer*). The importance of zooplankton is now probably less than indicated because the introduction of a mysid shrimp into the lake has resulted in the near elimination of the larger species. [From Moyle (1976a), modified from Miller (1951).]

and buffalofishes are mobile, bottom-feeding species that are most likely to be found close to shore at night. Predatory catfishes from the Deep-Water Benthic Zone may move into shallow water at night to prey on the juvenile centrarchids and small minnows that are the most abundant fishes in the shallow areas.

The **Open-Water Zone** is host to most reservoir species at some stage in their life cycle, but it is characterized consistently by plankton-feeding shad (*Dorosoma*) and predatory fishes that feed on the shad, typically white bass (*Morone chrysops*) but often striped bass (*M. saxatilis*), walleye, or sauger. Large crappie may also be found in this zone, feeding on both zooplankton and shad. In addition, in the Mississippi drainage, large plankton feeders, such as freshwater drum and bigmouth buffalo (*Ictiobus cyprinellus*), are generally present. If a reservoir stratifies every summer, the fishes mentioned above are found in the epilimnion, while trout and/or kokanee salmon are found in the hypolimnion. More often than not, the salmonid populations are not self-sustaining and must be supplemented each year by plants of fish.

The **Deep-Water Benthic Zone** contains mainly predatory catfishes and fishes that subsist on detritus or detritus-feeding insect larvae. The most common catfishes are channel catfish (*Ictalurus punctatus*) and flathead catfish (*Pylodictus olivarus*). The detritus-oriented species are typically suckers (Catostomidae) of the genera *Catostomus, Moxostoma*, and *Ictiobus*, and carp. It is worth noting that in most reservoirs detritus-oriented fishes, including bullheads and other species more characteristic of the Inshore Zone, make up a majority of the fish biomass (Cherry and Guthrie 1975; Jenkins 1975).

Supplemental Readings   Carlander 1955; Colby and Wigmore 1977; Hall 1971; Kozhov 1963; Kuzin 1968; Jenkins 1975; Lane 1967; Loftus and Regier 1972; J. Moyle 1956; P. Moyle 1976a; Poddubny 1971; Wetzel 1975; Zhadin and Gerd 1961.

αααααααααααααααααααααααααααααααααααααααααααααααααααααααααααααααααααααααααα
~~~~~~

Tropical Freshwater Lakes and Streams

The fishes of tropical areas are affected by the same factors that affect temperate freshwater fishes, so patterns of distribution and abundance can often be explained by making comparisons to the much better known temperate fish communities. On the other hand, the enormous number of fish species found in tropical fresh waters (see Chapters 24 and 26 for details), the extraordinary specializations for feeding and reproduction many of them possess, and the nature of the tropical environments themselves mean that tropical freshwater fish communities have many unique characteristics. These communities are just beginning to be understood (Lowe-McConnell 1975) at a time when they are also being severely disrupted by human activities, such as dam building (Balon and Coche 1974), introduction of exotic species (Zaret and Paine 1973), and commercial fishing (Turner 1977). One of the generalities that seems to be emerging from recent studies is that within a tropical lake or stream system, biological factors are usually more important than physical and chemical factors in determining fish distribution and abundance, although physical and chemical factors retain their importance for explaining broad distributional patterns. The main reason for the importance of biological factors is the general climatic stability of tropical areas. Temperatures are warm all year around and food production, at least in rain forest areas, tends to be continuous. In many areas the alternation of wet and dry seasons produces considerable environmental fluctuation, although the fluctuations tend to be more regular and are less likely to be as extreme as those found in temperate areas. Coupled with the climatic stability is geological stability, so that many of the lakes and streams of the tropics are quite old, giving plenty of opportunity for many highly specialized species to evolve to take advantage of localized physical, chemical, and trophic conditions (Lowe-McConnell 1975).

428

Physical Factors   The physical factors which seem to have the most noticeable impact on the distribution of tropical freshwater fishes are temperature, water level fluctuations, gradient, stream order, and turbidity.

Temperature.   The fishes that live in large tropical lakes and rivers live in environments that are warm all year and have comparatively little temperature fluctuation.   As a consequence, they tend to have rapid growth and short life cycles. Temperature is not a particularly important environmental cue for movements and reproduction.   However, the further a body of water is located from the equator, the more likely the cycles of reproduction, growth, and movements are to be affected by local temperature regimes. While seasonal low temperatures place broad distributional limits on tropical fishes (most do not seem to be able to survive temperatures below 15°C for extended periods of time), local distribution patterns are much more likely to be affected by high temperatures.   In Lake Victoria (Africa), the young of two genera of cichlids sort themselves out in shallow water on hot days according to their ability to tolerate high temperatures; *Tilapia* spp. are found in the hottest (to 38°C), shallowest water, while *Haplochromis* spp. are found in slightly cooler and deeper water (Welcomme 1964).   In Sri Lanka the ability of the native stream fishes to survive in pools during the dry season seems to be largely a function of their tolerances to high temperatures (Senanayake 1977).

Water level fluctuations.   In contrast to temperature, annual fluctuations in water levels are extremely important cues to tropical fishes. With the advent of the rainy season, intermittent streams in the drier areas start flowing again, stagnant jungle pools and backwaters on the flood plains are flushed out, lake levels rise, and the flows of major rivers greatly increase.   As a consequence of the flooding of land and the flushing of terrestrial nutrients into the rivers, habitats and food resources for fish expand greatly (Fig. 30.1). It is thus not surprising to find that reproduction and growth are often strongly related to rising water levels.   Many tropical riverine fishes make extensive upstream spawning migrations at this time or move out into the flood plain to spawn.   In either case, the young hatch rapidly and find abundant food for rapid growth. Adult fish also find food abundant and do most of their growing during this period. The seasonal differences in growth rates are often striking enough so that annual rings are deposited on scales and other bony structures, making it possible to age the fish (Lowe-McConnell 1975).

The seasonal fluctuations in water levels have interesting effects on the interactions among the species of fishes.   During the wet season food is superabundant, so there is considerable overlap in the diet of the various species.   As water levels drop and the fishes are confined together in pools, competition for limited resources is presumably intense. Zaret and Rand (1971) found that food overlap, as a consequence,

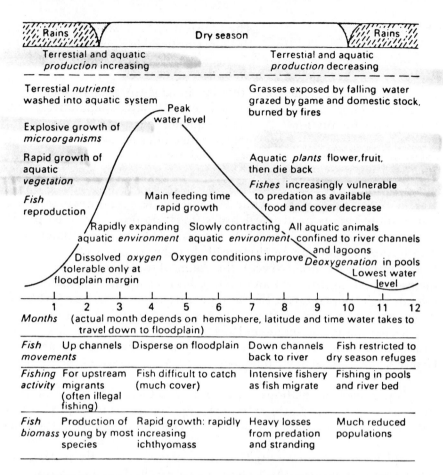

| Rains | Dry season | Rains |

Terrestial and aquatic *production* increasing

Terrestial and aquatic *production* decreasing

Terrestial *nutrients* washed into aquatic system

Peak water level

Grasses exposed by falling water grazed by game and domestic stock, burned by fires

Explosive growth of *microorganisms*

Rapid growth of aquatic *vegetation*

Aquatic *plants* flower, fruit, then die back

Fishes increasingly vulnerable to predation as available food and cover decrease

Fish reproduction

Main feeding time rapid growth

Rapidly expanding aquatic *environment*   Slowly contracting aquatic *environment*   All aquatic animals confined to river channels and lagoons

Dissolved *oxygen* tolerable only at floodplain margin   Oxygen conditions improve   *Deoxygenation* in pools

Lowest water level

| Months | 1 2 3 4 5 6 7 8 9 10 11 12 |

(actual month depends on hemisphere, latitude and time water takes to travel down to floodplain)

Fish movements	Up channels	Disperse on floodplain	Down channels back to river	Fish restricted to dry season refuges
Fishing activity	For upstream migrants (often illegal fishing)	Fish difficult to catch (much cover)	Intensive fishery as fish migrate	Fishing in pools and river bed
Fish biomass	Production of young by most species	Rapid growth: rapidly increasing ichthyomass	Heavy losses from predation and stranding	Much reduced populations

FIGURE 30.1 The seasonal cycle of events in a tropical flood-plain river. (From Lowe-McConnell, 1975.)

is minimal at this time. However, other studies have found that food overlap may actually be greatest at this time because the amount and variety of food is so limited (Lowe-McConnell 1975). In rivers with extensive flood plains the particular combination of species found may vary from one jungle pool or lake to another as the result of more or less random mixing while water levels are high.

Gradient and **stream order**, which are usually strongly interrelated in their effects on fish distribution, seem to have the same general kind of effects on tropical fishes as they do on temperate fishes. In high-gradient headwater streams, the typical fishes are streamlined cyprinids (Africa and Asia), the highly specialized hillstream fishes (Homalopteridae, Asia), and specialized catfishes (South America). As gradient decreases and stream order increases, the variety of body shapes increases, as do feeding specializations. In the headwater streams, most fishes feed either on terrestrial invertebrates or detritus. In higher-order streams, piscivorous forms become common and often seem to make up an extraordinarily large percentage of the fish biomass (Lowe-McConnell 1975).

Turbidity. While the lakes and most of the smaller streams of the tropics are usually quite clear, the large rivers are usually turbid with suspended or dissolved materials (or both). Often there is considerable seasonal variation in turbidity, with the clearest water flowing during the dry season. One impact of high turbidity has been the radiation of fish groups in rivers that do not rely primarily on vision for prey capture, particularly electric fishes (the gymnotoid fishes of South America and the Mormyridae of Africa) and catfishes. These fishes also are mostly nocturnal in habit, which presumably reduces the amount of interaction with day-active cyprinids, characids, and other fishes. In clear water, bright colors seem to have an advantage for communication among the fishes, and most of the brightly colored "tropical" fishes favored by aquarists come from lakes and clear streams (Roberts 1972).

Chemical Factors

Three chemical factors seem to have the most profound influence on fish distribution and abundance in tropical waters: dissolved oxygen, pH, and dissolved nutrients. These three factors interact with each other and with turbidity to produce three general types of stream environments: white water, clear water, and black water (Roberts 1972; Sioli 1975).

White waters are characterized by high turbidity due to suspended material, pH values around neutrality (7), moderate levels of dissolved oxygen, and high nutrient levels. Since whitewater rivers also tend to be the main rivers of most tropical systems, their flooding creates the flood-plain lakes and pools. When the rivers recede, these lakes and pools become more transparent as the suspended material settles out. If the light is not blocked by trees, the high nutrient levels and clear water result in large blooms of plankton. However, the large amount of decaying organic matter present results in low oxygen levels. Nevertheless, these environments often contain large numbers of fish. It is not surprising to find that many, if not most, of the fish are either air breathers or small fishes capable of utilizing the oxygen present in a thin band of water at the surface. In addition, the commonness of species that are livebearers, oral incubators, or nest builders in this type of habitat suggests that such methods may have developed to protect eggs and young from low oxygen levels (Roberts 1972).

Clear waters range in pH from 4.5 to 7.8 but typically are slightly acidic. They are transparent jungle streams with moderate to low gradients and usually flow into large whitewater rivers by way of a mouthbay. The current in mouthbays is usually so slow that they are more like lakes than rivers. Oxygen levels in clearwater streams are high enough to support abundant fish life, although the food chains are based primarily on organic matter of terrestrial origin. The frequent presence of abundant aquatic insect life in these streams increases the complexity of the food webs, and the variety of fishes, particularly small, brightly colored forms, is often considerable. Many of these streams may also be important as spawning streams for main-river and flood-plain fishes during the wet seasons. One of the more curious aspects of South American clear waters is that the mouthbays are now lower in dissolved nutrients and fish numbers than might be expected. Fittkau (1970) has speculated that this might be due to the elimination of the caiman (*Melanosuchus niger*) by hunting. The caimans formerly preyed heavily on the fishes passing through the mouthbays to spawn in the streams. The wastes of the caimans presumably fertilized the water, greatly increasing the production of the mouthbays, and thereby providing more resources for resident fishes.

Black waters are transparent but dark brown in color (they appear black from a distance) because of dissolved organic humic matter. They are extremely acidic, with pH values often lower than 4.5, and contain almost no dissolved nutrients. The decay of organic matter present on the bottom of slow-moving stretches greatly reduces the amount of dissolved oxygen available. Levels are essentially zero at the bottom, so aquatic insect life is almost nonexistent. Obviously, such water is not conducive to the support of fish life, and even the larger black waters, such as the Rio Negro (the largest tributary of the Amazon), contain comparatively few fish. The fish that do live there are concentrated around the edges, especially in flooded vegetation, where terrestrial invertebrates are likely to be found. In the Amazon Basin there are a number of fishes that are largely confined to black waters and seem to be able to spawn only in waters with extremely low pH values (Roberts 1972). Fish kills occur in black waters when strong winds cause the oxygenless bottom waters to upwell (Geisler 1969).

Biological Factors   Because the number of fish species is so high in tropical environments, the interactions among them are complex. Curiously enough, aquatic invertebrate faunas in tropical waters containing fish seem to be comparatively simple, greatly limiting the complexity of fish–invertebrate interactions (in contrast to coral reefs, where the diversity of fish–invertebrate interactions is highest). Because of the general predictability of tropical environments through time, the evolutionary results of predator-prey, competitive, and symbiotic interactions are often expressed as extraordinary morphological and behavioral specializations. These are most extreme in the cichlid fishes of the Great Lakes of eastern Africa, although the specializations of many stream fishes are almost as bizarre.

Predator-prey relationships. Tropical fish communities may be complex, and the large number of species they contain may give them a certain resilience, but their structure is governed by the same "rules" that govern the structure of temperate communities. Thus, human tampering with predator–prey relationships can severely strain them. Addition of exotic predators such as the peacock cichlid (*Cichla ocellaris*) and largemouth bass (*Micropterus salmoides*) to Central American lakes has greatly altered their trophic structure by the elimination, through predation, of a number of small fish species (Zaret and Paine 1973). Even the zooplankton community has changed. In Gatun Lake, Panama, one of the dominant zooplankters has "horned" and "unhorned" forms. The unhorned form normally exists only in shallow water where the plankton-feeding fishes cannot feed on it, despite the considerable reproductive advantage it has over the horned form. However, the horned form is much more resistant to predation. With the elimination of the main planktivorous fish from Gatun Lake by the exotic predators, the unhorned form quickly became abundant in the open waters of the lake (Zaret and Paine 1973). On the other hand, reduction in the populations of piscivorous fishes in a tropical lake can cause a great increase in plankton-feeding fishes, as was illustrated by the increase in the biomass of native herrings (Clupeidae) in Lake Tanganyika following the depletion by fishing of the populations of three species of *Lates* (Centropomidae) (Coulter 1976).

In the absence of human disturbance, predator–prey relationships in tropical waters are presumably fairly stable. Nowhere, except on coral reefs, does one find fishes with more remarkable adaptations that reflect the coevolution of predators and prey. The abundant small catfishes of various families have a wide variety of antipredator features, including heavy bony armor, stout spines that lock in place, cryptic coloration, and nocturnal activity. Other forms seem to thrive by being small and living in environments too shallow, too low in oxygen, or too hot for large predators (e.g., Cyprinodontidae, small characins). The piscivorous predators have evolved many mechanisms to overcome the defenses of their prey, such as the cryptic coloration and behavior of the patient leaffishes (Nandidae), the stunning ability of the electric catfish (*Malapterurus electricus*) and electric eel (*Electrophorus electricus*), and the formidable teeth and jaws of piranhas (*Serrasalmus*) and African tigerfish (*Hydrocynus*).

Since in tropical, as in temperate waters, predation is probably the ultimate cause of death for most fish, it has been hypothesized that it has been a major factor contributing to the development of the large number of species in tropical waters, especially in lakes (Lowe-McConnell 1969). Predation could increase isolation by making it difficult for fish with specific habitat requirements to move from one patch of habitat to another, and thus could promote speciation. The large number of piscivorous fishes that seem to be typical of tropical lakes and streams may also permit potentially competing species to coexist by keeping the populations of the competitors low enough so that the resources are never limiting. Another way predators may permit two competitors to coexist is to prey selectively on the species that has a competitive advantage over the other. While no conclusive examples of this are yet known in tropical fishes, differential predation may be responsible for the coexistence of color morphs of the Midas cichlid (*Cichlasoma citrinellum*) in Lake Nicaragua (Barlow 1976).

Competition. As is true for predator–prey interactions, the most dramatic examples of competitive interactions in tropical fishes occur with introduced species. When *Tilapia zilli* was introduced into Lake Victoria, Africa, their young displaced the young of *T. variabilis* from crucial nursery areas, causing a severe decline in the population of *T. variabilis* (Lowe-McConnell 1975). As for temperate systems, it is the results of presumed competition that are most conspicuous in tropical lakes and streams, particularly the extreme morphological specializations (see Chapter 29). These specializations are most extreme among the cichlid fishes of the great lakes of Africa, which seem to be able to use them to minimize competition for food and space. Although extraordinary specializations are also found among stream fishes, many of the species that live together appear to be relatively unspecialized and have broadly overlapping diets. Saul (1975), for example, was impressed with the lack of feeding specializations among the 50 species he studied in some streams and small lakes in the upper Amazon; most fishes fed predominantly on plant matter of terrestrial origin or terrestrial insects, especially ants. Part of the explanation for this overlap may be that terrestrial food is superabundant during the rainy season and so the species may segregate mainly during the dry season, when food is less abundant (e.g., Zaret and Rand 1971). Segregation by habitats (including microhabitats) may also be important. In the River Gombak in Malaysia, the 27 species present seem to segregate fairly nicely through a combination of morphological specializations and food, habitat, and microhabitat preferences (Table 30-1), much as would be found in a temperate stream, although with a much greater dependence on food of terrestrial origin (Bishop 1973).

While segregation among the fishes of smaller tropical streams may follow the pattern of that of temperate streams, the large rivers and their flood plains with their large numbers of species cannot be explained so easily. Roberts (1972) points out that there *is* considerable diversity of habitat and food preferences among these fishes, indicating that more detailed studies should bring out the differences among similar coexisting species. Yet most studies of the feeding habits of tropical stream fishes partition the fishes into groups with similar feeding habits, bringing to mind the guilds of ecologically similar fishes found on coral reefs (see Chapter 34). Another characteristic of these fish communities seems to be that species vary considerably in abundance from location to location, even though ecological conditions seem to be similar. Such distribution patterns may be the result of the more or less random scattering of the young of the fishes by seasonal floods. It is thus possible, as Sale (1975) has found for some coral reef fishes, that mem-

TABLE 30-1

Ecological Characteristics of the Common Fishes of Gombak River, Malaysia

Species	Zones Where: Abundant	Present	Main Food	Feeding Location	Special Adaptations
Betta pugnax	1	3	C	Surface	Small air breather
Tor soro	1, 2	(3)	F	Midwater	Torpedo shaped, day active
Mastacembelus maculatus	1, 2	(3)	D	Bottom	Eel-like with proboscis; day-active
Acrossocheilus deauratus	1, 2	(3)	F	Midwater	Torpedo-shaped
Silurichthys hasseltii	2	1, (3)	C	Surface	Long barbels
Glyptothorax major	2, 3	1	D, A	Bottom	Adhesive disc
Puntius binotatus	3	1, 2	B	Midwater, pools	Deep-bodied, small
Channa gachua	—	1	E, D	Bottom	Air breather
Macrones wyckii	—	1, 2, 3	E	Bottom	
Glyptothorax platypogonoides	—	1	D	Bottom, rifles	Ventral adhesive disc
Mastacembelus armatus	2, 3	2, 3	D	Bottom	Eel-like, with proboscis
Mystacoleucus marginatus	2, 3	—	B	Midwater, pools	Deep-bodied
Rasbora sumatrana	2, 3	—	C	Midwater	Small, schooling
Clarias batrachus	—	2, 3	D, E	Bottom	Air-breathing catfish
Osteochilus hasseltii	3	2	A	Bottom	Large; deep-bodied, with papillose mouth
Hemiramphodon pogonognathus	—	2	C	Surface, edges	Halfbeak with long lower jaw
Doryichthyes deokhathoides	—	2, (3)	C	Surface	Pipefish, sucking mouth
Channa striata	—	(2), 3	E	Bottom	Air breather
Hampala macrolepidota	—	2, (3)	E	Midwater	Cyprinid rover-predator
Fluta alba	—	3	E, F	Bottom, edges	Eel-like air breather
Dermogenes pusillus	3	2	C	Surface	Small halfbeak
Poecilia reticulata	3	—	D	All	Guppy, introduced

Zones are indicated as follows: 1—headwater zone; 2—middle reaches; 3—lowlands.

Food types are indicated as follows: A—detritus; B—plant material; C—terrestrial arthropods; D—aquatic invertebrates; E—fish, frogs, and decapods; F—omnivorous.

Source: Information from Bishop (1973).

bers of guilds of similar species compete for limited resources, especially during the dry seasons. No one species is ever able to become completely dominant because young fish are randomly distributed by floods to the suitable habitats.

Symbiosis. There are few examples of symbiotic interactions among tropical freshwater fishes, although this is not surprising when one considers how poorly known the habits of tropical fishes are in general. Mutualistic relationships among schooling fishes are probably common, given the frequency with which small South American characins seem to be found together and the mixtures of cichlid species found in the Great Lakes of Africa. In Central America cichlids guarding a school of their own young have been observed to "adopt" young of other cichlid species in a manner which may reduce predation on their own young, while giving the foreign young some protection as well and the opportunity for more rapid growth (McKaye 1977). At least one example of cleaning symbiosis is known. Wyman and Ward (1972) have shown that one species of the Indian cichlid genus *Etroplus* cleans members of another species. On the opposite extreme, parasitic relationships among tropical fishes are fairly common. A number of species of small South American catfishes of the families Cetopsidae and Trichomycteridae enter the gill chambers of larger fish, where they feed on the gill filaments and blood. At least one of the Trichomycteridae feeds mainly on the scales of other fishes, a feeding adaptation found as well in many South American characins and African cichlids (Roberts 1972). Still other cichlids and characins, including most members of the African family Ichthyoboridae, feed primarily by taking bites out of the fins of other fishes.

Fish Communities

Because the fish species of tropical fresh waters are so numerous and diverse and because few tropical freshwater environments have received much detailed study, it is difficult to find a body of water whose fish communities can be said to be typical of anything but itself. The three bodies of water discussed here are therefore presented mostly to give an idea of the range of types of fish communities and interactions that are possible in tropical fresh waters: (1) the Gombak River in Malaysia; (2) Lake Malawi; and (3) Lake Kainji, a recently constructed reservoir in Nigeria.

The **Gombak River** is a small, permanent river draining jungle-covered hills in West Malaysia that was intensively studied by Bishop (1973). On the basis of gradient and surrounding countryside, the river can be divided into Upper, Middle, and Lower Zones. The Upper Zone has a steep gradient and consequently has swift, well-oxygenated water, although there is also much quieter water in small tributaries draining the surrounding jungle and along the river's edge. The Middle Zone occurs in the foothills, where gradients are much less, so that the river consists of shallow riffles and short pools. The river in this area flows through mixed jungle and rubber plantations. The Lower Zone river flows through areas of rice cultivation and is sluggish and turbid. Oxygen levels are often low, as a result of both natural conditions and pollution. While each zone has its characteristic fish species (Table 30-1), there is considerable overlap in species composition.

The Upper Zone was dominated by two active, streamlined species of cyprinids, a bottom- and edge-dwelling mastacembelid eel and, in small jungle tributaries, a small, air-breathing anabantid (*Betta*). In the riffles there were two species of hillstream fishes (Homalopteridae) which have a ventral sucker for holding onto rocks. The abundant cyprinids and *Betta* fed mainly on terrestrial invertebrates and detritus, while the other species fed mainly on aquatic invertebrates. The only piscivorous species present was a snakehead (*Channa*, Channidae), which was not abundant.

The Middle Zone contained a variety of fishes, including small, schooling cyprinids (*Rasbora*), a highly specialized detritus feeder (*Osteochilus*), several species of predatory snakeheads, catfishes (*Clarias*, *Silurichthys*), halfbeaks (*Hemiramphodon*, *Dermogenes*) specialized for capturing insects on the water's surface, pipefish (*Doryichthyes*), and mastacembelid eels. Also present in abundance was one of the hillstream fishes.

The Lower Zone contained the same species as the Middle Zone, with the addition of a synbranchid eel and the guppy (*Poecilia*), an introduced species. The most abundant species in this zone, especially in polluted areas, were air breathers or small species capable of obtaining oxygen from the air–water interface. The most abundant fishes of this zone also are livebearers (*Dermogenes*, *Poecilia*), bubble nest builders (*Fluta*, *Betta*), or those with other adaptations that permit breeding in oxygen-poor waters.

Lake Malawi is about 2 million years old and partly as a consequence contains at least 250 species of fish, most of them endemic to the lake. The actual number of species present may be in excess of 500, depending on how taxonomists classify the many new types of cichlids being observed in the lake. The large number of species is also due to the size of the lake (560 km long by 80 km wide, with a maximum depth of 772 m) and to the fact that most of the species are cichlids. The well-developed parental and territorial behavior patterns of the cichlids seem to make them particularly subject to isolation and hence speciation. Also, the highly developed pharyngeal "jaws" of cichlids have permitted extraordinary feeding specializations to evolve (Liem 1974). Lake Malawi can be divided up into five broad habitat types, each with its characteristic fish community: (1) shallow bays and lagoons; (2) rocky-bottomed inshore areas of the main lake; (3) mud- or sand-bottomed shore areas of the main lake; (4) open water; and (5) deep-bottom water (Lowe-McConnell 1975).

The shallow bays and lagoons are a relatively small part of the lake, yet they are the most productive of food fishes. They contain a complex of *Tilapia* species (Cichlidae) that feed on small invertebrates. Associated with these interesting cichlid species are two species of *Corematodus,* one of which mimics *Tilapia* so that it can feed on *Tilapia* scales, and the other of which mimics *Lethrinops,* upon which it preys. Other species found in this habitat are large cyprinids and large predatory catfishes.

The rocky-bottomed inshore areas, which may have a steep profile, contain perhaps the most ecologically diverse group of fishes found anywhere in the world in such limited habitat. Most of the fishes are cichlids, especially of the genus *Haplochromis* (of which there are over 120 species in the lake). There actually seem to be more fish species present than there are basic types of resources to exploit, so species with similar feeding habits segregate by depth, size of food, method of feeding, and other subtle ways. Cichlids have also developed many ways to feed on other cichlid species. Among the basic feeding types listed by Fryer and Iles (1972) (Fig 30.2, see pp. 440–41) are:

1. Epilithic algae feeders live by scraping algae from the rocks. There are a number of different species in this group, with mouths modified variously for scraping diatoms (e.g., *Pseudotropheus tropheops*), for combing out filamentous algae (e.g., *Petrotilapia*), or for nipping off strands of algae (e.g., *H. guentheri*).
2. Periphyton collectors that feed mostly on algae, etc., scraped from the leaves of higher plants. These species typically have a pointed snout with scraping teeth on the sides of the jaws. They feed by grabbing the leaf and then moving down it sideways, scraping as they go. Such activity does not harm the leaf.
3. Leaf choppers (e.g., *H. similis*) feed by taking chunks out of leaves with their stout teeth.
4. Mollusc feeders are of two types: shell crushers and foot grabbers. Shell crushers suck in small molluscs and crush them with their stout pharyngeal teeth. Foot grabbers (e.g., *H. sauvagei*) grab the foot of a snail and somehow pull the snail out of its shell.
5. Invertebrate pickers (e.g., *Labidochromis vellicans*) pick small invertebrates from algae beds with long, forcepslike teeth. These species also have the large eyes necessary for precision feeding. Other species (e.g., *Aulonocara nyassae*) are more generalized predators on large invertebrates, possessing protractile mouths and bands of inward-directed teeth inside their mouths.
6. Zooplankton feeders consist of a number of species with sucking mouths and long gill rakers. While they feed in open water, they seldom venture far from rocky or sandy areas.
7. Scale eaters have a scraping type of mouth similar to those of epilithic algae feeders, so they can scrape small scales (usually from the

caudal peduncle region) of other cichlids and also of cyprinids. Each species typically seems to specialize in a particular type of host-prey. Other scale eaters devour large scales which they obtain by sliding their lower jaw under a scale, clamping down with the upper jaw, and then jerking out the scale.

8.   Fin choppers sneak up on their prey, presumably in part by mimicry, and take bites out of their fins.

9.   Piscivorous cichlids appear in a number of standard forms from rover-predator to pikelike lie-in-wait predator.

10.   Egg, embryo, and larval fish eaters seem to live mainly on the young of other species of cichlids, with different species apparently specialized for feeding on different stages of development. Since most cichlids they prey on are mouthbrooders, they must have some means of getting the brooding fish to jettison their young. It is possible that such predation is an important means of population control and that the susceptibility of adults to releasing their eggs or young might depend on the population density.

11.   The eye biter (*Haplochromis compressiceps*) is a lie-in-wait predator with a narrow profile and an elongate snout that is famous for biting out the eyes of large fish, although it also eats whole small fish.

The muddy- and sandy-bottomed areas have their own highly specialized cichlids as well as various cyprinids and catfishes (Mochochidae). Among the cichlids are species of *Lethrinops* specialized with shovel-like lower jaws and stout gill rakers for digging in the sand and filtering out invertebrates. The different species feed on different sizes and types of prey. Other species of cichlids feed on organic deposits on the bottom, scrape periphyton from aquatic plants, or feed on the plants themselves. Piscivorous cichlids are also abundant.

The open waters of the lake are dominated by a species flock of zooplankton-feeding *Haplochromis* (which tend to be localized in their distribution near shore or rocky reefs) and the small pelagic cyprinid *Engraulcypris sardella*. These fishes are preyed upon by a number of large cichlids, catfishes, and cyprinids.

The deep bottom water contains a poorly known group of fishes that live at depths as great as 100 m, below which the water is anoxic. The species are a mixture of catfishes, cyprinids, cichlids, and at least one electric fish (Mormyridae). Many of these species are piscivorous, and they may feed by moving into shallow water or moving up into the water column, perhaps after dark.

While the picture of Lake Malawi presented here, as an environment whose resources are extraordinarily finely subdivided among its fishes, has been widely accepted, it is mostly based on studies of cichlid morphology. Ongoing studies in the lake itself, by Kenneth McKaye and others, indicate that while cichlid fishes do indeed exhibit many amazing morphological and behavioral adaptations, their actual feeding

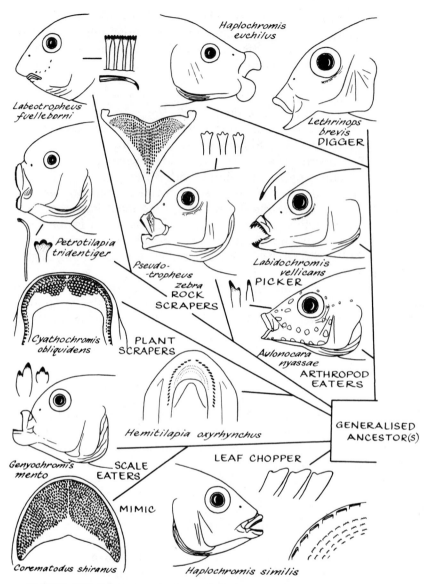

FIGURE 30.2 Feeding mechanisms of "mbuni" cichlids from Lake Malawi, showing adaptive radiation from a generalized ancestor. (From Fryer and Iles, 1972.)

is usually much less specialized than the morphology indicates. For example, the abundant zooplankton in the lake is an important food source for many of the cichlids, including the forms adapted for bottom feeding. It now seems likely that the extreme feeding specializations observed are an advantage mainly in times of food shortages, which, if they do not occur seasonally, may occur on an irregular basis over a longer time span.

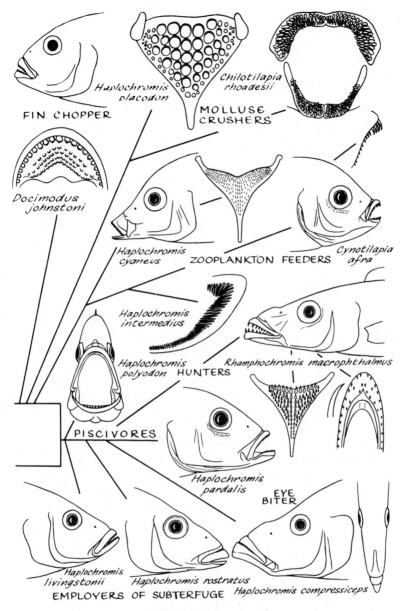

FIN CHOPPER

Haplochromis placodon

Chilotilapia rhoadesii

MOLLUSC CRUSHERS

Docimodus johnstoni

Haplochromis cyaneus

ZOOPLANKTON FEEDERS

Cynotilapia afra

Haplochromis intermedius

Haplochromis polyodon

HUNTERS

Rhamphochromis macrophthalmus

PISCIVORES

Haplochromis pardalis

EYE BITER

Haplochromis livingstonii

Haplochromis rostratus

EMPLOYERS OF SUBTERFUGE

Haplochromis compressiceps

FIGURE 30.2 (continued)

Lake Kainji was created by the closure of a dam in 1968 which turned 137 km of the Niger River into a 1280-km² lake (Lowe-McConnell 1975). Lake Kainji, like temperate reservoirs, seems to have three fish zones, although since 50 to 60 species occur in the reservoir, this may be a gross oversimplification. The Inshore Zone is shallow and contains considerable habitat diversity because of flooded trees and vegetation. It consequently contains most of the fish species and much of the fish production. The Open-Water Zone is dominated by pelagic clupeids and characins, as well as their predators, particularly the tigerfish (*Hydrocynus forskali,* Characidae). The Deepwater Benthic Zone is not well developed because of the shallowness of the reservoir but seems to contain mostly omnivorous characins, cyprinids, and catfishes. Despite this apparent general similarity of fish zones to those of temperate reservoirs, tropical reservoirs such as Kainji differ greatly from temperate reservoirs in that the number of species is much larger, the environment is likely to be more constant in terms of both temperature regimes and water level fluctuations, and there seems to be a greater predominance of piscivorous and omnivorous fish species.

One of the more interesting aspects of tropical reservoirs is the succession of fishes that takes place following the closure of the dams. The species that dominate such reservoirs are mostly native to the dammed rivers, yet the reservoir fish faunas are considerably different. The preimpoundment fish fauna of the Niger River was diverse but dominated by species typical of flowing water, mostly members of the families Mormyridae, Mochochidae (catfishes), and Citharinidae (moonfishes). As the reservoir filled up, there was initially a population explosion of one species of moonfish, followed by: (1) increases in the predatory tigerfish and the omnivorous characin *Alestes baremose;* (2) increases in species of the catfish family Schilbeidae; (3) a slight increase in members of the family Mochochidae, but with a dramatic change in species composition; and (4) a decline in the Mormyridae. As the reservoir aged further, (1) the moonfishes declined; (2) the characins continued to be abundant; (3) herrings (Clupeidae) became abundant in the open waters of the lake; (4) cichlids became abundant, especially *Tilapia;* and (5) the mormyrids started to increase in abundance again. In general, the species that became abundant in the reservoir were species that were relatively rare in the main river, being mostly characteristic of backwaters and swampy edges. The species that declined after the reservoir filled tended to be bottom feeders on aquatic insects or detritus feeders, while those that increased were piscivores, planktivores, and omnivores (Lelek 1973; Lewis 1974; Blake 1977).

One of the reasons that such changes are so fascinating is that most of them were unexpected, reflecting our general lack of knowledge of tropical fish ecology, but especially that for large rivers. For example, in Kariba Reservoir, on the Zambezi River, a number of the dominant species are now fishes that were formerly known only from above Victoria Falls, 100 km upstream (Balon 1974, 1978). Previously, this falls was thought to be a barrier to fish movement, both upstream and downstream. As Balon (1978) points out, the changes brought about by the creation of such larger reservoirs as Kariba are more often than not more detrimental than beneficial, not only to the local fauna but to the local people as well. An increase in fish production may be balanced by a decrease in animal production from the terrestrial systems, as well as a decrease in agricultural production (from the flooding of vast valleys). Highly predictable systems become unpredictable, as species replace one another in response to new perturbations to the systems. Given the rapidity with which tropical rivers are now being "developed," it is likely that significant parts of the unique endemic fish faunas of these rivers may disappear in the near future.

Supplemental Readings   Balon 1974; Bishop 1973; Lowe-McConnell 1969, 1975; Roberts 1972, 1976; Saul 1975; Thorson 1976; Whitton 1975; Whyte 1975; Zaret and Paine 1973.

ααααααααααααααααααααααααααααααααααααααααααααααααααααααααααααααααααααα
~~~~~~

Special Inland Environments

The interior basins and mountain ranges of the continents contain many unusual bodies of water with extreme physical or chemical characteristics. While these bodies of water tend to be hostile to most forms of aquatic life, a surprising number of them contain fish. These fish typically show unusual adaptations that enable them to cope with the harsh environment and to take advantage of the equally unusual invertebrates and plants found with them. Two such environments especially notable for their fishes are caves and small springs and streams of deserts.

Caves
Cave lakes, pools, and streams that contain fishes highly specialized for cave living occur primarily in temperate regions where the dominant rock is limestone (Poulson and White 1969). Limestone areas have the best-developed cave systems because limestone will dissolve in water charged with carbon dioxide (i.e., weak carbonic acid). The water consequently tends to be high in dissolved minerals and slightly basic. The aquatic environment of caves can be divided into three types of habitat: (1) lakes and streams in the twilight zone; (2) streams flowing in complete darkness; and (3) lakes and pools in complete darkness. Unique fishes can be found in all three environments, but most of the "true" cavefishes (troglobitic fishes) are found in the deep cave lakes and pools where the lighted world has little influence. However, even these latter habitats are dependent on nutrients washed in from outside for their energy, and most cave waters containing troglobitic fishes have at least intermittent connections to the outside. Even so, the nutrients present are typically in very limited supply. This is reflected in the energy-saving adaptations of the organisms present, particularly the fish, as well as in the simplicity of the cave ecosystems.

Cave-adapted fishes have evolved independently in various parts of the world and represent at least eleven families of fishes. Despite their different origins, the troglobitic species are remarkably similar in their adaptations. The eyes are reduced or absent, and other sensory systems (but particularly the lateral line system) are well developed; the scales are reduced or absent; pigmentation is absent, so that the fishes appear translucent white in color; the pelvic fins are reduced or absent; body size is small (less than 15 cm), and they are carnivorous. Since the cave environment is fairly constant in temperature and oxygen level, some troglobite fishes have reduced abilities to regulate metabolic rates in response to changing conditions.

The characteristics that involve a loss of some physical feature or metabolic ability presumably evolved as a means of conserving energy. Energy not put into growth or into development of features that are of little use to the fish can be put instead into features that will enhance its survival and reproductive potential. An idea of how completely some troglobitic fishes have adapted to the cave environment can be obtained by comparing the biology of *Amblyopsis spelaea* with that of *Chologaster agassizi*. Both species are members of the family Amblyopsidae, which is found only in caves and springs in eastern North America. *Amblyopsis* is found only in the absence of light, whereas *Chologaster* is found in the mouths of caves, in the "twilight zone" (Poulson and White 1969). *Amblyopsis* has tiny, nonfunctional eyes and no skin pigmentation; *Chologaster* has small (but barely functional) eyes and pigmented skin. The lateral line system is extremely well developed in *Amblyopsis* compared to *Chologaster* (Fig. 31.1). The metabolic rate of *Amblyopsis* is about half that of *Chologaster*. *Chologaster* is more efficient at locating food organisms at high densities, but when the density of food organisms is very low, as in a deep cave, the slow but constant activity pattern of *Amblyopsis* is more efficient. Escape responses from potential predators are well developed in *Chologaster* but absent from *Amblyopsis*. Both species incubate their eggs in their gill cavities, assuring high survival, but *Amblyopsis* lays larger and fewer eggs, which take longer to develop than those of *Chologaster*. The reproductive strategy of *Amblyopsis* not only consumes less energy but apparently reduces the incidence of cannibalism, which is an important source of mortality in *Chologaster* (Hill 1969).

Besides the family Amblyopsidae, cave fishes are known from four families of catfishes (Trichomycteridae, Ictaluridae, Pimelodidae, Clariidae) and from the families Cyprinidae, Characidae, Eleotridae, Symbranchidae, Gobiidae, and Ophidiidae. Six of these families are ostariophysan fishes, which is not surprising, since they are the dominant freshwater fishes. The catfishes in particular would seem to be good candidates for becoming isolated and surviving in cave habitats, since they are already adapted for a nocturnal existence. Of particular interest are two species of catfish (*Trogloglanis pattersoni* and *Satan eurystomus*)

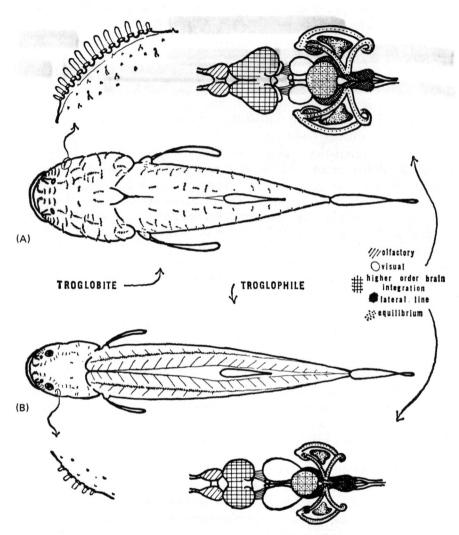

FIGURE 31.1 Adaptations of two species of amblyopsid fish from different cave habitats: (A) *Amblyopsis spelaea* lives in total darkness and has a well-developed lateral line system. The sections of the brain dealing with the lateral line system and equilibrium are also well developed. The head is larger and has more sensory canals for detection of obstacles and prey than that of *Chologaster agassiz* (B), which lives in caves that receive some light. The longer fins of *Amblyopsis* allow it to "row" slowly and efficiently about the cave in search of prey. [From Poulson and White (1969); copyright 1969 by the American Association for the Advancement of Science.]

known only from water brought up in artesian wells in Texas, from over 300 m beneath the surface of the earth (Hubbs and Bailey 1947). Among the Characidae there is a species of tetra (*Astyanax mexicanus fasciatus*) widespread in Mexico that has cave-dwelling populations that are eyeless and unpigmented. Most populations that do not live in caves have normal eyes and pigmentation, although some populations found near cave mouths contain many individuals with intermediate characteristics (Mitchell et al. 1977).

Regardless of the fish species, the ecosystems in which cave fishes are found are very simple in structure. The fish are typically the top carnivores, feeding on two to four species of small crustaceans (copepods, amphipods, isopods, decapods). The crustaceans in turn feed on each other and on detritus and its associated bacteria. Although cave fishes occasionally coexist with the larvae of cave salamanders, it is unusual to find two troglobite species of fish in the same cave pool or stream. Poulson and White (1969) indicate that in the Amblyopsidae, once a species is established in a cave, it may prevent other species from also becoming established, even though the other species may have access to the cave.

Desert Waters

The deserts of the world contain many unusual bodies of water, from saline lakes and seas to small springs, streams, and marshes. The latter waters contain some of the most extreme habitats in which fish manage to exist. As in caves, the severity of the environment greatly limits the number of species. Most small desert waters, if they contain fish at all, contain just one to five species, usually from the families Cyprinodontidae, Cichlidae, or Cyprinidae. Perhaps the best known of the desert fishes are the killifishes and pupfishes (Cyprinodontidae), small, deep-bodied fishes that inhabit a wide variety of desert habitats in North and Central America, Africa, and Eurasia. The range of conditions in which these fish manage to live is well illustrated by the habitats of the pupfishes of the Death Valley region of California and Nevada: Ash Meadows, Devil's Hole, Salt Creek, Cottonball Marsh, and Tecopa Bore.

Ash Meadows contains the most benign habitats for pupfishes in the Death Valley area, a series of freshwater springs[1] that range in size from Big Spring, which is 15 m in diameter and 9 m deep and has an outflow of about 5700 l/min, to Mexican Spring, which covers only 1.6 m^2, is only 2 cm to 5 cm deep, and has little outflow. The temperatures of the larger springs range from 21°C to 33°C, with annual variations of only 2°C to 7°C. The fish living in these springs are *Empetrichthys merriami* (now extinct) and *Cyprinodon nevadensis*. Because each spring is a stable, isolated environment, the pupfish present in each one are

---

[1]Many of these springs have been destroyed or disrupted by humans, resulting in the extinction of a number of distinctive forms.

morphologically distinct from those in other springs. As might be expected, the ecosystems of these springs are simple, and so the pupfish subsist largely on algae, supplemented with a few small invertebrates.

Close to Ash Meadows is Devil's Hole, which is the sole home of the Devil's Hole pupfish (*C. diabolis*). Although Devil's Hole is over 60 m deep, the fish are largely confined to a shallow shelf about 20 m^2 in area, giving the pupfish the smallest known range of any vertebrate animal. The pupfish, whose population fluctuates between 200 and 700 individuals, subsists on the sparse growth of algae on the shelf and on the small invertebrates associated with it. The temperature of the water is 33.9°C, with only minor fluctuations, which allows the pupfish to reproduce all year around. Like cave fishes, the pupfish in Devil's Hole have evolved a number of energy-saving features, such as small size (1.5 cm to 2.0 cm long), lack of pelvic fins, and reduced pigmentation. However, they have retained the typical cyprinodont characteristic of being able to tolerate about a 40°C range of temperatures (Brown and Feldmeth 1971).

In contrast to Devil's Hole, Salt Creek contains a large population of pupfish (*C. salinus*) that may fluctuate in size by a factor of 100 each year. The population builds up as water flows down the stream in the spring and then dies back in the summer as the stream dries up. Over the course of a year, the pupfish here are exposed to temperatures ranging from nearly freezing in the winter to 40°C in the summer and salinities ranging from that of sea water (35 ppm) to about half that value. Perhaps the most exceptional characteristics of the water containing these fish are the high levels of boron (39 ppm) and total dissolved solids (23,600 ppm).

The water from Salt Creek eventually may seep into Cottonball Marsh, on the floor of Death Valley, which is inhabited by yet another species of pupfish, *Cyprinodon milleri* (LaBounty and Deacon 1972). The salinity levels in the waters of Cottonball Marsh are often so high (up to 4.6 times that of sea water) that the rims of the shallow, exposed pools inhabited by the fish are encrusted with salt (sodium sulfate) and gypsum. Water temperatures range from nearly freezing in the winter to 40°C in the summer, with daily fluctuations of 14°C to 15°C common in the summer, although the more extreme values may be avoided by the fish seeking out the deeper parts of the pools. The pupfish feed on algae and its associated populations of small invertebrates.

Tecopa Bore is the freshwater outflow of an artesian well that was colonized by *Cyprinodon nevadensis* from a nearby marsh. It is a remarkable habitat that demonstrates how pupfish can thrive under near lethal conditions. Water flows out of the well at 47.5°C but cools down as it flows toward the floor of Death Valley. The maximum temperature the fish can withstand is 42°C and in the bore there tends to be a concentration of fish in water that is at this temperature. The reason for this is that the pupfish feed on filamentous bluegreen algae, which grows thickly in the section of the bore too warm for the fish. By remaining in water that is 42°C, the pupfish can make forays into the areas thick with algae when the wind temporarily causes the 42°C isotherm to move upstream (Brown 1971). Tecopa Bore is also remarkable for its high rate of fish production. Naiman (1976) has estimated that 17.5% of the primary production (algae) is consumed annually by the pupfish to produce 119 Kcal of pupfish per m^2 per year. This level of fish production is exceeded only in a few situations where herbivorous fishes are under intensive cultivation by humans.

Supplemental Readings

Caves: Norman and Greenwood 1975; Hubbs and Bailey 1947; Mitchell 1969; Poulson 1963; Poulson and White 1969; Thines 1969; Vandel 1965.

Desert Waters: Brown 1971; Brown and Feldmeth 1971; Deacon and Minckley 1974; Miller 1948; Moyle 1976a; Soltz and Naiman 1978.

αααααααααααααααααααααααααααααααααααααααααααααααααααααααααααααααααααααααααααααα
~~~~~~

Estuaries

Estuaries[1] are transitional environments between fresh water and salt water. Estuarine fish faunas, as a consequence, tend to be mixtures of euryhaline species from both environments, species migrating from one environment to another, and a small number of resident species. While the fluctuating physical and chemical environment limits the number of species in estuaries, the abundance of nutrients allows estuaries to support large concentrations of individuals. These individuals, more often than not, belong to important commercial species. Unfortunately for the fish, estuaries are also typically the focus of major urban areas and tend to be highly disturbed and polluted. Thus, they are worth considering in some detail because they present many interesting challenges to the fish, as well as to the biologists who study them. This chapter will consider: (1) characteristics of estuaries; (2) types of estuarine fishes; (3) factors affecting the distribution and abundance of the fishes; (4) estuarine food webs; and (5) estuarine fish communities.

Characteristics of Estuaries   The characteristics of each estuary depend on its size, shape, geological history, location, amount and quality of the inflowing fresh water, and the nature of the surrounding land; yet all estuaries have two important characteristics in common: the harshness of the physical and chemical environment and high concentrations of nutrients.

The harshness of the estuarine environment is caused by the mixing of fresh and salt water. This creates not only salinity gradients but also simultaneous temperature gradients because the salt water and fresh

---

[1] The term *estuary* as used in this chapter refers to "a semi-enclosed coastal body of water having free connection with the open sea and within which the sea water is measurably diluted with freshwater deriving from land drainage" (Cameron and Pritchard 1963).

water are rarely of the same temperature. The gradients created by the mixing are not stable phenomena but move up and down the estuary on a daily basis according to tidal cycles. They are also affected seasonally by the amount of fresh water entering the estuary and by oceanic storms that may push in more salt water. The inflowing water carries suspended organic and inorganic matter, which may create gradients of turbidity and dissolved oxygen as well. Not only are there strong gradients from the head of the estuary to its mouth, but there are also gradients in the water column as well because fresh water is less dense than salt water and tends to "float" on top.

The fluctuating nature of the estuarine environment means that estuarine fishes must expend considerable amounts of energy adjusting to the changing conditions either metabolically or by moving about in search of less stressful conditions. However, these energy costs are easily paid because the same factors that create the harsh environment also cause nutrients to become concentrated, and the nutrients support large populations of food organisms. The nutrients are mostly associated with detritus that is washed in with the fresh water or is created from the decay of plants in surrounding marshlands. Salt marshes (see Chapter 33) are particularly important as sources of nutrients in Atlantic and Gulf coast estuaries. Although the high turbidity of estuaries typically limits photosynthesis, phytoplankton may be another important source of energy input. Today, however, sewage is one of the most important sources! The constant mixing that occurs in estuaries assures that most of the nutrients are recycled in them and that major losses occur only during times of flood. At least as important as the mixing processes in the retention of nutrients in estuaries are the activities of the invertebrates. Estuaries have large concentrations of filter-feeding zooplankton, particularly copepods, that feed on detritus and phytoplankton in the water column and are preyed on by fish. The fecal pellets from the zooplankton and fish drop to the bottom, where they form part of the organic ooze that serves as food for the abundant benthic invertebrates such as amphipods and nereid worms. Often even more abundant on the bottom are clams and oysters, which filter-feed from the water column. Because estuarine currents typically concentrate nutrients and zooplankton in the upper, low-salinity (2 ppt to 12 ppt) parts of the estuary, benthic invertebrates and fishes often show a peak of abundance in this region as well. The same processes that concentrate nutrients in estuaries also concentrate pollutants, including pesticides and heavy metals. This may not only have direct adverse effects on estuarine faunas (which are often naturally under stress) but may render those organisms that survive inedible for humans.

Estuarine Fishes   Fishes found in estuaries are of five broad types: (1) freshwater; (2) diadromous; (3) true estuarine; (4) nondependent marine; and (5) dependent marine.

Typically an estuary has representatives of all five types, although their relative abundance varies from season to season and locality to locality.

Freshwater fishes may complete their entire life cycle in the upper reaches of estuaries, but most records of freshwater fishes from estuaries are probably fish that have washed in from upstream and are only temporary residents. Most "true" freshwater fishes will not be found at salinities higher than 3 ppt to 5 ppt, and even the most tolerant species are not found where salinities are much higher than 10 ppt to 15 ppt. Examples of freshwater fishes that will live in the upper reaches of estuaries are white catfish (*Ictalurus catus*), channel catfish (*I. punctatus*), mosquitofish (*Gambusia affinis*), and cyprinids such as Sacramento splittail (*Pogonichthys macrolepidotus*).

Diadromous fishes are found in estuaries in large numbers as they pass through on their way to either fresh or salt water. The estuaries frequently act as staging areas for anadromous fishes; for example, salmon and shad may remain in them for several days or weeks before finally moving upstream. For many anadromous species, estuaries also serve as nursery grounds for the young. Young American shad (*Alosa sapidissima*) typically spend the first few months to year of life in estuaries. Some of the most important estuarine fishes might best be labeled *semianadromous*, since they spawn just above the head of the estuary, use the estuary as a nursery area, and may or may not go out to sea. Examples of this are the striped bass (*Morone saxatilis*) and some sturgeons (*Acipenser* spp.).

True estuarine fishes are those that usually spend their entire life cycle in estuaries. While they may be important parts of the fish fauna of estuaries, there are few species in this category. In the great Sacramento–San Joaquin estuary of California, for example, only the Delta smelt (*Hypomesus transpacificus*) falls into this category. In east coast estuaries true estuarine fishes include the white perch (*Morone americana*) and spotted seatrout (*Cynoscion nebulosus*), both of considerable importance to sport fishermen.

Nondependent marine fishes are those species that are commonly found in the lower reaches of estuaries but do not depend upon them to complete their life cycles. These species may be important parts of estuarine ecosystems, but they are also important in shallow-water marine environments in general. On the Pacific coast of North America, three of the most abundant estuarine species are in this category: staghorn sculpin (*Leptocottus armatus*), starry flounder (*Platichthys stellatus*), and shiner perch (*Cymatogaster aggregata*).

Dependent marine fishes are those that usually spend at least one stage of their life cycle in estuaries, using them as spawning grounds, as nurseries for their young, or as feeding grounds for the adults. Species such as the herrings (*Clupea* spp.) that use the estuaries for spawning are relatively few and tend to attach their eggs to submerged plants or objects. The turbulence of estuaries is likely to create problems for eggs passively floating in the water column. The main advantage of laying eggs in estuaries is that the young hatch close to abundant supplies of food. Most marine species with young that take advantage of estuaries spawn outside the estuaries and have the young migrate into them. Examples of this strategy are common in Atlantic and Gulf coast estuaries, in groups such as the croakers (*Sciaenidae*) and menhadens (*Brevoortia* spp.). On the Pacific coast there are no estuarine dependent species with this strategy except the totoaba (*Cynoscion macdonaldi*). The totoaba lives in the Gulf of California and uses the estuary of the Colorado River as a nursery grounds. Unfortunately for the totoaba, the water in the river is now completely used by humans, and little river water reaches the estuary except that polluted by salts leached from soils by irrigation. As a result, the totoaba populations have collapsed (along with its fishery) and it is now considered to be an endangered species.

Adults of marine fishes also frequently move into estuaries to prey on the abundant invertebrates and small fishes, but only a few species do this as a normal part of their life cycle (e.g., adult croakers in Atlantic coast estuaries). The abundance of estuarine dependent marine fishes is one of the reasons that most estuaries show strong seasonal fluctuations in the numbers and kinds of fishes present.

Factors That Affect Distribution

The distribution and abundance of fishes found in estuaries are determined primarily by physical and chemical factors and only secondarily by biological factors. One of the main reasons for this is that most estuarine fishes are only part-time residents of estuaries. They move in when conditions are favorable to take advantage of the abundance of food, either for themselves or their young, but move out when physical and chemical conditions become too severe. Dahlberg and Odum (1970) noted that only about half the 70 fish species they collected from a Georgia estuary could be found there year-round. Results from other estuaries are similar (Fig. 32.1). The seasonality of estuarine fish populations seems to be created primarily by their responses to temperature and salinity, but oxygen levels, predation, and interspecific competition may also play a role.

Temperature is probably the single most important factor affecting fish distribution both between and within estuaries seasonally, although temperature effects are closely tied to the effects of other variables. The often striking differences between the summer and winter fish faunas of estuaries are probably due in large part to the temperature tolerances and preferences of the different species, as is the gradual change in the composition of estuarine faunas from north to south along the Atlantic coast of North America. For species resident in estuaries all year, temperatures have a profound effect on local distribution patterns. Temperature is also important in determining the distribution of gulf menhaden (*Brevoortia patronus*) in Gulf Coast estuaries; they are most abundant

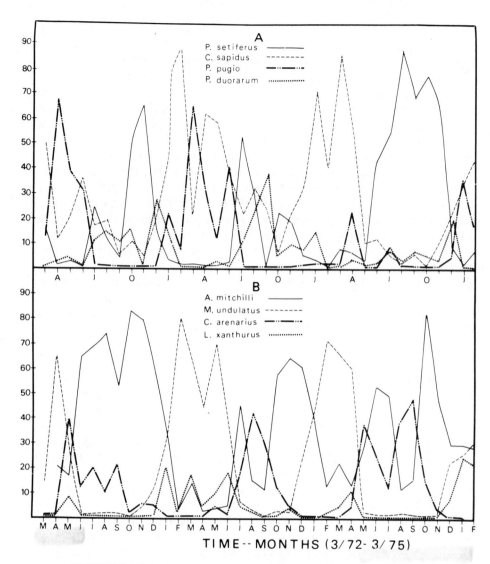

FIGURE 32.1 Relative importance (percentage of total caught) of four species of estuarine fishes (B) and four species of invertebrates (A) at different times of year in the Apalachicola Bay estuarine system, Florida. (From Livingston et al., 1975.)

at temperatures between 25°C and 35°C. However, the distribution of menhaden is also strongly influenced by salinity and food supply, since young menhaden seek out the upper reaches of estuaries, where salinities are low and detritus is abundant (Copeland and Bechtel 1974).

Salinity exercises a strong influence over the distribution of fishes within estuaries (Table 32-1). The intermediate and fluctuating salinities typical of estuaries help to keep the number of species down because

TABLE 32-1

Distribution of Common Fishes in the Navarro River and Its Estuary, California, in Relation to Salinity

Species	Classification[a]	Salinity (ppt)						
		0[b]	0[c]	1	3	9 to 10	23 to 25	30+
Sacramento sucker	1	X[e]	X	X				
California roach	1	X	X	X	X			
Prickly sculpin	2	X	X	X	X	X	X	X
Rainbow trout	3	X	X	X	X	X	X	R
Threespine stickleback	2 and 3	X	X	X	X	X	X	X
Starry flounder	4		X*	X*	X*	X*	X	X
Shiner perch	4			R*	R*	X*	X	X
Jacksmelt	4				R*	X*	X	X
Bay pipefish	4					X	X	X
Plainfin midshipman	4[d]					X	X	X
Penpoint gunnel	4						X	X
Pacific herring	4[d]						X	X
Surf smelt	4						X*	X
Northern anchovy	4						X	X
Ling cod	5							X*

[a]The species are classified according to their salinity tolerance as follows: 1—stenohaline, freshwater; 2—euryhaline, freshwater; 3—anadromous; 4—euryhaline, marine; 5—stenohaline, marine.

[b]More than 1 km upstream from first riffle.

[c]Just above first riffle.

[d]Spawning.

[e]X indicates that the fish were present and common, R that they were present but rare. An asterisk indicates predominantly young-of-year fish.

Source: From unpublished data of D.H. Varoujean and P.B. Moyle, 1973–1976.

they prevent stenohaline marine and freshwater fishes from penetrating far into estuaries. Most estuarine fishes are capable of living in a wide range of salinities, and the most tolerant species, such as striped bass, can survive abrupt transfers from fresh water to full-strength sea water. However, the ability to survive such transfers is generally more pronounced at higher temperatures. While some estuarine fishes will tolerate the abrupt salinity changes caused by sudden increases in freshwater inflow and stay in one area, other species, such as the spotted seatrout, move to more saline regions (Tabb 1966). The life history stages of a species may also differ in their ability to survive salinity changes. Sudden increases in freshwater inflow may cause mass mortalities of young fish unable to avoid the low-salinity waters, either by osmotic shock or by flushing them to less productive portions of the estuary, where they may starve.

Oxygen levels are usually high in estuaries because of the constant inflow and mixing of both fresh water and salt water, although the naturally high levels of organic matter may reduce oxygen levels during times of low flow. The modern practice of dumping sewage into estuaries increases the amount of organic matter in estuarine systems and may reduce oxygen levels to the point where fish are killed or, more subtly, where they will not enter the estuaries. In the highly polluted Thames estuary of England, fishes seem to move up and down the estuary at least partly in response to changing oxygen levels, avoiding areas where the water is less than 10% saturated with oxygen (Arthur 1975).

Predation is an important process in estuaries, because a majority of the species are carnivores. The populations of the carnivorous fishes are large, and the impact of their predation on both invertebrates and fish populations seems to be considerable. Large concentrations of predators may also locally deplete prey populations. For example, spot (*Leiostomus xanthurus*) may severely limit the density of benthic invertebrates on soft bottoms of Atlantic coast estuaries (Virnstein 1977). Pilots observing large schools of plankton-feeding menhaden frequently notice that the water is much clearer behind the school than ahead of it, presumably because the menhaden have filtered out most edible organisms (McHugh 1967). However, plankton production is often so high in estuaries that high densities are typically present despite intense predation, while the benthic invertebrates compensate for high predation rates through rapid growth and short generation times. Young fish also are subject to intense predation in estuaries, but the heavy mortality is apparently also compensated in part by their rapid growth rates. Rapid growth enables them to reach more quickly sizes at which they are less vulnerable to predation as well as to achieve adult (reproductive) status more quickly than they could in areas where food is less available. In general, the physical and chemical fluctuations of the estuarine environment seem to have a much greater influence on fish populations than predation.

Competition, like predation, does not seem to be as important in regulating the distribution and abundance of estuarine fishes as the fluctuations of the environment. Most studies of food habits of estuarine fishes show a high degree of overlap among all the species present. One reason for this is that the number of species of abundant invertebrates in an estuary is typically low. For example, the dominant detritus/ phytoplankton filtering organism in the Sacramento–San Joaquin estuary is the opossum shrimp (*Neomysis mercedis*). This organism is important in the diet of almost all the fishes in the estuary at one life history stage or another. Nevertheless, it can be argued that the staggered use of estuaries by estuarine dependent marine fishes may be at least partially a mechanism for the species to reduce interspecific competition for food by their young (Livingston 1976). In the York River estuary, Virginia, ten species of croaker (Sciaenidae) manage to segregate partially on the basis of feeding habits (as reflected in body shape and mouth structure) and partially on the basis of differences in distribution within the estuary and timing of use of the estuary (Chao and Musick 1977).

Food Webs   Food, particularly in the form of detritus, detritus-feeding invertebrates, and small fishes, is abundant in estuaries, but the availability of any particular type of food is likely to show considerable fluctuation in even short periods of time. As a consequence, most estuarine fishes are not specialized feeders. Each species or life history stage shows a preference for some general type of food, such as small fish or benthic invertebrates, yet sooner or later almost every potential source of energy will appear in the diet. Thus, in a Louisiana estuary, Darnell (1961) found that detritus and detritus-feeding invertebrates were important in the diet of most fishes but that zooplankton and phytoplankton were relatively unimportant. Other studies have shown that even plankton may be important in the diets of estuarine fishes, particularly planktonic juvenile fishes.

As a consequence of the flexibility of fish feeding habits, the food webs in estuaries are robust. At any given time it is unlikely that any source of food will not be utilized. The simplicity of estuarine food webs, compared to other inshore marine systems, is caused not only by the lack of extreme specialization of many species but by the small number of fish species that are abundant at any one time. For example, Dalhberg and Odum (1970) found that only 12 of 70 species in a Georgia estuary made up over 90% of the individuals and that at any given time only three to five of the common species were present in large numbers. In many estuaries the number of species increases in the summer, when conditions are most stable, but most of the species are relatively rare and probably do not have much impact on the structure of the food webs.

Fish Communities   The species making up estuarine fish communities change constantly, yet the basic structure of the communities is fairly stable, or at least predictable (Livingston 1976). This stability is the result of: (1) the regular distribution of species along gradients of salinity, temperature, and other variables; (2) the predictable seasonal movements of fishes in and out of the estuaries; (3) the dominance of estuaries by a relatively few but interchangeable (in terms of trophic role) species; and (4) the robust food webs. These aspects of estuarine fish communities can be illustrated by the fishes found in the estuaries along the coast of the Gulf of Mexico, which are among the best studied in North America.

Although the fishes of Gulf Coast estuaries do have definite preferred temperature and salinity ranges, these ranges tend to be broad, so that the alignment of species along environmental gradients is often hard to detect. Nevertheless, there are usually distinct differences between the fish communities at the upper ends of the estuaries and those of the more saline and less thermally fluctuating lower ends. The most numerous fishes at the upper ends are usually small planktivores, such as the bay anchovy (*Anchoa mitchilli*, a year-round resident) and juvenile menhaden (an estuarine dependent marine species). However, croakers, typically juveniles, are also abundant, along with some "true" estuarine species such as the hogchoker (*Trinectes maculatus*). Freshwater fishes are often present in low numbers, as are anadromous species such as shad (*Alosa* spp.) and sturgeon (*Acipenser oxyrhynchus*). As the water becomes more saline, nondependent marine fishes dominate the species list, but each species is generally uncommon. In terms of numbers of individuals the dominant species are still true estuarine forms and estuarine dependent marine species.

The exact composition of the fish community at any given place in a Gulf Coast estuary depends strongly on the season of year (Fig. 32.1). There is a tendency for the dominant species, particularly the different species of croakers, to peak in abundance at slightly different times of the year. The peaks are related mostly to the influx of young, although the exact timing of the peaks and the size of the peaks are also related to natural fluctuations in the estuarine environment, as well as to disturbances. Both dependent and nondependent marine fishes also show seasonal patterns of abundance in estuaries. In a Georgia estuary, sea catfish (Ariidae) were found almost exclusively in the summer, while hake (Gadidae, *Urophycis* spp.) were found only in the winter (Dahlberg and Odum 1970). The seasonal use of estuaries by fish species may show considerable variation from one estuary to another. For example, sand trout (*Cynoscion nothus*) are found only in the summer in the Georgia estuary just described but are most common in Texas estuaries in the winter.

The most numerous fishes in Gulf Coast estuaries are usually juveniles that are feeding on plankton, but the biomass is often dominated by larger individuals that are feeding on fish, benthic invertebrates, detritus, or all three. Despite changes in the fish fauna with the seasons, no major source of food is neglected. In Apalachicola Bay, Florida, bay anchovy are usually the dominant planktivore in the summer, while juvenile Atlantic croaker (*Micropogon undulatus*) are dominant in the winter (Livingston et al. 1975). Similarly, the data of Perret and Caillouet (1974) indicate that benthic feeding individuals (over 10 cm long) of at least one species of croaker are always present in a Louisiana estuary.

While studies of Gulf Coast estuaries, as well as estuaries elsewhere, have shown that the fishes have predictable (more or less!) patterns of distribution and abundance in estuaries, it is worth pointing out that estuarine fish populations can change dramatically (and permanently) in the face of severe disturbances to the systems, particularly those disturbances that are the result of human activities. Estuarine fishes and food webs are very hardy and flexible, but the low diversity of fishes found in many urban estuaries today attests to the fact that even estuarine fishes have limits to their tolerances to extreme environmental conditions.

458

Supplemental Readings

Bechtel and Copeland 1970; Dahlberg and Odum 1970; Darnell 1961; Douglas and Stroud 1971; Green 1968; Lauff 1967; Livingston 1976; Livingston et al. 1975; McErlean et al. 1973; Odum et al. 1974; Odum 1970; R.F. Smith et al. 1966.

ααααααααααααααααααααααααααααααααααααααααααααααααααααααααααααααααααααααααα
~~~~~~

Coastal Habitats

Most marine fishes are found on or near the edges of the continents, from the intertidal regions to the edge of the continental shelf. Within this region there are a wide variety of habitat types, each inhabited by a distinctive set of fishes. Because of the large numbers of individuals and species of fish, the variety of habitats, and the general difficulty of studying much of the inshore region, our knowledge of the ecological relationships of these fishes is not great. As this chapter should illustrate, the amount of information available on the fish communities increases in proportion to their closeness to shore, their closeness to institutions devoted to the study of marine biology, their attractiveness to divers, and their commercial value. In this chapter, the fish communities associated with the following habitat types will be briefly discussed: (1) rocky intertidal areas; (2) exposed beaches; (3) mudflats; (4) salt marshes; (5) mangrove swamps; (6) seagrass flats; (7) kelp beds; (8) near-shore rocky bottoms; (9) near-shore soft bottoms; and (10) miscellaneous minor systems. The important inshore communities of tropical reefs and the polar regions are discussed in separate chapters. The various coastal habitats grade into one another, and many fishes are found in several different habitats or move between them. However, the categories above do represent the most abundant and conspicuous habitat types found in coastal regions, and each does have distinct types of fishes associated with it.

Rocky Intertidal Areas   Much of the coastline of the world is rocky and subject to the rise and fall of tides. The farther north one goes, the greater the tidal fluctuation. The environment in these rocky areas is a harsh one, subject to crashing surf, strong currents, and daily exposure to the air, yet the fauna is quite diverse. This diversity, combined with the region's accessibility to observers, has made it perhaps the most studied of marine environments, although invertebrates have received most of the attention. However, the fishes have not been entirely neglected, and they present an interesting complex of adaptations to a harsh environment.

Intertidal rocky areas, as well as other intertidal environments, have four basic kinds of fishes: true residents, partial residents, tidal visitors, and seasonal visitors (Gibson 1969). **True residents** are found in the intertidal zone all year around and have the greatest degree of specialization for living in this environment. Typical representatives of this group in temperate areas are members of the families Cottidae (sculpins), Blenniidae (blennies), Gobiesocidae (clingfishes), Gobiidae (gobies), Stichaeidae (pricklebacks) and Pholidae (gunnels). The wide, flattened head, large pectoral fins, and smooth body of sculpins serve them just as well for a bottom-hugging existence in intertidal areas as they do in swift streams. The blennies tend to be laterally compressed and elongate, so that they can easily fit into crevices and holes. The gobies are similar to the sculpins although not as dorsoventrally flattened. They have their pelvic fins modified into a sucker for holding on to the rocks. The clingfishes also have a pelvic sucker but are extremely flattened dorsally, which allows them to live in areas of high turbulence. The gunnels and pricklebacks, in contrast, are eel-like fishes that avoid turbulence by squeezing into narrow crevices and cracks or by living underneath the rocks.

Partial residents are fishes that are consistently found in the intertidal areas but are also found in deeper water. Typically these fishes are juveniles of species with large adults, and they are often representative of the same families that make up the true residents (e.g., Cottidae, Pholidae). However, partial residents may also be small, deep-bodied forms (e.g., Clinidae, Embiotocidae, Labridae). **Tidal visitors** are fishes that move into the intertidal region to feed as the tide moves in. These fishes can be almost any of the species that inhabit the more stable regions below the intertidal region. **Seasonal visitors** are often fishes that use the intertidal region for spawning, but the species that use the rocky areas in this manner are few. Tidal visitors are often seasonal visitors as well, since the inshore fish fauna in general shows seasonal changes in composition.

The dominant fishes of the rocky intertidal areas are the residents and partial residents, and their distribution patterns strongly reflect the physical, chemical, and biological aspects of their environment. Since there are generally strong, fluctuating gradients of temperature and general environment severity from the upper intertidal areas to the lower intertidal areas, the species distribution patterns tend to reflect their tolerance for these conditions. In the upper intertidal areas the species must have special adaptations to survive the harsh environment, such as a tolerance for fluctuating salinities and the ability to breathe air (Wright and Raymond 1978). In the lower intertidal areas interactions among the fish species may play an important role in determining distribution patterns, but usually similar coexisting species have strong preferences for particular environmental conditions that enable them to avoid competition. For example, two common intertidal species of sculpin (*Oligocottus maculosus* and *O. snyderi*) show segregation on the basis of habitat selection and temperature tolerances. *O. snyderi* selects habitats with plenty of cover (eelgrass) and low temperatures, while *O. maculosus* shows a preference for shallow water and has a tolerance for a wide range of temperatures and salinities (Nakamura 1976). Since intertidal species often tend to align themselves along various environmental gradients, there is a succession of species from the upper to the lower intertidal regions, but the strong zonation so often demonstrated by the invertebrates is usually difficult to find.

Although much of the ecological segregation present among intertidal fishes is on the basis of responses to the physical environment, fishes with overlapping distributions also tend to segregate on the basis of feeding habits. Most are carnivores, but herbivores and omnivores are not uncommon. One of the more remarkable omnivores is the amphibious pejesapo (*Sicyases sanguineus*), a clingfish of the rocky intertidal areas of the Pacific coast of South America. It lives where wave action is heavy and scrapes a wide variety of invertebrates and algae from the rocks, occupying a dominant grazer/predator role normally occupied by invertebrates in the upper intertidal zone (Paine and Palmer 1978).

The dominance of rocky intertidal areas by specialized acanthopterygian fishes indicates that the present environment has been in existence for a long time, but such areas are nevertheless locally unstable. Local fish faunas consequently fluctuate as a result of environmental disturbances, such as unusually cold water temperatures or destruction of sections of coastline by earthquakes or other natural phenomena. Jones and Clarke (1977) and Thomson and Lehner (1976) noted that unusually cold winter sea temperatures reduced the number of species present in the communities they studied. In both situations a core of tolerant species survived the unusual conditions with few ill effects, and the populations of affected species recovered with varying degrees of speed. The ability of intertidal fish communities to recover from highly localized disasters is also remarkable. Small areas that have had all the fishes removed experimentally with poisons are generally back to normal within a year. The commonness of natural local depletions of fish populations is demonstrated by the existence of fugitive species, such as the bay blenny (*Hypsoblennius gentilis*). This species is excluded from stable areas by two other species of *Hypsoblennius* but quickly colonizes areas from which the other species are absent (Stephens et al. 1970). The bay blenny has thrived in recent years as a consequence of the constant creation by humans of new habitats, such as breakwaters. An important factor contributing to the ability of the bay blenny and other intertidal

462

species to colonize uninhabited areas quickly is that many, if not most, such fishes have pelagic larvae which have strong substrate preferences when they settle out (e.g., Marliave 1977). Once established in an area, however, many intertidal fishes become territorial, reducing the probability of additional colonization by larvae of their own and, perhaps, similar species. Such fishes usually also have strong homing abilities and quickly return to their territories if displaced (Gibson 1969).

Exposed Beaches   The fishes associated with exposed coastal beaches live in the turbulent environment of the surf. The turbulence and currents would seem to require high energy expenditures by most of the fishes that live there, just to maintain themselves. On the other hand, the turbulence also provides a constant source of small, disoriented invertebrates that are exceptionally vulnerable to capture by fish. Thus, the surf zone is inhabited by a small but select group of fishes, often in surprisingly large numbers, mostly of the following types: (1) small, active plankton feeders; (2) roving substrate feeders; (3) flatfishes; (4) migratory species; (5) beach spawners; and (6) piscivores. Most species found in the surface are widely distributed in coastal habitats; few are found primarily in the surf.

Small, silvery, streamlined planktivores, such as silversides (Atherinidae), anchovies (Engraulidae), and herrings (Clupeidae), are often the most numerous fishes in the surf. Along the Atlantic and Gulf coasts, species specialized for feeding on the peculiar invertebrate fauna that lives in the sand may also be abundant. Examples of roving substrate feeders are the Atlantic threadfin (*Polydactylus octonemus*), with its specialized pectoral fin rays used for poking into the sand to find prey, and the gulf kingfish (*Menticirrhus littoralis*), a typical member of the bottom-feeding family Sciaenidae, with their sensitive barbels. The flatfishes in the surf also feed largely on benthic invertebrates. The flattened bodies of flounders and rays, particularly stingrays (Dasyatidae), enable them to avoid being swept about by the turbulence in the water column. Fishes that migrate along the coast in the surf zone and fishes that spawn on beaches typically do not feed in the surf, so their distinctive behavior patterns probably developed in large part to reduce their vulnerability to predation. The best-known examples of fishes that migrate through the surf are mullets (*Mugil* spp.), whose large schools can often be observed from shore. Fishes that spawn on beaches are few, but one of them, the California grunion (*Leuresthes tenuis*) attracts hordes of people to witness the spawning and collect the fish to eat. Their spawning is remarkably predictable because the fish move inshore on high tides following a new or full moon at certain times of the year. The grunion allow themselves to be washed in by the waves and in between breakers the females burrow into the sand, lay their eggs, and have them fertilized by the males. The eggs hatch on the next series of high tides, and the larvae are washed out to sea.

Considering the variety and abundance of fishes found in the surf, it is not surprising to find that piscivorous fish make excursions into the region to feed. Typical examples are bluefish (*Pomatomus saltatrix*) and various members of the family Carangidae. On the New England coast, one such predatory fish is the silver hake (*Merluccius bilinearis*), which is found in the surf in the fall and winter. Since they frequently become stranded on the beaches while pursuing their prey, they are known as frost fish to the people who go down to the beaches in season to pick them up. Occasionally, even large predators such as great white sharks are present in the surf, in pursuit of the large piscivorous fishes or marine mammals.

Many factors can affect the abundance and species of fish found in the surf. Many of the species move in to feed at certain times of the day and then move out again to less energetically demanding environments. This is particularly true of the predatory fishes. The occurrence of mullets in the surf is often a seasonal event, related to their migration patterns. The fishes of the surf also respond to such factors as temperature, tidal fluctuations, and salinity (Anderson et al. 1977).

Mudflats   Mudflats that are exposed by the falling tides are associated with backwaters, bays, or other features that allow sediment to accumulate. When exposed, they appear barren of life, yet they are extremely productive of polychaete worms, clams, and other burrowing invertebrates. As a consequence, as the tide moves in to cover the flats, large numbers of fish move in to feed. The species are those mobile forms that are typical of bays, estuaries, and other inshore environments: flounders from various families, skates and sharks, drum (Sciaenidae), and deep-bodied forms such as the surfperches (Embiotocidae).

These species find their prey with a variety of mechanisms. Rays often flap their "wings" rapidly to remove sediment covering clams. Some sharks go about biting off the protruding siphons of tube-dwelling worms. Many bony fishes search the substrate carefully, either by sight or with barbels, to find individual prey. Although most mudflat fishes are tidal visitors, there are a small number of species that are full-time residents of mudflats, aside from the few small tidal visitors that manage to survive in shallow drainage channels. These true tide flat residents are mostly small forms that can live in the burrows of marine invertebrates. Gobies (Gobiidae) are particularly well known for this trait. One species of goby, the longjaw mudsucker (*Gillichthys mirabilis*), has developed the ability to breathe air by having a highly vascularized bucco-pharyngeal chamber. If conditions in an invertebrate burrow or mudflat pool become too severe, the mudsucker is capable of "walking" with its pectoral fins across the muddy surface to a more favorable spot. Other species of gobies presumably manage to survive in the water that remains in the invertebrate burrows.

Salt Marshes   When mudflats are present in sheltered coastal areas, particularly bays and estuaries, for long periods of time, they are invaded by salt-tolerant plants and become salt marshes. On the Atlantic and Gulf coasts, salt marshes and their associated networks of drainage channels and embayments are major coastal habitats. On the Pacific coast, thanks to its steepness and rockiness, such marshes are much less abundant, but those that exist appear to be ecologically similar to those of the Atlantic coast (Lane and Hill 1975). Like other intertidal environments, salt marshes are subject to extreme daily and seasonal changes of water levels, salinity, and temperature. They are nevertheless one of the most productive environments known, and estuarine salt marshes are important sources of nutrients for estuarine systems. Salt marshes also support large fish and invertebrate populations of their own, and the standing crops (grams per square meter) of these organisms may be among the highest of any coastal system.

As in other intertidal systems, the fishes of salt marshes are a mixture of true residents, partial residents, tidal visitors, and seasonal visitors. At any given time the number of species present in a salt marsh is likely to be small, typically less than 15, but over the course of a year more are likely to be found, for example, 20 in a New England marsh (Nixon and Oviatt 1973) and 55 in a Florida marsh (Subrahmanyam and Drake 1975). The **true residents** of North American salt marshes, those fishes that complete their entire life cycle in the marshes, are mostly killifishes of the genera *Fundulus* and *Cyprinodon*. Most of these killifishes can live at salinities ranging from near 0 to several times that of sea water and at temperatures from near freezing to 35°C to 40°C. If stranded by the falling tide, some species such as the common mummichog (*F. heteroclitus*) will bury themselves in the mud or flop toward the receding water. As the tide rises, the killifishes typically penetrate into the marsh as far as they can, in order to feed on the abundant invertebrates associated with the marsh vegetation.

The main **partial residents** of Atlantic and Gulf coast salt marshes are silversides (*Menidia*). These fishes are found associated with the marshes throughout the year as juveniles. However, the adults tend to school along sandy or gravelly beaches or among beds of eelgrass. In Gulf Coast estuaries, juvenile spot (*Leiostomus xanthurus*) and pinfish (*Lagodon rhomboides*) may also be present in salt marshes all year around. **Tidal visitors** are typically larger fishes, such as adult sciaenids, flounders, and halfbeaks (Exocoetidae), that move into the salt marshes at high tide to feed on the abundant juvenile fishes and invertebrates. The species that play this role vary from season to season (Table 33-2).

Seasonal visitors are species that use the salt marshes as spawning or nursery areas or as seasonal refuges from predators. In both the Atlantic and Pacific coasts, the main salt marsh spawners are sticklebacks (Gasterosteidae). In the spring they build nests in the vegetation where the water is more or less permanent. The most important seasonal visitors

TABLE 33-1

Ecological Characteristics of 16 Common Fishes in Two Northern Florida Salt Marshes

	Life History Stage[a]	Main Food[b]	Type[c]	J	F	M	A	M	J	J	A	S	O	N	D
Longnose killifish	A,J	S,D	TR	X	X	X	X	X	X	X	X	X	X	X	X
Gulf killifish	A,J	S,M,D	TR		X	X	X		X	X	X	X	X	X	X
Sheepshead minnow	A,J	D	TR		X	X			X	X	X	X	X	X	X
Diamond killifish	A,J	?	TR		X								X	X	X
Sailfin molly	A,J	D,S	TR?					X	X	X	X	X	X	X	X
Rainwater killifish	A,J	S,D	TR?			X	X	X	X				X	X	X
Tidewater silverside	J	S,D	PR	X	X	X	X	X	X	X	X	X	X	X	
Spot	J	D,S	PR	X	X	X	X	X	X	X	X	X	X	X	X
Pinfish	J	D,S	PR		X	X	X	X	X		X	X	X	X	X
Pinfish	A	S,M,D	TV					X	X	X	X				X
Spotfin mojarra	J	S	SV							X	X	X	X	X	X
Bay anchovy	J	S	SV			X	X	X	X	X		X		X	
Striped mullet	J	D	SV		X				X	X	X	X	X	X	X
Halfbeak	A	S,D	TV	X				X	X	X		X	X	X	
Atlantic needlefish	A	C,S	TV	X		X		X	X	X	X	X	X	X	
Sand seatrout	J	C,F	TV					X	X	X			X		
Atlantic threadfin	A,J	S	TV				X		X	X	X	X	X		X

[a] A—adults; J—juveniles.
[b] S—small invertebrates; D—detritus; M—molluscs; C—crabs and other large invertebrates; F—fish.
[c] TR—true resident; PR—partial resident; SV—seasonal visitor; TV—tidal visitor.
Source: Information from Subrahmanyam and Drake (1975).

to southern Atlantic coast and Gulf coast salt marshes are juvenile drum, anchovies, mullet, and mojarras (Gerreidae). They spend several months in the marshes, taking advantage of the abundance of food and warm temperatures that promote rapid growth. The nursery function of salt marshes appears to be less important in northern Atlantic marshes, although Nixon and Oviatt (1973) noted that juvenile menhaden concentrated in a New England salt marsh embayment in late summer, largely to avoid predators.

Although the fish communities of salt marshes are often dominated in terms of biomass by the true residents, they show considerable fluctuations in both species composition and numbers, as well as total numbers of fish. The fluctuations are caused not only by movements of fishes related to reproduction and tides but also by the differing responses of the fishes to changes in salinity and temperature and to the abundance of both predators and prey. For example, Subrahmanyam and Drake (1975) found that the abundance of killifishes in a Florida salt marsh was related to warm temperatures, the abundance of pinfish was associated with high salinities, and the abundance of spot was related to low temperatures and high salinities together. Although the fluctuating nature of the salt marsh environment undoubtedly exacts high energy costs from the fishes that live there, the abundance of food usually more than makes up for these costs. Fishes that can take advantage of the food supply are largely detritus feeders, small invertebrate pickers (from the bottom or plants), and piscivores (Table 33-1). The most abundant species are typically invertebrate pickers, but the detritus they ingest while capturing their prey may also be a significant source of nutrition (Darnell [1967]; but see Prinslow et al. [1974]). Invertebrate feeders such as the common mummichog may be so abundant and so efficient at utilizing the invertebrates associated with salt marshes that they can significantly affect the species abundance and size distributions of the invertebrate populations (Vince et al. 1976). At the same time they may achieve extremely high production of their own species (Valiela et al. 1977). This high production of killifish in turn allows a large number of predators (birds and fish) to exist by feeding on them. Since the predatory fish (e.g., bluefish, white perch) are important sport and commercial fishes, the high productivity of salt marshes gives them a high value to humans, even apart from their importance as nursery areas.

Mangrove Swamps   On tropical coastlines the sea–land interface is, more often than not, covered with dense thickets of mangroves. The mangroves create rich swamps that may extend for miles inland along estuaries or form narrow belts along coastlines (Kuenzler 1974; Lugo and Snedaker 1974). In subtropical regions, such as Florida, they may also be important, but their distribution is less extensive. The shallow water beneath the mangroves ranges from hypersaline to fresh and from moving (by tidal currents or freshwater outflow) to stagnant. Intersecting the mangroves are usually muddy drainage channels a meter or so deep. Mangrove swamps thus provide a wide variety of aquatic habitats. Although variations in salinity, temperature, and dissolved oxygen levels can make the environment a hostile one, fish, particularly juveniles of marine fishes, abound wherever there is much exchange of the water. There are two main reasons for this: Mangrove swamps are among the most productive ecosystems in the world, and the interconnecting root systems and shallow water provide extensive cover. The mangroves support large populations of aquatic animals, mainly through a detrital food chain, since few of the invertebrates feed on the mangroves themselves. The detritus-feeding invertebrates are fed upon by each other and the fish. In Florida, W.E. Odum (1971) found that many game fishes have young that may spend part of their life cycle among the mangroves. Some of the more important species are tarpon (*Megalops atlantica*), ladyfish (*Elops saurus*), snook (*Centropomus undecimalis*), and grey snapper (*Lutjanus griseus*).

Mangrove swamps frequently show zonation in the vegetation, based on the different tolerances of the various mangrove species to factors such as salinity and water depth. Not surprisingly, there often is a zonation of animals that follows that of the vegetation. The areas that are important as nurseries for marine fishes are on the edges of the swamps or in the estuaries, where flow prevents stagnation and limits temperature extremes. The more severe interior environments of mangrove swamps are usually occupied by fishes such as the cyprinodonts (mollies [*Poeciliia*], and killifishes [*Cyprinodon*]) and, in tropical regions, mudskippers (*Periopthalamus*). Mudskippers are often extremely abundant in mangroves, especially along muddy drainage channels, since they are capable of breathing air, of "walking" across exposed mudflats, and even of climbing the exposed roots of the mangroves.

Seagrass Flats

The intertidal mudflats, salt marshes, and mangrove swamps of bays, estuaries, and other shallow coastal areas often grade into another habitat that is also extremely productive of fish: the subtidal, muddy-bottomed flats upon which grow beds of seagrass. There are 35 to 50 species of grass that can characterize these beds, but the dominant species in temperate regions is eelgrass (*Zostera marina*). In tropical regions the dominant grass is usually turtle grass (*Thalassia testudinum*), which is often associated with flats around coral reefs (see Chapter 37). Seagrass beds are among the most productive plant communities in the world, comparing favorably with corn and other intensively cultivated crops and with plankton blooms in areas of upwelling (Thayer et al. 1975). As a consequence of this high productivity, they support large populations of fish, which find both food and cover in the grass. These fishes are principally either juveniles of large species or species with small (less than 200 mm) adult sizes. However, because seagrass beds are located in shallow coastal areas such as estuaries, the water is subject to both seasonal and daily changes in temperature and salinity, although the salinity changes are seldom as dramatic as the temperature changes. As a consequence of these environmental fluctuations, the number of species found in a bed is likely to be small and the species composition resembles that of nearby or associated estuaries and salt marshes. Adams (1976a) collected only 39 species of fish in two North Carolina eelgrass beds over a one-year period, and 15 of the species were collected only once. Of the biomass of the two beds, 45% and 67%, respectively, was just one species, the pinfish. A similar pattern was found for New York eelgrass beds, except that there were two dominant species rather than one: Atlantic silverside (*Menidia menidia*) and fourspine stickleback (*Apeltes quadracus*) (Briggs and O'Connor 1971).

The number of fish in a seagrass bed fluctuates both diurnally and seasonally. Adams (1976a) found that densities of fish in eelgrass beds in the summer were highest at night, when temperatures were lowest. Since movement into the beds he studied was apparently not related to feeding, it may well have been to avoid nocturnal predators. The movement out of the beds in the morning permitted the fish, particularly larger individuals, to avoid potentially stressful temperatures. On a seasonal basis, densities of fish are highest in the summer, when the waters are warm and the eelgrass beds thickest. Again temperature seems to be the key factor regulating the movement of fish into and out of the beds. When the water cools down in the winter, many of the fishes seek slightly warmer deep water away from the beds, just as in the summer they may seek cooler water when the water around the beds becomes excessively warm. Regardless of the temperature of the beds, however, there always seem to be at least some fishes present, usually representatives of the same four or five species. During the summer, not only does the number of individuals increase, but the number of species increases as well, mostly as a reflection of the use of eelgrass beds as nursery grounds.

Seagrass beds are important as nursery areas because they are such a rich source of food for young fish. While the grass itself is rarely eaten, the detritus it produces is consumed by the fishes either directly or indirectly through detritus-feeding invertebrates. Given the abundance of food in eelgrass beds, it is not surprising to find that the diets of the various species overlap considerably. Nevertheless, there are four basic feeding types that can be found in the beds: detritivores, carnivores, planktivores, and omnivores. Usually, the most abundant fishes are carnivores which feed on the abundant invertebrates and small fishes associated with the grass, although omnivorous species such as pinfish may actually be the most numerous fishes, particularly in the more southern eelgrass beds (Adams 1976b). The omnivores include not only invertebrates, fish, and algae in their diets but also substantial amounts of detritus. Species that feed predominantly on detritus throughout their life cycle, such as spot, are few, although detritus is at times the dominant item in the diet of juveniles of many species. Such juveniles, particularly during their youngest stages, also frequently consume large amounts of zooplankton, which thrives in the nutrient-rich waters around the eelgrass beds.

Overall, the structure of the fish communities of seagrass beds is very similar to that of salt marshes. Both environments are highly productive, and both are dominated by large populations of a few species of small, tolerant fishes capable of utilizing a wide spectrum of food resources.

Kelp Beds

Kelp beds are undersea forests of brown algae, typically found in temperate waters between 6 m and 30 m. The kelp are anchored to rocky or sandy bottoms with holdfasts and have fronds extending to the surface, forming a dense canopy. The kelp forests provide a variety of habitats for invertebrates and fishes (Fig. 33.1) and are located in naturally productive waters, so they support an abundant and diverse fish fauna. However, relatively few species are exclusively kelp dwellers, although many are most abundant among the kelp. The most spectacular and most studied of the kelp bed fish communities are those found in the beds of giant kelp

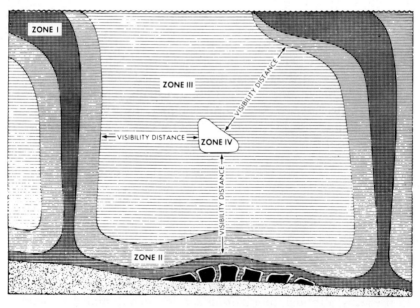

FIGURE 33.1 Major fish habitat zones in a kelp forest. Zone I is the surface of the kelp stalks, fronds, and holdfasts. Zone II is the water immediately above Zone I. Zone III is the water column out to the limits of visibility. Zone IV is the open water beyond the limits of visibility of the kelp plants. The fishes occupying each zone are given in Table 33-2. (From Quast, 1968.)

(*Macrocystis*) off the California coast (North and Hubbs 1968). This section will consequently deal largely with the ecology of these beds.

Most fishes associated with kelp beds are acanthopterygians, particularly of the orders Perciformes and Scorpaeniformes, and the number of species can be quite high. Off California, probably most of the 150+ inshore subtidal species can be found in kelp beds at one time or another, but only 50 to 60 of these are common and only 15 to 20 are abundant and conspicuous enough so that they are easily observed by divers (Quast 1968). The exact species composition of a kelp bed fish community will vary from place to place and time to time, depending on such factors as ambient water temperatures, depth of the beds, bottom type, season, water clarity, and the amount of turbulence created by wave action.

Because the species composition of kelp beds is likely to vary, most of the species have considerable flexibility in their living arrangements and are able to coexist with a wide variety of other species. At the same time, the variety of body shapes and behavior patterns indicate that a certain amount of specialization is also the rule. Quast (1968) found that the fishes segregated to a large degree on the basis of the part of the kelp plant with which they associated (holdfast, stalk, fronds), the distance they typically maintained from the kelp, where they foraged, and feeding behavior (Table 33-2). Species with similar habitat preferences and feeding behavior segregated further by the size and type of prey eaten. Quast (1968) divided the fish up into: (1) microcarnivores, which feed on microscopic (to us) prey, such as copepods and other zooplankters; (2) mesocarnivores, which feed on invertebrates and fish up to 30 cm long; and (3) megacarnivores, which consume invertebrates and fish longer than 30 cm. As Table 33-2 indicates, within each microhabitat there are groups of species (guilds) that are micro- or mesocarnivores. Close examination of the guilds shows that the species further segregate from each other on the basis of type of prey, method of prey capture, size of prey, and time of feeding. For example, the pile perch (*Rhacochilus vacca*) and the rubberlip perch (*R. toxotes*) are superficially similar to each other and even school together. However, the pile perch feeds during the day on large, hard-shelled molluscs, whereas the rubberlip perch feeds on smaller, thin-shelled invertebrates, apparently at night (Alevizon 1975). Similar segregation has been noticed among the microcarnivores that forage on zooplankton around the kelp beds. The day-active fishes are specialized for feeding on small zooplankters, and the night-active fishes have developed large eyes and other adaptations that allow them to prey on the larger zooplankters available at night (Hobson and Chess 1976). The complexity of the interactions possible in the kelp beds is indicated by the fact that two species, the senorita (*Oxyjulis californica*) and the kelp perch (*Barachyistius frenatus*), frequently clean ectoparasites from other fishes as well as foraging for small invertebrates on the kelp (Bray and Ebeling 1975).

TABLE 33-2
Niches of Common Adult Kelp Bed Fishes of Southern California

Zone I.   Fishes in nearly continuous contact with substrate
    A. Bottom
      1. Microcarnivores: painted greenling, sculpins, island kelpfish, spotted kelpfish
      2. Mesocarnivores: California moray, California scorpionfish, treefish, gopher rockfish, starry rockfish, calico rockfish, cabezon, lingcod
    B. Kelp holdfast
      1. Microcarnivores: various blennies, spotted kelpfish, reef finspot, black pricklefish, rock pricklefish, slimy snailfish, California clingfish
    C. Kelp column and canopy
      1. Microcarnivores: kelp clingfish, giant kelpfish, striped kelpfish(?), kelp gunnel, kelp pipefish

Zone II.   Inhabited by fishes that roam continuously over the substrate, from which they feed and which they use for refuge
    A. Bottom
      1. Microcarnivores: black surfperch, senorita, opaleye, halfmoon
      2. Mesocarnivores: kelpbass, garibaldi, halfmoon, California sheepshead, rubberlip seaperch, pile perch
      3. Megacarnivore: giant seabass
    B. Kelp holdfast
      1. Microcarnivores and megacarnivores same as for bottom (IIA)
    C. Kelp column and canopy
      1. Microcarnivores: kelp perch, halfmoon
      2. Mesocarnivores: kelpbass, halfmoon, olive rockfish
      3. Megacarnivore: giant seabass

Zone III.   Inhabited by fishes which use the open-water spaces to the limit of landmark visibility
    A. Bottom
      1. Microcarnivores: blacksmith, senorita, halfmoon
      2. Mesocarnivores: kelpbass, halfmoon, olive rockfish
      3. Megacarnivore: giant seabass
    B. Kelp column and canopy
      1. Microcarnivore: topsmelt (top 5 m only), senorita, blacksmith, halfmoon
      2. Mesocarnivores: kelpbass, senorita, halfmoon, olive rockfish
      3. Megacarnivore: giant seabass

Zone IV.   Beyond visibility range of fishes in kelp forest; region of pelagic fishes and foraging region for zooplankton-feeding kelp bed fishes.

Habitat zones are shown in Fig. 33.1.
Source: From Quast (1968).

Near-Shore Rocky Bottoms

Shallow (less than 50 cm) rocky-bottomed areas, from cliff faces to flat shelves, have fish communities similar to those of kelp beds. The reason for this is partly that kelp beds grow mostly on rocky bottoms and partly that, to a fish, the two habitats have similar attributes. Both habitats contain a diversity of microhabitats where small fishes can hide and large fishes can forage; both provide substrate for the attachment of sessile invertebrates and cover for small, active forms, thus providing a diverse and abundant supply of food. The differences between the two habitats are mostly in the relative abundances of the different species. Kelp beds are likely to contain larger numbers of plankton-feeding fishes, such as blacksmith (*Chromis punctipennis*), that use the beds for shelter between forays into the water column, while rocky areas are likely to have a higher density of crevice-dwelling forms, such as sculpins, blennies, gunnels, and pricklebacks. The most conspicuous fishes in both habitats are invertebrate pickers that roam over the substrate in schools or loose aggregations, feeding on small invertebrates. Such fishes are mostly members of the Embiotocidae (surfperches), Scorpaenidae (mostly *Sebastes*, rockfishes), Labridae (wrasses), Sparidae (porgies), and Sciaenidae (drums). Such fishes are often the object of sport fisheries, but most sought after are the fishes that prey on them, such as lingcod (*Ophiodon elongatus*) and striped bass (*Morone saxatilus*).

Most fishes that favor rocky bottoms have pelagic larvae (as do the invertebrates). As a result, new areas can be rapidly colonized. Off southern California, sewage outfall pipes that extend for several kilometers across muddy-bottomed areas have become spectacular, if narrow, reefs with large populations of fishes that otherwise would be rare in the area (Allen et al. 1976). It is now a common practice to create artificial reefs deliberately from concrete, old tires, automobile bodies, and old ships to increase the fish populations in muddy-bottomed bays (e.g., Dewees and Gotshall 1974).

The fish fauna of rocky areas deeper than 30 m to 50 m is poorly known because of the difficulty of sampling the habitat and because of its inaccessibility to divers. It is likely that many species of fish now considered to be rare because of their infrequency in fish collections are abundant in such habitats, especially members of such families as the Cottidae (sculpins), Zoarcidae (eelpouts), and Ophidiidae (cusk-eels). Some of the better-known species that are associated with deep rocky-bottomed areas are various species of rockfish (*Sebastes*), which feed in the water column and so are taken by fishermen. Among these species are two of high commercial value that have (or had, prior to overexploitation) enormous populations: Pacific ocean perch (*S. alutus*) and Atlantic redfish (*S. marinus*). The Pacific ocean perch is typically associated with gullies and canyons at depths of 150 m to 460 m (Major and Shippen 1970). They generally stay on or close to the bottom during the day and move up the water column at night to feed on large planktonic crustaceans, squid, and small fish, where they are caught by commercial fishermen. It has been estimated that the standing crop of Pacific ocean perch in the Gulf of Alaska was once over 1 *billion* kg. In just 6 years (1963–1968), this stock was reduced by 60% by commercial fishing!

Near-Shore Soft Bottoms On the continental shelf and slope, a majority of the bottom is soft and relatively featureless, covered with a layer of sand, silt, broken shells, and other fine materials in various proportions. The number of fish species found in a given soft-bottomed area is usually low; 40 to 60 species may be expected if the area is sampled for several years, with 15 to 20 occurring on a regular basis, and 2 to 5 making up most of the fish biomass. However, the most abundant species are often of major commercial importance. In particular, the trawl fisheries for various species of flatfish (Pleuronectiformes) and codfish (Gadidae) are largely associated with soft bottoms. Despite the importance of these fisheries, it is worth noting that the actual standing crops of fishes are not particularly high when compared to such productive areas as salt marshes and estuaries. The ease of fishing over soft bottoms and the large areas they cover, coupled with the fact that many of the important species concentrate at certain times of the year, make up for the low overall productivity. Furthermore, it is often possible to be fairly selective in a fishery over soft bottoms, because the different species show different patterns of distribution, depending on bottom type, depth, oceanographic conditions, pollution, and interactions with other fish species.

Bottom type.   Commercial fishermen have long known that the presence of a particular species of fish in an area can often be predicted on the basis of bottom type. As Bigelow and Schroeder (1953) note, the bottoms where cod (*Gadus morhua*) and hake (*Urophycis* spp.) are found "are so distinct that a long line set from a hard patch out over the soft surrounding ground will often catch cod at one end, hake at the other" (p. 184). Since most fishes can readily move from one bottom type to the next, the consistent association of a species with a particular bottom type (e.g., clay, silt, sand) is likely to be related to feeding habits. For example, bottoms with a high percentage of silt, support a diverse "infauna" of benthic invertebrates, which in turn support fishes specialized for feeding on them. However, the association of species with bottom types may also be coincidental, the result of their responses to other factors such as depth or oceanographic conditions. Thus, Day and Pearcy (1968) found that the associations of fishes found at different depths off the Oregon coast were also associated with distinct bottom types. Similar patterns have been found in areas as diverse as the coastal areas off South America and western Africa (Lowe-McConnell 1977).

Depth.   Most species of bottom-oriented fishes have fairly narrow depth ranges (Fig. 33.2), and on both the Atlantic and Pacific coasts of North America distinct associations of fish found within depth intervals have been recognized (e.g., Day and Pearcy 1968; Haedrich et al. 1975). Usually on soft bottoms between depths of 50 m and 2000 m there is a gradual decrease in the number of fish species, in the overall abundance of fish, and in fish biomass, although the average size of the fish tends to increase. At depths less than 50 m trends are less predictable. Off southern California the number of species, fish abundance, and fish biomass all decrease in waters shallower than 50 m, as does mean fish size (Mearns and Smith 1975). The causes of the observed depth distributions of fishes are poorly known, but the fact that they frequently vary

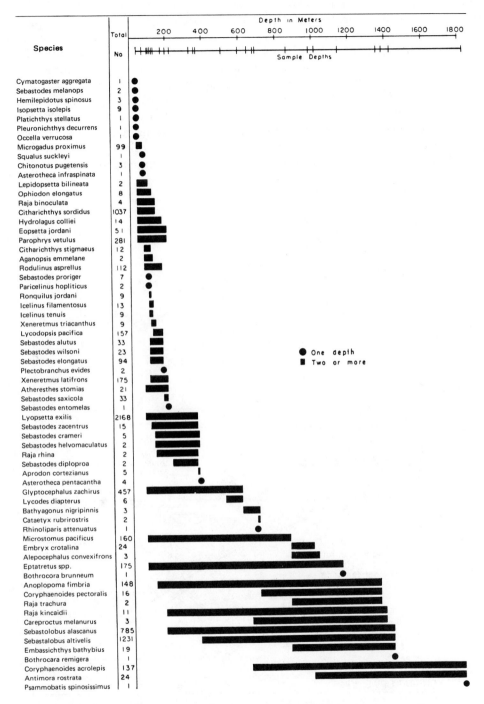

FIGURE 33.2 Depth ranges of benthic fishes collected off the central coast of Oregon. (From Day and Pearcy, 1968.)

with season indicates that responses to oceanographic conditions play at least a partial role.

Oceanographic conditions. Perhaps the most famous example of a benthic fish species whose distribution is limited by oceanographic conditions (principally temperature) is the tilefish (*Lopholatilus chamaeleonticeps*) off the coast of New England, which is restricted to water with temperatures between 8°C and 12°C, at depths between 90 m and 200 m; this species dies off in large numbers when conditions in its habitat change (Bigelow and Schroeder 1953). Off southern California, upwelling, which brings close to shore deep water that is low in temperature and oxygen

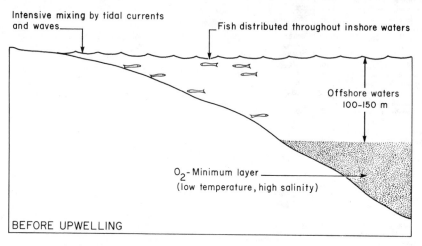

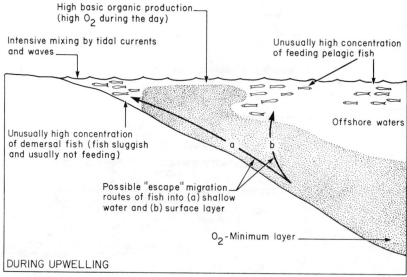

FIGURE 33.3 Impact of upwelling on the distribution of benthic and epipelagic fishes along the coast of southern California. (Used by permission of Southern California Coastal Water Research Project.)

and high in salinity, causes dramatic changes in the distribution patterns of the inshore fishes (Fig. 33.3). Seasonal changes less dramatic than upwelling also have a profound effect on the soft-bottomed fish fauna. Tyler (1971) noted that in the shallow waters (less than 55 m) of the Atlantic coast, there are four types of fishes in terms of their seasonal occurrences: year-round regulars, summer periodics, winter periodics, and occasionals. The latter group consists of species found in low numbers on an irregular basis. The relative proportions of these components in a local fish fauna seems to depend on the amount of annual temperature fluctuation. Where the temperature fluctuation is low, the regular component is more abundant than the seasonal component; where it is high, the seasonal component (and the occasional component) is much more important than the regular component (Fig. 33.4). Seasonal movements of fish, presumably in response to oceanographic conditions, have also been noted in deep water. For example, witch flounder (*Glyptocephalus cynoglossus*) off Newfoundland aggregate to spawn in waters 500 m to 700 m deep in the spring (the young use the continental slope as a nursery area), but they move into the Gulf of St. Lawrence in the summer and back into deeper water in the winter (Bowering 1976).

Pollution. The effluents from cities are increasingly having a significant impact on the inshore fish communities. In the most extreme cases, such as areas where the wastes from New York City have been dumped repeatedly, areas of anoxic or near-anoxic "wasteland" have been created. In less extreme situations the composition of the fish communities may be changed, the abundance and diversity of fishes reduced, and the incidence of disease increased. For example, off Los Angeles the fish com-

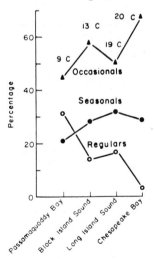

FIGURE 33.4 Percentages of fish species that are found on a year-round basis (regulars), seasonally, and irregularly (occasionals) in coastal waters at different latitudes in eastern North America. Annual temperature ranges are shown at top of graph. (From Tyler, 1971.)

munity appears to have shifted from one associated with sand bottoms to one associated with silt bottoms as a result (at least in part) of the deposition of sewage on the bottom. In the immediate vicinity of waste-water discharge sites, the diversity of fishes is low, even though some species, such as white croaker (*Genyonemus lineatus*) and Dover sole (*Microstomus pacificus*), may actually be attracted to the discharges. In addition, there is a high incidence of disease, particularly fin erosion disease, in the benthic fishes of the area, apparently as a result of contact by the fish with toxic materials on the bottom (Mearns 1973).

Species interactions. Competition and predation undoubtedly play an important role in determining the structure of soft-bottomed fish communities, although there is little direct evidence. However, the indirect evidence is compelling. The succession of similar species with depth would seem to indicate that some sort of competitive exclusion takes place, based in part on physiological specializations for different combinations of temperature and depth (pressure). Along the northern portions of both coasts, for example, flounders of the genus *Glyptocephalus* tend to replace other species of flounders in water deeper than 150 m. The impact overfishing has on fish communities also indicates that the presence of one species may result in the exclusion of others. On the Georges Bank overfishing of the haddock (*Melanogrammus aeglefinus*) led to their replacement by the yellowtail flounder (*Limanda ferruginea*). Overfishing of the flounder in turn led to their replacement by red hake (*Urophycis chuss*) (Rounsefell 1975). Another line of evidence indicating the importance of competitive exclusion, at least over long periods of time, is that studies of the feeding habits of coexisting fishes consistently show partitioning of the food resources available among the species (Tyler 1972). Overall, it appears that fishes on soft bottoms are specialized in terms of both habits and habitat requirements but that a number of them are flexible enough to take advantage of situations created when a normally dominant species is absent.

Zonation. Although the fishes of the continental shelf and slope may show seasonal patterns of movement, especially in relation to reproduction, it is usually possible to detect distinct fish zones in relation to depth. As in freshwater streams, these zones appear to be broad areas where the distributions of species with more or less similar habitat requirements overlap. Species frequently inhabit more than one zone (often at different times in their life cycle), but within zones segregation by feeding habits seems to be the rule. Off most coasts, five basic habitat zones can be recognized: (1) shallow-water; (2) inner continental shelf; (3) outer continental shelf; (4) upper continental slope; and (5) middle continental slope.

The Shallow-Water Zone is typically found in water less than 50 m deep and includes bays and other sheltered areas. Within this zone, of course, are the other coastal ecosystems discussed previously.

The Inner Shelf Zone is typically found between 50 m and 100 m to 150 m. The bottom is often sand, or mixed sand, silt, and broken shells, and is flat and featureless, although interrupted by submarine canyons and islands or rocky reefs. The dominant fishes here are such forms as hagfishes (Myxinidae), flounder, codfishes (Gadidae), rockfishes, and skates.

The Outer Shelf Zone, usually between 150 m and 400 m in depth, is similar in many respects to the previous zone, although the bottom tends to contain more silt and clay. The fishes are also similar but are usually of different species. In addition, members of families such as the Ophidiidae (cusk-eels) and Zoarcidae (eelpouts) are more common. It is worth noting the species determined to be "dominant" are dominant in the catches of the sampling gear used and not necessarily dominant on the bottom itself. Photographs taken by cameras lowered to the bottom in such areas often reveal quite different patterns of species abundance than those determined from sampling programs.

The Upper Slope Zone generally shows an increase in gradient from the previous zone, dropping from about 440 m to 1200 m. The bottom is mixed clay and silt. Along the Atlantic coast the fishes are mostly true deepwater forms that are rarely seen in shallower water: grenadiers (Macrouridae), longnose eel (*Synaphobranchus kaupi*), a small hake (*Phycis chesteri*), and eelpouts. Although species tend to be year-round residents in this zone, one other common species, the witch flounder, uses the zone as nursery grounds so the young flounder eventually move up onto the continental shelf (Markle and Musick 1974; Haedrich et al. 1975). Off the Pacific coast many distinct deepwater forms are also present in this zone, but the dominant species seem to be some of the same species of rockfish, flounders, and hake abundant on the shelf.

The Middle Slope Zone is similar in most respects to the Upper Slope Zone, but the number of species is much fewer and all are largely confined to the continental slope. The benthic fish fauna of this zone is remarkably similar in both the Atlantic and the Pacific, with the dominant fishes in trawl catches often being grenadiers (especially *Coryphaenoides*) and flatnoses (Moridae, *Antimora*). The fishes of this zone and of the Upper Slope Zone are discussed in more detail in Chapter 35.

Miscellaneous Systems   There are many coastal habitats which do not fit nicely into any of the categories previously discussed. This is particularly true of limited habitats characterized by extreme physical or chemical conditions that may form interesting, if highly localized, ecosystems. Examples of such systems are: (1) tidal inlets; (2) bluegreen algal mats; (3) hypersaline lagoons; and (4) salt ponds.

Tidal inlets are narrow channels into bays through which the water rushes at high velocities during incoming and outgoing tides. In rocky areas such channels may have the appearance of a whitewater rapids on a large stream. Tidal inlets are of interest because they contain a mixture of intertidal and subtidal invertebrates in high concentrations that filter-feed on the flowing water. There appear to be few fishes that are permanent residents in such areas, but during slack tides the local bay fishes move in to feed in large numbers (Odum et al. 1974).

Bluegreen algal mats occur in warm, protected, very shallow waters, especially along the Gulf of Mexico. The algal mats are the dominant feature, and because the water is subject to extreme variations in temperature, salinity, and oxygen, few animals are associated with them. Not surprisingly, however, one group of organisms that can thrive in this environment are the cyprinodont fishes, especially the sheepshead minnow (*Cyprinodon variegatus*). These fishes not only can live under extreme conditions but can feed on the algae as well.

Hypersaline lagoons are shallow embayments in arid regions in which high evaporation rates, combined with poor oceanic circulation and low freshwater inflow, result in salinities frequently exceeding 40 ppt. The number of fish species in a hypersaline lagoon is typically low, but if the fluctuations in temperature and salinity are not too extreme, the fish populations can be quite large. The most abundant fishes are typically juveniles of the same species that characterize local estuaries and other shallow-water environments. In the Gulf of Mexico, where such lagoons are common, characteristic species are sea catfish, sheepshead minnow, tidewater silverside, striped mullet, pinfish, southern flounder (*Paralichthys lethostigma*), and various species of croakers (Sciaenidae). Most of the fishes are planktivores or predators on other fishes, although the sheepshead minnow, mullet, and some drum do browse on algae and detritus (Copeland and Nixon 1974).

Salt ponds, like hypersaline lagoons, are semi-isolated shallow embayments, but they are located in nonarid regions so that their salinities are seldom greater than that of the local sea water, and often less. The fishes are the same species found in local eelgrass beds and bays: silversides, pipefish, stickleback, killifish, and other small species, as well as the young of various larger species. Some salt ponds seem to be quite important locally as nursery grounds for inshore fishes. On the Hawaiian Islands there are numerous low-salinity ponds formed by lava flows into the ocean. These ponds are inhabited by a wide variety of euryhaline fishes that have accidentally been washed into them by storm waves or have moved into them through outlet streams. The ponds apparently are not used as nursery areas, but they are often good producers of fish for human consumption (Brock 1977).

Supplemental Readings Bigelow and Schroeder 1953; Gibson 1969; Hart 1973; Hoese and Moore 1977; Hubbs 1968; Leim and Scott 1966; Nixon and Oviatt 1973; North and Odum et al. 1974; Oviatt and Nixon 1973; Rounsefell 1975.

ααααααααααααααααααααααααααααααααααααααααααααααααααααααααααααααααααααααα
~~~~~~

Tropical Reefs

For sheer diversity of fish life, tropical reefs are unbeatable. Somewhere between 30% and 40% of all fish species are associated with such reefs in one way or another, and anywhere from 250 to 2200 species are likely to be found in, on, or near a major complex of reefs. The number of species found in even one small area is often amazing; Smith and Tyler (1972) collected 75 species from an isolated coral dome that was only about 3 m in diameter and 1.6 m high. Most of the fishes found on reefs are acanthopterygians with an extraordinary array of adaptations for maintaining themselves in a crowded environment. The few nonacanthopterygian species associated with reefs are largely adapted either for preying on the other fishes (e.g., moray eels, sharks) or for feeding on plankton above the reef (e.g., herrings). While the diversity of reef fishes has been appreciated for a long time, it is only in recent years that the development of scuba gear and modern transportation systems has made reefs readily accessible to biologists. These developments have also made them open to exploitation, so there is a real need to study the various reef systems of the world while their fish communities are still intact. One of the major challenges of the present time to ecologists and evolutionary biologists is the development and testing of hypotheses to explain how reef communities evolved and how they maintain their complexity. This chapter will summarize some of the progress that has been made in this area in recent years by describing: (1) the reef habitat; (2) the types of reef fishes, based on feeding habits; (3) life cycles of reef fishes; (4) species interactions; (5) activity patterns of reef fishes; and (6) community structure.

The Reef Environment   Coral reefs are found between latitudes 30° north and 30° south, in shallow water (usually less than 50 m deep) that is warm enough to support the growth of corals and clear enough to allow photosynthesis at moderate depths. This means that the water in reef areas rarely drops below 18°C (it is usually around 23°C to 25°C) and that underwater visibility is usually in excess of 10 m to 20 m. Although corals are typically associated with tropical reefs and are famous for their reef-building habits, many so-called coral reefs have largely been built up by calcareous algae. In addition, there are many rocky coastal areas and reefs that support a complex fish and invertebrate fauna similar to that of the coral and algae reefs. Most tropical reefs are surrounded by nutrient-poor oceanic waters, so their extremely high productivity is surprising. It can be attributed to a combination of: (1) a high degree of recycling of nutrients within the reefs; (2) the photosynthetic activity of attached algae under optimal light and temperature conditions; and (3) nitrogen fixation by bluegreen algae on the reefs (Wiebe et al. 1975).

There are four major regions of the ocean that have tropical reefs: (1) the Indo-Pacific Region; (2) the Eastern Pacific Region; (3) the Western Atlantic (West Indian) Region; and (4) the Eastern Atlantic (West African) Region. The Indo-Pacific Region includes the Indian Ocean and the Western Pacific and consequently most of the large reef systems, especially coral reefs. The Eastern Pacific Region includes the rocky reef communities of Baja California and the coral reef communities off Central and South America. The Western Atlantic Region contains the diverse reefs in the Gulf of Mexico as well as those around the tip of Florida, Cuba, and the West Indies. The Eastern Atlantic Region is made up of scattered patches of reef along the coast of western Africa, which, perhaps because of their isolation, have the least diversity of tropical reef fishes.

While the wide distribution of tropical reefs means that they exhibit a great variety of shapes and sizes, each reef does have a series of habitat zones with distinctive fish and invertebrate faunas (Hobson 1974; Goldman and Talbot 1976). Six major zones can be recognized, although all are not present on every reef: (1) off-reef floor; (2) reef drop-off; (3) reef face; (4) reef surface; (5) reef flat; and (6) lagoon. The **off-reef floor** is the shallow sea bottom around a reef. It is typically sandy and often supports beds of seagrass and thus may be an important foraging area for reef fishes. Many reefs are not surrounded by a sandy floor but drop off abruptly, often to great depths. The **reef drop-off** in its upper 50 m to 60 m is favored by large numbers of fishes which can find shelter on the cliff face and abundant plankton immediately off it. The **reef face** above either the floor or the drop-off is often the richest habitat for fishes and invertebrates. The complex growths of coral and calcareous algae provide innumerable cracks and crevices for protection, and the abundant invertebrates and epiphytic algae provide an abundant source of food. The **reef surface** is also a rich habitat for life, but the organisms that live there must be able to withstand the constant surge of the waves and, in some areas, the rise and fall of the tides. Behind the main reef, toward shore, there is often a sandy-bottomed **reef flat** containing scattered chunks of coral. The reef flat may be a protected area bordering a lagoon or a flat, rocky area between the reef and shore. In the former case the number of fish species living in the area is often the highest of any reef zone. Many coral reefs completely surround an area, creating a quiet-water **lagoon,** which usually contains small patches of reef within it as well.

Although the zones on a reef are fairly stable phenomena and most reefs presumably have a long history, the topography of a reef is constantly changing. Each reef is made up of irregular patches of algae, sessile invertebrates, and bare rock and sand. The size, shape, and relative abundance of these patches changes from year to year, in response to the various factors that may favor one type of patch over another. On a larger scale tropical storms may knock out big pieces of reef and cause boulders on sandy areas to move around. These changes, whether large or small, are essentially unpredictable and thus provide a habitat for reef fishes that is continually changing on a local scale, even if the overall environment seems quite benign and stable (Sale 1977; Connell 1978).

Types of Reef Fishes There are many ways reef fishes can be classified, but for understanding the structure of the fish communities, it is best to classify them by feeding habits. Following Hobson (1974) in good part, we can place reef fishes into three general feeding categories: generalized carnivores, specialized carnivores, and herbivores.

Generalized carnivores. These fish are classic rover-predators in body shape, with large, flexible mouths well suited for seizing large prey (Fig. 34.1). By and large, they prey on mobile fishes and invertebrates. The generalized carnivores are of three basic types: nocturnal, crepuscular, and diurnal (Hobson 1974). The **nocturnal predators** are specialized to the extent that they have large eyes and typically feed either on benthic crustaceans that move about the reef at night or on the large zooplankters that are found in the water column at night. The **crepuscular predators** are classic piscivores, representing such families as the Serranidae, Carangidae, and Lutjanidae. These fishes become active during twilight because the low light levels offer a certain amount of concealment to the predators while still enabling them to see their prey, particularly schooling fishes. **Diurnal predators** are similar to crepuscular predators in their body shape and preferences for fish. They obtain their prey by slowly cruising over the reef or by lying in concealment. In either situation, they must wait until a nearby fish makes a defensive mistake, such as moving too far from cover or becoming separated from a school.

484

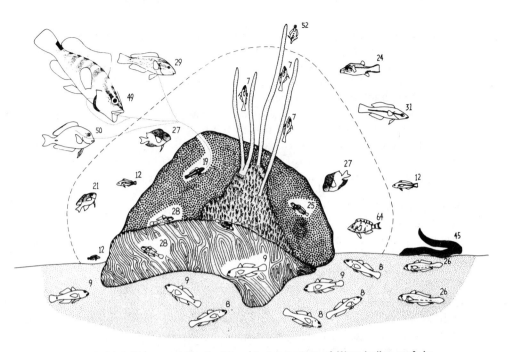

FIGURE 34.1 Fishes associated with an isolated piece of West Indian reef, in which a cleaner goby (19, *Gobiosoma*) has a station. Waiting to be cleaned are a herbivorous parrotfish (29, *Scarus*), a generalized carnivore (49, a grouper, *Epinephelus*), and a herbivorous surgeonfish (50, *Acanthurus*). Associated with the reef surface are diurnal planktivores (27, a damselfish, *Pomacentrus;* and 12, a wrasse, *Thalassoma*), a territorial herbivore (21, a damselfish, *Pomacentrus*), a herbivorous parrotfish (64, *Sparisoma*), small, plankton-feeding (?) goby (7, *Coryphopterus*), and a small filefish (52, *Monacanthus*). Visiting the patch to feed on occasion are a diurnal feeder on hard-shelled invertebrates (24, a puffer, *Canthigaster*), a diurnal invertebrate picker (31, a wrasse, *Halichoeres*), and a crevice feeder (45, a moray eel, *Muraena*). Associated with the sand around the coral and the coral itself are a guild of gobies (8, 9, 25, 26, 28), feeding variously on algae, detritus, and small invertebrates, often at night. (From Smith and Tyler, 1972.)

Specialized carnivores are fishes adapted for taking a particular type of prey or for feeding in a particular manner or in a particular microhabitat (Hobson 1974). A majority of reef fish species belong in this category, but the number of individuals of any one species is likely to be small on any one reef. Although many of the specializations are extraordinary, it is not unusual to find several species on the same reef with about the same specializations. As will be discussed later, these similar species form feeding guilds whose members interact with each other through competition. On a broader basis, the specialized carnivores can be divided into seven types: (1) ambushers; (2) water column stalkers; (3) crevice predators; (4) concealed-prey feeders; (5) diurnal predators on benthic invertebrates; (6) cleaners; and (7) diurnal planktivores.

Ambush feeding is one of the principal methods of prey capture of generalized reef carnivores, from which the specialized ambushers differ in their extreme use of camouflage, necessary for capture of prey during the day. Among these fishes are the lizardfishes (Synodontidae), various scorpionfishes (Scorpaenidae), and flounders (Bothidae). Such fishes match their backgrounds so well that they are frequently overlooked by divers (and prey!). The scorpionfishes, such as the deadly stonefish (*Synanceja*), are particularly famous for their ability to be "invisible."

Another group of fishes that specializes in making themselves invisble to potential prey are the water column stalkers. These fishes are silvery, elongate forms, with long, pointed snouts full of sharp teeth. A head-on view often belies their large size. They drift through the water column toward a small fish and then seize it with a sudden lunge, propelled by a fin structure typical of lie-in-wait predators. Examples of this group are barracudas (Sphyraenidae), needlefishes (Belonidae), and cornet fishes (Fistulariidae).

In contrast to the preceding two groups of ambush feeders, crevice predators actively seek their prey, mostly fishes that are hiding in the numerous crevices and small caves characteristic of reefs. The main specializations of this group are elongate bodies and small heads that allow them to penetrate into crevices to find their prey. Examples are moray eels (Muraenidae) and reef brotulas (Ophidiidae).

Concealed-prey feeders also actively seek prey hidden on or about the reef, taking both active invertebrates and small fish. This group consists mainly of the goatfishes (Mullidae), an abundant and conspicuous group of reef dwellers. They have long chin barbels with which they probe the reef surface or sandy bottoms around a reef. Once a goatfish has located a prey organism with its barbels, it sucks it up with its flexible, slightly subterminal mouth. Depending on the species, goatfishes can be either nocturnal or diurnal (Hobson 1974).

Among the most spectacular reef fishes, in terms of both body morphology and bright color patterns, are the members of the next group, the diurnal predators on benthic invertebrates. This group differs from the goatfishes in that they use vision, rather than touch, to find their prey and, while some of them also feed on concealed prey, many of them feed on the more conspicuous reef invertebrates, such as sponges, corals, tunicates, sea urchins, and snails. By doing so, they provide some of the more spectacular examples of coevolution of predators and prey. The invertebrates that are preyed on have, over the course of several million years of predator pressure, evolved a formidable array of defense mechanisms, mostly various combinations of spines, toxins, heavy armor, and adherence to the substrate. In the same period of time the predatory fishes have evolved many mechanisms for overcoming the defenses of the invertebrates. One means for overcoming heavy armor is to have strong, hard jaws, such as the heavy beaks possessed by most members of the order Tetraodontiformes (puffers, boxfishes, etc.) and the strong pharyngeal teeth of many of the wrasses (Labridae). These fishes crush various hard-shelled invertebrates. Other species get around the problem of armor by biting off exposed pieces of flesh, such as the polyps of coral and the "fans" of sessile polychaete worms. Many of the species which feed in this manner are the deep-bodied, brightly colored butterfly fishes (Chaetodontidae), which have elongate snouts equipped with a small mouth containing tiny (but sharp) teeth, with which they can clip off pieces of invertebrates. Other butterfly fishes use the same type of feeding mechanism for seizing prey that is deep in crevices, such as small crustaceans or even encrusting sponges. The depth to which a species can reach into a crevice is reflected in the length of its snout, which in some species may be over 25% of the body length. Yet another way some butterfly fishes feed is by scraping the surface of living coral, thereby obtaining mucus secreted by the coral, small, attached invertebrates, and algae.

Diurnal predators that feed on small, concealed invertebrates also have many specializations, although they tend to be more behavioral than morphological. Some species of wrasse with small mouths feed by carefully searching the reef surface and then picking up invertebrates that are too small for most other species to feed on. Other wrasses will use their snouts to overturn chunks of rock and coral on the reef edge in order to expose hidden invertebrates. Some tetraodontids obtain invertebrates in sandy-bottomed areas by uncovering them with a jet of water blown from their mouth. Fishes that feed in such a manner often elicit following behavior by other fishes, who also attempt to feed on the exposed invertebrates. Following behavior is also elicited by schools of herbivorous fishes which disturb the substrate or even by foraging moray eels, which may send small fish fleeing from cover and into the mouths of other predators (Strand 1978).

Many of the benthic invertebrate feeders engage, mostly as juveniles, in another specialized form of invertebrate feeding, that of picking ectoparasites and dead and diseased tissue from other fishes. For some species, such as gobies of the genus *Gobiosoma* of western Atlantic reefs and wrasses of the genus *Labroides* of Indo-Pacific reefs, material picked from other fishes is the main food of the adults as well. The distinctive behavior and bright coloration of cleaner fishes attracts other fishes to them. Fishes will express their receptivity to cleaning by entering a trancelike state, with fins held rigidly, opercula flared, and mouths open. Such fish often exhibit special contrasting color patterns as well. The cleaner then swims about the fish, picking off ectoparasites from the sides and, for larger fishes, often from the mouth cavity as well. They will also apparently "clean" wounds, eat loose scales, consume mucus, and nibble off pieces of healthy fin. Cleaner fishes either work from stations on the reef to which fishes come to be cleaned or move freely about the reef during the day, stopping to clean territorial fishes (Ehrlich 1975). In the latter case they will apparently also steal eggs from nests being guarded by the territory holders (Losey 1978).

While all the preceding groups of specialized carnivores find their food mostly on the reef itself, another very abundant group uses the reef mainly for cover and feeds on zooplankton in the water column during the day. These fishes are more specialized than their nocturnal counterparts because (1) their prey is either very small (copepods) or gelatinous (larvaceans, chaetognaths, fish eggs, etc.); and (2) they must be able to escape diurnal predators (Hobson 1974). These factors have resulted in fishes from different families (e.g., Pomacentridae, Serranidae, Acanthuridae) evolving quite similar morphologies: streamlined bodies, deeply forked or lunate tails, and small, upturned mouths. The first two features enable the fishes to dive quickly into the cover of the reef at the approach of a predatory fish. However, it should be noted that their body shape, while streamlined, is more or less a compromise between the rover-predator shape and the deep-bodied shape, since a deep body is useful for hovering in the water column and picking out the plankton. The small mouth enables the fish to capture small prey, while its upturning apparently functions to shorten the snout, which gives the fish binocular vision at close range, enabling it to pinpoint its small prey (Hobson 1974).

Herbivores.   Compared to the number of carnivorous fish species on a reef, the number of herbivorous species is small (22% of all species, according to Sale 1977). However, what the herbivores lack in species they make up for in numbers and in conspicuousness, as well as in their impact on the appearance of reefs. Herbivores are often the most noticeable fish on reefs. Small, brightly colored damselfishes vigorously defend their territories, while schools of large parrotfishes (Scaridae) and surgeonfishes (Acanthuridae) browse over the reef surface. Other herbivores (or partial herbivores) are scattered through the various families of reef fishes, such as Kyphosidae, Chaetodontidae, Blenniidae, Pomacanthidae, and Siganidae (Ehrlich 1975). The main sources of food for these are the filamentous algae that coats a reef and, to a lesser extent, the seagrasses and algae that grow on reef flats. The herbivorous fishes (and invertebrates as well) keep the algae on the reef cropped down to a thin mat, only 1 mm to 2 mm thick, and can create a ring around reefs up to 10 m wide that is bare of vegetation (Randall 1961, 1965). The reduction of attached algal abundance by herbivores is apparently also important for the well-being of reef-building corals and algae, since patches of reef from which herbivores are excluded quickly become covered with thick growths of filamentous and leafy algae (Ogden and Lobel 1978).

The plants are eaten in various ways by the fishes, such as scraping by parrotfishes and plucking by damselfishes, but, overall, the diets of the various herbivores seem to differ little from species to species. The smaller herbivores, such as the damselfishes, may protect their share of this food supply by defending sections of reef against their own kind as well as other species of fish. This aggressive defense results in heavier

488

growths of algae (and invertebrates) in the territories than outside them (Brawley and Adey 1977). In order to take advantage of these growths, some herbivores will move into a territory as a school, overwhelming the defender (Robertson et al. 1976).

Life Cycles

Given the variety of fishes present on reefs, the variety of life cycles is surprisingly small (Sale 1977). Spawning may take place all year around in equatorial regions and may last 4 to 6 months in the higher latitudes. Because of the crowded conditions of reefs, competition for mates in most species is intense. As a result, elaborate mating systems have evolved that rival (or exceed) those of mammals and birds in their complexity, including the use of territories, leks, and harems (Robertson and Hoffman 1977). During the spawning periods individuals may spawn frequently, even daily in some species (Sale 1977). Eggs may be either planktonic or attached to the substrate, in which case they are protected by territorial adults (usually the males).

The reproductive strategy adopted by a particular species is closely tied to the species' use of the reef for other purposes, as well as to its density on the reef (Fig. 34.2). The larvae are almost invariably planktonic, drifting in the currents for 2 to 10 weeks. This assures a fairly wide dispersal of most species. One of the main advantages of pelagic larvae is that they live away from concentrations of predators associated with the reefs (Johannes 1978). Nevertheless, most of these larvae are eaten, either while they are planktonic or shortly after they settle out and either cannot find suitable habitat or find all the suitable habitat already occupied by other fishes. The presence of established fishes is particularly important, since most reef fishes are surprisingly flexible in their habitat requirements once they are in a generally suitable area, such as a reef zone.

Species Interactions

Because tropical reefs are both a physically benign and ancient environment, the fish fauna is complex, with some of the most complex patterns of interactions among fish species known. These interactions are very important determinants of community structure and fall into four basic categories: predator-prey interactions, competition, symbiosis, and mimicry.

Predator-prey interactions. The variety of ways in which reef fishes act as predators has already been discussed. However, reef fishes also serve as prey for each other and certain reef invertebrates, so they consequently have many means, both morphological and behavioral, of protecting themselves. Most reef fishes possess a formidable array of spines, which often are venomous or can be rigidly locked in place. Many have cryptic or disruptive color patterns as well to confuse predators. Behaviorally, small reef fishes protect themselves from predators either

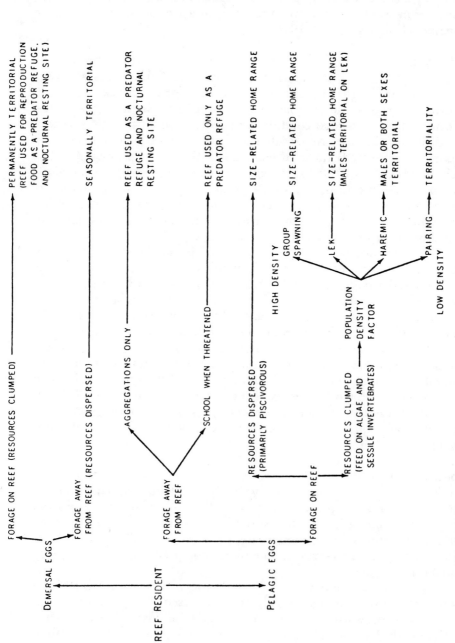

FIGURE 34.2 Relationships between egg type, feeding habits, and space utilization among reef fishes of the Gulf of California. (From Strand, 1978.)

by schooling or by hiding in reef crevices. Many reef fishes spend most of their lives in one small area so they have well-known hiding places instantly available. Others may roam the reef, typically in schools, but return to specific areas to hide during the times when they are not actively feeding (Ogden and Ehrlich 1977). While resting, small fishes are still vulnerable to crevice predators, so many fishes cram themselves into the smallest hiding places possible and wedge themselves in with erect spines. Parrotfish can secrete a cocoon of mucus about themselves while resting, which seems to provide protection against predators that find hidden prey by smell or touch (Hobson 1974). While it is obvious that predator–prey interactions have had a tremendous impact on the evolution of reef fishes, their impact on fish community structure is not well understood. Because it is usual to find groups of ecologically similar species coexisting on reefs, Goldman and Talbot (1976) speculate that predators may limit the populations of such forms to the point that they never build up large enough numbers to cause competitive exclusion. However, vacant spaces on a reef never remain so for long, so it seems likely that piscivorous fishes are taking mainly young, ailing, or displaced fishes that have been unable to find a place to live or established fishes that have made a rare defensive mistake. In either case, predation would not have much impact on the structure of reef communities. One important role that predators may play is in bringing nutrients from the water column to reefs, since many piscivores and planktivores feed away from reefs but rest on them, where they deposit feces.

Competition. Competition, like predation, has undoubtedly been an important process shaping the fish communities of tropical reefs, and character displacement resulting from competition is no doubt responsible for many of the bizarre shapes and colors of reef fishes, such as the butterfly fishes with different snout lengths found on Hawaiian reefs (Hobson 1974). Despite the high diversity and age of reef communities, there is considerable evidence that competition among species for scarce resources, particularly space, is a common phenomenon on reefs. As Ehrlich (1975) points out, reefs are "crammed" with both species and individuals, and they appear to crop the available food resources heavily. The filamentous algae on reefs have even been characterized as overgrazed (Randall 1961). Furthermore, despite the many specialized fishes on reefs, there are even more that are generalists in their feeding habits. At the same time, within habitat zones there seems to be surprisingly little spatial specialization; most species can be found wherever conditions are broadly suitable (Sale 1977). Guilds of ecologically similar species are common on reefs, and the members of the guilds seem to recognize each other's signals. Thus, a damselfish defends its territory not only against its conspecifics but against members of other damselfish species (Sale 1977). Ecologically, each guild behaves much as a species would in less complex communities.

Symbiosis.   Of the types of symbiosis, only mutualism and commensalism are common among reef fishes, although some of the cases of aggressive mimicry (see below) could be classified as parasitism if a broad definition is used, as could some interactions between large fish and small invertebrates (see Chapter 27). The classic example of mutualism among fishes is the interaction among cleaner fishes and the fishes being cleaned; the former are fed and the latter have parasites removed. Another example is the schools made up to two or more species often found on reefs, which confer on the cooperating species the advantages of schools larger than any of the species could produce by themselves (Ehrlich and Ehrlich 1973). Mutualistic relationships may also form between invertebrates and fish, the classic example being the anemone fishes (*Amphiprion*) and their anemones. These fishes are protected from predators by the stings of the anemone (to which the fish are acclimated), while the anemone feeds partially on food brought in by the fish. Other fish–invertebrate interactions are commensal in nature, such as those exhibited by the fishes that hide among the spines of sea urchins and starfish or hide in the hollow tubes of sponges. An example of commensalism among fish species is the following behavior of fishes seeking prey stirred up by other fishes, although there may be mutualistic aspects of this behavior as well, if fright behavior of following fishes warns the fish being followed of the approach of a predator (Strand 1978). A purely commensal relationship, however, is that of some cornet fish (Fistulariidae) and parrotfishes (Eibl-Eibesfelt 1965). The long, narrow cornet fish "rides" on top of the parrotfish, essentially using the parrotfish as a mobile cover from which it can ambush small fishes.

Activity Patterns

One way that reef species avoid interactions with other species is to have periods of activity that do not overlap those of potential competitors or predators.   Indeed, one of the striking aspects of reef fish communities is the difference between night and day on a reef. During the day the deeper cracks, crevices, and caves of a reef are filled with night-active fishes, whereas at night they are filled with day-active fishes (Fig. 34.3). The changeover from diurnal to nocturnal fishes and then back again is a fascinating and complex phenomenon (Hobson 1975).

During the day the surface of the reef is a busy place, since most of the brightly colored, specialized carnivores are active at this time, feeding, defending territories, and spawning.   Immediately above the reef are schools of small plankton-feeding fishes, which are under the surveillance of various piscivorous fishes.   Closer to the reef are large, relatively inactive schools of nocturnal planktivores and other nocturnal fishes that do not feed on the reef. Deep within the reef are other nocturnal fishes, often red in color with large eyes, such as the squirrelfishes (Holocentridae), cardinalfishes (Apogonidae), and bigeyes (Priacanthidadae).

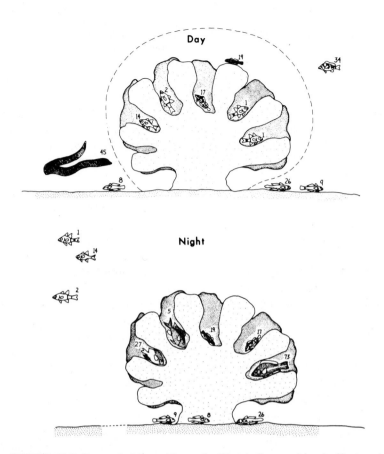

FIGURE 34.3 Day and night residents of a West Indian coral head. Nocturnal planktivores (1, 2, 14, cardinalfishes, Apogonidae), a cleaner goby (19, *Gobisoma*), a predatory blenny (17, *Labrisomus*), a piscivore (34, *Hypoplectrus*), various gobies (8, 9, 26, Gobiidae), a crevice feeder (45, moray eel, *Muraena*), diurnal planktivores (5, 27, damselfishes, Pomacentridae) and a diurnal herbivore (73, a parrotfish, *Sparisoma*). (From Smith and Tyler, 1972.)

As twilight approaches, the transition between day and night fish faunas begins (Hobson 1975). The dominant behavior patterns of the diurnal fishes are cover-seeking. As the light dims, the diurnal planktivores come closer to the reef, while the specialized carnivores become less active and seek out their nighttime hiding places. Fishes that roam the reef during the day stream back to their regular resting places. Most of these fishes are in place 15 to 20 minutes after sunset (Hobson 1975), and for the next 20 minutes or so the reef is remarkably quiet, since the nocturnal fishes have not yet emerged. One reason for this general hiatus in fish activity is presumably that during this time of low light intensity, piscivorous fishes are most active and most effective at capturing prey. The quiet period ends when the nocturnal planktivores emerge in large numbers from their hiding places and swim up into the water column. By this time it is nearly dark. On the surface of the reef small, unspecialized predators begin to move about, feeding on small crustaceans that have also emerged from hiding. Nocturnal piscivores such as conger eels (Congridae) and some goatfishes also become active at this time, seeking out hidden diurnal fishes. Despite this activity, the number of active fishes on the reef itself is smaller at night than during the day. As dawn approaches, the process observed in the evening reverses itself, and the diurnal fishes once again resume their activities.

Community Structure The complexity of the interactions among the fishes of tropical reefs makes the overall structure of the fish community very difficult to comprehend. Smith (1978) observed that the nature of reef fish communities is strongly influenced by three factors: (1) most reef fishes are highly specialized, with complex adaptations to a complex environment; (2) there are many more fish species in a region than can possibly fit into a reef patch or a reef of a size that can be effectively studied; and (3) among reef patches there appears to be a great deal of variation in the composition of the fish fauna. When reef patches are surveyed repeatedly over long periods of time, some species of fish (presumably habitat specialists) are always present whereas other species (habitat generalists) appear to come and go in an unpredictable fashion. There are two basic views to explain these observations. The traditional view is that the fish community is largely made up of specialized fishes that interact in a myriad of subtle ways to subdivide food and space, perhaps with predation acting to increase complexity by allowing competitors to coexist in some situations. In this view, reef communities are in a state of equilibrium with a fish fauna that should be highly predictable in its composition once the interactions among the species are understood. Another view is that of Peter Sale (1977), who proposes that in fact there is considerable competition among reef fishes, particularly for space, and that competitors do not eliminate one another because of the constant yet unpredictable alterations of reef topography and the unpredictable mortalities of resident fishes. Similar species belong to guilds in which the individuals, no matter what the species, essentially interact as if they were one species. When a vacant space occurs on a reef, the members of a guild all participate in a lottery. The winner of the lottery is the juvenile fish that happens to be the right size, at the right place at the right time. Since all the species have long spawning periods and planktonic larvae, which species finds the vacant spot is largely a matter of luck. Once a place is occupied, however, the resident fish has the considerable advantage of defending its "home" against intruders of similar species and size. For example, when Sale (1975) examined a guild of eight species of herbivorous damselfishes on an Australian reef, he found that they all had basically similar habitat requirements, although two of the spe-

494

cies appeared to specialize in living in one reef zone. Dale (1978) offers an alternative to Sale's lottery model to explain the guilds. His "money-in-the-bank" model suggests that guild members all have habitats in which they occur in the absence of other guild members (the bank) and that the larvae that settle in the multispecies areas are surplus larvae from the single-species habitats. For both models this picture is complicated somewhat by the presence of member species of some guilds that seem to be able to dominate the other species as adults and by the presence of other member species that act as fugitive species. Overall, the picture that emerges is one of a community that is not in a state of equilibrium but is changing constantly, and this constant change results in a great diversity of species (Connell 1978).

The two views of community structure are not mutually exclusive, since there is a considerable amount of both spatial and feeding segregation among reef fishes, even among closely related species. For example, Hobson (1974) found that six species of goatfishes (Mullidae) on a Hawaiian reef differed in part from each other according to whether they fed during the day or night, or whether they fed on sandy bottoms or on the reef itself. The differences between this type of observation and those of Sale (1975) can be partially explained by the differences in the kinds of fishes involved; damselfishes defend their space, but goatfishes do not. However, the commonness of ecological overlap in reef fishes makes Sale's hypothesis very attractive for helping to explain the extremely high diversity that exists on reefs, much higher than would seem to be possible given the resources available and the variety of feeding mechanisms known. Nevertheless, it should be pointed out that the validity of the Sale hypothesis depends on the members of a guild being equal in all aspects of their life histories, including fecundity, mortality rates, and ability to defend a territory. Similarly, the validity of the equilibrium hypothesis depends on demonstrating that the similar species do in fact segregate ecologically or else are limited by predators. Such information for both views is largely incomplete.

Supplemental Readings   Barlow 1974; Collette and Earle 1972; Dale 1978; Ehrlich 1975; Goldman and Talbot 1976; Hobson 1974, 1975; Ogden and Lobel 1978; Sale 1975, 1977; Smith 1978.

ααααααααααααααααααααααααααααααααααααααααααααααααααααααααααααααααααα

Epipelagic Zone

The surface waters of the ocean provide an enormous, if nearly feature-less, habitat for fishes. Lack of habitat diversity limits the number of species that occupy this region (Epipelagic Zone) to less than 2% of all known fish species, and the region itself contains vast expanses of nutrient-poor midocean water that can support few fish. As a consequence, epipelagic fishes tend to be concentrated above the continental shelf or in oceanic areas where upwelling increases the productivity of the water. They are also found almost entirely in the upper 100 m of the water column, where light can penetrate and permit phytoplankton to grow and where visual predators can see their prey. Despite their inability to use much of the habitat open to them and despite the limited number of species, epipelagic fishes are overall the most valuable group of fishes to humans because they either occur in enormous numbers (herrings, anchovies) or are particularly favored as food fishes (tunas, salmon). As a direct consequence of their value, the biology of epipelagic fishes has been intensively studied, although the difficulty of such studies means that many basic questions about them are still unanswered. In this chapter, this information will be summarized by discussing: (1) adaptations for pelagic life; (2) ecological types of epipelagic fishes; (3) factors affecting distribution and abundance; (4) migrations and movements; and (5) life history of a representative species, the Pacific sardine (*Sardinops sagax*).

Adaptations for Pelagic Life Most epipelagic fishes belong to families of fishes whose members have streamlined bodies that permit continuous, often rapid, swimming, such as (1) the galeomorph sharks (mackerel sharks, requiem sharks, whale shark, etc.); (2) clupeiform teleosts (herrings, anchovies); (3) Salmonidae (salmon); (4) atherinid teleosts (flying fishes, halfbeaks, sauries, etc.); and (5) perciform teleosts, most notably Carangidae (jacks), Coryphaenidae (dolphins), Bramidae (pomfrets), Sphyraenidae (barracudas), Scombridae (tunas), Xiphiidae (swordfishes), and Istiophoridae (billfishes). Most of these fishes school and are visual predators on zooplankton or fish, although a number are filter feeders on plankton. The predators typically have smooth, fusiform bodies, deeply forked tails, and large mouths. Both prey and predators reduce their visibility by being silvery in color, which scatters the incoming light, and by being countershaded.

Filter-feeding epipelagic fishes have the same general morphological features as the predatory fishes, and many of them are in fact facultative predators; they will pick individual invertebrates and small fish out of the water column or filter-feed on phytoplankton, depending on which mode is energetically most advantageous. However, all fishes capable of filter feeding have a well-developed apparatus for straining small organisms from the water, usually long, fine gill rakers. It is interesting to note that the largest (whale sharks, basking sharks) and smallest (anchovies) adult epipelagic fishes are filter feeders.

Ecological Types

Epipelagic fishes can be divided, for convenience, into two basic ecological types: oceanic forms, those that spend all or part of their life cycle in the open ocean that is not above the continental shelf, and neritic forms, those that spend all or part of their life cycle living pelagically in the waters above the continental shelf. The two categories are not mutually exclusive, since many epipelagic fish are both oceanic and neritic, often at different stages in their life cycle.

The oceanic epipelagic fishes can be divided into true, partial, and accidental residents of the open ocean. The true residents spend their entire life cycle there and are of two basic types, those that are free-swimming and those associated with drifting seaweed. The number of species that are true residents is small, mainly a few species of shark, tuna, flying fishes, sauries, dolphins, swordfish, billfishes, and ocean sunfish, plus the commensal remoras (Echeneidae) and pilotfish (Carangidae). Most of these fishes make extensive migrations across the open ocean and occasionally come close to the continents. Drifting seaweed, particularly pelagic *Sargassum*, provides abundant cover and food in some areas for epipelagic fishes and even supports its own unique fish fauna, including the endemic sargassum fish (*Histro histrio*) and the young of many filefishes (Monacanthidae) and jacks (Carangidae). Dooley (1972) found that 54 species from 23 families inhabited the pelagic *Sargassum* off Florida. Many of these fishes were juveniles of neritic species that used the weed for shelter and fed on the abundant fish and invertebrates associated with it. Such juvenile partial residents are also found free-swimming, although most partial residents are adult fish such as salmon, dolphin, flying fish, and whale sharks. These fishes spawn in inshore areas (or in streams), and the young use similar areas as nursery grounds. Another group of partial residents are deepsea fishes, such as the lanternfishes (Myctophidae), that often migrate up into the Epipelagic Zone at night. Occasionally the true and partial residents of the zone are joined by adults and juveniles of species that are more properly associated with inshore and deepsea environments but that have been carried by currents into the zone by accident.

Neritic epipelagic fishes are among the most abundant fishes in the world, since this group includes herrings, sardines, anchovies, and menhaden, as well as the predators on them, such as sharks, tunas, mackerel, jacks, billfish, and salmon. Such fishes take advantage of the high productivity of inshore water caused by upwelling and shoreline productivity, and most can complete their entire life cycle in the region. However, some are partial residents that spawn in bays, estuaries, or streams or on the bottom. It is also not unusual to find among these fishes species that are really characteristic of other inshore habitats but that have been carried into the open water by currents and storms.

Factors That Affect Distribution and Abundance

Physical factors. Although the open ocean appears featureless physical factors nevertheless are probably the most important determinants of fish distribution and abundance in the Epipelagic Zone. The principal physical factors are temperature, light, oceanographic features, and islands and banks.

Sea temperatures have a strong relationship to the distributional patterns of epipelagic fishes. The 8°C to 10°C isotherm, for example, loosely separates the cold ocean water dominated by salmonids and the warm ocean water dominated by tunas and billfishes. Many epipelagic fishes, but particularly the tunas, move north as the water warms up and south as it cools, so that the arrival of commercially important species in some waters can be predicted on the basis of sea temperatures (Blackburn 1965). Similarly, changes in the average sea temperatures in the region of even 2°C to 3°C can cause a dramatic change in the fish fauna (Radovich 1961). As will be discussed later in this chapter, temperature is also important because it interacts with other physical and chemical factors and can affect processes such as predation and competition.

Light is important to most epipelagic fishes because they are visual feeders. Tuna fishing is often best when the water transparency, as measured by a secchi disc, is 15 m to 35 m (Blackburn 1965), but water that is too clear probably contains little food. On the other hand, some of the most productive waters are rather turbid from plankton blooms and consequently favor filter-feeding planktivores and smaller piscivores than are found in clear water. Light is also important because vision is a principal cue fishes use for schooling, so that schools tend to break up in the evening. One of the more curious aspects of schooling epipelagic fishes is their tendency to associate with drifting objects (flotsam). The main reason for this association appears to be that flotsam serves as "a visual stimulus in an optical void" (Hunter and Mitchell 1966, p. 27). Flotsam is particularly important to juvenile fishes, which may find that it offers some protection from predators.

Although light and temperature do have considerable independent influence on the ecology of epipelagic fishes, they usually act in concert with oceanographic conditions, particularly those associated with upwelling and currents. Upwelling is a phenomenon found along coastlines and in midocean convergences of deep, strong currents, whereby cold, nutrient-rich deep water is brought to the surface. This water supports large blooms of phytoplankton, which in turn support zooplankton and many of the world's most important fisheries. When the upwelling fails or is reduced in an area, the fisheries fail as well. This is well illustrated by the Peruvian anchoveta (*Engraulis ringens*) fishery, once the largest fishery in the world. When oceanographic conditions change and upwelling is reduced, the anchoveta populations decline precipitously, the fishery fails, and sea birds, which also depend on the anchoveta, die by the millions. Ocean currents also play a major role in concentrating fishes, since they form distinct, if fluctuating, boundaries to oceanic regions. At times these boundaries are even visible, but more typically they are detectable as rapid changes in temperature, salinity, and turbidity. Depending on the species, fish may concentrate along these current boundaries or avoid them. For example, Nakamura (1969) indicates that albacore (*Thunnus alalunga*) in the northern Pacific have a northern limit determined by the cold North Pacific Current and a southern limit determined by the North Equatorial Current and that within this broad area between these two current systems, their distribution is determined by the Kuroshio Current, which flows at varying strengths according to the season. Many epipelagic fishes also use currents for reproduction, spawning "upstream" so that the eggs and young will drift into suitable areas for feeding and eventually wind up in the adult feeding areas.

Besides currents and areas of upwelling and shoreline productivity, the features most likely to concentrate epipelagic fish are islands and banks. Although fishermen are grateful for this fact, the exact reasons for it are not known. Part of the answer may be concentrations of small fish and invertebrates that are associated with productive reefs and banks and thereby provide an additional source of food for pelagic predators. There is also some evidence that large eddies may form on the downwind or down-current side of islands, concentrating plankton and consequently fish (Blackburn 1965).

Chemical factors. The surface waters of the oceans are well mixed and well oxygenated, so it is seldom that salinity or oxygen have much effect on the distribution of epipelagic fishes. Pollutants are chemical factors which may also be affecting the populations of epipelagic fishes in unknown ways. However, as Longhurst et al. (1972) pointed out, the effects of pollutants so far have been largely masked by the natural fluctuations in fish populations in response to changing oceanographic conditions, coupled with heavy exploitation by humans.

Biological factors. Competition, predation, and symbiosis undoubtedly are all important in regulating the fish populations of the Epipelagic Zone, but their roles are poorly understood because of the difficulty of studying such processes in large, widespread fish populations and because the populations do respond so strongly to changes in oceanographic conditions and to the intense fishing effort directed at them.

Competition among members of the same species appears to be one of the more important processes regulating the size of the populations, allowing each population to adapt to changing oceanographic conditions and exploitation (see the Pacific sardine example at the end of this chapter). Basically, intraspecific competition for limited food among adult fish leads to limited growth and smaller sizes and hence to decreased fecundity. Intraspecific competition among larval fishes for food also leads to slower growth, which in turn results in increased mortality, particularly from predation. Its role in interspecific interactions is less certain, since many rather similar species seem to coexist in the open oceans. For example, in the tropical and subtropical Pacific Ocean there are four species of tuna with wide, broadly overlapping ranges and ecological requirements. Often two species even school together. In the neritic epipelagic regions of the world, there are usually two or more species of clupeids present in each area. Each species appears to have a competitive advantage over the other(s) under the appropriate oceanographic conditions, so the dominant species may change with time. For example, in the English Channel, herring (*Clupea harengus*) was replaced in the 1930s as the dominant planktivore by pilchard (*Sardinops pilchardus*), but the situation was reversed in the 1970s (Cushing 1978). The change was accompanied by many other oceanographic and biological changes. Similar shifts between clupeid species have been recorded in a number of other areas of the world. The actual mechanisms that allow one species to become dominant over the other are poorly understood and are complicated by the presence of large schools of other plankton-feeding fishes that may coexist with the clupeids while seeming to exploit the same food supply (Murphy 1977).

Because oceanographic conditions exert a powerful influence on the populations of plankton-feeding fish, the populations of piscivorous fish (and other animals) may be strongly affected by the environmentally induced fluctuations of their prey. Thus, when upwelling is reduced off Peru and the anchoveta populations crash, millions of sea birds die of starvation. Off California, changes in the abundance of brown pelicans seem to show a direct relationship to the changes in local abundance of

500

their main prey, the anchovy. The influence of predator and prey populations on each other in the Epipelagic Zone is buffered somewhat by the fact that most predators are capable of preying on a wide range of organisms and will switch prey if the population of one prey species declines. Regardless of such buffering effects, there is little doubt that predation has been a major factor in shaping epipelagic fish communities. One of the strongest indications of this is that schooling is the dominant mode of behavior. Large schools of small fishes offer protection from predators, while schools of predatory fishes presumably have an advantage in finding prey.

Given the small number of species that inhabit the epipelagic zone, examples of symbiosis are surprisingly common, although, as with competitive and predatory interactions, the exact nature of the relationships between the coexisting species is poorly known. Examples of symbiosis in epipelagic fishes are: (1) multispecies schooling; (2) tuna and porpoise; (3) remoras and large fishes; (4) pilotfish and sharks; and (5) fish that live in association with floating invertebrates (Parin 1968). Schools of fish made up of more than one species are common, especially among the tunas and clupeids. Presumably much of the advantage of such relationships is an increase in school size, which results in an increase in protection from predators or an increase in probability of locating a patch of prey. These advantages would be particularly beneficial to a rare species that schooled with an abundant one. Among the clupeids the ability of one species to school with another may be one of the main methods by which a species that is at a competitive disadvantage can maintain small populations among the much larger ones of its competitor (Radovich 1979). The tuna–porpoise relationship is a special case of two species schooling in close association. It seems to be a commensal relationship, with the schools of tuna following the schools of porpoise (or perhaps vice versa). The relationship is not obligatory for either species. How the two species benefit is not known, but the tuna may be taking advantage of the ability of the porpoise to find schools of small fish through the use of this mammal's sonar. At present, however, this relationship is detrimental to both species, since tuna fishermen set nets around schools of porpoise to capture the associated tuna and kill porpoises in the process.

In contrast to the first two examples, where animals of equal size (usually) are schooling together, remoras and pilotfish are small fish that live with large pelagic fishes in relationships that have elements of commensalism and parasitism. Remoras have a special suckerlike apparatus that they use to attach themselves to sharks and other large fishes, turtles, and whales. The remora uses the host for transportation and protection, leaving it only for short pursuits of the small fishes and invertebrates upon which it feeds. Remoras often act as cleaners, picking parasites off the host fish, but it is doubtful if this benefit compensates for the energy expended by the host in carrying the remora around. Pilotfish (*Naucrates*) have a relationship to their host similar to that of remoras, only they swim in the friction layer of water around the host and are consequently pulled along by the host's swimming (Parin 1968).

Small epipelagic fishes are also commonly found in association with jellyfish, siphonophores, and pelagic tunicates (*Tetragonurus* in tunicates), living in the body cavity or among the tentacles. The man-of-war fish (*Nomerus*) is always found among the tentacles of the man-of-war siphonophore. Presumably, this fish has a mutualistic relationship with the man-of-war much like that anemone fish have with their hosts on coral reefs.

Migrations and Movements

Most epipelagic fishes move freely from one area to another in search of food, for spawning, or in response to changing oceanographic conditions. In large predators, such as tuna and salmon, these movements can cover many thousands of miles, from one side of an ocean to the other and back (Fig. 35.1). When spawning is involved, the overall migration pattern typically follows a triangular pattern (Harden-Jones 1968). The adults migrate in a direction opposite that of surface currents to areas suitable for spawning and close to waters that support the high concentrations of plankton needed by the larval fish. The adults then return to their feeding area, while the larvae drift in the surface currents to a nursery area. As they grow, the juvenile fish actively migrate to the adult areas. This pattern reduces competition for food among the different life history stages of a species, as well as reducing the incidence of cannibalism. A classic example of the triangular pattern is found in the herring of the North Sea. They migrate to spawning grounds off the coast of Great Britain, where the eggs are deposited on stones and gravel. The larvae hatch and drift over to the coast of Germany and Denmark, where shallow waters serve as nursery areas. After one to two years, at a length of 9 cm to 10 cm, they move off the coast toward the North Sea, where they eventually join the adults (Harden-Jones 1968).

Pacific Sardine

As commercial fishermen are well aware, the local populations of epipelagic fishes undergo considerable fluctuation from year to year, as well as over much longer periods of time. These fluctuations often seem to be unpredictable, but this is mainly because their causes are complex. Fish populations are simultaneously affected by oceanographic conditions, interactions with other species (predators and competitors), and fisheries. What is more, such factors may act in different ways and at different intensities on the various stages of a fish life cycle. The factors may also act in concert, either in opposition to one another or synergistically. An idea of the complexity of the interactions can be

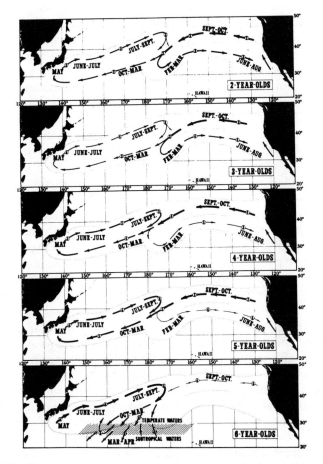

FIGURE 35.1 Presumed albacore migration patterns in the northern Pacific Ocean, by age groups. (From Otsu and Uchida, 1963.)

obtained by examining the history of the Pacific sardine, one of the most studied of epipelagic fishes (Murphy 1966, 1977; Ahlstrom and Radovich 1970). The study of the sardine was stimulated by the sudden collapse of the fishery for them in the 1940s, a disaster caused by over-fishing and unfavorable oceanographic conditions acting together, compounded by apparent competition from the northern anchovy (*Engraulis mordax*).

Sardines spawn off the coast of California and Baja California, at temperatures between 13°C and 19°C (mostly 15°C to 18°C). The larvae hatch from the drifting, translucent eggs in two to three days. They then drift for another 40 to 45 days, absorbing the yolk sac and capturing organisms they bump into, until they develop the capability to swim actively. At this stage they begin to move inshore and grow rapidly on a diet of zooplankton and diatoms. By the end of the first year they typically reach lengths of 11 cm to 12 cm, the second year 17 cm to 18 cm, the third year 19 cm to 20 cm. They often live 6 to 7 years and reach lengths of 25 cm. Prior to the collapse of the populations, the larger fish moved north in the summer, as far as British Columbia, and moved south again in the winter, although the timing and extent of these movements depended on oceanographic conditions. The main oceanographic feature that affected the sardines was the California current, which flows southward along the coast, bringing with it cold water from the Gulf of Alaska. During years when the current flowed strongly, water temperatures were lower and the sardine did not move as far north, although increased upwelling presumably provided more food for the populations in the south. When the current was weak, water temperatures were warmer and the sardine was found farther to the north. It was also noted that the "warm" years were those in which the sardine had high reproductive success, while the opposite was true of the "cold" years. Despite the variations in reproductive success, prior to the heavy fishery the sardine appeared to be able to maintain large populations off California, even through a series of unfavorable years. However, when a heavy fishery was coupled with a long series of such years (1944-1956), the populations collapsed.

The reasons for the collapse are not known for certain, but Murphy (1961, 1966) presents evidence that the key is in survival of the larvae. Each female sardine produces 100,000 to 200,000 eggs in a season, but less than 0.1% survive through the drifting larval stage. Murphy hypothesized that the main cause of death of the larval sardines was predation by invertebrates such as arrow worms and copepods. According to this hypothesis, despite the enormous numbers of larval sardines likely to be present in a spawning area, they are a relatively small part of the total plankton and consequently a small part of the total diet of the invertebrate predators. Therefore, the number of sardines that are eaten depends on the density of predators and on the length of time the larvae are exposed to predation. In unfavorable years productivity increases, so that the zooplankton and invertebrate predator populations increase. At the same time, the sardine larvae take a few days longer to reach the point where they can actively avoid the invertebrate predators. These two factors result in much lower survival of the sardine larvae during the cold years. If the sardine population is large, so many eggs and larvae are produced that enough can probably survive to maintain the population or at least to keep the population decline minimal regardless of oceanographic conditions. If the sardine population is small, however, it will stay small and probably become even smaller, particularly if the cold years and fishery continue (which they did). Because of the high fecundity of the sardines and the high survival rates during warm years, a small adult population can lead to a large adult population again, if there is no fishing and there are a series of years favorable to larval survival (Fig. 35.2).

504

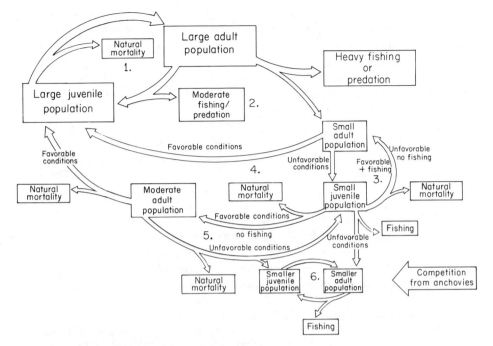

FIGURE 35.2 Some possible population cycles in the Pacific sardine: (1) the no- or light-exploitation cycle, in which large populations maintain themselves regardless of fluctuations in oceanographic conditions; (2) the heavy exploitation cycle, under favorable oceanographic conditions; (3) the cycle for maintaining a small but significant population; (4) the cycle for restoration of large populations following overfishing, during years of favorable oceanographic conditions; (5) the cycle resulting from unfavorable oceanographic conditions following overfishing; and (6) the permanently small population cycle resulting initially from overfishing an already depleted population during unfavorable oceanographic conditions but now maintained by competition from a large northern anchovy population and incidental capture of sardines in other fisheries. These cycles are only a few of the combinations possible, since the relationship between larval survival and adult populations is very complex and may be affected by several factors simultaneously. For example, Cycle 1 can revert directly to Cycle 6 even in the absence of fishing if the right combination of oceanographic and biological conditions exists.

While Murphy's predation hypothesis is an attractive one, another hypothesis, developed by Lasker (1978) to explain population fluctuations in the ecologically similar northern anchovy (*Engraulis mordax*), may offer an even better explanation of the fluctuations of sardine populations in response to oceanographic conditions. By this hypothesis, the critical factor for survival of the larvae is the availability of food of the proper size, abundance, and nutritional value during the first few days of feeding. Sardines (and anchovies) at this stage are weak swimmers, have high metabolic rates, have small mouths, and feed only during the day. This means that small organisms (probably dinoflagellates) must be available in high densities if the larvae are going to be able to capture enough during the day not only to avoid starving to death at night but also to grow quickly to a size at which a larger size range of prey is available. The best conditions for early larval survival therefore seem to be warm, stable oceanographic conditions that produce blooms of organisms of the proper size and nutritional value. Storms or upwelling may disperse such organisms to a point where their density is too low for the larvae to survive on. Upwelling may greatly increase the total abundance of organisms, but the diatoms that result are too small, while the invertebrates are too large and active. However, upwelling may be beneficial for older larvae that are large enough to capture copepods and other invertebrates.

Whether it was predation, starvation, a combination of both, or other factors coupled with overfishing that caused the decline of the sardine, competition from the northern anchovy may be now keeping the sardine populations at low levels. Following the decline of the sardine, the anchovy became the dominant planktivore, using a substantial part of the food and space resources once used by the sardine.

Supplemental Readings
Blackburn 1965; Blaxter and Holliday 1963; Cushing 1968, 1978; Gulland 1977; Harden-Jones 1968; Hart 1973; Murphy 1966; Nakamura 1969; Parin 1968; Radovich 1979; Rounsefell 1975.

ααααααααααααααααααααααααααααααααααααααααααααααααααααααααααααααααααα
~~~~~~

Deepsea Habitats

In the Epipelagic Zone the water is well lighted, well mixed, and capable of supporting actively photosynthesizing algae. Below this zone conditions change rapidly. Between 100 m and, on the average, 1000 m (the Mesopelagic Zone) the light gradually fades to extinction and temperatures fall through a more or less permanent thermocline to 4°C to 8°C. Nutrient levels, dissolved oxygen, and rate of circulation also fall, while pressure increases. Below 1000 m (the Bathypelagic Zone) conditions are more uniform until the bottom (Deepwater Benthic Zone) is reached, characterized by complete darkness, low temperatures, low nutrients, low dissolved oxygen levels, and great pressure. This environment is the most extensive aquatic habitat on the earth: with the mean depth of the oceans being about 4000 m, about 98% of their water is found below 100 m and 75% below 1000 m (Marshall 1971). The vastness of this environment, coupled with its probable stability through geological time, has led to the development of a diverse and often bizarre fish fauna, making up about 11% of all known fish species. Probably the most numerous fishes in existence are the small (less than 10 cm) pelagic forms, particularly bristlemouths of the genus *Cyclothone*. These fishes form much of the "deep-scattering layer" of the ocean, so called because sonar reflects off the millions of airbladders, often giving the impression of a false bottom.

The diversity and abundance of deepsea fishes is indicated by the result of midwater trawling. In a 12-km² area off Bermuda 1500 trawl hauls produced 115,000 fish from 46 families and 220 species (Fitch and Lavenberg 1968). Similarly, Brewer (1973) reported catching 56,000 fish in 61 hauls in the eastern Pacific, representing 49 families and 113 species. In both studies, over 90% of the fishes belonged to two families, the Gonostomatidae (bristlemouths) and the Myctophidae (lanternfishes).

Most of the species were quite rare, represented in the collections by one to 20 individuals. Large and diverse collections of deepsea fishes are made primarily in the tropical and subtropical regions of the oceans, particularly near continents. The bathypelagic fish fauna in particular becomes depleted in high latitudes, and it appears to be totally absent from the arctic region and represented by about only 30 species in the antarctic region. Regardless of where they are found, one of the more curious aspects of deepsea fishes is the scarcity of acanthopterygian species among them. Deepsea fishes are represented mostly by the orders Anquilliformes (eels), Notacanthiformes (spiny eels), Salmoniformes (bristlemouths, hatchet fishes, viperfishes, dragon fishes, etc.), Myctophiformes (lanternfishes, barracudinas, etc.), Gadiformes (grenadiers, brotulas, eelpouts), and Lophiiformes (anglerfishes). The acanthopterygian forms are mainly in the "ancestral" orders Lampridiformes and Beryciformes.

By the standards of the lighted world, all of the above fishes are very peculiar in appearance, and one of the challenges of deepsea ichthyology is to determine the value of strange structural features to the fishes. Inference is the main tool used in this endeavor, since trips to the deepsea habitat are extraordinarily difficult. Similar problems exist in attempting to study the distribution and ecology of deepsea fishes using trawls that are towed several km beneath a ship. Nevertheless, these fishes are so fascinating that they are responsible for a large literature, which will be sampled in this chapter by looking at (1) adaptations to the deepsea environment; (2) reproductive strategies; (3) factors affecting distribution; and (4) ecology of the three major habitat zones. This brief account owes much to the writings of N. B. Marshall (1954, 1960, 1966, 1971). These works are classics of clarity that have integrated the diverse information on deepsea fishes with many original insights and observations.

Adaptations

The fishes that inhabit the Mesopelagic, Bathypelagic, and Deepwater Benthic Zones are in many respects remarkably different from one another in structure, even though there are often closely related species in the different zones.

Mesopelagic fishes are adapted for an active life under low light conditions. Most of them make extensive vertical migrations, often moving into the Epipelagic Zone at night, where they prey on plankton and each other, and then moving down several hundred meters during the day. These fishes have muscular bodies, well-ossified skeletons, scales, well-developed central nervous systems, well-developed gills (especially in forms that inhabit oceanic regions with low oxygen supplies), large hearts, large kidneys, and, usually, swimbladders. Since they are primarily visual predators, their eyes are large, often with high concentrations of photosensitive pigments in the rods of the retina, giving the fishes extreme sensitivity to light. Many mesopelagic fishes also have tubular eyes, typically pointing upwards, with large lenses, which permit binocular vision (Marshall 1971). Such visual capabilities, coupled with short snouts, enable the fishes to pick out small planktonic organisms in dim light. Most mesopelagic fishes lack spines, so their main defense from predators is concealment. In color they are either black (lie-in-wait predators) or silvery, with countershading (migratory forms that encounter low light levels). In addition, many of them have rows of ventrally placed photophores, producing light that helps to break up the silhouette of the fish to predators peering up into the downward-streaming light. However, Muntz (1976) suggests that the special nature of bioluminescence has permitted some mesopelagic predators to overcome this camouflage by having yellow lenses that filter out the ambient light, leaving the bioluminescence visible. Since photophores are well developed in other locations on mesopelagic fishes, they may also serve other functions, particularly intraspecific signaling for schooling and reproduction. Ecologically, mesopelagic fishes can be divided up into zooplankton feeders, which have small mouths and fine gillrakers, and piscivores, which have large mouths and coarse gillrakers.

Bathypelagic fishes, in contrast to the mesopelagic fishes, are largely adapted for a sedentary existence in a habitat with low levels of food and no light other than bioluminescence. These fishes generally have poorly developed, flabby muscles, weak skeletons with minimal ossification, no scales, poorly developed central nervous systems (except those parts associated with the lateral line and olfactory systems), small gills, small kidneys, small hearts, and reduced or absent swimbladders. These features allow the fishes to remain suspended in the water column with almost no expenditure of energy, since they have achieved nearly neutral buoyancy without having to maintain a gas-filled swimbladder in a high-pressure environment. Their eyes are small and may be nonfunctional. The most important sensory system is usually the acousticolateralis system, although the olfactory system may also be well developed (but especially in male anglerfishes, which locate females by smell). Bathypelagic fishes are uniformly black in color and have only a few small photophores. Among anglerfishes photophores are usually confined to the lures they use for attracting prey. Because of the scarcity of food, anglerfishes and other bathypelagic predators consume whatever invertebrate or fish that comes close enough to be grabbed. This means that the fishes have to be able to capture a wide size range of prey. This is accomplished by having a large mouth with sharp teeth for the capture of large prey combined with well-developed, overlapping gillrakers that prevent the escape of small prey that have been swallowed (Ebeling and Caillet 1974).

Deepwater benthic fishes are similar to mesopelagic fishes in that they have muscular bodies and well-developed organ systems. However, they are more variable in many of their characteristics. Photophores

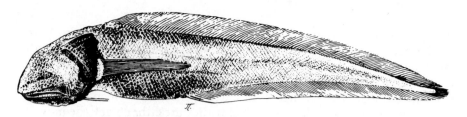

FIGURE 36.1 *Abyssobrotula galatheae,* the deepest-living fish known. (From Nielson, 1977, used by permission Scandinavian Science Press Ltd.)

may be present but are usually absent. Eyes range from being well developed to being absent, as do swimbladders. The fishes are also variable in size, with large species (in excess of 1 m) being fairly common. Curiously enough, many, if not most, deepsea benthic fishes are elongate, many of them being eels or at least eel-like. The most abundant, or at least the most conspicuous, forms seem to be rattails (Macrouridae) and brotulas (Ophidiidae), although a wide variety of other families such as the Myxinidae (hagfishes), Zoarcidae (eelpouts), Chloropthalmidae (greeneyes), eels (various families), Cyclopteridae (lumpfishes), and Ogocephalidae (batfishes) are also well represented. The commonness of eel-like forms may be related to the importance of the lateral line as sensory system, since an elongate body results in long lateral line canals. The sense of smell is also important in many of these fishes, as indicated by the rapidity by which a trap baited with dead fish is found by the local fishes. Smell, combined with touch and well-developed cephalic lateral line canals, may also be important to these fishes for locating invertebrates of the deepsea benthos that, together with carrion, are the main items in their diets. The deepest-living fish known (Ophidiidae: *Abyssobrotula galatheae,* Fig. 36.1) is a blind, elongate fish that feeds on benthic invertebrates (Nielson 1977). However, members of the

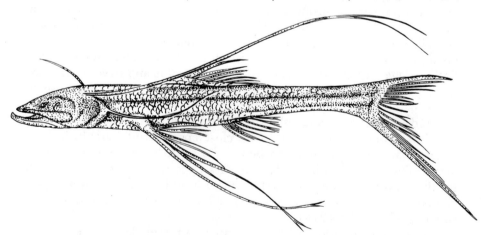

FIGURE 36.2 *Bathypterois oddi,* a predator of benthopelagic organisms. (After Sulak, 1977, used by permission Scandinavian Science Press Ltd.)

CH. 36 DEEPSEA HABITATS

common, widely distributed genus *Bathypterois* (Chloropthalmidae, spider fishes), which also are nearly blind, feed on the community of benthopelagic zooplankton that lives within a meter or so of the bottom. These fishes have elongate rays on the caudal and pelvic fins that permit them to "stand" on the bottom, presumably facing into currents, and grab passing zooplankters (Fig. 36.2) (Sulak 1977).

Reproductive Strategies   Among the more remarkable adaptations of deepsea fishes are their methods of reproduction.   Since densities of many species are extremely low, just finding a mate is a major problem. As a consequence, many unconventional reproductive strategies have evolved. These developed mainly in the piscivorous and bottom-feeding fishes, since the vast schools of mesopelagic planktivorous species, such as the bristlemouths, lanternfishes, and hatchet fishes, can rely on mass spawning and epipelagic eggs and larvae to maintain their populations. Most of the mesopelagic and bathypelagic predators also have epipelagic larvae, which they produce in large numbers.   A female anglerfish, for example, may contain as many as 5 million eggs (Menzies et al. 1973). The main problem is finding a mate to fertilize the eggs. To facilitate this process, female anglerfishes apparently release a species-specific pheromone into the water, which male anglerfish can detect and follow to the female. In many species, once the female is found, the male anglerfish attaches himself to her with specially equipped jaws and assumes a parasitic mode of existence. In species in which this strategy is best developed, the gonads of both sexes do not mature until the female has been parasitized by a male (Pietsch 1976).   An additional advantage of this strategy is that the energy required for reproduction is reduced, but not at the expense of fecundity (Marshall 1971). Presumably also because of the energetic advantages, most species of mesopelagic and bathypelagic fishes have males which are smaller than females. In some of these species (e.g., Idiacanthidae), the males do not feed, although they are free-living. An even more extreme solution to the energy and mate-finding problems is to be hermaphroditic. This is characteristic of a number of deepsea predators such as the lancetfishes (Alepisauridae) and the barracudinas (Paralepididae), although it is not known whether these fishes are capable of self-fertilization (Mead et al. 1964).

In deepsea benthic fishes, finding a mate seems to be less of a problem than assuring that the young will settle in suitable habitats. The grenadiers (Macrouridae) and brotulas (Ophidiidae) apparently can produce sounds with their swimbladders and thereby attract mates over some distance. Bioluminescence may also play a role in this regard in other fishes. Deepsea eels, such as longnose eels (*Synaphobranchus*), may aggregate for spawning through the use of smell, although homing to a hereditary spawning ground may also play a role (Menzies et al. 1973). Although the eels all have pelagic leptocephalus larvae, most deepsea benthic fishes seem to have relatively short larval stages. Many species produce large, benthic eggs, resulting in large, active larvae, which settle out quickly. Some of these species, especially among the eelpouts (Zoarcidae), may have parental care as well, although direct evidence is lacking. Other species are viviparous, most prominently chimaeras and other deepsea chondrichthyian fishes, but also species of brotulas and eelpouts. Regardless of how the young are produced, they probably remain close to the spawning area. As a result, there is a much higher incidence of species that are confined to one ocean basin than is true for bathypelagic and mesopelagic fishes, many of which are nearly cosmopolitan in their distribution.

Factors That Affect Distribution

Physical factors. The main physical factors affecting the distribution of deepsea fishes are temperature, light, pressure, features of the ocean floor, and currents. Temperatures of the deep ocean are rather stable, between 4°C and 8°C, so it seems unlikely that temperature has much of an impact on the local distribution patterns of deepsea fishes. However, the great reduction in diversity of bathypelagic and mesopelagic fishes at high latitudes may be partially a function of the slightly lower temperatures that exist there. Backus et al. (1977) were able to divide up the Mesopelagic Zone of the Atlantic Ocean into zoogeographic regions, noting that faunal changes coincided with changes in physical conditions, particularly temperatures at about 200 m. Many mesopelagic fishes nevertheless show a great tolerance for temperature changes and may migrate through the permanent thermocline on a daily basis, encountering temperature changes of 10°C to 20°C.

Light, in contrast to temperature, is extremely important in determining the local distributions of deepsea fishes. Indeed, the distinction between Mesopelagic and Bathypelagic Zones and the adaptations of the fishes that live in the zones are directly or indirectly related in large part to light levels. In the Mesopelagic Zone the movements of the fishes that make vertical migrations are cued to light, the fishes following the receding light levels up in the evening and then moving down in the early morning as light levels in the surface waters increase.

Pressure, like light, has a major impact on the vertical distributions of deepsea fishes, since it increases at the rate of 1 atm per 10 m. The absence or reduction of the swimbladder in so many deepsea fishes is undoubtedly related to the energy costs of filling the bladder at great depths. One indication of this is that the swimbladders of some deepsea fishes are functional when the fishes are juveniles living in the Epipelagic Zone, but they regress or become fatfilled when the fishes change to their adult habitat (Horn 1970). Mesopelagic fishes that make extensive vertical migrations apparently expend some energy deflating the swimbladder as they move up and inflating it as they move down. Even fishes that inhabit nearly anoxic waters at the bottom of the migratory cycle manage to reinflate their swimbladders with oxygen (Douglas et al. 1976). At great depths, pressure may be a limiting factor to fishes, although other factors, such as scarcity of food, are also important. Bathypelagic fishes are usually not found below 3000 m, and the greatest depth record for benthic fishes is about 8370 m (Nielson 1977).

Features of the ocean floor and currents often act together in determining both local and worldwide distribution patterns of deepsea fishes, particularly benthic fishes. Although much of the deep ocean floor is a featureless plain covered with sediment, many deepsea benthic fishes are associated with rock outcroppings or canyons, which also have distinct invertebrate communities. On a broader scale, benthic fishes are also more diverse and numerous on the continental slope, presumably due to a combination of greater food supply and greater habitat diversity. On an even broader scale, undersea mountain ranges and ridges often form barriers to fish movement, as well as boundaries of distinct sets of oceanographic conditions. Thus, Brown (1974) found that three basins off southern California separated by ridges each had distinctive elements in its mesopelagic fish fauna that reflected in part the currents that flowed into the basins. One basin (Rodriguez Dome) was influenced by the California current flowing in from the north, while another (Santa Cruz) was influenced by currents from the south. The third (Santa Barbara) was close to the coast and greatly influenced by runoff and upwelling. These differences were enough so that 11% to 16% of the fish collected in each basin by Brown were not found in the other basins. When such patterns are examined for entire oceans, regions of endemism can be noted, particularly for benthic fishes, which do not disperse as easily over geologic barriers as do pelagic fishes.

Chemical factors. Since the ocean is so well mixed chemically, salinity and oxygen levels are the main chemical factors likely to influence the distribution of deepsea fishes. Although the water masses with which distinct deepsea fish faunas are associated often differ slightly in their salinities, it seems unlikely, given the small differences that exist (1 ppt to 2 ppt), that salinity by itself limits the distribution of any of the species. Oxygen, in contrast, is probably very important, since there exists in many areas, often at depths between 100 m and 1000 m, an oxygen minimum layer, where dissolved oxygen levels may be almost undetectable. While these layers undoubtedly act as barriers to movement of some fishes, they are often inhabited by large numbers of mesopelagic fishes for at least part of the day. Below the oxygen minimum layers, oxygen levels are also usually low, between 5 ppm and 6 ppm, which when combined with the low temperatures that also exist at these depths undoubtedly limits the activities of the fishes.

Biological factors. Because the deepsea environment is so hard to study, predatory, competitive, and symbiotic interactions among species are poorly understood. Predation is undoubtedly the most common type of interaction, since all deepsea fishes known are carnivorous and many of the behavioral and structural adaptations of the fishes can best be explained as mechanisms either to help avoid being eaten or to increase the probability of capturing a suitable prey. In the Bathypelagic Zone, most fishes do not appear to be selective in their feeding habits, so who eats whom seems to depend largely on size. Even this rule does not always hold, for a number of anglerfishes, blackdragons (Idiacanthidae), and viperfishes (Chauliodontidae) are capable of swallowing fishes considerably larger than themselves, through the use of distendable stomachs and "hinged" heads.

Competition, like predation, has undoubtedly been an important "pressure" shaping the deepsea fish communities, as indicated by the surprisingly high diversity of the communities and the striking morphological differences between closely related species that occupy different habitat zones. On the other hand, within zones there are groups of coexisting species that all seem to do about the same thing, such as the small plankton feeders of the Mesopelagic Zone, the anglerfishes of the Bathypelagic Zone, and the various rattailed fishes of the Deepwater Benthic Zone. Tyler and Pearcy (1975) noted that the diets of three species of mesopelagic lanternfishes were broadly similar but indicated that, nevertheless, there was some segregation by food habits, perhaps related to slightly different depth distributions. Johnson and Glodek (1975) speculate that observed distributional differences between similar species of mesopelagic pearleyes (Scopelarchidae) is related to differential tolerances to low oxygen levels, so that one species has a competitive superiority only when oxygen levels are low because of its longer gill filaments. In the Bathypelagic Zone there are about 100 widely distributed species of anglerfishes, many of which occur together. Although these species present an extraordinary series of morphological variations on the basic anglerfish theme, they all apparently consume whatever prey is available, including (presumably) each other. How these fishes manage to share the scarce food resources of the zone is not known, but it can by hypothesized that it is done through a combination of spatial (depth) preferences combined with the widespread dispersal of the epipelagic larvae. As Sale (1977) hypothesized for coral reef fishes, these larvae may be part of an anglerfish lottery, in which the winner is a larva that happens to settle out in an area not occupied by another anglerfish or predator (regardless of species) and so grows instead of being eaten. Given the apparent rarity of anglerfishes in general, long-term success of an individual would depend in large part on "winning" (i.e., consuming or avoiding) the rare encounters with other bathypelagic predators, as well as encountering enough prey to avoid starvation.

The deepsea floor, like the Bathypelagic Zone, is a stable environment with scarce food and a wide array of ecologically similar species. Most of the fishes apparently roam the floor in search of food, either in the form of invertebrates (which are surprisingly diverse) or in the form of carrion that has dropped from the waters above. While it is likely that there is some segregation among the fishes, based on depth and food preferences, there also appears to be a considerable amount of overlap among coexisting species. For example, photographs of species visiting areas baited with dead fish indicate that it is not unusual for five to six species of fish to be attracted to the bait in a few hours. Dayton and Hessler (1972) speculate that the large number of predators/scavengers that roam the deepsea floor may be responsible for the high diversity of benthic invertebrates, since the predators may depress the invertebrate populations so much that food or other resources never become limiting for the invertebrates. How the predators maintain their own diversity is not known, especially since the apparent use of mucous secretions by hagfish to coat dead fish, thereby making them inedible to other fishes, indicates that there may be direct competition for this type of resource.

Because of the difficulty of making behavioral observations in the deepsea environment, there are few recorded cases of symbiosis involving fish from this zone. The snubnose eel (*Simenchelys parasiticus*) is reported to be parasitic on large fishes, since fishermen occasionally find one burrowed into a fish caught on the bottom (Bigelow and Schroeder 1953). However, it is more likely that these eels burrow into a fish after it is already helpless in a net or on a hook, much as hagfishes do.

Ecology   Mesopelagic Zone. The most conspicuous feature of the ecology of the Mesopelagic Zone is that many of the fishes make nightly vertical migrations into the Epipelagic Zone. This enables them to take advantage of the abundant zooplankton in this zone (which also often moves upward at night) and to avoid the epipelagic predators as well. Where an oxygen minimum layer exists, the migrating mesopelagic fishes may further avoid large predators by seeking refuge in it. The result of these migrations seems to be a net export of energy downwards (Rogers and Grandperrin 1976). Much of this energy may be recycled in the Mesopelagic Zone through predaceous fishes and through copepods that filter-feed in part on fecal material, although some is lost downwards (and supports the bathypelagic fishes) and some is recycled upwards, through squid and other epipelagic nocturnal predators that forage in the mesopelagic zone. The importance of energy recycling within this zone is indicated by the large populations of fishes that do not make vertical migrations or that migrate on an irregular basis. Many of these species are predators that simply wait in the water column and prey upon passing migratory fishes and zooplankters.

The pattern of energy flow through the Mesopelagic Zone combined with the abundance and diversity of fishes found there indicate that the community structure is complex. Since little is known about annual fluctuations in abundance of the mesopelagic species, it is not known whether the diversity of fishes is maintained through extremely complex specializations or through differential responses to environmental fluctuations, which prevent any one species in a group of potential competitors from becoming dominant. Although the evidence is scanty, it does seem to favor the latter hypothesis. Feeding and distributional studies of similar species generally do indicate some segregation by depth and food types, but a great deal of overlap is also found (Dewitt and Cailliet 1972; Tyler and Percy 1975). The potential fluctuations in local mesopelagic fish populations are indicated by the study of Brewer (1973), who in his extensive sampling of the Mesopelagic Zone of the Gulf of California failed to capture a single specimen of bristlemouth (*Cyclothone*), although they had been found there in abundance a few years earlier.

Bathypelagic Zone. If the most conspicuous feature of the Mesopelagic Zone is the movement of the fishes, the most conspicuous feature of the Bathypelagic Zone is the sedentary nature of the fishes. The dominant fishes of this zone, anglerfishes and bristlemouths, seem to spend most of their time suspended in the water column, waiting for prey organisms to pass by or to be lured to them by their photophores. Bathypelagic fishes are extreme generalists in their feeding, which is necessary because of the scarcity of food. The limited energy available in this zone all comes from above, from fecal material, detritus, and an occasional mesopelagic fish or invertebrate. The scarcity of bathypelagic fish below 3000 m presumably reflects in part the small amount of food that makes it through the water column above. Considering the amount of energy probably flowing through the zone, it is a wonder that bathypelagic fishes exist at all, much less in such diversity.

Deepwater Benthic Zone. Compared to the fishes of the Bathypelagic Zone, the fishes of this zone are active and often quite abundant. Energy (in the form of organic matter) enters this zone through a number of pathways, originating either on the continents or in the water column (Sedberry and Musick 1978). Organic matter from the continents can move into the zone through migrations of fish and invertebrates, through the sinking of terrestrial plant material and "seaweed" such as eelgrass, and through currents that flow down and along the continental shelf and slope. That these are among the most important sources of energy for deepsea benthic organisms is indicated by the gradual decrease in fish and invertebrate numbers and biomass with distance from the continents. Organic matter from the water column enters in the form of: (1) particulate matter raining from above, particularly where the Deepwater Benthic Zone and the Mesopelagic Zone meet; (2) dead fish and other large "particles" that sink to the sea floor; and (3) mesopelagic fishes that approach the bottom during their vertical migrations. The organic matter from these various sources is consumed, broken down, and recycled by both invertebrates and fish. Fish are considered to be especially important in this recycling process, since they consume the dead material that falls to the bottom and crop the invertebrates, and then through their fecal material quickly distribute the organic matter rather evenly over the ocean floor (Dayton and Hessler 1972).

In order to play this role effectively, deepsea benthic fishes should be relatively unspecialized, consuming whatever prey they can encounter. This has in fact been found to be largely the case, although the fishes do specialize to the extent that they feed mostly on pelagic organisms, on invertebrates that are on the surface of the bottom (epifauna), on invertebrates that burrow into the substrate (infauna), or on carrion (Sedberry and Musick 1978). On the upper continental slope some of the more abundant fishes, such as longfinned hake (*Phycis chesteri*) and cutthroat eel (*Synaphobranchus kaupi*), feed mostly on mesopelagic fishes. What is surprising is that mesopelagic fishes and invertebrates are also common in the stomachs of benthic fishes found well below the intersection of the Mesopelagic Zone with the bottom. Since the benthic fishes are rarely captured more than a meter or so off the bottom, it is likely that they are taking advantage of mesopelagic forms that become resident in deep water either seasonally or at certain stages of their life cycles (Sedberry and Musick 1978). An additional pelagic component to the diet of these fishes consists of invertebrates, such as copepods, that live within a meter of the bottom, feeding on the suspended material associated with bottom sediments.

The fishes that feed on benthic invertebrates are usually the most abundant ones in the Deepwater Benthic Zone. As indicated previously, these fishes consume whatever invertebrates they can capture. There is some specialization based on prey size (reflected in mouth size of the fish), depth distribution, and preference for epifauna or infauna. The infauna feeders often have large amounts of sediment in their digestive tracts as well as the small infaunal invertebrates they were presumably seeking. The nutritional value of the sediments to the fish is not known (Sedberry and Musick 1978). The infauna is also important as a secondary food source for fishes that are scavengers, such as hagfish and snubnose eels. When dead fish are placed on the bottom with a camera suspended over them, the scavengers, both vertebrate and invertebrate, quickly congregate. If the dead fish is large, many of the scavengers will burrow into it and consume it from the inside out. Large numbers of other fishes, such as grenadiers, are also often attracted to such bait stations, but they may be feeding primarily on scavenging amphipods and other invertebrates rather than on the bait itself.

The overall picture that develops from the study of the ecology of fishes of the three deepsea zones is that they are part of complex and highly efficient systems that waste little of the energy available and that they are the links that connect the energy pathways (food webs) of the various zones.

Supplemental Readings

Clarke and Wagner 1976; Dayton and Hessler 1972; Douglas et al. 1976; Ebeling and Cailliet 1974; Fitch and Lavenberg 1968; Grassle et al. 1975; Marshall 1954, 1971; Menzies et al. 1973; Phleger 1971; Pietsch 1976; Rogers and Grand-perrin 1976; Sedberry and Musick 1978.

αααααααααααααααααααααααααααααααααααααααααααααααααααααααααααααααααααααα
~~~~~~

Polar Regions

The aquatic environments of the Arctic and Antarctic are often compared to those of the deep sea, in part because these environments are uniformly cold and in part because polar organisms have many of the same adaptations as deepsea benthic organisms. However, there are more differences than similarities because of the unique features of the polar environments, such as long summer days that make high levels of primary production possible and long winter nights that create and maintain the ice cover. Temperatures are also colder than those found in the deep sea, typically between $+1.0°C$ and $-1.9°C$. The two polar regions also differ greatly from each other in their environmental characteristics, and this is reflected in the differences in their fish faunas. The Arctic consists largely of an ice-covered sea of low productivity which is surrounded by land that greatly limits the exchange of water with the Atlantic and Pacific oceans. The Antarctic, in contrast, is a continent surrounded by highly productive seas that have "free" interchange with the world's oceans, although unique oceanographic conditions have effectively kept the fish fauna of the continental shelf of Antarctica isolated from other faunas. As a result, the Antarctic has a comparatively diverse fauna characterized by a high degree of endemism, while the Arctic shares much of its limited fauna with the northern Atlantic and Pacific Oceans. Because of these differences, the Arctic will be treated only briefly in this chapter, but the Antarctic will be discussed in some detail.

Arctic Fishes The Arctic is rich in neither species nor numbers of fish. In arctic America there are less than 110 species (Legendre et al. 1975, plus records of D. E. McAllister, National Museum of Canada, 1979). The total for the entire Arctic is probably not much greater. Presumably because of the coldness

519

and low productivity of the environment, a majority of the species belong to families of predominantly sluggish, bottom-dwelling fishes, such as the Cyclopteridae (lumpfishes and snailfishes, 15 species), Cottidae (sculpins, 14 species), Zoarcidae (eelpouts, 10 species), Gadidae (cods, eight species), Stichaeidae (pricklebacks, six species), Anarhichadidae (wolffishes, four species), Agonidae (poachers, four species), and Pleuronectidae (right-eye flounders, six species). Because of the grinding of arctic shores by sea ice, most of these fishes rarely venture into shallow water, and only sculpins of the genus *Myoxocephalus* occur on a regular basis in the intertidal or subtidal regions. However, there are fifteen species of euryhaline or anadromous salmonids and three species of smelt (Osmeridae) known from the Arctic, which, along with herring, may be of some importance in bays during the short summer months and in the midwaters above the shelf.

Perhaps the most distinctive and abundant arctic fishes are two species of endemic codfishes, the polar cod (*Arctogadus glacialis*) and the arctic cod (*Boreogadus saida*). These fishes differ markedly from most other cods in that the mouth angles slightly upwards, rather than being terminal or subterminal, and the barbels are greatly reduced in size. Such adaptations reflect the association of such cods with pack ice and the fact that they feed largely on the peculiar amphipods and diatoms found in or on the undersurface of the ice. The only other fish found on a regular basis in association with the ice are juvenile sand-lances (*Ammodytes*), which may actually hide in holes in the ice (McAllister 1977). The community of organisms associated with the ice (which has its parallel in the Antarctic) is known as the cryopelagic community (Andriashev 1970). The cods are abundant enough so that flocks of kittiwakes will follow icebreakers to capture the fish thrown up in the wakes. They are also quite important in the diets of seals and whales that feed under the ice.

The presence of a cryopelagic community and the predominance of benthic fishes in the Arctic indicate the strong selective pressures the harsh environment must exert on the fishes. McAllister (1977) has observed that arctic fishes also tend to have larger eyes than equivalent species found further south, presumably a response to the reduced light found under the ice, in deep water, and seasonally. One of the most interesting adaptations of benthic fishes of the Arctic, which links them with deepsea and Antarctic fishes, is their basic reproductive strategy. Most lay a small number of large eggs which are (presumably) cared for by one or both parents, until hatching or beyond. According to Marshall (1953) this strategy has the advantages of reducing competition among the larvae and of producing large, active young with a wide range of food items available to them. Such larvae are either pelagic or benthic, depending on the species.

Antarctic Fishes   Depending on the taxonomic analysis accepted and on where the line separating the Antarctic from other regions is drawn, antarctic fish are 65% to 96% endemic. The best estimate of endemism seems to be that of DeWitt (1971), who found that 86% of the fishes (excluding deepsea forms) south of the Antarctic Convergence were found nowhere else. The Antarctic Convergence separates the "true" antarctic fauna (or at least the shallow-water fauna) from the fauna of the rest of the southern ocean because it is a remarkably stable oceanographic feature that surrounds the Antarctic continent. It is characterized by clockwise flows that tend to keep drifting organisms away from the continental area by spinning them off in a northward direction. In addition it presents a distinct temperature boundary, marking the region where the cold antarctic surface water sinks beneath the warmer subantarctic surface water. The convergence is strictly a surface phenomenon, so the deep-water fauna shows a much lower degree of endemism than the shallow-water fauna.

South of the Antarctic Convergence there are 90 to 100 species of fishes found at depths of less than 800 m, mostly close to the Antarctic continent. Most of these fishes, by both species and numbers, belong to four families in the perciform suborder Notothenioidei: Nototheniidae (antarctic cods), Harpagiferidae (plunder fishes), Bathydraconidae (antarctic dragonfishes), and Channichthyidae (icefishes). Other families represented in the Antarctic are Rajidae (skates), Muraenolepididae (eel cods), Zoarcidae (eelpouts), Cyclopteridae (snail fishes), and Bothidae (left-eye flounders). Most of these fishes show remarkable adaptions to the peculiar features of the antarctic environment. The rest of this chapter will therefore be devoted to a discussion of: (1) morphological, physiological, and reproductive adaptations; (2) factors affecting distribution; and (3) fish communities.

ADAPTATIONS   **Morphological adaptations.**   Perhaps the most striking feature of the body morphology of antarctic fishes is the comparative lack of variety. Most of the fishes are bottom-oriented visual predators, and their basic external features reflect this. The dominant notothenioids have large, flattened heads with large mouths and large eyes, which are often located toward the top of the head. The bodies tend to be elongate, often tapering to a small tail, with large pectoral fins, small pelvic fins, and long dorsal and anal fins. The swimbladder is absent. With the conspicuous exception of the skates, other antarctic fishes deviate from this theme by either having more eel-like bodies, with continuous dorsal and anal fins, or by having more fusiform bodies, such as in the pelagic antarctic herring (Nototheniidae, *Pleuragramma antarcticum*).

Physiological adaptations. The remarkable nature of the physiological adaptations of antarctic fishes is indicated by two observations. First, many of the fishes have been observed to be active at temperatures very close to the freezing point of salt water ($-1.9°C$); some of these species are actually associated with ice on a regular basis, either resting on anchor ice or swimming among floating ice platelets. Second, the icefishes are without hemoglobin in their blood, so their gills are cream-colored rather than pink, while some other antarctic fishes have reduced amounts of hemoglobin.

Resistance to freezing seems to be accomplished either by living in deep water or by having "antifreeze" in the blood (DeVries 1970). Fishes that live in water below 30 m actually have body fluids that will freeze at temperatures higher than the water in which they are living! These supercooled fish survive because of the absence of ice crystals in the water to "seed" body fluids and start ice forming internally. However, when such fish are caught in traps and brought up to the surface, they freeze just as soon as they enter the ice-laden surface waters (DeVries 1970). The notothenioid fishes that live in the shallow waters where ice crystals are present have glycoproteins in the blood that give the body fluids freezing points lower than that of the surrounding water (Chapter 6). Further, some species have been shown to be extremely sensitive to minor temperature changes and to actively avoid "warm" temperatures (Crawshaw and Hammel 1971).

Reproductive adaptations. Antarctic fishes have large, yolky eggs, so Marshall (1953) predicted that the eggs would be laid on the bottom. In a study of a plunderfish (*Harpagifer bispinis*), Daniels (1978) found that this was indeed the case and discovered further that this fish lays the eggs in a nest which is guarded for about four months. This is the longest period of nest guarding known for any species of fish, but the behavior is probably common among antarctic fishes, since such parental care is also characteristic of many antarctic invertebrates as well. The eggs are laid during early winter, usually while there is still ice cover, and hatch when the ice breaks up and the spring plankton bloom begins. The larvae swim upwards soon after hatching and join the plankton, upon which they feed. The planktonic stage may last as long as one year.

FACTORS THAT AFFECT DISTRIBUTION The distribution patterns of antarctic fishes are still poorly known. For example, only about 20% of the species are known to be circumpolar, a percentage which should increase considerably as fishery investigations increase. The known distributional limits of most species seem to be associated with physical factors, particularly temperature, currents, depth, and ice. The annual range of temperatures in antarctic waters is usually less than $7°C$ or $8°C$, but the apparent sensitivity of the fishes to even small temperature changes means that temperature is an important environmental cue. The departure of many fishes from the food-rich inshore areas in the autumn may be largely a response to dropping temperatures (but perhaps cued by the changing light regime) and ensures avoidance of water containing ice crystals. On a broader scale, the restriction of most antarctic fishes to the polar region is probably a reflection of their stenothermy, with the Antarctic Convergence providing a particularly strong temperature barrier. The convergence is also a region of strong currents, which may limit the distribution of the fishes as well. The depth distributions of the fishes seem to be related to a combination of factors, but principally temperature and substrate. The presence of anchor ice in shallow water (less than 33 m) and the depth of the continental shelf around Antarctica results in the greatest number of species occurring between 200 m and 600 m. In this region substrates are varied, benthic invertebrates are abundant, and temperatures are fairly constant. The fishes that are permanent residents of water less than 40 m deep are mostly species with antifreeze compounds in their blood.

FISH COMMUNITIES   The fishes of the Antarctic fall into three broad ecological groups: pelagic fishes, fishes of the continental shelf, and deepsea fishes. The divisions between the groups are not sharp, however.

Pelagic fishes.   The open surface waters of the Antarctic are dominated by crustacean krill (*Euphausia*), which support (or supported) large populations of whales, seals, penguins, and other marine birds. Fish, except as larvae, are surprisingly uncommon here, even though krill is an important item in the diet of many species. The bodies of the pelagic notothenioid fishes are more fusiform than those of bottom-dwelling species, yet their large fins and other features still give them the appearance of bottom-dwelling species. The species most specialized for pelagic life is the antarctic herring, which is one of the few antarctic fishes with a forked tail. One rather specialized component of the pelagic fauna is the cryopelagic fish community, which feeds on invertebrates associated with the underside of fast ice or the sides of icebergs. While the antarctic herring is a component of this community, it also includes a number of species of antarctic cod (*Trematomus*). The *Trematomus* species live on sides of icebergs by clinging to them with their pectoral fins or by living in crevices, much as a benthic fish would use a rocky cliff (Andriashev 1970). In many instances it appears that only young fish are pelagic or cryopelagic, while the adults are bottom-dwelling.

Fishes of the continental shelf.   By both numbers of individuals and numbers of species, most antarctic fishes live on the continental shelf. It is not unusual to find 10 to 20 species, many in quite large numbers, at one location. The reason for this appears to be that the shelf is a very stable environment, with large populations of invertebrates that serve as prey for the fishes. This food supply is nearly constant all year around, in marked contrast to the strong seasonality exhibited by the availability of food in the pelagic regions (Fig. 37.1). As a result,

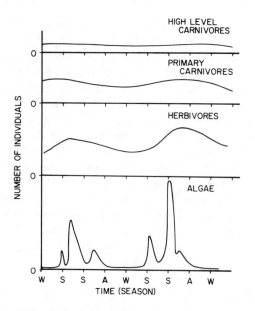

FIGURE 37.1 Seasonal changes in the flora and fauna of the Antarctic. Most fishes are high-level carnivores. (Diagram by R. A. Daniels.)

the benthic communities are quite complex. The fishes feed largely on invertebrates that are themselves largely carnivorous, and the fishes in turn may be taken by seals, birds, and other fishes. Thus food chains with seven or eight links are likely. The energy for this system is derived from the plankton blooms and growths of benthic algae that occur during the austral summer, coupled with presumably efficient recycling of nutrients (ultimately through detritus) in the winter.

The efficiency of the system is indicated by the specializations of the fishes. To begin with, there is considerable segregation by depth preferences, most conspicuously the separation of fishes with antifreeze in the blood from those without it. Because of the differences in the depth distributions of the fishes, it is possible to divide the shelf fish fauna into about three species associations based on depth (Nybelin 1947; DeWitt 1971), although overlaps among the groups are extensive. Among species coexisting at the same depth, there seems to be considerable specialization in type and size of prey consumed, as well as in method of feeding. Although some species are generalists, feeding opportunistically on whatever prey is available, many specialize by feeding largely on just one or two taxa of invertebrates, such as amphipods or polychaete worms. The degree of specialization is illustrated by the feeding behavior of *Harpagifer bispinis,* which feeds mostly on amphipods and scaleworms. When feeding on scaleworms, the fish captures them by ambushing a passing individual. It removes the scales from each worm by spitting it out and sucking it in repeatedly, presumably scraping off the scales on its palatine teeth (R. A. Daniels, personal communication).

It should be pointed out here that despite their abundance, these benthic fishes are very poor candidates for exploitation. The fishes are very slow-growing (a 25-cm fish is likely to be 5 to 10 years old), so replacement of fish taken would be extremely slow. Although comparatively little is known about the community structure of the continental shelf benthos, the complexity and apparent long-term stability of the communities may mean that a new stress (fishing) could severely disrupt them. In addition, since the method of fishing most likely to be used is bottom trawling, the fishing could severely disturb the reproductive success of some species, by disrupting nests and removing the parental guardians.

Deepsea fishes. The deepsea fishes of the antarctic region are poorly known, especially south of the convergence. The fish fauna of the continental slope and deeper areas is a mixture of notothenioid fishes and representatives of the typical deepsea fish families, such as the Macrouridae. A number of the species are endemic, but many are more widely distributed. The bathypelagic and mesopelagic fish faunas are made up of about 50 species (Andriashev 1965). Although many of the species are endemic, they all belong to widespread families. The mesopelagic lanternfishes (Myctophidae, about 14 species) are particularly abundant, taking advantage of the abundant krill as a food source.

Supplemental Readings   Andriashev 1965, 1970; Daniels 1978; Dell 1972; DeWitt 1971; Dunbar 1968; Holdgate 1970; Marshall 1953; Menzies et al. 1973; Walters 1955.

ααααααααααααααααααααααααααααααααααααααααααααααααααααααααααααααααααααα
~~~~~~

Conservation

One of the biggest problems facing ichthyologists, fishery biologists, or anyone else interested in fish is that of conservation. As humans increase their exploitation of fish populations, as they increase their use of the water fish live in, as they pollute the oceans and fresh waters, and as they change the nature of the air and land which interact with the waters, they cause populations of fishes to change. A few species may actually increase in abundance, but most will decline, some only to the point where they can no longer be harvested at high levels, but others to extinction. Under such pressure fish communities change dramatically, and the diversity of fish life decreases. Whether such changes are good, bad, or simply of no consequence depends on one's value system and state of hunger, but nevertheless the changes *are* taking place and the future welfare of humankind and that of most fishes are closely linked. An earth turned into a wasteland for fish will equally be a wasteland for humans. On the other hand, wise utilization of the waters and the life within them can provide benefits for humankind for the indefinite future. It is therefore important to understand the changes that are taking place, to monitor them, and to regulate them if conservation is to be possible. Thus, this chapter will briefly discuss: (1) human-related causes of change; (2) the reasons for conserving fish resources and non-resources; and (3) recommendations for the future.

Causes of Change The aquatic environment is changing constantly, even where it is not affected by humans. As the previous ten chapters indicate, fish species are often alternately abundant and rare, on an irregular basis, in response to natural environmental fluctuations. Species also naturally become extinct in time, and new ones are formed. In a sense, then, the pressures humans put on fish populations are nothing new. On the other hand, humans are placing stress on fish populations in many environments to an extent they have never experienced before in such a short period of time. This stress, because it is in addition to those naturally acting on fish populations, results in greatly accelerated rates of extinction and other apparently irreversible changes. The human-related stress can be divided into four components, which often act on fish populations simultaneously: (1) exploitation; (2) introduction of exotic species; (3) habitat alterations; and (4) pollution.

EXPLOITATION   Exploitation is the single biggest cause of changes in fish populations and communities, since there are few waters in the world today in which a fishery of some sort does not exist. The most dramatic changes are those brought about by overfishing, which may bring about the near elimination of fishable stocks of fish, such as the sardines off California (Chapter 35). Such disasters are best known for the economic hardships they frequently bring to fishing communities, but comparatively little attention is paid to the impact they have on the biotic communities of which the overexploited species are part. The collapse of the anchoveta fishery off Peru was also accompanied by a permanent collapse of the huge populations of sea birds that once depended on the anchoveta. Overexploitation of fishes low on the food chain may similarly lead to the decline of predatory fishes that prey upon them, such as tuna and mackerel. Species whose populations are fished to low levels are often (but not always) replaced by other species that are ecologically similar although often differing somewhat in their life history characteristics and desirability to humans. Thus California's sardines were replaced by anchovies; on the Georges Bank, haddock were replaced by yellowtail flounder, which were in turn replaced by red hake (Chapter 33). It is important to note that these effects have been recorded because of their spectacular nature, but they surely were accompanied by other, unrecorded effects as well, such as changes in the species composition of the zooplankton or benthos or changes in the abundance of nonexploited species. These are the kinds of effects we barely understand, and we have little idea of their reversibility. However, it is also worth noting that overexploitation rarely leads to the extinction of a species or population of fish, since fishing usually stops when the populations get too low. Thus, many of the changes wrought by overexploitation should in theory be reversible because the components of the original system are usually still present. The main exceptions to the "rule" that overexploitation of fish does not lead to extinction are with fishes of unusually high value that are unusually easy to catch, such as the salmons and sturgeons. Even these species can recover from severe overexploitation when their value becomes so high that it pays to have them artifically propagated.

Another exception to the "rule" that overexploitation will not lead to extinction in the wild is the fishery for tropical freshwater fishes for the aquarium trade. Because of their cash value to poverty-stricken peoples, such fishes are being intensively collected in many parts of the tropics. Especially vulnerable to collection by nets are species that become confined to isolated pools during the dry season, so that few fish can escape a serious collecting effort. Even more damaging is the use of poisons to collect aquarium fish; here the basic technique is to pour some toxic substance into a stream and collect the largest and most valuable fishes as they appear at the surface in distress. Most will survive if placed immediately in fresh water. Such collecting, of course, kills nearly everything in the stream not collected, so it is not unusual to find streams, especially in southeast Asia, with greatly depleted faunas as a result of such collecting. Because of depletion in the wild and high demand by aquarists, many species of aquarium fish are now cultured. However, it should be emphasized that fishes in such populations reflect selection processes aimed at producing fish capable of thriving under aquarium conditions, as well as fish that have color patterns favored by aquarists. Such fish may be poorly suited for returning to the wild, even if restoration of lost or damaged fish faunas ever does become a reality.

Although the effects of overexploitation are most obvious, even light exploitation of a fish population can have far-reaching effects. Removal of a few large, predatory bass from a farm pond may cause a population explosion and subsequent stunting in the bluegill population; removal of large, predatory trout from a stream may similarly cause an increase in the numbers of their former prey. Even the selective removal of large piscivorous fishes from complex coral reef communities can cause major shifts in the kinds of fishes of other species that are most abundant. On the other extreme, light to moderate fishing for major prey species, such as anchovy, may reduce their populations to the point where the feeding on them by predatory fishes, birds, and mammals is much less efficient, causing a downward shift in the numbers of predators and perhaps a shift in the relative abundances of the prey species as well.

INTRODUCTION OF EXOTIC SPECIES   Exotic fish species are those species that have been introduced by humans, either deliberately or inadvertently, into waters to which they are not native. Their impact has been greatest in inland waters, but the presence, in abundance, of striped bass, American shad, and two species of gobies in the coastal waters of California and the invasion of the Mediterranean Sea, via the Suez Canal, of Red Sea fishes, indicates that exotic species can be important in marine environments as well. It is obvious that the very presence of an exotic species in a "new" (to it) environment represents a major change in the fish community, although more often than not exotic species are successful in environments that have been severely altered by humans, so that the native species have already been placed under stress or are gone. Thus, in the Central Valley of California, the streams are usually still dominated by native species except where they have been dammed or otherwise altered. In these situations exotic species dominate. Nevertheless, exotic fishes can have severe impacts on native fish populations through predation, competition, and hybridization.

Predation can result in rapid and drastic changes in a fish fauna when an exotic piscivore is introduced into a community of fishes not adapted to its style of predation. Thus, the sea lamprey was able to virtually wipe out the populations of large fishes in the upper Great Lakes in less than 20 years (Chapter 13), and the peacock bass and largemouth bass have been able to eliminate most fish species from large lakes into which they have been introduced in Central America (Chapter 30). Predation by largemouth bass has also been implicated as one of the causes of the declines in some isolated populations of pupfish (*Cyprinodon*), now on the U.S. Fish and Wildlife Service threatened species list (Moyle 1976a).

Competition from exotic fishes as a factor causing the decline of native fish populations is very difficult to demonstrate, yet it is undoubtedly very important. For example, in the Great Lakes the decline of many, if not most, of the plankton-feeding whitefish species (*Coregonus*) was related to the establishment of the alewife in the lakes, which not only reduced the populations of large zooplankters in the lake but crowded into whitefish "space" at critical times of the year (see Chapter 17). Often the competitive superiority of an exotic species over a native form is related to habitat change. Species which evolved in a stream environment typically decline in numbers if the stream is impounded and exotic, lake-adapted fishes are introduced. Some species may actually change the environment themselves. Thus in the Mississippi drainage, native bottom-feeding species, such as buffalofishes (*Ictiobus* spp.), may disappear from shallow lakes once carp become established, root up the bottom, and decrease the water clarity.

Hybridization results in the elimination of a native form when members of a closely related species are introduced and breed with the endemic form, resulting in a hybrid swarm. If the hybrid (intermediate) phenotypes then have some competitive or reproductive disadvantage compared to the phenotypes that are closest to the exotic form, the intermediate phenotypes will gradually be eliminated from the population. Gradually, the population will increasingly resemble the "pure" exotic species. This mechanism has apparently been responsible for the elimination of many interior cutthroat trout populations by rainbow trout. However, one of the best documented cases is the virtual elimination of the Mojave tui chub (*Gila bicolor mohavensis*) from the Mojave River in California through hybridization with the arroyo chub (*G. orcutti*) (Hubbs and Miller 1942).

HABITAT ALTERATIONS   Habitat alteration by humans in inland waters (including estuaries) is the single biggest cause of faunal change and is increasingly becoming a major factor in the marine environment as well.

Every time a stream is dammed, a streambed channelized, a watershed logged or heavily grazed, a lakeside marsh filled in, or any other type of alteration, major or minor, takes place, the fish fauna changes, although often very subtly. Removing large trees that shade a salmon spawning stream may greatly increase salmon production, by increasing the amount of sunlight on the water and hence the stream's productivity. However, if such a logging operation causes the stream to become too warm or is accompanied by the silting in of the spawning gravels, minnows, suckers, and other nongame species may increase in numbers instead. On a more extreme scale, most of our major river systems have been so altered by dams, locks, channelization, urbanization, wetland drainage, etc., that their fish faunas bear little resemblance to the ones that were present originally. Once common species have become rare and uncommon species abundant, along with exotic species. One of the most severely altered rivers is the Colorado, whose unique minnow and sucker fauna has been almost totally replaced with lake-adapted exotics in reservoirs, cold-water exotics in waters below dams, and other exotics elsewhere. Many of the native species are prominent on the U.S. endangered species list. The fact that many river-dwelling fishes in North America are threatened species is a tip-of-the-iceberg indication of the extent to which the river fish communities have changed.

In the oceans, shipwrecks and other debris of civilization have created numerous new reefs where none existed before, often greatly increasing the abundance and diversity of local fish faunas. In many coastal areas, such reefs are now being created deliberately. On the other hand, the destruction of intertidal habitats by the construction of breakwaters, marinas, etc., and filling in of vital coastal habitats such as salt marshes, mangrove swamps, and estuaries is causing declines not only in the fishes unique to such areas but also in the populations of offshore fishes that require such areas as nurseries for their young.

POLLUTION Pollution is really a type of habitat alteration, but it nevertheless deserves separate consideration because of its extent and frequently subtle action. Of course, the best-known effects of pollution are not subtle at all. Releases of toxic chemicals have caused massive kills in hundreds of miles of major river systems, as well as in lakes and estuaries. Many streams in mining areas are devoid of fish life because of acidic water draining from the mines; many mountain lakes are losing their fish faunas as they become acid from material carried by air in the smoke of distant industries. Large amounts of sewage in lakes and streams cause depletion of the oxygen supply, killing all but the hardiest fish, or forcing them to move elsewhere. Fortunately, fishes are by and large very adaptable and have the reproductive potential to recolonize quickly areas from which they have been eliminated, once the cause of their initial disappearance is gone. For example, Atlantic salmon have returned to spawn in the Penobscot River in Maine, after

CH. 38 CONSERVATION

a decade-long absence, following a successful effort to "clean up" polluting industries and towns. Permanent elimination of species by pollution occurs either where the populations are highly localized (endemic) or where the pollution is continual and severe.

While direct kills of fish by pollution are of obvious concern, in the long run changes that are equally, or perhaps more, significant are changes caused by the sublethal effects of pollution. Power plants that use water for cooling may raise the temperatures of the stream, lake, or estuarine regions into which they draw and discharge the water. While such thermal pollution may kill fish directly, more often it causes local shifts in the composition of the fish fauna. From a fisheries point of view, these shifts may even be at times desirable, since in cool weather game fishes (and hence fishermen) may be attracted to the warmer water associated with power plants. However, other fishes may avoid the warmer water, just as they may avoid water with reduced oxygen concentrations, increased turbidity, or gooey bottoms due to pollution. The overall effect in such situations is typically decreased numbers of species, accompanied by an increase in such tolerant species as carp. Similar effects may result from sublethal levels of toxic compounds such as pesticides, especially if the toxins accumulate in the flesh of the fish. In such cases, they may reduce temperature tolerances, change behavior patterns, and generally reduce growth and survival rates. Since such toxins typically accumulate through food chains, predatory game fishes are especially likely to be affected. For example, mosquitofish (*Gambusia affinis*) living in waters adjacent to cottonfields may develop extraordinary tolerances to pesticides and so survive. However, predatory fishes that would normally prey on the mosquitofish are now largely absent from such areas, presumably poisoned by their prey.

Resources and Nonresources

For the purposes of management, fish can be divided into resource species and nonresource species.

Resource species include all fishes harvested by humans, plus the organisms they depend upon for food or other purposes. It should be recognized that these represent a rather small percentage of the total number of fish in either fresh or salt water. Most economically important species are rather eclectic in their food habits, within the limits of their morphology and size, yet even so the total number of species upon which they are likely to depend for growth and survival is likely to be fairly small. In a few environments, such as cold-water streams, temperate lakes, and the Epipelagic Zone of the ocean, 50% or more of the species can be identified as having direct value to humans, as food. However, these environments are not especially species-rich. The more complex the environment, usually the smaller the proportion of species harvested by humans. It is likely, for example, that less than 10% of the species found on coral reefs or in tropical rivers are harvested by humans, with the possible exception of those taken for the aquarium trade.

What resource fishes lack in number of species, they make up for in number of individuals. It is estimated that together, the marine species alone can yield to fishermen, on a sustained basis, between 90 million and 100 million metric tons of fish per year (Rounsefell 1975). This figure, which is about the level at which the resources are being harvested now, assumes reasonable management practices to sustain it. Since such practices, if they exist at all, have for the most part only been recently applied, the harvestable total can be expected to decline. However, a hopeful sign has been the extension by coastal nations of their management jurisdiction over fishery resources to at least 200 miles from the coastline. International agreements have not been particularly successful in managing marine fishery resources, so this action permits unilateral action in fishery management by all nations. In the United States the 200-mile limit was established on March 1, 1977, as a result of the Fisheries Management and Conservation Act of 1976 (PL 94-265). This act not only established the limits and the means to regulate fishing within them but also established a National Fisheries Management Program, complete with noble objectives and regional management councils. This, of course, is in addition to the management agencies of each state, plus the various federal agencies with an interest in fisheries management. Resource species, on paper at least, thus appear to have many people looking after their welfare.

Nonresource species are those of no known economic value to humankind (Ehrenfeld 1976). For better or worse, a majority of fish species belong in this category. These species could apparently disappear completely without the welfare of humankind being greatly affected. They therefore represent the biggest challenge in conservation, since it is likely that many of these species will indeed disappear if active measures are not taken to conserve them and their habitats. Why save such species? Ehrenfeld (1976) lists nine arguments that are commonly given: (1) recreational or esthetic values; (2) undiscovered or undeveloped values; (3) ecosystem stabilization values; (4) examples of survival; (5) environmental baseline and monitoring values; (6) scientific research values; (7) teaching values; (8) habitat reconstruction values; and (9) conservation value (avoidance of irreversible change). It is worthwhile to examine each of these arguments in detail to see how they apply to nonresource fish species.

The **recreational and esthetic values** of nonresource species have long been recognized by aquarists, and this very recognition has turned quite a number of small or unusually attractive fishes into resources with definite economic value. Although the demand for exotic fishes by aquarists seems to be insatiable, often to the detriment of wild populations, aquarists are rather selective in their tastes. Sterba (1959) lists over 1600 species that have been kept in aquaria in Europe at one time or another, and a generous estimate would put the worldwide total at perhaps double that number. Many of these species, of course, have been kept by a few individuals or public aquaria only for their curiosity value and would be unlikely to have the steady market demand necessary for making them a true resource. Unfortunately, many fishes are unlikely to have even fleeting value as curiosities (except to scientists). Examples might be the many rather similar species of minnows and darters in North American streams, the small benthic fishes of the Antarctic, or the numerous similar species of sculpins, blennies, and other forms found in tidepools.

In recent years the popularity of snorkeling and scuba diving, particularly on tropical reefs and in rocky coastal areas of temperate regions, has greatly increased public awareness and appreciation for nonresource fishes (at least in Western countries). However, even in areas popular with divers, a majority of the species are rarely seen because they are either nocturnal, cryptically colored, or very small. In any case, often the most popular fish for viewing are the large predatory fishes that also have commercial value. Overall, it appears that many fishes do have value to people for recreation or esthetics. However, putting a dollar value on this is very difficult (and not really even desirable), so esthetic values are likely to be considered secondary to economic ones (such as ripping up a reef to install an oil refinery).

Fish species with **undiscovered or undeveloped values** are probably not many, yet every time some obscure species becomes extinct, whatever potential value that species may have had is lost forever. Heading the list of potential uses for nonresource species is aquaculture, which is becoming an increasingly sophisticated and worldwide occupation. There is still a real need for fishes that can fit particular local conditions, such as alkaline waters or fluctuating temperatures, that can convert agricultural byproducts and "undigestible" bluegreen algae into fish flesh, or that can fit into polyculture operations. Another potential value is in natural "drugs" or other compounds produced by fish that may serve humans for medicines or other uses. A fascinating recent discovery of this sort is the shark-repellent substance secreted by the Moses sole (*Pardachirus marmoratus*) (Clark and George 1979). Of course, given that modern processing techniques can turn practically any fish into a patty of anonymous flesh, fish meal, or fish protein concentrate, any fish that can be caught, regardless of its size or abundance, does potentially have commercial value. However, the very anonymity of the processing means that species really do not matter, only pounds of flesh!

The **ecosystem stabilization value** argument for preserving individual species is a rather weak one, although frequently used. It is based on the hypothesis (often stated as an axiom) that the more species present in a system, the more stable that system should be. A corollary of the hypothesis is that the removal of species from an ecosystem should destabilize it. The main problem here is mostly that the relationship between diversity and stability is not all that straightforward, if there is any at all (see, for example, Connell 1978). Most ecosystems have been shown to be remarkably robust, and in coral reefs, the most complex of all aquatic environments, there appears to be considerable duplication of function among the various fishes present (see Chapter 34). If anything, the most complex systems are the most vulnerable to destabilization, especially through human actions. Nevertheless, it is worth noting that a certain degree of complexity appears to be highly desirable in aquatic systems, since species change as the environment changes. As the shifting abundances of benthic and epipelagic fishes of commercial importance indicate, a fish that is of little value today because of its rarity may become extremely abundant if environmental conditions favor it over its competitors.

The **examples of survival** argument is based on the idea that natural communities are living examples of long-term persistence under constant change. Thus, by studying natural communities and their constituent species we can better learn how to design artificial systems that will have the same resiliency. This argument has particular value for people interested in developing aquaculture systems that involve several species or for those who are interested in farming the sea floor.

The **environmental baseline and monitoring values** argument says that species and significant samples of natural systems should be preserved as a way of determining the amount and kind of change brought about by human activities. Obscure species are particularly valuable in this context because some measure of species diversity is probably the best indicator of environmental change (especially degradation). Non-resource species may be important here as well because their very lack of value means that they will not have been exploited, so that population changes can be related more easily to changes in environmental conditions. Thus, the sculpins living in a trout stream may be a better long-term indicator of the stream's health than the trout, since they are not subject to vagaries of fishing pressure. Similarly, the amount of pesticides in the flesh of a small, sedentary bottom fish may be more indicative of local problems than the amount in the flesh of a more mobile species that is being harvested.

The **scientific research values** of fish are obvious to ichthyologists, who find all fish intrinsically interesting. Fortunately for ichthyologists, who are relatively few in number (at least in their pure form), many other scientists find fish interesting as well. Sticklebacks and poeciliids have proven to be invaluable for studies of evolution, behavior, and genetics that are of general interest. The study of reef fish ecology has provided considerable insight into the structure and function of complex ecosystems. Lampreys have proven to be invaluable for studies of neurophysiology. Important though fish already are in basic research, their potential for experimental and *in situ* studies is just beginning to be realized.

The teaching values of fishes are also obvious. They are the one group of vertebrates in which it is really possible to maintain large populations in the laboratory for observation and experimentation. Many varieties are readily available for dissection, giving an easy overview of the many types of adaptations possible in vertebrates. Most important of all, they typically can be found in large numbers and diversity in waters fairly close to most educational institutions, so that many types of ecological demonstrations can be made. Fishes have the right combination of availability, size, and ease of handling to make them the most desirable group of vertebrates for comparative classroom studies of ecology, behavior, evolution, and anatomy and to be very valuable in other areas, such as genetics and physiology, as well.

The value of saving species for habitat restoration is based on the assumption that we may someday want to reconstruct habitats or ecosystems in areas from which they have been eliminated. A faithful reconstruction, of course, would only be possible if an entire example of habitat to be reconstructed had been set aside. The habitat restoration value is very similar to the conservative value, which is simply the belief that no ecosystem, habitat, or species should be allowed to disappear completely because one never knows if such an irreversible change might have some long-term negative impact on human survival. As Ehrenfeld (1976) states, this value means we should "preserve the full range of natural diversity because we do not know the aspects of that diversity upon which our long-term survival depends" (p. 650).

At present, these arguments are used mostly in relation to preserving endangered or threatened species and their habitats. Endangered species are those in immediate danger of extinction if some active conservation measures are not taken, while threatened species are those that are likely to become endangered in the near future. In the United States in 1978, the U.S. Fish and Wildlife Service's Office of Endangered Species listed 41 taxa (species or subspecies) that are officially recognized as endangered or threatened species. The American Fisheries Society Endangered Species Committee (Deacon et al. 1979) lists 182 taxa of fishes found north of Mexico that deserve endangered, threatened, or "special concern" status. The latter category includes fishes about which too little is known to include them in a "higher" category or fishes that are borderline threatened species. These fishes are the ultimate nonresources because most of them are rather obscure forms that are already so rare that they would hardly be missed if they disappeared altogether.

Can the above nine arguments be successfully applied to such nonresource species? The best answer is, sometimes! The problem with the arguments is that directly or indirectly they are an effort to turn nonresource species into resource species, with a real, if hard to define, economic value (Ehrenfeld 1976). Unfortunately, these values are so nebulous and/or complex that they will usually seem small when compared to the very real economic values that can be gained from the short-term exploitation of an environment or a species. A well-known confrontation between these values came with the efforts to stop the construction of Tellico Dam on the Little Tennessee River, to protect the endangered snail darter (*Percina tanasi*). The Endangered Species Act of 1973 was invoked successfully all the way through the U.S. Supreme Court to protect the species, but Congress subsequently changed the law to make exemptions possible. The reason for the change is easy to understand. The original law was passed after a majority of Congress was presumably persuaded by such arguments as those just given, plus the noneconomic argument of saving the more spectacular symbols of the disappearing American wilderness, such as bald eagles, wolves, and whooping cranes. Once the law passed, however, it quickly became evident that it had opened up a Pandora's Box of problems for many elements of the U.S. economy; the list of endangered or threatened species is rapidly growing longer and longer as not only small, obscure fish but also invertebrates and plants are added.

Thus, it increasingly appears that while long-term value arguments can be used to save some species and habitats, they can be easily overcome in a majority of cases. This means that the preservation of diversity will ultimately depend on the development of convincing noneconomic arguments, which will essentially appeal to a sense of morality. The simplest of these is just that nonresource organisms should be allowed to continue to exist because they have existed for a long time and therefore have as much right to continued existence as we have. "Existence is the only criterion of value, and diminution of the number of existing things is the best measure of decrease of value" (Ehrenfeld 1976, p. 654). Ehrenfeld suggests that this should be called the Noah Principle after its first practitioner. Elton (1958) pointed out that this reason for preserving species is basically a religious one. Unfortunately, it also seems to run counter to the prevailing cultural and religious values in our present society. As Ehrenfeld (1976) states:

> If nonresource arguments are ever to carry their deserved weight, cultural attitudes will have to be changed. Morally backed missionary movements, such as the humane societies, are doing quite well these days, but I have no illusions about the chance of bringing about an ethical change in our Faustian culture without the prompting of some general catastrophe. What sort of change in world view would favor the conservation of nonresources? Nothing less than a rejection of the heroic, Western ethic with its implicit denial of man's biological roots and evolved structure.
>
> Not all problems have acceptable solutions; I feel no constraint to predict one here. On the one hand, conservationists are unlikely to succeed in a general way using only the resource approach; and they will often hurt their own cause. On the other hand, combination of resource and nonresource arguments may also fail, and if it succeeds it will probably be because of forces that the conservationists neither expected nor controlled. But in this event we will at least be ready to

take advantage of favorable circumstances—and will have had, whatever the outcome, the small, private satisfaction of having been honest for a while [pp. 655–56].

Recommendations for the Future

Although the above conclusion is rather pessimistic, it does not mean that the preservation of diversity is not worth working for. In the United States and Canada and in northern European countries there is actually reason for cautious optimism, since changes in public and official attitudes toward nonresource biota have resulted in many positive measures being taken to ensure their continued survival. However, one can only be pessimistic about the future of the biota of most other countries, as human populations expand and habitats from tropical streams and lakes to coral reefs are exploited, polluted, and severely disturbed by activities of peoples trying to survive in the present and unable to worry about the future. Regardless of location, there is much that should be done as soon as possible, such as the following:

1. Perhaps the first task in any region where conservation is a possibility is to inventory the fishes. Successful management will ultimately depend on knowing what species are where, what their general habitat requirements are, and how they interact with other species.

2. Monitoring programs need to be established that will let scientists and legislators know on a regular basis the status of particular habitats, communities, and species.

3. Research programs are needed to show how both resource and nonresource species can be managed more effectively, preferably together. A broad outline of research needs in fisheries is given in Moyle et al. (1979).

4. Plans for regional management that follow natural rather than political boundaries are needed. For fresh water, it is becoming increasingly obvious that drainage systems have to be treated as units, since a development in one place is likely to affect the entire system. It is unfortunate that often waterways have been selected as boundaries between political units, making the management of these waters especially difficult. In salt water, fish have been notorious for not respecting political boundaries, resulting in a number of international management plans for some commercially important species. Similar international efforts are needed for the conservation of oceanic resources and nonresources in general.

5. Fish communities and habitats should start being managed as units. Although multispecies management strategies are likely to be extremely complex, they should nevertheless be tried as a way not only of increasing total fish production but as a way of conserving nonresource species, as well as the complex set of interactions each community represents. The need to get away from the present species-by-species man-

agement approach is becoming more and more apparent, as more species are exploited and more species are added to endangered and threatened species lists. The conflicting goals of many of these individual plans can only be resolved if a much broader approach to management is taken.

It is obvious that even to begin really doing something with these rather utopian recommendations, a rather large commitment of capital on the part of the developed nations will be required. Yet the total investment would in all probability be considerably less than funds put into moon shots and other monuments of our era, and the chances of such investments paying handsome dividends (economic and moral) in the future are quite good.

Supplemental Readings   Deacon et al. 1979; Ehrenfeld 1976, 1978; Moyle 1976a; Rounsefell 1975.

Bibliography

ABLE, K.W. 1976. Cleaning behavior in the cyprinodontid fishes *Fundulus majalis, Cyprinodon variegatus,* and *Lucania parva. Ches. Sci.* 17(1):35–39.

ACKERMANN, W.C., WHITE, G.F., and WORTHINGTON, G.B., eds. 1973. *Manmade lakes: their problems and environmental effects.* Geophys. Monogra. 17. 847 pp.

ADAMS, S.M. 1976a. Ecology of eelgrass, *Zostera marina* (L.) fish communities. I. structural analysis. *J. Exp. Mar. Biol. Ecol.* 22:269–291.

ADAMS, S.M. 1976b. Feeding ecology of eelgrass fish communities. *Trans. Amer. Fish. Soc.* 105(4):514–519.

AHLSTROM, E.H., and RADOVICH, J. 1970. Management of the Pacific sardine. Pages 183–193 *in* N.C. Benson, ed. *A century of fisheries in North America.* Amer. Fish. Soc. Spec. Publ. 7.

ALBERS, C. 1970. Acid-base balance. Pages 173–208, *in* W.S. Hoar and D.J. Randall, eds. *Fish physiology.* Vol. IV. New York: Academic Press.

ALEEV, Y.G. 1963. *Function and gross morphology in fish.* Jerusalem: Israel Prog. Scientific Trans.

ALEVIZON, W.S. 1975. Spatial overlap and competition in congeneric surfperches (Embiotocidae) off Santa Barbara, California. *Copeia* 1975(2):352–355.

ALEXANDER, R.M. 1966a. Structure and function in catfishes. *J. Zool.* (London) 148:88–152.

ALEXANDER, R.M. 1966b. Physical aspects of swimbladder function. *Biol. Rev.* 41:141–176.

ALEXANDER, R.M. 1967. *Functional design in fishes.* London: Hutchinson Lib. 160 pp.

ALEXANDER, R.M. 1970. Mechanics of the feeding action of various teleost fishes. *J. Zool.* (London) 162:145–156.

ALLAN, J.D. 1975. The distributional ecology and diversity of benthic insects in Cement Creek, Colorado. *Ecology* 56(5):1040–1053.

ALLEN, G.R. 1972. *The anemone fishes.* Neptune City, N.J.: TFH Publ. 288 pp.

ALLEN, K.R. 1969. Distinctive aspects of the ecology of stream fishes: a review. *J. Fish. Res. Bd. Canada* 26:1429–1438.

ALLEN, M.J., PECORELLI, H., and WORD, J. 1976. Marine organisms around outfall pipes in Santa Monica Bay. *J. Water Poll. Cont. Fed.* 48(8):1881–1893.

ALLEY, D. 1976. *Bioenergetic significance of microhabitat selection by two fishes in a Sierran foothill stream.* Unpublished M.S. thesis, Univ. Calif., Davis. 378 pp.

ALM, G. 1949. Influence of heredity and environment on various forms of trout. *Ann. Rpt. Inst. Freshw. Res.* (Drottningholm) 29:29–34.

AMUNDSRUD, J.R., FABER, D.J., and KEAST, A. 1974. Seasonal succession of free-swimming perciform larvae in Lake Opinicon, Ontario. *J. Fish. Res. Bd. Canada* 31(10):1661–1665.

ANDERSON, W.D., DIAS, J.K., DIAS, R.K., CUPKA, D.M. and CHAMBERLAIN, N.A. 1977. *The macrofauna of the surf zone off Folly Beach, South Carolina.* NOAA Tech. Rpt. NMFS SSRF-704. 23 pp.

ANDREWS, J.W., and STICKNEY, R.R. 1972. Interactions of feeding rates and environmental temperature on growth, food conversion, and body composition of channel catfish. *Trans. Am. Fish. Soc.* 101:94–99.

ANDRIASHEV, A.P. 1962. Bathypelagic fishes of the Antarctic 1. Family Myctophidae. *Akad. Sci. USSR Zool. Inst., Expl. Fauna Seas* 1(9):216–294.

ANDRIASHEV, A.P. 1965. A general review of the Antarctic fish fauna. Pages 491–550 *in* P. van Oye and J. van Mieghem, eds. *Biogeography and ecology in Antarctica.* Monogr. Biol. 15.

ANDRIASHEV, A.P. 1970. Cryopelagic fishes of the Arctic and Antarctic and their significance in polar ecosystems. Pages 297–304 *in* M.W. Holdgate, ed. *Antarctic ecology.* New York: Academic Press.

APPLEGATE, V.C. 1950. *Natural history of the sea lamprey (Petromyzon marinus) in Michigan.* U.S. Fish. Wildl. Serv. Spec. Sci. Rept. 555:1–237.

ARON, W.I., and SMITH, S.H. 1971. Ship canals and ecosystems. *Science* 174 (4004):13–20.

ARTHUR, D.R. 1975. Constraints on the fauna in estuaries. Pages 514–537 *in* B.A. Whitton, ed. *River ecology.* Berkeley: Univ. Calif. Press.

ASPINWALL, N. 1974. Genetic analysis of North American populations of the pink salmon, *Oncorhynchus gorbuscha*, possible evidence for the neutral mutation-random drift hypothesis. *Evolution* 28(2):295–305.

ATCHLEY, W.R., GASKINS, C.T., and ANDERSON, D. 1976. Statistical properties of ratios. I. Empirical results. *Syst. Zool.* 25(2):137–148.

ATEMA, J. 1971. Structures and functions of the sense of taste in the catfish (*Ictalurus natalis*). *Brain, Behavior and Evolution* 25(4):273–294.

AVISE, J.C., SMITH, J.J., and AYALA, F.J. 1975. Adaptive differentiation with little genic change between two native minnows. *Evolution* 29(3):411–476.

BABEL, J.S. 1967. Reproduction, life history, and ecology of the round stingray, *Urolophus halleri* Cooper. *Calif. Dept. Fish. Game Fish. Bull.* 137:1–104.

BACKUS, R.H. 1957. The fishes of Labrador. *Bull. Amer. Mus. Nat. Hist.* 113 (4):273–338.

BACKUS, R.H., CRADDOCK, J.E. HAEDRICH, R.L., and ROBISON, B.H. 1977. Atlantic mesopelagic zoogeography. Pages 266–287 *in* B.F. Nafpaktitus et al., eds. *Fishes of the western North Atlantic, part seven.* Mem. 1, Sears Found. Mar. Res.

BACKUS, R.H., et al. 1968. *Ceratoscopelus maderensis*: peculiar sound-scattering layer identified with this myctophid fish. *Science* 160:911–993.

BAGENAL, T.B. 1978. Aspects of fish fecundity. Pages 75–101 *in* S.D. Gerking, ed. *Ecology of freshwater fish production.* New York: Wiley.

BAILEY, R.M., and six others. 1970. *A list of common and scientific names of fishes from the United States and Canada.* 3rd ed. Amer. Fish. Soc. Spec. Publ. 6. 150 pp.

BAINBRIDGE, R. 1958. The speed of swimming of fish as related to size and to the frequency and amplitude of the tail beat. *J. Exp. Biol.* 35:109–133.

BAINES, G.W. 1975. Blood pH effects in eight fishes from the teleostean family Scorpaenidae. *Comp. Biochem. Physiol.* 51A:833–843.

BALON, E.K. 1974. Fish production of a tropical ecosystem. Pages 253–748 *in* E.K. Balon and A.G. Coche, eds. *Lake Kariba: a man-made tropical ecosystem in Central Africa.* The Hague: W. Junk.

BALON, E.K. 1975a. Reproductive guilds in fishes: a proposal and definition. *J. Fish. Res. Bd. Canada* 32(6):821–864.

BALON, E.K. 1975b. Terminology of intervals in fish development. *J. Fish. Res. Bd. Canada* 32(9):1663–1670.

BALON, E.K. 1977. Fish gluttons: the natural ability of some fishes to become obese when food is in extreme abundance. *Hydrobiologia* 52:239–241.

BALON, E.K. 1978. Kariba: the dubious benefits of large dams. *Ambio* 7(2): 40–48.

BALON, E.K. 1979. The theory of saltation and its application in the ontology of fishes: steps and thresholds. *Env. Biol. Fish* 4:97–101.

BALON, E.K. 1980. Saltatory processes and altricial to precocial forms in the ontogeny of fishes. *Amer. Zool.* 20. In press.

BALON, E.K., and COCHE, A.G. 1974. *Lake Kariba: a man-made tropical ecosystem in central Africa.* The Hague: W. Junk. 767 pp.

BANARESCU, P. 1975. *Principles and problems of zoogeography.* Springfield, Va.: Nat. Tech. Info. Serv. 214 pp.

BARBER, W.E., and MINCKLEY, W.L. 1966. Fishes of Aravaipa Creek, Graham and Pinal Counties, Arizona. *Southw. Nat.* 11(3):313–324.

BARBOUR, C.D., and BROWN, J.H. 1974. Fish species diversity in lakes. *Amer. Nat.* 108(962):473–488.

BARDACH, J.E. 1959. The summer standing crop of fish on a shallow Bermuda reef. *Limnol. Oceanogr.* 4:448–462.

BARDACH, J.E., JOHNSON, G.H., and TODD, J.H. 1969. Orientation by bulk messenger sensors in aquatic vertebrates. *Ann. N. Y. Acad. Sci.* 163:227–235.

BARDACH, J.E., RYTHER, J.H. and McLARNEY, W.O. 1972. *Aquaculture.* New York: Wiley-Interscience. 868 pp.

BARDACH, J.E., and TODD, J.H. 1970. Chemical communication in fish. Pages 205–240 *in* J.W. Johnson et al., eds. *Advances in chemoreception.* Vol. 1. New York: Appleton-Century-Crofts.

BARLOW, G.W. 1961. Causes and significance of morphological variation in fishes. *Syst. Zool.* 10(1):105–117.

BARLOW, G.W. 1972. The attitude of fish eye-lines in relation to body shape and to stripes and bars. *Copeia* 1972(1):5–12.

BARLOW, G.W. 1973. Competition between color morphs of the polychromatic Midas cichlid *Cichlasoma citrinellum. Science* 179:806–807.

BARLOW, G.W. 1974. Contrasts in social behavior between Central American cichlid fishes and coral-reef surgeon fishes. *Amer. Zool.* 14(1):9–34.

BARLOW, G.W. 1976. The Midas cichlid in Nicaragua. Pages 333–358 *in* T.B. Thorson, ed. *Investigations of the ichthyofauna of Nicaraguan Lakes.* Lincoln: School of Life Sci., Univ. Nebraska.

BARRETT, I., and WILLIAMS, A.A. 1965. Hemoglobin content of the blood of fifteen species of marine fishes. *Calif. Fish and Game* 51:216–281.

BEAMISH, F.W.H. 1964. Respiration of fishes with special emphasis on standard oxygen consumption. II. Influence of weight and temperature in respiration of several species. *Can. J. Zool.* 42:177–188.

BEAMISH, F.W.H. 1970. Oxygen consumption of largemouth bass, *Micropterus salmoides,* in relation to swimming speed and temperature. *Can. J. Zool.* 48: 1221–1228.

BEAMISH, R.J. 1974. Loss of fish populations from unexploited remote lakes in Ontario, Canada as a consequence of atmospheric fallout of acid. *Water. Res.* 8:85–95.

BECHTEL, T.J., and COPELAND, B.J. 1970. Fish species diversity indices as indicators of pollution in Galveston Bay, Texas. *Cont. Mar. Sci.* 15:103–132.

BEHNKE, R.J. 1970. The application of cytogenetic and biochemical systematics to phylogenetic problems in the family Salmonidae. *Trans. Amer. Fish. Soc.* 99(1):237–248.

BELL, M.A. 1976a. Evolution of phenotypic diversity in *Gasterosteus aculeatus* superspecies on the Pacific coast of North America. *Syst. Zool.* 25(3):211–227.

BELL, M.A. 1976b. Reproductive character displacement in threespine sticklebacks. *Evolution* 30(4):847–850.

BELLAMY, D., and CHESTER-JONES, I. 1961. Studies on *Myxine glutinosa*. I. The chemical composition of the tissues. *Comp. Biochem. Physiol.* 3:175–183.

BENNION, G.R. 1968. *The control of the function of the heart in teleost fish.* M.S. thesis, Univ. British Columbia, Vancouver. 53 p.

BEN-TUVIA, A. 1966. Red Sea fishes recently found in the Mediterranean. *Copeia* 1966(2):254–275.

BEN-TUVIA, A. 1978. Immigration of fishes through the Suez Canal. *NOAA Fish. Bull.* 76(1):249–255.

BEN-YAMI, M., and GLASER, T. 1974. The invasion of *Saurida undosquamis* (Richardson) into the Levant Basin—an example of biological effects of interoceanic canals. *NOAA Fish. Bull.* 35:359–372.

BERG, L.S. 1940. *Classification of fishes both recent and fossil.* Ann Arbor, Mich.: J.W. Edwards. 517 pp.

BERG, L.S. 1949. *Freshwater fishes of the U.S.S.R. and adjacent countries.* Jerusalem: Israel Prog. Sci. Transl. 510 pp.

BERG, T., and STEEN, J.B. 1965. Physiological mechanisms for aerial respiration in the eel. *Comp. Biochem. Physiol.* 15:469–484.

BERTELSEN, E., and STRUHSAKER, P.J. 1977. The ceratioid fishes of the genus *Thaumatichthys.* Osteology, relationships, distribution, and biology. *Galathea Rpt.* 14:7–40.

BEYENBACH, K.W., and KIRSCHNER, L.B. 1975. Kidney and urinary bladder functions of the rainbow trout in Mg and Na excretion. *Am. J. Physiol.* 229: 389–393.

BIGELOW, H.B., and SCHROEDER, W.C. 1948. Sharks. Pages 59–546 *in* J. Tee-Van et al., eds. *Fishes of the Western North Atlantic.* Mem. Sears Found. Mar. Res. 1.

BIGELOW, H.B., and SCHROEDER, W.C. 1953. Fishes of the Gulf of Maine. *U.S. Fish. Wildl. Ser. Fish. Bull.* 74:1–577.

BINOTTI, I., GIOVENCO, S., GIARDINA, B., ANTONINI, E., BRUNORI, M., and WYMAN, J. 1971. Studies on the functional properties of fish hemoglobins. II. The oxygen equilibrium of the isolated hemoglobin components from trout blood. *Arch. Biochem. Biophys.* 142:274–280.

BISHOP, J.E. 1973. Limnology of a small Malayan river, Sungai Gombak. Monograph. Biolog. 22. The Hague: W. Junk. 435 pp.

BJERRING, H.C. 1973. Relationships of coelacanthiforms. Pages 179–206 *in* P.H. Greenwood, R.S. Miles, and C. Patterson, eds. *Interrelationships of fishes.* London: Academic Press.

BLACKBURN, M. 1965. Oceanography and the ecology of tunas. *Oceangr. Mar. Biol. Ann. Rev.* 3:299–322.

BLAKE, B.F. 1977. The effect of the impoundment of Lake Kainji, Nigeria, on the indigenous species of mormyrid fishes. *Freshw. Biol.* 7:37–42.

BLAXHALL, P.C. 1972. The haematological assessment of the health of freshwater fish. *J. Fish Biol.* 4:593–604.

BLAXHALL, P.C., and DAISLEY, K.W. 1973. Routine haematological methods for use with fishblood. *J. Fish Biol.* 5:771–782.

BLAXTER, J.H.S. 1970. Light, fishes. Pages 213–320 *in* O. Kinne, ed. *Environmental factors 1, Marine ecology 1.* New York: Wiley-Interscience.

BLAXTER, J.H.S. 1974. *The early life history of fish.* New York: Springer Verlag. 765 pp.

BLAXTER, J.H.S., and HOLLIDAY, F.G.T. 1963. The behavior and physiology of herring and other clupeids. *Adv. Mar. Biol.* 2:261–393.
BODZNIK, D. 1978. Calcium ion: An odorant for natural water discriminations and the migratory behavior of sockeye salmon. *J. Comp. Physiol.* 127:157–166.
BONAVENTURA, J., BONAVENTURA, C., and SULLIVAN, B. 1975. Hemoglobins and hemocyanins; comparative aspects of structure and function. *J. Exp. Zool.* 194(1):155–174.
BONE, Q. 1966. On the function of the two types of myotomal muscle fibre in elasmobranch fish. *Fish. J. Mar. Biol. Assoc. U. K.* 46:321–349.
BOOTH, J.H. 1978. The distribution of blood flow in the gills of fish: application of a new technique to rainbow trout. *J. Exp. Biol.* 73:119–129.
BOULENGER, G.A. 1907. *Zoology of Egypt: fishes of the Nile.* London: Hugh Rees. 578 pp.
BOULENGER, G.A. 1910. Ichthyology. I. History of literature down to 1880. Pages 243–250 *in Encyclopedia Brittanica.* 11th ed. Vol. 14.
BOWERING, W.R. 1976. Distribution, age and growth, and sexual maturity of witch flounder (*Glyptocephalus cynoglossus*). *J. Fish. Res. Bd. Canada* 33(7):1574–1584.
BRAUM, E. 1978. Ecological aspects of fish eggs, embryos, and larvae. Pages 102–136 *in* S. Gerking, ed. *Ecology of freshwater fish production.* New York: Wiley.
BRAWLEY, S.H., and ADEY, W.H. 1977. Territorial behavior of threespot damselfish (*Eupomacentrus planifrons*) increases reef algal biomass and productivity. *Env. Biol. Fish* 2(1):45–51.
BRAY, R.N., and EBELING, A.W. 1975. Food, activity and habitat of three "picker-type" microcarnivorous fishes in the kelp forests off Santa Barbara, California. *NOAA Fish. Bull.* 73(4):815–829.
BRAY, R.N., and HIXON, M.A. 1978. Nightshocker: predatory behavior of the Pacific electric ray (*Torpedo californica*). *Science* 200:333–334.
BREDER, C.M. 1934. Ecology of an oceanic freshwater lake, Andros Island, Bahamas, with special reference to its fishes. *Zoologica* 18:57–88.
BREDER, C.M., and ROSEN, D.E. 1966. Modes of reproduction in fishes. Garden City, N.Y. *Nat. Hist. Press,* 941 pp.
BREDER, C.M., Jr. 1976. Fish schools as operational structures. *NOAA Fish. Bull.* 74(3):471–502.
BRETT, J.R. 1971. Energetic responses of salmon to temperature. A study of some thermal relations in the physiology and freshwater ecology of sockeye salmon (*Oncorhynchus nerka*). *Am. Zool.* 11:99–113.
BRETT, J.R. 1975. The swimming energetics of salmon. *Sci. Amer.* 212:80–85.
BRETT, J.R. 1979. Environmental factors and growth. Pages 599–675 *in* W.S. Hoar, D.J. Randall, and J.R. Brett, eds. *Fish physiology,* Vol. 9. New York: Academic Press.
BRETT, J.R., and GROVES, T.D. 1979. Physiological energetics. Pages 279–352 *in* W.S. Hoar, D.J. Randall, and J.R. Brett, eds. *Fish physiology.* Vol. 9. New York: Academic Press.
BRETT, J.R., SHELBOURN, J.E., and SHOOP, C.T. 1969. Growth rate and body composition of fingerling sockeye salmon, *Oncorhynchus nerka,* in relation to temperature and ration size. *J. Fish. Res. Bd. Canada* 26:2363–2394.
BREWER, G.D. 1973. Midwater fishes from the Gulf of California and the adjacent eastern tropical Pacific. *Los Angeles Co. Mus. Nat. Hist. Contrs. in Sci.* 242:1–47.
BRIDGES, W.W., CECH, J.J. Jr., and PEDRO, D.N. 1976. Seasonal hematological changes in winter flounder, *Pseudopleuronectes americanus.* *Trans. Am. Fish. Soc.* 105:596–600.
BRIGGS, J.C. 1974. *Marine zoogeography.* New York: McGraw-Hill. 475 pp.
BRIGGS, J.C. 1979. Ostariophysan zoogeography: an alternative hypothesis.

Copeia 4:111–118.

BRIGGS, P.T., and O'CONNOR, J.S. 1971. Comparison of shore-zone fishes over naturally vegetated and sand-filled bottoms in Great South Bay. *N. Y. Fish. Game J.* 18(1):15–41.

BROCK, R.E. 1977. Occurrence and variety of fishes in mixohaline ponds of the Kona, Hawaii, coast. *Copeia* 1977(1):134–139.

BROCKSEN, R.W., and COLE, R.E. 1972. Physiological responses of three species of fishes to various salinities. *J. Fish. Res. Bd. Canada* 29:399–405.

BRODAL, A. and FÄNGE, R., eds. 1963. *The biology of the myxine.* Oslo: Scand. Univ. Books. 588 pp.

BROOKS, J.L. 1968. The effects of prey size selection by lake planktivores. *Syst. Zool.* 17(3):272–291.

BROOKS, J.L., and DODSON, S. 1965. Predation, body size, and composition of plankton. *Science* 150:28–35.

BROTHERS, E.B., MATHEWS, C.P., and LASKER, R. 1976. Daily growth increments in otoliths from larval and adult fishes. *NOAA Fish. Bull.* 74:1–8.

BROWN, D.W. 1974. Hydrography and midwater fishes of three contiguous oceanic areas off Santa Barbara, California. *Los Angeles Co. Mus. Nat. Hist. Contr. Sci.* 261:1–30.

BROWN, J.H. 1971. The desert pupfish. *Sci. Amer.* 225(5):104–110.

BROWN, J.H., and FELDMETH, C.R. 1971. Evolution in constant and fluctuating environments; thermal tolerance of desert pupfish (*Cyprinodon*). *Evolution* 25 (2):390–398.

BRYAN, J.E., and LARKIN, P.A. 1972. Food specialization by individual trout. *J. Fish. Res. Bd. Canada* 29:1615–1624.

BUCKLEY, J.A. 1977. Heinz body hemolytic anemia in coho salmon (*Oncorhynchus kisutch*) exposed to chlorinated wastewater. *J. Fish. Res. Bd. Canada* 34:215–224.

BUDKER, P. 1971. *The life of sharks.* New York: Columbia Univ. Press. 222 pp.

BULLOCK, T.H. 1973. Seeing the world through a new sense; electroreception in fish. *Amer. Sci.* 61(3):316–325.

BURGER, J.W. 1962. Further studies on the function of the rectal gland in the spiny dogfish. *Physiol. Zool.* 35:205–217.

BURGER, J.W., and HESS, W. 1960. Function of the rectal gland in the spiny dogfish. *Science* 131:670–671.

BURGESS, T.J. 1978. The comparative ecology of two sympatric polychromatic populations of *Xererpes fucorum* Jordan and Gilbert (Pisces: Pholididae) from the rocky intertidal zone of central California. *J. Exp. Mar. Biol. Ecol.* 35:43–58.

BURGGREN, W.W. 1978. Gill ventilation in the sturgeon, *Acipenser transmontanus:* Unusual adaptations for bottom dwelling. *Resp. Physiol.* 34:153–170.

BURGGREN, W.W., and RANDALL, D.J. 1978. Oxygen uptake and transport during hypoxic exposure in the sturgeon *Acipenser transmontanus. Resp. Physiol.* 34:171–183.

BURTON, G.W., and ODUM, E.P. 1945. The distribution of stream fish in the vicinity of Mountain Lake, Virginia. *Ecology* 26(1):182–293.

BUSSING, W.A. 1976. Geographic distribution of the San Juan ichthyofauna of Central America with remarks on its origin and ecology. Pages 157–175 *in* T.B. Thorson, ed. *Investigations of the ichthyofauna of Nicaraguan lakes.* Lincoln: Univ. Nebraska.

CAMERON, J.N. 1970a. Blood characteristics of some marine fishes of the Texas gulf coast. *Tex. J. Sci.* 21:275–283.

CAMERON, J.N. 1970b. The influence of environmental variables on the hematology of pinfish (*Lagodon rhomboides*) and striped mullet (*Mugil cephalus*). *Comp. Biochem. Physiol.* 32:175–192.

CAMERON, J.N. 1971a. Oxygen dissociation characteristics of the blood of rain-

544

bow trout, *Salmo gairdneri*. *Comp. Biochem. Physiol.* 38A:600–704.

CAMERON, J.N. 1971b. Methemoglobin in erythrocytes of rainbow trout blood. *Comp. Biochem. Physiol.* 40A:743–749.

CAMERON, J.N. 1975. Morphometric and flow indicator studies of the teleost heart. *Can. J. Zool.* 53:691–698.

CAMERON, J.N. 1976. Branchial ion uptake in arctic grayling: resting values and effects of acid-base disturbance. *J. Exp. Biol.* 64:711–725.

CAMERON, J.N. 1978. Chloride shift in fish blood. *J. Exp. Zool.* 206:289–295.

CAMERON, J.N., and DAVIS, J.C. 1970. Gas exchange in rainbow trout (*Salmo gairdneri*) with varying blood oxygen capacity. *J. Fish Res. Bd. Canada* 27: 1069–1085.

CAMERON, J.N., RANDALL, D.J., and DAVIS, J.C. 1971. Regulation of the ventilation–perfusion ratio in the gills of *Dasyatis sabina* and *Squalus suckleyi. Comp. Biochem. Physiol.* 39A:505–519.

CAMERON, W.M., and PRITCHARD, D.W. 1963. Estuaries. Pages 306–323 *in* M.N. Hill, ed. *The sea.* Vol II. New York: Wiley-Interscience.

CAPRA, M.F., and SATCHELL, G.H. 1977. The differential haemodynamic responses of the elasmobranch, *Squalus acanthias*, to the naturally occurring catecholamines adrenaline and noradrenaline. *Comp. Biochem. Physiol.* 58C: 41–47.

CAREY, F.G., and LAWSON, K.D. 1973. Temperature regulation in free-swimming bluefin tuna. *Comp. Biochem. Physiol.* 44A:375–392.

CAREY, F.G., and TEAL, J.M. 1966. Heat conservation in tuna fish muscle. *Proc. Nat. Acad. Sci. U. S.* 56:1461–1469.

CAREY, F.G., TEAL, J.M., KANWISHER, J.W., LAWSON, K.D., and BECKETT, J.S. 1971. Warm-bodied fish. *Am. Zool.* 11:137-145.

CARLANDER, K.D. 1955. The standing crop of fish in lakes. *J. Fish. Res. Bd. Canada* 12(4):543–569.

CARLANDER, K.D. 1969. *Handbook of freshwater fishery biology.* Vol. 1. Ames: Iowa St. Univ. Press.

CARLSON, H.R., and HAIGHT, R.E. 1972. Evidence for a home site and homing of adult yellowtail rockfish, *Sebastes flavidus. J. Fish. Res. Bd. Canada* 29: 1011–1014.

CARRIER, J.C., and EVANS, D.H. 1976. The role of environmental calcium in freshwater survival of the marine teleost, *Lagodon rhomboides. J. Exp. Biol.* 65:529–538.

CASTEEL, R.W. 1976. *Fish remains in archaeology and paleo-environmental studies.* New York: Academic Press. 180 pp.

CATLETT, R.H., and MILLICH, D.R. 1976. Intracellular and extracellular osmoregulation of temperature acclimated goldfish: *Carassius auratus* L. *Comp. Biochem. Physiol.* 55A:261–269.

CECH, J.J., Jr., BRIDGES, D.W., ROWELL, D.M., and BALZER, P.J. 1976. Cardiovascular responses of winter flounder, *Pseudopleuronectes americanus* (Walbaum), to acute temperature increase. *Can. J. Zool.* 54:1383–1388.

CECH, J.J., Jr., MITCHELL, S.J., and MASSINGILL, M.J. 1979. Respiratory adaptations of Sacramento blackfish, *Orthodon microlepidotus* (Ayres), for hypoxia. *Comp. Biochem. Physiol.* 63A:411–415.

CECH, J.J., Jr., and WOHLSCHLAG, D.E. 1973. Respiratory responses of the striped mullet, *Mugil cephalus* L., to hypoxic conditions. *J. Fish Biol.* 5:421–428.

CECH, J.J., Jr., and WOHLSCHLAG, D.E. 1975. Summer growth depression in the striped mullet, *Mugil cephalus* L. *Contr. Mar. Sci.* 19:91–100.

CECH, J.J. and WOHLSCHLAG, D.E. 1981. Seasonal patterns of respiration, gill ventilation, and hematological characteristics in the striped mullet, *Mugil cephalus*, L. *Bull. Mar. Sci.* 31(in press).

CHANCE, R.E., MERTZ, E.T., and HALVER, J.E. 1964. Nutrition of salmonoid fishes, XII. Isoleucine, leucine, valine and phenylalanine requirements of chinook salmon and interrelations between isoleucine and leucine for growth. *J. Nutr.* 83:177–185.

CHAO, L.N., and MUSICK, J.A. 1977. Life history, feeding habits, and functional morphology of juvenile sciaenid fishes in the York River estuary, Virginia. *NOAA Fish. Bull.* 75(4):657–702.

CHEN, L., and MARTINICH, R.L. 1975. Pheromonal stimulation and metobolite inhibition of ovulation in zebrafish *Brachydanio rerio. NOAA Fish. Bull.* 73(4):889–894.

CHERRY, D.S., and GUTHRIE, R.K. 1975. Significance of detritus or detritus-associated invertebrates to fish production in a new impoundment. *J. Fish. Res. Bd. Canada* 32(10):1799–1804.

CHESLEY, L.C. 1934. The concentrations of proteases, amylase and lipase in certain marine fishes. *Biol. Bull.* 66:133–144.

CLARK, E., and GEORGE, A. 1979. Toxic soles, *Pardachirus marmoratus* from the Red Sea and *P. pavonius* from Japan, with notes on other species. *Env. Biol. Fish* 4(2):103–123.

CLARKE, T.A., and WAGNER, P.J. 1976. Vertical distribution and other aspects of the ecology of certain mesopelagic fishes taken near Hawaii. *NOAA Fish. Bull.* 74(3):635–645.

COHEN, D.M. 1970. How many recent fishes are there? *Proc. Calif. Acad. Sci.* 37(17):341–346.

COHEN, D.M., and NIELSEN, J.G. 1978. Guide to the identification of genera of the fish order Ophidiiformes with a tentative classification of the order. *NOAA Tech. Rept. NMFS Circ.* 417:1–72.

COLBY, P.J. 1971. Alewife dieoffs; why do they occur? *Ambios* 4(2):18–27.

COLE, L.C. 1954. The population consequences of life history phenomena. *Q. Rev. Biol.* 29:103–137.

COLLETTE, B.B., and EARLE, S.A., eds. 1972. Results of the Tektite Program: ecology of coral reef fishes. *Bull. Los Angeles Co. Nat. Hist. Mus.* 14. 180 pp.

COLT, J., and TCHOBANOGLOUS, G. 1978. Chronic exposure of channel catfish, *Ictalurus punctatus*, to ammonia: effects on growth and survival. *Aquaculture* 15:353–372.

COMPAGNO, L.J.V. 1973. Interrelationships of living elasmobranchs. Pages 15–62 *in* P.H. Greenwood, R.S. Miles, and C. Patterson, eds. *Interrelationships of fishes.* New York: Academic Press.

COMPAGNO, L.J.V. 1977. Phyletic relationships of living sharks and rays. *Amer. Zool.* 17(2):303–322.

COMPAGNO, L.J.V. 1979. Coelacanths: shark relatives or bony fishes? *Occ. Pap. Calif. Acad. Sci.* 134:45–52.

CONNELL, J.R. 1978. Diversity in tropical rain forests and coral reefs. *Science* 199:1302–1310.

COPELAND, B.J., and BECHTEL, T.J. 1974. Some environmental limits of six Gulf coast estuarine organisms. *Cont. Mar. Sci.* 18:169–204.

COPELAND, B.J., and NIXON, S. W. 1974. Hypersaline lagoons. Pages 312–330 *in* H.T. Odum et al., eds. *Coastal ecological systems of the United States.* Washington, D.C.: The Conservation Foundation.

COPELAND, B.J., and BECHTEL, T.J. 1974. Some environmental limits of six Gulf coast estuarine organisms. Cont. Mar. Sci. 18:169–204.

COULTER, G.W. 1976. The biology of *Lates* species (Nile perch) in Lake Tanganyika, and the status of the pelagic fishery for *Lates* species and *Luciolates stappersii. J. Fish Biol.* 9:235–259.

COURTNEY, W.R., SAHLMAN, H.F., MILEY, W.W., and HERRMA, D.J. 1974. Exotic fishes in fresh and brackish waters of Florida. *Biol. Cons.* 6(4):292–302.

CRACRAFT, J. 1974. Continental drift and vertebrate distribution. *Ann. Rev. Ecol., Syst.* 215–261 pp.

CRAWSHAW, L.I., and HAMMEL, H.T. 1971. Behavioral thermoregulation in two species of antarctic fish. *Life Sci.* 10(17)1009–1020.

CROIZAT, L. 1958. *Panbiogeography.* Caracas: privately published. 1973 pp.

CROIZAT, L., NELSON, G., and ROSEN, D.E. 1974. Centers of origin and related concepts. *Syst. Zool.* 23(2):265–287.

CRONIN, L.E., and MANSUETI, A.J. 1971. The biology of the estuary. Pages 14–39 in P.A. Douglas and R.H. Stroud, eds. *A symposium on the biological significance of estuaries.* Washington, D.C.: Sport Fish. Inst.

CUMMINS, K.W. 1972. What is a river? a zoological description. Pages 33–52 in R.T. Oglesby et al., eds. *River ecology and man.* New York: Academic Press.

CUSHING, D.H. 1968. *Fisheries biology: a study in population dynamics.* Madison: Univ. Wisc. Press. 200 pp.

CUSHING, D.H. 1978. Biology of fishes of the pelagic community. Pages 317–340 in D.H. Cushing and J.J. Walsh, eds. *The ecology of the seas.* Philadelphia: Saunders.

CUTHBERT, A.W., and MAETZ, J. 1972. The effects of calcium and magnesium on sodium fluxes through gills of *Carassius auratus. J. Physiol.* 221:633–643.

DAHLBERG, M.D., and ODUM, E.P. 1970. Annual cycles of species occurrence, abundance, and diversity in Georgia estuarine fish populations. *Amer. Midl. Nat.* 83(2):382–392.

DALE, G. 1978. Money-in-the-bank: a model for coral reef fish coexistence. *Env. Biol. Fish* 3(1):103–108.

D'AMICO MARTELL, A.L., and CECH, J.J., Jr. 1978. Peripheral vascular resistance in the gills of the winter flounder *Pseudopieuronectes americanus. Comp. Biochem. Physiol.* 59A:419–423.

DANIELS, R.A. 1978. Nesting behavior of *Harpagifer bispinis* in Arthur Harbour. Antarctic Peninsula. *J. Fish Biol.* 12:465–474.

DANIELS, R.A. 1980. *Aspects of the biology of Antarctic fishes.* Unpublished Ph.D. thesis, Univ. Calif., Davis. 78 pp.

DANIELS, R.A. and MOYLE, P.B. 1978. Biology, distribution, and status of *Cottus asperrimus* in the Pit River Drainage, Northeastern California. *Copeia* 1978(4):673–679.

DARLINGTON, P.J. 1957. *Zoogeography: the geographical distribution of animals.* New York: Wiley. 673 pp.

DARNELL, R.M. 1961. Trophic spectrum of an estuarine community, based on studies of Lake Pontchartrain, Louisiana. *Ecology* 43(3):553–568.

DARNELL, R.M. 1967. Organic detritus in relation to the estuarine ecosystem. Pages 376–382 in G.R. Lauff, ed. *Estuaries.* AAAS Publ. 83.

DARNELL, R.M., and MEIEROTTO, R.R. 1962. Determination of feeding chronology in fishes. *Trans. Amer. Fish. Soc.* 92:313–320.

DAVENPORT, H.W. 1974. The AC of acid-base chemistry. 6th ed. Chicago: Univ. Chicago Press. 124 pp.

DAVIS, G.E., and WARREN, C.E. 1965. Trophic relations of a sculpin in laboratory stream communities. *J. Wildl. Manag.* 29:846–871.

DAVIS, J.C. 1970. Estimation of circulation time in the rainbow trout, *Salmo gairdneri. J. Fish. Res. Bd. Canada* 27:1860–1863.

DAVIS, R.M. 1973. *Benthic macroinvertebrates and fish populations in Maryland streams influenced by acid mine drainage.* Univ. Maryland Nat. Res. Inst. Contr. 528. 103 pp.

DAXBOECK, C., and HOLETON, G.F. 1978. Oxygen receptors in the rainbow trout, *Salmo gairdneri. Can. J. Zool.* 56:1254–1259.

DAY, D.S., and PEARCY, W.G. 1968. Species associations of benthic fishes on the continental shelf and slope off Oregon. *J. Fish. Res. Bd. Canada* 25(12):

2665–2675.

DAYTON, P.K., and HESSLER, R.R. 1972. Role of biological disturbance in maintaining diversity in the deep-sea. *Deep-sea Res.* 19:199–208.

DEACON, J.E., and MINCKLEY, W.L. 1974. Desert fishes. Pages 385–488 *in* R.W. Brown, ed. *Desert biology.* Vol. 2. New York: Academic Press.

DEACON, J.E. and 24 others. 1979. Fishes of North America endangered, threatened, or of special concern: 1979. *Fisheries* 4(2):29–44.

DEAN, B. 1895. *Fishes, living and fossil.* New York: Macmillan. 300 pp.

DELL, R.K. 1972. Antarctic benthos. *Adv. Mar. Biol.* 10:1–216.

DeMARTINI, E.E. 1969. A correlative study of the ecology and comparative feeding mechanism morphology of the Embiotocidae (surf perches) as evidence of the family's adaptive radiation into available ecological niches. *Wassman J. Biol.* 27(2):177–247.

DENTON, E.J., and SHAW, T.J. 1963. The visual pigments of some deep-sea elasmobranchs. *J. Mar. Biol. Assoc. U. K.* 43:65–70.

DENTON, E.J., and WARREN, F.J. 1956. Visual pigments of deep-sea fish. *Nature* 178:1059.

DeRENZIS, G., and MAETZ, J. 1973. Studies on the mechanism of chloride absorption by the goldfish gill: relation with acid-base regulation. *J. Exp. Biol.* 59:339–358.

DeVLAMING, V.L. 1972a. The effects of temperature and photoperiod on reproductive cycling in the estuarine gobiid fish, *Gillichthys mirabilis. NOAA Fish. Bull.* 70:1137–1152.

DeVLAMING, V.L. 1972b. Reproductive cycling in the estuarine gobiid fish, *Gillichthys mirabilis. Copeia* (2):278–291.

DeVLAMING, V.L. 1972c. The role of the endocrine system in temperature-controlled reproductive cycling in the estuarine gobiid fish, *Gillichthys mirabilis. Comp. Biochem. Physiol.* 41A:697–713.

DeVRIES, A.L. 1970. Freezing resistance in Antarctic fishes. Pages 320–328 *in* M.W. Holdgate, ed. *Antarctic ecology,* I. New York: Academic Press.

DeVRIES, A.L. and WOHLSCHLAG, D.E. 1969. Freezing resistance in some Antarctic fishes. *Science.* 163:1073–1075.

DEWEES, C.M. and GOTSHALL, D.W. 1974. An experimental artificial reef in Humboldt Bay, California. *Calif. Fish, Game.* 60(3):109–167.

DeWILDE, M.A., and HOUSTON, A.H. 1967. Hematological aspects of the thermoacclimatory process in rainbow trout, *Salmo gairdneri. J. Fish. Res. Bd. Canada* 24:2267–2281.

DeWITT, F.A., and CAILLIET, G.M. 1972. Feeding habits of two bristlemouth fishes, *Cyclothone acclinidens* and *C. signata* (Gonostomatidae). *Copeia* 1972 (4):868–871.

DeWITT, H.H. 1971. *Coastal and deep-water benthic fishes of the Antarctic.* Amer. Geogr. Soc. Antarctic Map Folio Series 15. 10 pp.

DIJKGRAAF, S. 1962. The functioning and significance of the lateral-line organs. *Biol. Rev.* 38:51–105.

DIJKGRAAF, S., and KALMIJN, A.J. 1963. Untersuchungen über di Funktion der Lorenzinischen Ampullen an Haifischen. *Z. Vgl. Physiol.* 47:438–456.

DIZON, A.E., HORRALL, R.M., and HASLER, A.D. 1973. Long-term olfactory "memory" in coho salmon, *Oncorhynchus kisutch. NOAA Fish. Bull.* 71: 315–317.

DOBBS, G.H., LIN, Y., and DeVRIES, A.L. 1974. Aglomerularism in Antarctic fish. *Science* 185:793–794.

DOBZHANSKY, T., AYALA, F.J., STEBBINS, G.L., and VALENTINE, J.W. 1977. *Evolution.* San Francisco: Freeman.

DONALDSON, E.M., FAGERLUND, U.H.M., HIGGS, D.A. and McBRIDE, J.R. 1979. Hormonal enhancement of growth. Pages 455–597 *in* W.S. Hoar, D.J.

Randall, and J.R. Brett. *Fish Physiology.* Vol. 9. New York: Academic Press.

DOOLEY, J.K. 1972. Fishes associated with the pelagic *Sargassum* complex, with a discussion of the *Sargassum* community. *Contr. Mar. Sci.* 16:1–32.

DOUGLAS, E.L., FRIEDL, W.A., and PICKWELL, G.V. 1976. Fishes in oxygen-minimum zones: blood oxygenation characteristics. *Science* 191:957–959.

DRUMMOND, R.A., SPOOR, W.A., and OLSON, G.F. 1973. Some short-term indicators of sublethal effects of copper on brook trout, *Salvelinus fontinalis. J. Fish. Res. Bd. Canada* 30:698–701.

DUNBAR, M.J. 1968. *Ecological development in polar regions.* Englewood Cliffs, N.J.: Prentice-Hall. 118 pp.

DUMAN, J.G., and DeVRIES, A.L. 1974a. Freezing resistance in winter flounder *Pseudopleuronectes americanus. Nature* 247:237–238.

DUMAN, J.G., and DeVRIES, A.L. 1974b. The effects of temperature and photoperiod on antifreeze production in cold water fishes. *J. Exp. Zool.* 190:89–97.

DURBIN, A.G., and DURBIN, E.G. 1975. Grazing rates of the Atlantic menhaden *Brevoortia tyrannus* as a function of particle size and concentration. *Mar. Biol.* 33:265–277.

EATON, J.W., KLOPIN, C.F., and SWOFFORD, H.S. 1973. Chlorinated urban water: a cause of dialysis-induced hemolytic anemia. *Science* 181:463–464.

EBELING, A.W., and CAILLIET, G.M. 1974. Mouth size and predator strategy of midwater fishes. *Deep-sea Res.* 21:959–968.

ECHELLE, A.A., and SCHNELL, Gary D. 1976. Factor analysis of species associations among fishes of the Kiamichi River, Oklahoma. *Trans. Amer. Fish. Soc.* 105(2):17–31.

EDDY, F.B. 1971. Blood gas relationships in the rainbow trout *Salmo gairdneri. J. Fish. Res. Bd. Can.* 24:2267–2281.

EDDY, F.B. 1973. Oxygen dissociation curves of the blood of the tench, *Tinca tinca. J. Exp. Biol.* 58:281–283.

EDDY, S., MOYLE, J.B., and UNDERHILL, J.C. 1963. The fish fauna of the Mississippi River above St. Anthony Falls as related to the effectiveness of this falls as a migration barrier. *J. Minn. Acad. Sci.* 30(2):111–115.

EDDY, S., and UNDERHILL, J.C. 1978. *How to know the freshwater fishes.* Dubuque: W.C. Brown. 215 pp.

EHRENFELD, D.W. 1976. The conservation of nonresources. *Amer. Sci.* 64: 648–656.

EHRENFELD, D.W. 1978. *The arrogance of humanism.* New York: Oxford.

EHRLICH, P.R. 1975. The population biology of coral reef fishes. *Ann. Rev. Ecol. Syst.* pp. 211–247.

EHRLICH, P.R., and EHRLICH, A.H. 1973. Coevolution; heterotypic schooling in Caribbean reef fishes. *Amer. Nat.* 107:157–160.

EHRLICH, P.R., TALBOT, F.H., RUSSELL, B.C., and ANDERSON, G.R.V. 1977. The behavior of chaetodontid fishes with special reference to Lorenz's "poster colouration" hypothesis. *J. Zool. Soc.* (London) 183:213–228.

EIBL-EIBESFELDT, J. 1965. *Land of a thousand atolls.* New York: World Publ. Co. 194 pp.

EISLER, R. 1965. Erythrocyte counts and hemoglobin content in nine species of marine teleosts. *Chesapeake Sci.* 6:119–120.

EKMAN, S. 1953. Zoogeography of the sea. London: Sedgewick and Jackson. 417 pp.

ELLIS, A.E. 1977. The leucocytes of fish: a review. *J. Fish Biol.* 11:453–491.

ELTON, C.S. 1958. *The ecology of invasions by animals and plants.* London: Methuen. 181 pp.

EMERY, A.R. 1973. Preliminary comparisons of day and night habits of freshwater fish in Ontario lakes. *J. Fish. Res. Bd. Canada* 30:761–774.

ENDLER, J.A. 1977. Geographic variation, speciation, and clines. *Princeton Univ.*

Mono. in Pop. Biol. 10:1–246.

ENDLER, J.A. 1978. A predator's view of animal color patterns. Pages 319–364 *in* M.K. Hecht, W.C. Steere, and B. Wallace, eds. *Evolutionary biology.* Vol. 11. New York: Plenum Press.

ENSOR, D.M., and BALL, J.N. 1972. Prolactin and osmoregulation in fishes. *Fed. Proc.* 31:1615–1623.

ERMAN, D.C. 1973. Upstream changes in fish populations following impoundment of Sagehen Creek, California. *Trans. Amer. Fish. Soc.* 102(3):626–629.

EVANS, D.H. 1967a. Sodium, chloride and water balance of the intertidal teleost, *Xiphister atropurpureus.* 1. Regulation of plasma concentration and body water content. *J. Exp. Biol.* 47:513–518.

EVANS, D.H. 1975. Ionic exchange mechanisms in fish gills. *Comp. Biochem. Physiol.* 51A:491–495.

EVANS, D.H. 1977. Further evidence for Na/NH_4 exchange in marine teleost fish. *J. Exp. Biol.* 70:213–220.

EZZAT, A.A., SHABANA, M.B., and FARGHALY, A.M. 1973. Studies on the blood characteristics of *Tilapia zilli* (Gervais). 1. Blood cells. *J. Fish Biol.* 6:1–12.

FÄNGE, R. 1968. The formation of eosinophilic granulocytes in the esophogeal lympomyeloid tissue in the elasmobranchs. *Acta Zool. Stockh.* 49:155–161.

FÄNGE, R. 1976. Gas exchange in the swimbladder. Pages 189–211 *in* G.M. Hughes, ed. *Respiration of amphibious vertebrates.* London: Academic Press.

FARMER, G.J., and BEAMISH, F.W.H. 1969. Oxygen consumption of *Tilapia nilotica* in relation to swimming speed and salinity. *J. Fish. Res. Bd. Canada* 26:2807–2821.

FAY, R.R., KENDALL, J.I., POPPER, A.N. and TESTER, A.L. 1974. Vibration detection by the macula neglecta of sharks. *Comp. Biochem. Physiol.* 47A:1235–1240.

FEDUCCIA, A., and SLAUGHTER, B.H. 1974. Sexual dimorphism in skates (Rajidae) and its possible role in differential niche utilization. *Evolution* 28(4):164–168.

FELDMETH, C.R., and JENKINS, T.M., Jr. 1973. An estimate of the energy expenditure by rainbow trout (*Salmo gairdneri*) in a small mountain stream. *J. Fish. Res. Bd. Canada* 30:1755–1759.

FERGUSON, H.W. 1976. The ultrastructure of plaice leucocytes. *J. Fish Biol.* 8:139–142.

FERRIS, S.D., and WHITT, G.S. 1978. Phylogeny of tetraploid catostomid fishes, based on the loss of duplicate gene expression. *Syst. Zool.* 27(2):189–206.

FINE, M.L., WINN, H.E., and OLLA, B.L. 1977. Communication in fishes. Pages 472–518 *in* T.A. Sebeok, ed. *How animals communicate.* Terre Haute: Indiana Univ. Press.

FINN, J.P., and NIELSON, N.O. 1971. Inflammatory response in rainbow trout. *J. Fish Biol.* 3:463–478.

FISHER, R.A. 1930. *The genetical theory of natural selection.* New York: Dover Books.

FITCH, J.E., and LAVENBERG, R.J. 1968. *Deep-water fishes of California.* Berkeley: Univ. Calif. Press. 155 pp.

FITTKAU, E.J. 1970. Role of caimans in the nutrient regime of mouth-lakes of Amazon affluents (an hypothesis). *Biotropica* 2(2):138–142.

FITZSIMMONS, J.M. 1972. A revision of two genera of goodeid fishes (Cyprinodontiformes, Osteichthyes) from the Mexican Plateau. *Copeia* 1972(4):728–756.

FORNEY, J.L. 1974. Interactions between yellow perch abundance, walleye predation, and survival of alternate prey in Oneida Lake, New York. *Trans. Amer. Fish. Soc.* 103(1):15–24.

FORREST, J.N., SILVA, P., EPSTEIN, A., and EPSTEIN, F.H. 1973. Effect of rectal gland extirpation on plasma sodium in the spiny dogfish. *Bull. Mt. Des. Biol. Lab.* 13:41–42.

FORSTER, R.P., and BERGLUND, F. 1956. Osmotic diuresis and its effect on total electrolyte distribution in plasma and urine of the aglomerular teleost, *Lophius americanus. J. Gen. Physiol.* 39:349–359.

FOURIE, F. LeR., and HATTINGH, J. 1976. A seasonal study of the haematology of carp (*Cyprinus carpio*) from a locality in the Transvaal, South Africa. *Zool. Africana.* 11:75–80.

FOX, D.L. 1978. *Animal biochromes and structural colors.* Berkeley: Univ. Calif. Press,

FREADMAN, M.A. 1979. Role partitioning of swimming musculature of striped bass, *Morone saxatilis* Walbaum and bluefish, *Pomatomus saltatrix* L. *J. Fish Biol.* 15:417–423.

FREY, D.G. 1969. A limnological reconnaisance of Lake Lanao. *Verh. int. Verein. Limnol.* 17:1090–1102.

FRICKE, H.W. 1970. Ecological and ethological field observations on colonies of the garden eels *Gorgasia sillneri* and *Taenioconger hassi* (in German). *Zeit. Tierpysch.* 27(9): 1076–1099.

FRYER, G., and ILES, T.D. 1972. *The cichlid fishes of the Great Lakes of Africa.* Edinburgh: Oliver and Boyd. 641 pp.

GANNON, B.J., and BURNSTOCK, G. 1969. Excitatory adrenergic innervation of the fish heart. *Comp. Biochem. Physiol.* 29:765–773.

GARDNER, G.R., and YEVICH, P.P. 1969. Studies on the blood morphology of three estuarine cyprinodontiform fishes. *J. Fish. Res. Bd. Canada* 26:433–447.

GAREY, W.F. 1962. Cardiac response of fishes in asphyxic environments. *Biol. Bull.* 122:362–368.

GARMAN, S. 1913. *The Plagiostoma (sharks, skates, and rays).* Mem. Mus. Comp. Zool. Harvard 36. 528 pp.

GASCON, D., and LEGGETT, W.C. 1977. Distribution, abundance, and resource utilization of littoral fishes in response to a nutrient/production gradient in Lake Memphremagog. *J. Fish. Res. Bd. Canada* 34(8):1105–1117.

GEE, J.H. 1974. Behavioral and developmental plasticity of buoyancy in the long-nose *Rhinichthyes cataractae*, blacknose, *R. atratulus* (Cyprinidae) dace. *J. Fish. Res. Bd. Canada* 31(1):35–41.

GEE, J.H., and NORTHCOTE, T.G. 1963. Comparative ecology of two sympatric species of dace (*Rhinichthys*) in the Fraser River System, British Columbia. *J. Fish. Res. Bd. Canada* 20(1):105–118.

GERALD, J.W. 1971. Sound production during courtship in six species of sunfish (Centrarchidae). *Evolution* 25:75–87.

GERKING, S.D. 1966. Annual growth cycle, growth potential and growth compensation in the bluegill sunfish in northern Indiana lakes. *J. Fish. Res. Bd. Can.* 23:1923–1956.

GERY, J. 1969. The fresh-water fishes of South America. Pages 828–848 *in* E. Fittkau et al., eds. *Biogeography and ecology in South America.* Monogr. Biol. 19(2). The Hague: W. Junk.

GIBSON, R.N. 1969. The biology and behaviour of littoral fish. *Oceangr. Mar. Biol. Ann. Rev.* 7:367–410.

GILBERT, C.R. 1977. Status of the western south Atlantic apogonid fish *Apogon americanus*, with remarks on other Brazilian Apogonidae. *Copeia* 1977(1):25–32.

GILBERT, P.W., MATHEWSON, R.F., and RALL, D.P., eds. 1967. *Sharks, skates, and rays.* Baltimore: Johns Hopkins Press. 624 pp.

GILES, M.A., and VANSTONE, W.E. 1976. Ontogenetic variation in the multiple hemoglobin of coho salmon (*Oncorhynchus kisutch*) and the effect of environmental factors on their expression. *J. Fish. Res. Bd. Canada* 33:1144–1149.

GILLEN, R.G., and RIGGS, A. 1971. The hemoglobins of a fresh-water teleost,

Cichlasoma cyanoguttatum (Baird and Girard). I. The effects of phosphorylated organic compounds upon the oxygen equilibria. *Comp. Biochem. Physiol.* 38B: 585–595.

GILLESPIE, A.L. 1898. Changes in the digestive activity of the secretions of the alimentary canal of the salmon in different conditions. *Fish. Bd. Scotland Rep. of Investig. Life Hist. Salmon* 4:23–35.

GOLDMAN, B., and TALBOT, F.H. 1976. Aspects of the ecology of coral reef fishes. Pages 125–153 *in* D.A. Jones and R. Endean, eds. *Biology and geology of coral reefs.* Vol. 3(2). New York: Academic Press.

GOLDSTEIN, L., JANSSEN, P.A., and FORSTER, R.P. 1967. Lungfish *Neoceratodus forsteri:* activities of ornithine-urea cycle and enzymes. *Science* 157: 316–317.

GOODE, G.B., and BEAN, T.M. 1895. *Oceanic ichthyology.* Smithson. Inst. Spec. Bull. 2. 540 pp.

GORDON, B.L. 1977. The secret lives of fishes. New York: Grosset & Dunlap. 305 pp.

GORLICK, D.L., ATKINS, P.O., and LOSEY, G.S., Jr. 1978. Cleaning stations as water holes, garbage dumps, and sites for the evolution of reciprocal altruism. *Amer. Nat.* 112:341–353.

GOSLINE, W.A. 1966. The limits of the fish family Serranidae, with notes on other lower percoids. *Proc. Calif. Acad. Sci.* 33(6):91–112.

GOSLINE, W.A. 1971. *Functional morphology and classification of teleostean fishes.* Honolulu: Univ. Hawaii Press. 208 pp.

GOSLINE, W.A. 1978. Unbranched dorsal fin rays and classification in the fish family Cyprinidae. *Occ. Pap. Mus. Zool., Univ. Mich.* 634:1–21.

GRAHAM, J.B. 1971. Temperature tolerances of some closely related tropical Atlantic and Pacific fish species. *Science* 172:861–863.

GRANT, P.R. 1972. Convergent and divergent character displacement. *Biol. J. Linn. Soc.* 4:39–68.

GRASSLE, J.F., SANDERS, H.L., HESSLER, R.R., ROWE, G.T., and McLELLAN, T. 1975. Pattern and zonation; a study of the bathylmegafauna using the research submersible *Alvin. Deep-sea Res.* 22:457–481.

GRAYTON, B.D., and BEAMISH, F.W.H. 1977. Effects of feeding frequency on food intake, growth and body composition of rainbow trout (*Salmo gairdneri*). *Aquaculture* 11:159–172.

GREANEY, G.S., and POWERS, D.A. 1978. Allosteric modifiers of fish hemoglobin: in vitro and in vivo studies of the effect of ambient oxygen and pH on erythrocyte ATP concentrations. *J. Exp. Zool.* 203:339–349.

GREEN, J. 1968. *The biology of estuarine animals.* Seattle: Univ. Wash. Press. 401 pp.

GREEN, J.M. 1971. High tide movements and homing behavior of the tidepool sculpin *Oligocottus maculosus. J. Fish. Res. Bd. Canada* 28:383–389.

GREENE, C.W. 1926. The physiology of the spawning salmon. *Physiol. Rev.* 6:201–241.

GREENWOOD, P.H. 1976. Fish fauna of the Nile. Pages 127–141 *in* J. Rzoska, ed. *The Nile, biology of an ancient river.* The Hague: W. Junk.

GREENWOOD, P.H. 1977. Notes on the anatomy and classification of elopomorph fishes. *Bull. Brit. Mus. (Nat. Hist.) Zool.* 32(4):65–102.

GREENWOOD, P.H., MILES, R.S., and PATTERSON, C., eds. 1973. Interrelationships of fishes. New York: Academic Press. 536 pp.

GREENWOOD, P.H., ROSEN, D.E., WEITZMAN, S.H., and MYERS, G.S. 1966. Phyletic studies on teleostean fishes, with a provisional classification of living forms. *Bull. Amer. Mus. Nat. Hist.* 131(4):341–455.

GREGORY, W.K. 1933. Fish skulls. *Trans. Amer. Philosoph. Soc.* 23(2):75–481.

GRIGG, G.C. 1969. Temperature-induced changes in the oxygen equilibruim curve of the blood of the brown bullhead, *Ictalurus nebulosus. Comp. Biochem. Physiol.* 28:1203–1223.

GRIGG, G.C. 1974. Respiratory function of blood of fishes. Pages 331–368 *in* N. Florkin and B.T. Scheer, eds. *Chemical zoology.* Vol. 8. New York: Academic Press.

GROSSMAN, G. 1979. Demographic characteristics of an intertidal bay goby (*Lepidogobius lepidus*). *Environ. Biol. Fish* 4:207–218.

GROSSMAN, G. 1980. Food, fights, and burrows: the adaptive significance of intraspecific aggression in the bay goby (Pisces: Gobiidae). *Oecologia* 45:261–261.

GROSSMAN, G., COFFIN, R., and MOYLE, P. 1980. Feeding ecology of the bay goby (Pisces: Gobiidae). Effect of behavioral, ontogenetic, and temporal variation on diet. *J. Exp. Mar. Biol. & Ecol.* 44:47–59.

GROTHE, D.R., and EATON, J.W. 1975. Chlorine-induced mortality in fish. *Trans. Am. Fish. Soc.* 104:800–802.

GRUBER, S.H. 1977. The visual system of sharks: adaptations and capability. *Amer. Zool.* 17:453–470.

GRUBER, S.H., and COHEN, J.L. 1978. Visual system of the elasmobranchs: state of the art 1960–1975. Pages 391–417 *in* E.S. Hodgson and R.F. Mathewson, eds. *Sensory biology of sharks, skakes and rays.* Washington, D.C.: Off. Naval Res. Publ.

GRUBER, S.H., GULLEY, R.L., and BRANDON, J. 1975a. Duplex retina in seven elasmobranch species. *Bull. Mar. Sci.* 25:353–358.

GRUBER, S.H., HAMASAKI, D.I., and DAVIS, B.L. 1975b. Window to the epiphysis in sharks. *Copeia* (2):378–380.

GULLAND, J.A. ed. 1977. *Fish population dynamics.* New York: Wiley. 372 pp.

GUNTER, G. 1957. Predominance of the young among marine fishes found in fresh water. *Copeia* 1957(1):13–16.

GUPPY, M., and HOCHACHKA, P.W. 1978. Skipjack tuna white muscle: a blueprint for the integration of aerobic and anaerobic carbohydrate metabolism. Pages 175–181 *in* G.D. Sharp and A.E. Dizon, eds. The physiological ecology of tunas. New York: Academic Press.

HAAS, R. 1976a. Sexual selection in *Nothobranchius guentheri* (Pisces: Cyprinodontidae). *Evolution* 20:614–622.

HAAS, R. 1976b. Behavioral biology of the annual killifish, *Nothobranchius guentheri. Copeia* 1976(1):80–91.

HAEDRICH, R.L., and HAEDRICH, S.O. 1974. A seasonal survey of the fishes in the Mystic River, a polluted estuary in downtown Boston, Massachusetts. *Est., Coast. Mar. Sci.* 2(1):59–73.

HAEDRICH, R.L., ROWE, G.T., and POLLONI, P.T. 1975. Zonation and faunal composition of epibenthic populations on the continental slope south of New England. *J. Mar. Res.* 33(3):191–212.

HAGEN, D.W. 1967. Isolating mechanisms in threespine sticklebacks (*Gasterosteus*). *J. Fish. Res. Bd. Canada* 24:1637–1692.

HAGEN, D.W., and McPHAIL, J.D. 1970. The species problem within *Gasterosteus aculeatus* on the Pacific coast of North America. *J. Fish. Res. Bd. Canada* 27:147–155.

HAHN, G. 1960. Ferntastsinn and Stromungssinn beim augenlosen Hohlenfisch *Anoptichthys jordani* Hubbs and Innes im Vergleich zu einigen Teleosteern. *Naturwissenschaften.* 47:611.

HALL, C. 1972. Migration and metabolism in a stream ecosystem. *Ecology* 53 (4):585–604.

HALL, F.G. 1929. The influence of varying oxygen tensions upon the rate of oxygen consumption in marine fishes. *Amer. J. Physiol.* 88:212–218.

HALL, F.G., and McCUTCHEON, F.H. 1938. The affinity of hemoglobin for oxygen in marine fishes. *J. Cell. Comp. Physiol.* 11:205–212.

HALL, G.E., ed. 1971. *Reservoir fisheries and limnology.* Amer. Fish. Soc. Spec. Pub. 8. 511 pp.

HALSTEAD, B.W. 1967. *Poisonous and venemous marine animals of the world* Vols. 2, 3: Vertebrates. Washington, D.C.: U.S. Govt. Printing Off.

HALSTEAD, L.B. 1968. *The pattern of vertebrate evolution.* San Francisco: W.A. Freeman. 209 pp.

HALVER, J.E. 1957. Nutrition of salmonoid fishes. IV. An amino acid test diet for chinook salmon. *J. Nutr.* 62:245–254.

HALVER, J.E. 1972. The vitamins. Pages 29–103 *in* J.E. Halver, ed. *Fish nutrition.* New York: Academic Press.

HALVER, J.E. 1976. Formulating practical diets for fish. *J. Fish. Res. Bd. Canada* 33:1032–1039.

HALVER, J.E., DeLONG, D.C., and MERTZ, E.T. 1957. Nutrition of salmonoid fishes. V. Classification of essential amino acids for chinook salmon. *J. Nutr.* 63:95–105.

HALVER, J.E., and SHANKS, W.E. 1960. Nutrition of salmonoid fishes. VIII. Indispensable amino acids for sockeye salmon. *J. Nutr.* 72:340–346.

HAMASAKI, D.I., and STRECK, P. 1971. Properties of the epiphysis cerebri of the small spotted dogfish shark, *Scyliorhinus caniculus* L. *Vision Res.* 11:189–198.

HAMILTON, W.J. III. 1973. *Life's color code.* New York: McGraw-Hill. 238 pp.

HANKIN, D.G. 1978. New fluorescent fish scale marker. *Prog. Fish. Cult.* 40:163–164.

HANSEN, K., and HERRING, P.J. 1977. Dual bioluminescent systems in the anglerfish genus *Linophryne* (Pisces: Ceratoidea). *J. Zool.* (London) 182:103–124.

HANSON, D. 1967. *Cardiovascular dynamics and aspects of gas exchange in Chondrichthyes.* Ph.D. thesis, Univ. Wash., Seattle.

HARDEN-JONES, F.R. 1968. *Fish migration.* London: E. Arnold Pub. 325 pp.

HARDER, W. 1975. *Anatomy of fishes.* Pt. *II.* E. Schwelzerbart'sche Verlabsbuchhandling. Stuttgart. 132 pp.

HARDISTY, M.W., and POTTER, I.C., eds. 1971. *The biology of lampreys.* Vols. 1 and 2. New York: Academic Press.

HARRINGTON, R.W. 1961. Oviparous hermaphroditic fish with internal self-fertilization. *Science* 134:1749–1750.

HARRIS, A.J. 1965. Eye movements of the dogfish, *Squalus acanthias* 1. *J. Exp. Biol.* 43:107–130.

HART, J.L. 1973. *Pacific fishes of Canada.* Fish. Res. Bd. Canada Bull. 180. 740 pp.

HARTMAN, G.F. 1965. The role of behavior in the ecology and interaction of underyearling coho salmon (*Oncorhynchus kisutch*) and steelhead trout (*Salmo gairdneri*). *J. Fish. Res. Bd. Canada* 22(4):1035–1081.

HARTMAN, G.F., and GILL, C.A. 1968. Distributions of juvenile steelhead and cutthroat trout (*Salmo gairdneri* and *S. clarki clarki*) within streams in southwestern British Columbia. *J. Fish. Res. Bd. Canada* 25(1):33–48.

HARTMAN, W.L., and BURGNER, R.L. 1972. Limnology and fish ecology of sockeye salmon nursery lakes of the world. *J. Fish. Res. Bd. Canada* 29(6):699–715.

HASLER, A.D. 1966. *Underwater guideposts.* Madison: Univ. Wisc. Press. 155 pp.

HASLER, A.D., HORRALL, R.N., WISBY, W.J., and BRAEMER, W. 1958. Sun orientation and homing in fishes. *Limnol. Oceanogr.* 3(4):353–361.

HASLER, A.D., and SCHOLZ, A.T. 1978. Olfactory imprinting in coho salmon (*Oncorhynchus kisutch*). Pages 356–369 *in* K. Schmid-Koenig and W.T. Keeton, eds. *Animal migration, navigation, and homing.* Berlin: Springer Verlag.

HATTINGH, J., LeROUX FOURIE, F., and VAN VUREN, J.H.J. 1975. The transport of freshwater fish. *J. Fish Biol.* 7:447–449.

HAWKINS, A.D., and RASMUSSEN, K.J. 1978. The calls of gadoid fish. *J. Mar. Biol. Assn. U. K.* 58:891–911.

HAY, D.E., and McPHAIL, J.D. 1975. Mate selection in threespine sticklebacks (*Gasterosteus*). *Can. J. Zool.* 53:441–450.

HAYDEN, J.B., CECH, J.J., Jr. and BRIDGES, D.W. 1975. Blood oxygen dissociation characteristics of the winter flounder, *Pseudopleuronectes americanus* (Walbaum). *J. Fish. Res. Bd. Canada* 32:1539–1544.

HELFMAN, G.S. 1978. Patterns of community structure in fishes: summary and overview. *Env. Biol. Fish.* (3)1:129–148.

HELFMAN, G.S. 1981. The advantage to fishes of hovering in shade. *Copeia* 1981: 392–399.

HENDRICKSON, W.A., LOVE, W.E., and MURRAY, G.C. 1968. Crystal forms of lamprey hemoglobin and crystalline transitions between ligand states. *J. Mol. Biol.* 33:829–842.

HENNIG, W. 1966. *Phylogenetic systematics.* Urbana: Univ. Ill. Press.

HERALD, E.S. 1959. From pipefish to seahorse — a study of phylogenetic relationships. *Proc. Calif. Acad. Sci.* 26(13):465–473.

HERALD, E.S. 1961. *Living fishes of the world.* New York: Doubleday. 304 pp.

HEVESY, G., LOCKNER, D., and SLETTEN, K. 1964. Iron metabolism and erythrocyte formation in fish. *Acta Physiol. Scand.* 60:256–266.

HILDEBRAND, S.F. 1946. *A descriptive catalog of the shore fishes of Peru.* U.S. Nat. Mus. Bull. 189. 530 pp.

HILDEMANN, W.H. 1970. Transplantation immunity in fishes: Agnatha, Chondrichthyes and Osteichthyes. *Transplant. Proc.* 2:253–259.

HILL, L.G. 1969. Feeding and food habits of the spring cavefish, *Chologaster agassizi. Amer. Midl. Nat.* 82(1):110–116.

HINEGARDNER, R., and ROSEN, D.E. 1972. Cellular DNA content and the evolution of teleostean fishes. *Amer. Nat.* 106(951):621–644.

HOAR, W.S. 1976. Smolt transformation: evolution, behavior, and physiology. *J. Fish. Res. Bd. Canada* 33(6):1234–1252.

HOAR, W.S., and RANDALL, D.J., eds. 1969. *Fish physiology.* Vol. 3. New York: Academic Press.

HOBSON, E.S. 1974. Feeding relationships of teleostean fishes on coral reefs in Kona, Hawaii. *NOAA Fish. Bull.* 72(4):915–1031.

HOBSON, E.S. 1975. Feeding patterns among tropical reef fishes. *Amer. Sci.* 63 (4):382–392.

HOBSON, E.S., and CHESS, J.R. 1976. Trophic interactions among fishes and zooplankters near shore at Santa Catalina Island, California. *NOAA Fish. Bull.* 74(3):567–598.

HOCUTT, C.H., and STAUFFER, J.R. 1975. Influence of gradient on the distribution of fishes in Conowingo Creek, Maryland and Pennsylvania. *Ches. Sci.* 16 (1):143–147.

HODGSON, E.S., and MATHEWSON, R.F. 1978. Electrophysiological studies of chemoreception in elasmobranchs. Pages 227–267 *in* E.S. Hodgson, and R.F. Mathewson, eds. *Sensory biology of sharks, skates, and rays.* Washington, D.C.: Naval Res. Publ.

HOESE, H.D., and JONES, R.S. 1963. Seasonality of larger animals in a Texas turtlegrass community. *Publ. Inst. Mar. Sci., Univ. Tex.* 9:37–46.

HOESE, H.D., and MOORE, R.H. 1977. *Fishes of the Gulf of Mexico.* College station: Texas A. & M. Univ. Press. 329 pp.

HOGARTH, P.J. 1973. Immune relations between mother and foetus in the viviparous poeciliid fish, *Xiphophorus helleri* Haeckel. III. Survival of embryos after ectopic transplantation. *J. Fish Biol.* 5:109–113.

HOGMAN, W.J. 1968. Annulus formation of scales of four species of coregonids reared under artificial conditions. *J. Fish. Res. Bd. Canada* 25:2111–2112.

HOLDGATE. M.W., ed. 1970. *Antarctic ecology.* New York: Academic Press. 604 pp.

HOLETON, G.F. 1970. Oxygen uptake and circulation by hemoglobinless Antarctic fish (*Chaenocephalus aceratus* Lonnberg) compared with three red-blooded Antarctic fish. *Comp. Biochem. Physiol.* 34:457–471.

HOLETON, G.F. 1976. Respiratory morphometrics of white and red blooded Antarctic fish. *Comp. Biochem. Physiol.* 54A:215–220.

HOLMES, W.N., and DONALDSON, E.M. 1969. The body compartments and the distribution of electrolytes. Pages 1–89 in W.S. Hoar and D.J. Randall, eds. *Fish physiology.* Vol. 1 New York: Academic Press.

HOPKINS, C.D. 1974. Electric communication in fish. *Amer. Sci.* 62(4):426–437.

HORN, M.H. 1970. The swimbladder as a juvenile organ in stromateiod fishes. *Breviora* 359:1–9.

HORN, M.H. 1972. The amount of space available for marine and freshwater fishes. *NOAA Fish. Bull.* 70(4):1295–1297.

HORN, M.H. 1975. Swimbladder state and structure in relation to behavior and mode of life in stromateoid fishes. *NOAA Fish. Bull.* 73(1):95–109.

HORN, M.H., and ALLEN, L.G. 1978. A distributional analysis of California marine fishes. *J. Biogeography* 1978(5):23–42.

HORN, M.H., GRIMES, P.W., PFLEGER, C.F., and McCLANAHAN, L.L. 1978. Buoyancy function of the enlarged fluid-filled cranium in the deep-sea ophidiid fish *Acanthonus armatus. Mar. Biol.* 46:335–339.

HORN, M.H. and RIGGS, C.D. 1973. Effects of temperature and light on the rate of air breathing of the bowfin, *Amia calva. Copeia* 1973(4):653–657.

HOUSSAY, S.F. 1912. *Forme, puissance, et stabilité des poissons.* Paris: Herman. 372 pp.

HOUSTON, A.H., and CYR, D. 1974. Thermoacclimatory variation in the hemoglobin systems of goldfish (*Carassius auratus*) and rainbow trout (*Salmo gairdneri*). *J. Exp. Biol.* 61:455–461.

HOUSTON, A.H., and DeWILDE, M.A. 1968. Thermoacclimatory variations in the hematology of the common carp, *Cyprinus carpio. J. Exp. Biol.* 49:71–81.

HOUSTON, A.H., and RUPERT, R. 1976. Immediate response of the hemoglobin system of the goldfish, *Carassius auratus,* to temperature change. *Can. J. Zool.* 54:1737–1741.

HOWELL, J.B., BAUMGARDNER, F.W., BONDI, K., and RAHN, H. 1970. Acid-base balance in cold blooded vertebrates as a function of body temperature. *Amer. J. Physiol.* 218:600–605.

HOY, J.B., KAUFMAN, E.E., and O'BERG, A.G. 1972. A large-scale field test of *Gambusia affinis* and Chlorpurifos for mosquito control. *Mosquito News* 32(2):163–171.

HUBBS, C.L. 1955. Hybridization between fish species in nature. *Syst. Zool.* 4:1–20.

HUBBS, C.L. 1964. History of ichthyology in the United States after 1850. *Copeia* 1964(1):42–60.

HUBBS, C.L. 1974. Review of *Marine zoogeography* by J.C. Briggs. *Copeia* 1974 (4):1002–1005.

HUBBS, C.L., and BAILEY, R.M. 1947. Blind catfishes from artesian waters of Texas. *Occ. Pap. Univ. Mich. Mus. Zool.* 499:1–17.

HUBBS, C.L., and HUBBS, L.C. 1932. Apparent parthenogenesis in nature, in a form of fish of hybrid origin. *Science* 76:628–630.

HUBBS, C.L., IWAI, T., and MATSUBARA, K. 1967. External and internal characters, horizontal and vertical distribution, luminescence, and food of the dwarf pelagic shark, *Euprotomicrus bispinatus. Bull. Scripps. Inst. Oceanogr.* 10:1–64.

HUBBS, C.L., and LAGLER, K.F. 1964. *Fishes of the Great Lakes region.* Ann

Arbor: Univ. Mich. Press. 213 pp.

HUBBS, C.L. and MILLER, R.R. 1942. Mass hybridization between two genera of cyprinid fishes in the Mohave Desert, California. *Papers Mich Acad. Sci. Arts., Letters.* 28:343–378.

HUBBS, C.L., and POTTER, I.C. 1971. Distribution, phylogeny, and taxonomy. Pages 1–65 *in* M.W. Hardisty and I.C. Potter, eds. *The biology of lampreys.* Vol. 1. New York: Academic Press.

HUBBS, Clark. 1957. Distributional patterns of Texas freshwater fishes. *Southw. Nat.* 2(2–3):89–104.

HUCKABEE, J.W., GOODYEAR, C.P., and JONES, R.D. 1975. Acid rock in the Great Smokies: unanticipated impact on aquatic biota of road construction in regions of sulphide mineralization. *Trans. Amer. Fish. Soc.* 104(4):677–684.

HUET, M. 1959. Profiles and biology of Western European streams as related to fish management. *Trans. Amer. Fish. Soc.* 88:155–163.

HUGHES, G.M. 1963. *Comparative physiology of verbebrate respiration.* Cambridge: Harvard Univ. Press. 146 pp.

HUGHES, G.M., and GRIMSTONE, A.V. 1965. The fine structure of the secondary lamellae of the gills of *Gadus pollachius. Quart. J. Micro. Sci.* 106:343-353.

HUNTER, J.R., and MITCHELL, C.T. 1966. Association of fishes with flotsam in the offshore waters of Central America. *NOAA Fish. Bull.* 66(1):13–30.

HUTCHINSON, G.E. 1957. *A treatise on limnology.* Vol. 1, Geography, physics, and chemistry. New York: Wiley. 1015 pp.

HYNES, H.B.N. 1970. *The ecology of running water.* Toronto: Univ. Toronto Press. 555 pp.

IDLER, D.R., and BITNERS, I. 1959. Biochemical studies on sockeye salmon during spawning migration. V. Cholesterol, fat, protein and water in the body of the standard fish. *J. Fish. Res. Bd. Canada* 16:235–241.

INGER, R.F., and CHIN, P.K. 1962. The freshwater fishes of North Borneo. *Fieldiana (Zool.)* 45:1–268.

IVLEV, V.S. 1961. *Experimental ecology of the feeding of fishes.* New Haven: Yale Univ. Press. 302 pp.

JANSSENS, P.A., and COHEN, P.P. 1966. Ornithine-urea cycle enzymes in the African lungfish, *Protopterus aethiopicus. Science* 152:358–359.

JARA, Z. 1957. On the morphology and function of the so-called palatal organ in the carp (*Cyprinus carpio* L.) *Preeglad Zoologiczny* 1:110–112.

JARVIK, E. 1977. The systematic position of acanthodian fishes. Pages 199–225 *in* S.M. Andrews, R.S. Miles, and A.D. Walker, eds. *Problems in vertebrate evolution.* Linn. Soc. Lond. Symp. 4.

JAYARAM, K.C. 1974. Ecology and distribution of fresh-water fishes, amphibia, and reptiles. Pages 517-584 *in* M.S. Mani, ed. *Ecology and biogeography of India.* The Hague: W. Junk.

JENKINS, R.E., LACHNER, E.A., and SCHWARTZ, F.J. 1972. Fishes of the central Appalachian drainages: their distribution and dispersal. Pages 43–117 *in* P.C. Holt, ed. *The distribution history of the biota of the southern Appalachians.* Virg. Poly. Inst. Res. Div. Mono 4.

JENKINS, R.M. 1965. Bibliography on reservoir fishery biology in North America. *U.S. Bur. Sport Fish. Wildl. Res. Rept.* 68:1–57.

JENKINS, R.M. 1968. The influence of some environmental factors on standing crop and harvest of fishes in U.S. reservoirs. Pages 298–321 *in* C.E. Lane, ed. *Reservoir fishery resources symposium.* Bethesda, Md.: Amer. Fish. Soc.

JENKINS, R.M. 1975. Black bass crops and species associations in reservoirs. Pages 114–124 *in* H. Clepper, ed. *Black bass biology and management.* Washington, D.C.: Sport Fishing Inst.

JENKINS, R.M., and MORALIS, D.I. 1971. Reservoir sport fishing effort and harvest in relation to environmental variables. Pages 371–384 *in* G.E. Hall, ed. *Res-*

ervoir fisheries and limnology. Amer. Fish Soc. Spec. Publ. 8.

JENKINS, T.M. 1969. Social structure, position choice, and distribution of two trout species (*Salmo trutta* and *Salmo gairdneri*) resident in mountain streams. *Anim. Behav. Monogr.* 2(2):57–123.

JENSEN, A.C. 1966. Life history of the spiny dogfish. *NOAA Fish. Bull.* 65(3): 527–554.

JENSEN, D. 1966. The hagfish. *Sci. Amer.* 214(2):82–90.

JESSEN, H.L. 1973. Interrelationships of actinopterygians and brachiopterygians: evidence from pectoral anatomy. Pages 227–232 *in* P.H. Greenwood, R.S. Miles, and C. Patterson. eds. *Interrelationships of fishes.* London: Academic Press.

JOHANNES, R.E. 1978. Reproductive strategies of coastal marine fishes in the tropics. *Env. Biol. Fish* 3(1):65–84.

JOHANNES, R.E., and LARKIN, P.A. 1961. Competition for food between redside shiners (*Richardsonius balteatus*) and rainbow trout (*Salmo gairdneri*) in two British Columbia lakes. *J. Fish. Res. Bd. Canada* 18(2):203–220.

JOHANSEN, K. 1968. Air-breathing fishes. *Sci. Amer.* 219:102–111.

JOHANSEN, K., and HANSON, D. 1967. Hepatic vein sphincters in elasmobranchs and their significance in controlling hepatic blood flow. *J. Exp. Biol.* 46:195–203.

JOHANSEN, K., and HANSON, D. 1968. Functional anatomy of the hearts of lungfishes and amphibians. *Am. Zool.* 8:191–210.

JOHANSEN, K., LENFANT, C., SCHMIDT-NIELSEN, K., and PETERSON, J.A. 1968. Gas exchange and control of breathing in the electric eel, *Electrophorus electricus. Z. Vergl. Physiol.* 61:137–163.

JOHANSON-SJOBECK, M., and STEVENS, J.D. 1976. Haematological studies on the blue shark, *Prionace glauca* L. *J. Mar. Biol. Assn. U. K.* 56:237–240.

JOHN, K.R. 1964. Survival of fish in intermittent streams of the Chiricahua mountains, Arizona. *Ecology* 45(1):112–119.

JOHNSON, A.G., and HORTON, H.F. 1972. Length-weight relationship, food, habits, parasites, and sex and age determination in the ratfish, *Hydrolagus colliei. NOAA Fish. Bull.* 70(2):421–430.

JOHNSON, D.L., and STEIN, R. A. 1979. *Response of fish to habitat structure in standing water.* N. Cent. Div. Amer. Fish. Soc. Spec. Publ. 6.

JOHNSON, D.S. 1967. Distributional patterns in Malayan freshwater fish. *Ecology* 48:722–730.

JOHNSON, G.B. 1977. Assessing electrophoretic similarity: the problem of hidden heterogeneity. *An. Rev. Ecol. Syst.* 8:309–328.

JOHNSON, L. 1976. Ecology of arctic populations of lake trout, *Salvelinus namaycush*, lake whitefish, *Coregonus clupeaformis*, arctic char, *S. alpinus*, and associated species in unexploited lakes of the Canadian northwest territories. *J. Fish. Res. Bd. Canada* 33(11):2459–2488.

JOHNSON, R.H., and NELSON, D.R. 1973. Agonistic display of the gray reef shark, *Carcharhinus menisorrah*, and its relationship to attacks on man. *Copeia* 1973(1):76–83.

JOHNSON, R.K., and BARNETT, M.A. 1975. An inverse correlation between meristic characters and food supply in mid-water fishes: evidence and possible explanations. *NOAA Fish. Bull.* 73(2):284–298.

JOHNSON, R.K., and GLODEK, G.S. 1975. Two new species of *Evermanella* from the Pacific Ocean, with notes on other midwater species endemic to the Pacific Central or the Pacific Equatorial water masses. *Copeia* 1975(4):715–730.

JONAS, R.E.E., SEHDEV, H.S., and TONLINSON, N. 1962. Blood pH and mortality in rainbow trout (*Salmo gairdneri*) and sockeye salmon (*Oncorhynchus nerka*). *J. Fish. Res. Bd. Canada* 19(4):619–624.

JONES, D., and CLARKE, J. 1977. Annual and long-term fluctuations in the abundance of fish species inhabiting an intertidal mussel bed in Morecambe Bay, Lancashire. *Zool. J. Linn. Soc.* 60(2):117–172.

JONES, E.C. 1971. *Isistius brasiliensis*, a squaloid shark, the probable cause of crater wounds on fishes and cetaceans. *NOAA Fish. Bull.* 69(4):791–798.

JONES, J.R.E. 1964. *Fish and river pollution.* London: Butterworths. 204 pp.

JORDAN, D.S. 1895. The fishes of Sinaloa. *Proc. Calif. Acad. Sci.* 5:378–513.

JORDAN, D.S. 1922. *The days of a man.* Vols. I, II. New York: World Book Co. 1616 pp.

JORDAN, D.S., and EVERMANN, B.W. 1900. *The fishes of North and Middle America.* Bull. U.S. Nat. Mus. 47, parts I–IV. 3313 pp. + 392 plates.

JORDAN, D.S., and EVERMANN, B.W. 1903. The aquatic resources of the Hawaiian Islands. *Bull. U.S. Fish. Comm.* 23:1–765.

JORDAN, D.S., and STARKS, E.C. 1895. The fishes of Puget Sound. *Proc. Calif. Acad. Sci.* 5:785–855.

JORDAN, H.E., and SPEIDEL, C.C. 1930. Blood formation in cyclostomes. *Am. J. Anat.* 46:355–392.

JORDAN, J. 1976. The influence of body weight on gas exchange in the air-breathing fish, *Clarius batrachus. Comp. Biochem. Physiol.* 53A:305–310.

KALMIJN, A.J. 1971. The electric sense of sharks and rays. *J. Exp. Biol.* 55: 371–383.

KALMIJN, A.J. 1974. The detection of electric fields from inanimate and animate sources other than electric organs. Pages 147–200 *in* A. Fessard, ed. *Handbook of sensory physiology.* Vol. 3(3). Berlin: Springer Verlag.

KALMIJN, A.J. 1977. The electric and magnetic sense of sharks, skates, and rays. *Oceanus* 20:45–52.

KALMIJN, A.J. 1978a. Electric and magnetic sensory world of sharks, skates, and rays. Pages 507–528 *in* E.S. Hodgson and R.F. Mathewson, eds. *Sensory biology of sharks, skates, and rays.* Washington, D.C.: Off. Naval Res. Publ.

KALMIJN, A.J. 1978b. Experimental evidence of geomagnetic orientation in elasmobranch fishes. Pages 347–353 *in* K. Schmidt-Koenig and W.T. Keeton, eds. *Animal migration, navigation, and homing.* Berlin: Springer Verlag.

KAMOHARA, R.H. 1964. Revised catalog of fishes of Kochi Prefecture, Japan. *U. S. A. Mar. Biol. Stat.* 11(1):1–99.

KAPOOR, B.G., EVANS, H.E. and PEVZNER, R.A. 1975. The gustatory system in fish. *Adv. Mar. Biol.* 13:53–108.

KAPOOR, B.G., SMIT, H., and VERIGHINA, I.A. 1975. The alimentary canal and digestion in teleosts. *Adv. Mar. Biol.* 13:109–239.

KAVALIERS, M. 1979. Pineal involvement in the control of circadian rhythmicity in the lake chub, *Couesius plumbeus. J. Exp. Zool.* 209:33–40.

KEAST, A. 1965. Resource subdivision amongst cohabiting fish species in a bay, Lake Opinicon, Ontario. *Univ. Mich. Great Lakes Res. Div. Publ.* 13:106–132.

KEAST, A. 1966. Trophic interrelationships in the fish fauna of a small stream. *Univ. Mich. Great Lakes Res. Div. Publ.* 15:51–79.

KEAST, A., and WEBB, D. 1966. Mouth and body form relative to feeding ecology in the fish fauna of a small lake, Lake Opinicon, Ontario. *J. Fish Res. Bd. Canada* 23(12):1845–1874.

KERSTETTER, T.H., and KIRSCHNER, L.B. 1972. Active chloride transport by the gills of rainbow trout, *S. gairdneri. J. Exp. Biol.* 56:263–272.

KEYS, A.B. 1933. The mechanism of adaptation to varying salinity in the common eel and the general problem of osmotic regulation in fishes. *Proc. Roy. Soc. Lond. B.* 112:184–199.

KHANNA, S.S., and SINGH, H.R. 1966. Morphology of the teleostean brain in relation to feeding habits. *Proc. Nat. Acad. Sci., India* 336:306–316.

KHOO, H.W. 1974. Sensory basis of homing in the intertidal fish *Oligocottus maculosus* Girard. *Can. J. Zool.* 52:1023–1029.

KICENIUK, J.W., and JONES, D.R. 1977. The oxygen transport system in trout (*Salmo gairdneri*) during sustained exercise. *J. Exp. Biol.* 69:247–260.

KINNE, O. 1960. Growth, food intake, and food conversion in a euryplastic fish exposed to different temperatures and salinities. *Physiol. Zool.* 33:288–317.

KISCH, B. 1948. Electrocardiographic investigation of the heart of fish. *Expl. Med. Surg.* 6:31–62.

KLINE, K. 1978. *Aspects of digestion in stomachless fishes.* Unpublished Ph.D. dissertation, Univ. of Calif., Davis. 78 pp.

KLONTZ, G.W. 1972. Haematological techniques and immune response in rainbow trout. Pages 89–99 *in* L.E. Mawdesley-Thomas, ed. *Diseases of fish.* Symp. Zool. Soc. Lond. No. 30. London: Academic Press.

KNAPP, F.T. 1953. *Fishes found in the fresh waters of Texas.* Brunswick, Ga.: Ragland Printing. 166 pp.

KOBAYASHI, S., YAMADA, J., MAEKAWA, K., and OUCHI, K. 1972. Calcification and nucleation in fish scales. Pages 84–90 *in* H.K. Erban, ed. *Biomineralization research reports.* Stuttgart: Schattauer Verlag.

KOZHOV, M. 1963. *Lake Baikal and its life.* Monogr. Biologicae 11. The Hague: W. Junk. 344 pp.

KREBS, J.R. 1978. Optimal foraging: decision rules for predators. Pages 23–63 *in* J.R. Krebs and N.B. Davies, eds. *Behavioural ecology, an evolutionary approach.* Oxford: Blackwell.

KREBS, J.R., and DAVIES, N.B., eds. 1978. *Behavioural ecology, an evolutionary approach.* Oxford: Blackwell. 494 pp.

KROGH, A. 1939. *Osmotic regulation in aquatic animals.* London: Cambridge Univ. Press.

KROPF, A. 1972. The structure and reactions of visual pigments. *In* M.G.F. Fuortes, ed. *Handbook of sensory physiology.* 7(2), Physiology of photoreceptor organs. Berlin: Springer Verlag.

KUCHNOW, K.P. 1971. The elasmobranch pupillary response. *Vision Res.* 11:1395–1406.

KUEHNE, R.A. 1962. A classification of streams illustrated by fish distribution in an eastern Kentucky creek. *Ecology* 43(4):608–614.

KUENZLER, E.J. 1974. Mangrove swamp systems. Pages 346–371 *in* H.T. Odum, B.J. Copeland, and E.A. McMahan, eds. *Coastal ecological systems of the United States.* Washington, D.C.: The Conservation Foundation.

KUHN, W., RAMEL, A., KUHN, H.J., and MARTI, E. 1963. The filling mechanism of the swimbladder, generation of high gas pressures through hairpin countercurrent multiplication. *Experientia* 19:497–511.

KUZIN, B.S., ed. 1968. *Biological and hydrological factors of local movements of fish in reservoirs.* New Delhi: Amerind Publ. 389 pp. (Trans. from Russian.)

LaBOUNTY, J.F., and DEACON, J.E. 1972. *Cyprinodon milleri*, a new species of pupfish (family Cyprinodontidae) from Death Valley, California. *Copeia* 1972 (4):769–780.

LAGIOS, M.D. 1979. The coelacanth and the chondrichthyes as sister groups: a review of shared apomorph characters and a cladistic analysis and reinterpretation. *Occ. Pap. Calif. Acad. Sci.* 134:25–44.

LAGLER, K.F., BARDACH, J.E., MILLER, R.R., and PASSINO, D.R.M. 1977. *Ichthyology.* 2nd ed. New York: Wiley. 506 pp.

LAKE, J.S. 1971. *Freshwater fishes and rivers of Australia.* Melbourne: Thos. Nelson. 61 pp.

LANE, C.E., ed. 1967. *Reservoir fishery resources symposium.* Bethesda, Md.: Amer. Fish. Soc. 569 pp.

LANE, E.D., and HILL, C.W., eds. 1975. Marine resources of Anaheim Bay. *Calif. Dept. Fish, Game Fish Bull.* 165:1–195.

LANZING, W.J.R., and BOWER, C.C. 1974. Development of colour patterns in relation to behaviour in *Tilapia mossambica* (Peters). *J. Fish Biol.* 6:29–41.

LARIMORE, R.W., CHILDERS, W.F., and HEKCROTTE, C. 1959. Destruction and reestablishment of stream fish and invertebrates affected by drought. *Trans. Amer. Fish. Soc.* 88:261–285.

LARKIN, P.A. 1956. Interspecific competition and population control in freshwater fish. *J. Fish. Res. Bd. Canada* 13(2):327–342.

LASKER, R. 1978. The relation between oceanographic conditions and larval anchovy food in the California current: identification of factors contributing to recruitment failure. *Rapp. P.-v. Reun. Const. Int. Explor. Mer.* 173:212-230.

LAUFF, G.H., ed. 1967. *Estuaries.* Amer. Assoc. Adv. Sci. Publ. 83. 757pp.

LEBEDEV, N.V. 1969. *Elementary populations of fishes.* Jerusalem: Israel Prog. Sci. Trans. 224pp.

LeCREN, E.D., KIPLING, C., and McCORMACK, J.C. 1972. Windermere: effects of exploitation and eutrophication on the salmonid community. *J. Fish. Res. Bd. Canada* 29(6):819-832.

LEE, R.F., PHLEGER, C.F., and HORN, M.H. 1975. Composition of oil in fish bones: possible function in neutral buoyancy. *Comp. Biochem. Physiol.* 50B: 13–16.

LEE, R.M. 1920. A review of the methods of age and growth determination in fishes by means of scales. *Fish. Invest.,* Ser. II. 4(2):1–32.

LEGENDRE, V., HUNTER, J.G., and McALLISTER, D.E. 1975. French, English and scientific names of marine fishes of arctic Canada. Syllogeus 7. Ottawa: Nat. Mus. Nat. Sci. Canada. 15 pp.

LEGGETT, W.C. 1977. The ecology of fish migrations. *Ann. Rev. Ecol. Syst.* 8:285–308.

LEGGETT, W.C., and CARSCADDEN, J.E. 1978. Latitudinal variation in reproductive characteristics of American shad (*Alosa sapidissima*): evidence for population specific life history strategies in fish. *J. Fish. Res. Bd. Canada* 35:1469–1478.

LEGGETT, W.C., and WHITNEY, R.R. 1972. Water temperature and the migrations of American shad. *NOAA Fish. Bull.* 170(3):659–670.

LEIM, A.H., and SCOTT, W.B. 1966. *Fishes of the Atlantic coast of Canada.* Fish. Res. Bd. Canada Bull. 155. 485 pp.

LEIVESTAD, H., and MUNIZ, I.P. 1976. Fish kill at low pH in a Norwegian river. *Nature* 259:391–392.

LELEK, A. 1973. Sequence of changes in fish populations of the new tropical man-made lake, Kainji, Nigeria, West Africa. *Arch. Hydrobiol.* 71:381–420.

LEWIS, D.S. 1974. The effects of the formation of Lake Kainji, Nigeria, upon the indigenous fish population. *Hydrobiologica* 45(1–3):281–301.

LI, H.W., and MOYLE, P.B. 1976. Feeding ecology of the Pit sculpin, *Cottus pitensis. Bull. S. Calif. Acad. Sci.* 75(2):111–118.

LIEM, K.F. 1963. *The comparative osteology and phylogeny of the Anabantoidei (Teleostei, Pisces).* Ill. Biol. Monogr. 30. 149 pp.

LIEM, K.F. 1974. Evolutionary strategies and morphological innovations: cichlid pharyngeal jaws. *Syst. Zool.* 22:425-441.

LIGHTHILL, M.J. 1969. Hydromechanics of aquatic animal propulsion. *Ann. Rev. Fluid Mech.* 1:413–446.

LINDBERG, G.U. 1971. *Fishes of the world.* New York: Wiley. 545 pp.

LINDSEY, C.C., and HARRINGTON, R.W., Jr. 1972. Extreme vertebrate variation induced by temperature in a homozygous clone of the self-fertilizing cyprinodontid fish, *Rivulus marmoratus. Can. J. Zool.* 50(6):733–744.

LINEAWEAVER, T.H., and BACKUS, R.H. 1969. *The natural history of sharks.* New York: Lippincott. 256 pp.

LISSMAN, H.W. 1963. Electric location in fishes. *Sci. Amer.* 152:1–12.

LIVINGSTON, R.J. 1976. Diurnal and seasonal fluctuations of organisms in a north Florida estuary. *Est., Coast. Mar. Sci.* 4(3):373–400.

LIVINGSTON, R.J., KOBYLINSKI, G.J., LEWIS, F.G., and SHERIDAN, P.F. 1975. Long-term fluctuations of epibenthic fish and invertebrate populations in Apalachiola Bay, Florida. *NOAA Fish. Bull.* 74(2):311–321.

LOFTUS, K.H., and REGIER, H.A., eds. 1972. Symposium of salmonid communities in oligotrophic lakes. *J. Fish. Res. Bd. Canada* 29(6):613–986.

LONGURST, A., COLDBROOK, M., LeBASSEUR, R., LORENZEN, C., and SMITH, P. 1972. The instability of ocean populations. *New Sci.* 1972:1–5.

LOOS, J.L. and WOOLCOTT, W.S. 1969. Hybridization and behavior in two species of *Percina* (Percidae). *Copeia* 1969(2):374–385.

LOSEY, G.S., Jr. 1978. The symbiotic behavior of fishes. Pages 1–31 *in* D.I. Mostofsky, ed. *The behavior of fish and other aquatic animals.* New York: Academic Press.

LOTRICH, V.A. 1973. Growth, production, and community composition of fishes inhabiting a first-, second-, and third-order stream of eastern Kentucky. *Ecol. Monogr.* 43(3):377–397.

LOVE, M.S., and CAILLET, G.M. 1979. *Readings in ichthyology.* Santa Monica: Goodyear 525 pp.

LOVE, R.M. 1970. *The chemical biology of fishes.* London: Academic Press. 547 pp.

LOWE-McCONNELL, R.H. 1962. The fishes of the British Guiana continental shelf, Atlantic coast of South America, with notes on natural history. *J. Linn. Soc. (Zoology).* 44:669–700.

LOWE-McCONNELL, R.H. 1969. Speciation in tropical freshwater fishes. *Biol. J. Linn. Soc. (Zool.).* 45:103–144.

LOWE-McCONNELL, R.H. 1975. *Fish communities in tropical freshwaters.* London: Longman. 337 pp.

LOWE-McCONNELL, R.H. 1977. *Ecology of fishes in tropical waters.* London: Ed. Arnold. 64 pp.

LUGO, A.E., and SNEDAKER, S.C. 1974. The ecology of mangroves. *Ann. Rev. Ecol. Syst.* 5:39–64.

LURIE, E. 1960. *Louis Agassiz: a life in science.* Chicago: Univ. Chicago Press. 390 pp.

LYTHGOE, J., and LYTHGOE, G. 1971. *Fishes of the sea.* New York: Doubleday. 320 pp.

MacGINTIE, G.E. 1939. The natural history of the blind goby (*Typhlogobius californiensis* Steindachner). *Amer. Midl. Nat.* 21:489–508.

MAETZ, J. 1974. Origine de la difference de poietiel electrique transbranchiale chez le poisson rouge *Carassius auratus.* Importancie de l'ion Ca. *C. R. Hebd. Siance Acad. Sci. Paris.* 279:1277–1280.

MAETZ, J., and GARCIA ROMEU, F. 1964. The mechanism of sodium and chloride uptake by the gills of a freshwater fish, *Carassius auratus.* II. Evidence of NH_4^+/Na^+ and HCO_3^-/Cl^- exchanges. *J. Gen. Physiol.* 50:391–422.

MAETZ, J., SAWYER, W.H., DICKFORD, G.E., and MAYER, N. 1967. Evolution de la balance minerale du sodium chez *Fundulus heteroclitus* au cours du transfert d'eau de mer en eau douce: effects de l'hypophysectomie et de la prolactine. *Gen. Comp. Endocrinol.* 8:163–176.

MAJOR, P.F. 1978. Predator–prey interaction in two schooling fishes, *Caranx ignobilis* and *Stolephorus purpureus. Anim. Behav.* 26:760–777.

MANI, M., ed. 1974. *Ecology and biogeography in India.* Monogr. Biologicae 23. The Hague: W. Junk. 773 pp.

MANSUETI, R.J. 1961. Effects of civilization on striped bass and other estuarine biota in Chesapeake Bay and tributaries. *Proc. Gulf. Carib. Fish. Inst.* 14:110–136.

MANWELL, C. 1958. On the evolution of hemoglobin of the California hagfish, *Polistotrema stouti. Biol. Bull.* 115:227–238.

MANWELL, C., BAKER, C.M.A., and CHILDERS, W. 1963. The genetics of hemoglobin in hybrid. I. A molecular basis for hybrid vigor. *Comp. Biochem. Physiol.*

10:103–120.

MARKERT, J.R., HIGGS, D.A., DYE, H.M. and MacQUARRIE, D.W. 1977. Influence of bovine growth hormone on growth rate, appetite, and food conversion of yearling coho salmon (*Oncorhynchus kisutch*) fed two diets of different composition. *Can. J. Zool.* 55:74–83.

MARKLE, D.F., and MUSICK, J.A. 1974. Benthic-slope fishes found at 900 m depth along a transect in the western North Atlantic ocean. *Mar. Biol.* 16:225–233.

MARLIAVE, J.B. 1977. Substratum preferences of settling larvae of marine fishes reared in the laboratory. *J. Exp. Mar. Biol. Ecol.* 27(1):47–60.

MARSHALL, N.B. 1953. Egg size in arctic, antarctic and deep-sea fishes. *Evolution* 7:328–341.

MARSHALL, N.B. 1954. Aspects of deepsea biology. London: Hutchinson's. 380 pp.

MARSHALL, N.B. 1960. Swimbladder structure of deep-sea fishes in relation to their systematics and biology. *Discovery Rept.* 31:1–122.

MARSHALL, N.B. 1962. Some convergences between the benthic fishes of polar seas. Pages 273–278 *in* R. Carrick, M.W. Holdgate, and J. Prost, eds. *Symposium on Antarctic biology.* Paris: Hermann.

MARSHALL, N.B. 1966. *The life of fishes.* New York: Universe Books. 402 pp.

MARSHAL, N.B. 1971. *Explorations in the life of fishes.* Cambridge: Harvard Univ. Press. 204 pp.

MATTY, A.J., and CHEEMA, I.R. 1978. The effect of some steroid hormones on the growth and protein metabolism of rainbow trout. *Aquaculture.* 14:163–178.

MAYR, E. 1963. *Animal species and evolution.* Cambridge, Belknap Press. 797pp.

MAYR, E. 1976. *Evolution and the diversity of life: selected essays.* Cambridge: Harvard Univ. Press. 721 pp.

MAZEAUD, M., MAZEAUD, R., and DONALDSON, E.M. 1977. Primary and secondary effects of stress in fish. Some new data with a general review. *Trans. Amer. Fish. Soc.* 106:201–212.

McALLISTER, D.E. 1963. *A revision of the smelt family, Osmeridae.* Bull. Nat. Mus. Canada 91. 53 pp.

McALLISTER, D.E. 1977. Ecology of the marine fishes of arctic Canada. Pages 49–65 *in* Section II. *Marine ecology.* Ottawa: Proc. Circumpolar Conf. on Northern Ecology.

McCOSKER, J.E. 1979. Inferred natural history of the living coelacanth. *Occ. Pap. Calif. Acad. Sci.* 134:17–24.

McCOSKER, J.E., and DAWSON, C.E. 1975. Biotic passage through the Panama Canal, with particular reference to fishes. *Mar. Biol.* 30:343–351.

McCOSKER, J.E., and LAGIOS, M.D., eds. 1979. The biology and physiology of the living coelacanth. *Occ. Pap. Calif. Acad. Sci.* 134. 175 pp.

McDOWALL, R.M., and ROBERTSON, D.A. 1975. Occurrence of galaxiid larvae and juveniles in the sea. *N. Z. J. Mar., Freshw. Res.* 9(1):1–9.

McDOWALL, R.M., and WHITAKER, A.H. 1975. The freshwater fishes. Pages 277–299 *in* G. Kuschel, ed. *Biogeography and ecology in New Zeland.* The Hague: W. Junk.

McEACHRAN, J.D., and MUSICK, J.A. 1974. Distribution and relative abundance of seven species of skates (Pisces: Rajidae) which occur between Nova Scotia and Cape Hatteras. *NOAA Fish. Bull.* 73(1):119–136.

McELMAN, J.F., and BALON, E.K. 1979. Early ontogeny of walleye, *Stizotedion vitreum,* with steps of saltatory development. *Env. Biol. Fish* 4:309–348.

McERLEAN, A.J., O'CONNAR, S.G., MIHURSKY, J.A., and GIBSON, C.J. 1973. Abundance, diversity, and seasonal patterns of estuarine fish populations. *Est. Coast. Mar. Sci.* 1(1):19–36.

McFARLAND, W.M. 1963. Seasonal changes in the number and the biomass of fishes from the surf at Mustang Island, Texas. *Publ. Inst. Mar. Sci. Texas.* 9: 91–105.

McFARLAND, W.N., and MUNZ, F.W. 1965. Regulation of body weight and serum composition by hagfish in various media. *Comp. Biochem. Physiol.* 14:383–398.

McGOWAN, J.A. 1974. The nature of oceanic ecosystems. Pages 9–28 *in* C.B. Miller, ed. *The biology of the oceanic Pacific.* Corvallis: Oregon St. Univ. Press.

McHUGH, J.L. 1967. Estuarine nekton. Pages 581–620 *in* G.H. Lauff, ed. *Estuaries.* AAAS Publ. 83.

McKAYE, K.R. 1977. Defense of a predator's young by herbivorous fish: an unusual strategy. *Amer. Nat.* 11(978):310–315.

McKAYE, K.R., and BARLOW, G.W. 1976. Chemical recognition of young by the Midas cichlid, *Cichlasoma citrinellum. Copeia* 1976(2):276–282.

McLAUGHLIN, R.H., and O'GOWER, A.K. 1971. Life history and underwater studies of a heterodont shark. *Ecol. Monogr.* 41:271–289.

McPHAIL, J.D. 1969. Predation and the evolution of a stickleback (*Gasterosteus*). *J. Fish. Res. Bd. Canada* 26:3183–3208.

McPHAIL, J.D. 1977a. A possible function of the caudal spot in characid fishes. *Can. J. Zool.* 55(7):1063–1066.

McPHAIL, J.D. 1977b. Sons and lovers: the functional significance of sexual dichromatism in a fish, *Neoheterandria tridentiger* (Garman). *Behaviour* 64:329–339.

McPHAIL, J.D., and LINDSEY, C.C. 1970. *Freshwater fishes of northwestern Canada and Alaska.* Fish. Res. Bd. Canada Bull. 173. 379 pp.

MEAD, G.W., BERTELSEN, E., and COHEN, D.M. 1964. Reproduction among deep-sea fishes. *Deep-sea Res.* 11(4):569–596.

MEARNS, A.J. 1973. Southern California's inshore demersal fishes: diversity, distribution, and disease as responses to environmental quality. *CalCOFI Rpt.* 17:141–148.

MEARNS, A.J., and SMITH, L. 1975. Benthic oceanography and the distribution of bottom fish off Los Angeles. *CalCOFI Rpt.* 18:118–124.

MENDELSON, J. 1975. Feeding relationships among species of *Notropis* (Pisces: Cyprinidae) in a Wisconsin stream. *Ecol. Monogr.* 45(3):199–230.

MENON, A.G.K. 1973. Origin of the freshwater fish fauna of India. *Curr. Sci.* 42(16):553–556.

MENZIES, R.J., GEORGE, R.Y., and ROWE, G.T. 1973. Abyssal environment and ecology of the world oceans. New York: Wiley. 488 pp.

MIHURSKY, J.A., and KENNEDY, V.S. 1967. Water temperature criteria to protect aquatic life. Pages 20–32 *in* E.L. Cooper, ed. *A symposium on water quality criteria to protect aquatic life.* Amer. Fish. Soc. Spec. Publ. 4.

MILLER, D.J., and LEA, R.N. 1972. *Guide to the coastal marine fishes of California.* Calif. Dept. Fish, Game Fish Bull. 157. 249 pp.

MILLER, R.G. 1951. *The natural history of Tahoe fishes.* Unpublished Ph.D. dissertation, Stanford Univ. 160 pp.

MILLER, R.J. 1964. Behavior and ecology of some North American cyprinid fishes. *Amer. Midl. Nat.* 72(2):313–357.

MILLER, R.J., and EVANS, H.E. 1965. External morphology of the brain and lips in catostomid fishes. *Copeia* (4):467–487.

MILLER, R.R. 1948. The cyprinodont fishes of the Death Valley System of eastern California and southwestern Nevada. *Mus. Vert. Zool., U. of Mich. Misc. Publ.* 68:1–155.

MILLER, R.R. 1958. Origin and affinities of the freshwater fish fauna of western North America. Pages 187–222 *in* C.L. Hubbs, ed. *Zoogeography.* Washington, D.C.: AAAS.

MILLER, R.R. 1966. Geographical distribution of Central America freshwater fishes. *Copeia* 1966(4):773–802.

MILLER, R.R., and HUBBS, C.L. 1969. Systematics of *Gasterosteus aculeatus*, with particular reference to intergradation and introgression along the Pacific Coast of North America: a commentary on a recent contribution. *Copeia* 1969:52–69.

MILLOT, J. 1955. The coelacanth. *Sci. Amer.* 193(6):34–39.

MILNE, R.S., and RANDALL, D.J. 1976. Regulation of arterial pH during fresh water to sea water transfer in the rainbow trout *Salmo gairdneri*. *Comp. Biochem. Physiol.* 53A:157–160.

MINCKLEY, W.K. 1963. *The ecology of a spring stream Doe Run, Meade County, Kentucky.* Wildl. Monog. 11. 124 pp.

MINCKLEY, W.K., and DEACON, J. 1968. Southwestern fishes and the enigma of "endangered species." *Science* 159:1424–1431.

MITCHELL, R.W. 1969. A comparison of temperate and tropical cave communities. *Southw. Nat.* 14(1):73–88.

MITCHELL, R.W., RUSSELL, W.H., and ELLIOTT, W.R. 1977. *Mexican eyeless characin fishes, genus Astyanax: environment, distribution and evolution.* Texas Tech. Mus. Spec. Publ. 12. 89 pp.

MOODIE, G.E.E., and REIMCHEN, T.E. 1976. Phenetic variation and habitat differences in *Gasterosteus* populations of the Queen Charlotte Islands. *Syst. Zool.* 25:49–61.

MOORE, W.S. 1976. Components of fitness in the unisexual fish *Poeciliopsis monacha occidentalis*. *Evolution* 30(3):564–578.

MORGAN, M.D., THRELKELD, S.T., and GOLDMAN, C.R. 1978. Impact of the introduction of kokanee (*Oncorhynchus nerka*) and opossum shrimp (*Mysis relicta*) on a subalpine lake. *J. Fish. Res. Bd. Canada* 35:1572–1579.

MORIN, J.A., HARRINGTON, A., NEALSON, K., KRIEGER, N., BALDWIN, T., and HASTINGS, J. 1975. Light for all reasons: versatility in the behavioral repertoire of the flashlight fish. *Science* 190:74–76.

MORSE, D.H. 1977. Feeding behavior and predator avoidance in heterospecific groups. *Biosci.* 27(5):332–339.

MOSELEY, F.N., and COPELAND, B.J. 1969. A portable dropnet for representative sampling of nekton. *Contrib. Marine Sci. Univ. Texas* 14:37–45.

MOSS, S.A. 1977. Feeding mechanisms in sharks. *Amer. Zool.* 17:355–364.

MOYLE, J.B. 1956. Relationships between the chemistry of Minnesota surface waters and wildlife management. *J. Wildl. Mgmt.* 20(3):303–320.

MOYLE, J.B., and CLOTHIER, W.D. 1959. Effects of management and winter oxygen levels on the fish population of a prairie lake. *Trans. Amer. Fish. Soc.* 88:178–185.

MOYLE, P.B. 1969. *Ecology of the fishes of a Minnesota lake, with special reference to the Cyprinidae.* Unpublished Ph.D. dissertation, Univ. Minnesota. 169 pp.

MOYLE, P.B. 1973. Ecological segregation among three species of minnows (Cyprinidae) in a Minnesota lake. *Trans. Amer. Fish. Soc.* 102(4):794–805.

MOYLE, P.B. 1976a. *Inland fishes of California.* Berkeley: Univ. Calif. Press. 405 pp.

MOYLE, P.B. 1976b. Some effects of channelization on the fishes and invertebrates of Rush Creek, Modoc County, California. *Calif. Fish, Game* 62(3): 179–186.

MOYLE, P.B. 1977. In defense of sculpins. *Fisheries* 2(1):20–23.

MOYLE, P.B., and KOCH, D.L., eds. 1975. Symposium on trout/non-game fish relationships in streams. *Univ. Nev. Cent. Water Resources. Res. Misc. Pub. No.* 17:1–81.

MOYLE, P.B., and LI, H.W. 1979. Community ecology and predator–prey relationships in warmwater streams. Pages 171–180 *in* H. Clepper, ed. *Predator-prey systems in fisheries management.* Washington, D.C.: Sport Fish. Inst.

MOYLE, P.B., and NICHOLS, R. 1973. Ecology of some native and introduced fishes of the Sierra-Nevada foothills in Central California. *Copeia* 1073(3): 478–490.

MOYLE, P.B., and NICHOLS, R. 1974. Decline of the native fish fauna of the Sierra-Nevada foothills in central California. *Amer. Midl. Nat.* 92(1):72–83.

MOYLE, P.B., and five others. 1979. Research needs in fisheries. *Trans. 44th N. Am. Wildl., Nat. Res. Conf.* pp. 176–187.

MOY-THOMAS, J., and MILES, W.S. 1971. *Paleozoic fishes.* New York: J. Saunders. London: Associated Book Publishers Ltd. 259 pp.

MUIR, B.S., and KENDALL, J.I. 1968. Structural modifications in the gills of tunas and other oceanic fishes. *Copeia* (2)388–398.

MUNTZ, W.R.A. 1976. On yellow lenses in mesopelagic animals. *J. Mar. Biol. Ass. U. K.* 56:963–976.

MUNZ, F.W. 1971. Vision: visual pigments. Pages 1–32 *in* W.S. Hoar and D.J. Randall, eds. *Fish physiology.* Vol. 5. New York: Academic Press.

MUNZ, F.W., and McFARLAND, W. 1964. Regulatory function of a primitive vertebrate kidney. *Comp. Biochem. Physiol.* 13:381–400.

MURDAUGH, H.V., and ROBIN, E.D. 1967. Acid-base metabolism in the dogfish sharks. Pages 249–264 *in* P.W. Gilbert, R.F. Mathewson, and D.P. Rall, eds. *Sharks, skates and rays.* Baltimore: Johns Hopkins Press.

MURPHY, G.I. 1961. Oceanography and variations in the Pacific sardine population. *CalCOFI Rpt.* 8:55–64.

MURPHY, G.I. 1966. Population biology of the Pacific sardine (*Sardinops caerules*). *Proc. Calif. Acad. Sci.* 34(1):1–84.

MURPHY, G.I. 1968. Pattern in life history and the environment. *Amer. Nat.* 102:390–404.

MURPHY, G.I. 1977. Clupeiods. Pages 283–308 *in* J.A. Gulland, ed. *Fish population dynamics.* New York: Wiley.

MURRAY, R.W. 1960. The response of the ampullae of Lorenzini of elasmobranchs to mechanical stimulation. *J. Exp. Biol.* 37:417–424.

MUUS, B.J. 1967. *Freshwater fish of Britain and Europe.* London: Collins. 222 pp.

MYERS, G.S. 1938. Fresh-water fishes and West Indian Zoogeography. *Smithson. Rpt.* 1937:339–364.

MYERS, G.S. 1951. Fresh-water fishes and East Indian zoogeography. *Stanf. Ichthy. Bull.* 4(1):11–21.

MYERS, G.S. 1960. The endemic fauna of Lake Lanao and the evolution of higher taxonomic categories. *Evolution* 14:323–333.

MYERS, G.S. 1964. A brief sketch of the history of ichthyology in America to the year 1850. *Copeia* 1964(1):33–41.

MYRBERG, A.A., Jr. 1978. Underwater sound—its effect on the behavior of sharks. Pages 391–417 *in* E.S. Hodgson and R.F. Mathewson, eds. *Sensory biology of sharks, skates, and rays.* Washington, D.C.: Off. Naval Res. Publ.

NAFPAKTITIS, B.G. 1978. Systematics and distribution of lanternfishes of the genera *Lobianchia* and *Diaphus* (Myctophidae) in the Indian Ocean. *Los. Ang. Co. Nat. Hist. Mus. Sci. Bull.* 30:1–92.

NAIMAN, R. 1976. Productivity of a herbivorous pupfish population (*Cyprinodon nevadensis*) in a warm desert stream. *J. Fish Biol.* 9:125–137.

NAKAMURA, H. 1969. *Tuna distribution and migration.* London: Fishing News Books. 76 pp.

NAKAMURA, R. 1976. Experimental assessment of factors influencing microhabitat selection by the two tidepool fishes *Oligocottus masculosus* and *O. snyderi. Marine Biol.* 37:97–104.

NAKANO, T., and TOMLINSON, N. 1967. Catecholamine and carbohydrate concentrations in rainbow trout (*Salmo gairdneri*) in relation to physical disturbance. *J. Fish. Res. Bd. Canada* 24:1701–1715.

NEILL, W.H., CHANG, R.K.C., and DIZON, A.E. 1976. Magnitude and ecological implications of thermal inertia in skipjack tuna, *Katsuwonus pelamis* (Linnaeus). *Env. Biol. Fish* 1:61–80.

NEILL, W.H., and MAGNUSON, J.J. 1974. Distributional ecology and behavioral thermoregulation of fishes in relation to heated effluent from a power plant at Lake Monona, Wisconsin. *Trans. Am. Fish. Soc.* 103:663–710.

NEILL, W.H., MAGNUSON, J.J., and CHIPMAN, G.G. 1972. Behavioral thermoregulation by fishes: a new experimental approach. *Science* 176:1443–1455.

NELSON, G.J. 1969. Gill arches and the phylogeny of fishes, with notes on the classification of vertebrates. *Bull. Amer. Mus. Nat. Hist.* 141(4):475–552.

NELSON, G.J. 1972a. Comments on Hennig's "Phylogenetic Systematics" and its influence on ichthyology. *Syst. Zool.* 21(4):364–374.

NELSON, G.J. 1972b. Observations on the gut of the Osteoglossomorpha. *Copeia* 1972(2):325–329.

NELSON, G.J. 1975. Anatomy of the male urogenital organs of *Goodea atripinnis* and *Characodon lateralis* (Atheriniformes: Cyrpinodontoidei) and *G. atripinnis* courtship. *Copeia* 1975(3):475–482.

NELSON, J.S. 1968. Hybridization and isolating mechanisms between *Catostomus commersoni* and *C. macrocheilus* (Pisces: Catostomidae). *J. Fish. Res. Bd. Canada* 25:101–150.

NELSON, J.S. 1976. Fishes of the world. New York: Wiley-Interscience. 416 pp.

NEVILLE, C.M. 1979. Sublethal effects of environmental acidification on rainbow trout (*Salmo gairdneri*). *J. Fish. Res. Bd. Canada* 36:84–87.

NICHOLS, J.T. 1943. The fresh-water fishes of China. New York: Amer. Mus. Nat. Hist. 322 pp.

NICOL, J.A.C., and ZYZNAR, E.S. 1973. The tapetum lucidum in the eye of the big-eye *Priacanthus arenatus* Cuvier. *J. Fish Biol.* 5:519–522.

NIELSON, J.G. 1977. The deepest living fish *Abyssobrotula galatheae*, a new genus and species of oviparous ophidioids (Pisces, Brotulidae). *Galathea Rpt.* 14:41–48.

NIKOLSKY, G.V. 1937. On the distribution of fishes according to the nature of their food in rivers flowing from the mountains of Asia. *Verh. Int. Verein. Theor. Angew. Limnol.* 8(2):169–176.

NIKOLSKY, G.V. 1954. *Special ichthyology.* Jerusalem (1961): Israel Prog. Sci. Trans. 538 pp.

NIKOLSKY, G.V. 1963. *The ecology of fishes.* New York: Academic Press. 352 pp.

NILSSON, N.A. 1963. Interaction between trout and char in Scandanavia. *Trans. Amer. Fish. Soc.* 92(3):276–285.

NILSSON, N.A. 1967. Interactive segregation between fish species. Pages 295–313 *in* S.D. Gerking, ed. *The biological basis of freshwater fish production.* New York: Wiley.

NIXON, S.W., and OVIATT, C.A. 1973. Ecology of a New England salt marsh. *Ecol. Monogr.* 43(4):463–498.

NORMAN, J.R., and GREENWOOD, P.H. 1975. *A history of fishes.* 3rd ed. New York: Halstead Press. 467 pp.

NORTH, W.J., and HUBBS, C.L., eds. 1968. Utilization of kelp-bed resources in southern California. *Calif. Dept. Fish, Game Fish. Bull.* 139:1–264.

NORTHCOTE, T.G., ed. 1969. *Symposium on salmon and trout in streams.* H.R. MacMillan lectures in fisheries. Vancouver: Univ. B. C.

NORTHCUTT, R.G. 1977. Elasmobranch central nervous system organization and its possible evolutionary significance. *Amer. Zool.* 17(2):411–430.

NORTHCUTT, R.G. 1978. Brain organization in the cartilaginous fishes. Pages 117–193 *in* E.S. Hodgson and R.F. Mathewson, eds. *Sensory biology of sharks, skates, and rays.* Washington, D.C.: Off. Naval Res. Publ.

NOVACEK, M.J., and MARSHALL, L.G. 1976. Early biogeographic history of the ostariophysan fishes. *Copeia* 1976(1):1-12.

NYBELIN, O. 1947. Antarctic fishes. *Sci. Res. Norweg. Ant. Expeds.*, 1927-28 26:1-76.

O'BRIEN, W.J., SLADE, N.A., and VINYARD, G.L. 1976. Apparent size as the determinant of prey selection by bluegill sunfish (*Lepomis macrochirus*). *Ecology* 57:1304-1310.

O'DAY, W.T. 1974. Bacterial luminescence in the deepsea fish *Oneirodes acanthias* Gilbert (1915). *Los Ang. Nat. Hist. Mus. Contr. in Sci.* 255:1-12.

ODUM, H.T., COPELAND, B.J., and McMAHAN, E.A., eds. 1974. *Coastal ecosystems of the United States.* Vols I-IV. Washington, D.C.: Conservation Foundation.

ODUM, W.E. 1970. Insidious alteration of the estuarine environment. *Trans. Amer. Fish. Soc.* 99(4):836-847.

ODUM, W.E. 1971. Pathways of energy flow in a south Florida estuary. *Univ. Miami Sea Grant Tech. Bull.* 7:1-162.

OGDEN, J.C., and EHRLICH, P.R. 1977. The behavior of heterotypic resting schools of juvenile grunts (Pomadasyidae). *Marine Biol.* 1977:273-280.

OGDEN, J.C., and LOBEL, P.S. 1978. The role of herbivorous fishes and urchins in coral reef communities. *Env. Biol. Fish* 3(1):49-64.

OGLESBY, R.T., CARLSON, C.A., and McCANN, J.A., eds. 1972. *River ecology and man.* New York: Academic Press. 465 pp.

OGURI, M. 1964. Rectal glands of marine and fresh-water sharks: comparative histology. *Science* 144:1151-1152.

OHNO, S. 1974. Protochordata, cyclostomata and pisces. Pages 1-91 *in* B. John, ed. *Animal cytogenetics.* Vol. 4. Berlin: Bortraeger.

OHNO, S., CHRISTIAN, L., ROMERO, M., DOFUKU, R., and IVEY, C. 1973. On the question of American eels, *Anguilla rostrata* versus European eels, *Anguilla anguilla. Experientia* 29:1-891.

OLMSTED, L.L., and CLOUTMAN, D.G. 1974. Repopulation after a fish kill in Mud Creek, Washington County, Arkansas, following pesticide pollution. *Trans. Amer. Fish. Soc.* 103(1):79-87.

ORVIG, T., ed. 1968. Current problems of lower vertebrate phylogeny. New York: Wiley-Interscience. 539 pp.

OTSU, T., and UCHIDA, R.N. 1963. Model of the migration of albacore in the north Pacific Ocean. *NOAA Fish. Bull.* 63:33-44.

OTTAWAY, E.M., and SIMKISS, K. 1977. "Instantaneous" growth rates of fish scales and their use in studies of fish populations. *J. Zool.* (London)181:407-419.

OVIATT, C.A., GALL, A.L., and NIXON, S.W. 1972. Environmental effects of Atlantic menhaden on surrounding waters. *Chesapeake Sci.* 13:321-323.

OVIATT, C.A., and NIXON, S.W. 1973. The demersal fish of Narraganset Bay: an analysis of community structure, distribution, and abundance. *Est. Coast. Mar. Sci.* 1:361-378.

PAINE, R.T., and PALMER, A.R. 1978. *Sicyases sanguineus:* a unique trophic generalist from the Chilean intertidal zone. *Copeia* 1978(1):75-81.

PANELLA, G. 1971. Fish otoliths: daily growth layers and periodical patterns. *Science* 173:1124-1127.

PARIN, N.V. 1968. *Ichthyofauna of the epipelagic zone.* Jerusalem: Israel Prog. Sci. Trans. 206 pp.

PARTRIDGE, B.L., and PITCHER, T.J. 1979. Evidence against a hydrodynamic function for fish schools. *Nature* 279(5712):418-419.

PATTEN, B.C. 1964. The rational decision process in salmon migration. *J. Cons. Cons., Perma. Int. Explor. Mer.* 8:410-417.

PATTERSON, C. 1973. Interrelationships of holosteans. Pages 233-305 *in* P.H. Greenwood, R.S. Miles, and C. Patterson, eds. *Interrelationships of fishes.* New

York: Academic Press.

PATTERSON, C. 1977. The contribution of paleontology to teleostean phylogeny. Pages 579–643 *in* M.K. Hecht, P.G. Goody, and B.M. Hecht. *Major patterns in vertebrate evolution.* New York: Plenum Press.

PATTERSON, C., and ROSEN, D.E. 1977. Review of the ichthyodectiform and other mesozoic teleost fishes and the theory and practice of classifying fossils. *Bull. Amer. Mus. Nat. Hist.* 158:81–172.

PEDEN, A.E., and CORBETT, C.A. 1973. Commensalism between a liparid fish, *Careproctus* sp. and the lithodid box crab, *Lopholithodes foraminatus. Can. J. Zool.* 51:555–556.

PELLEGRIN, J. 1921. Les poissons des eaux douces de l'Afrique du Nord Française etc. *Mem. Soc. Sci. Nat. Maroc.* 1(2).

PERCY, L.R., and POTTER, I.C. 1976. Blood cell formation in the river lamprey, *Lampetra fluviatilis. J. Zool.* (London) 178:319–340.

PERRET, W.S., and CAILLOUET, C.W. 1974. Abundance and size of fishes taken by trawling in Vermilion Bay, Louisiana. *Bull. Mar. Sci.* 24(1):52–75.

PERUTZ, M.F. 1978. Electrostatic effects in proteins. *Sci.* 201:1187–1191.

PFLIEGER, W.L. 1975. *The fishes of Missouri.* Missouri Dept. Cons. 343 pp.

PHLEGER, C.F. 1971. Biology of macrourid fishes. *Amer. Zool.* 11:419–423.

PIC, P., MAYER-GOSTAN, N., and MAETZ, J. 1974. Branchial effects of epinephrine in the seawater-adapted mullet. I. Water permeability. *Am. J. Physiol.* 226: 698–702.

PIETSCH, T.W. 1974. Osteology and relationships of ceratioid anglerfishes of the family Oneirodidae, with a review of the genus *Oneirodes* Lutken. *L. A. Co. Nat. Hist. Mus. Sci. Bull.* 18:1–113.

PIETSCH, T.W. 1976. Dimorphism, parasitism, and sex: reproductive strategies among deepsea ceratoid anglerfishes. *Copeia* 1976(4):781–793.

PIETSCH, T.W. 1978a. Evolutionary relationships of the seamoths (Teleostei: Pagasidae) with a classification of gasterosteiform families. *Copeia* 1978(3): 517–529.

PIETSCH, T.W. 1978b. The feeding mechanism of *Stylephorus chordatus* (Teleostei: Lampridiformes): functional and ecological implications. *Copeia* (2): 255–262.

PIETSCH, T.W., and GROBECKER, D.B. 1978. The compleat angler: aggressive mimicry in an antennariid anglerfish. *Science* 201:369–370.

PIIPER, J., MEYER, M., WORTH, H., and WILLMER, H. 1977. Respiration and circulation during swimming activity in the dogfish, *Scyliorhinus stellaris. Resp. Physiol.* 30:221–239.

PITCHER, T.J., PARTRIDGE, B.L., and WARDLE, C.S. 1976. A blind fish can school. *Science* 194:963–65.

PODDUBNY, A.G. 1971. *Ecological topography of fish populations in reservoirs.* New Delhi: Amerind Publ. 414 pp.

POLUHOWICH, J.J. 1972. Adaptive significance of eel multiple hemoglobines. *Physiol. Zool.* 45:215–222.

POPPER, A.N., and FAY, R.R. 1973. Sound detection and processing by teleost fishes: A critical review. *J. Acoust. Soc. Amer.* 53:1515–1529.

POPPER, A.N., and FAY, R.R. 1977. Structure and function of the elasmobranch auditory system. *Amer. Zool.* 17:443–452.

POTTS, W.T.W., and FLEMING, W.R. 1971. The effect of environmental calcium and ovine prolactin on sodium balance in *Fundulus kansae. J. Exp. Biol.* 54: 63–75.

POULSON, T.L. 1963. Cave adaptation in amblyopsid fishes. *Amer. Midl. Nat.* 70(2):257–290.

POULSON, T.L., and WHITE, W.B. 1969. The cave environment. *Science* 165: 971–981.

POWLES, P.M., and KOHLER, A.C. 1970. Depth distribution of various stages of the witch flounder (*Glyptocephalus cynoglossus*) off Nova Scotia and in the Gulf of Lawrence. *J. Fish. Res. Bd. Canada* 17:2053–2062.

PREJS, A., and BLASZCZYK, M. 1977. Relationships between food and cellulase activity in freshwater fishes. *J. Fish Biol.* 11:447–452.

PRIEDE, I.G. 1976. Functional morphology of the bulbus arteriosus of rainbow trout (*Salmo gairdneri* Richardson). *J. Fish Biol.* 9:209–216.

PRINSLOW, T.E., VALIELA, I., and TEAL, J.M. 1974. The effect of detritus and ration size on the growth of *Fundulus heteroclitus* (L.). *J. Exp. Mar. Biol. Ecol.* 16(1):1–10.

PYKE, G.H., PULLIAM, H.R., and CHARNOV, E.L. 1977. Optimal foraging: a selective review of theory and tests. *Q. Rev. Biol.* 52:137–154.

QUAST, J.C. 1968. Fish fauna of the rocky inshore zone. Pages 35–55 in W.J. North and C.L. Hubbs, eds. *Utilization of kelp-bed resources in southern California.* Calif. Dept. Fish, Game Fish. Bull. 139.

RADAKOV, D.V. 1972. *Schooling in the ecology of fish.* New York: Wiley. 173 pp.

RADOVICH, J. 1959. Redistribution of fishes in the eastern North Pacific Ocean in 1957 and 1958. *CalCOFI Rpts.* 7:163–171.

RADOVICH, J. 1961. Relationships of some marine organism of the northeast Pacific to water temperatures, particularly during 1957–1959. *Calif. Dept. Fish, Game Fish Bull.* 112:1–62.

RADOVICH, J. 1979. Managing pelagic schooling prey species. Pages 365–376 in H. Clepper, ed. *Predator–prey systems in fisheries management.* Washington, D.C.: Sport Fishing Inst.

RANDALL, D.J. 1968. Functional morphology of the heart in fishes. *Am. Zool.* 8:179–189.

RANDALL, D.J. 1970. The circulatory system. Pages 133–172 in W.S. Hoar and D.J. Randall, eds. *Fish physiology.* Vol. 4. New York: Academic Press.

RANDALL, D.J., and CAMERON, J.N. 1973. Respiratory control of arterial pH as temperature changes in rainbow trout *Salmo gairdneri. Amer. J. Physol.* 225(4):997–1002.

RANDALL, J.E. 1961. Overgrazing of algae by herbivorous reef fishes. *Ecology* 42(4):1–812.

RANDALL, J.E. 1965. Grazing effect on sea grasses by herbivorous reef fishes in the West Indies. *Ecology* 46(2):255–260.

RAVEN, P.H., BERLIN, B., and BREEDLOVE, D.E. 1971. The origins of taxonomy. *Science* 174:1210–1213.

REGAN, C.T. 1914. Fishes. British Antarctic Expedition, 1910. Natural History Report. *Zoology* 1:1–54.

REGAN, C.T., and TREWAVAS, E. 1932. *Deep-sea angler fishes (Ceratoidea).* Dana Rpt. 2. 123 pp.

REMANE, A., and SCHLIEPER, C. 1971. *Biology of brackish water.* New York: Wiley-Interscience. 372 pp.

RENFRO, J.L., and HILL, L.G. 1970. Factors influencing the aerial breathing and metabolism of gars (*Lepisosteus*). *Southw. Nat.* 15(1):45–54.

REPETSKI, J.E. 1978. A fish from the upper Cambrian of North America. *Science* 200:529–531.

RICHARDS, S.W. 1963. The demersal fish population of Long Island Sound. *Bull. Bingham Ocean. Coll., Yale Univ.* 18(2):1–101.

RICHERSON, P.J., WIDMER, C., and KITTEL, T. 1977. The limnology of Lake Titicaca (Peru, Bolivia), a large high altitude tropical lake. *Univ. Calif., Davis, Inst. Ecol. Publ.* 14:1–78.

RIGGS, A. 1970. Properties of fish hemoglobins. Pages 209–252 in W.S. Hoar and D.J. Randall, eds. *Fish physiology.* Vol 4. New York: Academic Press.

RIGLEY, L., and MARSHALL, J.A. 1973. Sound production by the elephant-nose fish *Gnathonemus petersii* (Pisces, Mormyridae). *Copeia* 1973(1):134–135.

RINGLER, N.H. 1979. Selective predation by drift feeding brown trout (*Salmo trutta*). *J. Fish. Res. Bd. Canada* 46:392–403.

ROBERTS, J.L. 1975. Active branchial and ram gill ventilation in fishes. *Biol. Bull.* 148:85–105.

ROBERTS, J.L., and GRAHAM, J.B. 1979. Effect of swimming speed on the excess temperatures and activities of heart and red and white muscles in the mackerel, *Scomber japonicus*. *NOAA Fish. Bull.* 76:861–867.

ROBERTS, T.R. 1969. Osteology and relationships of characoid fishes, particularly in the genera *Hepsetus*, *Salminus*, *Hoplias*, *Ctenolucius*, and *Acestrophynchus*. *Proc. Calif. Acad. Sci. Ser. 4* 36(15):391–500.

ROBERTS, T.R. 1971. Osteology of the Malaysian phallosteid fish, *Ceratostethus bicornis*, with a discussion of the evolution of remarkable structural novelties in its jaws and external genitalia. *Bull. Mus. Comp. Zool., Harvard* 142:393–418.

ROBERTS, T.R. 1972. Ecology of fishes in the Amazon and Congo basins. *Bull. Mus. Comp. Zool., Harvard* 143(2):117–147.

ROBERTS, T.R. 1976. Geographic distribution of African freshwater fishes. *Zool. J. Linn. Soc.* 57:249–319.

ROBERTSON, D.R., and HOFFMAN, S.G. 1977. The roles of female mate choice and predation in the mating system of some tropical labroid fishes. *Zeit. fur Tierpsych.* 45:298–320.

ROBERTSON, D.R., SWEATMAN, H.P.A., FLETCHER, E.A., and CLELAND, M.G. 1976. Schooling as a mechanism for circumventing the territoriality of competitors. *Ecology* 57:1208–1220.

ROBERTSON, D.R., and WARNER, R.R. 1978. Sexual patterns in the labroid fishes of the Western Caribbean. II: The parrotfishes (Scaridae). *Smithson. Contr. Zool.* 255:1–26.

ROBERTSON, J.D. 1954. The chemical composition of the blood of some aquatic chordates including members of the Tunicata, Cyclostomata, and Osteichthyes. *J. Expt. Biol.* 31:424–442.

ROBERTSON, J.D. 1957. The habitat of early vertebrates. *Biol. Rev.* 32:156–187.

ROGERS, C., and GRANDPERRIN, R. 1976. Pelagic food webs in the tropical Pacific. *Limnol. Oceano.* 21(5):731–735.

ROMER, A.S. 1966. *Vertebrate paleontology.* Chicago: Univ. Chicago Press. 468 pp.

RONSIVALLI, L.J. 1978. Sharks and their utilization. *Marine Fish. Rev.* 40(2):1–13.

ROOT, R.W. 1931. The respiratory function of the blood of marine fishes. *Biol. Bull.* 61:427–456.

ROSEN, D.E. 1964. The relationships and taxonomic position of the halfbeaks, killifishes, silversides, and their relatives. *Bull. Amer. Mus. Nat. Hist.* 127(5): 217-268.

ROSEN, D.E. 1973. Interrelationships of higher euteleostean fishes. Pages 397–513 *in* P.H. Greenwood, R.S. Miles, and C. Patterson, eds. *Interrelationships of fishes.* New York: Academic Press.

ROSEN, D.E. 1974. Phylogeny and zoogeography of salmoniform fishes and relationships of *Lepidogalaxias salamandroides*. *Bull. Amer. Mus. Nat. Hist.* 153(2): 267-325.

ROSEN, D.E. 1975a. Doctrinal biogeography, a review of *Marine zoogeography* by J.C. Briggs. *Quart. Rev. Biol.* 50(1):69–70.

ROSEN, D.E. 1975b. A vicariance model of Caribbean biogeography. *Syst. Zool.* 24(4):437–464.

ROSEN, D.E., and BAILEY, R.E. 1963. The poeciliid fishes (Cyprinodontiformes), their structure, zoogeography, and systematics. *Bull. Amer. Mus. Nat. Hit.* 126(1):1–176.

ROSEN, D.E., and GREENWOOD, P.H. 1970. Origin of the Weberian apparatus and the relationships of ostariophysan and gonorynchiform fishes. *Amer. Mus. Novit.* 2428:1–25.

ROSEN, D.E., and GREENWOOD, P.H. 1976. A fourth neotropical species of synbranchid eel and the phylogeny and systematics of synbranchiform fishes. *Bull. Amer. Mus. Nat. Hist.* 157(1):1–69.

ROSEN, M.W., and CORNFORD, N.E. 1971. Fluid friction of fish slimes. *Nature* 234:49–51.

ROSSI-FANELLI, A., and ANTONINI, E. 1960. Oxygen equilibria of hemoglobin from *Thunnus thynnus. Nature* 186:895–896.

ROTHSCHILD, B.J. 1965. Hypotheses on the origin of exploited skipjack tuna (*Katsuwonus pelamis*) in the eastern and central Pacific Ocean. *U.S. Fish, Wildl. Serv. Spec. Sci. Rept. Fish.* 512:1–20.

ROUNSEFELL, G.A. 1957. Fecundity of the North American Salmonidae. *U.S. Fish, Wildl. Serv. Fish. Bull.* 57:451–468.

ROUNSEFELL, G.A. 1975. Ecology, utilization, and management of marine fisheries. St. Louis: C. V. Mosby. 516 pp.

ROVAINEN, C.M. 1979. Neurobiology of lampreys. *Physiol. Rev.* 59(4):1007–1077.

ROYCE, W.F. 1972. Introduction to fishery science. New York: Academic Press. 351 pp.

RUSSELL, F.S. 1976. *The eggs and planktonic stages of British marine fishes.* London: Academic Press. 524 pp.

RYDER, R.A. 1965. A method of estimating the fish production of north-temperate lakes. *Trans. Amer. Fish. Soc.* 94(3):214–218.

RYDER, R.A. 1977. Effects of ambient light variations on behavior of yearling, subadult, and adult walleyes (*Stizostedion vitreum vitreum*). *J. Fish. Res. Bd. Canada* 34(10):1481–1491.

SAILA, S.B. 1961. A study of winter flounder movements. *Limnol., Oceanogr.* 6:292–298.

SALE, P.F. 1971. Apparent effect of prior experience on a habitat preference exhibited by the reef fish, *Dascyllus aruanus* (Pisces: Pomacentridae). *Anim. Behav.* 19:251–256.

SALE, P.F. 1975. Patterns of use of space in a guild of territorial reef fishes. *Marine Biol.* 29:89–97.

SALE, P.F. 1977. Maintenance of high diversity in coral reef fish communities. *Amer. Nat.* 111(978):337–359.

SALE, P.F., and DYBAHL, R. 1975. Determinants of community structure for coral reef fishes in an experimental habitat. *Ecology* 56(6):1343–1355.

SATCHELL, G.H. 1965. Blood flow through the caudal vein of elasmobranch fish. *Aust. J. Sci.* 27:241–242.

SATCHELL, G.H. 1971. *Circulation in fishes.* London: Cambridge Univ. Press. 131 pp

SATCHELL, G.H. 1976. The circulatory system of air-breathing fish. Pages 105–123 *in* G.M. Hughes, ed. *Respiration of amphibious vertebrates.* London: Academic Press.

SAUL, W.G. 1975. An ecological study of fishes at a site in upper Amazonian Ecuador. *Proc. Phila. Acad. Sci.* 127(12):93–134.

SAVITZ, J. 1971. Effects of starvation on body protein utilization of bluegill sunfish (*Lepomis macrochirus* Rafinesque), with a calculation of caloric requirements. *Trans. Amer. Fish. Soc.* 100:18–21.

SAWYER, W.H., BLAIR-WEST, J.R., SIMPSON, P.A., and SAWYER, M.K. 1976. Renal responses of Australian lungfish to vasotocin, angiotensin, II, and NaCl infusion. *Amer. J. Physiol.* 231:593–602.

SCHAEFFER, B. 1967. Comments on elasmobranch evolution. Pages 3–35 *in* P.H. Gilbert, R.W. Mathewson, and D.W. Hall, eds. *Sharks, skates, and rays.*

Baltimore: Johns Hopkins Press.

SCHAEFFER, B. 1973. Interrelationships of chondrosteans. Pages 207–227 *in* P.G. Greenwood, R.S. Miles, and C. Patterson, eds. *Interrelationships of fishes.* London: Academic Press.

SCHAEFFER, B., and ROSEN, D. 1961. Major adaptive levels in the evolution of the actinopterygian feeding mechanism. *Amer. Zool.* 1:187–204.

SCHALLES, J.F., and WISSING, T.E. 1976. Effects of dry pellet diets on the metabolic rates of bluegill (*Lepomis macrochirus*). *J. Fish. Res. Bd. Canada.* 33: 2443–2249.

SCHMIDT, J. 1922. The breeding places of the eel. *Phil. Trans. Roy. Soc. London,* Ser. B. 211:179–208.

SCHMIDT, P.Y. 1950. *Fishes of the Sea of Okhotsk.* Jerusalem: Israel. Prog. Sci. Trans. 392 pp.

SCHMIDT-NIELSEN, K. 1975. *Animal physiology, adaptation and environment.* London: Cambridge Univ. Press. 699 pp.

SCHOLANDER, P.F. 1954. Secretion of gases against high pressures in the swimbladder of deep sea fishes. II. The *rete mirabile. Biol. Bull.* 107:260–277.

SCHOLZ, A.T., HORRALL, R.M., COOPER, J.C., and HASLER, A.D. 1976. Imprinting to chemical cues: the basis for home stream selection in salmon. *Science* 192:1247–1249.

SCHULTZ, R.J. 1971. Special adaptive problems associated with unisexual fishes. *Amer. Zool.* 11:351–360.

SCHULTZ, R.J. 1973. Unisexual fish: laboratory synthesis of a "species." *Science* 192:1247–1249.

SCHWARTZ, F.J. 1972. World literature on fish hybrids with an analysis by family, species, and hybrid. *Gulf Coast Mar. Lab. Mus.* 33:1–328.

SCOTT, T.D. 1962. *The marine and freshwater fishes of South Australia.* Adelaide: Govt. Printer. 338 pp.

SCOTT, W.B., and CROSSMAN, E.J. 1973. Freshwater fishes of Canada. *Fish. Res. Bd. Canada Bull.* 184:1–966.

SEABURG, K.S., and MOYLE, J.B. 1964. Feeding habits, digestion rates, and growth of some Minnesota warm water fishes. *Trans. Amer. Fish. Soc.* 93(2): 269–285.

SEDBERRY, G.R., and MUSICK, J.R. 1978. Feeding strategies of some demersal fishes of the continental slope and rise off the mid-Atlantic coast of the U. S. A. *Marine Biol.* 44:337–375.

SEEGRIST, D.W., and GARD, R. 1972. Effects of floods on trout in Sagehen Creek, California. *Trans. Amer. Fish. Soc.* 101(3):478–482.

SEKHON, S.S., and MAXWELL, D.S. 1970. Fine structure for developing hagfish erythrocytes with particular reference to cytoplasmic organelles. *J. Morph.* 131: 211–236.

SENANAYAKE, F.R. 1977. *An ecological appraisal of malaria resurgence in Sri Lanka.* Unpublished M. S. thesis, Univ. Calif., Davis. 47 pp.

SHARP, G.D., and DIZON, A.E. 1978. *The physiological ecology of tunas.* New York: Academic Press. 485 pp.

SHAW, E. 1970. Schooling in fishes: critique and review. Pages 453–480 *in* R.L. Aronsen et al., eds. *Development and evolution of behavior.* San Francisco: W. Freeman.

SHAW, E. 1978. Schooling fishes. *Amer. Sci.* 66:166–175.

SHELDON, A.L. 1968. Species diversity and longitudinal succession in stream fishes. *Ecology* 49(2):194–198.

SHELL, E.W. 1959. *Chemical composition of the blood of smallmouth bass.* Unpublished Ph.D. dissertation. Cornell Univ.

SIEBERT, G., SCHMITT, A., and BOTTKE, I. 1964. Enzymes of the amino acid metabolism in cod musculature. *Arch. Fisch. Wiss.* 15:233–244.

SILBA, P., and five others. 1977. Mechanism of active chloride secretion by shark rectal gland: role of Na-K-ATPase in chloride transport. *J. Physiol.* 233F:298–306.

SINGH, B.N. 1976. Balance between aquatic and aerial respiration. Pages 125–164 *in* G.M. Hughes, ed. *Respiration of amphibious vertebrates.* London: Academic Press.

SINHA, V.R.P., and JONES, J.W. 1975. *The European freshwater eel.* Liverpool: Liverpool Univ. Press. 146 pp.

SIOLI, H. 1975. Tropical river: the Amazon. Pages 461–488 *in* B.A. Whitton, ed. *River ecology.* Berkeley: Univ. Calif. Press.

SMALL, J.W. 1975. Energy dynamics of benthic fishes in a small Kentucky stream. *Ecology* 56(4):827–840.

SMITH, C.L. 1978. Coral reef fish communities: a compromise view. *Env. Biol. Fish* 3(1):109–128.

SMITH, C.L., and POWELL, C.R. 1971. The summer fish communities of Brier Creek, Marshall County, Oklahoma. *Amer. Mus. Nov.* 2458:1–30.

SMITH, C.L., RAND, C.S., SCHAEFFER, B., and ATZ, J.W. 1975. *Latimeria,* the living coelacanth is ovoviviparous. *Science* 190:1105–1106.

SMITH, C.L., and TYLER, J.C. 1972. Space sharing in a coral reef fish community. *Bull. Los Ang. Co. Mus. Nat. Hist.* 14:125–170.

SMITH, D.G. 1970. Notacanthiform leptocephali in the Western North Atlantic. *Copeia* 1970(1):1–9.

SMITH, F.M., and JONES, D.R. 1978. Localization of receptors causing hypoxic bradycardia in trout *Salmo gairdneri. Can. J. Zool.* 56:1260–1265.

SMITH, H.M. 1945. The freshwater fishes of Siam, or Thailand. *Bull. U.S. Nat. Mus.* 188:1–622.

SMITH, H.W. 1929. The excretion of ammonia and urea by the gills of fish. *J. Biol. Chem.* 81:727–742.

SMITH, H.W. 1961. *From fish to philosopher.* New York: Doubleday. 293 pp.

SMITH, J.L.B. 1949. *The sea fishes of Southern Africa.* Capetown: Central News Agency. 580 pp.

SMITH, J.L.B. 1956. *The search beneath the sea.* New York: H. Holt and Co. 260 pp.

SMITH, P.W. 1971. Illinois streams: classification based on their fishes and an analysis of factors responsible for the disappearance of native species. *Ill. Nat. Hist. Surv. Biol. Note* 76:1–14.

SMITH, R.F., SWARTZ, A.H., and MASSMAN, W.H., eds. 1966. *A symposium on estuarine fisheries.* Amer. Fish. Soc. Spec. Publ. 3:1–154.

SMITH, S.H. 1968. Species succession and fishery exploitation of the Great Lakes. *J. Fish. Res. Bd. Canada* 25(4):667–693.

SMITH-VANIZ, W.F. 1968. *Freshwater fishes of Alabama.* Auburn, Ala.: Auburn Univ. Ag. Exp. Stat. 211 pp.

SNEDECOR, G.W., and COCHRAN, W.G. 1967. *Statistical methods.* Ames: Iowa St. Univ. Press. 593 pp.

SOLTZ, D., and NAIMAN, R. 1978. The natural history of the native fishes of the Death Valley system. *Nat. Hist. Mus. Los Ang. Co. Sci. Ser.* 30:1–76.

SONNIER, F., TEERLING, J., and HOESE, H.D. 1976. Observations on the offshore reef and platform fish fauna of Louisiana. *Copeia* 1976(1):105–111.

Southern California Coastal Water Research Project. 1973. *The ecology of the Southern California bight: implications for water quality management.* El Segundo, Calif.: SCCWRP TR 104. 531 pp.

SPALL, R.D. 1970. Possible cases of cleaning symbiosis among freshwater fishes. *Trans. Amer. Fish. Soc.* 99(3):599–600.

SPRINGER, S. 1979. A revision of the catsharks, family Scyliorhinidae. *NOAA Tech Rpt. NMFS Cir.* 422:1–152.

SPRINGER, S., and GILBERT, P.W. 1976. The basking shark, *Cetorhinus maximus*, from Florida and California, with comments on its biology and systematics. *Copeia* 1976(1):47–54.

STARRETT, W. 1951. Some factors affecting the abundance of minnows in the Des Moines River, Iowa. *Ecology* 32(1):13–27.

STEARNS, S.C. 1976. Life history tactics: a review of the ideas. *Quart. Rev. Biol.* 51(1):3–47.

STEEN, J.B. 1971. *Comparative physiology of respiratory mechanisms.* New York: Academic Press. 182 pp.

STEEN, J.B., and BERG, T. 1966. The gills of two species of hemoglobin free fishes compared to those of other teleosts—with a note on severe anaemia in an eel. *Comp. Biochem. Physiol.* 18:517–527.

STEIN, R.A., and KITCHELL, J.F. 1975. Selective predation by carp *Cyprinus carpio* (L.) on benthic molluscs in Skadar Lake, Yugoslavia. *J. Fish Biol.* 7(2): 391–399.

STEIN, R.A., REIMERS, P.E., and HALL, J.D. 1972. Social interaction between juvenile coho (*Oncorhynchus kisutch*) and fall chinook salmon (*O. tshawytscha*) in Sixes River, Oregon. *J. Fish. Res. Bd. Canada* 29(12):1737–1748.

STEPHENS, J.S., JOHNSON, R.K., KEY, G.S., and McCOSKER, J.E. 1970. The comparative ecology of three sympatric species of California blennies of the genus (*Hypsoblennius*) Gill (Teleostomi, Blenniidae). *Ecol. Monogr.* 40:213–233.

STERBA, G. 1959. *Freshwater fishes of the world.* London: Vista Books. 878 pp.

STEVENS, E.D. 1968. The effect of exercise on the distribution of blood to various organs in rainbow trout. *Comp. Biochem., Physiol.* 25:615–625.

STEVENS, E.D. 1979. The effect of temperature on tail beat frequency of fish swimming at constant velocity. *Can. J. Zool.* 57:1628–1635.

STEVENS, E.D., BENNION, G.R., RANDALL, D.J., and SHELTON, G. 1972. Factors affecting arterial pressures and blood flow from the heart in intact, unrestrained lingcod (*Ophiodon elongatus*). *Comp. Biochem., Physiol.* 43A:681–695.

STEVENS, E.D., and RANDALL, J.R. 1967. Changes in blood pressure, heart rate, and breathing rate during moderate swimming activity in rainbow trout. *J. Exp. Biol.* 46:307–315.

STEVENSON, M.M., SCHNELL, G.D., and BLACK, R. 1974. Factor analysis of fish distribution patterns in western and central Oklahoma. *Syst. Zool.* 23(2): 202–218.

STEWART, N.E., SHUMWAY, D.L., and DOUDOROFF, P. 1967. Influence of oxygen concentration on the growth of juvenile largemouth bass. *J. Fish. Res. Bd. Canada* 24:475–494.

STICKNEY, R.R., and SHUMWAY, S.E. 1974. Occurrence of cellulase activity in the stomachs of fishes. *J. Fish Biol.* 6:779–790.

STRAHN, R. 1963. The behavior of *Myxine* and other myxinoids. Pages 22–32 *in* A. Brodal and R. Fange, eds. *The biology of the myxine.* Oslo: Scand. Univ. Books.

STRAND, S.W. 1978. *Community structure among reef fishes in the Gulf of California; the use of reef space and interspecific associations.* Unpublished Ph.D. dissertation, Univ. Calif., Davis. 144 pp.

STRASKRABA, M. 1965. The effect of fish on the number of invertebrates in ponds and streams. *Mitt. Int. Ver. Limnol.* 13:106–127.

SUBRAHMANYAM, C.B., and DRAKE, S.H. 1975. Studies of animal communities of two north Florida salt marshes. Part I. Fish communities. *Bull. Mar. Sci.* 25(4):445–465.

SULAK, K.J. 1977. The systematics and biology of *Bathypterois* (Pisces, Chloropthalmidae) with a revised classification of benthic myctophiform fishes. *Galathea*

Rpt. 14:49–108.

SUTTERLIN, A.M. 1969. Effects of exercise on the cardiac and ventilation frequency in three species of freshwater teleosts. *Physiol. Zool.* 42:36–52.

SUTTERLIN, A.M. 1975. Chemical attraction of some marine fish in their natural habitat. *J. Fish. Res. Bd. Canada* 32:729–738.

SVARDSON, G. 1949. Natural selection and egg number in fish. *Ann. Rpt. Inst. Freshw. Res., Drottningholm* 29:115–122.

SWINGLE, H.S., and SMITH, E.V. 1940. Experiments on the stocking of fish ponds. *Trans. N. Amer. Wildl. Conf.* 15:267–276.

SYMONS, P.E.K. 1976. Behavior and growth of juvenile Atlantic salmon (*Salmo salar*) and three competitors at two stream velocities. *J. Fish. Res. Bd. Canada* 33(12):1766–2773.

SZALAY, F.S. 1977. Ancestors, descendents, sister groups, and testing of phylogenetic hypotheses. *Syst. Zool.* 26(1):12–18.

TABB, D.C. 1966. The estuary as a habitat for spotted seatrout, *Cynoscion nebulosis*. Pages 59–67 *in* R.F. Smith et al., eds. *A symposium on estuarine fisheries.* Amer. Fish. Soc. Spec. Publ. 3.

TAGATZ, N.E., and DUDLEY, D.L. 1961. Seasonal occurrence of marine fishes in four shore habitats near Beaufort, N. C. 1957–60. U.S. Fish, Wildl. Serv. Spec. Sci. Rpt.

TALBOT, G.B. 1966. Estuarine environmental requirements and limiting factors for striped bass. Pages 37–49 *in* R.F. Smith et al., eds. *A symposium on estuarine fisheries.* Amer. Fish. Soc. Spec. Publ. 3.

TAVOLGA, W.A. 1956. Visual, chemical, and sound stimuli as cues in the sex discriminatory behavior of the gobiid fish, *Bathygobius soporator*. *Physiol. Zool.* 31:259–271.

TEICHMANN, H. 1962. Was leistet der Geruchssinn bei Fischen? *Umschau Wiss. Tech.* 62:588–591.

TEMPLEMAN, W. 1976. Transatlantic migrations of spiny dogfish (*Squalus acanthias*). *J. Fish. Res. Bd. Canada* 33(11):2605–2609.

TESCH, F.W. 1977. *The eel: biology and management of anguillid eels.* London: Chapman and Hall. 434 ppp.

TEYLAUD, A.R. 1971. Food habits of the goby *Ginsburgellus novemlinaetus*, and the clingfish, *Acros rubiginosis*, associated with echinoids in the Virgin Islands. *Caribb. J. Sci.* 11:41–45.

THAYER, G.W., WOLFE, D.A., and WILLIAMS, R.B. 1975. The impact of man on seagrass systems. *Amer. Sci.* 63(3):288–296.

THIBAULT, R.E. 1978. Ecological and evolutionary relationships among diploid and triploid unisexual fishes associated with the bisexual species, *Poeciliopsis lucida* (Cyprinodontiformes: Poeciliidae). *Evolution* 32(3):613–623.

THINES, G. 1969. *L'evolution regressive des poissons cavernicoles et abyssaus.* Paris: Masson et Cie. 394 pp.

THOMPSON, W.F., and VAN CLEVE, R. 1936. Life history of the Pacific halibut. *Rpt. Int. Fish. Comm.* 9:1–184.

THOMSON, D.A., FINLEY, L.T., and KERSTITCH, A.N. 1979. *Reef fishes of the Sea of Cortez.* New York: Wiley. 302 pp.

THOMSON, D.A., and LEHNER, C.E. 1976. Resilience of a rocky intertidal fish community in a physically unstable environment. *J. Exp. Mar. Biol., Ecol.* 22 (1):1–29.

THOMSON, K.S. 1969. The biology of the lobe-finned fishes. *Biol. Rev.* 44:91–154.

THOMSON, K.S. 1972. The adaptation and evolution of early fishes. *Quart. Rev. Biol.* 46(2):139–166.

THOMSON, K.S. 1973. New observations on the coelacanth fish, *Latimeria chalumnae*. *Copeia* 1973(4):813–814.

THOMSON, K.S. 1975. On the biology of cosmine. *Peabody Mus. Nat. Hist. Bull.* 40:1–82.

THOMSON, K.S. 1977. On the individual history of cosmine and a possible electroreceptive function of the pore-canal system in fossil fishes. Pages 247–269 *in* R.M. Andrews, R.S. Miles, and A.D. Walker, eds. *Problems in vertebrate evolution.* Linn. Soc. Lond. Symp. Series 4.

THORSON, T.B. 1958. Measurements of the fluid components of four species of marine chondrichthyes. *Physiol. Zool.* 31:16–23.

THORSON, T.B., ed. 1976. *Investigations of the ichthyofauna of Nicaraguan lakes.* Lincoln: School of Life Sci., Univ. Nebraska. 663 pp.

THRESHER, R.E. 1977. Eye ornamentation of Caribbean reef fishes. *Z. Tierpsychol.* 43:152–158.

TILZEY, R.D.J. 1976. Observations on interactions between indigenous Galaxiidae and introduced Salmonidae in the Lake Eucumbene catchment, New South Wales, Aust. *J. Mar. Freshw. Res.* 27:551–564.

TIPPETTS, W., and MOYLE, P. 1978. Epibenthic feeding by rainbow trout (*Salmo gairdneri*) in the McCloud River, California. *J. Anim. Ecol.* 47:549–559.

TODD, E.S. 1968. Terrestrial sojourns of the longjaw mudsucker, *Gillichthys mirabilis. Copeia* 1968(1):192–194.

TOPP, R.W. 1969. Interoceanic sea-level canal: effects on the fish faunas. *Science* 165:1324–1327.

TOWLE, D.W., GILMAN, M.E., and HEMPEL, J.D. 1977. Rapid modulation of gill $Na^+ + K^+$-dependent ATPase activity during acclimation of the killifish *Fundulus heteroclitus* to salinity change. *J. Exp. Zool.* 202:179–186.

TREVINO-ROBINSON, D. 1959. The ichthyofauna of the lower Rio Grande, Texas and Mexico. *Copeia* 1959(3):253–256.

TROTT, L.B., and TROTT, E.E. 1972. Pearlfishes (Carapidae: Gadiformes) collected from Puerto Galera, Mindoro, Phillipines. *Copeia* 1972(4):839–843.

TSAI, C. 1973. Water quality and fish life below sewage outfalls. *Trans. Amer. Fish Soc.* 102(4):281–292.

TSAI, C., and ZEISEL, R.B. 1969. Natural hybridization of cyprinid fishes in Little Patuxent River, Maryland. *Ches. Sci.* 102(2):69–74.

TURNER, J.L. 1977. Changes in the size structure of cichlid populations of Lake Malawi resulting from bottom trawling. *J. Fish. Res. Bd. Canada* 34(2):232–238.

TYLER, A.V. 1971. Periodic and resident components in communities of Atlantic fishes. *J. Fish. Res. Bd. Canada* 28(7):935–946.

TYLER, A.V. 1972. Food resource division among northern, marine, demersal fishes. *J. Fish. Res. Bd. Canada* 29(7):997–1003.

TYLER, H.R., and PEARCY, W.G. 1975. The feeding habits of three species of lantern-fishes (Family Myctophidae) off Oregon, U.S.A. *Marine Biol.* 32:7–11.

UTIDA, S., and HIRANO, T. 1973. Effects of changes in environmental salinity on salt and water movement in the intestine and gills of the eel, *Anguilla japonica.* Pages 240–278 *in* W. Chavin, ed. *Responses of fish to environmental changes.* Springfield, Ill.: Chas. C. Thomas.

UYENO, T., and SMITH, G.R. 1972. Tetraploid origin of the karyotype of catostomid fishes. *Science* 175:644–646.

VALENTINE, J.W. 1971. Plate tectonics and shallow marine diversity and endemism, an actualistic model. *Syst. Zool.* 20(3):253–264.

VALIELA, I., WRIGHT, J.E., TEAL, J.M., and VOLKMANN, S.B. 1977. Growth, production, and energy transformation in the salt-marsh killifish, *Fundulus heteroclitus. Mar. Biol.* 40:135–144.

vanDAM, L. 1938. *On the utilization of oxygen and regulation of breathing in some aquatic animals.* Unpublished dissertation, Univ. Groningen.

VANDEL, A. 1965. *Biospeleology.* Oxford: Pergamon Press. 524 pp.

VANICEK, C.D., and KRAMER, R.H. 1969. Life history of the Colorado squawfish, *Ptychocheilus lucius*, and the Colorado chub, *Gila robusta*, in the Green River in Dinosaur National Monument, 1964–1966. *Trans. Amer. Fish. Soc.* 98(2):193–208.

VINCE, S., VALIELA, I., BACKUS, N., and TEAL, J.M. 1976. Predation by the salt-marsh killifish *Fundulus heteroclitus* (L.) in relation to prey size and habitat structure: consequences for prey distribution and abundance. *J. Exp. Mar. Biol. Ecol.* 23:255–266.

VINCENT, R.E., and MILLER, W.H. 1969. Altitudinal distribution of brown trout and other fishes in a headwater tributary of the South Platte River. *Ecology* 50(3):464–466.

VIRNSTEIN, R.W. 1977. The importance of predation by crabs and fishes on benthic infauna in Chesapeake Bay. *Ecology* 58(6):1199–1217.

VLADYKOV, V.D. 1973. *Lampetra pacifica*, a new nonparasitic species of lamprey from Oregon and California. *J. Fish. Res. Bd. Canada* 30(2):205–213.

VLADYKOV, V.D., and FOLLETT, W.I. 1958. Redescription of *Lampetra ayersii* (Gunther) of western North America, a species of lamprey (Petromyzonidae) distinct from *Lampetra fluviatilis* (Linnaeus) of Europe. *J. Fish. Res. Bd. Canada* 25(5):1067–1075.

VLADYKOV, V.D., and KOTT, E. 1979. Satellite species among the holarctic lampreys (Petromyzonidae). *Can. J. Zool.* 57(4):860–867.

VOLYA, G. 1966. Some data on digestive enzymes in some Black Sea fishes and a micromodification of a method for the identification of a trypsin, amylase and lypase. In "Fisiologia morskikhyzhitvotnykh." *Nauka.* (in Russian).

von ARX, W.S. 1962. An introduction to physical oceanography. Reading, Mass.: Addison-Wesley. 422 pp.

von GELDERN, C., and MITCHELL, D.F. 1975. Largemouth bass and threadfin shad in California. Pages 436–449 *in* H. Clepper, ed. *Black bass biology and management.* Washington, D.C.: Sport Fish. Inst.

VRIJENHOEK, R.C. 1978. Coexistence of clones in the heterogeneous environment. *Science* 199:549–552.

VRIJENHOEK, R.C., and SCHULTZ, R.J. 1974. Evolution of a trihybrid unisexual fish (*Poeciliopsis* Poeciliidae). *Evolution* 28(2):306–319.

WAINWRIGHT, S.A., VOSBURGH, F., and HEBRANK, J.H. 1978. Shark skin: function in locomotion. *Science* 202:747–749.

WALBURG, C.H. 1971. Loss of young fish in reservoir discharge and year-class survival, Lewis and Clark Lake, Missouri River. Pages 441–448 *in* G.E. Hall, ed. *Reservoir fisheries and limnology.* Amer. Fish. Soc. Spec. Publ. 8.

WALKER, B.W. 1960. The distribution and affinities of the marine fish fauna of the Gulf of California. *Syst. Zool.* 9(3–4):123–133.

WALKER, B.W. 1966. The origins and affinities of the Galapagos shore fishes. Pages 172–174 *in* R.I. Bowman, ed. *The Galapagos.* Berkeley: Univ. Calif. Press.

WALLS, G.L. 1942. *The vertebrate eye and its adaptive radiation.* Bloomfield Hills, Mich.: Cranbrook Inst. Sci.

WALTERS, V. 1955. Fishes of western arctic America and eastern arctic Siberia. *Bull. Amer. Mus. Nat. Hist.* 106(5):255–368.

WARDLE, C.S. 1971. New observations on the lymph system of the plaice *Pleuronectes platessa* and other teleosts. *J. Mar. Biol. Ass. U. K.* 51:977–990.

WARDLE, C.S. 1975. Limits of fish swimming. *Nature* 255:725–727.

WARDLE, C.S., and REID, A. 1977. The application of large amplitude elongated body theory to measure swimming power in fish. Pages 171–191 *in* J.H. Steel, ed. *Fisheries mathematics.* London: Academic Press.

WARNER, R.R., and ROBERTSON, D.R. 1978. Sexual patterns in the labroid fishes of the western Caribbean. I. The wrasses (Labridae). *Smithson. Contrib. Zool.* 254:1–27.

WATERMAN, T.H., and FORWARD, R.B., Jr. 1972. Field demonstration of polarotaxis in the fish *Zenarchopterus*. *J. Exp. Zool.* 180:33–54.

WATSON, L.J., SCHECHMEISTER, I.L., and JACKSON, L.L. 1963. The hematology of goldfish (*Carassius auratus*). *Cytologia* 28:118-130.

WEATHERLY, A.H. 1972. *Growth and ecology of fish populations.* New York: Academic Press. 293 pp.

WEBB, P.W. 1971. The swimming energetics of trout. I. Thrust and power at cruising speeds. *J. Exp. Biol.* 55:489–500.

WEBB, P.W. 1975a. Hydrodynamics and energetics of fish propulsion. *Bull. Fish. Res. Bd. Canada* 190:1–159.

WEBB, P.W. 1975b. Acceleration performance of rainbow trout (*Salmo gairdneri*) and green sunfish (*Lepomis cyanellus*). *J. Exp. Biol.* 63:451–465.

WEBB, P.W. 1978a. Fast-start performance and body form in seven species of teleost fish. *J. Exp. Biol.* 74:211–226.

WEBB, P.W. 1978b. Temperature effects on acceleration of rainbow trout, *Salmo gairdneri*. *J. Fish. Res. Bd. Can.* 35:1417–1422.

WEBB, P.W., and BRETT, J.R. 1972. The effects of sublethal concentration of whole bleached kraftmill effluent on the growth and food conversion efficiency of underyearling sockeye salmon (*Oncorhynchus nerka*). *J. Fish. Res. Bd. Canada* 29:1555–1563.

WEBER, D.D., and RIDGWAY, G.J. 1962. The deposition of tetracycline drugs on bones and scales of fish and its possible use for marking. *Prog. Fish. Cult.* 24:150–155.

WEBER, D.D., and DeWILDE, J.A.M. 1975. Oxygenation properties of haemoglobins from the flatfish plaice (*Pleuronectes platessa*) and flounder (*Platichthys flesus*). *J. Comp. Physiol.* 128:127–137.

WEBER, R.E., and LYKKEBOE, G. 1978. Respiratory adaptations in carp blood: influences of hypoxia, red blood cell organic phosphates, divalent cations, and CO_2 on hemoglobin-oxygen affinity. *J. Comp. Physiol.* 128:127–137.

WEIHS, D. 1973. Hydromechanics of fish schooling. *Nature* 24(5387):290–291.

WEINREB, E.L. 1958. Studies on the histology and histopathology of the rainbow trout, *Salmo gairdneri iridius*. I. Haematology under normal and experimental conditions of inflammation. *Zoologica* 43:145–154.

WEINREB, E.L., and WEINREB, S. 1969. A study of experimentally induced endocytosis in a teleost. I. Light microscopy of peripheral blood cell response. *Zoologica* 54:25–34.

WELCOMME, R.L. 1964. The habitats and habitat preferences of the young of Lake Victoria *Tilapia* (Cichlidae). *Revue Zool. Bot. Afr.* 70:1–28.

WELCOMME, R.L. 1967. The relationship between fecundity and fertility in the mouthbrooding cichlid, *Tilapia leucosticta*. *J. Zool. Lond.* 151:453–468.

WELLS, L. 1968. Seasonal depth distribution of fish in southeastern Lake Michigan. *NOAA Fish. Bull.* 67(1):1–15.

WELLS, L. 1970. Effects of alewife predation on zooplankton populations in Lake Michican. *Limnol. Oceanogr.* 15(4):556–565.

WERNER, E.E., and HALL, D.J. 1974. Optimal foraging and the size selection of prey by the bluegill sunfish (*Lepomis macrochirus*). *Ecology* 55:1042–1052.

WERNER, E.E., and HALL, D.J. 1976. Niche shifts in sunfishes: experimental evidence and significance. *Science* 191:404–406.

WERNER, E.E., HALL, D.J., LAUGHLIN, D.R., WAGNER, D.J., WILSMANN, L.A., and FUNK, F.C. 1977. Habitat partitioning in a freshwater fish community. *J. Fish. Res. Bd. Canada* 34(3):360–370.

WERNS, S., and HOWLAND, H.C. 1976. Size and allometry of the saccular air bladder of *Gnathonemus petersi* (Pisces: Mormyridae): implications for hearing. *Copeia* 1976(1):200–202.

WESTOLL, T.S. 1949. On the evolution of the Dipnoi. Pages 121-184 *in* G.L. Jepsen et al. *Genetics, paleontology, and evolution.* Princeton: Princeton Univ.

Press.

WETZEL, R.G. 1975. *Limnology*. New York: W. G. Saunders. 743 pp.

WHEELER, A. 1975. *Fishes of the world, an illustrated dictionary*. New York: MacMillan. 366 pp.

WHITESIDE, B.G., and McNATT, R.M. 1972. Fish species diversity in relation to stream order and physicochemical conditions in the Plum Creek drainage basin. *Amer. Midl. Nat.* 88(1):90–101.

WHITLEY, F.R.Z. 1959. The freshwater fishes of Australia. Pages 136–149 *in* A. Keast, R. Crocker, and C.S. Christian, eds. *Biogeography and ecology of Australia*. The Hague: W. Junk.

WHITTON, B.A., ed. 1975. *River ecology*. Berkeley: Univ. Calif. Press. 725 pp.

WHYTE, S.A. 1975. Distribution, trophic relationships and breeding habits of the fish populations in a tropical lake basin (Lake Bosumtwi, Ghana). *J. Zool. Lond.* 177:25–56.

WICKLER, W. 1968. Mimicry in plants and animals. New York: McGraw-Hill. 255 pp.

WIEBE, W.J., JOHANNES, R.E., and WEBB, K.L. 1975. Nitrogen fixation in a coral reef community. *Science* 188:257–259.

WILEY, B., and COLLETTE, B. 1970. Breeding tubercles and contact organs in fishes: their occurrence, structure, and significance. *Bull. Amer. Mus. Nat. Hist.* 143(3):145–216.

WILEY, E.O. 1978. The evolutionary species concept reconsidered. *Syst. Zool.* 27:17–26.

WILLIAMS, G.C. 1966. Adaptation and natural selection. Princeton, N.J.: Princeton Univ. Press. 307 pp.

WILLIAMS, G.C. 1975. *Sex and evolution*. Monogr. Pop. Biol. 8, Princeton Univ. 200 pp.

WILSON, B.L., DEACON, J.E., and BRADLEY, W.G. 1966. Parasitism in the fishes of the Moapa River, Clark County, Nevada. *Calif. Nev. Wildlife* 1966:12–23.

WINN, H.E. 1958. Comparative reproductive behavior and ecology of fourteen species of darters (Pisces-Percidae). *Ecol. Monogr.* 28:155–191.

WINTROBE, M.M. 1934. Variations in the size and hemoglobin content of erythrocytes in the blood of various vertebrates. *Folia Heamat., Lpz.* 51:32–49.

WITTENBERG, J.B., and HAEDRICH, R.L. 1974. The choroid rete mirabile of the fish eye. II. Distribution and relation to the pseudobranch and to the swimbladder rete mirabile. *Biol. Bull.* 145:137–156.

WITTENBERG, J.B., and WITTENBERG, V.A. 1962. Active secretion of oxygen into the eye of the fish. *Nature* 194:106–107.

WOHLSCHLAG, D.E. 1960. Metabolism of the antarctic fish and the phenomenon of cold adaptation. *Ecology* 41:287–292.

WOHLSCHLAG, D.E. 1961. Growth in antarctic fish at freezing temperatures. *Copeia* 1961(1):11–18.

WOHLSCHLAG, D.E., CAMERON, J.N., and CECH, J.J., Jr. 1968. Seasonal changes in the respiratory metabolism of the pinfish (*Lagodon rhomboides*). *Contr. Mar. Sci.* 13:89–104.

WOHLSCHLAG, D.E., and WAKEMAN, J.M. 1978. Salinity stresses, metabolic responses and distribution of the coastal spotted seatrout, *Cynoscion nebulosus. Contr. Mar. Sci.* 21:173–185.

WOOD, C.M., and SHELTON, G. 1975. Physical and adrenergic factors affecting systemic vascular resistance in the rainbow trout: A comparison with branchial vascular resistance. *J. Exp. Biol.* 63:505–523.

WOOD, S.C., JOHANSEN, K., and WEBER, R.E. 1972. Haemoglobin of the coelacanth. *Nature* 239:283–285.

WOOTEN, R.J. 1973. The effect of size of food ration on egg production in the female three-spined stickleback. *J. Fish Biol.* 5:89–96.

WOOTEN, R.J. 1977. *The biology of sticklebacks.* New York: Academic Press. 388 pp.

WOURMS, J.P. 1977. Reproduction and development in chondrichthyan fishes. *Amer. Zool.* 17(2):379–410.

WRIGHT, W.G., and RAYMOND, J.A. 1978. Air breathing in a California sculpin. *J. Exp. Zool.* 203:171–176.

WU, T.Y., and YATES, G.T. 1978. A comparative mechanophysiological study of fish locomotion with implications for tuna-like swimming mode. Pages 313–337 *in* G. Sharp and A.E. Dizon, eds. *The physiological ecology of tunas.* New York: Academic Press.

WYMAN, R.K., and WARD, J.A. 1972. A cleaning symbiosis between cichlid fishes *Etroplus maculatus* and *E. suratensis.* I. Description and possible evolution. *Copeia* 1972(4):834–838.

YOUNG, W.D., and OGLESBY, R.T. 1972. Cayuga Lake: effects of exploitation and introductions on the salmonid community. *J. Fish. Res. Bd. Canada* 29(6): 787–794.

ZARET, T.M. 1972. Predators, invisible prey, and the nature of polymorphism in the Cladocera (Class Crustacea). *Limnol. Oceanog.* 17(2):171–184.

ZARET, T.M. 1977. Inhibition of cannibalism in *Cichla ocellaris* and hypothesis of predator mimicry among South American fishes. *Evolution* 31(2):421–437.

ZARET, T.M., and PAINE, R.T. 1973. Species introduction in a tropical lake. *Science* 182:421–437.

ZARET, T.M., and RAND, A.S. 1971. Competition in tropical stream fishes: support for the competitivie exclusion principle. *Ecology* 52(2):336–342.

ZENKIVITCH, L. 1963. *Biology of the seas of the U.S.S.R.* London: Geo. Allen and Unwin. 955 pp.

ZHADIN, V.I., and GERD, S.V. 1961. *Fauna and flora of the lakes and reservoirs of the U.S.S.R.* Jerusalem: Israel Prog. Sci. Trans. 626 pp.

ZYZNAR, E.S., and NICOL, J.A.C. 1973. Reflecting materials in the eyes of three teleosts, *Orthopristes chrysopterus, Dorosoma cepedianum* and *Anchoa mitchilli. Proc. Royal Soc. Lond. B.* 184:15–27.

Index

Acanthodii, 179
Acanthopterygii, 17, 189, 276, 285
Acanthuridae, 316, 488
Acid-base balance, 85
Acid waters, 400, 431
Acipenseridae:
  characteristics, 17, 222
  distribution, 342
  evolution, 187
  gills, 165
  spawning, 115
Acipenseriformes, 187, 222
Acoustico-lateralis system, 137
Actinopterygii:
  classification, 8, 222, 226
  evolution, 4, 186, 191
Adrianichthyidae, 283
Aggression, 161, 404
Aglomerular kidney, 80, 84
Agnatha:
  classification, 176, 194
  evolution, 176
  hemoglobin, 58
  ion regulation, 77
  osmoregulation, 74, 75
  reproduction, 110, 198, 200
  structure, 195, 196, 200
Agonidae, 17, 299, 360, 520
Air-breathing, 46, 72, 183, 218, 224, 225, 437
Alaska, 344
Albacore, 499, 503
Albulidae, 227, 230
Alepisauridae, 267, 511
Alepocephalidae, 245
Alevin, 244
Alewife, 389, 411, 418, 419
Algal mats, 480
Alosa (see Shad)
Amazon molly, 281
Amazon River, 434
Amblyopsidae:
  characteristics, 269, 446

distribution, 342, 349
ecology, 445
navigation, 143
spawning, 120
Ameiruridae, 259
Amiidae:
  distribution, 342
  evolution, 188
  respiration, 48, 224
  structure, 224
  vision, 148
Amino acids, 92
Ammocoetes, 196, 198
Ammodytidae, 313, 520
Amphioxus, 176
Ampullae of Lorenzini, 144
Anabantidae:
  characteristics, 319
  distribution, 334, 338
  respiration, 47, 72
  spawning, 117, 118
Anabantoidei, 319
Anablepidae, 15, 121, 147, 283, 336
Anabolism, 92, 100
Anadromy, 242, 332
Anarhichadidae, 520
Anatomy:
  external, 13
  internal, 20, 111
Ancestral, defined, 3
Anchovy (see also Engraulidae)
  northern, 503, 505
  Peruvian, 499, 527
Anemone fishes, 169, 307, 492
Angelfishes, 305
Anglerfishes (see Lophiiformes)
Anguillidae:
  hemoglobin, 59
  ion regulation, 80, 82
  migration, 152, 154, 230, 332
  olfaction, 135
  osmoregulation, 76